GOOD
IDEAS
FOR YOUR
GARDEN

READER'S DIGEST

GOOD
IDEAS
FOR YOUR
GARDEN

PUBLISHED BY THE READER'S DIGEST ASSOCIATION LIMITED
LONDON · NEW YORK · SYDNEY · CAPE TOWN · MONTREAL

GOOD IDEAS FOR YOUR GARDEN
was edited and designed by
The Reader's Digest Association Limited,
London.

First Edition
Copyright © 1995
The Reader's Digest Association Limited,
Berkeley Square House, Berkeley Square,
London W1X 6AB.
Copyright © 1995
Reader's Digest Association Far East Limited.
Philippines Copyright © 1995
Reader's Digest Association Far East Limited.

Printed in France
ISBN 0 276 42141 8

The typeface used in this book
is Plantin Light.

EDITOR
Judith Taylor

ART EDITOR
Judy White

CONTRIBUTORS

The publishers would like to thank the following people
for their contributions to this book:

CONSULTANT EDITOR
Allen Paterson, M HORT (RHS), MED, FLS

CONSULTANT PLANTSMAN
Kenneth A. Beckett, VMM

MAJOR CONTRIBUTORS
John Brookes, FSGD
Susanna Brown
Nigel Colborn
Sue Fisher
Angela Kirby
Allen Paterson
Geoff Stebbings

ARTISTS
Julia Bickham
Leonora Box
Wendy Bramall
Kevin Dean
Nick Hardcastle
Royston Knipe
Gill Tomblin
Barbara Walker
Anne Winterbotham
John Woodcock

CALLIGRAPHER
Gabrielle Izen

PHOTOGRAPHERS
Jonathan Buckley
Stephen Robson

The publishers would also like to thank the following
for their help in the preparation of this book:

Peter Barnes
Helen Baz
Jean and Francine Raymond
Martin and Jenny Thompson
Great Comp, Kent
Ham House, London
Ryton Organic Gardens, West Midlands
Snowshill Manor, Gloucestershire

CONTENTS

A Source of Inspiration

ONE OF THE JOYS of gardening is that there is always more to learn. It is rare to find a gardener who is not entranced by fresh ideas. They are not easy to come by and, indeed, are more often found by chance – seen from a car or train window, for example – than by diligent research.

The original approach of this gardening book, to be inspirational as well as factual, stems from understanding this difficulty. The book shows not only how to choose and care for the right plant in the right environment but also how to combine the plants and create a garden to match your dreams.

Throughout the 15 chapters, a bountiful array of designs and plantings is shown, not only in photographs but in original water-colours that bring to life schemes planned by the expert contributors. There are ideas, vividly described as well as illustrated, for transforming gardens of all shapes and sizes, no matter how unpromising they may seem at first. Many ideas aim to give delight with colour and scent, but others address particular needs – making a pretty place to sit, adding some drama to the garden, growing plants for flower arrangements and running a garden that is friendly to the environment.

For anyone about to make a new garden, much has to be thought out before planting begins. What shape and size is the plot? What is its soil type? How much time will you have to give to the garden? This book shows how to take stock of your plot as you find it – to evaluate its qualities and come to terms with its disadvantages – in order to turn it into the garden you have always wanted.

To help you through the changes, there is plenty of practical advice on making tricky tasks easier, saving money, choosing tools and accessories, rescuing plants in trouble and making the garden safe.

You may have been to visit one of Britain's grand country house gardens and admired a feature – a formal parterre, a flower-filled arbour or arch, or a lush conservatory – that you would like to have at home if you could only see how to adapt it for a smaller setting. To help you to do this, each chapter looks at a feature from a great garden and shows you how to rework it.

But while inspiration is important, it is the plants that finally make a garden. These are suggested in abundance throughout the book, and the conditions that suit them best are summarised in tables at the end, where there is also a general index.

The many strands in *Good Ideas for Your Garden* will help you to develop your garden to its full potential, treating it both as a blank canvas for your imagination and, ultimately, as a place for enjoyment and relaxation.

FIRST
IMPRESSIONS

THE FRONT GARDEN can gladden the heart or give a chilly greeting, for this most public part of your domain often receives little thought and it is the more private back garden that claims all the attention. But an attractive, easily maintained design creates a flattering frame for the house and welcomes you, and your guests, all the year round. Whether you have only a pair of tubs at the front door, hanging baskets and window boxes above a tiny strip of ground, or a more spacious area to develop, make the most of its potential and enjoy the result every time you come home.

Bergenias, Japanese anemones and a fuchsia make a sympathetic colour blend with a pink climbing rose, and their spreading, eager growth covers its leggy stems, to give a pretty finish to a stone cottage.

THE FRONT GARDEN'S ROLES

TOO OFTEN the front garden is dominated by the car and a gathering of dustbins while horticultural wonders are created round the back. Yet the front garden has several roles to play. It is a buffer against the world, offering the house privacy. It gives access to the main door and usually to the rear of the house; it is the service area for dustbin men, paperboy, postman and all deliveries – and it may be a car park as well.

The back garden is for relaxation, play and entertaining. It belongs mainly to the weekends and summer evenings, whereas the front one is used every day.

When it is successful, the front garden enhances the house and gives a lift to the spirits as well as performing its utilitarian functions. It also exposes the owner's personality and taste to public gaze and judgment and perhaps gardeners feel inhibited by this. But diffidence should be overcome for there is no right or wrong design; many different plans can work equally well in one plot.

There are, however, three broad guidelines that help to bring about a successful garden. Give it some unity with the lines and materials of the building, choose plants and features of suitable scale for the site, and stick to a style in keeping with the house's character. A rustic wheelbarrow full of pansies does little for a Georgian-style frontage; classical urns are much more its style. And an Italianate fountain never looks at home in front of a country cottage, which is suited to perfection by roses round the door.

WHAT GARDENERS WANT NOW

Front gardens have yet to be rethought to suit today's style of living, and Victorian habits of a century ago are still evident in shaved lawns, sharply trimmed at the edges and framed by perfect rows of bedding plants. But the ritual of summer bedding, autumn clearance, and a bare garden in winter is no longer welcome.

Although there is no consensus on a front-garden style for today, there are certain common needs shared by many gardeners – low-maintenance planting, some privacy from passers-by, security from intruders, and a space for off-street car parking.

Much enjoyment is to be had in creating the front garden that suits your needs and furnishing it, as you do the rooms indoors, to suit your taste – but with an eye to practical matters as well as appearance. Give the garden robust plants and tough structural materials that will stand up to daily traffic, and be sure to devise a plan that is easily kept in good order with a minimum of work. Then as you or your visitors approach the house, the front garden gives a satisfying first impression.

SYMPATHETIC STYLE This welcoming front garden has a well-marked path leading to the front porch, where there is a generous paved area for visitors. Each spring, bulbs such as *Narcissus* 'Thalia' and *Tulipa* 'Purissima' bloom under a canopy of the ornamental cherry, *Prunus* 'Tai Haku'.

HOUSE FRONT AND DOORWAY

A N ENCOURAGING ASPECT of any front garden is that its size is not everything. Shortage of space can be offset by ingenuity even where all you possess is a foot or two of soil beside the front door. Indeed there are many small-town side roads and many village streets where there is not even a strip of soil in front of a house and the building itself presents the only area where plants can grow.

A GARDEN ON A WALL

In such a situation, compose your garden from annuals, bulbs and dwarf shrubs in window boxes, vivid annuals in hanging baskets, and evergreens or colourful performers in tubs. Use inexpensive containers as much as you can since they are vulnerable to knocks, dogs and vandals.

If you do use an expensive pot, chain it to the railings or to a ring set in the wall, or cement the base to the spot but do not block the drainage holes. A chain can be hidden by plants trailing over the rim of the container, but a cheap container can be hidden in the same way and will cause you far less anxiety.

Glass fibre urns and Versailles boxes, now made in dark green plastic, keep down the cost. Galvanised buckets, plastic pots and even old paint tins make perfectly adequate containers provided they have drainage holes at the bottom.

Fix window boxes firmly on wall brackets, setting them with the rim a little below sill height. You do not want to see the back of a box through the window, nor to have plants blocking the light. Fill window boxes mainly with low-growing plants to look down on from indoors; flowers turn to face the daylight so you see only their outline if they are too high.

When the front of your house has only one ground-floor window, create a greater effect by fixing a window box and standing a deeper and wider trough on the ground under it. Use the same planting scheme in box and trough, putting trailers at the sides to link the two.

COLOURS TO ENHANCE A WALL

Mutual flattery between the plants and the building is more crucial than usual when they merge as one vertical surface. Put dark red or blue flowers against a strident red brick wall and they tend to

HANGING GARDENS Lack of soil need not be an obstacle to creating a colourful entrance display. Traditional summer bedding plants – pelargoniums, lobelias and petunias – fill hanging baskets and a window box.

MADE FOR EACH OTHER A coppery pink climbing rose, *Rosa* 'Meg', draws attention to the pretty brick detailing without obscuring it, and the paler colour of the rose is a perfect complement to the warm pink brickwork.

vanish, with neither party to the match gaining. But put pale flowers against it and they leap out with extra clarity while the wall serves as a strong foil.

Mellow old bricks usually mingle several colours. Emphasise their beauty with plants in slightly bolder versions of these shades in your tubs and baskets. For example, grow purple pansies and pink pelargoniums against rosy old bricks.

Rich, stained-glass colours look well against white walls in an informal setting,

PLANT A WINDOW BOX
FOR A YEAR OF PLEASURE

USE A GLASS FIBRE BOX to reduce the weight and cut out the need for a waterproof liner. Mount it on brackets that are firmly fixed to the wall and strong enough to prevent the box from tilting. Instead of putting crocks in the bottom for drainage, use broken-up polystyrene packing. Plant up the box early in October.

1. Spread the base with the polystyrene pieces and cover them with 2 in (5 cm) of compost. Put three sets of three *Tulipa* 'Red Riding Hood' in place; mark with canes before filling with compost.

2. Plant three *Daphne cneorum* 'Alba' along the front, one in the centre and one at each corner. Push two groups of five or six snowdrop bulbs in at the back, setting their bases 3 in (7.5 cm) deep.

3. Tuck three perennial forget-me-nots (*Myosotis alpestris*) in each of the two gaps for early summer flowering. Remove the canes and plant a bronze winter pansy over each tulip group.

4. At the end of February carefully clear out the pansies to avoid a colour clash with the April-flowering tulips. Nip the seed heads off the snowdrops after they finish flowering.

5. In June, when the tulips are over and the leaves are yellowing, cut off the top growth and plant a *Convolvulus tricolor* 'Blue Flash' in each gap to flower through summer and into October.

6. Early in October, trim off any remaining forget-me-not foliage and carefully take out the convolvulus plants. In their place plant bronze winter-flowering pansies again.

whereas the greater formality of stuccoed city walls requires restraint – perhaps the architectural shapeliness of a fatsia, or trimly clipped conifers.

DOUBLING THE IMPACT

Twin plantings create a stronger image on the house front than a random assortment of single features. Have matched tubs of plants on either side of the door, matched hanging baskets on the walls and matched window-box plantings.

Double the size of your hanging baskets as well as matching them. There are bolster-shaped baskets that make long flowery panels. Some models have built-in water reservoirs to help to keep the compost moist. Fill them lavishly with petunias, pelargoniums and trailing lobelia, all eager bloomers that put on a long and brilliant display.

SOME GROUND TO PLANT IN

The merest strip of soil along the front of the house gives a welcome opportunity to get some roots in the ground. Separate your plot from the public pavement by a row of edging stones or tiles, or by raising the bed – not enough to get close to the damp-proof course or air bricks but enough to stop people treading on it.

Make the little strip a launching pad for flowering climbers or shrubs to train on the wall. Give the plants freedom to smother an ugly wall but always keep the house number plainly in view. If you have a wall of mellow stone, lovely old bricks or decorative detail it would be a shame to obscure it completely.

Pick plants to flatter the walls; harmony or contrast give equal satisfaction.

🌢 Against a white rendered wall, the Japanese quince (*Chaenomeles speciosa*) can show off its late winter blooms. If the bright red 'Rowallane' is too vivid for your taste, grow 'Pink Lady'.

🌢 For a sandy-buff modern brick wall, choose the apricot-coloured Japanese quince 'Geisha Girl'. The fragrant yellow fruits, like small apples, look good too.

🌢 Harsh red brick is cooled by the white stars and dark leaves of *Clematis armandii*, or the creamy clusters and fresh-looking foliage of *Hydrangea petiolaris*.

🌢 The hint of purple in a sandstone wall is picked up by a velvety purple *Clematis* × *jackmannii* 'Superba'.

🌢 Cool grey limestone is warmed by rosy-mauve wisteria or a crimson rose. On an unpretentious cottage grow violet everlasting sweet pea (*Lathyrus latifolius*).

BLUE SYMMETRY Double planting heightens the impact of glorious hydrangea specimens in elegant stone containers, particularly with this restrained colour scheme set against white walls.

SAFETY FIRST

ROSE WITHOUT THORNS

ROSES NODDING round the front door make even the plainest house pretty, but the thorns on stray shoots can scratch people as they go in and out. Combine beauty with safety by choosing *Rosa* 'Zéphirine Drouhin'; it is a rich pink, perpetual flowering, heavily scented – and has thornless stems.

PAIRED OFF IN PINK Window boxes are linked by a hanging basket with a unified planting theme – trailing pelargoniums, fuchsias and lobelias. The window boxes are placed low enough to avoid obscuring the windows.

❦ Honey-coloured stone is a perfect backdrop for a deep yellow rose such as 'Golden Showers'.

In general, deciduous climbers are best confined to stone or brick walls. Painted or rendered walls can look shabby when a plant is bare in winter, so grow an evergreen climber there to give year-round cover. Alternatively, you can grow annual climbers such as mauve morning glory (*Ipomoea*), orange black-eyed Susan (*Thunbergia alata*) or even scarlet runner beans, these all leave the walls bare in winter for repainting.

COMPANIONS FOR CLIMBERS

The bottom end of a climbing plant is rarely worth seeing. Conceal its ungainly feet with shrubs and perennials that complete a harmonious picture along the front of the building. Put together a fresh-looking scheme for a sunny setting with some yellow-centred white *Cistus × corbariensis* and lime-green flowered *Euphorbia characias* in front of a yellow-splashed ivy or a yellow-and-white flowered Japanese honeysuckle .

Make a warmer scheme with white lavender, pink London pride (*Saxifraga × urbium*) and the pink-and-white tipped

BEST PLANTS

WINDOW BOXES AND TROUGHS

Hugging the wall of the house, window boxes and many troughs are frequently sheltered from the rain. With only a small amount of soil where roots can seek water, the plants that thrive are those that like dry conditions.

• Alyssum (*Aurinia saxatilis*): broad heads of yellow flowers cover the low greyish shrub through high summer.

• Wallflower (*Erysimum cheiri* 'Tom Thumb Mixed'): scented, early summer flowers in golds and russets.

• *Convolvulus cneorum*: pink buds and white flowers adorn the silvery leaved shrub from spring to autumn.

• Pink (*Dianthus* × *allwoodii* 'Doris'): clove-scented pink flowers in early summer and again in September; 'Show Pearl' is white.

• Ivy (*Hedera helix* 'Tricolor'): trailing evergreen growth has pale green leaves with a white rim that flushes to red during winter.

• Dwarf iris (*Iris pumila*): short-stemmed large spring flowers in white, yellow or mauve.

• *Mesembryanthemum criniflorum*: pink, mauve, yellow and orange daisy flowers open when summer sun shines.

• Cotton lavender (*Santolina chamaecyparissus* 'Nana'): dwarf evergreen shrub with feathery silver leaves and yellow July flowers.

• *Sedum* 'Ruby Glow': perennial with blue-grey leaves and large crimson flower heads in high summer.

CITY SOPHISTICATION A smart frontage is made more welcoming by careful planting. An evergreen bay in a dark green Versailles box adds height while discreet touches of colour enliven a subdued scheme that is in keeping with the formal style of the house.

greenery of the climber *Actinidia kolomikta*. For stronger impact put mauve lavender between a purple clematis and the purple tradescantia 'Isis'.

Create a cool effect on a sheltered sunny wall with white jasmine, in bloom from June to October, and round its feet set *Ceanothus thyrsiflorus* 'Repens' for its abundant blue flowers in May and a sprinkling that continues into autumn.

Cotoneaster and bergenia give you strong greens with red autumn and winter tints, while a fringe of evergreen ferns and silver-edged little box bushes (*Buxus sempervirens* 'Elegantissima') is fresh and neat at the base of a fiery Virginia creeper or a fragrant, lemon-coloured rose.

PLAY SAFE NEAR THE ROAD

Pick your plants carefully for a little strip of garden alongside a street. While you may want to ward off passers-by, you do not want to hurt them. Thorny berberis and roses, poisonous laburnum seeds and yew are best kept within the garden.

On the margin put plants that do not mind being picked at and will not harm passers-by. Lavender and *Brachyglottis* 'Sunshine' have tough but attractive grey foliage, and lavender releases its invigorating scent when you touch it.

Where traffic is heavy, choose hearty evergreens. Build a raised bed like a brick box for them in front of the house – leave drainage slits at the base, and a little space between the box and the house wall to prevent damp in the house. Make the bed about knee high to prevent rubbish

SAVING PLANTS BY THE ROAD

DUST AND GRIME from traffic exhaust fumes build up on roadside plants until they fail from clogged pores and lack of light. On a roadside grow evergreens with leathery, glossy leaves (which are most tolerant of pollution) and use a gentle hosepipe jet on them frequently to free them of all traces of dirt.

from blowing in and stop people walking on the plants.

Filled with a humus-rich compost the bed will grow anything regardless of the local soil type, but devote it to skimmias and cotoneasters, laurels and dwarf conifers, evergreen viburnum and holly, all of which are tough, low-maintenance plants tolerant of traffic pollution. Add pansies or fuchsias for extra colour.

BRIDGES AND STEPS

In city streets, many doors are reached by a 'bridge' over the basement area. This is the spot for a capacious trough painted the same dark colour as a box at the window. Clipped standard bays or hollies in the trough with dark periwinkles and white-edged ivies between look smart. Echo the shape of the scheme with little balls of bay in the window box, again with periwinkles and ivies between. A few yellow spring hyacinths and golden summer and winter pansies add just enough splashes of bright colour.

Seize the opportunity offered by a flight of steps up to the door. It is a ready-made stage for a tumble of colour. Put pots on both sides of the steps if there is room, but do not be tempted to narrow the way too much. A flight of five or six steps with a pot at each side adds up to a generous display. Simple planting with a harmonious colour theme looks best.

HIGHLIGHTS AT THE DOORWAY

No matter how tiny or large your front garden, design it to focus attention on the house entrance – the centrepiece of your home. Dress up the (*continued on p.18*)

ON THE WAY UP On a sunny flight of steps vibrant mesembryanthemums give the main colour, with extra zest from plantings in wall boxes. This planting needs full sun; use bulbs and foliage plants for more shady spots.

RAISED GROWTH A walled bed in front of the house gives room for a planting of variegated shrubs. For an area exposed to the street use tough evergreens that are easy to maintain.

MAKING AN ENTRANCE

As well as securing your privacy and safety, the front door advertises your tastes, skills and attitudes. You can translate and vary the ideas shown here to suit you and your garden.

THE FRONT DOOR is far too important to treat casually. Keep a generous open space in front of the door where possible. It is where visitors wait to be greeted and where you step out to wish them farewell. A broad, level area allows this. By raising it a little as a wide step, you can emphasise it even more.

A porch always adds importance to a doorway. Just a mere shelf over the door increases its status, and a wide masonry or glass structure is an attractive addition to the frontage. Callers have a sheltered place to stand and, better still from a gardener's point of view, the porch is a support for climbing plants. Even where

there is no room for a real porch, a similar effect is easy to create with trellis and a few stout posts. It suits many kinds of house front and gives stronger definition to any door.

You can adapt the plant choices in these examples. Skimmia, for instance, could be substituted for azaleas where the soil is not acid, and the scheme for the Georgian-style door could be replaced in winter by another based on apricot pansies, hebe and ivy. None of the schemes, in fact, is intended for posterity. If the plants grow too big, or you want a change, simply put them into a flowerbed and start all over again.

Victorian decorum

Diamond tiling is the very symbol of the Victorian terrace. It is well suited to the autumnal berries of pyracantha and to the spring cascade of wisteria. A variegated cabbage palm (*Cordyline*) unites the scheme.

Winter welcome

Pyramidal bays surrounded by aucuba and trailing ivy are the year-round basis for this display, which in January is warmed by hanging baskets of pansies and periwinkle.

Rustic charm

Lack of a front plot is overcome by two half-barrels of begonias and lobelias and a pair of matching baskets above them. Canary creepers grow on trellis; as they are annual climbers choice can be varied each year.

Peak perfection

Grey Derbyshire stone backs the white spring flowers of the climber *Clematis armandii* with *Rosa* 'Albertine' to follow. Spreading alchemilla is backed on the left by irises and soaring hollyhocks and on the other side by *Caryopteris*.

cool shade

This shady door is framed by a climbing *Hydrangea petiolaris* during summer, fatsia flowers in autumn and jasmine in winter. Spring adds hellebore then polygonatum, and vinca and box give more evergreen colour.

Leafy estate

A hint of woodland is brought to a modern doorway by a tall *Amelanchier*. Ground cover is *Viburnum davidii*, vinca and juniper. A grey *Chamaecyparis lawsoniana* 'Gimbornii' fronts a screen of ivy.

Georgian grace

A neo-Georgian door inspires the light touch of the 18th century in this summer display of a standard marguerite rising from a bowl of ivy and busy lizzies. It is balanced by a basket of white pelargoniums in similar company.

Porch promotion

Tiles and brickwork are set off by terracotta pots of *Choisya ternata*, whose evergreen leaves are a foil for forsythia in spring; from May their white flowers will flatter a yellow scramble of 'Maigold' roses.

Fragrant greeting

In summer, honeysuckle, nicotianas and regal lilies in pots waft a scented welcome while viburnum adds extra depth. The containers can be moved and replaced with spring bulbs.

Eastern approach

An oriental flavour is conjured out of rock, cobbles and gravel. It is enhanced by a shrubby bamboo, *Shibataea kumasasa*, wisteria and azalea and, in July, by the spires of bells on the *Yucca flaccida*.

ROOM ENOUGH Even a small strip of soil has room for some plants to enhance the front of the house. Spring wallflowers spill over the path in a rich mixture of warm colours with the sweet bonus of unsurpassed fragrance.

FOCUS ON THE FRONT DOOR Creamy flowered honeysuckle draped around the doorway is the epitome of the country idyll. Hanging baskets at the height of their summer display focus attention on the entrance.

door with colour; not just with immaculate paint or gleaming timber but with bright flowers climbing round it, frothing out of tubs or tumbling from hanging baskets on either side.

On a decorous formal frontage, flank the door with elegant topiary. Dark green foliage in a matching green Versailles box looks sumptuous against stucco walls. Where there is no traffic grime and the walls are stone or brick, white boxes draw attention to the doorway, but dark plants still give the smartest effect.

Box or conifer pyramids and bay lollipops are conventional but holly is cheaper for both shapes – and it defends itself against vandals. Cut costs further, and reduce maintenance, by using a glass fibre Versailles box. It keeps its pristine looks with an occasional wipe down and needs no waterproof liner as wooden boxes do if they are not to deteriorate.

For a more light-hearted version at a country cottage entrance, grow topiary birds, teddy bears or cottage-loaf shapes in terracotta pots.

THE GARDEN PATH

THE LAYOUT of the front garden must make it quite clear where callers are to go. The solidity and width of a path give unmistakable clues as to which is the right way. Be sure to have the main path smooth and broad enough to walk along with ease – no wobbly cobbles or uneven slabs, and no plants, however pretty, that lean so far over the path that they snatch at people's clothes or legs. It may be a joy to brush against sun-baked lavender and release its fresh scent, but touching rain-drenched lavender is a nuisance.

The path to the back door can be noticeably narrower, but should still be wide enough to walk along easily, even when carrying a bag or parcel. A narrower entrance to the path also indicates its subsidiary role. At the point where it reaches the house front, set a pair of shrubs, a panel of trellis or a climber twining round a pillar to make casual visitors feel they cannot go further without invading private territory.

PROS AND CONS FOR GATEWAYS

Highlight the main path with a tall plant on each side of it at the boundary, or with an intricate gate. A gate finishes off the garden perfectly, completing the sense of privacy when you are within and, from the outside, framing the garden, focusing attention on the path and so leading the eye to the doorway.

For some households a gate is simply necessary to keep toddlers in, and dogs in or out. But gates also tell tales if they are not properly chosen and fitted. A gate left open for days when it is normally shut is a giveaway that you are on holiday. Hang it on rising buttress hinges, which have a spiral joint so they always swivel back to the closed position. And have a self-closing catch so that no positive effort is needed to operate it.

Unless you have a foolproof security system, do not have a gate so high and solid that it screens the garden totally and gives cover to intruders. You can avoid such risks by doing without a gate but having substantial gateposts.

Gateposts are especially satisfying as a frame for the house when linked by an arch or beam. Elegant wrought iron looks well over formal pillars, a wisteria-swathed beam is pretty over tall timber

PRECISION PLANTING A strongly rectangular framework is softened by conifers, shrubs, perennials and container plants. The clear brick path is separated from a gravel area by symmetrical edgings of clipped box that are used to create separate planting areas within the garden.

posts, a smothering of honeysuckle suits trelliswork or rustic poles and you can, with patience, train conifers or privet to meet in a clipped green arch.

Make a Green Soakaway

When a pathway runs along the front of the house, keep it an arm's length away from the wall. You never walk right up against the building and a hard surface there has its disadvantages: rainwater cannot run off unless the whole path tilts slightly from the house.

Run a narrow bed along between the wall and the path and rainwater simply soaks into it, but make sure that the soil finishes at least two rows of bricks below the damp-proof course. Green permanent plants in the bed improve an unprepossessing building with a soft fringe at the meeting of two hard surfaces. Keep

the growth mainly below windowsill level and do not let it spread forward so far that window-cleaning mops and cloths cannot reach the panes. Ferns such as hart's tongue (*Asplenium scolopendrium*) and soft shield fern (*Polystichum setiferum*) will love the bed if it is on the side of the house that gets most rain.

Ways to Deter Intruders

Gain double value from your bed against the house by filling it mainly with evergreens for year-round interest – and put prickly plants under the windows to ward off would-be thieves. Clipped holly, ferociously armed berberis and mahonia are hard to better. Add rose bushes to give colour while still repelling intruders.

Keep plants low near the door, or certainly not high enough to give cover to a housebreaker. Put any tall plants well to

the side of the door. At night, a light over the door or in the porch emphasises the main entry's status as well as welcoming visitors and illuminating the path. Fit a sensor high on the wall to switch on the light when anyone approaches the front door. A well-lit door is also an effective way of making an intruder pass by. Nor are thieves keen to negotiate a path of crunchy gravel, which declares every footfall and defies a silent approach.

Safe and Stylish Paths

Gravel scores well on a quite different measure of safety: it gives a nonslip surface, a vital feature for a garden path. There is a range of colours so you can choose one to tone with the building.

Concrete is a cheap, hard-wearing and trouble-free material for paths, and its surface does not have to be corrugated

to make it nonslip although this unattractive finish is often given to it. Sections of poured concrete imprinted with a small overall design give grip and are far more attractive. Subtle colour tints, to harmonise with the house, also improve it, but these refinements increase the cost.

Concrete slabs are available with a nonslip texture similar to pebbledash. Laid in a pattern inset with bands and blocks of bricks or cobbles, they make a pleasing surface – as do nonslip slabs of reconstituted stone used in similar ways.

Look for combinations that pick up the colours of the building to give the unity a satisfying design demands. For example, use slabs whose colour matches the house and inset red bricks if the roof is red-tiled, purple-grey if it is slate.

When their colour is close to the local natural stone of an area, reconstituted stone slabs look good on their own and improve with weathering to make an agreeable foil for plants.

Brick or tile paths are trickier. There are many more cracks for moss to grow in than large slabs offer. Moss creeping onto the surface of bricks or tiles makes them slippery, so use a stiff brush on them frequently. This keeps the surface clean without banishing entirely the soft green tracery in the cracks which adds charm in an informal or rural garden.

Whatever the path is made of, it must have a very slight camber to throw off water, and no hollows where pools collect. Water that does not run off forms an icy film on bitter days and a path is a bruising surface to fall on. A hardcore

TOPIARY THAT COSTS LESS

READY-SHAPED TOPIARY, so smart in a pot beside the door, is expensive to buy because it takes several years to train a plant. Slash the cost by growing your own pieces, and doing it quickly.

Use a ready-made frame – cone, double-sphere, spiral, lollipop – and grow two or three small-leaved ivies over it. They quickly cover the frame and clipping them to keep the shape distinct is not hard work.

SEVERELY STYLISH A successfully designed front garden is in keeping with the style of the house. Here the door arch is repeated in the path arch, and clipped shrubs add formality to a planting theme of restrained colour.

PRETTY AND PRACTICAL A small bed between the drive and the house lets rainwater soak away and conceals the hard line where the wall meets the ground. Here nicotianas flower robustly and scent the air round the door.

base packed down by a plate vibrator and topped with sand makes a stable platform for bricks and slabs. Without a sound foundation they can shift, making dents and dips to stumble on.

A path leading callers unerringly to the principal door need not be a straight central strip. Give it a diagonal route or build in a slight curve or angle. The variation gives more interesting shapes in the garden, but keep any bend slight so that callers can take virtually a straight line from gate to door without cutting across the lawn or a border.

CASUALLY CURVED In this mature garden a curved path softened by aubrietia leads to a door flanked by pots and canopied by an old pear tree. The massed informal planting suits the countryfied style of the house.

GARDENING ON AN ESTATE

R ECENTLY BUILT ESTATES of houses often have open plan front gardens, and giving a plot character without making it an eccentric misfit among its neighbours is a challenge.

It is vital to inject some variety into the flat rectangle. Doing without boundary hedges or fences – often a condition of sale – poses problems but the guiding principles for all successful garden design still apply: link the garden to the house in materials or shapes, keep the planting in scale with the site and match the character of the garden to its setting.

SPOT THE SHAPE TO DEVELOP

The ground pattern works best when it has details that echo those of the house itself, so that the two clearly belong together. For example, a pointed gable breaking the roofline or a pointed porch over the front door suggests a diamond or lozenge shape for a lawn and for decorative motifs in a path. If the house has a curve in a front door panel or at the top of the window or door frame, shape the lawn with curved ends – and insert arcs of brick into a concrete path.

CUTTING DOWN LAWN CARE

Quality turf is the best buy for a small lawn in a show position. The finest grass is short growing and does not turn into a waving meadow when you miss a cut or two. There is not much wear to withstand so the velvety green stays at its best.

If mowing is a problem or there is no access for a mower except through the house, keep the lawn very small; even at table-top size it gives that smooth green foil for the planted areas. Ten minutes with hand shears, or with a cordless powered trimmer is enough to cut it.

Consider artificial turf, which is not a bad copy of the real thing now – and it keeps its trim surface with regular hosing down or lifting to shake well. If you do not want a lawn at all, choose low-maintenance planting for the whole area. Gravel, or paving slabs of different sizes laid in a random pattern, are labour-saving alternatives to plant cover.

Choose hard materials that tone with, rather than match, the building. Too much of the same material and colour can be overwhelming. Just a few insets of

TROUBLE-FREE GROUND COVER

Varied leaf shape and colour, neat weed-smothering growth and some flowers and berries are on offer from these plants, all of them evergreen.

• *Arabis ferdinandi-coburgi* 'Variegata': small, ground-hugging mats of silver-splashed leaves.

• *Daphne retusa*: purple buds among dark leaves open to fragrant white flowers in spring with red berries following in autumn.

• *Euonymus fortunei* 'Silver Queen': wide spreading with firm, shrubby growth of dark cream-trimmed leaves.

• *Hebe buxifolia* 'Nana': a spread of little upright spires of neat leaves stacked horizontally on the shoots.

• Juniper (*Juniperus sabina* 'Tamariscifolia'): low, wide-spreading growths densely clothed with bright green needles.

• *Sarcococca confusa*: very fragrant cream flowers in winter hide among evergreen leaves and are followed by red berries that ripen to black.

• *Viburnum davidii*: grooved, evergreen leaves; white summer flower heads and turquoise berries if plants from different parents are mixed.

• Greater periwinkle (*Vinca major* 'Variegata'): bright green, cream-edged leaves have a scattering of mauve late-spring flowers.

PATHSIDE PLANTING For easy care, plant shrubs – *Juniperus × media* 'Pfitzeriana', low-growing *J. sabina* 'Tamariscifolia', red-leaved *Berberis* and box – and brighten them up with the flowers of *Osteospermum*.

NO MOWING OR WEEDING Hummocks of low-growing, spreading conifers define the boundary of this garden. A change of scale is given by more upright conifers and colour is added by flowering heathers. The close planting leaves no room for weeds to grow and there is no lawn to tend.

SMALL AND EASY GARDENS

Hard surfacing over most of the garden is the biggest labour-saver. Tiny patches of grass in an urban or formal setting need to be meticulously cared for. They are not suited by the casual scattering of daisies that looks so pretty on country lawns.

But immaculate grass is not achieved without the persistent maintenance most gardeners prefer to reserve for the back garden. Nor is it easy to manoeuvre a mower in a small area. It can soon seem too much trouble when the mower has to be brought through the house.

EFFECTS WITH HARD MATERIALS

Hard surfacing may sound unlikely to give the delight that plants do, yet an imaginative use of materials can create a satisfying pattern and colour harmony, two chief pleasures of any garden.

Apart from the many sizes and shades of paving slabs (in real stone, reconstituted stone and concrete), there are stone setts and a wide choice of bricks. Strong red, soft red, browns, buffs, greys and purples are available. Quarry or mosaic tiles, tiles in black and white, and the Victorian favourites of blue and red add to the range for making bold outlines.

To fill in, use less geometric materials that are much easier to manipulate.
- Fine gravel comes in shades from cool off-white and grey to warm rosy hues.
- Marble and flint chippings cover the same range and add greens and mauves.
- Shingle offers oval shapes as well as subtle colours. The larger cobbles set in mortar of matching or contrasting colour give a softer, quilted look.
- To negotiate curves or fill in angles, use roofing tiles pushed edge-down into mortar until flush with the surface, and fanning out like daisy petals; blues, greys, greens, browns and reds make up a varied palette.

Tiles are appropriate in a town garden, laid in straightforward chequerboard fashion or in a more decorative pattern focusing on one spot where a single plant commands attention. The plant may be in a pot or a bed; a standard rose or artemisia does well in either.

With a pot you can put different plants such as fuchsias, hydrangeas, palms and conifers on show at different

matching brick are enough for a visual link. Merge this hard surface with the path to give an impression of greater breadth, a less rigid form to the path and sharper definition to the planted areas.

HOW TO VARY THE FLATNESS

Give your garden some contours with the plantings, concentrating on foliage plants, which give much longer value than flowers. Put hummocks of knee-high plants at the edge to create the illusion of a boundary. Within, grow large swathes of a few ground-cover species rather than a mosaic of single plants.

Fill any gaps with clumps of spring bulbs and, when you give the garden its major clean-up as summer comes, buy a couple of trays of yellow and orange nemesia or red and white antirrhinum to plant in two or three pools of colour. For

an eye-catching focus, grow one tall item. A variegated holly clips into a handsome column while the slow-growing conifer *Chamaecyparis obtusa* 'Nana Gracilis' makes a head-high globe composed of dark fans of foliage held upright. The cider gum (*Eucalyptus gunnii*) makes a blue-grey bush if you cut it back hard each spring. The leaves have a lovely rosy tinge when new, and if you pinch back the shoots during the summer more new leaves keep coming.

Instead of an evergreen, try *Cornus alba* 'Spaethii'; its cream-splashed leaves fall in autumn but the bold red upright stems make a brilliant winter display. Finely cut golden foliage is the chief delight of the elder (*Sambucus racemosa* 'Plumosa Aurea'); before the leaves fall in autumn they glow even more than usual round clusters of little red fruits.

PLANS FOR A SMALL TOWN GARDEN

Lack of space does not mean lack of options. An astonishing number of variations can develop from a handful of basic designs. In this square plot an imaginative combination of materials is used to make bold designs. Choose the pattern that pleases you and put your own signature on the garden with the plantings.

COLOUR WITHOUT PLANTS

The straight herringbone path is set with terracotta bricks which, as a link, are also used to edge the decorative diamond. An attractive ground pattern is made combining hard surface materials – of blue slate set on edge, cobbles and blue flint chips – set into mortar as a mosaic. Four matching plants balance the diamond; these could be either clipped bay or standard roses.

HOT SPOTS IN COOL BLUE

The emphasis on marking the path clearly is cleverly achieved by using a basket-weave pattern of brick paving among grey flagstones. The planting is minimal and it is the decorative pattern of surfacing that is the strongest design element. The two parallel areas of planting soften the straight lines of the path and the slightly raised brick planter adds variation in height.

GREEN AND GOLD

Honey-coloured paving is used to make the warm-toned floor in a neatly squared-up plan given interest by a promontory jutting into it. The large pot next to the side plantings provides a focal point from the window and door and breaks up rigid geometric lines.

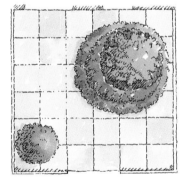

SIMPLE RINGS

The virtues of easy maintenance deriving from hard surfacing are apparent in this design of just two planted areas set within Cotswold coloured stone. The area of clear surface and the circular sweep of the greenery create a spacious air. Under the small tree are plants that create distinct tiers for vertical interest.

GROWING IN KNOTS

An angled path is defined by low hedges of box. A simple adaptation of the intricate formal knot garden makes a perfectly balanced triangular composition. Silvery-leaved santolina and a crimson-leaved berberis are the plants used within the hedging.

LIGHT AND SHADE A dramatic idea is based on the contrast of sharp lines and circles. Pots of coppery leaved cabbage palms (*Cordyline australis* 'Purpurea') stand on rippling circles of buff-coloured bricks which show up the movement of the spiky shadows under the summer sun.

into four by more box. Fill the sections with grey santolina for a cool scheme. For a warmer look use purple sage or variegated periwinkle with the box.

MODERN STYLE OUT OF TOWN

Away from town terraces, low-care small gardens are still easiest to create with a hard surface. A modern house allows a striking, simple design of bricks in concentric circles or rectangles, whichever suits the building's detail. A curved bay window or porch top, for example, suggests circles, while a square-cornered bay or porch calls for rectangles.

At the centre, plant a dramatic yucca, a fatsia, a New Zealand flax (*Phormium tenax*) with gold or orange stripes on its soaring sword-shaped leaves, or an evergreen *Mahonia japonica*, whose holly-like leaflets are paired on either side of long stalks, and whose yellow, scented flowers bloom in winter. Take care that the planting does not block the way to the front door. Push the pattern to one side of the garden area if the front door is at the centre of the house front.

Mortar the joints in the brickwork or fill them with fine gravel, matching the colour to the bricks. You could also lay porous plastic sheeting before the bricks to suppress weeds. An evergreen fringe of ferns and red-hot pokers (*Kniphofia caulescens*) softens the edges.

When the house walls are of brick that is too insistent in colour to repeat over the whole garden, space out the bands of brick with wide strips of gravel between. For a stone-built house, make the pattern of setts and encourage moss to fill the gaps. To lower the cost, space out the bands of setts with strips of gravel.

ADDING BEAUTY TO GRAVEL

Gravel as the main surface cuts down care but it looks dull on its own. In an informal country garden, inset it with stepping-stones meandering to pools of interest where groups of two or three boulders are fringed with smooth cobbles. Amid the main group of boulders make a bed just big enough for a dark cypress with a steel-blue prostrate juniper and pink and white heathers below it.

You can use millstones in place of groups of boulders, setting them down slightly or raising them up to give variation in contour. Alpines make a pretty green fringe round them and to increase the relaxed air, let alchemillas, pansies and helianthemums grow in the gravel.

seasons. If you decide to have a small bed, you need a plant such as an evergreen berberis or cotoneaster, with more than one period of interest, or a plant with the year-round sculptural quality of holly or the lobed-leaf × *Fatshedera lizei*.

STRONG PATTERNS FOR LONG-TERM PLEASURE

Lay two or three colours of tiles as a simple knot garden and its precision will give almost as much pleasure as a genuine knot, without the work of clipping and feeding. Interlaced squares or diamonds are easier to achieve than circles. Put a pot plant or a small bed with an evergreen where the motifs overlap to soften the effect. Neat grey hebes or santolinas look well with terracotta and blue tiles, while sarcococca or box give strong green to balance black and white tiles.

You can give variety of texture by using gravels of two or three different colours to fill in a pattern laid out in tiles or bricks that echo the colour of the building. If you are prepared to take on some hedge-clipping, you can make a pattern with low box hedging – perhaps a diamond set in a square – and fill in the enclosed sections with gravel. A standard rose, bay or holly in each section completes the formal design.

Start making such a garden by covering the ground with perforated plastic sheeting that suppresses weeds but lets water drain away. Make slits through which to plant the standards. Then cover the sheeting with the coloured gravels– which are not to be walked on except for clipping the plants; this is a garden for looking at rather than wandering in.

Simple parterres, in which an outline pattern of low hedging is filled with plants, require sprucing up a couple of times a year but give value with their permanence and satisfying geometry.

An easy plan to lay out and plant is a square outline of box hedging divided

LARGER GARDENS

THE CHIEF BOON of a larger front garden is that its plants do not have to work as hard as those in a small plot. The point of interest can shift from one part of the garden to another in a way that is not possible in a tiny space. Wallflowers need not follow bulbs, and penstemons and phlox follow roses, all in the same bed – with the problems of colour coordination that this raises. The garden still needs its strong framework of evergreen and other foliage plants, but these can provide the quiet, constant backcloth; they do not have to be the star performers as well.

A large front garden is not found only on substantial properties. When building land was not so scarce as it is now, little

RELAXED STYLE On this sloping site, shrubs and conifers in a range of shapes and a subtle blend of grey, green and purple ensure long-term interest. Angled steps and bountiful roses complete a well-composed garden.

country cottages, council houses, small town houses and modest surburban villas were often set well back from the road. The gardens of such houses now call for varied styles that are appropriate to today's needs as well as for the setting.

COTTAGE CHARMS UPDATED

The early tenants of country cottages were farm labourers and other rural workers who needed the garden for raising vegetables along with herbs for the pot. An artless miscellany of onions and leeks, edgings of strawberries and peas, a few cabbages tucked here and there and pyramids of runner beans, all flourishing among roses and hollyhocks (*Althaea rosea*), makes a charming picture still but may not be the dream garden of anyone whose country cottage is the base for daily commuting and all-too-short weekends for relaxing. Romantic rural images can be achieved with minimum effort, however, if you choose the right scheme.

Put your main effort into dressing up the door and keep the rest simple. Daisy-spangled grass flanking a crazy-paving path is charming in such a setting. Fringe

MOVABLE CLIMBERS

GROW CLIMBERS up a rendered house on trellis panels fixed to the wall with hinges at the bottom edge and secured by catches at the top. When the wall needs a fresh coat of paint, swing the top of the panel forward just enough to get a paint brush or roller in behind. The main stems at the base are scarcely disturbed.

OLD FAVOURITES In a larger garden an expanse of lawn with clipped hedges and shrubs makes a restful background for flowering plants. The roses and lupins, traditional cottage garden plants, flower year after year, maintaining the colourful show when the rhododendrons begin to fade.

TOOLBOX

ROOTING OUT WEEDS

LAWN ON PUBLIC VIEW in a front garden needs to be carefully tended, with weeds removed before they can spread. Push a weed-gripper straight down over a weed and as you pull the tool out, it tightens round the weed and removes it without disturbing the lawn.

it with purple, mauve, pink and white lavenders and plant a self-fertile apple tree for blossom and scent in late spring, fresh foliage and developing fruits to watch in summer, a crop in autumn and a shape full of character in winter; underplant a mature tree with bulbs. Plant up a wooden wheelbarrow with pelargoniums for summer colour.

If you want large areas of flowers, grow old favourites that appear every year – forget-me-nots, yellow daisylike doronicums, masses of peonies and poppies, spires of delphiniums, red valerian and blue cranesbills, spurred aquilegias, bell-flowered campanulas, honesty and love-in-a-mist. Contain them all with an edging of pinks and lady's mantle, and

thread the fence with a rose and a honeysuckle. Cut back the stems as blooms fade and pull out seedlings or pop them in beside their fellows to build up sizable drifts of each plant.

COUNTRY STYLE IN TOWN

This romantic, flowery image works in the gardens of old market towns and in leafy suburbs, too. Mix the perennials with evergreens for winter interest since there is no green countryside within view. Suitable candidates are dwarf conifers or the feathery green *Santolina rosmarinifolia*, and *Viburnum* × *burkwoodii* or a rhododendron, both of which carry their promising fat flower buds through the winter ready for generous displays in late

ON THE EDGE OF TOWN

Pleasing shapes and materials can be combined with tough but attractive plants in a variety of designs to suit suburbanites – and their cars.

AT THE FRONT of a standard edge-of-town house the challenge is to make a low-maintenance garden where the drive is integrated into the design rather than dominating it. Two principal objectives are to break up the dull square of grass and make a wide, welcoming space for alighting from the car and approaching the front door. The design can be given more interest with just a small change of level and a clear, bold shape.

Screening plants at the roadside give some privacy without masking the view of the door. In each scheme the planting focus is diagonally opposite the door so that it can be enjoyed from the house.

Balanced setting

The attractive curve over the door is echoed in the curve of lawn sweeping under the window, where the evergreen *Mahonia × media* 'Charity' gives constant interest. From the house, the gaze is drawn over the lawn to a balancing curve entered between two pots of clipped box. Within, there is a brick circle where colourful annuals spill out of a large pot. The screen of dark evergreens shuts out the road but the front of the house is not concealed from view.

Softened circles

Circles feature in the centrepiece of a sunken lawn, and in the raised area of solid brickwork that bites into it. This is the platform for the garden's focal point – an urn holding a dramatic, spiky phormium. A small tree at the edge of the drive adds height to the dense planting of shrubs which makes a softening fringe along the front fence and, for a good succession of colour, includes camellias, weigela and a mock orange.

Simply squared

This, the simplest of the options, draws its inspiration from the angular shapes of the window frames. The overlapped rectangles of the lawn, the square paving blocks and the straight clipped hedge add up to a unified linear design. This is softened by hummocks of hebe fronting the stretch of arching, leafy bamboos and spreading fatsias.

Clear angles

The shape of the bay window is repeated in the angled entrance to the lawn, which gains immensely in impact simply from being raised by the height of two courses of bricks. This raised edge is clear of planting. The plant interest focuses on a golden leaved tree, a robinia, set off by darker leaved rhododendrons, laurels and Mexican orange blossom.

WELL MATCHED Weathered paving is a good choice in front of this mellow stone-built house and as a background for foliage plants and pockets of flowers, with containers and staddle stones making sympathetic decoration. The random pattern of the paving merges gradually with the drive.

FORM AND FUNCTION A drive has to be solid and wide enough for cars, but does not mar the garden when it has an attractive surface pattern – as with these warm beige bricks set in fishscale panels with contrasting outlines.

spring. A lawn contributes a welcome stretch of green during winter, too.

A lawn comes into its own in a larger garden, where a green foreground flatters the house and is often regarded as the essential groundcloth on which to work the embroidery of plantings. A large lawn means work though, and hard surfacing can save much time and effort.

LARGE BUT LABOUR-SAVING

Labour-saving is not the same as bare and dull – far from it. Put together two or three principal features, plants that care for themselves and hard materials of lasting beauty and your garden will give constant pleasure. Since space is ample, you are free of the hunt for the miniature that tests the ingenuity of many gardeners.

Think on a large scale – full-size trees, spacious planters, big and bold paved areas. Use mainly large paving slabs, in a random pattern, and make an imperceptible rise from the sides to the centre so that water does not all run to the same point. A narrow rim of soil at the edge soaks up the water and fosters a luxuriant fringe of plants to soften the scheme.

Grow one or two trees well away from the house and put a very low wall, only two or three courses high, round each tree to avoid the difficulty of paving over thick root ridges near the trunk. Within the wall grow ferns, white-flowered lesser periwinkle and white-striped *Lamium maculatum* 'Album', but take care not to heap soil against the trunks.

To further the harmonious scheme the trees could be silver birches, magnolias, white lilacs or *Sorbus hupehensis*, the white-berried relative of rowan. To fringe the paving, grow low-care plants – lily-of-the-valley, Solomon's seal, variegated white honesty, Corsican hellebore and

Tiarella cordifolia for its foam of white flowers. Tulips, *Achillea* 'Moonshine' and potentilla will add lemon highlights.

PLANS FOR SUBURBAN GARDENS

Older suburban houses frequently have a long, narrow strip of front garden whose shape is a challenging one to make attractive. Some of the best solutions take a lead from grander, formal gardens and divide the strip into 'rooms'.

Buttresses of hedging running in pairs from the side boundary towards the path give a strong structure; and create distinct areas for different colour schemes. If you keep the hedges low, you can see all the rooms; raise them and some rooms are hidden, giving a chance to use uncoordinated, even clashing, colours.

Low clipped hedges grown in perfect squares among paving are another way of breaking up a long, narrow strip. Fill the squares with flowery perennials and low evergreens for a soft and pretty finish.

ABSORBING THE CAR

A larger garden usually has to provide space for a car, perhaps more than one, without looking like a car park. You cannot make the drive less intrusive by shrinking it. There must be enough width for you to open car doors on both sides without hitting a boundary wall or fence, or encountering a scratchy plant.

To reduce a drive's domination, give it an attractive surface, make the straight edges less noticeable from the house, and try to merge drive and garden in a satisfying overall design. As a surface, large areas of tarmac or concrete have no visual appeal and gravel tends to move. Paving offers better prospects, whether real or reconstituted stone, bricks or agreeably tinted clay or concrete blocks.

The way the surface is laid makes a big difference. Swirls of setts, or blocks shaped for laying in a fish-scale pattern are discreetly attractive. Combinations of materials work well: bands of brick set into paving, gravel or concrete break up the expanse and can echo a curve, angle or other detail from the house front.

You can make a gradual transition from drive to garden with pockets of low plants tucked up to the paving. Planting is the best way of all to dress up the drive. Even if it has to be straight-edged, you can blur the line with little promontories of hebe, aubrietia, *Stachys byzantina* and cistus spilling softly over the edge to help to absorb the drive into the garden.

ALONG THE SIDE Generous allowance is needed for car access but planting a raised bed alongside the drive is one way to mask its long straight edge without using too much of the ground space.

MERGING WITH GRAVEL Plants of gently sprawling habit beside the drive quickly spill out and dissolve rigid lines. These warm shades tone well with beige gravel and colour-washed bricks.

SIDE SHRUBS Flourishing cistus, a Japanese maple and *Euphorbia characias* add colour and texture to what would otherwise be a flat and stark area between the house and the drive.

INSPIRATION FROM

GREAT GARDENS

PACKWOOD HOUSE

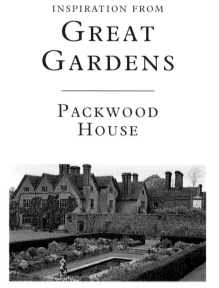

Elegant formality sets off a Tudor house.

Packwood House, wrapped in the glorious serenity of its gardens, lies south-east of Birmingham. The house, whose core dates from the late 16th century, was originally surrounded by the ancient Forest of Arden. It still lies in a vast spread of woodland but close to the house are formal gardens whose most renowned feature is the array of topiary where some of the statuesque, conical yews are thought to be more than 300 years old.

Far from excluding or blocking the way, the effect of a graceful open-work wrought iron gate is to entice; it draws the eye to what lies beyond. The example at Packwood House frames the grassy alley traversing the estate's most arresting feature, its topiary garden.

This is dominated by a mound at its southern end on which stands a single gigantic yew called the Master. Gathered about it are 16 more yews of impressive stature known as the Twelve Apostles and the Four Evangelists. Further away are about 80 more clipped yews, which are collectively christened the Multitude.

A tale widely believed is that the design and planting was carried out by the Fetherston family during the reign of Charles II as a representation of the Sermon on the Mount.

Recently, however, some garden historians have asserted that, though the Master, the Apostles and the Evangelists might well have been planted in Charles II's time, the space occupied by the Multitude was probably an orchard until the nineteenth century. Whatever the truth

GRACIOUS ENTRY An ornate 18th-century gate frames the formal avenue of clipped yews in the topiary garden at Packwood House.

behind the pieces of topiary, they go well with the garden's other long-established features. These include gazebos and terraces, a Carolean garden, a 20th-century sunken garden, herbaceous borders and purple-red walls. One wall is studded with recesses for bees and another has a flue along it to warm and ripen peaches.

FRAMING A FRONT ENTRANCE

An arch over an openwork gate dramatises the entrance to any garden, as well as being pretty in itself. A more rustic, less costly, alternative to wrought iron is a gate of open design in wood, completed by a pointed arch that echoes the shape of the porch over the front door. Jasmine (*Jasminum nudiflorum*), one of the most reliable of the winter-blooming shrubs, frames the gate with its yellow flowers from December to March. In summer, scented honeysuckle takes over.

Evergreen holly forms a stout hedge. *Ilex aquifolium* 'J.C. van Tol' has plentiful winter berries, and leaves with no spines to scratch passers-by. Winter-flowering *Cyclamen coum* adorns the base of the hedge. Beside the doorway, two cones of yew (*Taxus baccata* 'Fastigiata') enhance the symmetry and channel attention to the way in.

EMPHASISING A WARM WELCOME Sprays of winter-flowering jasmine grace the arch over the gate while, alongside, a dense holly hedge glowing with berries is underplanted with cyclamen.

DECORATIVE BOUNDARIES

ANY BOUNDARY, be it a tailored or carved hedge of rich green, a wall clothed with climbers or a fence softened with trailing plants, has a major role to play in your garden. It screens you from the outside world, creates welcome shade or a sheltered sun trap within and should be a perfect backcloth for the plants that grow near it. Whatever your practical needs – keeping children in or animals out, hiding ugly buildings nearby or making a frame for a view – there is no shortage of materials and means to choose from. Turn your back on the mundane and make your boundary work.

SPECIAL FEATURES

The autumn foliage of self-clinging Virginia creeper mingles with cream-rimmed ivy to weave a colourful network on a brick and trellis boundary.

THE DIVIDING LINE

GARDEN BOUNDARIES can do much more than simply mark the property line. Privacy and security are a priority for everyone, to shut unwanted visitors out, keep children and pets in and enjoy the garden without the eyes of the world looking in. But a boundary can also shelter plants and act as a windbreak or wind filter, it can screen an ugly view or direct the eye towards an attractive one, and it can be a feature in itself.

The boundary can be living or fabricated – a hedge, fence or wall – or a mixture. You can also tailor the boundary to suit the particular needs at various parts of the garden: erect a high, solid fence at the side to shut out the neighbours, plant a slow-growing hedge at the far end and keep an existing wall that extends from the house.

Homes with a view would gain more from a sunken boundary than from a raised one – as owners of grand gardens understood in the past. The view from stately homes was contrived so that it looked as if the owner's property extended as far as the eye could see. The ha-ha, a ditch with one steep side, kept strangers and animals out, without interrupting the view. Now ha-has are used more in zoos than in gardens because people tend to want to enclose their home. But privacy does not have to mean solid fences.

An informal screen of mixed shrubs or climbers on trellis creates an airy impression but gives a surprising degree of seclusion. You can combine a glimpse of the view and privacy with a formal boundary, too, perhaps by cutting circles like portholes out of a hedge or fence.

If you are lucky enough to have an old stone or mellow brick wall, enjoy it in all its glory, perhaps with just one or two espaliered or fan-trained fruit trees against it. But if you wish to disguise an ugly wall or fence, or use it as a backdrop for flower schemes, there is a host of suitable plants available to boost the design.

CLASSIC CHOICE One traditional boundary, still unbeatable, is a high wall made from local brick or stone with a border in front. Climbing roses and foliage make a pretty tracery on the mellow wall, while mauve irises and the bold, lime-green flower heads of *Euphorbia characias* enliven its base.

FENCES AND WALLS

◆

MANY ADVANTAGES go with a non-living boundary. It needs far less maintenance than a hedge. You have the option of growing plants up it if you wish and, if you do, it provides them with a firm support. A wall or fence also gives warmth and shelter and is reassuringly solid – it turns the garden into your own private haven.

Walls may give such a strong character to the garden that you want to reveal them rather than cover them with plants. Walls of local stone and old weathered bricks usually match the building materials of the house, linking indoors with outdoors. Stone walls may have crevices in which tough little plants will grow.

CONSIDER THE EFFECTS ON NEARBY PLANTS

Bear in mind that every solid boundary interacts with the wind. A semi-solid wall or fence that filters the wind is the kindest to your plants, as well as being the most stable. A solid wall or panelled fence creates shelter on the leeward side, but it increases wind turbulence in places.

The highest solid wall or fence you can put up now is 3 ft (1 m) fronting a road, or 6 ft 6 in (2 m) along any other boundary. Turbulence caused by a solid barrier 6 ft 6 in (2 m) high persists for at least ten times the height – a distance of about 65 ft (20 m) – on the leeward side with a strong swirl of wind created close to the barrier. A smaller eddy of wind occurs on the windward side. Delicate plants at the base of the barrier, on either side, may be flattened.

The traditional practice of surrounding a walled garden with trees combines the filtering effects of a hedge with the heat-storing capacity of the stones or bricks, which on cold nights protects plants growing against it.

USING TRELLIS FOR FENCES AND FEDGES

Fencing and trellis is now made in many variations on the standard panel and there are opportunities to make something more creative of the boundary.

Perhaps the most useful variation is a panel with a section of trellis on top, usually a 12 in (30 cm) strip. This lets you grow shrubs along the base and a climber

TRELLIS MADE TO ORDER You can commission a fence to specifications that fit your garden style, or even design one yourself. Dips or 'windows' prevent monotony and could frame a view. Decorative post tops add the finishing touch to trellis that is solidly constructed but airy.

such as jasmine, honeysuckle or clematis to make a swag of foliage and flowers at the top of the fence.

It is easier, and preferable for avoiding turbulence, to use a wind-filtering full-height trellis in the first place, even as an external boundary. And sometimes a flimsy screen that might topple over is more of a deterrent to thieves than a sturdy barrier which gives a foothold. A host of climbers can be planted on trellis, including variegated ivies, the delicate but vigorous *Clematis tangutica*, annual or everlasting sweet peas and canary creeper (*Tropaeolum peregrinum*).

A hybrid combination of fence and substantial plants is called a fedge. It may be a mix of an economical fence such as

TAKE CUTTINGS

MANY ROSES and shrubs can be easily increased by stem cuttings in autumn. As soon as the leaves fall, take stem cuttings 9 in (23 cm) long of new shoots that have just flowered. Retain two leaves at the top, and dip the bottom in hormone rooting powder. Plant the cuttings outdoors in 6 in (15 cm) of sharp sand and soil. Plant out the rooted new plantlets the following year during November.

chestnut paling with privet or beech, or it may be a thrifty curtain of ivy hiding angled metal stakes with horizontal wires running between them, or wire netting tied by wire to the same kind of stakes or stapled to chestnut or large poles. But a true fedge combines light, pretty fencing with beautiful plants such as tall and climbing roses or wall shrubs.

THE PERFECT PARTNER FOR TRELLIS

All climbing roses thrive on trellis. There is better air circulation here than against a house wall, and usually the soil is better in the garden than against the house.

The pink-flowered 'Queen Elizabeth' and yellow 'Chinatown' are good fedge choices because of their great vigour, but prune carefully as they have a tendency to flower at such a height that the blooms are out of sight. The hybrid musk roses 'Penelope' and 'Felicia' are less upright and are perfect in most respects.

A top variety for flower power combined with elegance and attractive foliage is *Rosa* × *odorata* 'Mutabilis'. The trellis provides a support for the plant to get a larger, more two-dimensional spread than is possible with a bush. The rose makes a large thicket and needs severe cutting back through the season to encourage the strong new purple shoots that are naturally growing along the trellis to produce more flowers. This is a multi-coloured rose, with flowers that change colour as they age. Single blooms open peachy yellow and are deep crimson as they fade. It is healthy and its only fault is a lack of scent.

CHOOSING THE MOST SUITABLE ROSE

As with all climbers, you should check a rose's ultimate height before buying. Where space is limited, choose moderate varieties such as 'Golden Showers', whose strong upright growth can almost be fan trained. Very strong growers like 'Seagull' and 'Rambling Rector', both white, are capable of growing arching stems of 30 ft (9 m) or more. They are suitable only for long expanses of trellis where you want a climber on the upper half to make a huge swag of flowers over shrubs or herbaceous plants below.

Look for the exciting new roses that have been bred to suit smaller gardens. Charmingly delicate adornments for an airy trellis are the miniature climbers – leafy, compact plants with masses of

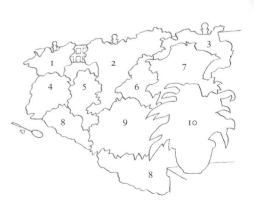

Open trellis gives extra height without gloom

BRINGING A PANEL FENCE TO LIFE

Where your garden flanks that of a neighbour, you usually want a solid fence. Lighten it with a trellis at the top and clothe it with plants.

A CLOSEBOARD FENCE 5 ft (1.5 m) high is tall enough for privacy, especially with 1 ft (30 cm) of trellis above it. Nail rigid netting to each post for climbers to reach the trellis – the mesh will not show once the plants have grown. A border 2-3 ft (60-90 cm) deep gives you room to plant shrubs and ground cover.

Start by choosing the climbers. Even for this north-facing fence, there is plenty of choice. The oval evergreen leaves of the coral plant give year-round cover. In late May or June, the globular orange-red flowers are on the point of coming out. Clematis deserves a central role and few varieties are lovelier than striped 'Nelly Moser'.

SCENT AND COLOUR ALL YEAR

A honeysuckle is on the post nearest the house so that its flowers scent the paved seating area nearby all summer long. It rambles through the viburnum in front, which flowers from November to March – there is always something to see and smell near the house. In the summer months, the pot-grown aspidistra marks the transition from paved area to lawn.

In front of the clematis are several shrubs that offer foliage interest. The Portugal laurel readily fills out within the shape you clip it to. The kerria provides apricot flowers in early summer and a sprinkling of blooms until its leaves fall in autumn. In June its leaves drape the fence behind the fatsia.

A mahonia bush fills in the corner. All mahonias have boldly shaped evergreen foliage; the variety 'Lionel Fortescue' has finer leaves than others and more leaflets to each leaf. In late autumn it thrusts out yellow flower racemes, making a splendid show at the end of the garden.

The carpeting cranesbill rapidly covers any bare soil, crowding out weeds. Its prettily veined flowers are in bloom throughout the summer.

Clematis and honeysuckle clothe the fence posts

Leafy evergreens break the stretch of bare wood.

Cranesbills add a summer-long ruff of ground cover

1. Coral plant (*Berberidopsis corallina*)
2. *Clematis* 'Nelly Moser'
3. Japanese honeysuckle (*Lonicera japonica* 'Aureoreticulata')
4. *Mahonia × media* 'Lionel Fortescue'
5. Portugal laurel (*Prunus lusitanica*)
6. *Kerria japonica* 'Variegata'
7. *Viburnum × bodnantense* 'Dawn'
8. Cranesbill (*Geranium × oxonianum* 'Claridge Druce')
9. *Fatsia japonica*
10. *Aspidistra elatior* (in pot)

A FEELING OF SPACE As an external boundary, trellis allows you glimpses of the view beyond. A border of low evergreens, including hellebore (*Helleborus foetidus*) with its two tones of green, gives a little privacy without excluding the wider horizons of the outside world.

vertical or horizontal wooden overlap is quick, easy and cheap. Supported by wooden or concrete posts, it shuts out the world effectively and is a barrier against wind. But its inflexibility can be a problem, as is plain to see on any day after a severe storm, which pushes the fence down. Solid panels resist the wind but offer no escape routes for it.

MAKE MORE OF YOUR FENCES

Consider some less resistant options. Cut heather stems have been used for centuries as a material for making brooms and for weaving into hurdle-type screening panels. The soft, pinkish brown wood is a useful colour in the garden, and the texture is interesting too. It is the perfect background to a border of heathers and conifers and a collection of foliage shrubs including bamboos.

Unpainted post and rail fencing looks rustic and informal, and it offers just enough support for a flowering hedge such as the purple-leaved *Berberis thunbergii*. Another choice is *Rosa rugosa*, with its healthy foliage, large single flowers in pink and white, and bright autumn hips. It makes a stable hedge up to waist height, but grows higher if you give it space to develop a broader base.

If you paint the posts and rails, making a more decorative feature, either herbaceous foliage plants or low-growing shrubs will make a sufficient decoration. Herbaceous need not mean short. Some grasses, such as miscanthus, are capable of making some 6 ft (1.8 m) of growth in a season, and the brown stems and leaves of many are attractive in the first months of winter before the weather begins to damage them.

HIDING HOMELY FEATURES

Wire strained between stout posts – called post and wire – makes a discreet support for a developing hedge or to train climbers against. Be sure that the wires are visible and that none is low enough to trip over. The same applies to post and chain fencing.

Concrete panels, in which concrete uprights hold horizontal slabs that slide into place, are very strong and secure but need immediate creative covering with trellis or a network of climbing plants such as jasmine or a Chilean potato-tree.

Chain-link fencing can be improved beyond recognition with a planting that covers it. It can even support herbaceous climbers in the summer, with golden

small flowers, clothed with foliage and blooms right down to the base. The orange 'Laura Ford' is typical in that it reaches a height of about 6 ft (1.8 m) and spreads about half that distance.

INSTANT BOUNDARIES

The joy of a fence is its immediacy. In a few days you can choose it, buy it and erect it, gaining instant privacy. New wooden fences tend to come in a rather lurid ginger, but this gradually mellows and plants in front of the wood soon

mask the colour. Once the fence is put in place, most gardeners want to plant it with climbers or shrubs. There are a few self-supporting climbers such as ivy, Virginia creeper and climbing hydrangea that can scale the fence themselves but they make maintenance of the panels difficult. It is best to attach horizontal supporting wires to the posts. A fan of canes fixed to the wires can support and train a host of plants, including fruit trees.

If your aim in putting up a fence is to block out the world and the wind, then

WOODEN FENCES TO
SUIT STYLE AND POCKET

Fences can be peep proof or see-through, head high or knee high, wooden or wire, painted or stained. With most garden centres offering only a limited selection it is wise to look at specialist shops and mail order catalogues for other options.

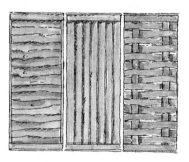

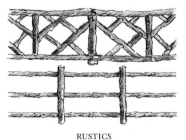

PICKET

The sight of white picket fencing, the tops pointed or more intricately shaped, conjures up visions of New England or country cottage gardens. Picket fencing looks good anywhere and need not be white. Sawn timber can be stained and preserved, in which case it will need less maintenance than painted fences.

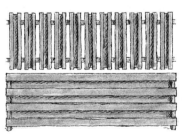

RUSTICS

Post and rail fencing (above) is easy to put up, and you can vary the rail and post spacing. It gives little in the way of shelter, but makes a useful boundary marker. For more interest, have larch or other attractive wooden poles (top) constructed to the post and rail design of your choice.

INTERFERENCE FENCING

Horizontal or vertical boards fixed to uprights with gaps between give a sturdy fence without blocking the view. When the panels alternate on both sides of the posts, they give a feeling of security and privacy but allow wind to filter through and give glimpses beyond the garden. The rails come in a range of lengths.

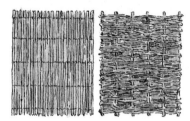

BAMBOO AND WATTLE

A bamboo screen (above left) gives a natural impression with a hint of the Orient. You can also grow a screen with bamboo plants. Suitable varieties range from dwarfs to tall, clump-forming kinds. Wattle fencing (above right) suits rural areas, where the woven stems blend into the surroundings. It is very sympathetic to wild flowers and cottage gardens and makes a good windbreak, but is not cheap or long lasting.

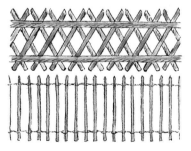

PALINGS AND LATTICE

Chestnut paling (above) is ideal as a temporary fence when planting hedges because it looks better than wire alone and is quite cheap. It is sold in rolled-up lengths. Softwood lattice (top) combines the virtues of post and rail and trellis, making a secure screen that filters the wind and enhances the look of the garden.

TRELLIS

Available usually in brown, green and white and in square or diamond pattern, trellis is sold in panels with a range of heights. You can order a bespoke version to be made up with your own design and decorative posts (top). You can also buy panels with arched, open or even fan-shaped tops. Trellis makes an attractive boundary in its own right but creative choices expand once you start growing plants up it.

CLOSEBOARD FENCING

Closeboard gives total privacy but needs to be softened with plants. Horizontal overlap (above left) is economical, but often has skimpy overlap; check for sound construction. Vertical overlap (above centre) is more expensive, but usually better made. The vertical boards are either feather-edged or square, which is the most expensive. Interwoven panels (above right) have timber strips which give a basket-weave pattern that filters the wind and is just see-through.

CREATING SWAGS OF COLOUR A two-tone climbing rose will transform a metal post and cable fence that marks the boundary between two gardens. The spectacular 'Climbing Masquerade', a reliable variety with a long flowering period, smothers the post before curving out to clothe the cables.

hops and everlasting peas the best choices. The purple-flowered *Clematis × jackmanii*, which can be trimmed almost to ground level in winter, makes a perfect companion to thread through the golden leaves of the hop.

Wrought-iron railings often mark the boundary of the front garden in a city dwelling. They are usually attractive in themselves and need only a little light planting in troughs or a shallow bed.

MAKING USE OF SMALL SHRUBS AND CLIMBERS

Many wall shrubs that need just a little support give their best against a fence, if the spot is not too draughty. Some wall shrubs are free standing, such as *Garrya elliptica*, while others, including *Solanum crispum*, sprawl just a little too much to be acceptable without something to hold them in place. In the early years train the main shoots of a solanum in the right direction, but after that just cut away the shoots growing away from the fence when the multitude of mauve flowers is over. A little pruning keeps the shrub fresh and young with successive growths to give the maximum cover. In winter it looks less appealing, so you may prefer the garrya, or you can grow both.

BE FIRM WITH CLIMBERS

If the original climber is getting too top heavy, cut it back ruthlessly. Avoid the temptation to plant another climber to cover the unclothed base. It will follow the first to the top of the fence in a rush to find the light, leaving you with the same problem. This is why wall shrubs often make better screens than climbers, whose nature is to grow fast to the top of the support, where their flowering and new growth happens out of sight.

When you combine climbers, choose those that can be maintained with ease. Climbing roses and clematis look lovely together, but make sure the clematis is one that can be pruned to near ground level each winter, as for example the late-flowering *Clematis viticella* or *C. texensis* hybrids can. Pruning and training are a nightmare when brittle clematis stems and thorny roses have to be separated.

Tangles of growth at the top of a fence, especially a light one such as trellis, can make it unstable and more likely to be damaged in gales. Avoid the very thickest honeysuckles such as *Lonicera japonica* 'Halliana', which is evergreen, and use deciduous sorts instead.

KNOW THE VIRTUES OF FACING NORTH OR SOUTH

The way that a wall or fence is positioned influences what grows well near it. One that runs from east to west has a south and a north-facing side. A wall to the north of the house faces south, which can be a big advantage. Many wonderful plants thrive in the warmth radiated and reflected by the wall. But on the north

PLANTING UP RAILINGS

If you are lucky enough to have ornamental railings at the front of your garden, draw attention to their decorative detail with some judicious planting. In a back garden, use plants to fill in the gaps in the ironwork and give more privacy.

IRON RAILINGS, some dating back to Georgian times when they first became popular, are more common in towns and cities than in rural areas. They are expensive to install, but give a garden a timeless, classic look. Formal planting schemes suit the geometric precision of railings. Climbing plants use the slender bars as supports, or you can make a narrow border in front of the railings and put in low-growing seasonal plants.

Railings require more maintenance than fences. Paint them frequently to prevent rust from getting a hold – and peeling paintwork quickly makes railings look shabby instead of smart.

Majestic spikes

The elegant semi-evergreen bear's breeches (*Acanthus mollis*) shows to advantage when planted alone. From July to September its spires of purple-and-white flowers are out, and for the rest of the year you can enjoy its large, deeply cut, glossy green leaves.

Summer glow

Humulus lupulus 'Aureus' twines up the railings. Cut back *Spiraea japonica* 'Goldflame' to encourage new, bright foliage. The cream flowers of *Philadelphus coronarius* 'Aureus' give off a scent of oranges; trim it to twice the height of the spiraea.

Purple splendour

In August and September, the feathery flower heads of *Liatris spicata* are at their best, set off by the darker leaves of the grapevine (*Vitis vinifera* 'Purpurea') and *Weigela florida* 'Foliis Purpureis'. While the colours harmonise, the shapes contrast – the stiff stems of the perennial liatris alternate with the bushy, arching forms of weigela, in turn interwoven with snaking vine tendrils. The weigela shrubs bring the bonus of rose-pink flowers as spring turns to summer.

A duet of roses

Few plant types offer such diversity of form as roses. Plant the ground-covering rose 'Surrey' (in the modern County series) to nestle at the feet of the faithful old-timer *Rosa* 'Albertine'. This triumph among ramblers looks its best in June, when the coppery buds burst into scented blooms. When it is not in flower, enjoy its vigorous growth and red young leaves, but beware the sharp thorns.

- *Hydrangea petiolaris* has lacy heads of small white flowers in summer.
- *Jasminum nudiflorum* has bright yellow flowers in winter and early spring.

WIDE CHOICE
FOR SOUTH-FACING WALLS

The southern aspect encourages early growth, but the risk of possible frost damage is offset by the advantage of a full growing season with good ripening of woody shoots in most years.

This gives the maximum flowering potential among plants from warmer climates such as fremontodendrons, with their flamboyant yellow saucer-shaped flowers, and the equally showy campsis, grown for its trumpet-shaped orange or red blooms.

- Ceanothus has racemes of blue flowers in late spring, early summer or autumn, depending on the type.
- *Chimonanthus praecox* bears fragrant, winter flowers that are cup-shaped and pale yellow with a purple centre.
- Pineapple broom (*Cytisus battandieri*) produces racemes of pineapple-scented yellow flowers in early to mid summer.
- Mimosa (*Acacia dealbata*) produces round, fragrant bright yellow flowers in spring. It is not very hardy.
- *Rosa banksiae* 'Lutea' bears fully double yellow flower rosettes in spring.

PLANTING AN
EASTERN OR WESTERN ASPECT

A wall or fence that runs north to south will have west-facing and east-facing sides. Of these the west-facing position is the easier to plant. Protected from easterly winds which are biting in winter, it is a relatively mild position, but not baking hot in summer like the south.

A west-facing wall supports a wide range of plants, though they may flower earlier than normal.

- False acacia (*Robinia hispida*) has hanging racemes of pink flowers in late spring and early summer.
- The Chilean potato-tree (*Solanum crispum* 'Glasnevin') bears clusters of lilac-purple flowers in summer.
- Wisteria produces drooping racemes of scented, pea-like mauve flowers in late spring or early summer.
- Honeysuckle (*Lonicera*) is grown for its deliciously fragrant flowers.
- *Jasminum officinale* has fragrant white flowers in summer and autumn.

The east-facing position can be cold and needs hardy plants. Since it receives

BEST PLANTS

ALPINES FOR
WALL CRANNIES

Alpines that by nature anchor deeply in rock crevices, scree, or pockets of gritty soil, are perfect for adorning a wall.

- *Aethionema* 'Warley Rose': evergreen sub-shrub with pink flowers in spring.
- *Alyssum montanum*: perennial with fragrant yellow flowers in summer.
- *Campanula poscharskyana*: spreading perennial with soft blue, starry summer flowers.
- Maiden pink (*Dianthus deltoides*): evergreen, mat-forming perennial with white or pink flowers in summer.
- *Erinus alpinus*: semi-evergreen perennial with purple, pink or white flowers in late spring and summer.
- *Parahebe lyallii*: semi-evergreen prostrate shrub with pink-veined white flowers in early summer.
- *Ramonda myconi*: evergreen perennial with blue or white flowers in late spring and summer.
- Saxifrage (*Saxifraga cotyledon*): evergreen perennial with yellow flowers in early summer.
- *Sempervivum montanum*: evergreen, mat-forming perennial with dark leaf rosettes and red flowers in summer.

PLANTING ON A WALL Tumbling grey-green aubrietia dresses the wall with purple flowers every spring while cushions of springy, white-flowered candytuft (*Iberis sempervirens*) bulge over the top. Both are evergreen.

side of the wall is an area that is shaded for most of the day. On a boundary this can cause problems if your new wall or fence shades your neighbour's sun-loving plants. In your own garden, regard shade as a positive boon. It creates a cool area to grow woodland plants. Indeed, they will grow in the shade of a wall far better than in most areas under trees which are too dry and full of tree roots.

A position on the cool north of a wall or fence causes plants to start into growth late in the season, which is a bonus since they are less likely to have their new shoots damaged by late frosts.

CHOOSING PLANTS
FOR NORTH-FACING WALLS

The colder north wall is the best place for frost-sensitive plants because temperatures fluctuate little and, after a frost, the thaw comes slowly. The morning sun on some frosted plants, particularly camellias, can do great damage, especially to flower buds and new growth.

Several intriguing plants are suited to a north-facing wall.

- Silk-tassel bush (*Garrya elliptica*) has grey-green catkins dripping from its branches from midwinter to early spring.

sun only until midday, unless skewed partly to the south, sun-loving plants do not thrive. Nor do plants that are sensitive to frost damage. But an east-facing wall or fence suits some plants, including clematis which suffers in full sun.

● *Clematis* 'Ernest Markham' has large single flowers with magenta petals and chocolate anthers.

● The flowering quince (*Chaenomeles japonica*) bears many orange-red flowers in spring, then spherical yellow fruits.

● *Kerria japonica* 'Pleniflora' has large, ball-like yellow flowers in spring.

CREATING IMAGINATIVE WALL DESIGNS

Walls give a garden a sense of maturity and stability, even when new. When you start a garden from scratch, few features look more satisfying than a wall made from the same natural stone as the house and other buildings of the region, or from the traditional local brick. And if you are not wedded to the standard form, there is plenty of choice.

Bricks are attractive in a honeycomb pattern that leaves a gap between each brick and the next. This way of laying bricks makes a strong boundary, filters wind and allows some of the outside world to be seen. You can incorporate honeycomb sections into the upper courses of a standard wall to give variety. Achieve a similar effect by building old roof tiles or drainage pipes into the wall to create decorative motifs.

Concrete screening walls have readymade gaps and motifs. They are the cheapest and easiest type of wall to build and they suit modern houses. The blocks are usually stack bonded (one directly above another) between concrete uprights but can also be used singly as an occasional feature let into a brick wall. They then give glimpses beyond the garden without loss of privacy.

ENJOYING TRADITIONAL BEAUTY

Reconstituted-stone walling, made in sections and fixed with an adhesive rather than mortar, creates a naturallooking wall that is easy for a reasonably handy person to set up. Stone does not always sit happily next to brick, so give thought to the overall effect.

Dry-stone walls, with their timeless beauty, best suit the areas of the country where they are used as field boundaries. Making such a wall is not a job to take on

GARDEN OF CONTRASTS Dark-painted trellis stands out against the warm-coloured wall, a contrast echoed in the planting. Yellow lupins look even brighter against the purple globes of allium, while irises echo both colours. Cranesbills and mixed herbs prettily fill the front of the border.

BLOOMS AGAINST THE BRICK Tone down the harshness of new brick by attaching trellis and growing a rose such as 'Climbing Pompon de Paris', which makes a wonderful display in June. The trellis alone, whether in its natural colour or stained, improves the appearance of the brick.

FILLING THE CRACKS A covering of moss adds even greater charm to a retaining wall of local stone. Choose flowers to suit the moist, shady bank and plant up the crevices as the wall is built – primroses form neat clumps.

MERGING A WALL AND HEDGE Grow a ruff of ivy over a stone boundary. Use rope swags to train the plant, clipping it ruthlessly to the shape that you want. Ivy is vigorous enough to grow back with renewed verve.

some that incorporate wall fountains. Some are made of reconstituted stone, others of terracotta or plastic. Give character with a Gothic grotto consisting of a pointed-arch niche in an ivy-covered wall and set with grotesque masks and gargoyles, carefully lit at night. Although such wall ornaments take a while to weather, fast-growing climbers quickly soften the outlines and make the feature look established.

USING PLANTS TO TRANSFORM A WALL

When you have a wall that is not an asset to the scene, convert it into an enviable feature with plants that give it full cover. The best plants are climbers such as Virginia creeper (*Parthenocissus quinquefolia*), Boston ivy (*P. tricuspidata*), ivy, *Schizophragma hydrangeoides*, *Hydrangea petiolaris* and the wall shrub pyracantha.

Clothe an ugly brick wall with ivy and then fix white, pale blue or natural wood-stained trellis over it. Stand chimney pots or tubs and urns of plants in front of the trellis for an additional feature.

PLAYING TRICKS WITH WALLS

Walls offer the best chance to use mirrors in the garden. Fix one on the wall of a small courtyard garden, grow ivy round it and the garden all of a sudden becomes twice the size.

Much can be done with paint. If you are skilled, re-create a scene from a holiday location or, if this sounds a little too ambitious, paint one single stretch of colour. A pale masonry paint, perhaps pink or stone-coloured, gives a new background to place your plants against.

Be bolder still and paint the wall yellow. This might be too startling for large areas, but is perfect for boundary walls enclosing patios which are as much part of the house as part of the garden. A yellow wall looks sunny all year and pushes purple foliage and red flowers to the height of their brilliance.

Follow the idea into pastels and use a soft mauve or lavender. This could be the basis of a pastel flower scheme of blue and lilac, or a backcloth for a white and grey border at the foot of the wall, the hint of colour making the monochrome planting even more ethereal.

A deep-blue boundary wall is the perfect home for a collection of sun and star wall plaques in Mediterranean style, and also for a border of sunny flowers in citrus tones of yellow and orange.

without the help of an expert. For a greater opportunity to plant, have a low double-skin wall with soil between. According to the height and width, a range of plants will grow. The lower and wider the walls the more choice you have; tall, narrow beds dry out fast and support only a few alpines. If the two walls share a concrete foundation, leave weep holes for water to drain away.

ADORNING THE WALL TO ADD CHARACTER

Whatever the style of a wall and the material it is made from, you probably want to dress it up with plants or ornaments. There is a wide range of heads and wall plaques available, including

HEDGES FOR NATURAL CHARM

HEDGES ARE POPULAR for their attractive appearance and because they are usually cheaper than fencing or walls. They demand less thought in planting, even though trimming requires more skill to make the most of the hedge as a decorative contribution to the garden.

All hedges are excellent wind filters, allowing some air through but sheltering plants – and people – from icy blasts. Most deciduous hedges have close to the ideal proportions of three-fifths solid material and two-fifths air space. The shelter hedges give garden plants is vital. It reduces damage to them and slows down the water evaporation from leaves that is increased by drying winds. The plants need less watering and the warmer, sheltered environment encourages growth.

REDUCING THE WIND FACTOR

In exposed gardens, especially near the coast, the prerequisite for making a garden of any kind is to establish a shelter belt of trees and shrubs that breaks the wind. Exceptionally windy gardens will benefit from a series of windbreaks to give a fair chance for plant growth.

Make up the outer windbreak from an informal, mixed belt of evergreen and deciduous plants of varied heights and vigour. The ragged profile filters wind much more effectively than a closely clipped hedge, which causes a certain amount of turbulence. The direction of a hedge in relation to the prevailing wind is important. The hedge is more effective when you plant it nearly at right angles to the wind. However, the individual locality is always a factor in the usefulness of any windbreak.

A hedge planted across a slope tends to trap cold air as it travels down the hillside. This may cause problems for plants in the garden immediately above the hedge, but it gives protection from frost damage to plants in the garden below.

MAKING PREPARATIONS

Think carefully about how a hedge is going to affect views, how easy it is to clip and how often it needs clipping.

If the hedge is to stand between you and a neighbour, check who is going to cut each side. You may need to put up a

---

BEST PLANTS

RELIABLE FORMAL HEDGES

These frequently seen hedges are popular for a reason – they are easy to grow and tolerate clipping.

• Box (*Buxus sempervirens* 'Suffruticosa'): a low-growing evergreen that needs trimming twice a year.

• Bush honeysuckle (*Lonicera nitida*): tiny glossy evergreen leaves; trim in summer. Good for small gardens.

• Common beech (*Fagus sylvatica*): the best deciduous hedge on well-drained soils, retaining foliage all year.

• Common hornbeam (*Carpinus betulus*): though deciduous, most of the rusty-brown leaves are retained through the winter on clipped hedges.

• Holly (*Ilex aquifolium*): excellent evergreen hedge. It grows slowly, but is long lived. Trim in late summer.

• Lawson cypress (*Chamaecyparis lawsoniana*): a huge range of evergreen shapes and colours.

• Privet (*Ligustrum ovalifolium*): its green, golden and variegated forms are evergreen except in the worst winters.

• Yew (*Taxus baccata*): ideal, long-lived evergreen hedge, well suited to topiary. Trim once a year in late summer.

EVERGREEN BACKDROP For a smooth, sleek curtain of colour, yew is hard to better. Trimmed to a peak, the hedge draws extra attention to the magnolia in front, and the light flowers are etched out of the dark drape.

TRIMMING AND TOPIARY Carrying a clipped theme from hedge through to terrace gives the garden a strong style. Neat spheres of box flank the approach to a carpeting lawn backed by holly trimmed into dramatic scoops.

of varieties ready for planting is greatest then. You can buy bare-rooted deciduous plants far more cheaply than the specimens in containers, which are all that is available in summer. Buy evergreens such as holly, laurel and escallonia from a reliable nursery as container-grown specimens or root-balled, with a ball of soil wrapped in hessian or plastic.

THE IDEAL HEDGE PLANTS

Select an appropriate hedging plant to ensure success. The ubiquitous Leyland cypress (× *Cupressocyparis leylandii*), for example, is widely available but you should think hard before choosing it. It rapidly achieves a height of 6 ft (1.8 m) but does not stop there, and requires very close clipping from an early age to make a small, dense hedge. Plain green forms of Lawson cypress are more suitable in small gardens.

Holly copes with some shade and pollution and so is good for an urban garden, but it requires formative pruning to ensure dense growth. Choose privet for year-round cover, remembering that its hungry roots can deprive neighbouring plants of water and nutrients. Do not plant yew within reach of livestock as the dried leaves and branches are poisonous to them. The berries will also poison humans, but there will be little fruit on well-trimmed hedges.

There is no need to stick to green for hedging. Copper or purple-leaved beech seedlings offer an unusual alternative to common beech, and are no more expensive. To accentuate the colour, plant a tapestry hedge of purple and green.

Osmanthus × *burkwoodii* is a slow-growing evergreen hedge worth planting for its sweetly scented flowers in late spring. As a garden shrub it is rather dull, but admirable as a fragrant, trimmed background. Clip it after flowering.

Cherry laurel (*Prunus laurocerasus*) has glossy leaves and fast growth. Laurel is one of the best large evergreen hedging plants. Clip in summer, using secateurs, as hedge trimmers leave unsightly ragged leaf edges. Grow it as a semiformal hedge or trimming can be daunting.

ENSURING SUCCESS WITH FORMAL HEDGES

To make a smooth, dense curtain of colour, a formal hedge must be clothed with branches down to ground level. These develop only when the plants are trimmed from a very early age. For this

TOOLBOX

CORDLESS TRIMMERS

EVEN EASIER TO USE than mains electric or petrol-driven hedge trimmers are cordless ones. The battery-powered trimmers work for about 45 minutes before they need recharging. They are safer, with no cables to get in the way, light to hold and a manageable size.

temporary boundary of chicken wire until the hedge grows. Where it is difficult to reach the back of the hedge for cutting, high fence panels may be best.

Bear in mind that a hedge is a row of shrubs – a fact often forgotten when it comes to planting and preparation. These shrubs are to be in place for many years and need thorough soil preparation if they are to be given the best chance of growing successfully.

Clear the site of weeds in summer, dig it in late summer incorporating plenty of organic matter, and plant in October or November. Mid to late autumn is the best time to plant most shrubs: the choice reason, start off with small, young plants. Apart from being cheaper, they have a chance to establish a widespread root system that anchors the hedge soundly. It can then withstand the rocking that wind causes on the block of top growth.

PRODUCTIVE TRIMMING

Conifers cannot stand such hard trimming just after planting as deciduous shrubs. Stems need clipping little and often as they develop. But leave the leading shoot of each conifer unpruned until the hedge is above the desired height, then cut it off about 3 ft (1 m) below the top. In subsequent years, the top of the hedge should fill out with sideshoots.

Apart from this, do not be impatient for an evergreen or deciduous hedge to reach its full height. A stronger and more stable hedge results from trimming to encourage bushy growth. A tall, spindly hedge does not give privacy or stop the wind, and it will probably need some support to prevent it from blowing over.

From the start, shape the hedge to be wider at the bottom than the top. This makes it stable and helps to stop heavy snowfalls opening up the top. More light reaches lower parts of the hedge, encouraging sturdy growth. It is a particularly appropriate shape for conifers, as it echoes their natural growth habit.

WHEN AND HOW TO TRIM

To create an even profile, make a pair of wooden frames that can be set over the hedge as guides while you cut. Join the frames with strings to run along the top edges of the hedge.

Hedge trimming is laborious, but it is far easier if done regularly. Privet and bush honeysuckle need trimming about once a month during the growing season to keep a neat finish. Established conifer hedges need trimming once a year, but look better if cut more often. Once a year is enough for yew, box and holly.

Hornbeam and beech both retain their dead leaves through the winter if trimmed yearly in late summer when the flush of growth is finished.

Nothing works as well as shears on soft growths like those of bush honeysuckle. An irregularly shaped evergreen hedge with large leaves needs trimming with secateurs. You are aiming to take out whole shoots and want to avoid cutting a leaf in half as the remnant will go brown. When you keep a hedge no taller than shoulder height, trimming presents no

FORMALITY WITH A DIFFERENCE Golden buttresses are spectacular against the more familiar dark green and reinforce the imposing style of a yew hedge. Yew is ideal for such treatment – its small evergreen leaves tolerate close trimming, which is best done once a year in late summer.

TIDY NEED NOT MEAN STRAIGHT Closely planted columnar forms of Lawson cypress introduce curves and character into a formal hedge, accentuated by attentive clipping. The dark conifers are brightened by mats of aubrietia at the foot of the hedge and by flowering cherry above.

EXAGGERATING THE CURVES Formal meets informal with the scalloped edge of cherry plum (*Prunus cerasifera* 'Pissardii'). The plant is more often seen as a tree but there are purple or green selections for hedges. Left untrimmed, it bears white flowers in February and March.

HEDGING ON STILTS A hedge need not be solid at the base. The technique of interlacing branches, called pleaching, requires different plants from hedging shrubs. Lime, which is pliable, is most often used. A pleached hedge is more a feature than a barrier, though it can serve both purposes.

SCULPTURAL QUALITY Once you master the art of clipping and pleaching, exploit your skills to the full. The hedge, pleached halfway up, and the green arch over the entrance look even better in winter, a rare achievement.

problem. Use electric or petrol-driven trimmers for ease on firm and twiggy growths. Always bear safety points in mind, preferably with someone else standing by to help and pass you tools.

🔹 Never use electric hedge trimmers in the rain or on a wet hedge.

🔹 Renew the cable if the insulation is damaged. Use a circuit breaker (RCD).

🔹 If a hedge is too tall to reach from the ground, work from a platform of scaffold boards between trestles or stepladders.

🔹 Never use trimmers with one hand; it is easier and safer to move the platform.

🔹 Never overreach when cutting.

HOW TO SHAPE THE TOP

There are many ways to brighten up the neat, even texture of a formal hedge. Enjoy the scope to express your individuality through topiary skills. The simplest form of topiary is variations in the height of the hedge in places, giving a castellated top. Because this requires regular, matching notches along the top, measure carefully first and mark out where you will let the hedge grow taller. You can mark with tape held by clothes pegs, or for greater accuracy, make a template from wooden battens that includes at least one upper area and two lower. Lay it against the hedge and move it along as you cut. The upper areas will need only light trimming to take the tips off the shoots and encourage bushiness.

The higher areas of the hedge do not have to be hard edged or regular. They could be specific shapes, perhaps triangles or semicircles. You can make sure they rise in the right places to block out unsightly views or objects.

Another straightforward top is a crown. Find four or five strong shoots growing together in the centre of the hedge at the top. Tie them together at the base, then tie them to a vertical cane as they grow upwards. When they are tall enough, take the tips and bend them gently round to the base, where they meet the hedge. Tie them securely, to give four or five loops. In subsequent years trim the foliage closely so that each shoot makes a dense ring.

MORE AMBITIOUS SHAPES

The easiest way to create topiary shapes is to make the basic form with chicken wire or to buy a ready-made frame and attach it firmly to a stout stake driven through the hedge in the desired spot.

Tie strong shoots to this frame in the correct position on the underside. They will grow through the frame to fill the upper surface. In time the frame will be covered. Trim the topiary a short distance outside the wire to keep it concealed.

Peacocks are a traditional shape for topiary, but you can cut more quirky, individual decorations – perhaps a ship or a car – into the top of an established hedge. Use clothes pegs to fix coloured tape in the desired outline. Push canes horizontally through the hedge to mark a matching outline on the other side, then peg tape in place on the second side. Clip down to the marked outline on both sides and then across the width. You can leave some taller features, such as the funnels of a ship or locomotive, in the middle.

PLEACHING A HEDGE

For pleaching – which involves training adjoining plants horizontally to form a hedge on sticks – you have to plant large specimens, but fewer are required. Put in a row of sturdy stakes tall enough to reach the top of the completed hedge, with horizontal wires fixed to them.

The shoots are trained sideways in the manner of an espaliered fruit tree. The distance between the horizontal tiers is usually 1-2 ft (30-60 cm). The height of the lowest wire depends on how much open space you want below the hedge. Place a further stake or scaffolding pole at the end of the hedge for extra strength. Run the top wire diagonally down to the ground and peg it in securely.

Under this hedge on legs, erect a white picket fence or a painted trellis supported by posts with carved finials on top. For a greener lower storey, plant the fence with shade-loving plants such as hellebores, periwinkle and cyclamen. This gives a definite boundary that is original and allows views of the outside world.

PATTERNS AND MESSAGES

Patterns cut into the side of a hedge give it individuality. They require less skill than pleaching and are definitely more vandal-proof than a row of peacocks on top of a boundary hedge.

You can even vary the pattern on each side of the hedge. On the inside it could be simple geometric shapes cut in relief or a favourite saying spelt out across the garden, and on the outside it could be the house number or name. This decoration works best on very fine-leaved hedges such as yew, bush honeysuckle

PLEACHING YEAR BY YEAR

RAISING A HEDGE on 'stilts' by pleaching gives it a new character. Glossy-leaved lime (*Tilia cordata*) is the best plant to use. Make the framework taut and strong as it must support the trees for at least three years until they are fully established.

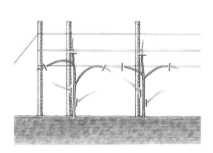

1. In the first winter after planting, tie the young trees securely to their upright supports. Tie any suitably placed branches to the horizontal training wires and cut off the end few inches to encourage bushiness. Remove all branches below the lowest horizontal branch, as close to the main trunk as possible. Shorten the leader (main vertical stem) so that it is just below the next horizontal wire. Even if it does not reach the wire, trim it back by a few inches to encourage strong new growth.

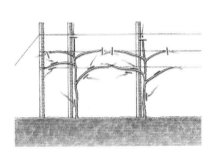

2. After a year, the first trained horizontal branches will have extended their growth. If they overlap, twist the stem tips together. Remove or severely shorten sideshoots to keep a clean framework of branches. There should now be two more branches to tie down to the second horizontal wire. Treat these in the same way as the ones the previous year, by removing the tips. Use the central, strongest shoot as the leader once again. Trim it just below the top wire. Remove any other stray shoots on the main trunk.

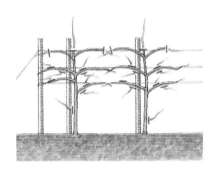

3. In the third year, the pleached trees will have reached the top of the support. Train two of the best side branches at the top horizontally as in previous years. Remove the leader as you no longer need it to extend the height. Continue to prune the horizontal shoots of previous years, shortening the sideshoots so that they are leafy and do not develop into woody growths that would interfere with the clean lines of the pleaching. In future years remove any strong upright shoots from the leader.

and conifers. Start off the trimming with mechanical hedge trimmers, and finish the details with one-handed shears.

Cut letter templates from cardboard strong enough to keep for several years. Use them every time you trim the plants. With the template laid against the hedge, cut round the letter, working with hand shears to avoid making mistakes.

Alternatively, clip a message in relief on the top of a flat hedge so that it can be seen from above, perhaps a secret line to a loved one which can be read only from an upstairs window. To make the hedge letters sturdy, lightly trim the tops of the

shoots after removing the template. The shoots will branch and interlock. After several seasons the letters will be clear.

As with all aspects of hedge care, the success of topiary depends on continuing attention. Occasional clipping is not enough. If you decide that the end does not justify the means there are other ways to give a distinctive touch to a hedge.

CREATING A LIVING ARCH

Most people's idea of an idyllic country cottage includes a rose arch, preferably over the front gate, but an arch of leafy plants is far more adaptable. Provided

HEDGE WITH ITS OWN FLOWERS It is easier to plant a flowering hedge than to apply colour later. A climbing rose that repeat flowers is excellent value, the more so if you save money by raising plants from your own cuttings.

tie in the shoots as they grow up the frame. Pinch out the tips as the shoots grow to encourage better branching, and trim the growths occasionally. Once the top is reached, let the shoots extend beyond the frame and carefully bend them over to cover the top. The living arch will take a couple of seasons to cover the structure and will soon blend in with the rest of the hedge.

Adapting this idea, you can increase the height of a hedge by several feet but still allow a few views into and out of the garden through 'windows' left in the hedge. Make wooden frames that can be fixed in the hedge. Instead of squares or rectangles, the windows could be circles or diamonds, which are simpler because the shoots can be more easily trained up and around the frame.

THE INFORMAL LOOK

If you would like a more casual-looking boundary, or if the prospect of regular trimming is too daunting, an informal hedge is for you. Although some initial trimming is necessary to form a sturdy framework, the plants can be left to develop their characteristic shapes, and to flower freely where appropriate.

Trimming an informal hedge is the same as if the shrub were growing elsewhere in the garden. For instance, trim *Berberis × stenophylla* in summer as soon as flowering is over to give the maximum bloom the following year.

If you take over a garden that has an overgrown hedge, take the opportunity to cut the plants back ruthlessly to renew the upper level. New growth is often very rapid, especially if you apply fertiliser, because of the substantial root system that exists. Such hard pruning is best done in early summer. New shoots then have a long growing season before the winter, whereas unripe, sappy stems can be damaged by frost.

COASTAL CONTENDERS

Elaeagnus × ebbingei is fast growing and attractive, with deep-green leaves and scented autumn flowers. It is prone to die back and not fully hardy in cold gardens, but it is ideal for coastal areas.

Escallonia 'Red Hedger' is upright and fast growing, with glossy evergreen leaves. It needs shelter inland but is perfect by the sea. Trim it in spring to remove any frost damage, and again in summer. If grown as an informal hedge it will flower more freely. *Griselinia littoralis*

your hedge is not too old and lacking in vigour you can make it grow into an arch over a gate or entrance.

A hedge of, for example, privet grows to 8 ft (2.5 m) and more, which is high enough for an arch, but it is not particularly stable at full height. Make a sturdy frame of wood about the desired size and shape of the hedging arch. The frame can be square, pointed or curved at the top, depending on your preference and woodworking skills. Give it a good coat of preservative intended for use in gardens and let it dry out thoroughly.

Tie it firmly to the main branches of the hedge or to metal rods driven into the ground and staple a layer of chicken wire to it. The wire netting makes it easier to

WHERE HEDGE MEETS BORDER Shrubs such as *Philadelphus* 'Beauclerk' bridge the gap between herbaceous plants and high hedge, giving a vigorous informal growth and a bountiful mix of flowers and heady scent.

is another choice for the coast. It is a dense evergreen shrub with light-green leaves on yellow stems, and it makes an excellent close-clipped formal hedge.

Too often restricted to coastal areas, where it is indeed ideal, is the tamarisk (*Tamarix pentandra*); its willowy stems of tiny leaves end in fluffy pink flowers. Prune after flowering as hard as necessary to create a semi-formal hedge.

Ornamental willows such as *Salix alba* 'Chermesina' and *S. daphnoides* make interesting informal hedges when at least half their growth is pruned annually to promote tall, upright stems. They screen well during summer, and in winter, when the leaves are not present, the young stems are brightly coloured.

THORNY HEDGE BARRIERS

Berberis × *stenophylla* grows strongly and is extremely prickly, making it suitable for keeping out animals and intruders. It occasionally suckers, which may be a nuisance, but the orange flowers in late spring are spectacular. Trim this evergreen informal hedge after flowering.

Hawthorn (*Crataegus monogyna*) produces a cheap deciduous hedge that tolerates hard clipping at almost any time of year. The white flowers are followed by red berries on the thorny stems. Hawthorn is a good hedge for attracting wildlife in rural areas – whether alone or mixed with privet, blackthorn and elder.

Blackthorn (*Prunus spinosa*) makes a dense deciduous hedge suitable for rural areas. As its name hints, blackthorn is impenetrably thorny. It needs a yearly trim in summer.

Common elder (*Sambucus nigra*) tolerates any soil, air pollution and some shade, and can be cut back hard. The two variegated forms with cream or white edges to the leaves make decorative semi-formal hedges if space is not too limited; they can be pruned at any time.

THE RIGHT FOREGROUND

Traditionally, a wall, fence or neatly clipped hedge is fronted by a border of other, lower-growing plants. To some gardeners a plain green hedge is a blank canvas on which to paint a picture. This is the purpose of the classic tall yew or beech hedge behind the herbaceous

NEAT ALL YEAR Choose bush honeysuckle (*Lonicera nitida*) for a trim, year-round hedge. For brighter colour, there is a yellow-leaved form, 'Baggesen's Gold', or you can enliven the base of the hedge with honesty.

HARDY HORNBEAM For a deciduous hedge, opt for common hornbeam (*Carpinus betulus*). It forms as good a hedge as beech; its leaves are more strongly veined, toothed and pointed, but as with beech they cling on in winter.

CHEAP AND CHEERFUL

IF YOU CANNOT WAIT for a hedge to grow and want a quick screen that need not be permanent, sow a row of sunflower seeds. They are fast growing and cheap. As well as the familiar tall yellow sunflowers there are strains with coloured or white flowers. The more branched plants are good for cut flowers as well as for a screen.

MIXING FLOWER AND FOLIAGE Growing a plant on the surface of a hedge adds an extra dimension to a plain backdrop. Starry pink *Clematis* 'Minuet' prettily partners 'Fletcheri', a grey-green Lawson cypress.

border. It provides a backdrop that throws the plants in the foreground into strong relief. But a hedge may run alongside the drive and is then a decorative feature in its own right. And it certainly needs to be this where it runs along the front of your territory and is the first thing you see every time you come home.

Where space allows, make the planted area against a hedge as deep as possible. The hedge blocks light from one side, making it inevitable that the plants against it reach forward to the light.

PLANTS TO COVER THE FEET OF THE HEDGE

The soil at the base of a hedge can be dry and poor, making it hard for any but the toughest plants to survive. There are many attractive contenders.

Small-leaved ivies (*Hedera helix*) in many guises – variegated, green or with delicately cut leaves – cover the ground in even the deepest shade. They also scramble up stems. Avoid the temptation to plant a patchwork of several different types which all vie for attention and may spoil the ordered form of the neat hedge.

Though the cyclamen looks so delicate and frail, *Cyclamen hederifolium* is a tough survivor. It is quite content under a hedge, especially if given a good mulch of compost during July, which is the only month it rests. August sees the start of its flowering and, soon after, the prettily marbled leaves make close clumps that last until the following June.

The periwinkles are often regarded as weeds, but they will grow anywhere, including dense shade, and are a blessing for alkaline soils. Their disadvantage is that they spread fast by creeping stems – or flying stems in the case of the large periwinkle – to colonise better places. The variegated kinds are especially attractive, and sometimes slower growing.

THREAD THE HEDGE WITH COLOUR

With a flowering hedge, you can combine more than one shrub type. A mixed screen that blends into smaller shrubs in the foreground, then perennials and edging is ideal for small gardens. Choose flowering times to coincide or to be staggered through the year, depending on whether you want a burst of seasonal glory or all-year interest.

If you already have a green hedge, give it colour by growing plants up it. Plants that thrive in poor soil are best. The climbing nasturtium (*Tropaeolum majus*) is especially suitable. This hardy annual grows far more luxuriantly when given rich soil but the plants can be very leafy at the expense of flowers. The roots of a hedge prevent any hint of lushness in the nasturtiums, so there is more flower and less leaf. If the plants need trimming at the top, just cut them back – you will do little harm to the flowers.

Equally good is the closely related canary creeper (*T. peregrinum*), with small leaves and less showy, dainty yellow flowers, but a greater ability to cling.

The everlasting pea (*Lathyrus latifolius*) makes a good show of warm rose-purple flowers, and will have set seed and be in need of a good trim by the end of August when the hedge needs clipping. Other vigorous annual climbers include

Mina lobata which has racemes of little red flowers that fade to orange then yellow, and the Chilean glory flower (*Eccremocarpus scaber*), which also has orange-red racemes.

The half-hardy cup-and-saucer vine (*Cobaea scandens*), with blooms that open yellow-green and age to purple, is another choice, or you could try the Japanese hop (*Humulus japonicus* 'Variegatus'), which has unusual foliage that is blotched and streaked with white.

DECIDUOUS FLOWERING SHRUBS

Fuchsia magellanica is the toughest of the hardy fuchsias, often retaining a woody framework all year. The small flowers are red and purple. The peeling rusty bark in winter is pretty and plants can reach 6 ft (1.8 m) or more in mild areas. The pink-flushed white 'Molinae' is a good alternative to the common form, and there are variegated kinds too.

Forsythias are a familiar delight of the urban landscape. When well pruned, by taking out old stems in lengths instead of trimming back to the same twiggy framework each year, they flower profusely.

Snowy mespilus (*Amelanchier*) is usually seen as a small tree, but it withstands pruning and makes a pretty screening plant in informal sites. Profuse white flowers in spring and brilliant autumn colour give it two periods of interest.

EVERGREEN WITH FLOWERS

Mexican orange blossom (*Choisya ternata*) creates a year-round hedge of medium height with small, scented flowers in spring and a few in summer. It withstands heavy trimming but may be damaged by very cold weather and wind.

Hebes are stout evergreens for coastal areas. Inland, some spectacular flowerers such as 'La Séduisante' and 'Midsummer Beauty' are not hardy, but *Hebe salicifolia* with long leaves and narrow flower spikes is suitable for tall hedges. Prune it in spring, when any branches damaged in winter can be removed.

Mahonia aquifolium is useful for shade but only grows to about waist height. It has holly-shaped leaves, clusters of lemon flowers and purple berries.

All the pyracanthas make superb hedges, trimmed formally or left to be more natural, when they produce more foamy cream flowers and scarlet berries. They perform well in cold and windy positions. Always plant named varieties, mixed if necessary, to ensure that the flowers and berries are what you wanted.

Among the huge group of viburnums is *Viburnum tinus*, which flowers very early in spring. It will put up with almost any conditions, and there are improved forms with bigger flowers, pink buds instead of the usual white, and attractively variegated leaves.

MINI-HEDGES

As a simple boundary marker rather than a screen for privacy, low hedges give you the scope to grow a wide range of plants.

🌣 Lavender can be clipped neatly and looks lovely around beds of pink and white roses, where the combination of

HEDGE OF GRASS The ornamental *Miscanthus sacchariflorus* reaches 10 ft (3 m) and is sometimes sold as a hedging plant. Cut down the dead stems in late winter and new growth makes a hedge as summer comes.

QUICK-FIX COLOUR Add ravishing colour to a screen by letting the long, flowering shoots of nasturtiums (*Tropaeolum majus*) trail over a hedge. Other suitable choices to blend with different colour schemes in nearby borders include sweet peas and purple morning glory.

IVY AS A HEDGE Clothe lengths of low trellis or wire netting with small-leaved ivy (*Hedera helix*) to form a vigorous green fedge that needs no clipping until the trailing growths travel too far. Ivy cuttings taken from pot-grown specimens are an economical way to plant up trellis.

colour and scent is a pleasure. 'Hidcote' and 'Munstead' are the most common varieties. Trim lightly from the outset to keep plants compact. There are also white and pink-flowered lavenders.

🌢 Use roses as a low hedge now that there are so many dwarf patio varieties to choose from.

🌢 *Brachyglottis* 'Sunshine', grown for its attractive grey leaves, makes a tough little evergreen hedge.

🌢 Cotton lavender (*Santolina*) has silvery foliage that tolerates regular clipping. It enjoys a site in the sun.

🌢 Culinary sage, an aromatic sun-lover, comes in gold-splashed or purple leaf forms as well as grey-green.

🌢 Hyssop, also an aromatic herb, has deep-green leaves and small blue flowers in summer, which you can leave or clip off for greater formality.

🌢 In shade dwarf box, neat and evergreen, is the best choice.

WAYS TO COMBAT DROUGHT

If all goes according to plan, your hedge will be a long-term boundary of beauty and utility. But things can go wrong.

In very dry conditions hedges suffer as much as any other plants. As a preventive measure, mulch with mushroom compost, garden compost, manure, or other organic matter to help conserve moisture and improve the soil.

If individual plants in a young hedge die of drought, replace them in autumn. First study the soil to try to discover the reason for failure, and improve the soil to foster good growth. Give the replacement plants every opportunity to thrive, with well-prepared soil and plenty of water. Unlike the original plants, they have to compete with strong root systems from the existing hedge. Cut away some branches of adjacent plants to let light and water reach the replacements.

MOVING A HEDGE

It is sometimes necessary to move large plants where the line of a hedge has to be shifted or a gate or path is to be altered.

Prepare the root system of the plants a year in advance. Cut the tap roots (main roots) to encourage new fibrous roots to form. Make the cuts in the dormant season, cutting down on both sides of the hedge with a spade and then removing a trench of soil so that you can cut under the plants to sever at least some of the taproots. Mix compost with the soil and replace it, watering well, and firming.

The following autumn the new site should be well prepared and dug ready to receive the plants. Have help and a large sheet ready to help to move the large rootballs. Digging up the plant should reveal some new roots in the enriched compost where the soil was dug the previous year. Cut back the branches where necessary to disentangle them.

Push the plant to one side in the trench, tuck the sheet under it, then pull the plant back again, unfold the sheet and drag or lift the plant without disturbing the roots too much. Check that the receiving hole is the correct size and depth

SAVING A BROKEN HEDGE

THE WORST DAMAGE to a hedge usually occurs if a traffic accident causes it to be broken at ground level. It is rare that any plants are killed altogether; if cut back, they often sprout again quite quickly. Water in a general fertiliser, put in temporary netting for security and trim back adjacent plants to let light and air reach the new shoots, and to let the old and new meld.

MIXED HEDGE Combine different shrubs for an informal boundary in a country setting. Two dogwoods, *Cornus alba* 'Elegantissima' and 'Westonbirt', give winter interest with red stems and remnants of autumn foliage.

before putting the plant in position. Carefully work the soil among the roots, lining the hedge up with the existing hedge. Firm the soil as you plant and then water well. Trim the plant as necessary. Support tall plants with stakes or guy ropes for the first season to prevent gale damage. Keep the soil moist.

REPAIRING SNOW DAMAGE

Heavy snow causes damage when it is left to lie on top of a flat hedge. The weight eventually becomes so great that the hedge splays open or falls to one side.

Take the damage as a warning that you have let the hedge reach too great a height too quickly. It is best to cut off the damaged section with a saw and loppers and allow it to regrow, regularly clipping back to promote bushy growth.

If conifer hedges splay apart, wire them together as they will not regrow from hard-pruned branches. Remove the centre stems to achieve a narrower profile and allow for fresh growth on the outside and a more stable shape.

Apart from rare problems, the boon of all boundaries, and living ones in particular, is that they improve with age. As hedging plants mature, the screen becomes denser. What starts out as a few stick-like saplings becomes an integral and creative part of the garden design.

ROSES ROUND THE GARDEN GATE The arching growth of *Rosa* 'Complicata' makes a thorny hedge that will reach at least head height. The cupped flowers are slightly fragrant and appear in profusion in midsummer.

INSPIRATION FROM

GREAT GARDENS

EDZELL CASTLE

Sandstone walls enclose a formal parterre.

The impressive grounds that originally surrounded the fine tower house near Edzell, in Tayside, were laid out almost 400 years ago and wrapped round by a red sandstone wall featuring heraldic devices and niches for statuary. Although the garden fell into disrepair, it has now been restored round the shell of the tower, and the wall again fulfils its original purpose – to display a coat of arms.

To GARDENERS resigned to a world of brick and rendering, there are few things more covetable than some well-matured wall of granite, limestone or sandstone, lichen-crusted and sprouting flowers, succulents and ferns from a dozen crevices.

Among the most striking of old walls are those which are heraldic in style, and the wall surrounding the garden at Edzell Castle is a fine example. The original tower is today without floors or roof, but the parterre of lawns, rose beds and topiary clipped to spell out family mottoes have been brought back to life over the past 60-odd years.

Around the whole stands a capped and banded sandstone wall depicting the armorial bearings of the man who laid out the garden in 1604 – Sir David Lindsay, Lord of Edzell. The arms of the Lindsays incorporate a broad horizontal chequered band in red, white and blue, with stars above. The stars are carved in relief on the wall, the red checks are the red of the stone, while the white and blue are supplied by pans of white and blue lobelia inserted into square niches left for the purpose. The flowers are provided by the gardens of the Palace of Holyroodhouse in Edinburgh.

YOUR OWN FLORAL WALL

Although there is little call these days for such a resplendent display of heraldry, the attractive honeycomb effect of the wall at Edzell Castle is easily reproduced in a less formal setting. A pyramid of terracotta troughs stacked in front of a bare stretch of wall at the end of the garden, for example, and filled with plants to provide cheerful summer colour adds an unusual decorative feature to a plot of any size.

At Edzell, the sympathetic tones of the sandstone wall form an attractive background for colourful annuals. Using terracotta containers to build a honeycomb wall capitalises on the same idea, as the warm hues of the troughs complement most shades of brickwork, although any type of sturdy, rectangular, stackable container works just as well.

In the example on the right, five troughs, each about 7 in (18 cm) deep, form the base of a pyramid which stands just over 2 ft (60 cm) high. The troughs are evenly spaced along the ground to give a firm base for the layers above. If there is any danger of the upper troughs

HERALDIC HONEYCOMB White and blue lobelia add the finishing touches to this stone representation of the Lindsays' coat of arms.

toppling over – because of adventurous children, maybe – simply screw the top layers to the wall.

Any number of plants are suitable for such a scheme, but perhaps the most effective are those chosen for their striking colours. Here, the red of the dwarf nasturtiums (*Tropaeolum majus*), yellow *Calceolaria integrifolia*, the orange pot marigolds (*Calendula officinalis* 'Orange King') and the rich purple petunias produce a brilliant tapestry on a sunny wall between June and September.

In some pots, purple basil (*Ocimum basilicum* 'Purpureum') provides greater height, while in others, purple-flushed leaves of *Tradescantia* reach down to link one layer of troughs to another.

SUMMER COLOUR An array of colourful
flowers in a pyramid of terracotta troughs
echoes the chequered honeycomb at Edzell.

THE LIE
OF THE LAND

S OME OF THE MOST INVENTIVE and exciting gardens are made on the most challenging of sites. Your garden may have steep slopes, an unpromising aspect, too much shade or simply be a featureless flat rectangle, but there are many imaginative solutions. You can introduce steps, terracing, rockeries, raised beds or sculpted mounds; less energetic measures will let the plants themselves do the work, perhaps with tall growers creating those missing contours, or roses and clematis scrambling over grassy banks.

A creamy burnet rose with prickly branches grows wild in a seemingly inhospitable coastal region.

IN SYMPATHY WITH THE SURROUNDINGS Make the most of a sloping site to give changes of level that add character. Choose plants that, if not native, are in tune with what grows wild locally.

SUITING GARDEN TO SITE

ONE OF THE HARDEST TASKS for any gardener is to pause from cultivating plants long enough to take stock of the land they grow on. Even with a new garden the temptation is to buy plants immediately and set them out. But a garden is about more than growing a collection of plants. The longer you take to weigh up what the site has to offer and what plants will establish themselves best, the more harmonious the result is, and ultimately the more satisfying.

Such restraint is the equivalent of living with a minimum of furnishings until you decide what will suit you and suit the room, rather than buying odd chairs and a table, then a sofa and a lamp, and finally having some curtains made to match. A room based on impulse buys seldom works as a visual entity, while one in which every piece of furniture fits into a strong scheme does. The same applies to the garden.

PLANNING AHEAD

Resolve what it is that you want from your garden tomorrow, next year and five years on. Look even further ahead if you have a large piece of ground to plan and plant, and if you intend to grow trees.

The growing garden represents a complex process of development. As it matures, so your needs, and even your tastes, may alter. Your garden requires well-thought-out management and some general principles or rules for its development to make it work.

In creating a garden, there are layers of considerations which, taken in proper sequence, help you to achieve your ambition. Things go wrong when you break or muddle the sequence.

What your own particular garden is for – the roles you require of it – comes first. Choosing specific plants comes last. In the middle comes the all-important accommodation between you and what nature decrees. What the soil is like, which way the garden faces, whether it is exposed or sheltered and whether the site is level or sloping are crucial to your plans. You can put money and effort into changing them, but for a garden that thrives and is easier to maintain you will do far better to recognise and work with the characteristics of the land.

GETTING TO KNOW THE SOIL

THE SOIL IN YOUR GARDEN is the end product of a particular climate of rain, wind, heat and cold that has worked upon rock over many millions of years. Whatever type of garden you ultimately achieve, you are dependent upon the soil. The best idea for your garden is to fall in with nature and follow its clues as to what you should grow.

WHERE SOIL COMES FROM

Wherever you live, the soil has had a long and complicated history, and so has the Earth's structure beneath it. What has been left over time is a remarkable diversity of ages and types of rock.

The harder rocks which did not move in a series of volcanic-type eruptions through the ages have become our mountain ranges and highlands. Areas of chalk are deposits carried from ancient seabeds and made up of the shells of myriad sea creatures. Deposits of clay,

COUNTRYSIDE PLANTS The wild dog rose (*Rosa canina*) is found on soils as diverse as clay, chalk and sand. Its generous flowering without any gardener's help indicates that it is a trouble-free choice for the garden.

boulders and gravel – drift materials as they are called – were carried far from their original bedrock and became the lowland landscapes.

Rain, frost and heat broke down the parent rocks into particles of various grades known as sands, silts or clay in which plants eventually grew – and died. The decomposing plants added organic matter to the rock particles, water and air clung to the organic matter, and the

whole created a layer of soil on the surface of the land. The more plants grew, the greater the amount of plant debris (humus) and the thicker the soil layer.

The types of plant that grew depended on soil and climate. In Britain temperate forest grew, and the earliest farming was all within the forest. Only slowly did settlers clear the forests to gain open land for arable crops and enclose areas for grazing. Each region developed

BRINGING NATURE INTO THE GARDEN Hybridised forms of species roses share the robust growth of their native cousins, but have been bred to give an even greater profusion of larger flowers. Make gardening easier by choosing shrubs and perennials that thrive in your soil of their own accord.

TESTING FOR SOIL TYPE

To TREAT YOUR SOIL successfully, it is crucial to know what type it is. Testing its pH tells you whether the soil is alkaline (chalk or limestone), neutral or acid (some loams, sand or peat).

Soil-testing kits are widely available. Fill the small container with soil from your garden and add a capsule and water or the solution from the kit. By matching the colour that the liquid turns against a chart you can see whether your soil is acid (orange), alkaline (dark green) or somewhere in between. Test soil from different parts of the garden because the pH can vary even over a short distance.

BLUEBELL GLADE A walk through woods in spring illustrates the ease with which bulbs will spread. Scatter a few native bulbs in your garden and plant them where they fall. In a few years you will have a carpet of colour.

its own character because of the nature of its underlying rock. In some areas the rock was suitable for building, and the colour and style of the buildings arose from it. Where the rock was not suitable, brick and timber were used, giving a quite different look from stone areas.

The colour and consistency of the soil, too, varied according to the rock that it originated from. Particular plant associations developed on different soils, emphasising the character already established by local building traditions. It is only comparatively recently that building materials, crops and garden plants have lost their strong local ties.

FROM FOREST TO GARDEN

No matter where your garden is, it was probably once covered by forest, and you are tapping into the basic soil that produced the forest. Understanding the

RUSSET WOODLAND Beech (*Fagus sylvatica*) can succeed in acid soils as well as in chalk; it thrives in all but heavy, wet soils. Beech makes a good hedge, or you can grow a weeping or coloured variety as a specimen tree.

HOW TO TREAT YOUR SOIL

SOIL TYPE	PROBLEMS	SOLUTIONS
Clay soil	Difficult to cultivate, cold and heavy in winter, dry and cracked in summer	• Add well-rotted organic matter to improve drainage, aeration and root penetration. It also feeds the soil and makes it easier to work. • Grow green manures such as field beans, alsike clover, mustard, grazing rye or winter tares. They aerate the soil, remove excess water and protect the soil from compaction. Dug in, they increase humus. • Add mulches to protect the structure of the soil, to conserve moisture and to prevent drying and cracking. They also help to keep soil warm in winter. • Improve drainage by double digging, breaking up compacted layers with an iron bar, adding grit at two bucketfuls per square yard or metre, introducing raised beds or digging a soakaway.
Sandy soil	In summer suffers from drought; in heavy rain susceptible to erosion and loss of valuable nutrients	• Add organic matter to feed the soil, to help to retain nutrients and water and to improve structure. • Grow any plants to prevent leaching of nutrients from the soil and erosion. • Grow green manures such as alfalfa, buckwheat, crimson clover, bitter lupins, phacelia, grazing rye and trefoil to protect the soil. Dig them in to enrich the soil. • Add mulches to reduce drying and to prevent the washing away of nutrients. • Add lime if your sandy soil has become acid, but apply with caution.
Peaty soil	May become waterlogged	• Construct raised beds to improve the drainage. • Grow green manures such as field beans, alsike clover, mustard, phacelia and grazing rye to reduce waterlogging. • Add lime with caution if soil is acid. • Improve soil drainage by adding grit at two bucketfuls per square yard or metre, or by digging a soakaway.
Chalk and limestone soils	Thin, dry, alkaline; lacks organic matter	• Construct raised beds to increase the depth of topsoil. • Grow green manures such as alfalfa, buckwheat, trefoil, grazing rye and phacelia to prevent leaching in deep beds and to add nutrients. • Add mulches to retain water, to prevent leaching in winter and to protect the soils from rain.

---

origin of a locality's character may strengthen the wish to preserve it. After all, one reason you live in an area is that you like its appearance. On the piece of ground you own you have the opportunity to maintain the existing look, so that your gardening seems at home in its site and does not impose something alien upon the land.

Apart from the pleasure of creating such a harmonious garden, there are practical benefits too. Lower maintenance is the major one; plants at home in the site need far less care than strangers. Go with the nature of your land and you make life easier. Fight it and you double the work. This is true whatever the size of your garden.

The land you work is the key to the garden you can devise – not only in terms of what will grow but also in its aspect and contours. Abrupt changes of level or a damp corner may seem insuperable challenges but take heart from the fact that no matter how bad you think your soil is, it does naturally grow something.

WHAT GROWS ON YOUR SOIL?

In the wild, nature does not dig, but lets the canopy of trees and the vegetation beneath take generations to develop. Nature abhors a void in its green carpet and tries to fill it up as soon as possible, whether in the wild or in a garden.

What grows first after soil has been disturbed or cleared, as for example on a building plot, is annual weeds. Their growth is encouraged by soil cultivation. If you leave this first growth alone, a generation of native perennials will then emerge and gradually take over. After the perennials come shrubs and eventually trees developing all the way up to forest vegetation. The natural state of much of the countryside before the land was disturbed can re-establish itself.

Each soil and situation, no matter how chalky, how clay or how acid, originally had its own range of plants. This range, from annual to forest tree, is called a plant sequence. It helps if you know what your area's natural sequence would have been, but you are not bound to copy it in the garden. It makes a valuable yardstick,

EASY COVER FOR SLOPES

Clothing banks with plants prevents soil slippage in the garden as efficiently as in the wild. Choose perennials and evergreens that need little care.

• *Cotoneaster dammeri*: prostrate evergreen shrub with dark green, glossy leaves, white flowers in June and red berries in autumn.

• Rose of Sharon (*Hypericum calycinum*): shrubby carpeter with bright green leaves, and golden flowers from June to September.

• *Rosa* 'Paulii': prickly thicket-forming shrub rose that roots as it spreads, with white fragrant flowers all summer.

• *Clematis heracleifolia*: sprawling growth bears purple-blue tubular flowers in August and September.

• Dead nettle (*Lamium maculatum* 'Beacon Silver'): mid-green leaves with overlay of silver, and pinkish-purple flowers in May.

• *Pachysandra terminalis*: hardy evergreen for shade, with rich green leaves and tiny white flowers in April.

• Lesser periwinkle (*Vinca minor* 'Aureovariegata'): unlimited spread of low growth with scattering of blue flowers all summer and yellow rims to the leaves.

• Blue fescue (*Festuca glauca*): ornamental grass for sunny banks with bristly blue-grey leaves, and little purple-grey flower spikes in summer.

• Bloody cranesbill (*Geranium sanguineum*): deeply lobed leaves with crimson flowers all summer. The variety 'Album' has white flowers.

• Lungwort (*Pulmonaria officinalis*): shade-lover with large, white-spotted leaves, and clusters of pink and blue flowers in spring.

HEATH AND MOORLAND Damp, acid soil on a scrubby moor, typical of regions such as the New Forest in Hampshire, provides ideal conditions for heath and ling. In other situations look for rhododendrons, which have spread from tended land into the wild, as indicators of soil acidity.

however, against which to check whether or not a plant is likely to settle comfortably where you want to put it.

LOOKING AT LOCAL PLANTS

Make your own survey of what grows naturally in your locality. Walk in local woods, study the open spaces, whether they are commons or patches of waste ground, and look closely at roadside verges. Any ground that is left virtually untended will give you clues as to which plants like the local soil. There might be a neglected churchyard, unkempt corners of fields, footpaths along the fringes of housing estates and sites that have waited years for some new road or building project. Railway embankments are often wonderful wildlife habitats, where trees and smaller plants are left undisturbed over a length of time.

For a garden receiving full light, use the open spaces as your guide and for a shady, tree-lined garden pay more heed to the wooded areas. A local field guide (usually available in a public library) helps with identifying the plants. Never take plants from the wild; take some close-up photographs instead for identifying plants later. It is surprising how many of their botanical names you will recognise as being similar to those of plants in your own garden.

Assess your site, particularly its soil, and keep at the back of your mind the range of plants that would grow naturally upon it. Stay close to this range and build up a collection of plants that grows with least fuss. You can veer either side of this, but knowing the list of what is suitable helps to control impulse buys of tempting exotics that will never like your site and will require a good deal of time and care to make them grow.

ACID OR ALKALINE?

Soil analysis is a basic requirement for making the right choices of what to grow. Uncultivated ground in your area is a good guide but when there is little of it use a soil-testing kit. A test also takes account of any treatment that may have altered the soil to some degree.

What greatly affects your soil is its acidity or alkalinity. Limestone in a soil creates alkalinity. The degree of alkalinity varies from chalky limestone, which has the highest count, through 'normal' soil having some lime, to soils totally free of

CLINGING TO A SLOPE Even the seemingly hostile environment of a shady rock-face is home to plants such as ferns and primroses, which adapt well to damp or craggy gardens. Hybrid forms of *Primula* come in colours other than yellow. Cowslips, a downland relative, prefer sunnier sites.

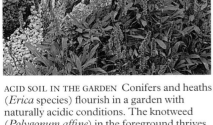

ACID SOIL IN THE GARDEN Conifers and heaths (*Erica* species) flourish in a garden with naturally acidic conditions. The knotweed (*Polygonum affine*) in the foreground thrives in any soil as long as it is moist.

lime, known as acid soils. A neutral soil is in the middle of this scale and gives a reading of pH 7 on a soil-testing gauge. Anything above is limy, while anything below gets progressively more acid. An ideal reading is pH 6.5.

Extreme acidity or alkalinity in a soil restricts the range of plants that grow, but helps to create the strongest regional idiom. Most plants, however, grow in most soils apart from the extremes. While it is possible to adjust a soil, this entails arduous work – and the work may be wasted, for the roots may eventually penetrate the unaltered layer beneath.

Far better than 'correcting' a chalky soil for growing acid-loving plants such as azaleas, rhododendrons and heathers is to buy compost that is suitable for acid-lovers (sold as ericaceous compost) and grow them in pots and tubs. Note that watering has to be of collected rainwater only, as tap water in chalky areas will be alkaline and will harm acid-loving plants.

SAND OR CLAY?

Other factors such as poor drainage or coldness are just as likely to inhibit growth as pH value. The soil's physical condition is important. The size of grain your soil is composed of depends on the source below ground. A coarse-grained

soil is usually sand, and often acid too. The finest grained soil is clay or silt. The grains stick together when wet in a way coarse grains never do. The result is that clay soil drains badly and is heavy to work. As it is close-textured, it contains little air and remains cold.

Sandy soil drains freely and its open texture contains plenty of air, so it warms up quickly. Sand is light to work, but often poor because all the nutrients as well as water drain through it quickly.

HOW TO IMPROVE THE SOIL STRUCTURE

A plant obtains nutrients in soluble or liquid form from the 'skin' of moisture round each grain of soil. In a light soil your task is to hold those nutrients around the plant; in clay you need to open the soil to let air between the grains and help the plant to put down its roots. On both light and heavy soils, organic matter improves the structure.

When you have a garden on a newly developed site, dig in some form of organic matter at an early stage. The decaying strands of vegetation in manure or compost bind a light sandy soil and push apart the close, often waterlogged, grains of a clay one. Organic matter also provides minerals to feed the soil. It enriches

BEST PLANTS

SUITED TO ALKALINE SOIL

There are plants of all types and sizes that thrive on chalk or limestone soil.

• Judas tree (*Cercis siliquastrum*): small, deciduous tree with pink flowers in spring, heart-shaped leaves and dark red pods in late summer.

• Juniper (*Juniperus × media* 'Pfitzeriana Aurea'): low, spreading conifer with golden-tipped foliage.

• Crab apple (*Malus sargentii*): spreading small tree with white spring flowers and deep red fruits in autumn.

• *Rosa rugosa*: vigorous rose with single purple-red flowers followed by large flask-shaped red hips.

• *Ceanothus impressus*: evergreen bush with deep blue flowers in spring and small crinkled dark green leaves.

• *Iris variegata*: bearded yellow iris with purple veining on the lower petals.

• Scabious (*Scabiosa caucasica* 'Clive Greaves'): perennial with summer-long violet-blue flowers with centres like pincushions .

• Maiden pink (*Dianthus deltoides*): ground-hugging evergreen with white or pink flowers in summer; good for rock gardens or banks.

• *Lavatera trimestris* 'Silver Cup': tall annual with trumpet-shaped, veined pink flowers from summer to autumn.

• *Triteleia laxa*: bulb with purple-blue flowers in early summer.

• *Cyclamen hederifolium*: spurred, pink flowers in autumn and ivy-shaped leaves with silver-green patterns.

NATURAL BEAUTY ON THE FRINGES Where weedkillers miss field edges, native plants spring up even when near urban areas. Corn camomile (*Anthemis arvensis*) and poppies (*Papaver rhoeas*) are common in the wild, so you can count on success when you plant garden varieties.

even a chalky soil, which is too porous to retain nutrients without regular and generous additions of humus. There may be a complex pattern of sublayers, where chalk overlies clay, or gravel overlies chalk. But still the best treatment you can give is to work in plenty of well-rotted organic matter.

The darker the colour of a soil, the richer it is in organic matter. Dark soil is also warmer than light, for it absorbs more heat from the sun. A warmer soil makes for earlier development of plants.

A handful of soil should be crumbly and dark, and should smell fresh. By the continued addition of organic matter to a soil over a long period you can bring even the poorest soil into 'good heart'.

OPEN CHALKY LAND

A specific soil and situation found in many regions is open chalky land. There is a similarity between limestone and chalk. Both contain lime and give a high pH reading but pure chalk is even more limy than limestone. The two have different consistencies, however. Chalk is soft

DECIDUOUS WOODLAND Under the dappled shade of leaf-shedding trees, the spring-blooming windflower (*Anemone nemorosa*) carpets the ground. In the garden, plant this delightful perennial in partial shade or sun.

and very soluble; limestone is harder and less soluble. Chalk is often considered to be difficult and unproductive in the garden, but it has one of the richest natural vegetations of annual and perennial flowers where it has been grazed. And a chalky soil with plenty of humus is one of the most fertile of all.

Even on roadsides with this soil type you can see milfoil (*Achillea*) and wild thyme (*Thymus*), salad burnet (*Poterium sanguisorba*), common rock rose or sun rose (*Helianthemum nummularium*) and bulbous buttercup (*Ranunculus bulbosus*). Cranesbill (*Geranium*), oxeye daisy (*Leucanthemum*), hoary plantain (*Plantago media*), small scabious (*Scabiosa columbaria*), and primrose and cowslip (*Primula*) are common sights; the original species grow in old cottage gardens.

CHALKY SITES IN SHADE

Where the site becomes shadier beneath native juniper (*Juniperus*), whitebeam (*Sorbus aria*), or wild cherry (*Prunus avium*), the plants that thrive include sanicle (*Sanicula europaea*), the wild rose (*Rosa canina*), wild privet (*Ligustrum*) and, growing through them, swathes of traveller's joy (*Clematis vitalba*). There is also native yew (*Taxus baccata*), but little grows beneath it. When you have a

FAVOURITES FROM THE WILD Some popular garden plants such as the blue meadow cranesbill (*Geranium pratense*) are natives of Britain; suitability to the climate and conditions is the key to their garden success. Yellow St John's wort (*Hypericum perforatum*) likes sunny well-drained soil.

SECRET GARDEN Railway sidings provide a haven of undisturbed ground for wild flowers. Foxglove (*Digitalis*) and broom (*Cytisus*) typically grow on sand but tolerate lime and so do equally well in chalky, alkaline soil.

chalky soil, exploring the many plants bred from these is a good starting point for selecting plants for the garden.

THE SCOPE OF SAND

Sandy soil, usually acidic, is easy to work, but nature's range is far thinner since such soil is a poor and hungry medium.

In open heathlands, ling, heathers and heaths thrive. Wild pansy (*Viola tricolor*), harebell (*Campanula*), heath speedwell (*Veronica officinalis*), foxglove (*Digitalis*), teasel (*Dipsacus*) and heath milkwort (*Polygala serpyllifolia*) grow among fine grasses. The shrubby vegetation includes tormentil (*Potentilla erecta*), broom (*Cytisus*) and bilberry (*Vaccinium*).

Above the shrubby profile, mountain ash (*Sorbus aucuparia*) grows with silver birch (*Betula pendula*) and, in Scotland, Scots pine (*Pinus sylvestris*).

PRODUCTIVE CLAY

Cultivation on clay is heavy work but the soil can become extremely productive. In the wild, plenty grows upon it even though no one digs it. Clay soil can be acid or alkaline or somewhere between, so its vegetation includes the plants from chalky and sandy soils. A further range of plants thrives since the soil can be water-logged at certain times of the year, and may be in woodland shade.

Ash (*Fraxinus excelsior*) is fairly wide-spread through the whole country. Oak (*Quercus robur*) grows, along with crab apple (*Malus sylvestris*), wild cherry and various forms of willow. Pussy willow (*Salix caprea*), grey willow (*S. cinerea*) and crack willow (*S. fragilis*) all thrive. In damper clay you see alder (*Alnus gluti-nosa*) and aspen (*Populus tremula*).

In boggy ground water avens (*Geum*), marsh marigold (*Caltha palustris*), water forget-me-not (*Myosotis palustris*), water mint (*Mentha aquatica*), yellow flag (*Iris pseudacorus*) and many reeds (*Phrag-mites*) and rushes (*Juncus*) grow.

There are also bulbs, which are often overlooked as natives. Tenby daffodil and Lent lily (both narcissi), fritillary, blue-bells and Solomon's seal all grow wild.

PUTTING PLANS INTO ACTION

MOST GARDEN EXPERTS now recommend that a new garden should be in close harmony with its setting. This gentle approach to a garden's design contrasts with the Edwardian tradition of the country house garden – the style you often see when visiting grand gardens that are open to the public.

These gracious gardens are very much of their time, with a formal style purposely at odds with the surrounding land. Why would persons of status want a cottage garden?

DRAWING ON A COMMON HERITAGE

The kind of garden the Edwardian gentry desired was formal in layout, with statues of Greek, French or Roman origin, and its chief merit in the owner's eyes – even above that of its layout – was the number of alien plants displayed in it. Imported species spoke of knowledge, travel and wealth as well as of a love of plants. The garden was protected by hedges, with the location all but blotted out in an attempt to realise a dream in which mundane considerations were not allowed to fetter the imagination.

Such gardens nearly a hundred years on are frequently period pieces of great beauty. They are reminiscent of an age when gardens were maintained by staff for owners, often highly informed ones, who vied with each other for supremacy in the size of their rhododendron collection, their camellias or the conifers in their pinetum. But is a garden of this kind a practical proposition for most garden owners today?

A SHIFT IN INTENTION

During the last hundred years there has been a shift in thinking on the nature of gardens. The wisdom of planning a garden based on alien species rather than native plants is questioned.

Not just the wisdom but the aesthetic and environmental value of such gardens is doubted by modern designers and a growing number of garden owners. For that style of garden and the wide range of foreign plants it contains is patently at odds not just with the landscape in which it sits, but with native flora and fauna. It entails suppressing the natural in layout

SEASIDE SURVIVORS A walk along the clifftops reveals the rich variety of plants that cope with the exacting conditions. Pink thrift, oxeye daisies, yellow kidney vetch and wild carrot hug the slope, flowering in the face of salt breezes on the Lizard peninsula at the tip of south-west England.

COASTAL GARDEN Thrift (*Armeria maritima*) rises to the challenge of an exposed seaside site. More familiar in the rockery or border front, its grassy cushions of leaves and dense flowers also suit a wilder part of the garden.

STEEP-SIDED PLANTING Take advantage of dramatic changes of level to grow plants such as tumbling yellow roses (*Rosa banksiae* 'Lutea') that relish a wall-top position. Tuck in pelargoniums for a dash of summery pink.

and plant material and replacing it with an unnatural form. In an age when a more easy-going style of living prevails, it is in keeping that a more 'natural' attitude to gardening should win favour.

An earthier approach to the garden did exist alongside the artificial styles imposed by the Edwardian well-to-do. Cottage-dwellers' employment, building materials and house style continued for generation after generation to come directly from the immediately surrounding land. Local work and materials were the only practical possibilities.

The garden too was largely dictated by practical demands, with vegetables and herbs growing alongside fruit trees, and flowers only one degree removed from the wild. Gardens such as this rarely survive now in Britain, and are a curiosity where they do. But the traditional cottage plots have more relevance to the current thinking on gardens than the grand Edwardian layouts. Their size compares more readily with the extent of average modern plots.

BLENDING HARD AND SOFT

Apart from establishing a broad theme of planting based upon your soil, you can link your garden to its locality by choosing appropriate hard materials. Look at old cottages in the district to see what material has been used to build the fence,

TEMPORARY TERRACING

WALLS, PATHS AND PAVING must be strongly constructed to stay sound. This can be costly and it is better to spread the work over a few seasons than have a quick job poorly done. Paths and paving have to take priority but you can make temporary low walls to create level areas on a slight slope.

Cut a slit in the slope, taking out the soil from the bottom to make level ground. Use a row of peat bales as the wall, securing them with short stakes driven in along the front. Level the upper surface with the soil taken from the lower level.

Nasturtiums, lobelia, aubrietia and other trailers cover the wall until the permanent one is built – and the bales' contents dress the soil. Railway sleepers or, for shallow terracings, breeze blocks, are alternatives to peat bales.

the outhouse, the steps, the path and its edging. Where the stone or brick used is now very expensive, use just a little of it as bands or insets among cheaper material that is in sympathy with your region. If there are no old cottages left try an older churchyard. One approach is to decide what would definitely not be right and then work backwards by elimination.

The larger your site the more influence the region should have upon your garden. In a smaller garden you can link the hard materials back to the house itself, choosing them to match or harmonise with brick or stone, with the colouring of walls or with the slates or tiles on the roof. These are the colours and textures to consider for a terrace, for steps, for path edgings or drive surfaces.

But before you design in detail, pause to think a moment longer. A garden is with you for a long time, and it is as well to get the look of it correct from the start. Although you can change a garden, you can do so only at a cost.

ASSESSING THE SITE

One way to cut the initial cost, especially in terms of labour, is to pay heed to what the site dictates. Must the site really be level, or will the garden be better with some dips and rises? If the site is already level, can you introduce some contours with skilful planting rather than embarking on major earth-moving? Which parts receive the most sun? Where does the prevailing wind strike?

Draw a plan of the garden, note down both what is there already, such as sheds and trees, and what influences there are from outside the garden, such as sun and wind. Include on your plan the views into and out of the site. Often with a light trim of a hedge you can enjoy a neighbour's pear tree in flower or catch a glimpse of a church spire.

SKILFUL USE OF WIND FILTERS

Removing a gloomy conifer opens up a site and lets sunlight into it, completely transforming the feel of the place. Similarly, bold clipping can improve Leyland cypress planted as a high hedge. Often, evergreen hedges have been planted to keep out the wind, but the necessary screen has now become far too high and can be reduced in its height by half. But bear in mind that opening up an outward view may bring gales in, particularly if you live in an exposed position or

---

SAFETY FIRST

THE RIGHT SITE FOR A TREE

BEFORE PLANTING A TREE be sure that you know its ultimate height and spread, below ground as well as above. Choose a site where the tree will not damage underground pipes and cables, or get caught in telephone wires overhead. Do not plant trees too near the house, especially on clay soils. Apart from shading the windows, some trees, especially poplars (*Populus*) and willows (*Salix*), have strong, far-reaching roots which can damage drains and a building's foundations.

FROM BARE PLOT TO BEAUTY

A blank plot can look unpromising, but starting from scratch gives you the chance to work with the site and the soil and put your imprint on the garden.

TAKE YOUR TIME in assessing the site at different times of day and in different weather conditions; consider what to hide and what to enhance – a few plants work wonders. Then list your priorities.

One urgent task is to clothe the stark new walls of the house with climbers, and few can match the intrepid Boston ivy. In late summer its leaves are beginning to redden, preparing for the spectacular autumn glow. On the shady side of the house, another ivy brightens the aspect with its variegated leaves.

The next task is to block the open view to the house next door. A panel fence and pyracantha hedge on one side of the drive and, at the other, two pyramidal hornbeams save the situation.

Virtually the whole garden is at the front of the house, looking straight onto the street, so the next priority is to shut out the traffic and give some privacy. Post and rails are quick to put up and mark the boundary but need their straight lines softened with plants.

COMPLETING THE CHANGES

After five years' growth, evergreen hebe and eleagnus have made an informal hedge, with swathes of caryopteris at the front. On the flat site, the higher rim of shrubs and the lower plants within add contours. The sweeping curve of the border lends movement to the otherwise static square layout.

The dull north-westerly corner turns into a shower of gold when the leaves of the fast-growing false acacias flutter in the breeze. As the wind is funnelled down the road from the north, the taller plants in the deep border serve as a filter for wind as well as noise.

The swoop of the lawn is reflected in a circular bed, a later addition which adds colour near the house with cluster-flowered (floribunda) roses that bloom all summer and into autumn.

BLANK CANVAS When taking on a new site, you can create the garden you want, rather than adapting someone else's ideas.

Enhancing the view

The neighbouring house is screened by a panel fence and a pyracantha hedge, close-clipped near the garage so as not to obstruct the doorway. Further away it is left to flower.

Blocking traffic noise and pollution

The front-line shrubs are sturdy evergreens, forming a mixed flowering hedge capable of filtering car fumes and muffling street sounds. The more the hedge matures the better it screens.

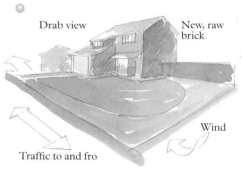

PINPOINTING DRAWBACKS List the plot's snags and decide what to do about them. Give these solutions priority before fine-tuning details.

Making the most of the sun

The house and garden face east, so morning sun is plentiful. By the afternoon, the house is casting shade over much of the garden. But keeping the style as open as possible, with no high evergreens to cast oppressive shadows, makes the garden seem light and airy.

Softening new bricks

Self-clinging climbers such as ivy quickly brighten a blank expanse of wall. Contrary to popular opinion, they do not harm the brickwork – so long as it is sound, they protect it from the elements.

Reducing the wind

The dense, shrubby border filters chilly breezes so that people and plants alike enjoy the sheltered conditions.

1. *Pyracantha atalantioides* 'Aurea'
2. Hornbeam (*Carpinus betulus* 'Fastigiata')
3. Boston ivy (*Parthenocissus tricuspidata* 'Veitchii')
4. Rose (*Rosa* Allgold)
5. Ivy (*Hedera colchica* 'Dentata Variegata')
6. False acacia (*Robinia pseudoacacia* 'Frisia')
7. *Hebe* 'Midsummer Beauty'
8. *Caryopteris* × *clandonensis* 'Kew Blue'
9. *Elaeagnus* × *ebbingei* 'Limelight'
10. *Hydrangea arborescens* 'Grandiflora'
11. Portugal laurel (*Prunus lusitanica*)

PLANTS FOR DAMP SITUATIONS Bugle (*Ajuga reptans*) grows most vigorously in wet ground so add it to your plant list if you need ground cover to clothe an awkward, boggy corner. Some species are evergreen, others semi-evergreen, and all are fully hardy and tolerate sun or shady conditions.

WINTER CHEER Many apparently wild plants have naturalised from gardens. They include the common snowdrop (*Galanthus nivalis*) and winter aconite (*Eranthis hyemalis*), two welcome signs of the new growing season.

near the sea. Before felling anything, ask yourself why it was planted.

Wind can be reduced by filtering it. Some standard trees with a light head, silver birches for example, near the house filter the wind as efficiently as a tall hedge planted a distance from it. Smaller town gardens and walled gardens often have to cope with a blast of air that whisks round a corner or between two properties; it may become a vortex when trapped in an enclosed space. Such wind tunnels need to be blocked, either by planting or, even better, by a wall or fence.

The vortex effect of the walled enclosure is harder to deal with. You cannot apply the best remedy, which is a shelter belt outside the enclosure to divert the wind over the top of the garden. A tall line of open plants to lift and filter as well is some help. If you are fortunate, a neighbour will grow such a belt and this will be much more help. Many small urban spaces are sheltered by neighbouring properties as well as their trees.

IMPROVING AN
URBAN VIEW AND SITE

In built-up areas, you can be troubled by views into your garden. A solid fence or hedge is one way of providing privacy, but an alternative is to position plants strategically as baffles within the site. This gives a feeling of greater space than an extensive barrier. Use baffles to block out headlights or to help to muffle traffic noise if you live on a corner.

Think very carefully about getting more light into the garden. By cutting down taller, older vegetation you allow more sun into your garden. But consider first where newly admitted sunlight will fall and whether it will be the right place for the layout that you are planning.

If you live in a town and your garden is surrounded by tall buildings, it can be sunny and sheltered in summer but very dark in winter when the sun never rises above your skyline.

Choose the plants with this firmly in mind; they must be tolerant of shade and unspoilt by full sun. If this will rule out too many plants you long to have, create permanent plantings of evergreens to suit the winter conditions and enliven the summer scene with pots and troughs of sun-loving plants. This is the plan to follow also in outer urban areas where trees in a neighbouring garden or on a railway bank blot out the low winter sun.

SUIT THE PLANTS TO THE SUN

The ideal garden has plenty of sun and little wind, but whether it is morning, noon or evening sun affects how you use your garden, where you like to sit and which plants you grow. Many plants like sun all day long, from sunrise in the east to sunset in the west. Herbs, flowering

SAFE AND STYLISH STEPS

All garden steps should be shallow for easy use, with plenty of room from front to back to give firm footing. They need to be soundly constructed with care to ensure that water drains off – otherwise steps become slippery in freezing weather. Suit the material to the house and the design to your style of garden.

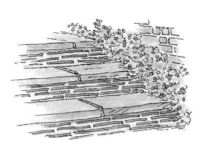

TILE AND STONE
Large tiles cemented together form the risers and stone slabs make stable treads in steps that suit any style of garden, casual or formal, large or small. Choose tiles with a slightly roughened, nonslip surface.

RUSTIC STONE
Where there is a local stone, chunky slabs of it fashioned into steps blend naturally with a rural or cottage-style garden. Provided the surface of the treads is generous and not too uneven, the steps are easy to negotiate.

LAYERS OF BRICK
For a sophisticated town-garden look, lay bricks side by side over a lower, lengthways layer. You could also set them in a running bond of alternating layers. Brick steps fit well next to a raised brick bed or retaining wall.

SLEEPERS AND GRAVEL
Railway sleepers make generously wide steps. Combined with gravel, they form a softer-looking feature than stone or brick steps, especially when edged with plants. This mixture of materials suits a modern, informal layout.

CRAZY PAVING AND BRICK RISERS
Steps can be rounded instead of straight-edged. It is easier to make the curve smooth with a material such as crazy paving which does not come in uniform slabs. A single layer of brick makes the shallow risers.

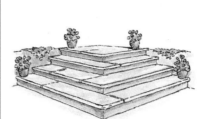

PAVING AND CONCRETE
Bring steps out to a point if there is a corner to tuck them in. Reconstituted stone or concrete slabs are much cheaper than natural stone, especially if you live in an area without a local stone.

TIMBER AND TILES
Prepared timber joists are narrower and smoother than sleepers, giving a sleek rather than rustic appearance. Pair them with smart tiles, softening the rigid lines with plants at the sides if you wish.

GRASS AND BRICK
Lead onto or from a lawn with springy steps of grass on brick risers. You have to clip with shears, but the effect is decorative. Matching low side walls of brick make a stronger feature of the short flight of steps.

shrubs and perennials require sun; bright flower colour is usually an indication of the need for ample sun. Few sites allow full sun; your house, a neighbouring house or a big tree probably gives partial shade at some time. Nearly all plants can cope with this, as long as they receive some hours of sunlight.

Some plants truly enjoy light shade all day. Shade-loving plants often have large leaves, which give them a greater area to catch light. All plants need some light to convert the nutrients taken from the soil into food. Flowers on shade-loving plants tend to be pale colours, to show up in the shade and attract pollinating insects.

Shade is urgently needed in many exposed new gardens. As well as giving somewhere pleasant to sit, it creates a point of interest and adds texture to the scene. A pool of shade in an otherwise sunny site always attracts the eye.

There is a small range of plants that open their flowers at night and have a fragrance to attract moths. Tobacco plants and evening primrose work this way and give great pleasure on summer evenings when planted near your garden seat.

COPING WITH POOR DRAINAGE

It is entirely possible that within a single garden you may have both well-drained land and a boggy area. The waterlogged patch may not be in a spot where you want a pond or bog garden and it may not respond sufficiently to your digging in coarse sand and liberal amounts of moisture-absorbing compost.

The solution could be to put in some drainage, but consider carefully before you take on the work. Few gardens need complex systems of drainage. The house

---

SAFETY FIRST

INSTALL A HANDRAIL

WHERE YOU HAVE a flight of more than three steps or a steeply sloping bank, think about putting up a handrail. The simplest way is to drive a series of posts into the ground and attach a length of rope, securing it to the top of each post. Alternatively, you can buy elegant, purpose-made handrails in wrought iron. For steps beside a wall, attach iron rings to the brick or stonework. Thread a stout rope through them, knotting it securely to each ring.

TRANSFORMING A NARROW GARDEN

Many family-sized houses have long strips of garden. The key is to break up the length, dividing it into 'rooms'. Turning an existing slope to your advantage helps to achieve this.

WHEN TAKING OVER A PLOT, start by analysing the site and the features that are already there.

The shade down the left-hand side of this garden is balanced by sun drenching the right. The rectangular shape of the site gives straight sides that need to be broken up. Mature trees bring the planting a step forward. All of them can stay except for the dominant conifer near the house, which makes the shadiest part of the garden seem gloomier and sucks up moisture in the nearby soil. A bank slanting across a third of the way down suggests a natural break in both style and function.

The owners want somewhere to sit and relax in the sun, a bit of lawn and a play area for the children, held together with a straightforward planting scheme – one that avoids fussiness in both looks and maintenance.

CHANGING LEVELS

A hard surface is laid for putting out sun loungers, chairs and a table. Concrete paving tones with the colour of the house. Shade-loving plants jut out from the left while herbs, conveniently near to the kitchen, soak up the sun that bathes the area on the right.

A flight of steps is cut across the slope, one of the many diagonal features in the new layout that help to make the shape seem wider and not so long. A solid handrail prevents the children – or anyone else – from falling over the drop, and a cupboard built in underneath the top level holds outdoor toys.

With a new level comes a new material – gravel. It is less formal than paving and breaks up the expanse of grass, providing a neat transition from hard surface to soft. The tone of the garden becomes more casual the further

away it is from the house. Another step down separates the children's 'room' from the rest of the lawn. The surrounding trees and shrubs are robust enough to take a few knocks as well as providing playhouses. Tucked away at the end of the garden, the children can run about without disturbing the adults, but the area is in view of a watchful eye from the terrace.

TAILOR-MADE PLANT SCHEME

The planting is designed to need a minimum of care. Ground-covering santolina, rosemary, senecio, cranesbill and hostas help to keep the weeds down, and shrubs and small trees need just an annual trim.

The yellow, blue and grey scheme is in sympathy with the yellow-beige of the house and hard surfaces. In June many of the plants are in bloom, but at other times of the year flowers come from viburnums and mahonia. Pyracantha gives autumn interest with its vivid red berries, and dogwood's red stems brighten the winter scene. The white-variegated foliage of ivy and silvery senecio is welcome all year, alongside the shimmering bark of silver birches.

THE EXISTING PLOT The owners take over a garden that contains the elements they want – paved area, lawn and room for the children to play – but it looks stark and has little charm.

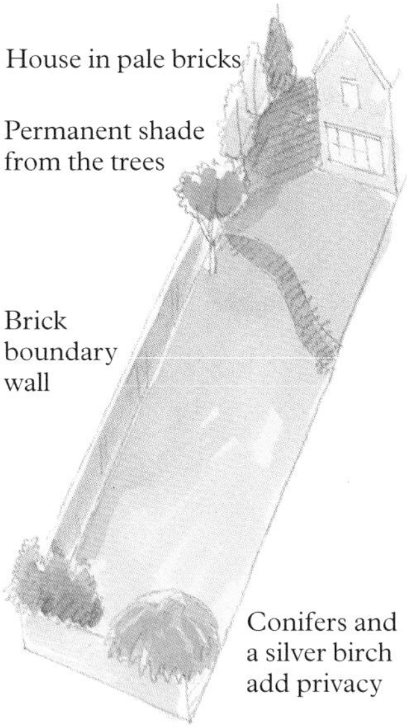

House in pale bricks

Permanent shade from the trees

Brick boundary wall

Conifers and a silver birch add privacy

ANALYSING THE GARDEN There are several features to make more of, and the drawbacks can be overcome.

In the shade

Graceful silver birches are open enough for plants to grow underneath. The shade-lovers chosen all fit the overall colour scheme. Yellow and silver suit the beige of the brick and paving, with blue adding lively splashes.

Sun trap

The warm, sheltered corner makes lounging and sunbathing a pleasure. Herbs native to the Mediterranean climate thrive in full sun and are near at hand to pick for use in the kitchen.

Using the slope

Take advantage of a slope to add character. The dynamic diagonal of the steps emphasises the drop, provides storage beneath and leads into a section entirely different in feel from the terrace.

Shaping the sides

The flowerbeds dip into the garden space, here deep, there shallow. In a symmetrical plot, irregular curves and unexpected angles make the shape seem livelier. The eye focuses on one area after another, rather than taking in the whole garden at once.

Play area

Where space allows, devoting a part of the garden to the children increases family harmony. Children want boisterous games, not pretty flowers, so for this area choose plants tough enough to withstand footballs and games of hide-and-seek.

1. Climbing hydrangea (*Hydrangea petiolaris*)
2. Lilies (*Lilium monadelphum* and *L. hansonii*)
3. Silver birch (*Betula pendula*)
4. *Hosta sieboldiana*
5. Cranesbill (*Geranium pratense*)
6. *Achillea* 'Moonshine'
7. *Iris sibirica*
8. Cherry (*Prunus serrula*)
9. Ivy (*Hedera helix* 'Glacier')
10. *Pyracantha atalantioides*
11. Dogwood (*Cornus alba*)
12. *Hydrangea arborescens* 'Annabelle'
13. Lawson cypress (*Chamaecyparis lawsoniana* 'Pembury Blue')
14. *Mahonia aquifolium*
15. *Viburnum rhytidophyllum*
16. Senecio (*Brachyglottis* 'Sunshine')
17. *Delphinium elatum*
18. *Santolina chamaecyparissus* and rosemary (*Rosmarinus officinalis*)
19. Mixed herbs: parsley, thyme, sage, basil, chives, rosemary
20. Mexican orange blossom (*Choisya ternata*)

itself is probably on a part of the land that is well drained, with a surrounding apron that is also dry even when it is built on low-lying land. There is then the problem of where to drain water to – and draining too well also takes away a plant's natural food, which is held in the water.

SIMPLE SOAKAWAY SOLUTIONS

Far more necessary than a complicated herringbone pattern of land drains are one or two soakaways in crucial positions – but they must be at least 16 ft (5 m) from the house. Site a soakaway at the trouble spot itself or conduct water to it with a pipe that receives excess water run-off from the trouble spot.

On heavy soil, pick up surface water this way from a terrace, for instance, or at the foot of a change of level such as a bank. Make sure a slight fall on the hard surface leads to a gully that drains into the pipe leading to the soakaway. Steps, too, need to throw off water easily or they will be covered with ice in frosty weather.

A house sitting on a hill gives you more serious problems with levels, for while water flows away from the house on one side, the flow is towards it on the other. You have to decide whether to treat the fall towards the house as one straight fall or as a series of terraces. You must also consider how you are going to catch water run-off at the bottom.

First of all you need a clear and level surround to the house. A gully between it and the sloping land can simply conduct water to right and left of the house; half-round piping concealed by gravel will suffice. It is illegal to lead rain run-off into the main drainage system.

How you treat the bank above the drain depends on its importance. If the drive has to lie on the slope you do not want it too steep. Anything with a gradient steeper than 1 in 3 will be hard to negotiate in wintry conditions. The junction with the road needs the gentlest slope. Where the land is steeper, consider taking the drive in a gentle curve across the site to give greater length, which then allows you to have a shallower gradient.

Terracing beside the drive gives many attractive possibilities for planting and need not take too much work to maintain. Grow large spreads of a few plants for the best effect. Make more terraces and keep the maximum slope 1 in 3 if the land is light and sandy or it may shift down. Where soil is heavy and sticky a gradient as steep as 1 in 2 will hold.

PLANTING A GRADIENT

For extra stability grow plants that root as they spread, and thus hold the incline. Ivy and periwinkle do this naturally. More decorative plants include the climbing hydrangea (*Hydrangea petiolaris*) and rambler roses whose tips, if pegged down, take root and put out more stems. Ramblers sprawl down or up a bank equally well and clematis clambers eagerly through them. Grass is another possibility; a fine, low-growing turf that you trim only a couple of times a year serves unless you want trimmed neatness – but this would require more care than ground-cover shrubs.

Some evergreens do not root as they go but spread out horizontally, keeping close to the ground and making excellent cover where the soil does not need to be stabilised. *Juniperus sabina* 'Tamariscifolia' or, for partial rooting, *Cotoneaster dammeri* are among the best.

Terracing is not a task to take on yourself unless the retaining walls are shallow. Any structure more than 3 ft (1m) high

SOFTENING STEPS Dwarf, spreading species such as *Campanula poscharskyana* are ideal for tucking in the crevices round steps and paths. The star-shaped blooms are usually blue – but almost white in the form 'E.H. Frost' which adorns the stone retaining wall behind these steps.

TO THE RESCUE

DRAINAGE TO A SOAKAWAY

WHERE WATER LIES on the ground, you can install a soakaway. Make it on the spot or, if it is near the house, at least 16 ft (5 m) away. Dig the soakaway 3 ft (1 m) square and deep. If it is at a distance from the damp spot, make a V-shaped trench 20 in (50 cm) deep at the wet place, sloping down to the soakaway. Lay perforated piping in the trench. Fill both trench and soakaway with rubble, gravel and then topsoil.

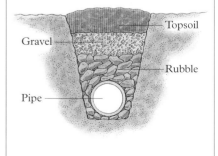

PERFECTING THE STEPS

To CHECK whether a surface is absolutely flat or on a slight slope, use a spirit level. Just lay it on the surface. The bubble in the spirit level is central on a flat surface, but moves right or left on a slope to whichever side is higher. Steps should have the tiniest slope down from back to front so that water runs off – the bubble should move nearer the back. If steps are flat or slope the wrong way, water forms pools on the tread making it slippery underfoot, especially in freezing weather.

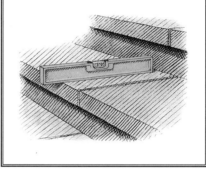

AVOIDING A FILM OF ICE Water may gather at the bottom of a flight of steps. Solve the problem by putting a narrow band of gravel up to 1 ft (30 cm) deep in front of the bottom step to act as a simple soakaway.

DRAMA FOR DAMP GARDENS Whether your garden is boggy by nature or design, there is scope for striking planting. White-sheathed arum lilies (*Zantedeschia*) behind mauve and white *Iris kaempferi* adorn the edge of a pond.

should be checked by a structural engineer. The weight of damp earth pushing against a retaining wall is enormous. Your retaining wall, whether it is of reinforced concrete alone or faced with brick or stone, must have both the correct depth of foundation and be the proper thickness to do its job. This is not work for the amateur.

BUILD IN CONTOURS FOR MORE APPEAL

A completely level garden takes on more character when you introduce contours. Raising one part by just one step, creating a small sunken area as a sun trap and using the spoil to make a bank for wild flowers in a corner adds not only drama but apparent size. The eye has different levels to dwell on instead of taking in the whole flat area in one sweep. When you can, construct mounds using surplus soil

from the excavation of, say, a pool, you save on removing it from the site. Make sure, however, that you remove any precious topsoil from the mound site before dumping your spoil and set aside the topsoil from the pool site also. It can be used again over the subsoil, but the depth may end up less than the original.

Grass can grow in a topsoil depth of 4-6 in (10-15 cm), whereas shrubs need at least 12 in (30 cm) if they are to thrive. Standard trees need an even greater depth of topsoil – 18 in (46 cm) or more.

Creating contour changes is one of the most satisfying jobs, for you achieve an instant effect. Try to make a finished mound or hollow look as natural as you can. Avoid too much regularity or too abrupt a change and blend the edges carefully with the natural level so that your creation does not seem to be a waste pit or a soil dump.

Where the garden is bordered by a noisy road, a mound can help to provide peace. A 7 ft (2 m) high mound will block noise if you are sitting in its lee. But the higher the mound, the greater the width needed at the base so it could easily dominate a small garden. And always remember that the more you go with the natural character of the land, the easier your garden will be to maintain.

INSPIRATION FROM

GREAT GARDENS

UPTON HOUSE

Late 17th-century order on steep ground.

Near Banbury in Oxfordshire,
handsome Upton House was the
comfortable home created by Sir
Rushout Cullen, a rich London
merchant. He built it in the 17th
century and laid out the bones of the
garden. In 1927 it was bought by the
2nd Viscount Bearsted, who greatly
extended it showing immense
ingenuity in developing a challenging
site on the steep, sloping
side of a valley.

U PTON HOUSE LIES in a sandstone area of abrupt ups and downs. You would not, however, suspect a sheer drop by taking in the view from the main door on the south front. From here a broad lawn with great cedars of Lebanon on the one hand, and mighty beeches and conifers on the other, leads the eye to the gently rising meadow at its far end, crowned in the distance by further groups of tall trees.

A stroll towards the meadow reveals an unexpected hindrance, in the form of a broad, deeply plunging valley between lawn and meadow that is completely invisible from the house. This territorial surprise has been put to use down the years and turned into a bonus, most especially by Lord Bearsted's development of the estate.

CREATING GARDEN SHELVES

He consolidated and improved upon the work of his predecessors – and built in a series of terraces whose dry-stone walls are draped with wisteria and roses and linked obliquely down the hillside by a series of stairs, with elegant balustrades

TERRACING ON A GRAND SCALE Shielded by ancient yews and curtained by wisteria and roses, flights of steps zigzag to the valley.

adding drama. The terraces, framed by stately yew hedges, all have their own distinct characters.

There are paved and rose gardens and a shubbery planted with brooms, laburnums, lilacs and other species. There is also a formal kitchen garden with trained fruit trees and orderly vegetable beds, and there are glorious herbaceous borders. Double flowerbeds line the steep grassy path to one side of the slope.

NEW VIEW AT EVERY TURN

The terraces look down on a rectangular pool below the kitchen garden while, round the corner, a second arm of the valley forms an L-shape to the west. Here, in the 17th century, a stream was dammed to make three fishponds. Above them, at the same time, terrace walks were created, defined by clipped yews. These once-disciplined plants have now grown into giants that obscure the steep face of the bank and reach up almost to the lawn above.

Of the ponds, one now contains goldfish, another has become a bog garden filled with bamboos, flowering shrubs and ferns, while the third has been transformed into a cherry orchard. Like the main valley, this one too is hidden from the outer world until you are standing almost on its brink.

The garden terraces are a brilliant exploitation of potentially difficult terrain and clearly illustrate how terracing can be used to transform into a most attractive asset of character what might otherwise be considered a liability.

EXPLOITING A CHANGE OF LEVEL IN A SMALLER GARDEN

Even where the scale is considerably smaller, a slope can make an eye-catching feature. The scheme shown here, for instance, was inspired by the terraces and steps at Upton but designed to suit a garden with a reasonably sharp drop of 4 ft (1.2 m) running across the middle.

Here an area some 12 ft (3.7 m) wide and the same from front to back is used to make a bold and attractive feature of generous steps and platforms providing room enough for sitting in the sun. They are made of concrete topped by quarry tiles. As at Upton, descending or ascending feet are directed to left or right of centre, most firmly in this case by an inset bed of of lavender and rosemary.

Two sentinel Irish yews (*Taxus baccata* 'Fastigiata') rise out of spreading grey-green clumps of prostrate juniper (*Juniperus* × *media* 'Pfitzeriana'). The mauve and yellow colour scheme is completed with ground-covering 'Tall Story' roses running down the slope.

GENEROUS LEVELS This adaptation of terracing retains the elegant air of the grand original and makes an easily maintained feature.

SETTING
THE STYLE

TIME AND PERSONAL TASTE are the key factors when you are making or reshaping a garden. The best garden is the one that suits your particular needs, so choose from the ideas of other gardeners and other ages to compose the style that pleases you. Have a garden that runs on a few hours' work a month or one that is an all-consuming passion. Design it to be childproof or to be easy for a disabled gardener to manage. Make it simple and modern or follow the cottage tradition; and if you want to experiment, create the mood of the Orient or the Mediterranean in a corner of your plot.

A classic symmetrical pattern of clipped box scrolls round a central urn
in a double image designed to be viewed from a higher level.

THE RIGHT STYLE FOR YOU

DECIDING HOW TO STYLE the plot is as exciting to a gardener as decorating a home is to someone who is passionate about interior design. There is a rich heritage to draw on, demonstrated in many great gardens of the past that have been maintained from their heyday or re-created in the style of the period.

Gardens in a modern style, suited to today's space and pace, also inspire with examples of architectural lines and hard surfaces softened by fuss-free plantings. Travel abroad, too, injects fresh ideas for touches of the exotic. Stimulated by influences from all sides, enthusiasm for growth and change is likely to mount ever higher, whether the garden is embryonic, in its infancy or mature.

You may like a rambly garden that is in keeping with the surrounding landscape or prefer everything in neat rows with clipped hedges and straight paths. As well as personal choice, the age and habits of those who use the garden, the tones of the local earth and stone are all factors affecting the choice of plants and materials, layout and mood.

REMAINING REALISTIC

You could combine areas of different styling, with perhaps a soothing Japanese corner, a sizzling Mediterranean hotspot and a Victorian kitchen garden plot. But it is vital to be practical, and to channel your fancies into the realms of the realistic. Remember that the enormous herbaceous border you saw in the garden of a stately home last June is maintained by expert staff, and may not look as good for the rest of the year.

The aim must be to stay within your bounds, so that when you achieve the desired image it is manageable and appropriate. It is a gardener's nature to aspire upwards, but too much grandeur, too many urns or hard stone benches, too many period planting schemes or mixtures of style can look pretentious and overdone in a private garden. So, if the chosen style is not quite working, resist the urge to add more bits – it is much better to take some away.

NOVEL WAYS TO GROW PLANTS A mulch of gravel over soil creates a marvellous growing medium for pockets of pansies and aromatic herbs, and you can walk on it. This informal style makes the most of hard materials without looking as severe as some modern architectural garden designs.

GARDENS TO SUIT TIGHT SCHEDULES

THE AMOUNT OF TIME you want to spend gardening is a factor in how elaborately you develop your design and, equally, in the style you decide on. Formal layouts, for instance, need the most time in clipping and restraining the plants, since you are imposing an unnatural idiom on a site.

Whether the garden is planned for low maintenance or is labour intensive, it saves you time in the long run to prepare the site thoroughly and construct the layout properly. Take the chance to banish perennial menaces when the plot is bare. The time to get rid of ground elder is when the decks are cleared, or it will plague you evermore. Silverweed and convolvulus are other weeds that are difficult to eradicate in a mature garden.

As well as putting in the hard work now, spend a sizable proportion of your garden budget on laying down hard surfaces solidly, with the correct base and sub-base. If you skimp on this, in a few years' time the paving will crack, wobble and be infested with weeds.

But the time to lay paving is often when the kitty is at its emptiest. You may have just bought the house and paid for its decoration. If the garden comes last in your financial priorities, do a small part of it well to start with. In the short term, seed the remainder of the garden with grass or, if it is in the shade of trees, plant it with a ground cover which you can remove later on. Dead nettle (*Lamium*) covers the ground fast, and so do ivy and periwinkle. You can complete the desired layout in successive years.

YOUR PERSONAL STYLE

When you have assessed the site, and thought about a style sympathetic to the house and what it is built of, turn your attention to the most important matter – what you want. If the garden is to be practical it should work for you. A list is probably the easiest way to clarify your needs, particularly when more than one person uses and tends the garden.

Perhaps include a second list with queries, such as who is going to look after particular parts of the garden? And how much time is available for it? If the answer is that you are the one who has to

EASY-CARE LAWN For the ultimate in undemanding lawns, lay artificial turf; it is untroubled by any site, from deep shade to arid roof garden. Use your limited time on raised beds and pots.

KEEP A GARDEN DIARY

A GARDEN DIARY helps you to keep track of what plants are where and is fun to look back on as your design develops. Make a note of each new plant, when you set it out and where it came from. Then you can repeat successes as well as learning from any mistakes.

Jot down, too, when different plants flower or look their best, to help you to plan new groupings or to extend schemes. It is also interesting to see from year to year how early or late the same plant flowers or bears fruit.

do the work, how much do you like gardening? The less time and enthusiasm you have the more you need a strong, simple layout with the minimum of frills. In any case, there is beauty to enjoy in a garden that is not always immaculate.

GARDEN PLANNER

Now, while the canvas is still bare, is the time to work out your styling ideas. To clarify your requirements, divide a sheet of paper in three. In one column write what you must have, in the second what you would like to be there and in the third what you do not want. Take one example.

What you must have:
Place for dustbins near the kitchen door, but covered up.
Place to hang clothes out to dry.
Convenient tap for watering and for a hose to wash the car.
Place to make compost, preferably in constructed bins.
Place for oil tanks, with easy access for filling them up.
Place for storing barbecue gear, play equipment for children and bicycles.

What you want to be there:
Place for a few herbs in summer.
Terrace to give somewhere to sit, read, sunbathe, entertain and eat.

SHORT CUT TO DRAMA Growing just a few huge plants cuts down on chores. For banana, red-flowered canna and variegated giant reed, you need a very sheltered, probably urban, garden which is not touched by frost.

Place for wild flowers – bulbs naturalised under a tree, perhaps.
Play space for children.

What you do not want:
Rock garden – requires too much site preparation at the outset.
Long grass – it is too untidy and takes up too much space in a small garden.
Fruit trees – not enough room.
Water – a hazard for children.

Most arguments are over the features you dream of having rather than those you must have. Once you have decided what you must keep in, what is desirable but not essential and what is definitely out, pencil in the items on a scaled plan of the garden. A plan helps you to resolve precisely what it is you want and how much you will be able to look after without the work getting on top of you.

Before you commit yourself to a design, get estimates for any work proposed. You can even have a design drawn up. Professional or homemade, it becomes the blueprint from which to work.

INCLUDING DREAM FEATURES

Gardens started from scratch often revolve round one particular feature that is coveted. Many gardeners long for a pergola, for instance. It conjures up pictures of dappled light filtering through the leaves of a climbing rose decked with scented flowers, of the evening fragrance of honeysuckle and bunches of grapes temptingly beyond reach. Provided that you get the dimensions right, a pergola will soften the abrupt transition from indoors to out.

Most gardeners hanker after a lawn when conditions allow. A typical, rectangular plot lends itself to a lawn with beds on either side. A few informal curves soften the rigid lines, but beware of too much weaving in and out as intricate shapes are tricky to mow.
🌢 Make sure that the lawn will be in sun or only partial shade, for the turf to thicken up satisfactorily. Otherwise seek out a turf or seed specifically designed for shade. Site the lawn away from large trees if possible.
🌢 Leave a grass-free strip all round the lawn, which makes edging much easier

than if it goes right up to a wall or a fence.
🌢 Lay paths to take the quickest route across the lawn, otherwise people will take short cuts and wear bare patches in the grass, making an unwanted path.
🌢 Banks should have a slope of less than 30°. It is hard to mow a steeper slope – grow ground-cover plants on it instead.

A pond is often another priority, and when well stocked and managed a water feature is a joy. The larger it is the more

SOW SEED FROM ANNUALS

THERE IS NO NEED to buy new plants each year. Save seeds of annuals such as cosmos or phlox and sow them thinly in early spring in washed-out yoghurt pots or ice-cream tubs filled with seed compost. Keep them on a warm windowsill until the danger of frost is over. The young plants may not be identical to the parent plants; you may have some colour surprises.

lavender and rosemary have foliage interest through winter. Grow them in blocks, not one through another, for roses need feeding and herbs do not.

● Shrub roses mixed with smaller roses add interest by way of autumn hips and give a variation in height.

● In a formal garden, alternate rose beds with beds of perennials or low shrubs to create a far more interesting place to stroll through.

KEEPING DOWN MAINTENANCE

For an easy-care garden tailor-made to your needs, think of what to leave out. Maybe you could forgo a lawn, and do without vegetables and soft fruit. Instead of a formal hedge choose an informal one that does not need clipping. Cover as much bare earth as possible with garden plants to keep out weeds. Roses, except shrub roses, need frequent care; perennials may need staking and dividing. You could instead have a garden of shrubs and trees alone.

After deciding where you want the items on your 'must have' list to go, think about incorporating some hard and soft features that bring visual interest without causing extra work – for example the mixing of surface textures, such as gravel with granite setts, paving slabs with bricks, or cobbles with tiles.

One of the joys of gardening today is the blurring of old distinctions between different types of border. Instead of separating herbaceous, bedding and woody plants, you can now mingle roses, shrubs, bulbs, perennials and annuals, and even edible plants. The mixed border gives all-year interest for little effort.

To minimise the workload, choose a few shrubs, preferably evergreen, and put clusters of the same species together. For instance, a group of rhododendron

easily you can establish enough flora and fauna to keep the water clear.

Where to put it is the next concern. A favourite spot is near a paved sitting area, where you can watch birds, insects and small mammals attracted by the water. Such a placement probably calls for a regular shape to work with a paved area's geometry, which in itself should echo the shapes and proportions of the house. This is the way to build up a relationship

of shapes which gives proper unity to a garden's design.

A plot for many people, particularly traditionalists, is not complete without a rose garden. The flowers of hybrid tea and floribunda roses (now called cluster roses) are superb, but the plants themselves are not. From autumn until late spring they offer only twigs. You can relieve this situation in several ways.

● Blend rose bushes with herbs – sage,

HOW TO DO IT

MAKING A RAISED
BED WITH RAILWAY SLEEPERS

A RAISED BED lets you garden from the comfort of a sitting position. When you build your own, you can make it the precise height you want.

Cut timber or railway sleepers blend with nearly all types of hard surface and provide a sympathetic frame for plants. Prepared cedar is sold at large garden centres and sleepers are available from suppliers around the country. Sleepers are stable but heavy and cumbersome – you can have them sawn in half before use. A two-layer raised bed requires no separate support, but a three-layer bed needs metal rods driven into the ground to brace the outside of the sleepers.

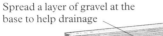

Spread a layer of gravel at the base to help drainage

Staggered layers make a strong frame

varieties needs little attention if you have acid soil, and has a unity of form enlivened with different flower colours and leaf detail. Add the occasional tree if there is the space. Use architectural plants such as *Yucca filamentosa* for interest against a shrub background, limiting massed colour to spring bulbs in tubs or summer annuals spilling from pots.

RAISED BEDS TO SAVE BENDING

Easy-care styles are well suited to older people as well as busy ones, and indeed to any gardener who likes to take it gently. Even devoted gardeners appreciate a layout that minimises the hard graft, leaving plenty of time for pottering. A garden made up entirely of raised beds fits the bill perfectly, as it cuts down bending or kneeling. It will probably be formal in its layout if the beds are hard edged, and would look good with either paving or gravel between the beds. For an informal mixture of plants, oval or kidney-shaped beds are more effective.

Give access to each raised bed from at least three sides if it is 5ft (1.5m) wide or more, so that you can reach across. Use brick, stone, railway sleepers or paving slabs on edge, with the soil level about 18-24 in (45-60 cm) above ground.

Grow roses, which will be at a good height for deadheading and pruning. Include herbs with them to conceal their legginess, which is even more noticeable

RETAINING WALL The low wall raises the bed so that low-growing plants such as aubrietia, arabis, lamium and pulmonaria are easy to see and tend. The weathered brick harmonises with the mellow wall at the back.

MODERN LOOK Compact raised beds filled with self-sufficient, spreading foliage plants such as lamb's tongue and tarragon leave you time to relax in the garden. Climbers will soften the wooden arch as they mature.

COASTAL PRIVILEGE If you live by the sea, and particularly on the western coast that is warmed by the Gulf Stream, take the chance to grow some frost-tender plants such as spiky *Echium pininana* and subtropical *Cordyline* which would perish in a colder site.

blue-green cabbages, broad beans and carrots is handsome enough to mingle with ornamental plants and herbs. Here is a case for a squared layout, if you want vegetable patches of a manageable size.

Raise vegetable beds by 12 in (30 cm) or so with a frame of timber. Raise the soil level to correspond by placing well-rotted organic matter on top, which has the added advantage of improving the vegetable-growing potential of poor soil. The effect of raising the bed is to make a feature of the vegetables, and they are a handy height for harvesting. Add an arch or two for runner beans and marrows and you create a stylish garden. Raised beds and arches give considerable concealment to a greenhouse or toolshed.

SOFT SURFACE IDEAS

A garden of raised beds, whether for vegetables, decorative plants or a mixture, needs no grass – the most common medium for the floor of a garden. The lawn is a British institution: it does not feature in the French, Italian or Japanese garden styles. It does not even feature in the cottage garden for, if you are surrounded by green fields, why have another on your side of the hedge?

There are ways to cover the ground with 'soft' surfaces other than close-cut lawn, which give your garden a different mood and involve lower maintenance. Try a chequerboard pattern of long and short grass, or insert an area of low ground cover. Swathes of periwinkle or ivy resemble a woodland floor and you can grow other plants through them.

ADAPTING AN EXISTING STYLE

Another range of considerations arises when a garden is not new but established, even neglected. What should you keep and what should you take out? It is best not to rush into a solution. Live with your new site to get the feel of what is needed in both summer and winter. Remember that a predecessor put things where they are for a reason. The cause may have gone now, or perhaps the solution is now too big, but check before removing it.

With out-of-hand shrubs, your best course is to cut them back hard after flowering. After a year you know when

WOODLAND GLADE At the other extreme from raised beds is a garden allowed to imitate nature, with bluebells carpeting the ground in spring. In a smaller garden, a few bluebells planted informally under a deciduous tree will soon spread by seed and bulblets to create a similar effect.

when they are raised. Herbs are valuable for both the kitchen and the ornamental garden; they are fragrant and decorative in flower and foliage, and need little care. Many herbs are evergreen – lavender, rosemary, hyssop and savory, for example – which reduces maintenance even further and provides winter interest. Alternatively, have a raised herbaceous

planting spilling over with woolly leaved lamb's tongue or blue-flowered catmint, or make a scree bed of shingle for alpines.

RAISED VEGETABLE PROFILE

When you have a vegetable plot, there is no need to banish it to the end of the garden, furthest from where you want to use it. The foliage of vegetables such as their best season is, and whether you like what they have to offer. Even if you are not won over by a shrub, it may be worth keeping as a backbone to a border.

When large trees need attention, check with the local planning office in case they have a protection order on them. Old trees may be taking light, using up too much space, or impoverishing the ground around them. Call a tree surgeon for technical advice before cutting down trees or lopping off branches.

An old greenhouse may be in place. If you do not want it and it is sound, sell it and use the old base as the foundation for a terrace. Do not keep a greenhouse and fit a garden plan round it when, after due thought, you find it an eyesore. The same applies to garden boundaries such as fences or hedges.

FINDING A STRONG THEME

When you take over someone else's plot, you often find that the basic concept has been diluted with a haphazard mixture of plantings, colours, periods and materials. Where this is the case, pick out the features you like best and build the garden round them.

Once you have decided what you are going to keep in the garden, draw up a scaled plan showing these features but excluding existing elements you want to remove. Make several copies on tracing or greaseproof paper and use them to try out the possible positions of new items. Try the most appropriate places and work out every possible permutation until you resolve the garden's layout.

This layout can be interpreted in a number of styles. The location of your property may give the first clue to the style. If you are surrounded by woodland, for instance, a garden of bulbs growing in the dappled shade cast by a blossom-covered fruit tree would be suitable. A coastal garden, too, may make the decisions for you. Trees such as pines, whitebeam and sycamore filter the wind, with escallonia, hebe and gorse growing underneath. Buddleia, cistus and fuchsia start to fill out the interest.

High or scree gardens also dictate the plants you grow. Some naturally thrive in shaded, north-facing places oozing with water; others prefer the hot, sunny face.

Develop any naturally boggy areas into ponds of water that can become wildlife sanctuaries; plant them with flag irises, reeds and rushes, and some early yellow-flowering marsh marigolds.

AN INFORMAL MODERN GARDEN

Beauty and practicality characterise this simple design. Swoops of plants punctuated by trees and imaginative use of the sloping site create a low-maintenance garden.

IMMEDIATELY OUTSIDE the house, an L-shaped terrace surfaced with decking provides a transitional room with steps leading to the rest of the garden. The straight lines of the timber contrast with the curving contours of the garden, where fluid lines lead the eye easily from one part to the next. Under the decking the shady stretch, studded with cobbles, makes an ideal environment for ferns.

A lawn carpets much of the garden. The mowing differs according to where the grass is and what its function is. Where the ground is flat, the grass is closely mown for easy walking. On the banks, rough grass is dotted with bulbs. Autumn crocus and cyclamen bloom in September, leading into groups of heaths and ling which provide year-round foliage and flower interest.

CREATIVITY WITH SHRUBS

Above the mid-garden bank, existing rowan trees have helped to set the route of the mown path that meanders alongside a substantial bed planted with rhododendrons. The shrubbery makes a pleasant vista, filters northerly winds and screens the neighbours from view.

The size of the shrubs varies from tree height to ground cover. Some of the leaves have differently coloured undersides, so you catch glimpses of brown, purple and blue-white. The theme continues with a group of azaleas, relatives of the rhododendron.

With evergreens blanketing much of the ground all year, there is hardly any weeding to do. Any 'weeds' that crop up in the grass banks can be left to mingle with the naturalised bulbs.

This garden is on sandy, acid soil, ideal for growing both heathers and rhododendrons. On a chalky, alkaline soil, a similar design could be carried out with whitebeam and viburnums.

Rowan trees are decked with bright autumn berries

Heathers nestle on the bank, giving colour all year

Azaleas clothe the slope with contrasts of foliage

1. Rowan (*Sorbus aucuparia*)
2. St Dabeoc's heath (*Daboecia cantabrica*)
3. Tree heath (*Erica arborea*)
4. *Rhododendron bureavii*
5. *Rhododendron calophytum*
6. Mixed bulbs (*Colchicum speciosum* 'Album' and 'Rosy Dawn'; *Crocus speciosus*; *Cyclamen hederifolium*)
7. Heath (*Erica × darleyensis*)
8. Ling (*Calluna vulgaris* 'H.E. Beale')
9. Ling (*Calluna vulgaris* 'Darkness')
10. Ling (*Calluna vulgaris* 'Cramond')
11. Ling (*Calluna vulgaris* 'Serlei')
12. Azalea (*Rhododendron* 'Lemonora')
13. Azalea (*Rhododendron obtusum*)

A FLAVOUR OF THE PAST

YOUR HOUSE is a great key to possible styles that would suit the garden. The date of the house might suggest a small piece of history in the layout, and a certain amount of period restoration lifts a garden out of the ordinary. True restoration requires attention to every detail. For the modern garden, a corner devoted to a particular period is enough to recall the past and echo the ambience of the house. A little knot garden of herbs such as santolina, hyssop, lavender or box pays homage to an original or mock Tudor house, for instance.

The style of your house gives some pointers to your garden plan, but the materials it is constructed from are equally important. Most people do not live in a period place, but in a brick, stone, pebble-dashed or rendered house. Using some of the materials of the house in pavings, edgings and garden buildings helps to unify the design.

Most gardens are maintained by one or two people pressed for time. When adapting ideas from an earlier period, it is possible to keep the flavour of the original without its continual round of chores. That is the secret of re-creating the past: interpreting it in an imaginative way that brings together the best of old and new.

ECHOES OF TUDOR TRADITIONS

The earliest surviving British gardens are medieval and Tudor. Enclosed from the harsh world, Tudor gardens symbolised paradise on Earth. Arbours and trellises were clothed in scented climbers (masking more unpleasant aromas), fountains and pools provided somewhere for the ladies to dabble their fingers, and lawns were strewn with flowering plants or made up of fragrant ground cover.

A camomile lawn makes an aromatic alternative to grass in the Tudor style, and needs mowing only once or twice a year. It has feathery fronds and a pleasantly sharp smell when crushed underfoot – but it is for the occasional stroll, not for regular hard wear, and looks dull in winter. Choose the form 'Treneague'

TRANSLATED IN TIME Tiny squares of clipped box filled in with pinks revive in miniature the grand schemes of Tudor knot gardens. Scale the design up or down depending on how much space you want to devote to one style.

COLONIAL DAYS The 16th and 17th centuries abroad saw the start of English colonies in what is now the United States. The settlers developed a pronounced style typified by white picket fencing, timber houses and spring bulbs in orderly rows, as seen in Williamsburg, Virginia.

TUDOR SPLENDOUR Formal knot gardens look their best seen from a raised vantage point where the pattern of plants clearly shows. An intricate design is labour intensive – you may need to be less ambitious in today's garden.

ORDERLY STYLE Retain a flavour of the 16th century by planting in blocks. Such a layout is particularly striking with low hedging plants but it is also suited to vegetables, which are decorative as part of a strong design.

which does not flower. Set out the plants about 6 in (15 cm) apart during spring in free-draining soil. Replant any bare patches that appear and weed as necessary. Pearlwort, thyme or clover can also be used as alternative lawn plants.

To make an arbour in Tudor mode, train an arch of old-fashioned roses and honeysuckle over a wooden frame, with lavender and pinks at the climbers' feet. For pleasant scent, mix *Rosa centifolia* and *R.* 'Alba Semiplena' with *Lonicera periclymenum* 'Belgica' for early summer flowering or 'Serotina' for later blooms. Place a bench underneath the arbour – perhaps a turf seat of camomile, so you are cushioned by its springy, aromatic greenery while you sit.

As the influence of the Renaissance spread, the focus of the garden shifted. Vistas, pathways and avenues created strong geometric shapes, linked by focal points such as fountains and sculptures – all ideas that are still fundamental to many of today's garden styles.

TRIM AND FORMAL SCHEMES

Seventeenth-century gardens were also formal, with much clipping and pleaching, using the basic material of yew or hornbeam almost as walls or colonnades. Gardens were trim and neat with rectangles, squares or canals of still water and hardly any flower colour. Topiary work was immensely popular – Hampton Court has over a thousand examples. If you adopt this soothing style, the time

you spend clipping hedging plants is countered by the hours you save on weeding and tending herbaceous plants. This is the garden for a pleached hedge (see p.49) as a boundary or divider, or for incorporating a water feature when the hard surfaces are put in.

While most urban gardens in the 17th century were quite small, they were gracious, fitting surroundings for the elegant houses. In Bath, the garden of an early 18th-century town house has been restored; it is still formal, with areas of paving and gravel, but borders of colour have crept in. If you feel more at home with flowers but like an ordered layout, adopt a similar style and combine a geometric design of hard surfaces set with pockets of bulbs, annuals and perennials.

ENHANCING A NATURAL LOOK

In the late 18th-century, British gardens reversed the principle of enclosing an idealised world within walls. In a celebration of wealth and property, landscaped parks were created – rolling pastoral land surrounding tranquil stretches of water. Reproduced on a smaller scale in the garden of today, this natural look becomes a haven for wildlife, planted with native species, particularly trees, and with a pond set in a meadow-like lawn dotted with wild flowers.

This so-called 'picturesque' movement had shifted from Classical order to a more Romantic phase. Appreciating rather than transforming nature was the

ROMANTIC FREEDOM The landscaped garden of the late 18th century let nature roam, but controlled by the hand of man. To capture something of this spirit, think of opening up a view hidden by a fence or dense shrubbery.

fashion of the day. The garden was regarded almost as a landscape painting, and buildings in the Gothic or Rustic styles completed the picture. You can give something of the same atmosphere by building a little folly or shell grotto or by adding fanciful detail to the garden shed.

The look changed after the turn of the century. In town gardens by the mid 19th century, gravelled paths were snaking through lawns edged with sombre shrubberies of laurel, box and aucuba.

DIFFERENT THEMES FOR LOVERS OF COLOUR

Slowly, the desire for colour which continues today crept in – not the soft tones of cottage garden perennials, but the vibrancy of geraniums and begonias set within edgings of alyssum and lobelia. The advent of the conservatory, heated by a steam boiler, allowed the production of half-hardy plants for the garden.

This love of 'bedding out' brightened summer scenes then as now, whether as warm colours in beds of circular or diamond shapes in parks, or as island beds or hedge-backed borders in a private garden. In a modern version of such a labour-intensive style, you can devote some of the space to permanent plantings. Introduce interest for winter with shrubs such as *Cotoneaster horizontalis* and pyracantha for their attractive berries, and mahonia for its flowers.

When reaction against industrialisation sparked off the changes known as the Arts and Crafts movement, garden design was rethought along with all other aspects of design. Designer-craftsmen and writers began to draw their followers away from vivid annual colour towards wild flowers and the cottage garden style.

Late Victorian gardeners included fruit trees with herbs and simple perennial flowers on a grand scale. The last great country houses to be built during the later 19th and early 20th centuries were surrounded by gardens in the form of hedged rooms decorated with non-native material mixed in the cottage way. The goal was to fill the garden with as many different foreign plants as possible – an ambition that long persisted.

At the end of the 20th century gardeners are questioning this precedent.

FORMAL AND ORDERLY In contrast to the Romantic look, gardens of the 19th century favoured symmetry. Immaculately clipped evergreen hedges enclosed colour-coordinated planting schemes and formed interesting pathways. Ornaments were placed at strategic points.

The emerging style is more concerned with native plants and a looser manner of growth. Informal plantings of native species fit into a strong basic design, which makes the garden functional, beautiful and not too time consuming.

PLANTING IN PERIOD STYLE

You can pursue the idea of planning a garden in the manner of an earlier epoch and choose plants that were in vogue during the period when the house was built. For instance, ferneries were very Victorian. They are excellent for northern manufacturing areas which grew up in Victorian times, and for any northern aspect. Many planting schemes in their day were nostalgic reminders of postings abroad. The moist, warm conservatory is reminiscent of Burma or India. Many conifers were introduced from British Columbia and rhododendrons from the Himalayas in the Victorian era.

Conifers proliferated and rhododendrons were hybridised extensively all through the early 1900s, while Japanese

CARPET BEDDING Victorian-style patterns of planting are fun to re-create. Try arranging blue *Echeveria* and purple *Iresine* among mixed foliage plants. An agave encircled with sempervivum graces the centre.

cherries arrived in the 1930s. The widespread × *Cupressocyparis leylandii* made its first appearance in the 1950s, while the gold *Robinia pseudoacacia* 'Frisia' was widely planted in the 1980s. Flower arrangers within the last 20 years have also popularised certain plants, such as variegated eleagnus, the blooms of astrantia and grey-green hosta leaves.

There is no need to be rigid in your selection according to era, but knowing when plants became popular casts an interesting sidelight on them. Observing the style of your house and corresponding materials and plants are pointers, not rules, to what gives a satisfying result.

COTTAGE OR COUNTRY-HOUSE STYLE?

A cottage may well come with an overgrown, mixed muddle of the nostalgic ideal – a medley of gnarled apple trees, rosemary, thyme and nasturtiums, holly, hawthorn and hollyhocks, campanulas, pinks and wallflowers, sweet williams and sweet peas. Such a garden will need extensive pruning and clearing but little stylistic change unless you want space for some new features.

Country-house style, on a larger scale than cottage plantings, alters according to period. The Victorian garden could be

TIMELESS AND AGELESS This cherub steps out of Classical myth but has a playful air that is equally suitable for a less controlled, Romantic style. Swathes of ivy make an appropriately wild and natural garden setting.

MAKING A FERNERY

MANY PLANTS cannot tolerate damp, dense shade. But do not despair if your garden has a boggy, dark corner; one group of plants – ferns – relish such a site. Ferneries were popular during the Victorian era so you can create a period piece at the same time.

Choose hardy ferns, for example royal fern (*Osmunda regalis*) and the sensitive fern (*Onoclea sensibilis*), for the boggiest areas, and *Adiantum venustum* – which needs neutral to acid soil – on slightly drier land. Dig rotted manure or compost into the soil before planting. Then enjoy the tender green and bronze-red young leaves, unfurling into rich green mature foliage.

COTTAGE GARDEN The charm of a small rural garden lies in its seemingly unplanned miscellany of old-fashioned, often scented, herbaceous plants including catmint, clary (*Salvia sclarea*), taller *Campanula latifolia* 'Alba' and foxgloves, backed by clambering honeysuckle and roses.

BEST PLANTS

LOW-ALLERGEN CHOICES

If you suffer from hay fever or similar allergic reactions to particular plants, choose from the many 'safe' species.

• Snowy mespilus (*Amelanchier lamarckii*): tree with leaves that unfold bronze, turn dark green then orange-red; sprays of white flowers in spring.

• Judas tree (*Cercis siliquastrum*): clusters of pink spring flowers and purple-red pods in late summer.

• Double wild cherry (*Prunus avium* 'Plena'): dark green foliage shaded red and yellow in autumn; reddish-brown bark and white flowers in spring.

• *Hebe* 'Autumn Glory': moderately hardy, with purple stems and violet-blue flowers from summer to autumn.

• *Viburnum tinus*: evergreen, with flat white, pink-budded flowers all winter and spring.

• *Weigela florida* 'Aureovariegata': golden-edged leaves; arching branches and pink flowers in early summer.

• *Delphinium* Elatum hybrids: closely packed upright spires of white, blue or purple flowers, usually with an eye of contrasting colour.

• *Campanula persicifolia*: forms spreading rosettes; nodding, bell-shaped papery white or blue flowers.

• *Bergenia cordifolia*: forms evergreen ground cover; large, rounded, crinkled leaves and pale pink spring flowers.

• *Epimedium perralderianum*: forms semi-evergreen ground cover; large, toothed glossy leaves and yellow flowers in spring.

either formal, with beds of annual colour round a central purple cordyline, or 'naturalistic', with gravelled paths sweeping through dense shrubberies.

The Edwardian look, inspired by the architect Sir Edwin Lutyens, has smaller areas within a garden divided by hedges of yew, holly or hornbeam. The garden pattern extends from the geometry of the house, using borders of perennials. Favourite flowers include asters, phlox, hollyhock and delphinium, in the manner of that doyenne of colour harmonies, the plantswoman Gertrude Jekyll.

Her style still works well when it is adapted to lessen the maintenance. Typical are wide paths, ending in a feature.

GARDENS WITHIN A GARDEN The Edwardians brought in the notion of outdoor 'rooms', where each compartment had a separate character or colour. The White Garden at Sissinghurst, Kent, is one room in a wider scheme – in a smaller garden, you could colour coordinate each section.

Borders on each side of the path are colour graded – strong in the foreground, paler in the distance. Pot-grown lilies and foxgloves supplement the borders.

In their original form, these borders lasted for six weeks, while a family was at its summer home. Such schemes are impractical today. Copy the adaptations that were devised in the 1950s and add shrubs to the perennials to make a mixed border and reduce the workload.

IN AND OUT OF TOWN

In town, smaller Edwardian terrace gardens were filled with similar flowers, and often had a vegetable patch at the furthest point from the house. Tilework was introduced into pavings separated from the plantings by a rope-type kerb or bricks set on edge to create a zigzag line. This is as charming now as it was then.

The style and form varied in the 1920s and 30s as more people took to gardening. Layouts dating back to those decades contain elements of the Victorian and Edwardian gardens before them, in a scaled-down form of gracious living.

In the 1960s, outside rooms, barbecues and play space for children became major requirements – as they continue to be. People with small urban gardens were readier to do without a lawn as they relished the convenience of hard surfacing, offset by architectural plants such as yucca and New Zealand flax. This style, too, is one to continue today.

Herbs, and their merits as garden plants, were appreciated as foreign dishes and healthier diets were discussed. The cycle is completed with these Tudor regulars again in high favour. Full sun is best for herbs, although chives and mint grow in shade too, and near the house is prudent for easy picking. Apart from their culinary use, herbs are lovely to brush against as you walk down the garden.

A GARDEN FOR CHILDREN

There is no need to turn your garden into an unbroken spread of lawn for children: formal hedges and knot gardens are superb for games of hide-and-seek and chase, while a cottage garden can cope with footballs landing in a flowerbed and the branches of a mature apple tree can be trimmed for safer climbing.

However, you may want to set aside one area for children and their toys. Apart from sunflowers, nasturtiums, radishes and a few other plants that offer

dramatic results, children tend to want an extended playroom, not flowers and foliage, scent and seasonal interest.

Grass provides the softest surface to fall on from swings, climbing frames and slides. Choose a hard-wearing mix of meadow grasses, timothy and crested dog's tail. A path can be a tricycle course, and paving a hopscotch area.

When the children grow up, it is easy to convert play areas into 'grown-up' features. Transform the sandpit, which you want near the house so that you can see what is going on, into a pool; use the swing and climbing-frame area for training runner beans and sweet peas, perhaps using the original features as supports.

THE ESSENCE OF A STYLE

Give your garden an instantly recognisable character inspired by distant places or times past. You can evoke the original with a single feature or a collection of plants.

TUDOR TIMES
An arch of sweet-smelling roses, a mulberry tree with crooked branches and intensely flavoured, late-summer berries, and a quince tree bearing pear-shaped or round fruit all conjure up the times of Henry VIII and Elizabeth I.

HOLLAND AND NORTHERN FRANCE
The royal garden of Versailles gave its name to a box much used in this formal style, often with a bay tree clipped into a standard 'mop-head' shape. Spirals were another popular topiary shape. Beds of tulips were a Dutch passion.

CLASSICAL ROME
Classical statues and a pebble-and-paving mosaic speak of the heyday of Rome, when it was the centre of artistic inspiration. Try out mosaic patterns on paper first, before buying pebbles in contrasting colours to make them up.

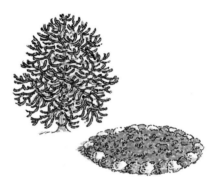

VICTORIAN PATTERNS
The distinctive monkey puzzle tree (*Araucaria araucana*), with its branches like furry tails, was introduced from Chile late in the 18th century and in vogue by Victorian times. Island beds of annuals in precise patterns also echo the era.

1980s OUTDOOR LIVING
The golden leaves of *Robinia pseudoacacia* 'Frisia' rustling in the breeze are one of the most visible legacies of the 1980s. The patio became an outdoor kitchen and living room, with built-in barbecue and places to sit.

MIDDLE EAST OASIS
Water gushing from an intricately shaped and inlaid fountain gives relief from the heat of the day. The Chusan palm (*Trachycarpus fortunei*) is hardy despite its tropical looks. A Persian rose opens wide in the warmth of the sun.

MEDITERRANEAN HEAT
In a sheltered sun trap, plant terracotta or ochre pots with an agave or an orange tree, plants often seen in southern France. A mural of gaily coloured tiles gives a white wall a Spanish flourish.

JAPANESE TOUCHES
Bonsai – miniature trees – are an intriguing Japanese idea that never fail to provoke comment. Raked shingle imitates the flow of water, dotted with 'islands' of rock under the aloof pose of a stone stork.

INFLUENCES FROM ABROAD

INSTEAD OF CREATING a piece of nostalgia, you might like to adopt the idiom of another country. As travel becomes easier, people see more styles and long to capture their character at home.

Gardens of northern France have a distinctive mood that is close to the formal styles in British tradition. Set the scene with gravelled paths and border them with clipped box standards and pyramids and low box hedges. Place a statue or ornament at the end of each vista. Fix painted shutters at the windows and set out matching café tables and folding chairs on a paved area.

Fill window boxes and pots with geraniums and find a place for a piece of French pottery. Install a stone trough for a centrepiece. Such a garden is far easier to lay out than an informal, rambling one, but it takes more time to maintain.

THE MEDITERRANEAN LOOK

Whether Spanish, Italian or Provençal, the Mediterranean look appeals to those who yearn for roasting summers, where the garden is hot and sunny and the owner likes to sunbathe. You need a site facing south or west. A seaside garden is ideal, as long as it is sheltered, because tender plants are easier to grow where hard frosts are rare, the light has a clearer quality – and the views are magnificent. Forget the lawn and have instead small corners of paving, partially shaded by pergolas draped with wisteria and vines. Add the cooling sound of trickling water and pack in some decorative terracotta pots brimming with pelargoniums.

Lay terracotta tiles on the terrace and grow vines over the white walls. Dot amphorae (two-handled, narrow-necked jars) about, filled with trailing plants or left empty and sculptural. A fig tree, sky blue plumbago (moved to a conservatory for the winter) and *Convolvulus cneorum* add to the southern atmosphere and culinary herbs with lavender, rosemary and cistus come into their own. Ceramic plaques make attractive wall features.

The Mediterranean look may surround a swimming pool, where flowers of clear blue and yellow work best. This is a tricky area to style, particularly if the pool is an insistent blue. Stick with brightness, which suits an area of action.

HOLIDAY HEAT Seeing the fleshy growth of cacti and succulents instantly transports you to hotter climates. Cacti and succulents store water in their tissues to carry them through dry spells and cope with infrequent watering even when grown in pots. Most need to come indoors for winter.

This is a good place to build a barbecue into the wall, for eating in the open air after a day of swimming and sunbathing.

ORIENTAL HARMONY

A highly popular style is that of Japan, although most of the gardens seen in this country under that name bear little relation to the original. Rock, water and plants are the core features and should evoke the natural landscape. Surface texture and subtle colouring contribute to their style and appeal as much as shape.

Make a restful oasis, planted with bamboo, other foliage plants and small-leaved evergreens, all set among drifts of gravel, pebbles and small boulders. Add a bonsai tree in a beautiful pot, a Buddha strategically placed or a stone lantern. Plants to give the right mood include the

JAPANESE SERENITY Rocks and stones are the most dramatic features in an area that is planned according to traditional Japanese style where space, texture and form predominate. Use rocks as a sculpture, in an asymmetric arrangement, to set beside paths and arid swirls of raked gravel.

BAMBOO CLOCHES

COMBINE FUNCTION and form in an Eastern-style garden with bamboo cloches. Place the cover over a plant for shelter from frost and wind. To give more protection, cover the cloche with horticultural fleece or newspaper held in place with clothespegs. The woven dome lets rain through while creating a warmer microclimate for the plant.

angelica tree (*Aralia elata*), with large, deeply divided leaves, and its relative, *Fatsia japonica*. Clipped Sawara cypress (*Chamaecyparis pisifera*), grasses, ferns and mosses are appropriate. A Japanese maple (*Acer palmatum*) adds autumn colour. The bamboo *Nandina domestica* and shrubby *Pinus mugo* – indeed all pines – add an Oriental air. Enhance it with azaleas clipped into hummocks.

In a Chinese garden, plants have significance beyond their visual appeal. Grow chrysanthemums for suggesting autumn, peonies for wealth and grace, magnolia, crab apple and laurel for wealth and contentment. The bamboo is flexible yet strong; the peach brings fertility and longevity. Intersperse plantings with mosaics of pebbles or tiles that depict plants or animals.

Indian and Persian gardens can be suggested in your own plot. Such gardens are always formal, with cisterns of water as centrepieces and gently playing fountains along the length. Pots of pelargoniums stand symmetrically around the water. A palm, cordyline or citrus tree in a tub helps to create the mood, although none of these is hardy unless placed in the most sheltered town garden. The only hardy palm is the Chusan palm (*Trachycarpus fortunei*).

Use precise, symmetrical plantings, perhaps in sunken beds with flowers at path height. Persian gardens are associated with roses, and the richness of all yellow roses has come from their *Rosa foetida* 'Persiana', a double yellow old-fashioned shrub rose. Eastern styles and plants suit a small, enclosed town garden.

MODERN STYLES AT HOME AND ABROAD

In the rocky landscape of Scandinavia, gardens created from natural stone groupings studded with silver birch are

MODERN MIX AND MATCH Plants such as shrubby potentilla provide plenty of detail to hold the interest. They soften the hard surfaces and need little weeding in their gravel mulch. Sleepers support changes of level.

COPPER TAGS

WHEN SETTING OUT new shrubs, it is wise to label them, particularly if you have selected a specific variety and want to remember its name.

For an unobtrusive but permanent marker, use a copper tag and tie, which weather to a greenish colour that blends in with the stems and foliage. Just write on the tag with a ballpoint pen and the name becomes indented. Attach it carefully to the chosen plant, making sure to leave plenty of slack for the shoot to thicken with age.

popular. To echo this easy-living style, make an informal arrangement of lawn, conifers and ground-cover plants, enlivened with spring bulbs and a few flowering shrubs. Add heathers for extra trouble-free planting if you have acid soil.

In a town, try a totally architectural garden, in the style of modern French designers. Emphasise the paths, walls and containers rather than the plants for a year-round, no-work garden. Put the plants you do include in raised beds for changes of level. For a satisfying shape choose *Mahonia lomariifolia*, *Juniperus × media* 'Pfitzeriana' or *J. scopulorum* 'Skyrocket'. Shrubs with good leaf colour include *Euonymus fortunei* 'Silver Pillar' and *Ilex × altaclerensis* 'Lawsoniana'.

You could make separate sections of the garden reminiscent of the styles of other countries. One section could have the contemplative character of Japan, another the formality of France and a hot area could have the flavour of Spain.

Gardeners are often conditioned by tradition to expect a certain look in a garden, and new ideas – even convenient ones – are accepted only slowly. The modern emphasis on subtle plantings overlaying hard surfacing is offering a distinctive new style which is catching on gradually just as bygone styles once did.

MOORISH COOLNESS The sound of playing water, so welcome in an arid climate, the arches created by the jets and the whispering of dark citrus leaves cool the sizzling atmosphere in a sun-drenched garden.

UNCLUTTERED LINES Unified by decking for surface, seating and planting, this up-to-the-minute garden has a no-frills simplicity. The fresh white argyranthemum and cheerful yellow chrysanthemum offset any starkness.

INSPIRATION FROM
GREAT GARDENS

PORT LYMPNE

Dutch colonial style links house to garden.

In 1973, John Aspinall bought the estate of Port Lympne, near the coastal town of Hythe in Kent, as a home for his growing collection of wild animals. The animals were installed in the surrounding park, and the house and garden were restored to their former colonial-inspired splendour.

P RAISED AS 'the last historic house to be built this century', Port Lympne was constructed in 1911 as the summer residence of Sir Philip Sassoon, merchant banker, statesman and soldier. He put his fortune to work on creating the house and grounds. The terraces of the garden are cut into the steep, south-facing slope that had been sea cliffs at the time when the English Channel occupied what is now Romney Marsh.

After the owner's death in 1939, Port Lympne was occupied by the RAF for the duration of the Second World War. Eventually, the wildlife collector John Aspinall came to the rescue.

WILD PARKLAND

Conservation is now the theme at Port Lympne – most famously of endangered wildlife species, but also of the highly individual house and garden. The outer parkland is reserved for the exotic animal species but even the fringes of the garden have an informal atmosphere and the plants are purposely left to grow with no treatment by sprays and fertilisers. This encourages native butterflies, bees and other insects vital to pollinating plants, and the insects attract birds, frogs and toads, newts and lizards. Rabbits come to feed on the greenery and foxes follow for the promising larder.

ORDERLY WITHIN

By contrast, the inner, enclosed garden is impeccably maintained, although a chemical-free regime is practised there, too. Many of the elements are typical of the colonial style: separate orchard areas for fruit trees, shipshape order in the flower gardens and plants popular with the North American colonists – cotton lavender, for example.

Much of the original garden has survived from Sassoon's day: the vineyard

LAVISH LABOUR Squares of red and white begonias interspersed with high-quality turf create a superb chequered display in summer.

and figyard (where native cowslips have self-seeded), the elaborately laid-out terraces, and the 125-step Trojan Stairway that looks out over Romney Marsh to the Channel and even the distant coastline of France, which is visible on a clear day.

PLANTING TRIUMPHS

Most dramatic of all, there is the geometric Chessboard Garden, surrounded by a yew hedge of such clipped perfection that it looks to be carved out of wood, sandpapered and painted. Evergreen hedges often enclosed colonial gardens.

Lines of brick mark out each row of squares in the 'board'. Half the squares are turfed and the remainder are planted with begonias, generally in contrasting red and white, although purple and pink have been used. Garden statistics tell of 400 begonias in each square, with the planting taking four gardeners five days.

Warming to their task each spring, the gardeners go on to re-create the Striped Garden. It differs each year, but was recently formed from African marigolds edged with silver-leaved plants. One year, it included a pattern like a Persian carpet, using ageratums, busy lizzies and lobelias. In true colonial tradition, a sundial forms the centrepiece for the Clock Garden, in which triangular beds of salvias, French marigolds and spider plant radiate from the focal point.

SCALED-DOWN CHESSBOARD

A smaller version will not be so labour intensive, or at least not once the basic pattern is established. Overall, 25 squares are envisaged, each area about 3 ft by 3 ft (1 m by 1 m), so the entire board takes up only 15 ft (5 m) square. Since clean-edged precision is vital, each area is outlined by a row of sunken bricks. Begonias are used here, too, but only to mimic the red squares, and a soft pink is used. The white squares are gravel, and the green contain the threadlike, green version of cotton lavender (*Santolina virens*), prevented from flowering by clipping.

The whole bed is surrounded by smooth turf, making a satisfying feature out of an everyday lawn. The view from the raised, paved area, edged by an inexpensive balustrade, is framed by a camellia, a little cypress (*Chamaecyparis obtusa* 'Nana') in an elegant container and a hedge of 'Iceberg' roses. At the far end a hedge and raised bed complete the setting for the chessboard.

SIMPLE PRECISION Using gravel instead of white begonias cuts planting time and care significantly. The feathery green cotton lavender needs clipping, but it takes far less time than mowing squares of grass.

GARDENING
BY DESIGN

FLOWERBEDS AND LAWNS, paving and gravel, paths and screens – what is the best combination for your garden? With so many possible shapes, patterns and textures, ideas abound for making a balance between the garden's major features. The plants will be the crowning glory, but the basic plan plays a crucial part in making your garden a success. It turns a static site into a dynamic design, builds in layer upon layer of interest and ensures that, as the seasons pass, the garden gives lasting delight.

A richly planted bed of pinks, foxgloves, roses and wallflowers is one component in a well-balanced composition of lawn, paving and flowers.

BEDS, BORDERS AND BETWEEN

CREATING A GARDEN happens over the years, reflecting the changing needs and tastes of its owner – and it is never finished. Some ideas come from gardens throughout the country that are opened to the public. These gardens are always above the ordinary as their design, plants and standard of maintenance are displayed to visitors. What works well here, however, can be adopted and adapted for sites that are often very different.

Several thousand gardens in Britain are open to visitors. But the number that can be seen is vastly increased by those glimpsed informally and these too can give you ideas for your own garden. Any walk down a leafy street or through a village provides ideas – the flow of a border, the materials of a path, or a particularly felicitous association of plants.

Back gardens are less easy to 'visit' and use. The best chance to see them is from a train, when you get flashes of all sorts of garden. Travelling from any major railway station, you see inner-city yards give way to the rectangular strips of commuter country and even to grand estates that were probably mature long before the coming of the railway.

REALISTIC PLANNING

Gardens often seem to have grown out of the lifestyles of the owners, partly by need and partly by intention. The two vital questions in garden-making – what do you want? and what do you have? – impinge upon each other. There is no point in craving romantically Edwardian herbaceous borders with long washes of colour when you have a small town courtyard – but colour harmonies are still important. Equally, it is futile to covet rhododendrons and camellias when you have chalk soil, but raised beds and containers of prepared lime-free compost can solve the dilemma on a small scale.

It helps to look at three major components of most gardens: grassed areas or their various alternatives; the beds and borders, specifically shaping, planting and edging them; and the features that link or screen, such as paths, internal hedges, pergolas and trellis. How these interact to form a satisfying whole is at the heart of garden design.

SHAPES AND SPACES Most gardens are developed around a choice of plants contained in a flowerbed or flower border – that strip of soil edging a lawn or path. Use the garden's shape imaginatively – for example, in a square, mow a daisy-free circle out of a round lawn surrounded by curving borders.

GREEN SURFACES

FOR MANY PEOPLE a lawn is central to the idea of a garden – it is where much activity takes place, both work and play. To maintain its perfect appearance it is fed, watered, mown every week for two-thirds of the year, raked, scarified and kept clear of weeds and pests. The banded billiard-table effect obtained is often its own justification – it is a design feature in which colour and texture are as consciously contrived as broadloom carpet indoors. Its edges are as impeccably finished as its surface.

Others, while admitting its beauty, regard such perfection as nearly unattainable and even unnecessary – and 'green' gardeners consider the chemicals commonly used to achieve it as ecologically unacceptable. But most gardens of any size have some form of lawn.

Like other ground surfaces, a lawn has several roles to play.

- It provides open, flat space which contrasts with the densely furnished borders that meet it.
- It is the best place from which to see the borders, and to work on them.
- It offers somewhere to stroll, lounge and play games.
- It leads the eye and the feet to other parts of the garden.
- More than other surfaces, lawn is yielding and soothing in feel and colour.

DIVIDING A LAWN INTO 'ROOMS'

Practising different patterns of cutting emphasises the separate parts of the garden. Typically, garden spaces progress from formality adjoining the house to ever-increasing informality where, for example, a bit of orchard meets the boundary hedge.

Give the first piece of grass, quite small in area, as much care as you have the time to provide, in order to link the outdoor and indoor carpet effects. This will demonstrate that the less carefully groomed effect elsewhere is intentional. After a division such as an arch, a pergola or an opening in an internal hedge or trellis, have a stretch of less pampered 'normal' grass.

Where there is space, let this in turn, after a further divider, lead into an 'orchard' area of fruit trees or specimen shrubs in rough grass. Such a meadow

HEART OF THE GARDEN A path flanked by spheres of box marks the entrance to the main 'room' of the garden – the lawn. The grass here should be smooth, but tough enough to walk on and take hard wear without damage.

effect, heightened by drifts of daffodils and pheasant's eye (*Narcissus poeticus* var. *recurvus*) from March to early June, oxeye daisies and lupins in summer and autumn crocus (*Colchicum*) to follow, makes a major feature in its own right.

Vary the planting to include your favourite bulbs and native species, which will determine how much maintenance the area needs. Usually meadow turf – in fact a mixture of plants, not all of the grass family – is maintained by just two high cuts, in early July and October. It needs no feeding, virtually no weeding unless some perennial gets out of hand,

GRASSY PATHS Like a ride through woodland, a strip of cut grass runs across a meadowlike area of long grass spangled with daffodils.

and certainly no spraying. Lovely as meadow grass looks, it is not easy to walk in, is slow to dry after rain and needs a path mown through it. Where there is room, make the path wide enough for two people to walk abreast. Single file makes for tedious strolls.

Remember that a path cut through high grass lets stems flop inwards across the path, especially in wet weather. This ruins the appearance and the convenience of walking. A band about 1 ft (30 cm) wide cut to intermediate height on each side of the path stops lank stalks brushing your legs and emphasises the role of the different grass heights.

WHERE LAWN MEETS BORDER

Just as long grass falls across paths, so plants bordering carefully tended lawns often flop. Plants tumbling forward in their natural habit show their beauty to the full but the grass underneath suffers.

Except in the most formal spots shrubs spilling onto the lawn do not matter, for the effect is year long and therefore the dead grass never shows. But removing herbaceous growth in autumn reveals entirely unacceptable edges and damaged turf that barely recovers by the following season. On the other hand, impeccably edged grass demands a boring bare rim of soil to the flowerbed before anything else appears. Edging the lawn is the answer.

Variations on low retaining walls can help to separate grass and border.
🌢 The Victorians were keen on using ceramic tiles to support beds. Their rope-topped pattern is in fashion again.
🌢 Make dwarf walls of local stone, roofing tiles or paving slabs set on edge.
🌢 Use railway sleepers or timber joists, or logs set vertically or horizontally.
🌢 Grow low hedges of box, thyme or *Teucrium chamaedrys*.

It does not matter if a raised edging is not itself very pretty because carefully chosen plants for the front row – arabis, aubrietia, *Gypsophila repens*, pinks – tumbling over the rim hide much of the face. But the advantage is that the edge plants do not meet the grass.

Even a bed-support that is only 3-4 in (7.5-10 cm) high lessens the problem; a support higher than this contributes in

MOWING MADE EASY A strip of paving bricks beside the lawn, butted up to terracotta edging, separates the soil and plants in the border from the grass. As well as looking neat, the arrangement greatly simplifies mowing.

TO THE RESCUE

A ROLL-OUT PATHWAY

IF YOU ARE GOING to and fro across the garden lawn with a wheelbarrow, perhaps with grass mowings or leaves, avoid making tracks or ruts in the lawn by using a lightweight instant pathway made of plastic. Simply hose the pathway down to clean it after use, and roll it up into a bundle for storage. It comes in 10 ft (3 m) and 20 ft (6 m) lengths.

INVITING AUTUMN APPEAL In wilder parts of the garden, a scattering of maple leaves adds informal charm. A stepping-stone path tempts you to stroll around the shrubs and gives a firm footing on the grassy slope.

other ways. Beds raised 1 ft (30 cm) above path or lawn level are markedly easier to weed. Raising bed edges is also a simple way to level sloping soil and to prevent heavy rain from washing earth and seeds down onto lawn or path.

MAKE LIFE EASIER WITH A MOWING STRIP

With a border edging, a hard vertical surface bars the mower blade from reaching the very edge of the grass, so you have to clip it by hand or use an electric trimmer. Insert a band of flat paving just below lawn level at the base of the dwarf wall or bed support and the problem is solved. This band, known as a mowing strip, is equally vital for a flat border.

Lawns require maintenance and the shape of a lawn can both determine and

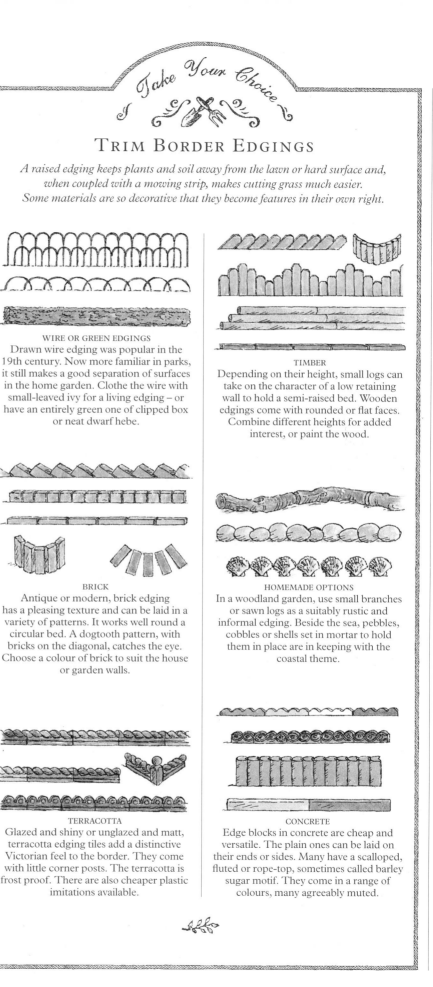

TRIM BORDER EDGINGS

A raised edging keeps plants and soil away from the lawn or hard surface and, when coupled with a mowing strip, makes cutting grass much easier. Some materials are so decorative that they become features in their own right.

WIRE OR GREEN EDGINGS
Drawn wire edging was popular in the 19th century. Now more familiar in parks, it still makes a good separation of surfaces in the home garden. Clothe the wire with small-leaved ivy for a living edging – or have an entirely green one of clipped box or neat dwarf hebe.

BRICK
Antique or modern, brick edging has a pleasing texture and can be laid in a variety of patterns. It works well round a circular bed. A dogtooth pattern, with bricks on the diagonal, catches the eye. Choose a colour of brick to suit the house or garden walls.

TERRACOTTA
Glazed and shiny or unglazed and matt, terracotta edging tiles add a distinctive Victorian feel to the border. They come with little corner posts. The terracotta is frost proof. There are also cheaper plastic imitations available.

TIMBER
Depending on their height, small logs can take on the character of a low retaining wall to hold a semi-raised bed. Wooden edgings come with rounded or flat faces. Combine different heights for added interest, or paint the wood.

HOMEMADE OPTIONS
In a woodland garden, use small branches or sawn logs as a suitably rustic and informal edging. Beside the sea, pebbles, cobbles or shells set in mortar to hold them in place are in keeping with the coastal theme.

CONCRETE
Edge blocks in concrete are cheap and versatile. The plain ones can be laid on their ends or sides. Many have a scalloped, fluted or rope-top, sometimes called barley sugar motif. They come in a range of colours, many agreeably muted.

be determined by the way it is mown. Large areas that require a sit-on mower need sweeping curves, not sharp corners. On a lawn cut with a smaller mower a rectangle is acceptable.

ALTERNATIVES TO GRASS LAWNS

Grass is the most adaptable living material for a lawn and is a plant family of amazing diversity. No other plants stand up to such foot traffic and wear. It is a delightful fancy to wander down the garden path in a haze of crushed thyme or camomile and, indeed, it can be done – occasionally. Both thyme and camomile (and pearlwort on heavier soils) have

their place: they can be introduced as additional species in a 'normal' lawn and combine and coexist with the finer grasses. Alternatively, put them in the gaps of paving and other hard surfaces.

Beyond this, 'turf' composed entirely of such broad-leaved species soon gets tired and tatty. Simplicity of maintenance is also a promise not borne out in practice. Regular mowing is not needed but grass becomes a persistent weed in such a lawn and selective herbicides for it are hard to come by.

For the ultimate in low maintenance, cover concrete with artificial turf. All it needs is the occasional hose down to get

rid of moss. Artificial turf is most suited to a roof terrace, where the garden is clearly an extension to the house – a carpeted room without a ceiling.

PLANTING GROUND COVER

Use ground-cover plants where lawn will not thrive – in damp, dark areas or thin, dry soils where you do not want to walk but would like to see an expanse of green. Make them into elements of the overall design, planting in geometric shapes, bold swathes or informal groups.

☙ Evergreen ivies, periwinkles and *Pachysandra terminalis* grow well in light or shade and in most soils. All three have variegated forms to add interest.

☙ Partridgeberry (*Gaultheria procumbens*), with red berries in autumn and bell flowers in summer, thrives in light shade and acid soil.

☙ In a sunny, drier place, try the silver *Hebe pinguifolia* 'Pagei', lamb's tongue (*Stachys byzantina* 'Silver Carpet'), thrift (*Armeria*), most pinks, helianthemums and two aromatics – camomile (*Chamaemelum nobile* 'Treneague') and creeping thyme (*Thymus serpyllum*) – all of which tolerate lime.

FRAMING A RECTANGLE OF LAWN Round a small area of grass, a mowing strip acts as a frame and gives a hard edge on which to turn without stepping in the soil. Border plants can dip forward without damaging the turf.

A SUCCESSFUL BLEND OF GRASSES Lawns need a mixture of many grass species; even an impeccable bowling green is made up of two or three. Avoid mixtures containing rye grass, which is fast growing but coarse.

HARD SURFACES

P AVED AREAS are likely to be permanent structures in the garden and so require the utmost thought and care about their positions and the materials they are made of. Balance aesthetic considerations – you look at these areas all the time – with convenience and ease of access. Surfaces need to be smooth but not slippery, quick to dry after rain, and easy to maintain.

The choice of materials, both natural and manmade, is vast – marble, slate or stone; bricks, granite setts, paving and tiles of all kinds; cobbles, pebbles, shingle, gravel and sand; timber decking, planks, railway sleepers, sections of tree trunks and wood or bark chippings. All are effective in the right setting.

ONE MATERIAL OR SEVERAL?

The use of similar materials throughout various areas and levels unifies the garden. Laying a range of surfaces, however, has the opposite effect; each part of the garden acquires subtle differences of character which are emphasised by the choice of plants and ornaments.

When you are mixing materials, lay the most formal, such as flagstones or brickwork, nearest the house. Further away, use a more casual surface such as gravel dotted with stepping-stones and informal plantings. Further away again, lead a path of, perhaps, railway sleepers to a dappled glade, where bluebells, primroses, ferns, hostas and other shade lovers grow through bark chippings.

IMAGINATIVE USE OF TILE, BRICK AND STONE

Tiles and paving stones of all kinds, natural or artificial, are made to suit every style and situation. Lay them close butted, pointed with mortar, or set between bands of timber, brick, cobbles, grass or low-growing plants. Leave some gaps to fill with bricks, cobbles or plants.

Use granite setts in a similar fashion. They are handy for curves and circular designs because of their small size. In a modest area, a circle is dramatic enough

SUBTLE WAYS WITH BRICK Lay materials to direct the eye or as a feature in their own right. The zigzag pattern of herringbone suggests movement down the path, while the circle draws attention to the central pedestal.

CONTRASTING SHAPES, TONES AND TEXTURES For a small garden, dispense with lawn and use an imaginative mixture of surfaces instead. Loose gravel lightens the brick in colour and form, with evergreens providing year-round shades of soft green on the ground and up poles and trellis.

to need little more than a few peripheral plants to set it off. Setts laid as a spiral sandwiching another spiral of, say, creeping thyme, like a swiss roll, dramatise a plant or ornament at the centre.

Bricks come in many colours, from the soft yellow of secondhand London stocks to the dark purple-blues of engineering bricks. When possible, use those which match the house walls, perhaps banded with another colour for relief on a large area. Match them with nearby plants, too. Honey-coloured London stock bricks and sombre grey-purple ones are happy with almost any flowers, but vibrant red brick, on the ground or as walling, fights with French marigolds and scarlet roses or pelargoniums.

There are many patterns of brick-work, from herringbone and basket-weave to simple courses, both straight and curved. Lay bricks alone or with any other surfacing material. Laying them diagonally or in overlapping squares and circles creates interesting effects, particularly useful when a break in pattern draws attention to a change of level.

If you can get it, local natural stone for paths and paving looks best. Many areas of the country have their own type to offer, such as sand-brown York stone or grey limestone. In an area of brick-built houses, use stone to relieve large expanses of brick surfacing outside.

Precast concrete slabs, which vary from York stone lookalike to unrelieved grey, can be almost as good. Use colours to harmonise with the plants and soften further with bands of other material.

Crazy paving is best laid as panels framed with brick or small regular stones to give form to the broken flags.

CREATIVE WAYS WITH CONCRETE

For large areas, poured concrete is comparatively inexpensive and very practical, needing no cutting or trimming to fit into tricky corners. It is the quickest material to lay, but hard to remove once in place. Concrete requires imaginative handling, even if coloured. It gains more character when interspersed with other materials. Its appearance is improved when it is given texture by brushing to expose the aggregate or raking to create shallow grooves, both of which also prevent it being slippery.

In a small informal garden, press shells, fossils, stones or tiles into the concrete just before it hardens, putting them in a variety of shapes and designs.

CHEQUERBOARD PATTERNS Lay concrete squares, filling some of the spaces between with smooth cobblestones and planting others with grasses and herbs. Add a central urn and you have a very sophisticated look.

Alternatively, stamp patterns into the concrete at the same stage by pressing down firmly on pastry cutters, shells, leaves or bits of ironwork. For fun, make hand prints or walk up the path in bare feet or flipflops (the larger the better). Fill the resulting impressions with some coloured gravel, or plant them with mind-your-own-business (*Soleirolia soleirolii*), moss, grass, stonecrops (*Sedum*) or creeping thymes, or leave them empty to hold water and reflect the sky.

There are other ways to cheer the starkness of concrete. Frame formal areas with bands of brick or stone (ideally exactly the same colour as those of the house), or insert panels of granite setts, cobbles, pottery shards or tiles.

In a modern setting, insert lengths of timber and panels of low-growing plants

PLAIN BUT BOLD The stronger the paving pattern, the simpler the planting should be to work with it. Furry leaves of lamb's tongue (*Stachys byzantina*) enliven the flat texture of brick and tone with the mainly grey stones.

CREVICE PLANTING

Soften the lines of a hard surface and keep the weeds out by sowing seeds of low-growing plants you want.

• Aubrietia (*Aubrieta deltoidea*): evergreen with pinkish-lavender flowers in spring.

• Maiden pink (*Dianthus deltoides*): evergreen and mat-forming with small white or pink flowers in summer.

• *Erigeron karvinskianus*: daisylike flowers open white, turn pink and fade to purple in summer and autumn.

• Violet cress (*Ionopsidium acaule*): lilac or white flowers flushed deep blue in summer and early autumn.

• Corsican mint (*Mentha requienii*): tiny semi-evergreen leaves smell of peppermint when crushed; little lavender-purple flowers in summer.

• *Pratia angulata*: evergreen, with star-shaped white flowers in late spring and purple-red berries in autumn.

• Pearlwort (*Sagina subulata*): mat-forming perennial with starry white flowers in summer.

• Creeping thyme (*Thymus serpyllum*): aromatic, with leaves from olive to bronze to yellow and silver; pinkish flowers in summer.

into concrete. Thymes are the classic choice, or try helianthemums, sedums, silenes and periwinkles. The Corsican mint (*Mentha requienii*) is so small that its flowers are virtually invisible from a standing position but they are strongly scented. There are even tiny annuals such as violet cress (*Ionopsidium acaule*) to pop in minuscule openings.

Brushed concrete is a comparatively cheap surfacing, created by watering and brushing newly laid concrete when it is nearly dry to expose its gravel aggregate. Poured concrete areas, unless reinforced with mesh or coarse chicken wire, should not be more than 10-13 ft (3-4 m) across, because the expansion and contraction that occurs in changing temperatures causes cracks. Create a pattern that makes allowance for the concrete to expand and contract, by containing it in separate areas framed by treated soft-wood or cedar strips, brick or slabs.

ORNAMENTAL USES FOR SAND, PEBBLES AND GRAVEL

Sand and gravel, being cheap, adaptable and easy to install and maintain, have few drawbacks, except that gravel is not kind to bare feet or high heels. Letting plants grow and self-seed through gravel gives a pleasing sense of change and development. Sand and gravel are much used in Japanese-style gardens – raked into swirling patterns about groups of plants and boulders to suggest the movement of water. As the patterns are broken when the area is walked upon, put in some stepping-stones or wooden 'bridges' for strollers to use.

Cobbles or disc-shaped stones make unusual paved areas. Smaller, flat stones, set on edge in mortar, make a charming circle for a central feature. Use clay tiles, also on edge, and sunk flush with the ground, to make circles and patterns among paving.

GRAVEL PRACTICALITIES

Gravel has been a staple covering for stretches of garden since gardens were made, and it remains useful yet cheap. There are local colours and textures. Take care not to use too great a depth or you end up with a shingle beach along which it is almost impossible to push a

WINNING COMBINATIONS Stone or concrete slabs can seem unwelcoming until rimmed with plants. Primroses, pansies, pinks and *Alchemilla mollis* quickly make a cold grey expanse look friendly and approachable.

loaded wheelbarrow. Loose gravel is also easily picked up underfoot and carried onto grass, where it subsequently meets the mower with a crash.

Some sort of bonding is essential; it can occur naturally with the type of un-washed gravel often called hoggin, although its name varies around the country. This, rolled in over a firm, level base, gives a hard-wearing, long-lasting surface. Resin-based bonding agents are also available to settle the layer of loose surface stones. Plants will seed them-selves into gravel, but they are easy to pull out. Do not pull too hastily or you risk losing desirable plants that appear. Many find an untrodden bit of gravel a perfect seedbed. Transplant them later, or even leave them where they are.

VARIETY IN WOOD

Timber is compatible with many garden styles and easily trimmed to size. Decking works for a level area, or to cover an unsightly screed. It can be laid in straight or diagonal runs, and small sections can be laid in squares. Planks of hardwood or of treated softwood make unusual hard surfaces in corners or damp places, especially at home in wild gardens. Discs cut from a tree trunk can be used in similar situations, winding among low plants. Decking has a nonslip coating, but planks, slices of tree and sleepers get mossy and very slippery.

Railway sleepers are effective with bold plants and groupings, and also make sturdy steps and low retaining walls. Two will bridge a small stream.

MIXING MATERIALS IN A COMPACT SPACE

Given enough space, most gardeners want a lawn. But in a small urban space you are better off mixing hard materials to create a courtyard atmosphere. This cuts down considerably on the labour, although the initial outlay is higher.

The smaller the space, the more im-portant it is to consider the winter months. Little lawns of muddy grass in a town garden are depressing, while crisp paving, with a winter-flowering cherry or winter jasmine, a beautiful camellia and some tubs promising wallflowers and bulbs, looks encouraging through the bleakest time of the year.

A mixture of squared old York stone and brick infill gives a classic look. Substitute reconstituted stone or slabs of

CONTRASTS IN SIZE Show-stopping plants such as gunnera are set off by rugged granite setts with moss between. Rising from a sea of foliage plants in a confined space, the vast leaves look all the more dramatic.

CURVES AND COLOUR In a garden disciplined by austere brick, straight lines and monochrome, contrive some pleasing curves and cheery accents with plants. Pink cranesbills tumble over the edging, pansies beam towards the light and the dusky red flowers of a clematis drape the wall.

TIMBER AND GRAVEL Railway sleepers are tough, and useful both for making strong lines in a design and to edge and contain gravel.

IN VOGUE WITH DECKING Timber decking is both stylish and comfortable; made with treated wood it will require little maintenance.

STONE PAVING In a chic, urban garden, match the elegance of stone with a symmetrical design, graceful foliage and clipped evergreens.

concrete to cut the cost while retaining the elegant style, and run rivulets of brick through to create a more mellow effect. Blended with soft herbs, paving and planting like this gives a Mediterranean air that lasts all year if you include plenty of evergreens.

STARKER COMBINATIONS

In the north of England and in Scotland, hard grey granite chips, granite setts and often whitened buildings create a starker mix than brick and stone. Materials from another region look out of place, and a stronger approach to the layout is necessary, although the ideas are the same.

For instance, to soften a design based on granite setts and grey chippings, plant low-growing *Pinus mugo*, a grey-leaved senecio (*Brachyglottis* 'Sunshine') or broom (*Cytisus*) with some low junipers. Introduce some annual or bulb colour in half-barrels set on the paving.

TAKE CARE OF THE DRAINAGE

Lay all paving on a well-tamped 4-6 in (10-15 cm) layer of coarse sand. In small areas this is usually all the drainage necessary, and plants grown in the cracks soften the scene.

The larger the area of paving, the greater the need to drain it. Slope it very slightly away from the house, picking up surplus water at the edge of the paving in a drain run below the soil in the flanking border. Lead it to a soakaway if the ground is not porous enough to absorb most of the water runoff.

PLANNING BEDS AND BORDERS

◆

BESIDES HOUSING PLANTS, beds and borders serve to surround and divide garden areas. The height and bulk of the plants protect you from wind, screen you from neighbours and even help to muffle traffic noise or children playing nearby. Frequently, borders are backed by a boundary or internal hedge or they run alongside paths.

What is seldom seen in photographs of grand country-house herbaceous borders, which appear so completely of a piece with the backing, is that a narrow service path runs between the hedge and the flowers. The hedge can be clipped without the plants being hurt, root competition is reduced and the border itself is easily maintained from both front and back. Even in a small garden the virtues of such a path hold good.

Similarly, in the country, garden borders frequently back onto pasture and people go to great trouble erecting barricades to prevent animals from browsing on their choice shrubs. Failure is frequent. It is much better to bring the border forward by, in effect, taking a yard or so off the lawn in front and slipping it in at the back. Maintenance is helped, weeds from the field no longer creep in and animals cannot reach the plants.

ACCESSIBLE ISLAND BEDS

An island bed does not have to follow a path or boundary, so it can be a more flowing shape. Cut two, three or more areas out of the lawn, and the areas between double as paths allowing passage for maintenance and appreciation.

The size of island beds is determined partly by the scale of the garden and partly by what you want to grow in them. Sweeping, flowing edges are more difficult to mow or to provide with a mowing strip, so aim for gentle curves. As with curved lawns, avoid irrational, fussy wiggles and swirls.

First sketch shapes of island beds on paper. Use garden hose or a piece of rope to try out the shape on the ground before you do anything irrevocable. When you

MIXED BORDER Compose a wide border with classic herbaceous perennials such as sedum, agapanthus, crocosmia, verbena and dahlias, backed by shrubs and yucca. Cordylines add a touch of the exotic in warmer gardens.

are cutting beds out of an existing lawn, you can help soil fertility by digging the turf in face down to rot gradually. You must remove some soil so that the final bed level is not much above that of the grass. Mounded beds are seldom successful; soil is apt to be washed down in periods of heavy rain.

Grade the height from the edge to the focus of the bed with plants. Island beds have clear advantages – as they are never backed by higher hedges or fences their plants are less likely to become 'drawn' and leggy. This virtually does away with the need to stake herbaceous perennials, especially when you choose plants with robust stems rather than the dwarf varieties which often lose the typical form and charm of the species.

An island bed looks all ways but has an open position. There is little need to be concerned with aspect unless its central plants are large enough to cast considerable shade. There is scope for surprise too. Break a too even grading of plants by placing some taller ones towards the front; make the choice from early-flowering plants so that, when they are over and clipped back, a shorter plant behind comes into view.

VISTA BORDERS

A view from a door or a window often needs framing so that the eye is led away – for a few strides or a hundred – to an eyecatcher at the end. That framing is wonderfully executed with a pair of narrow borders flanking a walk.

The walk itself, regardless of the size of garden, is unlikely to be less than 4 ft (1.2 m) wide, but the vista borders can be of any width. Narrow ones might hold just a single line of Hidcote lavender or, for August and September effect, *Caryopteris* 'Kew Blue' thickly underplanted with crocuses and *Scilla siberica* for spring. As with island beds, the open aspect of double-sided borders reduces the need for staking, especially where the central walk is hard and mowing strips on the outside edges act as a catch-all for front-row plants that flop forward.

PAY HEED TO THE ASPECT

Formal straight borders face a particular way. The aspect determines the range of plants a border is to hold.

Borders which face south especially where soil drainage is good (and it is well worth ensuring that it is), call for sun-loving plants. Choose species from

WALK OF DELIGHT The pleasure of wandering through a garden reaches new heights when Himalayan blue poppies (*Meconopsis × sheldonii*) flank the lawn. These short-lived perennials need plenty of water in summer.

COMBINING PLANTS Concentrations of colour against a permanent frame achieve the best result. The clematis provides a splash of pink between the background *Solanum crispum* and bluish grass *Helictotrichon sempervirens*.

MONEY · SAVERS
SEVERAL PLANTS IN ONE

WHEN YOU BUY young perennials in a pot, look for robust, bushy specimens. You can usually turn one such plant into at least three. At home, take the plant out of the pot. Tease the roots apart, and divide the plant with a sharp knife, making sure each section has plenty of root. Plant the pieces in separate holes in their flowering positions. Firm them down and water in well.

warm, Mediterranean climates such as cistus, the tree poppy (*Romneya coulteri*) from California, red-hot pokers from South Africa, as well as spring bulbs.

A north-facing border is the mirror image. When the soil does not dry out, it provides a happy home not just for all the subtly beautiful plants that accept shade but also for water-lovers, often thought of as the prerogative of gardeners with a pond. Waterside marginals such as primulas, rodgersias and astilbes flourish.

West-facing borders have many of the advantages of south-facing ones but never get as hot since the sun comes in mid afternoon. Plant sun-lovers such as *Jasminum officinale* and camellias. There is no need to restrict your choice to drought-resistant, Mediterranean types.

East has the chill of a north border but alleviated by morning sun which passes off before the full heat of the day. Plants to avoid are those that bloom early in the year such as peonies or camellias. Frosts may grip first thing in the morning and sun on frosted plants browns them. A clematis such as 'Ernest Markham' with magenta flowers in summer is suitable.

Fortunately, many garden plants will flourish in a wide range of conditions. However, no rhododendrons or camellias do well on chalk or limestone, and no sun-loving Mediterraneans thrive in ill-drained clay. Apart from basic concerns like these, the choice is up to you.

SHRUBS FOR THE BACKBONE OF THE BORDER

Develop your ideas bearing two points in mind. First, in Britain's climate no plants flower continuously. Second, green is a colour, not simply a backdrop. Accept that the form, texture and foliage effects of permanent plants often offer more to the garden scene than masses of temporary colour. Wonderful effects can be obtained with the formality of the simplest materials such as walks, hedges and topiary. Keep vibrant colour to annuals in pots, as in southern European gardens.

The most permanent of border plants are woody shrubs. Usually you make a choice because of the beauty or brilliance of flowers – for instance, golden forsythia for spring, the headily scented lilac or mock orange for early summer, buddleia for later. The transient season of each is part of the joy of the garden – one plant's moment of glory leading on to the next – but what about lilac or mock orange during the other 11 months of the year?

HOW TO DO IT

PROPAGATING INDOORS

YOU DO NOT NEED a greenhouse or a propagator to raise shrubs from your own cuttings – an indoor windowsill provides a protected environment.

Screw two cup hooks into the wall at either side of the window, about halfway up, and rest a cane across them. Set a short wooden board on the windowsill. Secure this shelf with strings attached to tacks on its underside and tied to the cane above. Lay foil, shiny side up, on the shelf and up the sides of the window recess.

Pot your cuttings up and place them on the shelf. Peg a sheet of heavy-gauge polythene to the cane, draping it over the front of the shelf. The cuttings soon take root.

North-east-facing window is best to avoid strong sun

Foil on shelf and sides reflects available light

Polythene keeps draughts out and moisture in

Consider whether an alternative would earn its keep for more of the year – a shrub such as *Mahonia aquifolium* with its glossy evergreen leaves which bronze in winter, and the bunches of purple fruit that follow the yellow flowers, gives 12 months of interest.

CHOICE OF A COLOUR SCHEME

Begin planning a bed by listing 'must haves' and their colour or ticking off irresistible plants in a catalogue. If you have no preconceived idea of the desired look,

study the list to see if any theme suggests itself – maybe a white border or a blue and grey bed.

Perhaps there are a number of yellow-flowering plants – forsythia, *Cytisus* × *praecox*, *Rhododendron luteum*, *Spartium junceum* – and a couple of pink or red shrubs such as weigela or *Rhododendron* 'Mars' on your list.

It is now a matter of choice whether you keep the happy miscellany or form a deliberate scheme. For instance, you could hold on to the yellows and instead

A SHOW FOR THE FIRST YEAR

Give a long-term border early character with annuals. Hardy types often self-seed and come up next year.

- Love-lies-bleeding (*Amaranthus caudatus*): bushy, with plush tassels of red flowers from summer to autumn.

- Pot marigold (*Calendula officinalis* 'Art Shades'): double apricot, orange or cream daisylike flowers.

- Cornflower (*Centaurea cyanus*): double, daisylike flowers in blue, pink, red, purple or white; good for cutting.

- Godetia (*Clarkia unguiculata*): generous trumpets of pink, salmon, red, purple or white flowers.

- *Convolvulus tricolor* 'Royal Ensign': intense dark blue saucer-shaped flowers, with yellowish-white throats.

- Californian poppy (*Eschscholzia californica*): cup-shaped, vivid yellow or orange papery flowers.

- Sunflower (*Helianthus annuus*): huge, daisylike yellow flowers with dark centres.

- Mallow (*Lavatera trimestris*): white, pink or red trumpet-shaped flowers.

- Love-in-a-mist (*Nigella damascena* 'Persian Jewels'): semidouble flowers in blue, pink or white; ferny leaves.

- Opium poppy (*Papaver somniferum*): large single or double flowers in red, pink, purple or white.

- Corn or field poppy (*Papaver rhoeas* 'Fairy Wings'): red, pink and white single and double flowers.

FILLED WITH COLOUR Pink lupin spikes tower over a clump of blue-purple *Centaurea montana* while, further along, poppies burst into bloom. Rustic poles allow for growing climbers at the back of the border.

of the pink flowers bring in *Cotinus coggygria* 'Royal Purple' and *Rosa glauca* to build up a picture in gold and purple. Continue such a theme by adding gold and purple herbaceous perennials to bulk up the scene at a lower level – still remembering the value of foliage.

You might consider *Acanthus spinosus*, gold-variegated *Yucca filamentosa* or the late-flowering purple-leaved form of *Cimicifuga racemosa* to put with a Michaelmas daisy or two. Provide spring interest with golden daffodils, coming through purple *Ajuga*, and 'Apricot Beauty' or 'Black Parrot' tulips above *Lysimachia nummularia* 'Aurea'. Plant the bulbs deeply to remain as permanent plants. A similar story can be pursued through any choice of colours.

BRIGHTENING THE BORDER IN THE FIRST TWO YEARS

The early days in a border's life can seem interminable before that mind's-eye picture starts to show, so temporary plants are the answer in the first two years.

Spring hardly lives up to its name in the garden without wallflowers (*Erysimum*), sweetly scented as nothing else. 'Harpur Crewe' fits the bill to perfection. Choose polyanthuses and primroses at the same time; they stay in flower for months if deadheaded regularly.

Brompton stocks (*Matthiola incana*) overlap with wallflowers and last into June. Like all true cottage garden plants they are strongly scented. In late summer perennials such as rudbeckia and sweet peas can take over. (*continued on p.120*)

DEVELOPING A BORDER

A border planted in the autumn is already taking shape the following spring. Bulbs and annuals flesh it out while the permanent shrubby and herbaceous planting matures.

THIS BORDER is the main planting area of the garden and extends about 12 ft (3.7 m) from the back fence. A low retaining wall separates the border from the lawn, and a path, which will be virtually hidden by the mature plants, lets you reach the middle and back of the border for weeding and pruning.

Shrubs form the framework of the planting, supplemented by perennials and bulbs, both of which flower reliably year after year. The taller shrubs are near the fence at the back, the smaller ones in front. Set out the young bushes one and a half times their mature spread apart, so you do not fall into the trap of planting too close. The colour theme is blue and purple with flame-bright accents. Purple and grey foliage complements, cools and contains the floral display. Planting relatively few species heightens the effect, so there are single plants of the large shrubs, several of the perennials and as many as possible of the bulbs.

Colour and even height can come from annuals and biennials in the first year but it is still vital that the permanent plants go in at once. The temporaries follow the planned colour scheme and these easy-come-easy-go plants help to give a foretaste of what the mature bed will be in its full glory.

The first spring

With autumn preparation and planting, you can expect colour and interest from early spring only four or five months later. The contribution of bulbs is individually short but spectacular. Bright red tulips and pastel-tinted daffodils and wallflowers reflect the overall colour scheme. Crocus and scilla provide earlier colour and forget-me-not comes into flower slightly later.

Silvery artemisia sets off purple sage

The first summer

In the first and second years there is ample space, until the shrubs fill out, to add splashes of summer colour. Annuals planted in early summer over the bulbs include cornflowers and Californian poppies, petunias, nasturtiums, annual mallow, cosmos and love-lies-bleeding. Even winter could show a few cushions of winter-flowering pansies in the same colours.

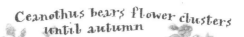

Ceanothus bears flower clusters until autumn

The third summer – mature growth fills and mellows the border

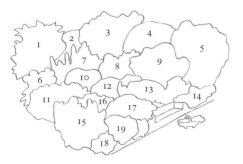

1. *Buddleia fallowiana* var. *alba*
2. Smoke tree (*Cotinus coggygria* 'Royal Purple')
3. Alpine snow gum (*Eucalyptus pauciflora* subsp. *niphophila*)
4. *Ceanothus × delileanus* 'Gloire de Versailles'
5. *Abutilon vitifolium* 'Veronica Tennant'
6. African lily (*Agapanthus* Headbourne Hybrids)
7. *Acanthus mollis*
8. Summer hyacinth (*Galtonia candicans*)
9. Tree poppy (*Romneya coulteri*)
10. Lavender (*Lavandula* 'Munstead')
11. *Artemisia absinthium* 'Lambrook Silver'
12. *Bergenia* 'Silberlicht'
13. Lamb's tongue (*Stachys byzantina*)
14. Alyssum (*Aurinia saxatilis* var. *citrina*)
15. Sage (*Salvia officinalis* 'Purpurascens')
16. *Hebe* 'Autumn Glory'
17. Hellebore (*Helleborus argutifolius*)
18. Aubrietia (*Aubrieta deltoidea*)
19. Broom (*Cytisus × kewensis*)

LINKS
AND DIVIDERS

TURNING A CORNER Inset strips of concrete are simple to lay round a curve and are easier and quieter to walk on than slightly shifting gravel.

FOUR-SQUARE FORMALITY All paths lead to the central focal point, and the continuous line of camomile adds a visual – and fragrant – lure.

BRICK MOTIF The brick pattern has a practical purpose – it stops gravel being carried onto the lawn. Sleepers make convenient steps.

PATHWAYS SHOULD BE just one part of a garden layout, not the reason for it. Imagine two identical neighbouring gardens. One has a T-shaped path to link the key elements of the layout, leaving three little plots to infill with grass, one on either side of the path and one along the top of the T. The other, filled with flowers and shrubs, has a single path weaving between the masses of colour and fragrance and joining every element of the design, without dominating it.

Either approach is valid, but regarding hard surfacing as just another element in a tapestry tends to produce a more versatile and less rigid layout, giving you scope to develop the garden.

There are no rules which state that a path has to be such and such a width, or even that it must be straight. The path may take a diagonal route across a wider paved area scattered with planting, or zigzag through shrubs.

THE BEST MATERIAL FOR A PATH

The length, and therefore cost, as well as the look you are seeking are factors in your choice of path. Service paths, which lead to, say, the dustbin and are in frequent use, need to be usable at all times of the year, preferably textured, and well drained so that they do not become slippery in winter. But bear in mind that stone paving, even when well laid, becomes slippery under trees or in shade unless you scrub it regularly.

Bricks take a lot of beating as a surface. Use wire-cut pavers, which are thinner and harder than building bricks. Building bricks need to be set on edge to expose their hardest sides, and are extravagant as pathways for that reason. The way you lay bricks influences how the eye sees the path.

🌣 Bricks laid lengthways emphasise a long, narrow look.

🌣 Bands of bricks laid crossways with another material break up the length, suggesting greater width.

🌣 A diagonal pattern acts like an arrow, urging walkers down the path.

Textured concrete or reconstituted stone slabs come in an enormous range, are nonslip and, where sympathetic to their surrounds, are pleasing to the eye. Edging is not necessary when you pave

with a hard surface, so long as the levels are correct on either side of it. But lay either a brick-on-edge or a wooden kerb when you use a fine path medium such as consolidated gravel or, in a woodland setting, pulverised bark.

PUTTING PATHS ON SLOPES

A path on a slope needs even greater care. Crossing a slope, any walkway should be horizontal, making in fact a terrace. Ground above the path must be graded gently so that soil does not wash down – quick ground-cover plants such as periwinkle, wild strawberry, *Lamium galeobdolon* or *Hypericum calycinum* help. Alternatively, the slope needs a retaining wall to support it. This results in one of the best and most convenient of all garden features, a raised bed. The path itself must also have sound support, such as bricks set in a cement base, on its lower side.

Paths on a slope have their own problems. Loose gravel or stone chips are unsuitable surfaces as they move under the feet and are washed away by heavy rain, though a diagonal gutter set across the path between two boards every so often helps. Surfaces can be slippery regardless of material once the slope exceeds about one in ten. There is then no alternative but for the path to have a step every stride or so.

SCREENS WITHIN THE GARDEN

Part of the function of borders is, as the word suggests, to 'border' – to edge a space. But they also link and divide garden areas. Think of the border across the garden that conventionally separates lawn and flowerbeds from a vegetable garden, wild garden or just compost and storage areas beyond.

A screen in this spot is often one of the first requirements of a new garden, but a fully living division takes several years to achieve. Some hedges are quite quick – Leyland cypress does the job wonderfully but never knows when to stop – but more satisfactory still for immediate effect is a built divider. Walls and fences, especially if they match or harmonise with existing buildings in their material, are seldom bettered.

Lighter screens are usually less expensive to construct but less permanent. Diamond-pattern or squared trellis has an honourable tradition – the grandest 17th-century gardens in Europe from Versailles downwards used latticework

END IN SIGHT Part of the function of a path is to divide borders, but it works doubly well heading for a distant object such as a bench.

DYNAMIC DIAMONDS The zigzag of gravel and slabs feels more energetic than a straight line, suitable for a path leading down the garden.

IN COTTAGE-GARDEN TRADITION Roses and catmint tumble softly over a path with a white picket gate at the end. Laying the bricks horizontally across the path makes it seem wider and, even with plants narrowing it, two people can comfortably walk along side by side.

UNDER A CANOPY Scented roses overhead add pleasure to a walk, with an intriguing glimpse of distant lawn and plants to draw you on.

extensively. When trellis is firmly anchored – perhaps as panels within a solid fence or wall frame, reducing visual weight and cost at the same time – it is to be highly recommended. It provides perfect support for climbers, the quickest of all plants to grow, making the screen between garden areas rapidly effective.

That end-of-garden area where all manner of unsightly objects, bits of equipment and piles of debris are stored needs to be screened, but also reached. A simple service path down one side of the main garden area – itself screened from general view – is one option. When the central lawn is intended to be impeccable such extra access is essential to stop a worn track developing, though wear can also be mitigated by paving flags set into the grass at vulnerable points.

But more often, you wish to take pleasure in passing from one area to another. Where there is only a yard or two between the screen and the end of the garden, frame an eye-catching pot on a plinth in the gap, giving just enough space to get a wheelbarrow to the compost or bonfire to left and right. When there are more spacious garden areas to go on to, make a bolder focal point such as a statue or large architectural plant.

Frame this important sight-line with the edges of a border, cut through by a path to provide access. Mark it with a matching pair of sentinel features, made from pillars, obelisks or simple posts or from statuesque plants. This is just the place to practise the gentle art of topiary, from a brace of simple obelisk yews to peacocks and other creatures, or abstract flights of fancy.

MAKING OVERHEAD FEATURES OF LINKS

Screens and paths act as frames for the garden as well as links and dividers. To complete the frame, link a screen to left and right with an overhead section. Join the top beams of a trellis, or train topiary pillars to become an arch.

Unlike a two-dimensional picture, a garden has real depth. You can project an arch backwards or forwards to become a pergola. At once you reintroduce the link between architecture and plants that makes gardening so satisfying.

Visits to large garden centres and flower shows demonstrate the range of materials from which to make garden screens, pergolas, arbours and tunnels. Stone, concrete, wood, iron and even

A FOLDING WHEELBARROW

LIGHTWEIGHT AND COMPACT, a folding wheelbarrow takes up hardly any storage space and is much less cumbersome than a conventional metal type. Despite the lightness of its woven fabric, the wheelbarrow is robust enough for most garden jobs and ideal for transporting weeds, prunings or lawn mowings. The fabric and the rubber wheel are replaceable, and the frame is rust resistant.

VERSATILE TRELLIS The open diamonds make an excellent garden divider – separating different areas without closing them off. Where the panels meet in an arch, clematis turns the trellis into a stunning feature.

PULLING TOGETHER The reward for meticulous planning is a garden where surfaces, borders and dividers all work to make a satisfying whole. The paving leads round soft plantings of euphorbias and yellow alyssum to the steps in the balustrade, which make the link to the raised lawn.

HERBAL LINK When a border is composed of large spreads of just a few species, it becomes more of a hedge than a flowerbed. Lavender and purple sage line the border, making a low hedge that divides the garden in two yet echoes the herbal knot garden and box circles near the house.

wire constructions are offered. Tie in your choice with existing features, what you expect its life span to be, what you expect to pay and, specifically, its job.

Is the feature to be a tunnel you walk through? Is it to support climbers or trained plants? If so, think very carefully about height; it should be 7 ft (2 m) to be sure that errant growths of climbing rose do not snatch at your hair. The width must be at least 4 ft (1.2 m) if you are not to get soaked by strands of sodden clematis. Do not choose a wire arch and expect it to support a wisteria, and be prepared for rustic poles to rot just when the plants they support are at their best. The better the quality, the more successful the tunnel will be.

SCREENS FOR PROTECTION

Pretty though a pergola is as a divider, it gives little shelter and many gardens need internal divisions that offer protection, usually from wind, sometimes from sun. Lightly clothed trellis casts a dappled shade that filters sun pleasantly but wind often takes more defeating.

Hedges or, for immediate protection, woven wattle hurdles securely fixed are better than a wall as they filter the wind and reduce its speed. High walls within a garden can block you in and look intimidating unless the area is very large.

Seaside gardens are often enviably frost free and many grow an almost subtropical range of plants. But taking advantage of the moderating influence of a maritime site is only possible once the sea-winds are tamed. Plant a screen of robust, wind-tolerant shrubs such as *Cotoneaster simonsii*, which has white flowers and orange-red berries, or the evergreen *Pittosporum tenuifolium*, with honey-scented, purple spring flowers, to shelter the patio or sitting-out place.

Other plants will flourish in their lee, many of them from the Southern Hemisphere – for example, escallonias, *Hebe salicifolia*, *H. brachysiphon* and the compact *H. × franciscana* 'Blue Gem', which flowers almost all year and looks wonderful in summer with catmint.

Keep in mind the need to select plants to suit each site, rather than attempting to change the site to suit the plant. There is a plant for every place and a place (though not necessarily in every garden) for every plant. Choosing plants that are already adapted to your conditions – shade or sun, dry soil or bog – increases your success in creating a garden.

INSPIRATION FROM

GREAT
GARDENS

BARNSLEY HOUSE

An inspired garden rings the mellow house.

*This late 17th-century
Gloucestershire house located just
north-east of Cirencester is home to
noted gardener and gardening writer
Rosemary Verey, who has
transformed the grounds round it.
The knot, herb and ornamental
kitchen gardens accord well with the
period of the house, while the little
Doric temple and the massed
plantings in the borders speak
eloquently of later centuries.*

Like everything else in Barnsley House's four acres, the laburnum walk must work for its living. Both tunnel and arbour, covered walkway and enclosed vista, it is in early June a vision of startling beauty. The chains of flowers are like a stilled golden cascade falling to meet crowds of mauve allium heads rising above a green river of hosta leaves. Later in the year, when the flowers have faded, the tunnel makes a deliciously cool contrast with the open, sunlit walk of pleached limes that leads up to it.

BLEND STYLES WITH SUCCESS

Barnsley is an expert's garden in which many themes – light and shade, long vistas and sudden surprises, antique and modern, disciplined beds and rough 'wilderness' – are orchestrated into a harmonious whole. Architectural features also serve as unifying elements, like the sundial that draws the eye to the end of

SUMMER BOWER An attractive feature in its own right, the flowery laburnum tunnel helps to link one part of the garden with another.

the laburnum walk. Far off to the right there is an 18th-century temple whose façade is reflected in a still pool, and to the left is a modern fountain.

Deep herbaceous borders, statues that peer from the shrubbery, a knot of box, rosemary, holly and silvery cotton lavender, a herb garden and a kitchen garden patterned with symmetrical plantings of vegetables, flowers and fruit provide a year-round unity of interest unrivalled by many larger gardens.

A feature that unites a few different elements – say, the lawn with a small orchard – is desirable in any garden, and the tunnel below owes much of its form to the example provided at Barnsley. It consists of metal hoops driven firmly into the ground on either side of a footpath. Golden hops planted on both sides twine up and over the front hoop. The second is occupied by honeysuckle, the third by white jasmine and the fourth by 'Buff Beauty' roses. *Alchemilla mollis* grows about the inner sides of each hoop, while *Galtonia candicans* and *Alstroemeria* fill the spaces on the outsides.

FRAGRANT ARCH Behind the golden hop, the daytime bouquet of *Lonicera × tellmanniana* gives way to night-scented *Jasminum officinale* 'Aureovariegatum' and, later, *Rosa* 'Buff Beauty'.

THROUGH THE WINDOW

SHIVERY WINTER DAYS and summer downpours alike put the garden out of bounds for all but the most devoted gardeners. Yet it is still there to be enjoyed. With well-thought-out planting, you can admire the dainty flowers of winter while sitting in your snuggest armchair, and in late spring have a grandstand view of the first butterflies basking on the rock plants. A landing window can give a quick glimpse of flowers too daringly gaudy for longer contemplation. Even dishwashing has more appeal when a few choice blooms are nodding at you through the kitchen window.

SPECIAL FEATURES

A sunlit vine frames the window outlook onto a
shady garden corner planted with red nicotiana.

THE GARDEN FROM INDOORS

WINDOWS ARE THE EYES of a home, opening on the world and seeing it from a unique point of view. But how many gardeners, as they are designing and planting a plot, give any thought to how it is going to look when viewed through the windows? Yet there are some parts of the garden that are far more frequently seen from inside the house than they are from outside.

Most people spend by far the greater proportion of their time indoors, even during the summer months. Whether preparing meals or washing up after them, relaxing in the sitting room or watching television, almost every indoor occupation, bar sleeping, is likely to be punctuated by glances or lengthy stares through the window. And in fact the first move in the morning is commonly to open the bedroom curtains and take a peek out to judge the state of the weather and check on that private small patch of the world outside.

BRIEF OR LINGERING LOOKS

Since gardens are so frequently viewed through windows, it makes sense to ensure that every pane of glass provides not merely an inoffensive view, but a tableau of delights that keeps up the pleasure through the changing seasons.

With a little forethought, a measure of imagination and a handful of clever ideas, you can make each window the frame for an absorbing picture of a section of the garden. Some windows are in sight for much of the day, while others seldom draw the eye. Some constitute the chief focus of a room used all day long, while others are seen often but only in passing. As you walk past a landing window, for example, you are unlikely to scan the view carefully, but one simple item of beauty that can be taken in at a glance provides enormous pleasure.

A window in more constant view, however, needs to give much more. Here you want a satisfying outline and a wealth of detail – and you expect it to please day by day through the seasons. A well-run garden has all-year interest built in, but the seasonal drama can be adapted to enhance the performance you watch from your favourite window.

CLOSE INTEREST As a focal point near the window, grow a plant that has a long decorative period and offers a pleasing shape, attractive foliage or fragrance. Hydrangea flower heads last for a long time and take on pretty rosy or metallic tints and a papery texture as autumn advances.

DESIGNING TO SUIT THE OUTLOOK

T HE TIME SPENT looking through a window is an influential factor in planning the scene outside, but not the only one. The window's size and shape cannot be ignored since they create the frame. Windows that are tall and narrow, round-topped, or broad and spacious all create specific design opportunities. A tiny light or porthole might need nothing more than a single pot plant outside, while a tall window can encompass a soaring, statuesque plant, and a huge picture window takes in virtually the whole of the garden.

Light levels outside windows are another unalterable fact to be heeded when you plan the picture.

ANGLES OF LIGHT AND SIGHT

The light may vary from the comparative gloom outside a basement window to the brilliance outside south-facing patio windows. Each situation has advantages to

MAKING · IT · EASIER

HIGH PLANTING

A PLANTER with attached trellis solves the problem of supporting tall plants or climbers on a roof garden or balcony, where you cannot drive in posts. Such elevated sites are surprisingly draughty and a flower-clothed trelliswork screen makes a pretty windbreak.

COLOUR IMPACT Planting the same types and shades of flower in big clumps and so creating blocks of colour makes far more visual impact than intermingling a few of this and that. Arrange perennials in drifts, sited to be seen through a side window in a swift but stunning glance.

offer, and the disadvantages need not lead inevitably to a disappointing view.

Bear in mind that strong light from one side encourages plants to bend towards it, so make allowance for this when positioning them. Many flowers – roses and daffodils, for example – generally turn to the sun; so if they grow to the south of a window, they face away from it.

Bright sun and hard shadows are unkind to delicate colours. Only the bold and bright make an impact in dazzling sun. Save your subtle palette for shadier spots. Many foliage plants love shade. Those with variegations make their own pool of light but intricate leaf shape, glossy surfaces and a bold outline overall give constant interest to a shaded scene.

Two or three windows may have the same dimensions or the same amount of light outside, but no two have exactly the same outlook. Indeed it is astonishing how two windows separated by only a yard or so of wall have quite different views into the same patch of garden. One shows the curving line of a lawn between jutting beds of tall plants, while its neighbour has a view between the beds into a recess that frames a fountain or a statue.

VIEWS FROM ABOVE OR BELOW

Perspectives change even more markedly from above. Much of the contour goes and plants lose their silhouette. More of the surface and the ground plan is visible, however, so you can enjoy placing plants as though they are patterns on a tapestry.

A lawn seen from above looks cool, green and weed-free. Its size and lines are exaggerated while the planted areas

MAKING PLANTS STAND TALL

UNOBTRUSIVE SUPPORT for a tall herbaceous plant ensures it holds its flowers up to be enjoyed from some distance rather than flopping in a bedraggled heap. For maximum benefit put the stakes in early, soon after the first growth appears.

Use stakes that link to form a flexible 'wall' which you can wind round or among the stems. As the plants shoot up and bush out, they quickly hide the supports from view.

shrink. On the other hand, 'carpet gardening' has an impact from above that is rarely equalled at ground level. A blend of low-growing thymes, with flowers of different purples and pinks, is dramatic from above and holds its impact when the leaf colours deepen in winter.

Equally effective from above are formal low hedges grown in squares round blocks of contrasting foliage or single-colour flowers.

When the garden is on a balcony, you have large windows or doors looking onto a tiny area. Plants are seen in close-up and space is tight but, with large enough boxes and troughs, you can create your own micro-jungle. A roof garden has still more potential, as you can add a layer of soil for small flower borders or a shrubbery – provided you check with the local planning officer.

If your window is looking up from a basement, relatively small objects such as plant pots or small shrubs become dominant because of their positions. This is something you can turn to advantage, adding drama to even the dullest spot.

FOLLOWING ORTHODOX STYLE

Although every window benefits from a specially tailored outlook, the design will be made up of the elements that go into any beautiful piece of scenery – line, form, layout and colour. You have to weigh up what it is in gardens that particularly satisfies you – be it long vistas, surprise views, secret corners, symmetrical or informal layout, artful touches of drama or well-composed colour schemes. Pleasing long views are easier to make for a window viewpoint. Even from a large window the view is more limited than when you stand outside. . This has the effect of making features that run away from a window more dominant. A path, a narrow lawn between borders, pairs of matched shrubs flanking ground-cover plants, or some pillars supporting climbers become special features when aligned with a principal window.

Where one of your windows looks out across a border to a lawn on the far side, carve a path to draw the eye through the border and set a sundial, birdbath or other small feature at its end.

A distant point of interest, perhaps near the boundary, is as effective as one close by. It draws the gaze farther, giving a sense of more space, and from it you can lead the eye across the garden with plants or structures, or lead it outside the boundary if there is a view beyond.

SOFT EDGES *Alchemilla mollis* is an ideal plant for softening hard lines of paving and cooling more showy companions. Its scalloped leaves and sprays of tiny lime-green flowers repay close scrutiny, especially when they are spangled with rain.

the interiors and the style of the house. Just a little effort with the foreground straightaway increases the sense that the garden is an extension of the room – especially where there are large windows or glass going to floor level. If the colour scheme in a room is, say, pink and blue, use sympathetic colours in a window box and in containers or beds nearby. To strengthen the link even more, have house plants on the windowsill inside that match the leaf form or echo the flower colour of the plants outside.

A period house usually looks better if its garden has at least a flavour of the same age and style. Small knot gardens, for example, have just the right blend of geometry and formality to view from a Tudor or Jacobean room. Victorian terrace houses, on the other hand, look comfortable with neat lawns and colourful flowerbeds in their gardens.

You can make harmonious links easily in modern houses. Patios or terraces, for example, are often separated from the interior by no more than large glass doors, so you can have great fun matching floor colour and clean-lined furniture inside and out, even before you plant up outdoor pots with hardy ferns and fatsias to echo the dainty ferns and tender fig (*Ficus benjamina*) indoors.

Above all, with large windows revealing all, your patio must remain attractive in winter. Plant some evergreens in the beds around it, even if you only have room for a few. Pots and tubs planted with winter pansies, hellebores and early-flowering bulbs sit happily on a sheltered patio giving it colour until spring.

VERSATILE CONTAINERS

Winter furnishing for patios is only one contribution containers make. Balconies, roof gardens and basements would be barren without an assembly of troughs, boxes, tubs, gracious urns and homely pots to grow plants in. The spread of city roofs can be masked or a canyon below ground made luxuriant with lovingly tended container plants.

At ground level, an elaborate empty pot or an overflowing tub of petunias or nasturtiums makes a focal point or lifts a dull area. Being movable, containers

Careful layout provides far more than focal points. You want to attract window gazers into absorbing the wider picture. Punctuate big, curvy borders with eye-catching plants at irregular intervals and put pleasing pools of colour round them for the eye to explore before being swept into the orbit of the next scene-stealer. You can even tantalise viewers by making a path or lawn curve from view.

Put your plants together with even more care than usual. It is the broad-brush effects that are visible from most windows, not the fine detail. Big clumps of plants, not tiny dots of this and that,

work best in the foreshortened view. Variations in height let the plants show their colours to advantage, and plenty of foliage makes pools of brightness stand out the more. Mercilessly evict any plant that does not pay its rent for the year with flowers, shape, fragrance, autumn berries, winter foliage or, preferably, several of these currencies.

HOW TO HARMONISE DESIGN

Garden design is much more successful when it fits in with its surroundings. Through-the-window design works best when it harmonises, to some extent, with

SHAPES AND SHADES This predominantly green and gold planting scheme is punctuated by striking architectural foliage plants – elegant hostas and a huge rheum. Busy lizzies, tall lilies and more distant white flowers create pools of light that draw the eye along the path.

enable you to ring the changes in providing beauty in close-up. The beauty may be of colour or shape but in summer, when windows are often open, best of all is scent. Place a couple of pots of mignonette or basil under a sheltered window and though not very colourful they give heavenly fragrance. Lilies, lavender and miniature roses all give you colour at the window as well as scent.

WAYS OF HIDING THE VIEW

Imaginative planting is often needed when a window view is spoilt by an eyesore, perhaps an intrusive streetlight or hoarding, or a neighbour's shed. You can hide most eyesores with the help of a cleverly positioned hedge and even an ingenious use of mirrors. With through-the-window gardening, subtler ploys can work. The objective is narrower when only the unique view from a particular window has to be considered.

You can arrange screening plants to line up with the window, then create a vista and take your eye to a distant focal point. A flowery or evergreen arch that leads nowhere or a tall white panel bearing a niche and a container plant will conceal a high eyesore. If a neighbour's window overlooks yours, place a single tree or shrub where it breaks the direct line of vision without blocking the light or the remaining view for either window.

PARTICULAR WINDOW SCENES

ALTHOUGH THE WINDOW must never be a tyrant, dominating the design outside, you can tailor the garden so that the views from particular windows give as much pleasure as a stroll outside.

Tall, narrow windows work best with a view that is long and thin, but it need not always be a narrow pathway, bordered by flowerbeds. Such windows are ideal for giving a fleeting glimpse of a beautiful object – an ornament, maybe, or patterned bark on a specimen tree – that comes into view only at certain angles.

Windows that come down virtually to floor level, whether sliding patio doors or french windows, do not cut off your view of the garden yards away but let it run right to the house. Create a foreground of small features – a shallow trough of tiny alpine plants, pots of winter bulbs and a long-flowering, dainty-leaved potentilla – as effective uplifters for any drab day, whatever the season.

FROM THE GROUND-LEVEL SITTING ROOM

From a favourite chair near the window, gardeners draw up new schemes during winter; in autumn, the year's progress with the scheme is reviewed; on summer mornings new blooms are welcomed and tasks for the day spotted. And on spring or summer evenings, there is nothing more pleasurable than watching the colours gently fade in the garden as the twilight deepens.

With a view that is so familiar, an observant eye spots the smallest changes, which tend to come from the planting rather than the design. Every day you notice slight alterations in colours as flowers emerge, or in outline as growth increases apace at midsummer. Larger changes are seasonal: the spring transition from duns to leafy green, or the big winter tidy-up when you put all that spent vegetation on a compost heap.

All the layout needs to do is provide a pleasing outline and an arrangement of beds, borders, pathways or features to show the plants to their best advantage from indoors. A window box gives sharp focus to the foreground. Fix the box low enough to let you look down onto the tops of the plants. Informal design gives the greatest scope for continuous interest

---

PLANT FRAMES

When possible, choose plant frames that are a feature in their own right as well as giving support and stability to climbers and ramblers. Viewed from indoors, a change of height varies the outline and lifts star plants up for enjoyment from a distance.

DIY PILLAR
Attach to a post two panels of trellis 6 ft (1.8 m) long by two squares wide, and top off with a finial. This gives the post width and a foothold for plants.

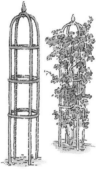

MAJESTIC OBELISK
Turn a flowering shrub into a triumph by training it up an obelisk. Tuck in a deciduous plant if you wish as the frame is handsome enough without winter foliage.

PYRAMID PROP
You can buy trellis shaped like a fan to attach to a wall. Turn four fans upside down and tie them together with twine to make a pretty pyramid for a climber.

UMBRELLA SPOKES
Use an umbrella frame for weeping shrubs or trailing roses as its shape mirrors their growth pattern. The frame is 4 ft (1.2 m), making it suitable for the smaller garden.

DOUBLE HOOP
Lax shrubs and herbaceous plants tend to collapse without support. Two simple hoops do the trick, disappearing from view once the ironwork is hidden by leaves.

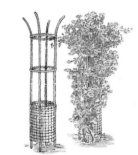

FOUNTAIN COLUMN
Ideal for sprawling climbers such as honeysuckle, this column makes an impressive sight with a height of 7 ft (2 m). A smaller version is also available.

in the middle distance and background. Arrange your curving borders, strategically placed trees, and lawn or paving in naturalistic lines that are easy on the eye.

If you opt for the formal design, take care that the picture is not too static. Let border plants grow free and unclipped – even if you impose a symmetrical layout and have such formal features as clipped hedges or pieces of topiary. Whatever the design, tall features give scale and contour to the scene. Plants on umbrella-shaped frames, pillars, obelisks and arches all act as punctuation marks.

There is often a hard surface outside the window – part of the drive or path at the front of the house, or a paved terrace

---

BEST PLANTS

CLIMBERS FOR TALL FRAMES

Strong foliage, profuse flowers and rich perfume are all on offer in plants that clamber high for viewing through the window.

• Kiwi fruit (*Actinidia deliciosa*): heart-shaped dark leaves studded in early summer with white flower-clusters that age to buff.

• Bird's-foot ivy (*Hedera helix* 'Pedata'): narrow-lobed, pale-veined evergreen leaves of metallic green.

• Maidenhair vine (*Muehlenbeckia complexa*): tangled reddish or dark purple stems with bright green leaves and tiny greenish flowers in summer.

• *Clematis montana* 'Elizabeth': covered with large clusters of pink flowers in May.

• *Clematis* 'Huldine': summer-flowering with large white blooms, mauve beneath.

• Rose (*Rosa* 'Albéric Barbier'): yellow buds opening to scented white blooms in high summer.

• Chilean potato-tree (*Solanum crispum* 'Glasnevin'): glossy semi-evergreen leaves and profuse purple flowers in midsummer with a scattering into autumn.

• Common honeysuckle (*Lonicera periclymenum* 'Graham Thomas'): sweetly scented cream flowers followed by red autumn berries.

• Star jasmine (*Trachelospermum jasminoides*): shiny evergreen leaves and heavily fragrant white flowers in summer followed by seedpods.

---

at the back – but it need not be bare and bleak. Just a few plants among the paving slabs or sprawling over the edge change the outlook completely.

PLANTS TO SOFTEN PAVING

Slip in some dwarf irises to blaze in spring and helianthemums to take over later. Strong reds and yellows stand out against the light tones of gravel and stone. Double helianthemums, such as the crimson 'Mrs Earle' or the yellow 'Wisley Primrose', are ideal because the flowers last a day longer. Singles are fine in the morning but on a hot day often shed their petals by afternoon; even so their long succession of flowers is a joy.

Saxifrages also thrive in crannies, as do flat mats of mountain avens (*Dryas octopetala*) and hummocks of the evergreen candytuft (*Iberis sempervirens*). These make pools of rich green in winter. For winter flowers plant *Cyclamen coum* and the early yellow crocus *Crocus ancyrensis* to shine out like little jewels.

COLOUR SCHEMES TO FRINGE PAVED AREAS

Round the edge of the hard surface you can add to the strong summer colour theme with shrubs such as the deep-rose flowering currant *Ribes sanguineum* 'Brocklebankii' whose leaves are golden yellow, and the yellow-leaved *Physocarpus opulifolius* 'Dart's Gold'. For winter, willow and dogwood look spectacular. The willow *Salix acutifolia* 'Blue Streak' has winter stems clothed with a bluish-white bloom, while the gold-leaved dogwood *Cornus alba* 'Aurea' has twigs that shine red in the winter sun. If you prune alternate shrubs every spring you get leafy displays in the summer followed by a forest of colourful wands in winter.

Herbaceous plants and bulbs complete the scheme through the year. Stick to a strict colour scheme against which bold spot plants stand out. Blue, gold and yellow with an occasional white flower is fresh without dominating.

After a February clean-up enjoy the cheerful yellow cups of winter aconites, nodding white snowdrops and the fresh foliage and yellow-spurred flowers of *Epimedium alpinum*. Fill out the spring scene with jonquils, yellow and blue primulas, long-lasting saucers of geums – especially creamy 'Lionel Cox' – and vivid yellow leopard's-bane (*Doronicum*). Soon after, euphorbias make an acid-yellow contrast for blue monkshood

---

A PICTURE WINDOW IN SPRING

When winter is almost over, but balmy days are rare, you still get great pleasure from a well-planned garden, and all without setting foot out of doors.

MARCH IS a confusing month. It brings with it some deceptively brighter days, but overall the weather is chill and bitter. So instead of venturing out, what could be nicer than surveying the garden from the comfort and warmth of your favourite armchair strategically placed beside the window?

To ensure maximum enjoyment of the outside from inside, bring the brave early blooms – low-growing little hepatica and cyclamen as well as the wide cups of hellebores – into close-up at the front of the bed near the window.

In sharp contrast, the twiggy viburnum and dark-leaved camellia tower over their low-lying companions. Their thrusting growth emphasises the soft floweriness around their feet.

COMPLETING THE PICTURE

More distant interest, the backdrop to closer delights, is not forgotten. Shape and texture are as valuable as colour.

The green solidity of a conifer stands out against the fading russet line of a hedge, both of them serving as a sympathetic foil for the brighter colours of the flowers at the front of the stage.

The pretty cherry tree in the centre of the lawn links the more neutral distance with the bright, busy foreground. It bears a delicate pale covering of blossom, which provides a reminder of the recent coverings of snow.

For extra interest close up, there are pots of flowers immediately in front of the window, raised on upturned plant pots to make sure that they are brought into full view.

The cheerful colours of the irises and hyacinths, the very essence of spring, brighten up the dreariest day. The attractively bushy woolly willow has its numerous twiglets crowded with swelling buds which hint at the display of the fluffy yellow catkins to come.

Palest pink cherry blossoms open throughout winter

Dainty cyclamen, hepatica and anemone fringe the raised bed

Green and pink hellebore cups face the window

Hyacinths and dwarf irises bloom close up

1. Autumn cherry (*Prunus × subhirtella* 'Autumnalis')

2. *Viburnum farreri*

3. *Camellia* 'Freedom Bell'

4. *Cyclamen coum, C. hederifolium* and *Hepatica transsilvanica*

5. Snowflake (*Leucojum vernum*)

6. *Pulmonaria saccharata*

7. Windflower (*Anemone blanda* 'Radar')

8. Lenten rose (*Helleborus orientalis* hybrids)

9. Woolly willow (*Salix lanata*)

10. Common hyacinth (*Hyacinthus orientalis* 'Ostara')

11. *Iris danfordiae*

PLANTING AND STAKING A TREE

TALL PLANTS such as trees catch the eye first in a scene through the window. Make sure that young trees get off to a good start. Supporting a newly planted tree with a short stake leaves most of the trunk free to bend with the wind. Such movement stimulates the production of a substance called lignin, which strengthens the trunk and gives the tree a speedier natural anchorage in the ground.

1. Dig the planting-hole wide and deep enough to accommodate the roots and sprinkle a handful of slow-release fertiliser at the bottom. Place the tree in the hole, spreading the roots to ensure they are not congested, and put enough soil on top to hold the tree upright.

2. Drive the sharp end of the stake in at a 45° angle with the point facing the same way as the prevailing wind. Drive it in until as much stake is in the ground as out.

3. Fill the hole with soil and tread it down firmly. Fit a tree tie, pushing the collar so the tie is tight round the stake but slightly loose round the tree, leaving room for expansion.

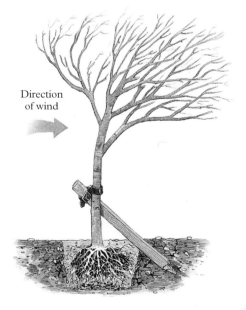

Direction of wind

ADJOINING CIRCLES Seen from a window above, pattern takes precedence in a garden while detail is obscured. This strong, simple design is based on repeated circles, reinforced by the directional setting of the paving stones.

(*Aconitum*) and Siberian iris. Plant lots of self-seeding blue pansies to spread where they will, with pale butter-coloured *Potentilla recta* 'Citrina', white scabious 'Mount Cook' and a scattering of evening primroses, blue cranesbills, campanulas and yellow achilleas to extend the gold and blue theme throughout the summer. In autumn, the colours will soften as the foliage turns a rusty colour and the plants die back.

VIEW FROM THE KITCHEN

In many houses the kitchen vies with the sitting room for the title of most used room since long hours are spent there every week on inescapable chores. Most of the planning and ploys used outside a sitting-room window work equally well outside the kitchen. But the kitchen has its own, often somewhat clinical, character that needs considering if the view from the window in front of the sink is to offer an escape for eye and imagination.

Soften the stark outline of kitchen windows by framing them with plants such as *Cotoneaster horizontalis*, climbing roses and *Viburnum rhytidophyllum*. These plants can do double service by giving support to early and late clematis species – such as *Clematis macropetala* 'Markham's Pink' and *C. viticella* 'Alba Luxurians'. For scent, plant lily-of-the-valley, lavender and old-fashioned pinks below the windows.

UPSTAIRS LOOKING DOWN

Most formal designs are seen to advantage from above, since their symmetry is at least as effective in two dimensions as in three. The pattern may be a knot or parterre, an arrangement of flower-filled circles with crescents round them, a rectangular assembly of clipped hedges, grass walks, gravels and carpet plantings, or pools, statues, topiary and paving.

Paving is one of the garden features that looks even better from above. An intricate pattern – whether of various-sized paving slabs or bricks in one of the traditional bricklayer's bonds such as Flemish or herringbone – gains impact when you see the overall design.

Formal designs and paving are particularly suitable for a front garden in town, which tends to be glimpsed rather than gazed upon. If you soften it with imaginative plantings it will stand a much longer look, and even make a satisfying layout for a small back garden.

The loose spires of pinky-red penstemons and the enthusiastic spread of frilly-leafed cranesbills, with saucers of pink or mauve floating above, instantly give a more airy feel – and cranesbills are repeat-flowering, so the effect is long lasting. Inject more soft colour and profuse flower and foliage with tender perennials such as white and pink *Argyranthemum*, mauve and purple salvia species, the more muted pelargoniums and lilac and rose-red verbenas. Let the plants tumble over the edge of their carefully shaped beds or froth at will within neatly clipped walls of box. For colour early on, plant bulbs – tulips especially, whose stateliness is lightened but not lost in the double and lily-flowered forms.

The pattern of beds looks equally good set in lawn, paving or gravel. Make clear paths through the beds, not just to emphasise the design from above, but to walk along for a closer enjoyment of the plants. A statue gives the perfect finish.

Informal layouts are more usual than formal ones now, but they do not make a satisfying picture from above when they

SWEEPING CURVES The sinuous expanse of lawn seen from above is more elegant than a rectangle and, at ground level, gradually unfolds the garden rather than revealing it at a glance. The small dovecote draws the eye across the lawn to explore the dense beds studded with focal plants.

present shapeless jumbles of flowerbeds, garden furniture, paths and tiny dabs of colour that merge into an overall blur.

Boldness and line are the crucial ingredients and the choices are almost infinite. The lines may be straight or curved, but they should create pleasing shapes balancing one side of the garden with the other. They should carry the eye towards points of interest – a giant clump of sunflowers, a still pool, a seat under a rose arch or a tree dripping with crab apples.

In the planting, use large sweeps of colour – a swirl of purple acanthus, a big circle of lupins, a patch of hostas wider than your outstretched arms, a whole bed of white petunias. It is only broad strokes

that stand out when you look from upstairs. The strong green circles of trees and shrubs stand out too, so use them to set off the brighter colours and to give a change of height sufficient to be evident from above. Amelanchier, Japanese maple, holly, magnolia, the large tulip tree (*Liriodendron*), the Judas tree (*Cercis siliquastrum*), rhododendrons and mahonias all give plenty of visual value.

SIDEWAYS GLANCES

A glimpsed view requires special treatment. Such a view is most likely to be seen through a window on the stairs or along a landing or passage. You pass it often but never linger. There is no time

FRAMING THE PICTURE Branches that change with the season make a pleasant outlook as you pass a window. When wisteria's blooms have faded and the leaves have fallen, the gnarled stems have a fascination of their own.

COMPOSING A SCENE Within the right setting, planting on a lavish scale is not necessary. Golden-leaved shrubs against a velvety dark-green hedge make an ideal backdrop for seasonal high spots such as stately tulips.

SAFETY FIRST

COVERING GARDEN CANES

IT IS EASY to forget there are canes in a garden bed when you are focusing on the plants beyond. A cane can cause very nasty injuries to the face or eye as you bend down. Protect yourself by fitting tops on all your canes. There are dark green PVC tops available

to see detail; simple, forceful features are all you take in as you move past.

A single branch of a tree can be sufficient for a landing window. The branch is always changing, sometimes bearing full blossom, sometimes in autumn colours, sometimes motionless, but more often moving gently to and fro in the breeze.

At ground level a few square feet of fertile soil widens the choice for giving a similar fillip to the senses. A statement that can be spotted, noted and enjoyed in an instant is vital, so plants need to shout to be noticed. Support the taller herbaceous plants for maximum effect and keep in mind year-round interest.

☙ A brilliant patch of tulips makes an eye-catcher for spring. The bolder the colour or mixture of colours, the better.

☙ For summer, choose the pillar-box red poppy 'Beauty of Livermere', or the double pink peony 'Sarah Bernhardt'.

☙ For autumn, plant double Michaelmas daisies such as red 'Andenken an Alma Potschke' or 'Harrington's Pink'.

☙ A Japanese maple offers pink buds and leaves in spring, a graceful form in summer and gorgeous autumn colour.

☙ Run a clematis up a tree that lacks summer appeal. Deep violet *Clematis × jackmannii* or the wine-red 'Madame Julia Correvon' once established swarm to the top of a small tree each summer.

☙ Grow a rose such as coppery pink 'Albertine' or golden 'Emily Gray' up a tree with handsome bark such as a cherry or hawthorn to enjoy in winter.

☙ If there is no soil but plenty of sun put a Chusan palm (*Trachycarpus fortunei*) in a large tub. Its pleated fans of leaves against a white wall are dramatic all year.

BASEMENT GARDENING

When you have a worm's-eye view of the world, the challenge is to make people want to look outside at all. However, with

A BASEMENT IN MAY

*Although often dismissed as gloomy
and impossible to work with,
a basement area becomes a verdant
little jungle when wisely planted.*

THE VIEW LOOKING OUT from most
basement windows is bare – not a
tempting canvas for a gardener, no
matter how keen. Take a practical
approach, however, and you can work
magic with greens and golds.

The key is to choose plants that thrive
in shade. Paint the wall pale blue to
suggest sky behind a selection of plants
with varied foliage textures.

The holly's sculptural form and
shapely, glossy leaves show up boldly
against the wall. The little tree contrasts
with the frilly edged and lacy ferns,
both evergreens that are now unrolling
their new season's refreshingly bright
green fronds.

Do not forget the changing seasons.
It is vital to create year-round interest,
within the limitations of the light and
space. Ensure there are always stars to
take centre stage.

In May the stars are the delicate,
almost luminous white and yellow
flowers of oxlips, the lily-of-the-valley
and the fluffy heads of the *Smilacina*.
The sweet perfume of the lily-of-the-
valley wafting in through the window
delights even the most jaded senses.

PLEASURES TO COME

During the summer, brilliant golden
Welsh poppies, yellow loosestrife, tall
creamy foxgloves and deep blue willow
gentians will take up the centre stage.
The ground-covering epimedium has a
bronze flush on the new spring leaves
then, after a green summer, it takes on
orange tints in autumn.

Chinese Virginia creeper looks
attractive throughout the year, but really
comes into its own in the autumn, when
its prettily variegated leaves turn a
glorious red. For now, in May, the
vigorous sky-seeking climber serves as a
backcloth for its more delicate and
earthbound companions.

*Virginia creeper
extends its tracery
with new shoots*

*Sculptured holly
leaves stand
out boldly*

*Lily-of-
the-valley
spreads a
rich scent*

*Fern fronds soften
the edge of the low wall*

1. Chinese Virginia creeper (*Parthenocissus henryana*)
2. Holly (*Ilex aquifolium* 'Madame Briot')
3. *Smilacina racemosa*
4. Lily-of-the-valley (*Convallaria majalis*)
5. Oxlip (*Primula elatior*)
6. *Epimedium × youngianum* 'Niveum'
7. Hart's-tongue fern (*Asplenium scolopendrium*)
8. Soft shield fern (*Polystichum setiferum* 'Acutilobum')

GARDENS BELOW To make a basement into a verdant jungle, build up a strong framework of evergreen architectural plants such as fatsia and mahonia. Ring the changes with containers of seasonal plants for highlights.

a little imagination and some prudent choices, your vertical garden can place a basement room in a green oasis.

The first task is to alleviate the gloom when a window is only two or three strides from a high wall, and sunshine is a brief or absent phenomenon. Go for light-coloured paving or tiles on the ground and paint the wall white or ice-blue, which not only reflects light but also provides a contrasting background for the plants. If you want a warmer effect, use lemon or pale ochre.

In such a restricted space, much of your garden is literally going up the wall. But it can also hang down the wall, so use some trailers as well as climbers. Plants that 'look down' because of their nodding flowers – as oriental hellebores do – or trail without being trained, are particularly useful for high spots.

Climbers respond best to a cool, roomy root run in rich soil, so a vertical garden needs fertile beds or capacious containers at the base of its wall. Where there is a narrow bed above the level of

TOOLBOX

UNSEEN EYES

MOST CLIMBERS need a support network. Vine eyes hammered into the mortar of a wall and linked with thin galvanised or plastic-coated wire are cheap, unobtrusive and effective. The eyes can be arranged so that the wires run horizontally between them, form a grid pattern, or spread in a fan shape.

the window, enrich it to make a nourishing home for trailing plants. *Clematis macropetala* dangles its blue bells, the broom *Cytisus × kewensis* make a creamy cascade and small-leafed ivies drape beautifully into evergreen curtains.

If there is no soil at the top of the wall, more ingenuity is needed. Hang small pots in brackets fixed to the wall and

plant them with aubrietia, saxifrage, lobelia and campanula. Fill some tall jardinières with exuberant falls of ivy-leaved pelargoniums. Do not forget the steps leading down to the basement; they are a ready-made stage for displaying pots of trailing plants.

Increase decorative value by making the practical and essential plant supports

GARDENS ALOFT
Balcony gardens can be exposed to drying winds, and plants will need big containers and frequent watering. These pelargoniums will not collapse as soon as they dry out and they have a long flowering period.

Although the choice of plants is wide, the whole arrangement is simplified since it has to be planned from the window point of view; no other viewpoint is possible.

The chief way of growing plants on a balcony is in containers, which you can shift around from time to time. With only a small area needing your time and care, you can afford to replace plants regularly for a fresh, healthy look all year. Each plant must be at its best to earn a place in this miniature garden.

The bigger and roomier the containers are, the better the plants do and the greater the number and variety you can grow. Small trees and shrubs need a particularly generous root space but, if grown in suitable planters, reward you with more growth and thus greater scope for pruning into a desired shape.

If you have room for a small tree Japanese maples, which have more than one period of interest, lend themselves to container culture. The trees stay healthy if fed regularly and placed in a well-lit part of the balcony. Prune to develop a mature shape by judicious removal of whole branches, by encouraging limbs to bend and arch as if with age, and by keeping the trunks as clean as possible.

Shrubs are easier to keep vigorous, especially if you select small kinds such as winter-flowering *Sarcococca confusa*, or spring-flowering *Daphne retusa*, both shade-tolerant evergreens with fragrant flowers. On a well-lit balcony, a wisteria gives generous rewards with the heaviest flowering after hard summer pruning.

Evergreens such as box or lavender make more solid shapes when clipped. Citrus trees are also candidates for clipping into glossy-leaved mop-heads, which will bear a few fruits; take them indoors for winter. Taller plants such as this vary the outline of a balcony garden, while easily changed perennials and annuals form the bulk of the planting.

For year-round pleasure vary the plants as much as you can.

🌶 Good-value perennials are perpetual-flowering carnations, pinks, penstemons, hostas and ornamental grasses.

🌶 For disposable summer planting, use salvias, helichrysums, petunias, nemesias, osteospermums and heliotropes.

🌶 'Angel' pelargoniums are especially

into design features. Trellis, for example, can create arches along the wall. You can make a side screen of trellis to mask dustbins, or bring the trellis arches forward a little to suggest greater depth.

Single spot supports, perhaps with wires between, can be adornments too. Wooden, china, metal or terracotta doorknobs are easily screwed into plugs driven into the joints in the wall. Invisible supports, such as wires held by vine eyes, may be your choice.

MAKING MORE OF A BALCONY

Balconies vary in size but, even with the roomiest, space is at a premium. And yet the opportunities for a little garden to give joy for the whole year are enormous.

valuable for balconies. Their profuse maroon, mauve and pink flowers appear over a long season and, being small, last longer in breezy conditions.

🌿 Herbs give you a pinch of fresh flavour for the kitchen and like poor, dry soil. A dark thyme, golden marjoram and purple sage make a pretty collection.

🌿 Plant bulbs for the 'off' seasons. Though pricey, they give a showy display for little effort. Unforced hyacinths are cheaper and, on a sheltered balcony, will bloom by March anyway.

🌿 Narcissi planted in several layers give dense colour and many are fragrant.

🌿 For more modest spring displays grow sweet violets or, if you can find them, double Parma violets. These like shade, are fragrant in winter and spring and provide posies for indoors.

🌿 Autumn bulbs for strong splashes of colour are the golden *Sternbergia lutea* and the lilac-blue *Colchicum speciosum*.

HOW TO IMPROVE SHADY OUTLOOKS

Dense, dry shade presents one of gardening's most taxing challenges – and one that confronts many gardeners since town houses so often have rooms at the back sunk below street level and looking out onto gardens thrown into perpetual shadow by fences or buildings. These not only block the daylight but keep the rain off as well. What can be done?

First try to reduce the severity of the conditions. Make the centre of the garden as open as possible to admit maximum light. Thin out overhanging trees or remove some that are not subjects of tree preservation orders. Next paint walls, fences and even ground surfaces a pale colour to help reflect what light there is. Instead of having a solid boundary fence or wall to head height, make the top strip from trellis, which admits some light while preserving privacy. You can dress it lightly with a pale climber.

Before making new plantings, feed and mulch the soil and perhaps lay on a 'ring main' of pierced hose for easy watering. Moist, well-fed soil gives the plants a better chance of matching your expectations of them.

Choose plenty of plants with pale or white flowers; they show up better in poor light. Large architectural foliage plants serve as invigorating contrast. Fragrant white lilies blooming above *Hosta sieboldiana* gives a summer mix of flower and leaf. The handsomest foliage belongs to *Gunnera manicata*, which in the wild grows vast, with a single leaf sometimes growing more than head high and spreading like a golf umbrella. This is a bold choice for a town garden and needs plenty of moisture but it would always draw your eye to the window and lend drama to the scene. If you fancy something less dominant, try *Rheum palmatum*, a relative of rhubarb, whose leaves are only the size of ladies' umbrellas but still make a superb showpiece. In the right conditions, *Rheum* sends up soaring spikes of white flowers.

Underplantings of snowdrops, the white snowflake (*Leucojum vernum*), the white Christmas rose (*Helleborus niger*)

Tassels of itea drape the side screen

REPAIRING A BROKEN POT

YOUR BALCONY OR BASEMENT garden can seem so much like an extra room that you forget your display of pots is exposed to the elements. If a wild wind blows a pot over or one that is not frost-proof is left out in an unexpected early or late frost, you may wake up one morning to find a broken pot.

Do not give up hope; the break is not difficult to repair and may be the spur you need to repot a root-bound plant. Once you have extricated the plant, tease out its roots and trim them back by a third before repotting it.

Then clean the broken pot thoroughly, moisten the edges to be bonded and coat them with an epoxy putty chosen to match the pot. Press together, letting any excess putty squeeze out of the crack. After an hour cut off any surplus with a sharp, wet knife then leave to harden overnight.

Next day wrap strong wire round the pot below the rim and twist the ends together with pliers to tighten it.

Scented, starry jasmine blossoms frame the door

Glossy, dark leaves set off the ripening lemons

Purple-centred clematis nods outside the window

1. Common white jasmine (*Jasminum officinale*)
2. *Itea ilicifolia*
3. *Salvia patens*
4. *Datura inoxia*
5. *Plectranthus coleoides* 'Variegatus', coral gem (*Lotus berthelotii*) and ivy-leaved geranium (*Pelargonium peltatum* 'L'Elégante')
6. Lemon tree (*Citrus limon* 'Meyer')
7. *Clematis florida* 'Sieboldii'

THE BALCONY AS A FRAGRANT OASIS

Gardening above the streets provides a unique opportunity for experimenting with plants that are less hardy, as well as enlarging and enhancing your living space.

IF YOUR OUTDOOR SPACE is a few floors above street level you can still make it feel like a more conventional garden. In fact you have a special advantage, because your balcony can easily be transformed into an extra room.

What could be more delicious than being overwhelmed with a rush of fragrance as soon as you open the french windows? Or looking out onto a soothing mass of lush green foliage, which counteracts the hustle, bustle and smells of the street below.

SUMMER BLUE AND GOLD

Plants framing the windows link the balcony and the room indoors while the stylish lemon tree in the carefully chosen container provides a strong focal point, and can be moved as the mood takes you. The mass of plants in the troughs lining the balcony rails screen off the outside world and provide protection against the strong breezes that always seem to swirl about keenly at this height.

Since this south-west-facing balcony, shown here in July, provides such good shelter, the container, which can be moved indoors during the winter, can be more ornate and delicate than one standing in an open garden. A stylish pot or urn becomes a part of the exuberantly decorative scene in its own right.

The trumpet flowers of the datura, with their rich, deep fragrance, and the sweetly scented lemon tree and jasmine will fill the room with their perfume.

The clematis resembling a passion-flower and the *Itea*, with its dramatic long catkins, are beautiful climbers, both adding an unusual touch to the scene.

The variety of colours and shapes are an irresistible draw. The plants are pleasing at a casual glance and their intricate details make them more interesting the closer up you see them.

PLANTING FOR YEAR-ROUND VIEWING

◆

PLANTING IS a creative art and, as in the other arts, a sense of beauty and an ability to imagine the finished result are a great help. Successful planting, however, does not need years of hard training. Even at the first attempt, you can produce satisfying results and that feeling of satisfaction continues to grow as your experience deepens.

In gardening, there is no need to bow to another's taste. You are free to choose the shapes, colours and textures that please you – provided the site suits them. Despite different tastes and aims, however, gardeners share the basic purpose of making their plot look good right now and at every other time of year. This is particularly important in through-the-window gardening, where you cannot move from one point of interest to another but must take the view presented. Forethought, practice and some corrective transplanting will compose scenes that work outside and from indoors.

HIGH-PERFORMANCE TREES

If there is room, plant a tree. There is no better way to capture attention from a distance. When your eye falls on an attractive or distinctive trunk it is drawn upwards, and then along the outline of the limbs until you enjoy the tracery of the smaller branches and twigs.

Look for trees with more than one attribute: the gleaming trunk of the Chinese cherry, *Prunus serrula*, resembles polished mahogany and is as outstanding in winter as in summer, but its blossoms are disappointing. *Prunus sargentii*, on the other hand, has a shapely outline, moderately shiny bark and looks beautiful all year. In spring, the foliage is dark russet as it emerges after the deep pink blossoms have faded. Autumn turns the leaves to orange and scarlet, and in winter the outline is shapely.

Among evergreens, generous berry bearers such as hollies – especially the extra heavy fruiting 'J.C. van Tol', or the variegated 'Handsworth New Silver' – give long-term value. In milder areas, a wonderful window tree is the slender *Eucryphia × nymansensis* 'Nymansay', which has shiny evergreen foliage and is smothered with white waxy blooms in

LEVELS OF INTEREST A clear area of paving creates a feeling of space which is extended towards the lawn as the urn draws the eye onwards. Two contrasting surfaces, hard and soft, are separated by a change of level, which adds a further dimension of interest.

and white crocus could brighten late winter. The evergreen shrub *Osmanthus × burkwoodii* keeps its glossy, dark leaves all winter and these make a backcloth for white spring blooms. Pale *Colchicum* 'Lilac Wonder' and *C. speciosum* 'Album', will carry the theme in autumn.

If you have paving, which suits the setting much better than sparse grass,

create highlights in the crevices with busy lizzies. *Impatiens* 'Accent White' lasts through summer, and you could slip in a golden sage to use all year in the kitchen.

Complete the summer scene with a climbing rose that thrives in the gloom. *Rosa* 'Madame Alfred Carrière' bears a copius succession of heavily scented white blooms.

autumn. Perhaps the most spectacular tree of all for mild areas is the Chilean fire bush (*Embothrium coccineum*), whose tall, narrow shape is perfect for viewing through a long window and whose light, glossy evergreen leaves disappear in high summer beneath a blazing mass of orange-red spidery blooms.

DISTINCTIVE SHRUBS

An arresting outline is the feature to look for in shrubs. The pleasing shapes of many dwarf conifers, for example, make bold, permanent features in the garden. And glossy, solid camellias, handsome all year but ravishing when in full bloom, also give a garden strong shape.

Position key species so that when viewed through the window, preferably from armchair level, they improve the garden's outline. To be sure you get the position just right, run some trials, pushing in canes as markers where the shrubs are to be. Keep nipping in and out of the house to make adjustments until you are sure you have positioned them to maximum advantage.

Later on you will be glad you took the trouble when you can admire from indoors a perfectly placed blossom-wreathed shrub rose, the long arrays of hollylike leaves on a *Mahonia* × *media* 'Charity' crowned with spires of yellow flowers, or the long, pale catkins of *Garrya elliptica* dancing among the dark-green leaves in the early spring breezes.

GENEROUS FILLINGS

Between high-profile specimen plants, the scenes need a constant groundwork of foliage. Although steady in its colours this groundwork gently increases in luxuriance as the growing season advances, and then falls back as it dies in autumn. Pulmonarias, with their silver-mottled foliage, and alchemillas, with light-green rounded leaves, are ideal. Bergenia leaves persist and colour up well in winter before vivid heads of pink blooms make a splash of early spring colour.

In partial shade, *Euphorbia amygdaloides* var. *robbiae* is a keen contributor, making a green carpet all year but giving its chief delight in spring, with lime-green blossoms of a shade as intense as you see anywhere when the sun falls on

them. The plant is invasive, so do not shrink from pulling it up if it goes too far.

Add more simple splashes of colour with quick, easy spreads of honesty, foxgloves, sweet williams and forget-me-nots. These all look as pretty from a distance as close to and they frequently develop into self-seeding colonies.

Include some plants with spectacular flowers, intense colours, outlandish or architectural shapes and, for summer when the window is open, a beguiling fragrance. Their function is to initiate the observing process – to clamour for attention but not hold it for long. They must

LONG LIFE FROM BULBS

WHEN BULBS have had their moment of glory in a pot, do not throw them away. If treated correctly, bulbs can be used again and again. Feed until the foliage has died, then lift the bulbs and strip off dead stems, leaves and roots. Plant any bulblets in a nursery bed to fatten. Leave the bulbs to dry, then store them in paper bags in a dry, cool place until it is time to pot them again.

SIGHTS OF SPRING The level of the earth next to this window means that planting can be brought up close and at eye level. Ideal are brilliant plants such as this blaze of tulips with primulas and arabis round their feet.

view of the window – raised on a plinth if necessary – planted with crocuses for late winter and hyacinths for spring. When planting up bulb bowls, cram in as many bulbs and corms as you can and stick to one kind for each bowl, but choose exceptional colours.

The purple-striped crocus 'Pickwick', for instance, could precede the soft blue hyacinth 'Myosotis' or, for a sharper change of colour, the apricot-coloured hyacinth 'Gipsy Queen'.

SUMMER STARS

To claim attention in summer, position fragrant plants beside an open window. A climber on the wall, preferably framing the window, will fill a room with fragrance and allow tantalising glimpses of the flowers. Summer jasmine is perfect for this, with its pretty flowers and strong fragrance. In shadier positions, use honeysuckle instead, especially the Japanese species. Look for the form *Lonicera japonica* 'Halliana'. Roses also make lovely window-frame plants; the pink, thornless 'Zéphirine Drouhin' does not snatch at you if you lean out and its flowers are intensely fragrant.

Lilies are elegantly formed flowers to see close up near a window; many are fragrant as well as lovely, and they are as happy in pots as in the ground. A more conventional, but still irresistibly eye-catching, planting for a container is a combination of pelargoniums, of fuchsias or of petunias. Look especially for some of the new cuttings-raised hybrid pelargoniums: 'Eroica', for example, is a hot, coconut-ice pink and 'Ecco' an intense orange scarlet semidouble with darkish foliage. A generous clump of any of these maintains its bold colour throughout the summer.

SUSTAINING THE DISPLAY

Windows in frequent use must offer constant interest, regardless of the season. You need some changes of mood and of colour, not only from season to season but from week to week.

Nowadays, bedding plants tend to be changed only twice a year – once in autumn for the spring display, and again in May or June for summer. The Victorians were far more adventurous, revising or replacing their schemes several times a season. This could be expensive on a large scale, but in a modest-sized planting, to sustain through-the-window interest, you could follow their example

INTO THE DISTANCE This garden is designed to accentuate distance and conceal its narrow bounds. The paving pattern adds breadth in the foreground while the honeysuckle arch tempts you into the alluring space beyond.

NATURAL TEXTURES Warm-toned gravel and mellow stone are a soft setting for sunny coloured shrubs and flowers. Lilies planted by the window join the display later in the year when their heady perfume drifts indoors.

not be too intrusive in the general design, but let the eye move away at leisure to other elements in the scene.

In winter, something as simple as a clump of snowdrops is spectacular if you choose the extra-large Crimean species, *Galanthus elwesii*, and bring them right up to the window so that they gleam in the light. The better oriental hellebore hybrids, especially with pale pink or white spotted flowers, are stunning in a raised bed near the window. Sun behind them gives them a particular glow. In a small courtyard, place a large bowl in

LONG SEASONS OF INTEREST

Trees and shrubs stand up well for viewing from a distance through the seasons and year after year. Many reward you with flower, foliage, hips and bark interest.

• Wedding-cake tree (*Cornus controversa* 'Variegata'): tiered growth, flat heads of white summer flowers and vivid autumn leaves.

• Red maple (*Acer rubrum* 'Scanlon'): slow-growing tree with a dense, conical crown and glowing autumn colour.

• Birchbark cherry (*Prunus serrula*): peeling trunk and branches show gleaming red-brown new bark, which is particularly good in winter.

• Rose (*Rosa moyesii*): tall shrub with red single flowers all summer and shiny scarlet flask-shaped hips to follow.

• *Fuchsia magellanica*: bushy shrub with a profuse show of dangling crimson and purple flowers from midsummer to October.

• Smoke bush (*Cotinus coggygria* 'Royal Purple'): feathery plumes of pink flowers in July and deep purple leaves lightening to red in autumn.

• Judas tree (*Cercis siliquastrum*): pink spring flowers followed by heart-shaped leaves flushed red at first, then yellow in autumn.

and pop in potted chrysanthemums for autumn, bulbs and pansies for winter, wallflowers and forget-me-nots or primulas for spring and knee-high sweet peas, pot marigolds, antirrhinums, busy lizzies or nasturtiums for summer.

Unconventional bedding plants, such as aubrietia, arabis or the speedy annual *Limnanthes douglasii*, contribute pools of clear colour to temporary plantings. Gladiolus, a summer-flowering corm, and especially the white and maroon, fragrant cultivar *Gladiolus callianthus* 'Murielae', is bold in colour and form.

Herbaceous plants that grow very tall very quickly can play a dual role. A peppering of tall mulleins, for example, provides a series of focal points when they flower, but before that their large rosettes of woolly foliage add distinctive texture to the general background. *Veratrum nigrum* is a slower-growing plant whose leaves, huge and pleated, add texture to

INVITING ASPECT The slightly random paving in the foreground and the circular shape of the central bed invites the onlooker to travel round the path and into the unknown. The canopy of foliage leaning in from both sides changes with the seasons, giving varied colour and light.

the scene before the curious, although not conventionally beautiful, brownish flowers are thrown up on towering stems in later summer.

THE BEST OF INSIDE AND OUT

Gardening through the window is a special culture with its own set of design and planting opportunities. You can tailor the garden to suit each unique window view, but the basic gardening principles still apply; only the point of view changes. With a shifting focus on star performers set against a general picture that develops over the seasons, the view through the window is constantly absorbing.

This does not detract from your outdoor design in any way at all. Indeed, the extra thought that goes into the planning is an improving factor for both indoor and outdoor viewing and the result is a garden of double delight.

INSPIRATION FROM

GREAT GARDENS

MOSELEY OLD HALL

Deceptive brickwork hides a Tudor gem.

The intricacies of the knot garden
at Moseley Old Hall near
Wolverhampton in Staffordshire are
best appreciated from an upstairs
window in this historic manor house,
now clad in Victorian brick.
Seen from there, the low box hedging,
the matched standard box trees,
the sanded paths and the
contrasting gravels in the scalloped
and circular beds unite
to form a perfect pattern.

KNOT GARDENS – so called because of their resemblance to the inter-weaving of silken knots or bows – first rose to popularity in Britain in the early 16th century. Their function was to provide a pleasant yet formal background for those strolling and chatting outside, a similar purpose to that served by the tapestries which lined the long gallery of a great house.

The pattern of a knot garden was outlined in low, clipped hedging, for which box, lavender and thyme were all widely used. In knots such as this one, the patterns were filled with coloured gravels or sand. Although most knot gardens were swept away by the more complex designs of the late 17th century, a few did survive, while others have been more recently re-created. The knot at Moseley Old Hall was constructed only in 1963 but it follows a design of 1640.

It works well as a kind of botanical and visual link with the house's great brush with history. In 1651, the fugitive Charles II sheltered here after the Battle of Worcester, although whether a knot existed beyond the window at the time of King Charles's visit is not now known. If it did it would surely have been close in both the style and the planting to that of the knot garden there today.

MODIFIED FOR TODAY

The orderliness and serenity of a knot garden still appeals as strongly as ever, and it is an intriguing way of constructing a small, formal garden.

In the example here, one segment has been plucked from the more complex knot at Moseley and adapted to work in a smaller space. It forms one part of a larger garden – an arch in the hedge of clipped yew (*Taxus baccata*) gives a glimpse of more beyond – although the design could just as well fill the whole of a town garden.

Low hedges of box (*Buxus*) border colourful beds filled with purple cranes-bill (*Geranium macrorrhizum* 'Bevan's Variety') and silvery, feathery *Artemisia* 'Powis Castle'. The beds could also be filled with some low-growing cluster-flowered (floribunda) roses, or even with pebbles to create a more authentic copy of the original.

Between the shaped beds lies a gravelled cruciform path with a standard rose, 'The Fairy', in the central circle, paying homage to the clipped standards

SIMPLE SYMMETRY The precise formality in the composition of this classic knot garden creates a feeling of welcome serenity.

of the original. The rose is trained over an umbrella-style frame about 4 ft (1.2 m) high and provides a focal point for the garden. It is underplanted with the delicate pansy *Viola cornuta* 'Alba' and finished at the base with a simple edging of brick. A surround of lawn sprinkled with daisies completes the picture, the whole sheltered from chilly breezes by the solidity of a yew hedge.

One virtue of such a garden is that its strong, shapely design is sustained throughout the winter months, thanks to the evergreen hedging. Both the planting and design can be varied to enhance any style of house or larger garden, but the end result is sure to provide a place for contemplation or a quiet, undisturbed read on a summer's day.

MODERN KNOT This knot garden echoes but simplifies the older scheme. It replaces clipped box and gravels with artemisias, cranesbills and a standard rose.

PLANTING TO PLEASE THE SENSES

ONE OF THE CHIEF JOYS of gardening is weaving together the colours you love most to create atmosphere and impact. Cool whites and lemons, gentle pinks and mauves, deep reds and crimsons, sophisticated greens or a fresh and jolly mixture may be what you long for, and with a little advice you can match your dream to your soil and size of garden. But gardens delight not only the eye; a drift of sweet fragrance as you stroll along a path, and plants that give a crisp rustle or a gentle sigh as they stir in the breeze add to the magic. And who can resist stroking a silky pulsatilla seed head, the soft plumes of fennel or the satin bark of a cherry tree?

*The deep colour of the fragrant sweet pea flowers emphasises
their velvety texture.*

EXPLORING EVERY DELIGHT

O F THE FIVE SENSES – touch, taste, hearing, smell and sight – the last sense is the most finely attuned, so it is no surprise that even the most creative gardener devotes most consideration to colour, shape, line, form and movement.

The sense of smell runs a close second to the joy in visual satisfactions, and as a result many gardeners devise planting schemes which incorporate the richest of scents from spring's awakening and summer's abundance right through to the late months of winter. There is more than just fragrance from flowers on offer; aromatic foliage, ripening fruit and pungent herbs all contribute to a garden's sensual atmosphere, and even the smell of gentle decay as the garden declines at the back end of the year can add its own sweet melancholy.

But is due respect paid to touch, sound and taste? Almost any planting scheme is enriched when it makes a point of including something to satisfy all three of these senses, as well as the two more dominant ones. Have you ever thought, for instance, of siting a bamboo where you can hear its whisperings through an open window; or of planting artemisia beside a favourite seat simply for the pleasure of running your hands through its silky foliage?

There are many simple, and cheap, design features that do much to intensify the sudden bursts of pleasure, the lifting of the spirits and the sheer delight engendered by a successful garden.

PLANNED TO SPARKLE Creamy-edged hostas, pink-tinged pansies and the heavily scented shrub *Viburnum carlesii* soften with their varied shades of white the monochrome effect of this planting scheme. The globes of the tulips, catching the light, seem to float out from the green background.

VISUAL SATISFACTIONS

COLOUR HAS INSTANT IMPACT, but shape gives its own subtle, enduring pleasure that should not be neglected. It may be the shape of individual plants or it may be the structure composed by the planting as a whole that satisfies the gardener's creative energies.

In the historic formal garden, such structures as pleached avenues, knots and parterres played a far greater role than colour. Patterns were bold and geometric, styles were rigid and the scale was usually stately. Strong geometry is just as effective in modern private gardens, however – even in small, informal ones.

Clever planting must lead the eye deliberately to specific points. To get people to look upward to a treasured plant, for example, guide the eye through a crescendo of lower ones, leading it to follow the outline higher and higher.

Contrasting shapes carefully put together enable rounded, tiered, upright or creeping plants to be enjoyed to the full. Colour then becomes an extra device used among the different shapes to highlight, embolden, tone down or shift the pattern with seasonal change.

When shape and colour are also combined with plants chosen for their special qualities – a strongly architectural feel, perhaps, or a hard and spiky foliage – a planting takes on yet another dimension.

PLANTS FOR TEXTURE

Use some of the bold, even brash, architectural plants that are irresistible to the eye. The giant thistle (*Onopordum nervosum*) grows at an impressive rate and has the most alluring soft felted leaves, although its spines are vicious. The plant scatters seeds prodigiously, but seedlings are easy to hoe out or transplant. The mullein, too, is grey-white and woolly, and its knee-high rosettes of large leaves throw up spires of crowded blooms resembling hollyhocks.

Plants with enormous leaves – gunnera, for example, or the rhubarb-like *Rheum palmatum* – make compelling shapes from a distance but are also fun to look at close up.

You can plan overall schemes which marry and enhance visual pleasures. The narrow grassy leaves of a brown sedge, for example, create a silky effect when

NATURAL SCULPTURE The expansive, eye-catching leaves of *Rodgersia tabularis* spread like a crowd of opened umbrellas over the dense mauve flowers of *Montia sibirica* which carpets the ground beneath.

combined with the foliage of Californian poppies (*Eschscholzia*), while the satiny, vivid orange poppy flowers give a bright edge to the bronze carex foliage.

The character of a planting changes according to season. The tender green growths of spring dry to crisp textures and starker brown shapes in autumn.

BEAUTY OF FORM WITHOUT FLOWERS

It is satisfying to compose plantings where flowers are not used at all, and where all the interest comes from leaf, stem and trunk, relying on their variations in outline, colour and texture.

A mixture of evergreen shrubs and woody plants with an attractive bark or pattern of bare twigs provides interest in the winter. Plants with lots of small leaves – the lesser periwinkle and low-growing hebes, for example – present a soft background for more conspicuous characters.

Tall fans of swordlike iris leaves, hard, spiky clumps of yucca and striped New Zealand flax, and huge purple hands of

KEEPING A FULL RECORD

AN INSTANT CAMERA keeps the best record of what is flowering and when in your garden. Take a series of shots over the seasons to use when planning what changes to make.

Before you make any decisions, spread the photographs out and place illustrations of promising plants, cut from catalogues, on them. This gives a good idea of what a new plant will look like in a certain position.

gleams the more brightly against the felted surfaces of *Ballota pseudodictamnus*, senecio (*Brachyglottis* 'Sunshine') or *Senecio cineraria*. A groundwork of light-leaved *Sedum spectabile* does wonders for the dark foliage of Portugal laurel or *Pittosporum*, while the lighter-leaved *Weigela* 'Florida Variegata' looks its best standing out from a dark underplanting of evergreen candytuft (*Iberis sempervirens*), common thyme, or even well-controlled plain ivy.

Bamboos combine shimmering leaves and graceful height. The glossy leaves of *Pleioblastus auricomus* shiver in the slightest breeze, drawing attention as they catch the light. In winter, little can divert the eye from the wildly twisting twigs of the corkscrew hazel (*Corylus avellana* 'Contorta'). Place this where you can see its fascinating silhouette and enjoy the dancing yellow catkins in February.

HOW TO MAKE COLOURS WORK

Different hues and combinations produce different effects on the viewer. Intense colour tends to heighten the emotions; gentle, pastel shades relax; reds and yellows are urgent and restless together; blues and whites create a cool setting but the warmer, primary contrast of blues and golden yellows is invigorating. Being aware of how colours work, together and on their own, helps you to achieve whatever effect you want.

The abrupt impact of a strident bed of hot tones, for example, distracts from a less than satisfactory outline or feature elsewhere in the garden. Conversely, a foliage garden with variations of green and subtle grey, lime or olive undertones merges into one dull mass unless something bolder is placed in it to make the viewer focus more sharply and then notice all the subtleties. A group of red tulips among spring greenery, for example, shouts for attention and invites the beholder to start a more searching look.

Once an initial flash of colour has drawn the eye, the viewer then begins to observe other colours and shapes, perhaps the browns and greys of tree trunks, the vivid spiky green of young crocosmia foliage and the pleasant contrast of softer, more muted green foliage behind.

USING COOL, PALE COLOUR SCHEMES

Pale colours, especially sharp lemons, blues and whites, work especially well in low light levels, gaining a luminosity that

---

ENDING A COLOUR CLASH

IF IT SUDDENLY strikes you that two flowering plants are clashing and you need to take one out, do not hesitate to do so. Simply dig out the offender with its roots and as much surrounding soil as you can lift and put it straight away into a prepared hole in a spot where it will show to greater advantage. Firm the plant in well and water it frequently until it is established.

Fill the gap left in the border on a temporary basis with a bland-coloured herbaceous plant such as a white pansy or petunia. Either of these will provide adequate ground cover until you find a permanent replacement.

CLEVER COLOURS A clump of bright pink *Geranium sanguineum* is planted in front of *Stachys macrantha* and the red *Knautia macedonica* in an unusual combination boldly coloured and dense enough to seize the gaze and keep it from an unattractive wall behind.

Rodgersia pinnata 'Superba' make dramatic shapes. Less commonly seen but equally striking are the toothed cream and dark green leaves of *Scrophularia aquatica* 'Variegata'.

Maples, and especially the Japanese species, also have beautifully shaped leaves in many subtle colours including gentle bronze, pink and purplish hues. The delicate points of the maples show to advantage above a spread of bolder, broader foliage. Hostas are good here, especially in fertile, moisture-retaining soil.

Try contrasts of pale and dark, shiny and matt, as well as contrasting shapes. The glossy sheen of holly and camellia

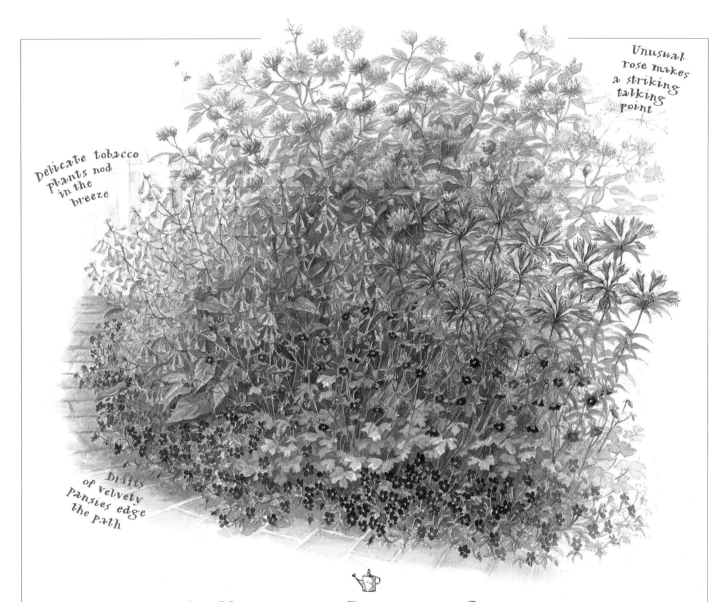

Unusual rose makes a striking talking point

Delicate tobacco plants nod in the breeze

Drifts of velvety Pansies edge the Path

AN UNEXPECTED PALETTE OF COLOURS

Startle the senses with an unashamedly novel slant on old favourites, in which green, red and, surprisingly, black mingle to create an effect that is strong yet harmonious.

A CARPET of self-seeding black pansies (*Viola tricolor* 'Bowles' Black') sets the tone for this adventurous corner. The small black flowers are dotted about the front of the bed, while tall tobacco plants, *Nicotiana langsdorffii*, with clusters of flaring green flower tubes, provide a contrast in colour and height.

The red-brown petal edges of the unusual green-flowered rose, *Rosa × odorata* 'Viridiflora', echo the combination of red and green in the flowers of *Alstroemeria psittacina* – which are also streaked with black. Under these two impressive examples of nature's way

with colour, the striking dark brown and green columbine *Aquilegia viridiflora* makes its early summer display.

EXTENDING THE THEME

Many other plants would fit into the scheme. The pansy 'Mollie Sanderson' has larger flowers and the dark tulip 'Queen of the Night' would add spring excitement to the border. Follow the aquilegia with bells of Ireland (*Moluccella laevis*), which looks like a short green delphinium, and consider the willow *Salix gracilistyla* 'Melanostachys', with black catkins, for a background shrub.

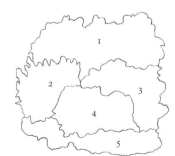

1. *Rosa × odorata* 'Viridiflora'
2. Tobacco plant (*Nicotiana langsdorffii*)
3. *Alstroemeria psittacina*
4. Columbine (*Aquilegia viridiflora*)
5. Pansy (*Viola tricolor* 'Bowles' Black')

COOLER TONES Glancing sun accentuates spires of white foxgloves, which enliven the intense blue of *Meconopsis betonicifolia.*

can be missing in the full glare of the sun. Flowers are important, but don't underestimate the contribution to be made by foliage plants. You can do nearly as much if you use some variegated plants contrasted with green or blue-green.

For spring, the coolest tulip variety is 'Spring Green', whose white petals have broad streaks of green on the back. Late white narcissus, especially the sweetly fragrant *Narcissus poeticus recurvus*, blend happily, but in gentle shade, the spreading perennial *Anemone sylvestris* with cup-shaped creamy white flowers makes a longer display and has attractive foliage. Add white sweet violets and primroses for extra charm, and plenty of small bulbs such as grape hyacinths (*Muscari armeniacum*) in both white and blue varieties, perhaps preceded in late winter by a flush of snowdrops.

Link spring to summer with a white-flowered honesty with cream-splashed leaves (*Lunaria annua* 'Alba Variegata') or with *Pulmonaria saccharata* 'Cambridge Blue', a beauty whose leaves are generously spotted with silver. Later, use the subtle tones of hostas to continue the cool theme throughout summer. Their flowers, usually lavender-mauve or near white, look wishy-washy in full sun, but in dappled shade lend much to the cooling theme. The bold, blue-grey foliage of *Hosta sieboldiana* is especially useful and

FRESH SPRING BLEND The distinctively green-streaked white *Tulipa viridiflora* 'Spring Green' rises above the daisylike flowers of *Anthemis cupaniana* and the fragrant cup-shaped flowers of *Anemone sylvestris.* This pale grouping is offset by the bright green of spring's emerging foliage.

contrasts well with variegated species such as 'Thomas Hogg' and 'Albopicta'.

Summer formal schemes are often composed of warm colours, but when the choice is restricted to a cooler range, the result is refreshing, even on a sunny site. Silver foliage works especially well; indeed many species that have evolved silvery filigree or felted foliage have done so as a defence against excessive sun.

COOL BUT NOT COLD

To avoid too white an effect, include at least one other cooling colour in the border. Supply more pale or mid blues with *Brunnera macrophylla*, forget-me-nots or bluebells in spring and, for late summer, the easiest of the gentians, *Gentiana septemfida.*

Lemon tones blend in well. Opt for *Achillea taygetea* or the variety 'Flowers of

Sulphur'. Seeds of the primrose yellow *Potentilla recta pallida* will produce progeny that bear pale yellow blooms. White *Cyclamen hederifolium* continues the scheme into autumn, and for late winter plant the pale forms of *Helleborus orientalis,* many of which are greeny white with just a hint of pink.

SKILFUL WAYS TO USE WHITE

The white garden works especially well on a small scale, occupying a single border or even just a small corner. By day the whites can be almost dazzling, and the viewer depends on contrasting foliage plants for relief, but in low light, the white border takes on a magical quality when the white flowers appear to float on invisible stems.

❀ Take care when combining white flowers. Shades range from the cream of

MAKING HOT COLOURS HOTTER A touch of cool contrast increases the intensity of a bright colour, as seen with these orange Californian poppies backed by blue *Geranium × magnificum*. Such striking colours are especially effective in full sunlight, which makes subtler hues insipid.

SUBTLE IMPACT A foaming urn of silvery artemisia makes a cool combination with the woolly leaved lamb's tongue at the base.

emerging white tulips to the pink flush found in most white roses and one shade can make another look soiled.

🌢 Roses that are particularly good for white borders include the hybrid musk 'Prosperity' and the floribunda 'Iceberg', both of which fade away gracefully. Deadhead frequently to prevent the petals of fading flowers showing up too markedly against the white background.

🌢 Keep the different plants apart with plenty of silver or grey foliage to lighten the display and ensure that one white flower does not make another look dirty.

🌢 Every ensemble needs to have its star performer, so be sure to have one white plant that is bigger, better and more dramatically showy than the rest – for example, the great heads of hydrangea or the sculpted stateliness of zantedeschia.

BRIGHT HERBACEOUS BEDS

Single colours are almost always more dramatic than a mix. Hot colours work exceptionally well against a drab, grey building or in a front garden that might otherwise be featureless. Abandon all thoughts of compromise and choose the boldest, brightest colours.

Vivid gold and orange French and African marigolds (*Tagetes patula* and *T. erecta*) are among the easiest half-hardy annuals to grow. They flower over a long period and are as good in single colours as in the more usual mixtures. Nonstop begonias in brilliant red, orange or yellow also thrive out of doors when they are treated as half-hardy annuals.

For a discordant but effective note, put pink with orange – *Alstroemeria* Ligtu Hybrids with poppies, perhaps – and pay special attention to foliage, crucial even in the brightest displays. Red blooms and purple-bronze foliage make the dahlia 'Bishop of Llandaff' an excellent centre plant for a fiery border.

BUILDING A HOT SCHEME WITH SHRUBS

Golden-leaved shrubs make an essential contribution to a glowing hot scheme, and the best are those that do not scorch in direct sunlight. *Physocarpus opulifolius* 'Dart's Gold' drops its golden leaves in autumn but has pleasing winter twigs with flaky tan bark, while the smaller, evergreen *Choisya ternata* 'Sundance' keeps its yellow leaves all year.

Choose shrubs that maintain the hot scheme in autumn when the herbaceous plants have disappeared. Berry bearers such as pyracantha or cotoneaster, dwarf maples with their rich autumn colour, or the dark, purple foliage of *Cotinus coggygria* which lightens to red in autumn are all eminently suitable.

Under the shrubs grow some euphorbias. Scarlet bracts make the statuesque

STAND-UP WEED BAG

A FREESTANDING OPEN BAG is ideal for tossing weeds and debris into as you work in the garden. Light, moisture proof and flexible, the bags have strong handles for transporting the contents to the dump or compost heap.

The bags are made in a number of shapes and sizes, with wide-top versions especially useful for those with poor aim. The shorter, wider bag is most suitable for a variety of waste from weeds to longer woody prunings.

Euphorbia griffithii 'Fireglow' and its stockier relative 'Dixter' attractive and the low-growing *Euphorbia polychroma* is smothered in spring with a profusion of tiny flowers in golden bracts.

MAINTAINING HOT COLOUR THROUGH THE YEAR

Euphorbias are interesting for most of the time, but peak in spring and early summer. Combine them with deep red blooms – the tulip 'Couleur Cardinal', perhaps, or scarlet anemones – to make an arresting highlight.

Wild North American columbines (*Aquilegia canadensis*) would do just as well in a hot planting, flaunting their bi-coloured red and yellow, long-spurred flowers in early summer. In midsummer, *Inula magnifica* grows vast foliage, throwing up 8 ft (2.4 m) stems topped with big yellow daisy flowers. In more restricted plantings, tiger lilies (*Lilium lancifolium*) are lovely in summer, coming in yellow, red or orange forms, and the Ligtu Hybrids of the Peruvian lily *Alstroemeria* offer a range of glowing salmon pink, scarlet and yellow flower shades from June to September.

Kniphofias and crocosmias are wonderful for a splash of orange in mid and late summer, perhaps with coreopsis to

precede them. Achilleas and golden rod enrich the yellow range, and are followed by chrysanthemums later in the season.

VIVID ANNUALS FOR A SUNSPOT

Sometimes a garden bed has fertile soil and receives almost constant sunshine. The range of plants that thrive in such conditions is vast but hardy annuals, many bred from cornfield or wasteland weeds, are particularly suitable.

An open, sunny site begs for a joyful mix of strong colours. The most obvious choices might be deep blue cornflowers traditionally teamed with flame-red poppies. Larkspurs in blue and pink add

VIVID CONTRASTS In strong sun, strident colours often work where pastel blends might be lost. The late summer combination of yellow rudbeckias and dusky pink chrysanthemums is striking in its own right, but also merges well with yellowing autumn foliage as the seasons change.

MELLOWER MIXES Colour schemes which are warm without being too insistent provide an early summer feast for the eye. A drift of red and gold aquilegias, rising from their dainty foliage, sprawls across the paving stones while richer notes are added by the purple of a group of irises.

BURNISHED REDS AND GOLDS Nasturtiums grown against a wall provide a vivid backdrop to a late summer bed of richly coloured flowers interspersed with cooler foliage. Reddish-orange heleniums contrast with spiky phormium leaves, and crocosmias and roses add bright shades of red. The orange blooms of the dahlia 'Ellen Houston' stand out against its purple-bronze foliage.

further vibrant shades, or choose the rich orange and yellow of marigolds for exuberant splashes of colour.

Colour clashes also work well in bright sunlight. The strong orange of Californian poppies, for instance, combines beautifully with the purple-blue of *Convolvulus tricolor* 'Blue Flash' and the deep yellow *Ursinia anethoides* blazes magnificently against blood-red dahlias.

To set off such colourfully contrasting flowers add the fast-growing castor oil plant (*Ricinus communis*) for the huge, palmate leaves, which are borne almost head high. The green form is strong and fresh in colour but there is also the option of bronze or red-purple foliage; the red-leaved 'Impala' would be striking among a display of vividly coloured annuals.

GENTLE AND ROMANTIC SCHEMES

Soft blends of pink and mauves spiked with a little blue are among the prettiest of colour combinations. Roses cannot be

PASTEL PRETTINESS Soft pink poppies (*Papaver orientale*) with frilled papery petals combine with the starry white flower heads of *Anthemis cretica*. Such ethereal colours come into their own in fading light.

TWILIGHT DRAMA Placing a large-flowered plant at the front of the border provides a powerful focal point to capture the attention. In this case, the pale spires of lupins rising from fresh green leaves contribute architectural interest and appear to draw the last of the light into themselves.

bettered as a centrepiece, and some old varieties are the most fetching. Their flowers are pinker than many modern counterparts and have a sweet fragrance.

Such historic varieties as the two-tone pink striped *Rosa gallica* 'Versicolor' and old forms of *Rosa alba* such as 'Maiden's Blush' and 'Queen of Denmark' have vigour, fine flower shape and rich scent. Since they have only one flush of flowers, mix them with modern shrub roses, which have all the charm of old roses and flower longer, but are less fragrant.

Underplant the roses with lavender, silver hummocks of *Stachys byzantina* and pinks, especially the crimson-eyed blush-pink 'Doris' and the maroon-laced 'Dad's Favourite'. At intermediate height, sweet williams (*Dianthus barbatus*) add an old-fashioned charm in midsummer. For extra foliage grow meadow rue, which has decorative finely lobed leaves.

For spring use bulbs, especially pink tulips such as 'Greenland' or the later 'Clara Butt', to follow spreads of purple crocuses and blue grape hyacinths.

PLANTS TO TOUCH AND TASTE

H ANDLING PLANTS just to see what they feel like is one of the great joys of gardening. Some are irresistibly silky, some velvety; there are trees with polished bark, flowers whose petals form firm bowls and leaves whose quilting of veins has to be traced with a finger.

Apart from stinging nettles and obviously spiny or thorny growth, most plants feel pleasant, but certain species are worth growing especially to touch. Many of them are pleasing to look at, too, and not just in the summer but right through the drabbest months of the year.

SOFT TO THE TOUCH

Eminently touchable plants are best placed near sitting areas or beside paths so that they can be plucked, tweaked or stroked by passers-by. Many grasses are especially useful here, but do be careful as some have sharp edges to their leaves. Among the silky grasses that are grand to look at and safe to run the fingers through are the Japanese *Hakonechloa macra* 'Aureola', with striped green and gold leaves, and *Helictotrichon sempervirens*, which is much taller. This excellent grass forms distinctive sage-green clumps and sports summer flower stems that move gracefully in the breeze.

The aptly named feather grass (*Stipa pennata*) bears its long silvery plumes

---

AWAITING RELEASE A generous bush of thyme encroaches on a garden seat, its profusion of delicate pink flowers above tiny leaves, inviting a sitter to grasp and gently squeeze a handful to release the herb's aroma. Behind, a purple French lavender makes a similar offer of delight.

BRILLIANT CONTRAST The white bark of *Betula utilis* var. *jacquemontii* stands out dramatically against the autumn foliage of an *Acer palmatum*. The leaves of this striking tree may turn clear yellow before they fall.

SKELETAL CONTORTIONS Once its summer foliage has gone, the corkscrew hazel, *Corylus avellana* 'Contorta', reveals its intricately twirling twigs, which are festooned in February with dancing yellow catkins.

SUMPTUOUS WINTER BARK The copper-tan bark of the Chinese cherry *Prunus serrula* shines as though treated to a daily polish, and provides a sturdy column of gleaming colour to warm the view in the colder months.

BEST PLANTS

A PLEASURE TO TOUCH

Grow one or several of the plants below so that you can enjoy the sensual, textural qualities they provide.

• Lamb's tongue (*Stachys byzantina*): low, mat-forming perennial with leaves like silver felt and woolly stems.

• *Prunus serrula*: a Chinese cherry whose glowing, satin bark peels off each year to reveal a new, shinier skin.

• *Abies pinsapo*: a conifer with stiff, blunt-ended needles which are like the teeth of a comb to run a thumb along.

• *Rosa* 'Zephirine Drouhin': a thornless rose, which makes it the most perfect climbing rose for pruning and training.

• *Carex flagellifera*: a grassy sedge with thin, brown or tan leaves and stems that feel almost like hair.

• Snapdragon (*Antirrhinum*): when the blooms are pinched gently at the sides, the petals open like jaws.

• *Verbascum bombyciferum*: the most densely coated of all mulleins, with rosettes of grey leaves and tall, woolly flower spikes the following season.

• Pussy willow (*Salix caprea* 'Kilmarnock'): a weeping willow with silky grey, and later yellow, catkins borne in early to mid spring.

• *Salix hastata* 'Wehrhahnii': a small willow with silver-grey catkins.

---

through midsummer, while *Pennisetum villosum* has creamy-white hairs fluffing out from the cylindrical flower head. Squirrel grass (*Hordeum jubatum*) waves long golden-tinged silky threads, but the white flower heads of hare's tail (*Lagurus ovatus*) have a furry softness.

It is the silky seed heads of the pasque flower (*Pulsatilla vulgaris*) that extend its beauty through May after the flowers have faded. The ferny leaves that accompany the seed heads are lovely to brush with the hand, too. The yellow-flowered *Clematis tangutica* offers its silky seed heads to be stroked in September.

It is a close-run thing between fennel and some artemisias as to which has the softer foliage. Fortunately you do not have to choose; the two make a beautiful combination when the bronze-purple fennel (*Foeniculum vulgare* 'Purpureum') soars above a foaming silver mass of *Artemisia schmidtiana* 'Nana'.

Altogether homelier is the sensation from touching lamb's tongue (*Stachys byzantina*), whose thick grey leaves have a comfortable fleecy feel, or the grey, woolly, erect catkins of the little ground-hugging *Salix apoda*, which resemble the Easter pussy willow.

The plush-covered young shoots of the stag's horn sumach (*Rhus hirta*, syn. *R. typhina*) are soon hidden by graceful ferny leaves that turn fiery when autumn comes. This small tree is keen to colonise the garden with suckers, however, so the velvet tassels of love-lies-bleeding (*Amaranthus caudatus*), which dangle in long crimson bunches from midsummer into autumn, may be preferable.

The chief joy in touching snapdragons (*Antirrhinum*) is to squeeze the sides of the flowers gently and see the 'face' open its mouth wide. With the Chinese lantern (*Physalis alkekengii*) it is the papery orange globe hiding the berry-like fruit that is so tempting, and with love-in-a-mist (*Nigella damascena*) it is the brown balloon of the seedpod.

More sedate pleasures are offered by magnolias and tulips, whose exquisitely smooth petals, gleaming slightly, form cool, firm goblets.

WINTER WOOD TO CARESS

Some trees and shrubs are so ravishing in winter that they are worth growing just for their twigs or bark.

The Chinese willow, *Salix fargesii*, has twigs like polished mahogany, with deep chestnut-red buds; *Acer griseum* has thin bark that peels off like rice paper; and several species of arbutus, especially *Arbutus menziesii*, have light-tan bark that gleams in the sun. The two trees with the loveliest winter bark are the Chinese cherry, *Prunus serrula,* with a gleaming copper-tan trunk, and the whitest of all birches, *Betula utilis* var. *jacquemontii.*

Trees like these are prettiest if the lower part of the branches are kept clean of shoots. This gives the maximum area of gleaming bark for your enjoyment.

GARDEN TASTES

As you stroll round the garden picking a growing tip here and there, it is tempting to test it with the tip of your tongue as well. Many plants are good to taste – not grown specifically as crops for the table but added to the ornamental garden for their decorative qualities. The cherry tomato is a sweet little mouthful to eat straight from a plant grown against a sunny wall. Tender green peas, mange-tout, broad beans, and french beans all make a crunchy titbit and grow contentedly in an informal bed. Even in the smallest garden you can find room for a dwarf pepper, and in a large one you might let a thornless blackberry sprawl along a boundary fence; you will have to be quick to beat the birds to the fruits.

Alpine strawberries are dainty plants to use as an edging to a bed, but to save stooping to pinch off the luscious fruits, grow them higher up, perhaps in a sink garden, at the front of a raised bed or even in a pair of hanging baskets. The fruits are incomparable for flavour, and both leaves and flowers are pretty.

PETALS AND LEAVES TO NIBBLE

More unexpected pleasures come from familiar flowers that are regarded as purely decorative. Pink rose petals and sweet violets are frequently crystallised to use as garnishes and have a sweet taste even before the sugary coating. Pale yellow primroses are edible, too; they are a traditional garnish on a pumpkin pie. Pansies and nasturtiums add a colourful flourish to a salad and the orange rays of pot marigolds, slightly bitter in taste, brighten a bowl of pale creamy soup.

Herbs are the most promising plants for plucking, sniffing and nibbling. Grow herbs beside a garden path where you brush against them as you pass, or plant a selection beside your favourite garden seat where you can pick off leaves with

---

GROW STRAWBERRIES IN A POT

CULTIVATING STRAWBERRIES in a strawberry pot or planter rather than in a bed keeps the fruit off muddy ground and away from slugs. A suitable variety for growing in a pot is Cambridge Favourite.

Make holes in a wooden barrel to grow the plants, or use a terracotta or plastic pot made for the purpose. If you want to, create a simple watering system for it. Place a length of perforated plastic hose or tubing down the centre of the container as you plant it up, leaving the top end clear. If you are going away for a few days, simply fill it with water.

1. Put a thick layer of crocks or broken polystyrene packing in the bottom of the pot, then fill it with John Innes potting compost No 2 up to the first holes.

2. Push the roots of a plant through each of the lowest holes, cover them with compost and firm it over the roots. Repeat for the holes further up the pot.

3. Once all the holes round the pot are planted, set several strawberry plants on the top, placing them about 6 in (15 cm) apart and firming into the compost.

4. Stand the pot on bricks or pot feet, for good drainage and in a light position. Water immediately after planting, and then water regularly during summer.

---

ease and rub them between your fingers.

Each of the many varieties of mint has its own flavour. Some are rather rank, others sweet; apple-mint and orange-mint are delicious when snipped into a salad or floated on a refreshing drink.

Basil is startlingly powerful tasted on its own, and lovage leaves have a sharp, celery flavour. Thymes are, without exception, decorative, so be sure to plant a selection, including golden or variegated forms. Lemon thyme, *Thymus × citriodorus,* is both aromatic and delicious.

Camomile and feverfew are good to nibble, though the latter leaves behind a bitter aftertaste. Young coriander foliage has an intriguingly peppery fragrance and, unlike so many herbs, tastes exactly as it smells. Be cautious, however, when nibbling, as some plants which smell tempting are quite unsuitable for culinary use. The curry plant, for example, smells of curry only by coincidence, and should not be used to flavour food at all.

Other plants are positively harmful. The dangers of rhubarb leaves, laburnum seeds and yew berries are well known, but stems and leaves of certain umbellifers – parsnips, carrots and the like – can also cause allergic reactions.

FRAGRANCE AND AROMA

WELL-PLACED FRAGRANCE The heady scent of the tall *Lilium regale* wafts out on the lightest breeze, spreading over the garden and inside the house when the window is open on a summer's day. The lily's impressive clusters of flowers stand out best when surrounded by foliage plants.

EVERYONE ACKNOWLEDGES the importance of fragrance in a garden, but few gardeners fully exploit this rich and rewarding resource. Scents are potent revivers of memories, the same smell evoking a different recollection in each person. Perfumed flowers are an obvious source of fragrance and herbs are familiar favourites but with a little gardening experience you can create a much wider range of sensations to savour.

Evergreen shrubs such as cherry laurel, holly and aucuba carry a mildly acrid aroma that goes with shady plantings. Box has a sharp smell – enjoyed by some, loathed by others – while walnut leaves smell spicy. Emerging poplar foliage has a hint of honey or musk, and on a hot day, eucalyptus produces a marvellous aroma, redolent of the tropics.

Certain plants, such as the oak-leaf pelargonium, have foliage so pungent that it overpowers the delicate scent of the flowers. A woodland planting where wild garlic predominates is unmistakable but not at all unpleasant, even in mid-summer when the garlic leaves are beginning to die down.

There are also quirky plants that are fun to grow for their unique aroma. If you have a large enough conservatory, grow the tender senna plant (*Cassia didymobotrya*), whose dark brown buds at the end of the flower spikes smell just like peanut butter. It is one of many flowers with a smell of food. In warm rain, sweetbriar foliage has the fragrance of ripe apples while the red-flowered *Salvia rutilans* has foliage that, when bruised, smells so strongly of pineapple that it makes your mouth water.

FRAGRANCE THROUGH THE YEAR

Even when you are planting chiefly for fragrance, do not forget that the overall aim in any garden is to delight all the senses. Sight and sound are as important here as anywhere, so careful planning is needed to create a garden that weaves these elements together – and not just for high summer but for the whole year.

Among the hundreds of beautiful and scented plants available there is something for every month, every week of the year, from winter-flowering shrubs such as witch hazel, to summer's sweet peas and Madonna lilies. It is always possible to have a flowering plant to provide fragrance either where it grows, or once it is picked and brought indoors.

WINTER AND SPRING SCENT

Most gardens have room for only one or two large shrubs or small trees. Choose one that bears scented blooms at a time when herbaceous plants are resting, such as *Viburnum × bodnantense* with pink winter flowers, or the equally fragrant white *V. farreri*. The intensely perfumed *Chimonanthus praecox* and the untidy winter honeysuckle (*Lonicera fragrantissima*) are good alternatives.

For spring, plant the evergreen *Osmanthus delavayi*, whose small white blooms are richly perfumed. The evergreen *Daphne laureola*, one of our most enchanting native shrubs, will surprise you in March, when its small green flowers exude a pervasive scent during mild afternoons. Strew the ground beneath the shrubs with a selection of violets, such as the vigorous *Viola odorata* 'Admiral Avellan' and the pink-flowered 'Coeur d'Alsace'.

SUMMER PERFUME

If you have the space, a philadelphus provides waves of orange scent in early summer, while a repeat-flowering rose such as 'Roseraie de l'Haÿ' or 'Fragrant Cloud' would be perfect for later.

Foliage makes a valuable foil for flowering fragrant plants, and if it is aromatic as well as decorative, so much the better. Rosemary and thyme meet both these requirements and mints, despite being rather invasive, excel in their aroma – especially the dark eau-de-cologne mint (*Mentha × piperita citrata*).

Lavenders keep their aromatic silver-grey leaves all through the year and make lovely companions for garden pinks. Mix old and modern pinks for flowers and scent. Old-fashioned varieties, such as *Dianthus* 'Dad's Favourite' or 'Sops in Wine', have a tang of cloves but tend to have only one flush of flowers, whereas modern border pinks – such as 'Doris' – are sweeter but less clove-like, and stay in flower for much longer.

Some peonies have a distinctive sweet smell, especially strong in the variety 'Sarah Bernhardt', while lupins have a spicy undertone. For late in the season plant the herbaceous *Clematis heracleifolia* whose small, pale blue flowers have a fresh narcissus-like scent. Scented-leaf

A BLEND OF APRICOT AND CHOCOLATE

When there is a moment to pause and reflect, a quiet spot planted to please all the senses is sure to lift the spirits.

IN THIS SUNNY CORNER, mouth-watering smells of chocolate mingle with a sweet, full fragrance reminiscent of tea, while shades of apricot yellow and velvet brown delight the eye.

The large, loosely formed flowers of the tea rose *Rosa* 'Lady Hillingdon' appear with gratifying regularity through the summer. When combined with the glossy buds and dark, velvety flowers of the sprawling chocolate cosmos (*Cosmos atrosanguineus*), which stretch up from the ground on a profusion of tall, spindly stalks, it completes a natural frame for a simple seat.

'Lady Hillingdon' is the most reliable of the climbing tea roses, and is hardy enough to grow anywhere, but does best on a sunny wall. Chocolate cosmos also flourishes in full sun, flowering through the summer season, but succumbing to the first moderate frost.

Light tea fragrance surrounds the rose

Velvety flowers release a chocolate aroma

WINTER SCENTS

Growing just two or three of these attractive, scented plants livens up the garden during the dull and dormant autumn and winter months.

• Sweet violet (*Viola odorata*): garden varieties such as 'Coeur d'Alsace' and 'Quatre Saisons' produce flowers in autumn, winter and spring.

• *Viburnum farreri*: a Chinese shrub with delicate, fragrant white blooms flushed with pink on leafless twigs.

• Witch hazel (*Hamamelis mollis*): a shrub with January flowers resembling yellow spiders; their warm fragrance has a slightly metallic undertone.

• *Mahonia japonica*: prickly evergreen shrub with sweetly fragrant yellow flowers in January. Its perfume is reminiscent of lily-of-the-valley.

• Winter sweet (*Chimonanthus praecox*): parchment-coloured flowers on bare twigs have the strongest fragrance of any winter shrub.

• *Sarcococca humilis*: low, evergreen shrub with tiny, cream, late winter flowers that smell distinctly of honey.

• *Daphne mezereum*: small shrub which produces purple flowers in late winter. Their fragrance is sweet and strong and hangs in mild, still air.

• Hyacinth (*Hyacinthus orientalis*): the scent of the numerous hybrids can be almost overpowering inside the house, but outdoors this bulb is a great contributor of fragrance.

A PLACE OF REPOSE A heavily scented honeysuckle *Lonicera × americana* temptingly overhangs a quiet seat tucked away in the garden against a sheltering wall. Cushions of lavender add further fragrance.

pelargoniums and verbenas can be put out for summer, but need overwintering indoors; there you can pinch the leaves to release their perfume whenever you wish.

Among annuals, little can match for strength and sweetness the fragrance of stocks and white nicotianas, which both release their scent in the evening. Even sharply odorous plants such as pot marigolds or tagetes enrich the general fragrance with their pungent aromas.

Bulbs for a scented border must include jonquils or pheasant's eye narcissus for late spring and species lilies for summer. *Lilium regale*, *L. candidum* and *L. speciosum* have outstanding beauty and a perfume that far surpasses that of hybrid lilies. In contrast to such sweetness a few species of allium add an arresting scent. In autumn, a bulb usually sold as *Acidanthera murielae* (but more correctly known as *Gladiolus callianthus* 'Murieliae') has a soft, clean fragrance.

CREATING A FRAGRANT BOWER

A bower is a bewitching, romantic spot – a seat for two under a canopy of fragrant climbers. The climbing rose 'New Dawn' is perfect for mid-year freshness of perfume, and white jasmine for late summer fragrance. In warm, sheltered gardens, where frost is a rarity, try the jasmine-like *Trachelospermum jasminoides*, which has evergreen foliage and delicious scent from its cream summer flowers.

In most of Britain, however, honeysuckles are more dependable flowers to grow over bowers, and of these *Lonicera japonica* 'Halliana' is the longest blooming. From mid June to late November, the sharply scented blossom just keeps coming. Other fine honeysuckles include

the earliest – *Lonicera periclymenum* 'Belgica' or 'Early Dutch', whose red, tubular flowers open to reveal a yellow centre – and *L. p.* 'Graham Thomas', whose lemon blooms fade elegantly to a deep shade of parchment.

A stronger-coloured rose than the shell-pink 'New Dawn' is needed to complement the honeysuckles. Grow the thornless climbing Bourbon 'Zéphirine Drouhin', which is vigorous with a succession of fragrant, deep-pink flowers.

At your feet grow camomile, lemon thyme or even coriander. The sharply citrus tang of its foliage gives a focus to all that sweetness, and the dusky pinkish white, lacy flowers are extremely pretty.

Place your bower in a bright spot, for the sun will then bring on the flowers of the climbers while the overhung seat is screened and cool. Stand a container or two of heliotrope or lemon verbena at the entrance to the bower in early summer, and replace it with a pot of lilies later.

AROMATIC RECIPES FOR SUNNY CORNERS

The favourite part of your garden is often the sheltered nook that traps most sunshine and where you take a stroll during a moment of leisure. Make it an extra source of pleasure by putting two or three well-chosen scented plants there.

Herbs are ideal for sun traps. Many of them are natives of hot, dry regions and give their best when these conditions are re-created for them. Traditionally herbs were utility plants, grown for their culinary and medicinal value but many have a discreet beauty.

Most herbs are aromatic rather than fragrant: their smell, and indeed flavour, is in the leaves. This is a bonus since the smell is not limited to flowering time but is much longer lived, waiting to be released by anyone brushing against or crushing the leaves.

Wild thyme is lovely for bright carpets of colour – in pink, purple and white – and is gently aromatic, especially in late spring. Its young foliage adds zest to the delicate fragrance of cowslip flowers.

In summer, place pots of Madonna lilies, with their clean perfume, among sage, tarragon, wormwood (*Artemisia absinthium*), lad's love (*A. abrotanum*) and

WINTER COLOUR AND SCENT Witch hazel brightens up the dreary months with a splash of colour early in the year. Its rather tangled looking threadlike yellow flowers spread a sweet scent with a sharp edge.

BEST PLANTS

SUMMER FRAGRANCE

Beautiful plants abound to keep your garden fragrant all spring and summer.

• Pheasant's eye narcissus (*Narcissus poeticus recurvus*): a white-petalled flower with a shallow, frilled red cup and a fresh, clean fragrance.

• Wallflower (*Erysimum cheiri* 'Harpur Crewe'): a double yellow form with twice the usual generous scent.

• Peony (*Paeonia delavayi*): an Asian tree peony whose blood-red single blooms have a powerful fragrance.

• Mock orange (*Philadelphus* 'Beauclerk'): a sharp, green, citrus-scented bloom, strong at early evening.

• *Rosa rugosa* 'Roseraie de l'Haÿ': a species rose whose purplish-pink blooms, produced in flushes all summer, have a strong, sweet scent.

• Sweet rocket (*Hesperis matronalis*): sweet scented with a spicy note, halfway between wallflower and stock.

• Pink (*Dianthus* 'Sops in Wine'): an old-fashioned pink, maroon with white markings, with an aroma of cloves.

• Lavender (*Lavandula angustifolia* 'Hidcote Pink'): one of the most powerfully scented of the lavenders with purplish-pink flowers.

• Summer jasmine (*Jasminum officinale*): a climber with white flowers and a rich, dark fragrance.

• Tobacco plant (*Nicotiana alata*): droops by day but lifts its white trumpets to blast out waves of rich fragrance by night.

• Golden-rayed lily (*Lilium auratum*): heavy fragrance wafts from the yellow-striped white flowers freckled with dark red spots.

---

rosemary – all of which delight with the silver and grey shades of their foliage, as well as with their different smells. Plant a purple sage underneath an old rose such as the Bourbon 'La Reine Victoria' for a softer summer look, adding a purple lavender for its flowers as well as its invigorating scent. Lavender also combines well with clove-scented garden pinks and an aromatic marjoram.

Stocks add a touch of spice, as do some other annuals such as mignonette (*Reseda odorata*) and sweet rocket (*Hesperis matronalis*). The fragrance of sweet

SWEET AND SPICY Sight and smell are engaged by this ravishing bed of clove-scented border pinks backed by *Rosa odorata*. The rose and the many varieties of pinks, which are treasured for their fragrance and lacy beauty, are a traditional combination in cottage-style gardens.

SOUND AND NOISE

HEARING IS THE SENSE least catered for in most gardens. Gardeners look, smell, touch, sample the taste, but seldom listen to a plant. And yet the ambiance of a garden is so important that you should consider sound at least as carefully as the other senses to make enjoyment as complete as possible.

In a water feature, for example, it is the tinkling of a fountain or waterfall that appeals just as much the appearance and, on a dreamy summer afternoon, it can be positively hypnotic.

Unwanted noise is an unfortunate feature of many gardens. There are ways of reducing noise with planting and of enhancing the natural sounds that help to distract from the unwelcome and make the garden a place of private enjoyment.

NATURAL SOUND EFFECTS

Plants make some remarkable sounds of their own accord – cranesbills release their seeds with a slingshot action that makes an audible ping, and broom pods pop in July sunshine like distant pistol shots. Most sounds, however, come from the action of the weather on plants.

Of all the elements wind has the most effect. Quaking aspen, for instance, is pretty for its shimmering foliage, but the patter of its leaves in a breeze sounds so like rain that hearing it makes you glance at the sky, even on a cloudless day. Grasses, especially those whose foliage persists in winter, whisper drily, while conifers sigh and mature willows moan, groan and creak.

The wind makes even sweeter music if you hang wind chimes where a gentle breeze blows, or set up a wind harp whose strings thrum as the air moves across them.

Rain also makes pleasant sounds, varying from soothing to sad. In classical Chinese gardens, it was common to plant broad-leaved species beneath the eaves of a building so that the sound of raindrops on them could be heard inside. To imitate this, plant *Rheum palmatum* or some of the larger hostas, such as 'Sum and Substance' and 'Snowden', near a window or door.

Birdsong, even in town gardens makes early mornings and spring evenings a joy. The main songsters that are found in

rocket carries strongly on still evening air. The flowers are in a range of delicate colours, from white through palest lavender to mauve and in twilight the pale hues show up well. The flowers make a pretty combination with a tall, purple fennel behind and round-leaved apple-mint pushing its way among them.

For an altogether bolder combination mix the vivid greens of basil and crisply curled parsley with the bright golds and scarlets of a non-trailing nasturtium.

PLANTING FOR SCENT AT DOORS AND WINDOWS

Seize every opportunity to place fragrant plants near the house. It is easy to concentrate on appearance when dressing up a doorway, but there is an added delight in garden scent wafting in through a door or window. Wherever there is a window that is opened in mild weather, plant a scented climber outside. All the favourite climbers – roses, honeysuckle, jasmine, clematis – work well for door or window framing.

To those you can add certain wall shrubs. Train winter sweet (*Chimonanthus praecox*) on a south or west-facing wall, where summer sun can ripen the twigs to ensure good flowering the next winter. Wisteria has a certain fragrance,

and the Japanese apricot (*Prunus mume*) on a warm, sheltered wall will sometimes release its gentle almond scent as early as February. To relieve the summer mediocrity of these shrubs, use their branches as supports for sweet peas, especially the strongly fragrant *Lathyrus odoratus* 'Painted Lady'.

Even routine summer bedding provides plenty of opportunity for fragrance at the door or under a window. Heliotrope has a rich, almost cloying scent and brooding purple flowers that look well dotted among a formal planting.

When you make a bed of pelargoniums, add a few scented-leaf kinds. There are many to choose from besides lemon-scented *Pelargonium* 'Graveolens'. Try the black-and-green-leaved *P.* 'Chocolate Mint' and the musky oak-leaved *P. quercifolium*, and do not overlook the most aromatic of them all, *P.* 'Fragrans'.

At the kitchen door grow something useful as well as fragrant. A big pot of eau de cologne mint, pineapple sage, or even something as pungent as chives, presents opportunities for pinching and sniffing. Keep a steady run of coriander seedlings germinating indoors through the winter months so that, as well as having fresh herbs to use, you enjoy their sharp fragrance every time you brush past them.

most gardens are blackbirds and song thrushes, followed closely by chaffinches, cooing collared doves and, in secluded gardens, by shy wrens.

The best songbirds are encouraged by soil and lawns in a healthy condition with a high worm population, plenty of cover and by branches to use as song posts. Blackbirds love rummaging about, under shrubs for example, but it is worth remembering that they can make quite a mess in the process, scattering mulches onto paths and lawns – and they are inveterate fruit robbers.

If the birds do not come, it is always possible to cheat with recordings of birdsong. Keep the volume low and you soon forget the stratagem in the relaxing atmosphere. The sound may help to attract the real thing.

The same trick can be used to create a playing fountain, a trickling stream or even the surge and retreat of the sea on a pebble beach. Just take care not to set up a cacophony: what to you is the pleasant trickle from a waterspout can be a persistent irritation to others.

BARRIERS TO DEADEN NOISE

Noise is different from sound. Noise is nuisance, something to be kept out of the garden, or to be masked if it cannot be shut out entirely. Unfortunately, it is

SHIMMERING SEED HEADS A dense growth of quaking grass (*Briza maxima*), with slender stems and dangling flower heads, will softly rustle as it responds to the elements – whether harsh winds or soft breezes.

BACKGROUND SOUNDS

Pleasant sounds can set the mood for lazy days in the garden. Warm air currents or summer rains can stir hanging chimes to life, the hypnotic hum of a wind harp is awakened by fresh breezes, and a simple birdhouse can attract cooing doves.

BELL CHIMES
Bell chimes are light, delicate and often Oriental in style. As the wind blows, so the clear, melodic tones of the bells chime, their unique sound evocative of Eastern temples.

DOVECOTE
The gentle cooing of doves is a sound reminiscent of warm summer afternoons. A dovecote contributes the low sounds of its inhabitants and makes a pretty focal point in the garden.

DEER SCARER
Originally Japanese, deer scarers feed water into pivoted hollow canes. Once full, the canes tilt over, empty and return to the original position, making a metallic chink as two studs strike each other.

WIND HARP
This ancient instrument is also known as an Aeolian harp, after Aeolus, Greek god of the winds. As the wind blows, the strings stretched across the simple, open box vibrate with a mellow hum.

WIND CHIMES
Wind chimes create a soothing atmosphere, the sound of the tinkling chimes varying according to the material used, whether glass, wood, terracotta or metal. They can be hung from trees, under a balcony or from a post in the garden.

seldom feasible to cut noise out altogether, so clever ways of insulating and masking it are essential. You can insulate your garden from outside noise without compromising the overall design.

The most obvious way is to develop barriers that soften or deflect sound. Walls, screens, hedges, even loose groups of shrubs and trees all help. You can make each of these barriers into a design feature, even a key focal point.

Try lining a wall or fence with a row of pillars linked by trellis panelling and smother it with climbing roses or wall plants. Together, the wall, trellis and planting create a triple layer of insulation that helps to muffle noises that come from outside the garden.

A straightforward evergreen hedge reduces noise well enough but can look rather ordinary. However, there are many alternatives to a standard hedge. A tapestry hedge is particularly attractive, made up of such different foliage plants as beech, holly and golden cypress. By incorporating flowering currant (*Ribes*), sweetbriar, escallonia and other flowering plants, you can make a mixed hedge to provide a pleasing view all year round as well as fulfilling the original intention of screening out unwelcome noise.

A tough species such as *Clematis montana* is too vigorous to thread in a mixed hedge, but you do need some extra-strong characters. *Chaenomeles speciosa* is a sturdy grower and is also a useful protection for a more delicate treasure such as the beautiful *Clematis florida* 'Sieboldii', with its resemblance to the passionflower. These plants look lovely grown against a screening wall, fence or thick, dark hedge.

Some roses love growing beneath trees, as long as they are not too densely shaded, but in poorer light evergreen viburnums, mahonias or low-growing cherry laurels are more suitable. At their feet, plant persistent perennials such as cranesbills, hellebores or the creeping *Euphorbia amygdaloides* var. *robbiae*. The denser the growth, the more effectively it will mop up intrusive noise.

RUSTLING GRASSES The tall, feathery stems of *Miscanthus sinensis* produce a soft whispering in the breeze while its graceful arched leaves produce a drier, rustling note. The fluffy, pale seed heads of *Pennisetum villosum* in the foreground add variety of height, texture and sound.

HARMONIES IN THE GARDEN

Planting to add a background of agreeable sounds gives the garden a dimension which is all too easily neglected, but completes the charmed world you are creating.

COMBINE THE VISUAL DELIGHT of a leafy corner with the sighs of foliage, the gentle rattle of stems, and the soothing trickle of water. Gentle sounds not only delight the ear but also help to distract attention from any intrusive noises beyond the boundary of the garden.

Tall bamboos stand guard at the back of this June border, screening the garden from the outside world. Their apple-green leaves sway on hollow stems that rub together, making quiet background chatter. A wren, light enough to perch on a leaf, adds its tune. Despite their slender appearance these evergreen bamboos are frost hardy.

The pots of grass and sedge and the dwarf bamboo behind contribute colour as well as rustling sound. The reddish-brown leaves of *Hakonechloa macra* 'Aureola' begin their life as yellow with green stripes – a bright complement to the small, white-striped bamboo.

The tree peony takes up the Eastern theme started by the bamboos. The huge, crimson-blotched lemon-yellow flowers are at their peak in June.

THE MUSIC OF WATER

The fountain, rising above glistening pebbles, also evokes the Orient, since water and shingle are an integral feature of many Japanese gardens. The water spouts just high enough to tinkle as it falls, and makes a 'sculpture' to punctuate the soft planting. A song thrush on the lookout for worms or snails is attracted by the light rain. The stone provides a hard surface on which the crack of snail shells rings sharply.

As raindrops fall, they plop satisfyingly onto the firm, fleshy foliage of the rheum and collect in the deeply veined leaves. Rain or shine, the orchestra in this lush, green corner lends a melodious note to the garden.

Tall bamboos click
busily in the breeze

Grass and small
bamboos whisper as they stir

A fountain
patters like
gentle rain

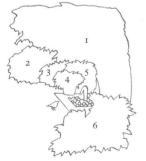

1. Muriel bamboo (*Fargesia murieliae*)
2. Tree peony (*Paeonia* 'Argosy')
3. Dwarf white-stripe bamboo (*Pleioblastus variegatus*)
4. *Hakonechloa macra* 'Aureola'
5. Sedge (*Carex flagellifera*)
6. *Rheum palmatum* 'Atrosanguineum'

CAPTURING A MOOD

MOST GARDENERS have a favourite time of year. For some, the fresh, sharp greens of spring have unmatchable beauty; others can never have enough of autumn's glowing colours. Cottage profusion is the essence of a garden to some people while, for others, orderly formality is crucial for giving the sense of peace they seek in the garden.

If your choice is a garden of several moods, with a single section or a corner devoted to each one, you can use a low barrier – a hedge, wall or fence – to divide a formal corner from a wild one or fresh greens from mellow golds. The barrier will make more changes from sun to shade, which will also help to establish different moods.

MEDITERRANEAN GARDEN

Where you have a dry bank, seize the opportunity to create a fragment of the Mediterranean. With gravel or pebbles of different sizes and discreetly placed stone or concrete pavers, you can intensify the arid nature of the site. Stones push summer ground temperatures up, intensifying the release of aromatic oils from the foliage of typical Mediterranean shrubs, among them many silver-leaved beauties such as *Convolvulus cneorum*, lavender, cotton lavender (*Santolina*) and artemisia.

For more spectacular herbaceous plants, choose from mulleins, blood-red poppies or some of the more dramatic irises. You could even step up the dry desert character with temporary planting during the summer. Bold, spiky-leaved plants such as agaves, aloes or the more fleshy aeoniums and echeverias, all grown in containers, can be plunged into the ground and the pots concealed with a top layer of gravel. Such plants will last for years if they are lifted, complete with pots, before the frosts to overwinter in a conservatory or greenhouse.

SPRING LEMONS AND GREENS

The fresh yellows and greens of spring that are so cheering after a drab winter can be continued, to prolong the mood of bright optimism. Allow foliage to predominate, and choose flowers to echo the colour theme. The spring plants are easy – variegated periwinkle and euonymus

ETERNAL SPRING The freshness of light green, golds and pale yellows makes spring a season to gladden the heart and lift the spirits. Here, a sunny combination of wallflowers and euonymus starts the year on a cheerful note.

MOOD IN MINIATURE If the autumnal colour range of russet shades gives you the greatest pleasure, create the same red-gold scheme throughout the year with a wooden tubful of pansies in gold, orange and brown.

OVERLAID WITH GOLD Yellow *Iris pseudacorus* 'Variegata' rises above the light green *Tanacetum parthenium* 'Aureum' in the foreground and golden *Filipendula ulmaria* 'Aurea' in the corner. The shrub *Philadelphus coronarius* 'Aureus' adds to the air of spring in this July border.

studded with winter aconites, doronicums, celandines, primroses and daffodils to give some height. As spring turns to summer, ferns such as the shuttlecock-shaped *Matteuccia struthiopteris* or, in drier sites, *Polystichum setiferum* or hart's-tongue (*Asplenium scolopendrium*) reveal a springlike green.

Grasses and bamboos prolong the feel of spring wonderfully. *Milium effusum* 'Aureum' has soft, waving foliage and feathery flowers in summer, and the dwarf bamboos *Pleioblastus auricomus* and *P. variegatus* look youthful all year, with their fresh green leaves.

Lady's mantle is an essential part of the scheme. Its lacy green flowers last for weeks. Lemon roses, potentillas, dahlias and chrysanthemums can maintain the mood into autumn.

SUMMER PURPLES ALL YEAR

The natural flower colours of summer in the wild are mainly in the mauve, purple and wine-red range, found in knapweeds, scabious, thistles, willowherb, tufted vetch and cranesbill. In a garden,

CHANGING SEASONS The warm colours so loved in autumn sing out in this late summer border, with red-hot pokers towering over dwarf red dahlias, bronze *Helenium*, orange crocosmia and golden rudbeckias.

summer purples and cerises are readily found in shrubby plants such as roses, buddleias and hebes, perennials such as centaurea and cranesbills, and bedding plants such as petunias and heliotrope.

The warm purples of summer look just as effective at other times of the year. In autumn, asters, colchicums and late Korean chrysanthemums such as the plum-pink 'Mei-kyo' take up the theme.

In spring, choose purple or cerise tulips – try the beetroot-purple 'Negrita' or lily flowered 'Springtime'. The easiest outdoor primula in cultivation is *Primula juliana* 'Wanda', whose bright purple-red blooms pop up in profusion from late February to late May.

The cow parsley *Anthriscus sylvestris* 'Ravenswing' is a contributor to this mood, producing dark ferny leaves in spring and then delicate, white lacy blooms. Rodgersias are perfect if you have plenty of moisture and space, and for drier conditions, *Euphorbia dulcis* 'Chameleon' is pretty, with deep bronze foliage and dainty green flowers.

The warm effect can be heightened by adding splashes of apricot and orange. In spring, the tulip 'Apricot Beauty' looks gorgeous with purple, and the gentle apricot rose 'Buff Beauty' or the foxglove strain 'Sutton's Apricot' makes

LATE SPRING PURPLES Although warm purple is a characteristic colour of a high summer garden it can be created equally effectively, as here, in late spring. Mauve wallflowers (*Erysimum* 'Bowles' Mauve') face a bed of bearded irises edged along the gravel with aubrietia.

EFFUSIVE COTTAGE GARDENS Foxgloves, delphiniums and lupins tower above a happy welter of colour and foliage in this typically generous cottage garden, where the plants spill out to take over the paths.

a ravishing summer companion. Yellow Welsh poppies and early spring pansies in warm orange are stunning with purple aubrietia, purple or mauve tulips and dark purple crocuses.

MELLOW FRUITFULNESS

The glowing tones of autumn foliage blunt the sting of approaching winter. Colour is warmest during these autumnal months, when green gives way to yellow, gold and red. The familiar late border plants, such as chrysanthemums, dahlias and orange and yellow crocosmias are particularly vivid.

Re-creating the red-gold scheme in other seasons is easiest in the summer. Red and yellow gaillardias flower for months on end and look good alongside the fiery scarlet of *Euphorbia griffithii*. In damp ground, orange and yellow Asian primulas – *Primula bulleyana*, *P. sikkimensis* and *P. florindae* – create the desired atmosphere. On drier ground, the red or bronze forms of swordlike New Zealand flax (*Phormium tenax*) have an autumnal air; choose 'Bronze Baby' or 'Aurora' for the warmest colours.

Winter is the most challenging period because there is so little foliage about – although you can compensate with gold-splashed evergreens. One of the brightest of these is the variegated holly 'Golden King' which is also a heavy berry bearer.

Berries and fruits that hang on through the winter warm the scene.

Cotoneaster horizontalis colours beautifully in autumn with little red leaves and copious berries clustered on the herringbone branches. One of the brightest winter shows is put on by the crab apple 'Red Sentinel' whose cherry-like red fruits hang on until the harshest February days and beyond.

In spring, deciduous azaleas come in a range of autumnal colours, many with the bonus of fragrance. Aquilegias now include several brilliant reds, pinks, yellows and combinations; choose *Aquilegia canadensis* and *A. formosa*.

COTTAGE GARDEN PRETTINESS OR FORMAL SYMMETRY

Whatever the mood you aim to create, bear in mind the potential of leaf, stem and fruit as well as flower. In a cottage garden, the end result should be a happy tumble of mixed plants, whereas a formal garden relies on shape, line and form as well as plant interest.

The bulk of cottage perennials flower between late May and mid July. Back up your main display with repeating late perennials such as penstemons, pelargoniums, osteospermums, verbenas and mignonette to have flowers that carry on into October. However, if these plants encroach on the space of late bloomers such as chrysanthemums, the autumn monkshood (*Aconitum carmichaelii*) and crocosmias, cut them back.

Lilies are outstanding among late performers, especially *Lilium auratum*. Plant gladiolus late – up to the end of April – for late flowering. Colchicums are useful too, and their foliage, following in spring, will fill gaps between such early flowers as crown imperials (*Fritillaria imperialis*) and honesty.

In a well-designed formal garden there is often as much scope for skilful planting as in an informal scheme. Every plant, including those for outline, can

GENEROUS SELF-SEEDERS

AMONG THE PLANTS that give the best value in the garden are the natural self-seeders which flourish in increasing numbers year after year. Many of these are found growing in the wild, adding colour to hedgerows and fields, but they look equally at home in a garden.

Foxglove (*Digitalis purpurea*) is a biennial which blooms once. If you leave the seeds to ripen and germinate, they provide a springtime display of large pink bells year after year.

TROUBLE-FREE CHOICES
A woodland flower that grows best in half shade and in clay soil is primrose (*Primula vulgaris*), which flowers from March to May, coming back stronger every year and producing seedlings. Deadhead some of the plants and they often provide a lesser display in autumn and winter.

For brilliant yearly colour Welsh poppies (*Meconopsis cambrica*) are not only persistent perennials, but also copious self-seeders. They germinate best in gentle shade, even in the poorest soil, their clear yellow or orange flowers popping up in cracks and crevices.

Love-in-a-mist (*Nigella damascena*) has deep blue or white flowers which turn into balloon-like seedpods that produce crowds more of the annuals the following year.

A prodigious self-seeder is forget-me-not (*Myosotis*) with blue flowers in April. Seedlings should be thinned out or moved to a nursery bed to grow on for September planting.

AN APPEALING FORMALITY Even in winter months, the orderliness of this parterre imparts a serenity, with obelisks set in clipped, shaped hedges forming a square frame round the variegated holly at the garden's centre.

provide interest. Knot gardens or small parterres with low box or lavender hedges and clipped hollies are set off by blocks of colourful plants. In spring, strengthen lasting performers such as winter pansies and dead nettle (*Lamium maculatum*) with tulips and wallflowers.

In summer, add height to nemesia, pelargoniums or annual osteospermum with late-flowering *Phlox paniculata*. As the summer bedding begins to tire in September, add polyanthus or more pansies to bloom as the senior partners – chrysanthemums and dahlias – reach their late autumn climax.

INSPIRATION FROM
GREAT GARDENS

NYMANS GARDEN

Wide lawns thread through garden 'rooms'.

*At Handcross, West Sussex,
only a short distance from the
hurtling traffic of the London to
Brighton road, there lies a gardening
oasis of great tranquillity. Here, four
generations of the same family have
devoted their time to assembling one
of the finest of all collections
of rare and exotic trees, plants
and shrubs. In the Rose
Garden, 139 old-fashioned roses
have been gathered together round
a small fountain.*

I N THE SEASON OF ROSES there is no finer way to celebrate the beauty of the flower than to stroll among and under the lavish blooms of old-fashioned climbers. Training them over columns and round hoops allows them to show off to greatest advantage their subtleties of colour and romantically sprawling growth habit.

The Rose Garden at Nymans is one of a number of horticultural 'rooms', all different, and each one of which would make a delightful, not over-large garden in its own right.

The Wall Garden, the first to be laid out in 1895 by the founder of Nymans, Ludwig Messel, features magnolias and other flowering trees, thousands of bulbs and a collection of rare South American plants. There is one of the first heather gardens to be established in Britain, filled with many varieties of heathers and rhododendrons. And towering above the garden as a whole is the shell of the main

house. It was gutted by fire in the late 1940s, but is now draped with fragrant honeysuckle, clematis, wisteria and roses.

The Rose Garden started to take shape in the 1920s with an assembly of old-fashioned roses from French and Italian sources. But by 1987 these were becoming gnarled and stringy, and it was decided to grub them out. The great storm in October of that year – which at Nymans alone demolished nearly 500 trees in a single night, as well as countless shrubs and plants – spelt the end of the original rose garden. In the winter of 1988, the construction of a new layout of pillars, pergolas and arches was begun.

This framework was planted up by the following spring, and in a relatively short time the garden reached its present glory. The profusion of rose blooms stands above a thick carpet of blue and white cranesbills, lavender-flowered and grey-leaved catmint (*Nepeta mussinii*) and the

OPULENT BOWER The rich scents and gentle colours of old-fashioned roses enclose the formal fountain with a screen of rare delight.

deep pink spikes of *Polygonum affine*. The finished garden is one of cheerful intimacy, with climbing roses spilling over their supports to form a most attractive surround for a tinkling bronze fountain.

A BOWER OF YOUR OWN

The fact that so much has been achieved in so short a time in the Rose Garden at Nymans is very encouraging when it comes to building a rose-scented bower on a more modest scale. Such a feature, constructed over a path in any size of garden, delights both the eyes and the nose, and is not difficult to make.

The framework is four stout oak posts, well driven in, and linked by an arched metal frame, obtainable from garden centres. At the foot of each post, plant the pink-bloomed, long-flowering, thornless climber 'Zéphirine Drouhin', tying in the shoots as they ascend the frame. To provide a dark red, velvety contrast, grow the vigorous scrambler 'Guinée' against two diagonally opposite posts of the frame.

Fill the side gaps between the posts by planting them with more roses – such as pink 'Cécile Brunner', white 'Francine Austin' and striped *Rosa gallica* 'Versicolor', all of which grow to about waist high. Signal the approaches to the bower with a selection of sweetly scented border pinks; a mixture of 'Gran's Favourite' and 'Mrs Sinkins' would be ideal.

Combined, the roses and pinks will illuminate and perfume the garden, and 'Zéphirine Drouhin' will continue to flower through to autumn. Even when the blossoms and leaves have faded and fallen, the domed bower, emphasised by the interlaced branches, makes a strong architectural feature in the garden during the winter months.

BLOOMS WITH A BOUQUET Thornless, gorgeously scented *Rosa* 'Zéphirine Drouhin' and the dark red 'Guinée', underplanted with pinks, riot over a bower in this echo of the rose garden at Nymans.

SOMEWHERE TO SIT

THERE IS NOTHING MORE RELAXING than sitting outside on a shimmering summer's day in the comfort of your own garden, so create a sunny haven for a picnic or afternoon tea, make a sheltered spot for breakfast where the early sun is warmest, or provide some shade to shield a Sunday gathering of friends and family from the lunchtime sun. A perfect patio for a quiet read, or a hideaway where you can improve your suntan, will make a focus for purely private pleasure. Whether your garden seat is permanent and weatherproof, elegant and fragile, or simple and homemade, find a place for it – and surround it with your favourite plants.

An elegant weathered bench, a trellis to provide shelter, and judicious plantings of scented flowers and shrubs that act as a screen create an invitation to linger at ease.

MAKING A HAVEN FOR LEISURE

◆

O F ALL THE PLEASURES that a garden has to offer, perhaps the greatest is the simplest, that of just sitting for a while and absorbing sights, sounds and scents.

Good garden furniture is an investment in comfort and enjoyment, and can be an added adornment. So take care over your choice of furniture – it should be in sympathy with the surrounding architecture and the overall atmosphere of the garden. The best furniture may be expensive, so allow time to consider the disadvantages, as well as advantages, of whatever takes your fancy.

The placing of this furniture is as vital as its style and construction. Most people are more relaxed sitting in an enclosed area – an arbour or a glade, for example. There are many ways of creating a sense of delicious intimacy, from simply surrounding your seat with scented plants, to placing it in a pool of soft light at dusk while all else is in shade.

While many garden owners see their plot as a retreat from the world, others have their most enjoyable gatherings with friends and family in a garden that serves as an extra room, complete with comfortable seats, a table to gather at for a meal and a barbecue for the cooking.

SITTING IN THE SHADOWS An accommodating chair in a shady spot on a hot day is the perfect place to enjoy the fruits of your gardening endeavours. From a quiet and secluded corner observe the dappled sunlight and the brightly lit stems of vivid yellow-green euphorbia.

CHOOSING AND CARING FOR SEATS

◆

B EFORE YOU BUY SEATS, think about storage space. If you have none, seats and tables will have to stay out all year, so must be sturdy. Where there is a little storage room, folding and stacking furniture is the most practical choice. When you have a garage or large shed where the pieces can overwinter, your choice is wider.

Some furniture comes complete with protective covers which help to keep it clean (particularly useful in town gardens and under trees) and to prolong its life, but the shrouded shapes give a rather gloomy feel to the garden in winter.

Those fortunate enough to have a summerhouse or a conservatory are free to choose all kinds of charming and delicate furniture which is enjoyed inside and brought out when the weather is mild.

SUITING THE SURROUNDINGS

Choose the furniture with as much thought for whether it suits its surroundings as you do when buying furnishings for the house. Plastic stacking chairs may seem brash on a formal terrace, while an ornate stone bench looks pretentious in a simple modern garden.

Any seat, no matter how comfortable, ruins the atmosphere of the garden if it is shoddily made, unbalanced in style or fitted with garish covers and cushions. Plain dark blue is particularly pleasing in the sun, whereas a splash of bright colour brings a shaded corner to life. By the sea or a pool, turquoise looks fresh while striped canvas is agreeable for deck chairs and hammocks; just two colours, and wide stripes, make for a crisp look. Floral patterns compete with nature's floral display but come off badly beside it.

APT FOR OCCASIONAL USE

Comfort is important, of course, but to varying degrees. A seat used as a temporary stopping-place, for a brief rest or to admire the view, need not have the same comfort-rating as one at a table used for meals outdoors, while seats used for sunbathing and drowsing need to be very comfortable indeed.

In a small garden, with room for just one seat, it is useful to have something that is easily moved. Movable furniture is

STATELY STONE Sunlight and shadow make an inviting pattern on the surface of a solid, curved stone seat. Stone is weighty and has to remain in one place, but it is robust enough to be left there permanently.

inconvenient if too heavy but lightweight furniture will have a shorter life if left outside. A handy compromise is a sturdy wooden seat with handles and wheels to make the moving easier.

DESIGNS IN STONE AND METAL

Benches and tables of stone and reconstituted or simulated stone can be left out in all weathers and look the better for it, becoming patterned with a textured layer of moss and lichen. To speed weathering, brush on a coat or two of yoghurt or diluted liquid manure.

Stone seats are handsome, durable and at home in most gardens, but cold, hard and virtually immovable once set in place – better for visual impact and occasional perching, than for comfort.

Metal furniture comes in an enormous range of designs. Pieces in cast iron are heavy, while those made of wirework or cast aluminium are lighter, but more likely to tip. Cast iron representing twining stems and flowers is uncomfortable unless covered with cushions – which ruins the visual effect. Without cushions, all metal seats are a little hard, except those with backs and seats of fabric, woven plastic or flexible metal strips.

Metal furniture can stay outside, but unless made from aluminium needs a yearly overhaul to keep rust at bay. Brush it briskly with a wire brush and repaint, using a rust-inhibiting primer, undercoat and exterior gloss, or a fast-drying alkyd paint to form a corrosion-resistant coat. Spray the metal framework of folding chairs with a rust-inhibitor before you put them away for the winter.

VARIETY IN DURABLE WOOD

There are designs in wood to suit both formal and cottage gardens, sturdy pieces to complement a modern, clean-lined style and informal seats for romantic, rambling gardens. Most are equally at home in town or country.

Picnic tables, which are rectangular with a fixed bench along either side, are stoutly made but are probably best kept

SCENTED SHADE Under a canopy of holly and roses this inviting bench has mellowed to a quiet silver grey. The weathered wood merges naturally with the underplanting of variegated ivy, the hosta and the white *Rosa* 'Nevada'.

SECURE FIXING FOR A SEAT

LIGHTER BENCHES, whether wooden or metal, will tip if children clamber on them, or if adults fling themselves back too heartily. The consequences can be painful, but you can prevent accidents by securing the seat to the ground with a galvanised iron bracket.

One end of the bracket fits over the rail of the bench and the other is hammered into the ground.

ROOM OUTSIDE A secluded sitting area has been created in a sunny spot, using trellis dividers, paving, careful planting and elegant metal benches. Clipped box in containers helps to define the perimeter of the area.

WHEN THE WEATHER SUITS Canvas chairs, being lightweight and folding, have the advantage of being easy to move, whether to position them in the sun, to be closer to a table or to be stored safe from wet weather.

TO THE RESCUE

NEW LIFE FOR A DECK CHAIR

SUN AND RAIN weaken the canvas on a deck chair. When it tears, replace it with new deck-chair canvas or double lengths of strong furnishing fabric sewn together. Fix it with a staple gun.

Canvas is available in ready-cut lengths – use the old piece as a pattern. Allow 3 in (7.5 cm) of extra material at each end to wrap round the rails.

Staple the fabric first to the bottom rail, at 1 in (2.5 cm) intervals, then wrap it once round the rail to cover the staples. Stretch the fabric as tightly as you can and turn under the raw edge before stapling it behind the top rail.

for a modern garden, a barbecue corner or where children are likely to clamber over any furniture.

Solid wooden furniture can be heavy, but is comfortable and strong. It lasts longer if kept under cover in severe weather. Seasoned hardwoods including teak, iroko, oak and elm give years of use, even when kept permanently outside. Most furniture labels tell you if the wood comes from a renewable source.

Oil can be rubbed into hardwood but its purpose is purely cosmetic – to restore a brown colour. It is not necessary for keeping the wood in good condition; untreated hardwood develops distinguished silvery tones as it ages.

Softwoods, except for cedar which weathers naturally, need to be treated with a decorative and preservative stain, exterior varnish or paint. When repainting, use primer, undercoat and exterior gloss, rubbing down between coats, or use a one-coat microporous paint, which allows the wood to 'breathe' through the paint layers, and helps to prevent flaking, peeling and bubbling.

SEA, TOWN OR COUNTRY STYLE

Folding 'steamer' chairs of slatted wood are sturdy and comfortable; some have armrests and legrests, as well as fitted cushions for added luxury. Adjustable loungers are even more comfortable; they are made from slats of hard or soft wood, sometimes with wheels, armrests and fitted cushions, and are at home on a large terrace or beside a swimming pool.

Café tables and folding chairs of wooden slats on metal frames are light, practical and look good in all but the grandest gardens, but they are strictly for sitting in demurely, not for lazy sprawling. The slats need to be varnished, stained or painted regularly, and metal parts need rustproofing and painting.

Rustic furniture particularly suits cottage gardens and those of the Victorian and Edwardian eras that have a matching rustic summerhouse. Rustic seats made from larch poles, with or without the bark left on, are sold at garden centres and by some timber merchants.

SIMPLICITY WITH CANVAS, CANE AND WICKER

Folding chairs of canvas on metal or wooden frames include the familiar deck chairs. Directors' chairs impose a more upright position than deck chairs but some have a tiltable backrest that

TAKING THINGS EASY

A place to sit adds to your enjoyment of a garden. Choose your seat with care to suit its setting and function, whether it is a lounger on the lawn, a seat to put in a secluded corner or a dining chair for a convivial meal out of doors.

VERSATILE WOOD
Wood is warm, solid, attractive and versatile. Hardwood furniture can be left out to weather with the seasons and take on a silver sheen. Café chairs with wooden slats fold up flat and can be stored in a small space for the winter.

LIGHT BUT TOUGH
Plastic chairs are inexpensive, light, strong and easily transportable. Those made of synthetic resin also withstand the elements. Stacking chairs are useful in saving space when not required for entertaining.

STURDY RUSTICS
A boot bench, a farmhouse bench and a countrified seat made from poles and planks all have an appropriate rustic charm for less formal gardens. They look well in cottage-style gardens and those with an air of old-fashioned profusion.

GENTLY SWINGING SEATS
The ulimate luxury in garden leisure is a seat that swings. Two sturdy trees will support a hammock; if you have no trees, use a hammock stand. Swinging chairs have the added indulgence of soft cushions and shade from the sun's bright rays.

TRADITIONAL FAVOURITES
This stylish selection includes a painted wooden barrow bench that can be wheeled to the most advantageous site, a sturdy and inviting wooden seat with wide armrests and a sloping back, and a wicker chair, an old favourite for appearance and comfort.

DURABLE ELEGANCE
Metal furniture, both wrought iron and cast iron, combines strength with an elegant fragility of detail. Long lasting, it can be left permanently in position to draw the eye and enhance a site, giving interest through the year.

RECLINING IN COMFORT
For putting your feet up to enjoy the warmth of a summer's day there is a vast array of choice in style and materials. Pick a classic wooden 'steamer' chair or a plastic frame with padded cushions that adjusts to varying degrees of inactivity.

SIMPLE CANVAS
Directors' chairs are comfortable and smart. Easily folded, they provide useful extra seats for entertaining. The adjustable deck chair is better suited to a more relaxed position. Both are readily transportable and storable.

LAZY DAYS You do not need a huge garden to enjoy the use of a hammock, just two branches strong enough to bear the weight and with enough space between them. Hammock stands can also be used though they are rather unwieldy and no substitute for the shade and sound of trees.

allows for some reclining. Similar to directors' chairs are campaign chairs, with arm and leg rests, a tiltable canopy and sometimes slots in the arm for a glass.

All look unpretentious, suit any style and take up little room when folded. Move them indoors for the winter and in wet weather to stop the canvas rotting. Varnish, stain or paint the wooden parts annually, and oil all hinges and other parts susceptible to rust.

Give individual style to your humble deck chair by abandoning bright stripes and fitting plain canvas lifted out of the ordinary by an appliquéd pattern. Cut out simple motifs such as leaves or scalloped circles from coloured fabric and oversew the edges to prevent fraying. Stitch the decorations to the canvas or fix them on with fabric glue.

Tender handling and winter cover is essential for cane and wicker furniture to make it last. Usually very comfortable although rather creaky, it looks well virtually anywhere you put it, including the conservatory. Both cane and wicker can be attacked by timber-beetles, so watch out for telltale holes and treat immediately with woodworm fluid.

Lloyd Loom chairs, looking like fine wicker but woven from paper-covered wire, are again as popular as they were 60 years ago. They are easily moved, and pretty sponged or stippled in two tones of paint under matt varnish. Add cushions and they are charming indoors or out, but do not leave them out in the rain.

THE VIRTUES OF PLASTIC

Furniture made from plastic or synthetic resin is comfortable, comparatively inexpensive, light and unharmed by being left outside unless it is blown about by strong winds. Some fixed designs are stackable, others are hinged to fold up or recline.

White furniture shows the dirt and stains but is easily cleaned by a wipe down with water and a little liquid detergent. This is the only care these chairs need. Other colours are now obtainable; black is sophisticated, brown is unobtrusive while dark green is restful.

With so many virtues, the furniture is on sale everywhere but it does not enhance an elegant period house or the romantic garden unless draped with a decorative shawl or 'throw' and given a cushion or two. It is perfectly at home in an informal garden and by the sea, while its lightness makes it useful for roof gardens and balconies.

FANCIFUL METAL AND CLAY

Metal is worked into some curious furniture, from 'rustic log' benches of cast iron, to filigree delicacies in galvanised wirework. Some designer-blacksmiths make seats to resemble giant vegetables, or composed entirely of horseshoes.

At a price, a local blacksmith will make up a seat of your own design – for

MAKING · IT · EASIER

STACKING CHAIRS

PLASTIC MOULDED CHAIRS, available from most garden centres, are cheap and comfortable, as well as being light and, most important, easy to stack. This is a great advantage as it means that they take up very little room when stored – four or six stacked chairs take up no more floor space than one.

example, a pair of hands, one for the seat and one for the back, or a spider's web chair complete with spider.

Drum-shaped stools and tables made of porcelain are very decorative on a small terrace or in an enclosed courtyard. Porcelain should be brought inside during the winter or it may crack.

You can design a chinoiserie setting to suit your porcelain seats, especially if they are blue and white. Set up a background of lattice screens, or an open timber pavilion, painted lacquer-red or to match the porcelain. In front, make a pool crossed by a small bridge or a few stepping-stones; add rocks and boulders and plant bamboos round them.

SOOTHING MOVEMENT

Swings have a hypnotic appeal for most people because the rhythmic motion induces a relaxed state. Metal-framed swing-seats with luxuriously thick cushions and a canopy are popular, and some have agreeably restrained colours.

There are stylish swing-seats available made from pine, pressure-treated with preservative to make the wood very durable. Their strong construction and simple design make them especially suitable for a contemporary or informal garden. A coat of wood preservative,

FOR ALL WEATHERS Cool green and cream ivy is a complementary background for this durable cast-iron bench with ornate detailing. An antique storage drum has been planted with the blue bells of campanula for added colour, and fragrance wafts from the mauve heliotrope behind.

applied every other year, is all they need by way of maintenance.

Much simpler and less costly is a plank of wood suspended by two lengths of rope from a sturdy bough. You can make a swing for two from an old wooden bench without its legs. Hang it by two lengths of rope at each end, to get the balance right, making sure that the bough is sufficiently strong to take the weight of two people. Alternatively, you could sling the bench from a crossbeam of a sturdy pergola.

A hammock is the ultimate in garden relaxation – once you master the art of getting in and out. If you do not have two stout trees to sling one from, buy a supporting frame – or hang it across the corner of two walls at right angles and train scented climbers around it.

SEAT WITH A VIEW Slabs of stone and a box shrub clipped to form a backrest make a low seat that is also a focal point to draw the eye down the grassy path. Situated at the end of a border of fragrant lavender the seat offers an invitation to sit and enjoy the sights and scents of summer.

QUIRKY AND UNEXPECTED SEATING

CURIOSITIES ARE FUN in an informal scheme, and even a formal garden may have a hidden corner where a quirky seat surprises and amuses. Junk shops, auctions, antique shops and car boot sales are all good hunting-grounds for potential treasures.

Trunks, tuck boxes, school benches, pub settles, tables and church pews turn up from time to time and all, with a little attention, make serviceable seats. Any low, wooden storage box has the makings of a seat; give it a back-rail, supported by two short uprights. It doubles as a place to hide boots, hoses and tools.

Slabs of slate or marble, including those from dismantled fireplaces and old washstands, become seats when raised on sturdy piers of brick or reconstituted stone. Practically anything in a strong flat length has potential. Lay it on concrete blocks, which are quickly concealed by twining ivy or clumps of perennials.

Let your imagination run free in transforming any junk-shop finds into outdoor chairs and tables. Strip the baize from an ancient card table and stick Victorian or Edwardian tiles in its place. Finish off with wooden beading. Store the table in a shed when it is not in use.

Choose paint colours and fabrics to build up an effect. Among bronze foliage and pink mallows put deep pink furniture with softer pink cushions. Put crimson seats with purple cushions beside matching fuchsias. For a hint of the East, use glossy scarlet or black paint on old chairs, decorate with gilded transfers and use an Oriental print for cushions.

TREE TRUNKS AND TOADSTOOLS

Weird seats and tables are easily made from oddly shaped tree trunks, roots and branches, the more bizarre and twisted the better, to resemble something from the tales of Grimm. Quirky furniture looks best in a wild or informal garden.

Such pieces would suit a 'gingerbread' garden house made from rustic logs (or logs nailed over an existing shed) decorated with garlands and pine cones stuck on with a glue-gun. Cover the floor with bark chips.

Children love such fantasy settings. Make 'toadstool' seats and tables for them from sections of logs. Nail a large flat slice on a longer, narrower length whose bottom half is soaked in preservative. Sink it into the ground and to secure it, firm it in with concrete.

MAKING SEATS FROM LOGS AND BARRELS

Chairs and benches are sometimes hacked out of upright sections of dead tree trunk, but a log seat is easier to make. All you need is a 3-4 ft (90-120 cm) length of tree trunk, approximately 18 in (45 cm) across, with any branches cut off flush with the trunk, and rubbed smooth. Lay it down in long grass and mow a path to it and a circle round it for a rustic perching place.

Use trunks of lesser girth as supports for planks or sanded floorboards. Cut two lengths of trunk about 2½ ft (75 cm) long for the supports and sink them by half their length into the ground. Nail on planks or floorboards with long galvanised nails. Or gouge hollows across the tops of the supports so that they cradle a length of tree trunk snugly.

Seats made from half-barrels look good everywhere apart from the most formal setting. Top them with a painted circle of marine ply and add a cushion.

GREEN, LIVING SEATS

'Green' seats date from medieval times. The simplest is just a low bank of turf on which to sit or sprawl. If you have a higher bank, then cut a seat directly into it and turf it over. Flat stones, concrete slabs and sleepers can also be used to form the base, sides and back of such a seat. They look particularly pretty with low plants trailing over them.

Another style of turf bench is easily made from a stone, brick or timber planter, about 18 in (45 cm) high and wide, and 36 in (90 cm) long. Fill two-thirds with rubble or bricks, finish off with topsoil and grow a cushion of turf on the top. Alternatively grow creeping thyme (*Thymus serpyllum*) or camomile (*Chamaemelum nobile*), both of them pleasantly aromatic. They are also attractive to bees when in flower, so look before you sit down on a living seat.

As a longer term venture, plant a hedge of box or *Lonicera nitida* in the outline of a sofa or armchair, minus the seat, clipping it into a comfortable-looking shape as it grows. Fill in the seat space with brick piers topped with stone slabs or thick, well-sanded planks.

MAKING A DRAWER SEAT

LOOK CLOSELY at any battered old chest of drawers in a jumble sale or junk shop. It is worth rescuing any with deep bottom drawers to transform them into seats.

Cut a piece of ¾ in (19 mm) marine plywood or medium-density fibreboard (MDF) to fit on top of the drawer space as a lid. Brass hinges make it easy to open to use the storage space inside.

Paint the piece of wood and drawer, inside and out, with gloss paint, allow to dry, then place a thick cushion on top.

SEATING AS SCULPTURE This topiary sofa of clipped box gains visual impact from its size and its setting. A dense, dark green hedge makes the background, while the foreground of large paving stones harmonises with the stone seat. Adapt the idea for green 'living seats' on a smaller scale.

TREE SEATS With some ingenuity and a few power tools, large logs and trunks can be adapted in a variety of different ways to serve as seats. This log seat makes a rugged perch for the short spells when the sun strikes it.

SAILOR'S REST The curved sides of half a boat upended create a sheltered seat for a seaside garden. Ivy planted at the base will, quite quickly, soften hard edges and make the boat seem a long-time feature of the garden.

SEATS FOR THE TIME OF DAY

WHERE YOU PLACE these carefully chosen seats depends not just on your garden but on your habits as well. Are you going to sit out during the day throughout the week, or only at the weekends? Do you eat breakfast or lunch on the terrace, or simply sip an evening aperitif on the garden bench? Are you an avid sun-worshipper, or does the heat make you seek cover?

A seat should be easy to reach, stable, welcoming and sheltered from the wind. A delightful view also helps. Put the seat in a luxuriant oasis and plan an attraction beside it – a fragrant shrub, the sound of water, or flowers to attract butterflies.

In a large garden, there may be room for two or three permanent seats for different times of day, but where space is limited you might have to settle for just one. Since it is likely to be a main focal point of the garden, make sure it is the most elegant and decorative piece you can afford. It can be backed up by a number of cheaper folding and stacking chairs when you have guests.

CATCHING THE MORNING SUN

There are few better ways to start a fine day than by strolling into the garden and sitting there for a while, enjoying the gentle warmth of the morning sun and noting each newly opened flower.

There is a lovely freshness, especially if rain has fallen in the night, and the scents are faint but sweet. Honeysuckle (*Lonicera periclymenum*), tobacco flowers (*Nicotiana alata* 'Evening Fragrance') and night-scented stocks (*Matthiola bicornis*) are still delicious in the morning. To take advantage of their last fragrance before the heat of the day suppresses it, place your seat among them facing east and back it with a protective semicircular wall or yew, beech or hornbeam hedge.

The fragrant white climbing rose 'Madame Alfred Carrière' will flower through the summer. It tolerates plenty of shade, so does well in an east-facing position. Plant the scented yellow day lily *Hemerocallis citrina* at its feet.

If you like to walk barefoot in the dew, set the seat on mown grass. The sedate can walk, well-shod, over a crisp path of gravel which dries out quickly and does not become slippery with moss and algae as flags and bricks tend to do when they receive only the morning sun.

IN SEARCH OF SHADE AT NOON

As the day becomes brighter and hotter, you have to choose between sun or shade. While tan-seekers are happy to stretch out on a deck chair or lounger placed in full sun, shade-lovers make for the lee of a north or east-facing wall, or plump instead for the filtered light beneath a tree. Seats that encircle a tree trunk come in a variety of styles made in delicate-looking ironwork or wood.

You can create extra places in the shade with imagination and patience.

🌢 When a tree is grown in a raised bed,

SCENTED BREEZES Permanent seating needs careful positioning. Consider the direction of the sun's rays in the morning and evening to make the most of early freshness or to savour the late warmth when perfumed plants such as these roses give off their strongest scent.

give the retaining wall a broad, flat coping so that it can be used as a seat.

🌷 Place timber decking round a tree and give it a raised surround of matching slats to serve as seating.

🌷 Grow a box or privet shrub as a tall standard in a container beside your favourite sitting place. Train and clip it over a frame into a neat parasol.

🌷 To prevent a seat on a south-facing terrace from becoming unbearably hot at midday, put up canvas blinds or awnings and create an airy space.

For the most easily portable shade, an outsize parasol is ideal. Parasols are easiest to move when they have a weighted base but some may be inserted into a sunken metal tube Many garden tables have a central hole to hold a parasol.

Even in a small garden, you can create a shady area. Many small spreading trees or large shrubs throw some shade, and do well in a container for some years. An Indian bean tree (*Catalpa bignonioides*), a golden-leaved robinia or a maple such as *Acer negundo* 'Auratum' or 'Flamingo', the graceful rowans *Sorbus cashmiriana*, *S. vilmorinii* and *S. hupehensis*, or the flowering crab apple *Malus × moerlandsii* 'Profusion', are all delightful.

Evergreens for warm gardens include the variegated privet *Ligustrum lucidum* 'Excelsum Superbum', the pineapple-scented broom *Cytisus battandieri* and *Ceanothus arboreus* 'Trewithen Blue'.

Plant resinous conifers and aromatic plants within reach of a garden seat. In the warmth of midday, artemisia, cistus, catmint, lavender, rosemary, lemon verbena (*Aloysia triphylla*), sage, thyme and many more release their fullest aromas in the hot sun.

HOARDING THE WARMTH FOR EVENING

A garden is often at its loveliest on a fine summer's evening when the light is soft, the air gentle and a host of flowers give off their delicious fragrances.

A west-facing corner is the perfect spot to watch the sun as it sinks, throws long shadows and gilds the trees. Here is the place for stone flags or brick paving, which stay free of the dew and retain some warmth from the day. However, any sheltering corner near the house gains warmth from the walls and makes a pleasant place to take an evening meal.

Where there is no sheltering wall or warm paving, set up movable screens of trellis, or arrange groups of container

MORNING WARMTH The colour and texture of warm stone paving is the foundation for a morning seating area screened by hurdles and brought to life by colourful planting. Plants include variegated ivy, alchemilla, London pride and the pink-splashed vine *Actinidia kolomikta*.

BEST PLANTS

SCENT TO WAFT ON THE AIR

Place scented plants so that their fragrance will carry on the breeze to the area around your seat.

• Mexican orange blossom (*Choisya ternata*): evergreen shrub with white spring flowers and a few in summer.

• Moroccan broom (*Cytisus battandieri*): silvery leaves, pineapple-scented yellow flowers in summer.

• Mock orange (*Philadelphus* 'Sybille'): mid-green leaves and white flowers in early to mid summer.

• *Rhododendron luteum*: yellow flowers in late spring.

• Sweet briar (*Rosa rubiginosa*): bright pink flowers in June, autumn hips.

• Lilac (*Syringa vulgaris*): deciduous shrub with large flower heads of white, mauve or purple in early summer.

• *Trachelospermum jasminoides*: evergreen climber with waxy, very fragrant white flowers in summer.

• *Buddleia alternifolia*: arching shrub with mauve flower-spikes in June.

• *Lilium* Pink Perfection: deep pink trumpet flowers borne in summer.

UNDER SPREADING BRANCHES In the heat of the midday sun a tree seat gives shady relief. In the morning and evening the rustle of leaves and the song of birds make it an ideal spot to enjoy extra pleasure in the garden.

plants, which you can change around for a succession of flowers and fragrance.

Plan a more permanent screen of fixed trellis clothed with roses, clematis and summer jasmine, then plant tobacco plants, night-scented stock (*Matthiola bicornis*) and sweet rocket (*Hesperis matronalis*) below them. Add a pot of lilies or verbena for even more scent.

To grow near the evening sitting place, choose as many white-flowered plants as you can because they glow magically in the dusk.

Subtle lighting transforms this scene once evening darkness falls. Up-lighters, down-lighters and side-lighters show off the plants, and strings of lights draped overhead and in the trees look pretty. Use lanterns, candles in firm holders, oil-lamps and flares to illuminate the table and paths, leaving other parts of the garden in mysterious pools of darkness.

A SPOT FOR ALL
TIMES AND ALL SEASONS

One of the most perfect places to relax is a conservatory. Make it as plain or fancy as your taste and purse dictate. Consult the local planning officer for planning consent before undertaking any work.

Crucial to your plan is the way the conservatory faces, for every direction has particular drawbacks and advantages. A south-facing position is brightest in winter but may prove unbearably hot in summer. An efficient form of shading and good ventilation have to be installed, but it then provides the conditions that are needed by many showy, exotic plants.

A north-facing site is comfortable enough in summer, and needs no shading, but some heating is needed to make the conservatory usable in winter. East or west-facing positions are best, having reasonable light but remaining a pleasant temperature for most of the day.

Make use of the conservatory walls and the roof area to increase the luxuriance of the planting without occupying too much of the floor space. Purple-leaved vines and crimson bougainvillea make a richly coloured start. Freshen it with the blue and white passion flower (*Passiflora caerulea*), pale blue *Plumbago auriculata* and the soft sky-blue hanging bells of *Sollya heterophylla* – all of which are happy in a conservatory, especially one that faces west.

For brilliant white flowers and rich scent grow the climbers *Jasminum odoratissimum*, *J. sambac* 'Maid of Orleans'

MOVABLE SHADE An airy, freestanding parasol can create a shady sitting area where previously the sun was too dazzling or scorching for sitting out in comfort. Plants in containers are used to delineate the raised area where chairs with slipover covers look fresh and inviting.

SUNNY SECLUSION Hedges and shrubs give privacy to a paved area that is softened by low plants. Flowers in containers add colour and leave the paving free for the best positioning of a seat to follow the sun.

and *J. grandiflorum* 'De Grasse'. Most pelargoniums rise to a reasonable height on a conservatory wall, while others, particularly the ivy-leaved *Pelargonium peltatum*, trail from hanging baskets, windowsills and shelving; *P. p.* 'La France' has pinkish-mauve double flowers and white-flowered *P. p.* 'L'Elégante' has pretty white-edged leaves. You will need to maintain a minimum winter temperature of 7-10°C (45-50°F) for all these flowering plants to flourish.

Complete the scene with foliage of contrasting sizes, shapes and shades. The golden feather palm (*Chrysalidocarpus lutescens*), the drooping combs of Kentia palm (*Howeia forsteriana*) and the glossy, crimped-edge shuttlecocks of bird's-nest fern (*Asplenium nidus*) all help to create lush green corners.

SOFT LIGHTS FOR SUMMER NIGHTS

When dusk falls and nights are balmy, illuminate your garden with the flattering glow of candlelight or flares. There are decorative ways of safeguarding the flame, though it is always sensible to have a bucket of water nearby as a precaution.

GARDEN FLARES
Flares are best used in a sheltered spot and are easily positioned for scenic lighting. Anchor them in the ground or in a pot. The protected candle inside split bamboo can also be hung from a tree.

DECORATIVE CAST IRON
Candles inside cast iron are sheltered and also show up the ornate tracery of the metalwork. A Victorian stove and an ornamental Japanese lantern are shown to advantage when lit from within.

POTS AND PAILS
Garden candles in pails and flowerpots can be used time and time again. They have a long burning time, and as some have an insect repellent included they are ideal for summer entertainments.

PROOF AGAINST BREEZES
A glass hurricane lamp and metal storm lantern provide candles with decorative shelter from garden breezes.

PARTY TIME
String up the lights for a festive occasion. Hanging on the rope are nightlight candles in coloured glass holders with wire handles. Ships' lanterns hang from support poles to give a stronger light.

UNUSUAL CANDLEHOLDERS
Search out some unusual candleholders that fit in with your own garden setting. A stone gargoyle candleholder adds a touch of grotesque drama, while an old-style metal birdcage is elegant and airy.

PRACTICAL AND ALLURING SETTINGS

A WELL-CHOSEN SEAT is only the first requirement for comfortable relaxation in the garden. You will also need shelter, privacy, something lovely to look at, fragrant plants nearby and perhaps some you can touch or crush to release their aroma. Screens and hedges, bowers and pergolas, pavilions and summerhouses all add form and depth of interest to the garden. Any one of them set in the right place and among elegant or informal plants, as befits them best, can become the garden's chief attraction.

MAKING PRIVATE CORNERS

An inexpensive way of creating a secluded glade is to design or reshape the lawn so that it flows out of sight round a corner into a small circular area screened by tall shrubs and perennials. Set the seat directly onto the grass or on a small area of paving at the edge of the lawn to avoid making the grass scuffed.

For a similar effect on a smaller scale, plant a low screen of lavender and herbs round a comma-shaped space at the end of a winding path. The path need only be short, with just one bend before it disappears behind the lavender.

Mark out the shape with a length of rope or hosepipe. Put the hose in the sun or run it off the hot tap for a few minutes to make it pliable.

In a paved garden, divide up the space with groups of plants in containers, using small trees and medium-sized shrubs for an instant transformation. A garden with parts screened off appears larger, as the eye is invited to travel round the plants into the unknown beyond. Include some evergreen plants in the screen – for example, bamboos, ceanothus, eleagnus, one or two conifers, fatsia, a strawberry tree (*Arbutus unedo*), *Rhamnus alaternus* 'Argenteovariegatus' and privet. Add a few deciduous shrubs and herbaceous perennials, with some pots of bulbs and annuals to keep up interest.

For areas of luxurious retreat, follow the well-established practice of dividing the garden into separate 'rooms' and give at least one of them a seat. The smallest garden is enhanced by such divisions.

Low clipped or informal hedges, pierced walls, fencing or trellises and low

TRELLIS TRANSFORMATION Charm and privacy can be created from an unpromising starting point. Trellis, a comfortable bench seat and skilful planting transform a low brick wall and paved yard. The bench is framed by twin containers of flowering annuals and by luxuriant hostas.

raised beds make satisfactory divisions and can take straight lines or a curve.

There are numerous plants suitable for a plant screen, from the larger hebes and smooth-leaved hollies, through the beautiful camellias and ceanothus to the elegant, whispering bamboos.

In a very small garden, surrounded by raised beds, one corner can be given a built-in seat and table to save space. The garden will appear larger if you plant the beds thickly to obscure the boundary walls and fences, so that it becomes unclear where the garden begins and ends.

Fast-growing plants for hiding the boundaries include *Phyllostachys aurea*,

Acer negundo 'Flamingo', *Cornus alba* 'Elegantissima', *Lavatera* 'Rosea' and *L.* 'Barnsley', *Ceanothus* and *Cotoneaster* × *watereri* 'Cornubia'.

A SHELTERED SPOT IN A WINDY GARDEN

For protection from the wind, screens of bamboo, brushwood or slatted wood, and woven hurdles of willow or hazel are extremely effective.

There are elegantly ornamental trellis panels on bracket feet, while others come with attached planting-troughs – both useful in paved areas, where climbers in containers or in the trough grow quickly

enough to decorate the panels. Two such screens set at a right angle will shelter a chair, three will shelter a bench.

Extra containers on either side, containing a small tree underplanted with scented annuals, give an illusion of permanence to the scheme.

White trellis is attractive, but consider other colours; black or dark green for sophisticates or a soft blue-green or dove grey for romantics.

A BREEZY SEASIDE PLOT

The best shelter for a seaside garden is a barrier of tough plants. The hardy sea buckthorn (*Hippophae rhamnoides*) has narrow silver leaves on spiny stems, and provided you grow male and female plants, the females bear a heavy crop of berries which the birds usually leave alone through autumn and winter. Sea buckthorn grows in sandy or chalk soils.

Evergreen *Griselinia littoralis* makes a pleasant hedge, as do two other evergreens, *Escallonia rubra* var. *macrantha* and *Euonymus japonicus*. On thin chalk soils *Escallonia* 'Iveyi' is the best choice.

While these plants are establishing themselves, make use of a three-sided windbreak of willow hurdles, fixed to four wooden stakes driven well into the ground. Set a chair inside the shelter with drifts of shells and cobbles for flooring. *Crambe cordifolia* on each side of the seat foams with tiny white flowers in summer. Grow sweet peas (*Lathyrus odoratus*) up the willow hurdles for exquisite scent.

Pots of the pink-flowered *Convolvulus althaeoides* make a charming alternative for such a spot; they like a dry, sunny site, but need to be brought in during the winter, except in the mildest areas.

For unorthodox shelter at the seaside use whatever is to hand. Folding screens of canvas on a metal frame, or grass matting, woven bamboo panels or tightly stretched hessian on an old wooden screen all make a movable shelter for a couple of deck chairs – and provide a hideaway for the bashful sunbather.

An old clothes horse covered with material makes a neat frame. Choose a fabric to match either the garden chairs or the colours of the plants.

FITTING IN THE BARBECUE

A barbecue needs to be conveniently near the house but, to make it an asset rather than an eyesore, screen it with plants or set it neatly in a rectangle of low walls and built-in seats. Make the walls

ROOM FOR ONE A niche in a raised bed is just the size for a bright chair that gives a private view of the geums and achilleas.

PART OF THE FITTINGS A permanent seat is built into a raised bed where marigolds can be appreciated at eye level.

THE WARMTH OF WOOD Timber decking is warm to the eye and the feet. Its organic origin gives it a particular affinity with a garden. Properly constructed from treated wood, decking is long-lasting and hard-wearing. Wooden loungers look well on this type of surface.

straight or diagonal runs, or in chevrons; ready-made squares create a chequer-board pattern. Straight runs that lead away from the house appear to lengthen a short garden, while those laid from side to side seem to broaden and shorten a long, narrow one.

Leave some gaps in the deck for trees or mature shrubs to grow through and raise a layer of decking round them to form a seat. Soften up all these strong lines with containers of lilies, hostas and perhaps a heavily perfumed, trumpet-flowered datura (*Brugmansia candida* 'Knightii') – beautiful but poisonous.

THE PLEASURE OF PERGOLAS AND VERANDAHS

Two rows of uprights, whether timber posts, metal poles, or pillars of brick and stonework, crossed by beams overhead and set far enough apart to accommodate a bench make a simple enough structure yet create a sense of gracious living. Entwine the pergola with roses and honeysuckle, clematis and jasmine and there is no more enticing place to enjoy airy privacy.

The pergola can be freestanding or set against the house, where it makes a link between the building and the garden. It needs just one row of uprights to support the crossbeams, the other end being fixed to joist hangers or to a stout bearer running along the wall.

In a south-facing garden a verandah, as it is covered, is a more welcome retreat than a pergola for those people who prefer to sit in the shade. Running along the wall like a wide, open porch, it has a sloping roof resting on posts that can be serviceable timber or elegant cast iron to suit the surrounding.

The floor, raised up a step or two above ground level, gives plenty of space for seating and for containers of shade-loving plants. Sun-lovers will thrive in a bed at the foot of the verandah steps, where climbers too can start the ascent up the posts and along the roof edge.

If you have an extension built on a south-facing wall, consider letting the upper storey jut out beyond the lower one. The shady gallery below – a loggia – with wooden or plaster pillars along it, is a comfortable spot for meals out of

double with a gap between to hold soil and use them for growing marjoram, rosemary, sage, thyme, lemon thyme, tarragon, chives, parsley and fennel for flavouring the barbecue food.

Make the seats of double walls, too, and top them with slabs, some of them left loose so that the space beneath can store the cushions in plastic bags, and all the barbecue fuel and equipment.

A similar design that is sunk into the ground is an unusual alternative. Make

the barbecue area circular, with built-in seating. At the centre put a round table large enough to contain or support a small grill. Grow herbs in the surrounding beds and add an outer circle of plants for a windbreak if necessary.

CLEVER DESIGNS WITH DECKING

A seating area is easily made into a strong feature when you use timber decking. It is particularly useful for making a level area on a sloping site. Lay the boards in

MAKING AN ARBOUR

A PRETTY PLACE to rest after the exertions of weeding is within an arbour. Whether freestanding or placed against a wall, it will look delightful, especially when covered by a rambling rose or another scented climber, with a simple seat set at its heart.

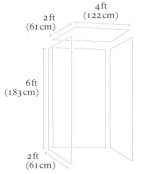

You need three 6 × 2 ft (183 × 61 cm) trellis panels to make the sides and roof, and a 6 × 4 ft (183 × 122 cm) panel for the back. Use four 6 ft (183 cm) lengths of 2 × 2 in (5 × 5 cm) timber for the uprights.

Make a three-sided box by nailing the side and back panels to the outside of the four uprights with galvanised nails (drill holes in the trellis panels before nailing to prevent splitting).

Cut down the roof panel to 4 ft (122 cm) long and nail it across the top in the same way.

Fix the arbour to a wall with screws and plugs, or hammer fixing irons over the bottom rim if it is to be freestanding. Top the corner posts with wooden finials and fit a shapely crest cut from marine plywood. Paint or stain the arbour.

DINING OUT This pergola provides support for climbing plants and some shade when the sun is overhead. The pleasures of eating outside are enhanced by the privacy created by the structure and the profusion of container plants including the fine yellow spikes of *Ligularia przewalskii*.

doors. In summer the loggia is likely to be shady, but at other times of the year the lower sun will light and warm it.

INTIMATE ARBOURS

Pergolas, loggias and verandahs may have space for several people but an arbour is made for one or two.

Ready-made arches of rustic poles, wooden trellis or wirework are sold at most garden centres and, when placed against a wall, hedge or fence, become an instant arbour. You can make your own with trellis panels and timber posts, then smother it with roses for the full romantic aura. In a semi-shaded site, clothe it with *Clematis alpina*, *C. macropetala*, runner beans or the colourful annual black-eyed Susan (*Thunbergia alata*).

Set the arbour among large-leaved plants such as fatsias, bergenias, the purplish ornamental rhubarb *Rheum palmatum* 'Atrosanguineum' and rodgersias. All have a solidity that emphasises the structure's delicate charms. For scent, add woodruff (*Galium odoratum*).

Turn a walled corner into an arbour by fixing a strong trellis panel across the top. Make it more distinctive by raising the ground a little and laying an approach of a couple of semicircular steps.

If the garden is very sheltered and south-facing, grow the evergreen climber *Trachelospermum jasminoides* which will look spectacular planted on each side of the arbour, where it will twine its way up wires and over the trellis. Its glossy, dark green leaves are attractive all year, while in summer, the small, star-like flowers produce the most ravishing fragrance. In more exposed areas, the evergreen and scented honeysuckle *Lonicera japonica* 'Halliana' is a good alternative. Put a silky-leaved *Artemisia absinthium* 'Lambrook Silver' at the foot of each honeysuckle as a finishing touch.

Against a white wall, an *Actinidia kolomikta* is lovely clambering up either side of the arbour. Its heart-shaped green leaves are generously splashed with white and pink, as if by a careless painter. To add flowers and swooning scent put a few pots on either side, thickly planted with pink and white lilies and tobacco plants.

SIMPLE GREEN BOWERS

A striking, permanently green bower is easily made with a strong timber frame covered with stapled-on chicken wire or plastic mesh. Cover it with ivies and it takes on an ancient rustic character.

Try dark green *Hedera helix* and *H. hibernica*, the yellow-variegated *H. helix* Goldheart' or some of the large-leaved ivies such as *H. colchica* 'Sulphur Heart', *H. c.* 'Dentata Variegata' and *H. algeriensis* 'Gloire de Marengo'.

Before the ivy makes enough growth, plant annual climbers, such as runner beans, sweet peas, the cup-and-saucer plant (*Cobaea scandens*) or morning glory (*Ipomoea hederacea*) round your bower.

Experiment with other evergreen frames for your seating.

❧ Plant a semicircle of box or conifer hedging behind a curved seat.

❧ Carve out an alcove from a well-established hedge. Be sure it is one that sprouts again after hard pruning, such as yew or privet.

❧ When planting a new hedge, set one section about 2-3 ft (60-90 cm) further back than the rest, making a natural recess long enough to take a bench.

❧ Plant a hedging conifer at each side of a garden bench and train and clip the two to meet in a round or pointed arch.

TREE BOWERS

Weeping trees make delightful natural arbours for a seat. The weeping ash is very hardy and thrives almost anywhere the soil is not waterlogged. In time it forms a medium-sized tree whose leafy branches trail to the ground, providing

TRANQUILLITY IN A SCENTED CORNER

By creating a calm but colourful corner, you can transform a terrace or patio into a special, private place where you can put a seat in sun or shade and relax totally.

DOZING OR READING in the dappled shade of the garden, surrounded by your favourite plants and soothed by scented flowers, is the summer equivalent of curling up on the sofa in front of a fire. A paved corner serves as an extra 'room' – an extension that opens up all the delights of living outdoors. Set against a backdrop of permanent ornamental planting it has the added bonus of flexibility: you can move furniture in and out as required and shift pot plants from garden to paving as the mood takes you.

This corner is set for one person to enjoy the solitude of a peaceful afternoon. The wooden fold-up chair is light and compact enough to be moved with ease. At present the chair faces east, cooled from afternoon rays by the partial shade of the climbing rose above and behind it.

The trellis panel gives privacy and divides the 'room' from the lawn, while on colder days the wall blocks out chill, northerly winds.

Creeping thyme relishes living among the paving, softening the look of the concrete and releasing a sweet aroma as you walk over it. Containers of scented plants clustered around the chair offer a feast for the senses, as you idly trail a hand through the lavender.

EXTENDING THE PLEASURES

When evening comes, the tobacco plants start to give out their scent, their pale flowers – and those of the lilies – looking almost luminous in the dusk.

More white tobacco plants grace the raised bed tucked against the wall. The bed gives scope to plant climbers, herbaceous plants and more herbs that can stay in place summer and winter, as well as creating interest at several

Climber-covered trelliswork keeps out breezes

Pot plants release a heady blend of scents

heights. A hanging basket of trailing pelargoniums adds another level to the display. Wind chimes tinkle and water trickles gently from a wall mask.

Despite its small size, the outdoor room is more than merely ornamental. The scarlet-flowered runner beans will yield several helpings. The herbs are also for picking. Snuggled up to the pot of marjoram, sage mingles with the tendrils of periwinkle draping the raised bed. Hard and soft features combine to make the most of a confined space.

Runner beans complete a colourful niche

A raised bed holds plants to frame the fountain

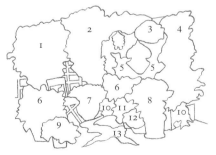

1. Rose (*Rosa* 'Aloha')
2. Honeysuckle (*Lonicera periclymenum* 'Serotina')
3. *Pelargonium* 'Mexican Beauty'
4. Runner bean (*Phaseolus coccineus*)
5. Ivy (*Hedera helix* 'Glacier')
6. Tobacco plant (*Nicotiana alata*)
7. Lavender (*Lavandula angustifolia* 'Munstead')
8. Lily (*Lilium longiflorum*)
9. Pink (*Dianthus* 'Houndspool Ruby')
10. Greater periwinkle (*Vinca major* 'Variegata')
11. Tricoloured sage (*Salvia officinalis* 'Tricolor')
12. Golden marjoram (*Origanum vulgare* 'Aureum')
13. Thyme (*Thymus serpyllum*)

the opportunity to trim away a small arch to frame the seat.

Weeping willows are suitable for similar treatment and look lovely by water. However, they become large trees so do not be tempted to plant them in a small garden – they lose their grace if they are chopped back. Much better are the weeping purple beech (*Fagus sylvatica* 'Pendula Purpurea') and the silver-leaved pear, *Pyrus salicifolia* 'Pendula', both of which make charming arbours, one darkly glowing, the other airily pale.

For a quick result plant two silver-leaved pears about 8 ft (2.5 m) apart, then tie the top branches together at the centre and prune away some of those underneath to make a shady 'cave'; a climbing rose such as 'Parade' or 'Pink Perpétué' and the purple-leaved vine (*Vitis vinifera* 'Purpurea') look beautiful growing up through the branches.

Most of the evergreens that are traditionally used for topiary – yew, laurel (*Prunus laurocerasus*), a fast-growing box (*Buxus sempervirens* 'Handsworthiensis') and honeysuckle (*Lonicera nitida*) – form green 'houses' with patience and careful clipping. Plant bushes in a round, rectangular or hexagonal shape, leaving one part open. Train the branches up and as soon as they have grown high enough, pull their tops over and tie them together to form the roof. Keep the bower well trimmed within. If you grow alternate green and gold privets in this way they make a striking striped 'tent'.

PAVILIONS AND SUMMERHOUSES

Similar to the living tent is a small garden pavilion, a pretty feature to look at in the garden as well as an elegant place to sit. Have two or all four sides with an opening and the pavilion becomes a gazebo, less sheltered in a breezy garden but less stuffy in a sunny one.

If you want something more substantial, invest in a summerhouse, in rustic, Gothic or sturdily modern style. One of these wooden houses makes a lovely spot to take tea in the summer or to retreat to on a sunny day in the winter, and it has great potential as a children's playhouse or a store for garden furniture.

COURTYARDS OR PATIOS

Not quite so enclosed is a courtyard or authentic patio. It is open to the sky but is sited within sheltering walls or fences.

Sometimes a courtyard has one wall, usually the back of a larger building, that

is tall and somewhat overwhelming, but the intimidating effect is lessened by placing your seating area at its foot, so that you face away from it.

First paint a large arch or rectangle on the lower part of the wall. To bring the eyes down, make a raised semicircular or rectangular seating area in front and edge it with a low wall. Place a bench in the centre with a pair of architectural plants – such as fatsias, figs, *Mahonia × media* 'Charity' or Mexican orange blossom (*Choisya ternata*) – on each side.

Instead of painting an arch, frame the seat by training a plant on the wall into a fan shape or by fixing a decorative panel of metalwork, trellis or simply bamboo screening. Or make a frame with a climber trained from each side to meet and form an arch. Fix a wall mask in the centre and, beneath it, install a raised pool with a wide, flat coping on which to sit and admire the fish or water lilies.

On the lower level round the raised seating area, plant a narrow bed with a low evergreen hedge of hebes, lavender or clipped box. Standard roses or fuchsias, or lollipop-shaped bays underplanted with pansies, give form and colour to admire from the seat, especially when backed by *Parthenocissus henryana* climbing on the remaining walls.

RETREAT ON THE ROOF

Every bit of potential garden space is an asset, so in towns, where space is at a premium, a roof garden is especially valued. Discover at the outset from your local planning officer and a surveyor what restrictions there are on the appearance, structures and weight.

As a flat roof is strongest at its perimeter, put the largest containers there. No matter how light the containers are themselves (plastic and glass fibre being particularly useful), the filling of compost weighs a considerable amount.

You need easy access to water and unimpeded drainage channels for rainwater to run off. Bear the drainage in mind when you choose the 'ground' surface. Artificial turf gives a welcome air of green open space and does not get too hot in summer. Lightweight tiles in a restful colour are good, while decking is particularly attractive and practical.

Give shelter from wind and sun with panels of trellis or slatted timber, which preserve the sense of space as well as being more effective than solid windbreak panels. Look for trellis made from

A SHADY BOWER Slabs of stone built into the wall in a curve are canopied by spreading *Cedrus atlantica* 'Pendula' trained over supports. This shady bower is both tempting to sit in and a focal point for the eye to rest on.

UP ON THE ROOF Climbers grown on a light fence screen the roof garden, giving shelter from the wind as well as some privacy. Plentiful watering is needed as containers dry out quickly from the effects of wind and sun.

CANOPY FOR OUTDOOR MEALS

ENSURE YOUR GUESTS and family eat in comfort by providing a cotton canopy for them to dine under. It can make all the difference to the success of a children's tea party, offering a private pavilion to keep the fair-skinned out of the heat of the sun.

Available from garden centres and mail order companies, canopies are made from showerproof cotton and lightweight galvanised steel tubing. They are simple and fast to set up.

CANOPY OF ROSES Diamond trellis is a strong framework for cascades of roses on this well-proportioned and airy arbour. Choose roses with a tumbling habit rather than upright growers to gain the best effect.

recycled polystyrene if you wish to be 'green'. Add canvas or bamboo screening on the most exposed side. A sense of security is needed as much as physical shelter; a vast expanse of sky is a little daunting. What you need is a feeling of space that is safely corralled.

Some kind of 'ceiling' helps. Dutch-blinds or pullout canvas awnings are pleasant and cheerful, while a lightweight pergola adds a more formal, structural note to the design. Pergola sounds rather grand, but a simple design suffices. Two posts fixed into neat, square, metal or brick 'shoes' mark the outer corners. A length of timber joins them at the top and another runs from the top of each post back to a joist fixed across the wall or to the screen. Two or three light beams across this framework complete the job.

PLANTS FOR THE HIGH LIFE

Train wind-tolerant climbers over the beams to create dappled shade; ivies will grow up in time and honeysuckle and *Clematis montana* add colour.

Most climbers do well on the house wall if the roof garden has one. Apart from climbers, spiky plants such as cordylines, phormiums and yuccas, and many grey-leaved plants (cistus, lavender, rosemary, hebe, *Convolvulus cneorum*) often do exceptionally well, giving a Mediterranean air. Suitable palms for a rooftop are restricted to *Trachycarpus fortunei* and *Chamaerops humilis*.

An exuberant atmosphere prevails when every container brims over with a riot of annuals in summer, but if you prefer a more restrained look, plant nothing but evergreen foliage plants.

Whatever your style of garden, create a space to suit your needs and fill it with those plants that give you most pleasure. Draw inspiration from as many sources as you can – look at books, magazines and other gardens. Whether you wish to stretch out in the sun or to meditate in the shade, there are sites and seats for all tastes – from the simple and conventional to the wild and whimsical.

BREAKFAST, LUNCH AND DINNER Eating meals outside with family or friends makes a special event out of an informal occasion. Allow a generous area of space and border it with plentiful foliage plants for constant interest.

INSPIRATION FROM
GREAT GARDENS

WALLINGTON HALL

A gravel terrace fronts the Classical façade.

Of the many charming features that make up the garden at Wallington Hall, near Cambo in Northumberland, most striking of all is the large and elegant conservatory. It is situated away from the house on a spacious terrace overlooking the walled garden. It dates from the earliest years of the 20th century and contains some remarkable old plants.

THE CONSERVATORY at Wallington Hall, built about 1908 by Sir George Trevelyan, holds a flourishing garden that can be enjoyed all year long. The impressive structure, with greenhouses at each end, stretches the length of a terrace to one side of the house.

From spring right through to autumn, a heady fragrance wafts through the conservatory, escaping outdoors during the summer months. A very pale, lavender-coloured heliotrope, established around 1940, is largely responsible; its clusters of small, scented flowers now clothe one of the central supports to the height of the roof. Pelargoniums, abutilon, plumbago

and a lemon verbena that was planted before the conservatory existed add colourful blooms to the display.

The conservatory also provides a home for a number of tree fuchsias of astonishing age. One of these, a strong-growing, almost hardy 'Rose of Castile Improved', with purple petals and flesh-pink sepals, was planted at the same time as the conservatory was built. Its trunk now measures 30 in (76 cm) across.

In among the plants are curiosities to catch the eye, many of them installed by Trevelyan himself. In one corner is a marble fountain whose design imitates that of a Roman tomb, while in another

EDWARDIAN GRANDEUR
Colourful shrubs, some established almost a century ago, scent the air in the conservatory at Wallington.

plot of land adjoining the house is able to create a smaller 'winter garden' with a glass extension to the house. It will bring a summer touch to autumn evenings and to the sunny but chilly days of winter.

WARMLY COLOURED ROOM

The plants in the modest heated conservatory below are as old-fashioned as those found at Wallington, and the predominating colours are just as rich. A *Stephanotis floribunda*, trained up the wall on the left, grows to a height of 10 ft (3 m) or so; it requires a minimum temperature of 10°C (50°F) to survive the winter. Here, its heavily scented white flowers frame the shapely, potted pink *Fuchsia* 'Display'.

A green backcloth for the flowers is given not just by the fuchsia's own rich green foliage but also by the dramatic,

elongated leaves of the paradise palm (*Howea forsteriana*), which takes pride of place in the foreground. Another potted *Fuchsia*, the carmine and magenta 'Gay Fandango', stands on the windowsill in the corner of the conservatory behind a comfortable Lloyd Loom chair.

Next to the chair is a column supporting a Victorian plaster bust, an affordable echo of the Roman-inspired marblework at Wallington. At its base are the lighter green ferns *Adiantum raddianum* 'Kensington Gem' and *Asparagus setaceus* 'Nanus', while the leaves of the fruiting purple vine, *Vitis vinifera* 'Purpurea', are silhouetted overhead. The vine's roots are in the soil outside, finding nourishment for the growth within, which spreads out over the inside of the roof, providing welcome shade on a hot day.

Around the bottom of the vine is the long-flowering, daisylike *Argyranthemum frutescens*. The red *Begonia*, 'Allan Langdon' tucked behind it is similar in shade to the deep red *Hibiscus rosa-sinensis* 'Holiday' which sits behind the bust. The two lend the conservatory a warm glow to offset the autumnal tints outside.

stands a marble bust of Antinous, a favourite of the Emperor Hadrian. The bust is particularly apt, because it was Hadrian who in AD 122 set in motion the building of the frontier wall, known as Hadrian's Wall, when Northumbria was the northern limit of the Roman Empire.

The profusion of plants, seating and ornaments turn the conservatory into an oasis of tropical lushness and vitality even on the gloomiest of winter days.

Few people have a large terrace on which to construct a full-scale conservatory, or indeed have plants in their garden that were established a century or more ago. But anyone with even a small

MODERN CHARM When frosts begin to tint the trees outside, draw inspiration from Wallington and warm your own conservatory with the rich purples and reds of vines, fuchsias and begonias.

FEATURES TO CATCH THE EYE

EVERY GARDEN BENEFITS from a touch of drama – and it takes so little to lift well-tended ordinariness into the memorable. There is a wealth of ideas to choose from, some simple and inexpensive, some grander and more costly, but all effective. You can draw the eye with a statue or a sundial, or with a striking corkscrew hazel or a monkey-puzzle tree. Curiosities will inject some fun, and plants or mementos that celebrate family occasions and favourite places will keep personal memories vivid.

Gazing down pensively amid a green sea of spotted laurel and lacy ferns,
a weathered statue steals the scene.

FINDING THE FOCUS

Only too often you look around the garden and feel vaguely dissatisfied. Despite the time and care lavished, the money spent, something seems to be lacking, but what? One or more decorative features are needed to create interest and pull the design together. An element of drama or wit lifts the garden from the passable to the delectable level, giving a satisfying visual climax which may also be a talking point. This focal point can be a statue, an outstanding plant, a curious object that holds memories for you, or some weathered hunk of wood.

The choice and siting of a centrepiece needs sensitivity. To install anything out of character, bitty or fussy makes for a restless feeling, while the line between the amusing and the kitsch is narrow.

A focal point should be in sympathy with the period and construction of the house. Happily, objects that are simple or excellent in themselves tend to fit into any well-planned design, just as a contemporary sculpture suits a Georgian house and an antique rug a modern flat.

When you choose the position for a main feature, it helps to photograph the garden from strategic points, including from the upstairs windows, and have the pictures enlarged. Try out the positioning of focal points on the photographs. Another trick is to cut out pictures of possible adornments and move them around over the photos of your garden. See if they fit the garden style and give the desired 'lift' to a problem area.

DRAWING THE EYE A living lattice frame of the evergreen climber *Trachelospermum* breaks up the expanse of brickwork on the high wall and provides a backdrop for the focus of the patio – the cherub statue. Raising the stone figure on a pedestal makes it even more noticeable.

FRONT AND SIDE GARDENS

WHEN YOU CONSIDER garden design, you tend to think of the main area for outside relaxation and entertainment – the back garden. But the front garden, and particularly the path to the front door, is the first part that you or your visitors see, so it is worth turning it into an arresting feature. If you have a flowerbed at the front or a central ornament to catch the eye, surround it with paving or gravel to accentuate it. Choose features which cannot be easily removed to deter the opportunist thief.

TOWN FRONT GARDENS

How best to make your front garden eye-catching partly depends on where you live. In the city you are likely to have less scope than in the countryside. But however little space you have, a plant or ornament can draw the eye.

For a scene-stealing central bed, plant one of the smaller magnolias, such as *Magnolia stellata*, or a camellia, perhaps the elegantly striped 'Contessa Lavinia Maggi'. If you are concerned about security, choose something prickly such as topiary work in holly. To set the stage, underplant with bulbs and seasonal bedding plants. An all-white bedding scheme, edged with clipped ivy, is pretty: hyacinths and tulips in the spring, followed by busy lizzies in the summer for a shaded aspect, or pelargoniums and silver foliage plants in the sun. In winter, white pansies take over.

DUAL-PURPOSE BOUNDARIES

For an even simpler scheme, pave or tile the ground and make a focal point of the boundary. Cut recesses in dark hedging and put a statue inside or plant a pale shrub within, such as the white standard roses 'Glamis Castle' or 'Iceberg', or a clump of *Cornus alba* 'Elegantissima'.

If the boundary is not a hedge, make the most of paving. Choose from slabs, bricks, quarry tiles or cobbles. Interplant with low-growing shrubs and perennials. A weeping standard rose, perhaps 'Debutante' or 'Princess Louise', makes a delightful centrepiece.

In shade, plant a weeping evergreen such as *Cotoneaster salicifolius* 'Pendulus' or *Ilex aquifolium* 'Argentea Marginata Pendula' – or choose the ferny leaved

Mask and jar catch attention

Dainty flowers set off bold foliage

WINTER CHARM IN THE SIDE GARDEN

With a well-thought-out design for the narrow strip between the boundary and the house wall, this unpromising spot becomes a corner of delight, even in winter.

WHITE WALLS and pale grey trellis give the confined space a more open feeling and make an attractive backdrop. The trellis gives scope for ivy to climb – types with variegated leaves add most colour.

Rectangular slabs laid across the whole area make the strip seem wider – even when pots and troughs are added, it is the area of paving that defines the width. Choose bergenia to form a foliage backbone of year-round interest, varying the detail with snowdrops and scillas in winter and spring, and petunias or red pelargoniums with hostas in summer.

The shortest wall is the most dramatic place for the *pièce de résistance*, a wall mask above a tall terracotta jar. Surround the jar with little pots of ivy. A barrel planted with a spiky phormium draws people from the main garden into the surprising beauty of the side strip.

In summer, hanging baskets full of annuals such as busy lizzies in a range of warm reds, pinks and purples brighten the area further. The mask and jar, too,

add more life to the scene then, as a water feature with a hidden pump circulating a trickle from the mouth of the mask into the jar and back again.

1. Ivy (*Hedera canariensis* 'Gloire de Marengo')
2. *Scilla siberica*
3. *Bergenia* 'Silberlicht'
4. Snowdrop (*Galanthus elwesii*)
5. Ivy (*Hedera helix* 'Glacier')
6. *Phormium* 'Dazzler'
7. Hart's-tongue fern (*Asplenium scolopendrium*)

TRAINING A LIVING PYRAMID

To GROW A PLANT in a topiary shape, choose one that grows slowly, is very dense and tolerates regular clipping. Ideal plants are box, privet, yew and holly. But you could also use sweet bay, hornbeam, hawthorn, pyracantha or even rosemary. There is no need to buy a ready-made frame for a simple shape like a pyramid.

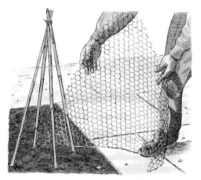

1. Choose four bamboo canes that measure the desired height of the topiary plus 6 in (15 cm). Tie the canes together with twine 2 in (5 cm) from the top and spread them to form a pyramid.

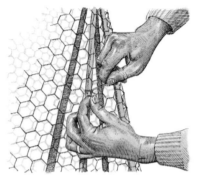

2. Use wire netting with holes larger than the plant's foliage. Wrap it round the frame, leaving 4 in (10 cm) free at the bottom. Tie the netting to each cane with twine at 5 in (12.5 cm) intervals.

3. Place the frame over the young plant in its container. Push the canes firmly into the soil so the frame will not be dislodged by the occasional knock. The netting should almost touch the soil.

4. As the plant grows, trim back any shoots that come through the wire. Use secateurs for cutting larger-leaved plants so that individual leaves do not suffer damage and turn brown.

5. Once the frame is filled by the plant, gently pull the canes out of the soil. Lift off the frame carefully. The plant will then need regular trimming, usually twice a year, to keep it in shape.

rose *Rosa xanthina* 'Canary Bird' which remains attractive after the small yellow flowers have finished their spring show.

FOCAL POINTS IN A MODERN OR COTTAGE SETTING

The strong lines of modern architecture are set off by ground cover, dramatised by a few specimen plants. Try sweeps of low-growing *Prunus laurocerasus* 'Otto Luyken', round plants of architectural interest. Aralia, fatsia and bamboos are all excellent in such a situation.

As a modern sculpture, make a group of boulders. Or sink five weathered timber posts of different lengths into the ground together as one pillar; before installation, treat the portion to be sunk underground with a wood preservative. Instead of timber you can use granite kerbstones. Set a large, smooth stone on each section of the pillar.

At the other extreme, in a cottage garden the features that delight are more cosy and familiar. Here is the spot to try your hand at some light-hearted topiary – a teddy bear, a teapot or a small, plump bird or two; if the shapes are a little lopsided, it adds to the charm. For flowering plants rather than green sculpture, use hollyhocks, delphiniums and sweet peas, or a long-flowering *Lavatera* 'Barnsley'.

BESIDE THE SEA

Seaside gardens give you the opportunity to use materials that are appropriate nowhere else. In a tiny garden use the surface itself as a centre of interest. Lay seashore pebbles in diamond shapes, outlined by others of different sizes and colours or, more ambitiously, lay them in a wave pattern and incorporate a gull, a fish or even a mermaid in the design.

For a living centrepiece in a sea of hard surfacing, plant prickly *Rosa rugosa*. Rugosas tolerate poor, sandy soils and the flowers are usually followed by large, colourful hips. 'Fru Dagmar Hastrup' grows to about 3 ft (1 m), has fragrant pink single flowers, huge red hips and leaves that colour up well in the autumn.

For a taller, shade-tolerant rugosa, 'Blanc Double de Coubert' is unrivalled. It reaches 6 ft (1.8 m), with fragrant, semidouble white flowers with golden stamen, and good leaf colour in autumn.

Figureheads were once familiar ornaments for seaside houses and gardens. Old ones are hard to come by, but why not carve and paint one yourself? As the originals were often crudely done, a little

CONTRASTING NOTE Hard edges and dense black make this Victorian stove stand out from the gentle planting round it. Hellebore leaves tickle the outside, their lobes rivalling the intricacy of the pierced metal.

clumsiness adds an air of authenticity – as does 'weathering' the paintwork. Rub bits of it away here and there, with fine sandpaper or wet-and-dry abrasive paper, to reveal the undercoat or the bare wood.

Failing a figurehead, use an anchor. Paint it black, bolt or cement it to a sunken concrete block and conceal the block with shingle. Frame the feature with a blue sea of catmint, then add groups of the silver and spiky plants that grow so well in such conditions – sea holly, globe thistle, artemisia and the little blue grass, *Festuca glauca*.

INTEREST IN THE SIDE GARDEN

The side garden is often a difficult area to make attractive. It may be little more than a wind tunnel running beside a garage or wall. Before considering ideas for turning drab, wasted space into a talking point, look at the paintwork. Think of houses seen abroad gaily painted in every possible combination of colours – the white walls and dark blue woodwork of the Greek islands, warm terracotta and burnt yellows in Italy, the clapboard houses of the Caribbean.

Take photographs of the house, and of the facing wall if there is one. Make tracings from these and colour in various schemes until you find one that pleases you. Try pale blue walls and dark blue woodwork, white walls with green woodwork, dark green or primrose-yellow walls with paintwork of sparkling white. A small porch or portico and some shutters make decorative features of doors and windows. Window boxes help too.

Trellis panels fixed to the wall add points of interest. The paint usually chosen for trellis is white or dark green, but try other colours and consider black for a sophisticated town garden. If the spot is gloomy, set a mirror (with a moisture-resistant film backing) behind the trellis to double what light there is.

Plant up a few space-saving plant holders such as hanging baskets, troughs or chimney pots or attach a wall plaque.

JOINED-UP HOUSES

Many terraced and semidetached houses have an L-shaped garden with a narrow leg where two buildings join. It is often shaded by a wall, but this is still valuable

CORNER OF DELIGHTS A lion's head fountain and box globes in gaily painted pots transform a dingy, narrow side-garden strip.

TOUCH OF THE EXOTIC A strappy purple-leaved cabbage palm always claims the limelight. *Cordyline australis* is a half-hardy species and can be grown outdoors in mild areas in the south and west.

space. You can brighten a bare expanse of wall in various ways.

🌢 Use a bit of false topiary. Train a small-leaved, pot-grown ivy up a wire spiral, or train a sphere, using a home-made frame of two mesh hanging baskets fixed together with strong fuse wire.

🌢 Train a climber up and around an arch or trellis. The larger-leaved ivies (*Hedera colchica* or *H. canariensis*) thrive in sun or shade. Those with variegated leaves do better in at least partial sunlight. They are all self clinging and fast growing once established.

🌢 Even simpler, paint an arch on the wall. Try a round-topped or pointed shape, making a template out of card or hardboard to guide you.

🌢 In front of the real or trompe l'oeil arch, position a statue or urn.

🌢 Plant up little beds at the foot of the wall. *Hydrangea petiolaris*, a self-clinging climber, is lovely in shade. It bears flat heads of lacy white flowers in summer.

ON A PEDESTAL

THE SIMPLEST ORNAMENT has more impact when raised. Keep costs down by using a piece of clay drainpipe, about a third taller than it is wide, for a pedestal. Lay a paving slab on a level bed of sand; cement the pipe on it. Fix a slightly smaller slab on top with cement and finish with an ornamental object such as a large seashell.

CHIMNEY POT CLUSTER Fill clay pots with *Verbena* 'Sissinghurst' or pelargoniums. Stand them against the wall, or on a step if you have one. A different level of interest and a splash of colour transform an unpromising area, turning a neglected side path into a pleasurable alley.

✿ For flower power in mild areas, the shade-tolerant 'Mermaid' is an excellent, nearly evergreen rose, with large, single creamy-yellow blooms until late autumn. Keep the growths tied in close to the wall; their thorns are vicious.

✿ For fragrance, plant the early and late Dutch honeysuckles, *Lonicera periclymenum* 'Belgica' and 'Serotina', both good in light shade.

At the other end of the narrow leg, where it joins the main garden, plant a couple of graceful shrubs such as *Acer palmatum* 'Bloodgood' or *Olearia virgata* on opposite sides, one a little ahead of the other. They invite you into the secret alley with a promise of delights to come.

SHOW STEALERS OUT OF TOWN

On the outskirts of towns there are many houses whose gardens are agreeably roomy. Often there is a garage at or joined onto one side of the house, presenting a large area of blank wall to a narrow side garden. If arches, niches or patterns of raised brickwork are incorporated at the building stage, they relieve the dullness. But when you inherit the wall you have to employ other methods.

A row of mop-headed, standard evergreens breaks up the base of a blank wall. *Elaeagnus pungens* 'Maculata' or silver-variegated *Ilex aquifolium* 'Argentea Marginata' give a light touch, while fast-growing privet is easy to train. Round their feet, grow half-square or half-circle 'containers' of clipped box or privet.

Alternatively, cover the wall with a plant 'trellis' trained and trimmed into a pattern of diamonds or squares copied from traditional trelliswork. Outline the pattern with strong wires stretched between vine eyes driven into the mortar, then tie in the young stems, clipping to shape as the plants grow. Pyracanthas or small-leaved ivies are suitable.

CLIMBERS FOR COVER

If two walls flank a wider area, train climbers to cover them and dangle overhead from a loggia or pergola of wooden beams, leading to the main garden. The Chinese gooseberry (*Actinidia deliciosa*) is suitable because it is hardy, happy in shade and grows in any well-drained soil as long as it is not too dry; it has vigorous, twisting stems and heart-shaped leaves.

Virginia creepers also do well in shade and turn a blank space and plain loggia into a living tapestry and ceiling. They climb by small tendrils with sucker-like

HIGHLIGHT ON A HOUSE WALL An espalier pear makes an elegant sentinel spreading its protective arms across the house. Clipped topiary pieces and a smart bench add to the soothing sense of order.

pads and have attractive leaves that colour up in autumn. *Parthenocissus tricuspidata* 'Lowii' has deeply cut leaves, *P. t.* 'Veitchii' turns a wonderful purple in autumn and *P. henryana* has pink-veined, bronzed leaves. For something less vigorous, grow a species clematis such as *Clematis flammula*, *C. chrysocoma* or evergreen *C. cirrhosa balearica*.

When one of the walls is sunny, make a central feature of a clematis, but shade its roots by tucking sun-lovers round the base, especially those that release their aroma as you brush past them: lavender, rosemary, purple sage, artemisia and *Cistus* × *hybridus* with dark foliage and large white flowers splashed with yellow.

SEASIDE PICTURE Add a breath of sea air to a bare wall by sticking shells and pebbles into wet plaster around a central tile or the head of a fountain. A coloured glass collage makes an inland substitute for beachcombing finds.

HIGHLIGHTS FOR THE SHADE

MOST GARDENS have areas of shifting shade throughout the day; others are in almost perpetual shadow. Shade is craved and created in a hot climate but in cooler regions care is needed if it is not to give a gloomy atmosphere.

Painting any walls in warm or sunny colours helps: a pinkish terracotta works well, as does a rich burnt cream or an acid yellow. Warm-coloured walls provide a pleasant backdrop for luxuriant groups of shade-tolerant plants. A surprising number prefer or even flourish in at least partial shade. Quite a few – aucuba, for instance – put up with very little light if given a soil that is fertile and reasonably moist but well drained.

ADDING VERVE TO A BASEMENT-FLAT ENTRANCE

Continual shade is most often found in towns, where tall buildings never let the sun reach the ground. One shaded area often encountered is the entrance to a basement flat, with steps leading down to the front area. A small rectangle of concrete may receive very little light, but it is a pity not to make something of it.

Build a sizable planter in at least one corner of the area, making sure it has drainage holes at the bottom. A shrub will grow comfortably in it for a few years before both compost and plant need replacing. Choose an evergreen to give year-round interest. Suitable plants include *Fatsia japonica*, *Choisya ternata*, *Viburnum tinus* and *Mahonia × media* 'Charity', which has striking leaves and scented yellow flower spikes throughout the winter. A rhododendron or a camellia needs a lime-free compost (described as ericaceous on the label). Illuminate the planter at night for extra pleasure.

For a more dashing scheme, paint the steps and the concrete with floor paint, in a strong blue, for example, then paint flowerpots or large tin cans a paler blue or perhaps yellow, and place one on each step. Fill the pots with ferns or trailing ivy. Be very daring and paint the walls sky blue, adding clouds, sun, birds and silhouettes of palm trees or huge cacti.

Paint planters, pots and window boxes to match; continue the green planting theme to soften the boldness with periwinkle, euphorbia, skimmia and hosta. Tie the door in with the scheme, painting the frame one colour and the panels another. Turn dustbins into a cheerful feature by painting them, either plain or in deck chair stripes.

DRAMA IN DEEP SHADE

Many of the ideas for basements can be applied equally well to back gardens. A shady garden gives scope for adventurous ornaments, and you can draw attention to sculptures and containers by fitting lanterns to shine on them. Paving comes into its own. Run a decorative edging round it and add a dramatic central motif. If the area has a smooth concrete base, use floor paint to create stencilled designs or a chequered pattern.

When the garden is enclosed by walls, painting them white or a bright colour helps to reflect and make the most of what light there is. For dramatic greenery, train a vigorous climber on ropes to hang in swags across one wall. More unusual than ivy or *Clematis montana* are

FOX AMONG THE FOLIAGE A surprise element such as a terracotta animal lurking in the undergrowth enlivens an area of ground-covering evergreens. Variegated *Lamium* keeps its white markings even in dense shade.

Schisandra rubriflora and, in mild areas, *Berberidopsis corallina*, both with deep red flowers. Within the swags, hang decorations, perhaps medallions of stained glass, ceramic plates, terracotta plaques or lead masks.

When there is not enough light and air to enable even shade-loving plants to flourish, use artificial means to liven things up. Tiles of black and white marble, terracotta, colourful ceramics from Spain and Portugal or crisp, white gravel lighten and brighten the ground. You might also consider artificial grass, choosing a soft olive-green.

Paint the walls white, give them a stencilled frieze and, as a central feature on each wall, paint a stylised bay, orange or lemon tree in a tub. At night, hang candle holders of plain or coloured glass on hooks round the walls and from an overhead trellis.

Alternatively, fix a frame of ornamental trellis on each wall round the painted tree. Instead of painting on plants, make

FOCUS ON THE SMALL SCALE Even the tiniest of shaded areas can give joy. All you need for the essence of a garden is a few bricks or tiles, a swirl of ivy across white-painted walls and an old stone trough brimming with alpines.

'trees' of twisted branches (available from many florists' shops), cementing them into pots or directly in the ground. Bricks, pebbles or dried moss hide the cement. A spotlight shows off the trees at night, or strings of the smallest Christmas-tree lights (exterior grade) add sparkle to the branches.

POTENTIAL OF LIGHT SHADE

In a garden where shadow is cast for part of the day or which is covered by the light shade of a deciduous tree, reflecting the available light brings the place to life.

Position a weather-resistant mirror so that it bounces any sunlight into the garden. When framed by a shallow arch of brick or latticed wood, this makes an attractive focal point in itself. The effect is doubled by placing something shiny,

BEST PLANTS

SHRUBS FOR SHADE

Evergreen shrubs make permanent features, and some can be clipped into shapes such as spires and drums.

• Privet (*Ligustrum lucidum* 'Excelsum Superbum'): large with yellow and creamy variegated leaves.

• Privet (*Ligustrum ovalifolium* 'Aureum'): medium height, yellow-green shrub good for topiary.

• Spotted laurel (*Aucuba japonica* 'Crotonifolia'): medium height with speckled leaves and scarlet berries.

• *Elaeagnus × ebbingei* 'Gilt Edge': yellow-edged leaves, silvery beneath.

• *Elaeagnus pungens* 'Maculata': large shrub with rich, yellow-centred leaves.

• *Skimmia japonica*: aromatic leaves and white flowers in spring; red fruits on female plants.

• Holly (*Ilex aquifolium* 'Argentea Marginata'): grows to a small tree unless checked; silver-margined leaves are shrimp-pink when young.

FLICKERS OF LIGHT White *Hydrangea macrophylla* shines like a beacon in a dimly lit garden. Twin pots of the shrub mark the pathway, drawing attention to the low step as well as dignifying the garden division.

LIGHT AND DARK Get the most from what light there is with pristine white metalwork, the more decorative the better. In the darkness of the corner and set off by the dark ivy, the ornamental arches shine like torches. Matching stone figures frame the centrepiece, leading the eye towards it.

COTTAGE GARDEN CORNER An old cartwheel gives a rustic air propped against the wall, where it doubles as a support for climbers. In front, the herb marjoram (*Origanum vulgare*) offers the twin rewards of flowers and flavour.

such as a metal sculpture, or something pale, such as a marble bust, in front of the mirror, where it will be highlighted by the reflected sunshine. Soften the edges of the arch with climbers and feathered clumps of bamboo or a pair of the silvery privets, *Ligustrum sinense* 'Variegatum'.

Another trick is to make a focal point of plants whose glossy leaves reflect light or whose flowers and foliage give an impression of light. Plants with gold, silver or variegated leaves are useful and white flowers look almost luminous, especially in the evening. Some golden plants, such as *Robinia pseudoacacia* 'Frisia' and the golden hop, tend to lose a degree of their brightness in the shade but, in compensation, take on soft green-yellow tints. Other yellow-leaved plants, such as the fragrant *Philadelphus coronarius* 'Aureus' and Bowles' golden grass (*Carex elata* 'Aurea') prefer shade for part of the day.

Where space is limited, let one small tree or large shrub with a long season of interest take a starring role. For instance, you could start with the yellow form of common elder, which has lacy white flowers in summer followed by small, dark fruit in the autumn. More elegant is its relative, *Sambucus racemosa* 'Plumosa Aurea'. Underplant this with a strappy-leaved day lily (*Hemerocallis*), which has yellow flowers, set within a semicircle of a low-growing evergreen such as *Euonymus fortunei* 'Emerald 'n' Gold'.

DEALING WITH SMALL AREAS

In a small garden a focal point needs particularly careful placing. Set either against the far boundary or somewhere along one of the sides, it draws the eye over the whole area, giving a feeling of more space, rather than halting the gaze in the middle of the garden.

A winding 'stream' of shingle, stone chippings and pebbles over sand between clumps of ground cover fits in a tiny corner and creates an element of wit. Outcrops of rocks, cobbles, small shells and patches of flat, slate pebbles make textural additions to the stream. Alternatively, make a 'pool' of a variegated ivy (*Hedera helix*) among some small boulders and gravel. In a long, narrow garden, two groupings of plants and statuary set on opposite sides, one just in front of the other, act as magnets, drawing you into a gentle meander down the length of the garden.

ACCENTS IN GREENERY

There is much to be said for the all-green approach, relieved only by touches of white – in seats, trellis, statues, flowers – for the eye to light on. In towns especially, such a scheme makes for an oasis, cool in summer, retaining its charm all winter and glimmering in twilight.

For a formal garden, you could give pride of place to a camellia, the rich green holly *Ilex* 'Camelliifolia' or the glossy dark privet *Ligustrum lucidum*. Underplant the privet with *Hedera hibernica*, which has large, mid-green leaves.

If the layout of the garden allows, make everything round. Concentric circles lead the eye to a crowning glory in the middle, made even more dramatic if it is an island of white amid green. Grow *Dicentra spectabilis alba* as the white centrepiece in a circular raised bed. Ring its retaining wall with paving.

White ornaments as well as white-flowered plants give a flicker of light. A white statue against a wall is bound to catch the eye. It attracts even more notice

PONIES ON PARADE High-stepping ponies add an unexpected accent tucked into a niche clipped in the boundary hedge. A pair of lead storks, statues or boulders works equally well, depending on the garden style.

TO THE RESCUE

STEADYING A STATUE

IT IS OFTEN HARD to get an ornament such as a statue to stay straight when it is freestanding in a flowerbed or border rather than on a solid plinth or a hard surface. The problem is usually worse after heavy rain or frost or in boggy soil. If your statue keeps lurching over, give it a level base.

Use a concrete paving slab bedded on sand if the base is hidden by flowers or foliage. A square of bricks is more decorative but needs a stable concrete foundation if the site is soggy.

HIGH AND MIGHTY An imposing pot is raised on an ivy-clad pedestal, and its warm terracotta is enhanced by the fat red winter buds of *Skimmia japonica* 'Rubella' and the rosy blooms of *Viburnum* × *bodnantense*.

MAKING COLOUR AND FORM STAND OUT The odd light or bright touch catches the eye all the more against a uniform backdrop. Beside the *Argyranthemum frutescens* and *Tulipa* 'Purissima', an empty jar stands in state – its shape, texture and colour contribute enough without plants.

in younger plants. Remove any shrubs obscuring a plant of such character and prune surplus growth from the lower branches so the dramatic shape emerges. Privet, lilac, euonymus and magnolia are candidates for this treatment.

Even a tree or shrub past its best can be transformed. Thread a climbing rose up through aged trees, choosing the shell-pink 'New Dawn' or 'Félicité Per-pétue' whose cream buttonhole blooms are red-flushed in the bud.

PLANTS THAT FLOURISH IN DEEPEST SHADE

The modern climbing rose 'Bantry Bay' thrives in the shade. With a succession of scented pink flowers, it thrives even in a pot and has an open-faced, relaxed look. A pair, planted on either side of the front door and intertwined with blue clematis, make an informal focus.

Honeysuckle evokes the rural past. Try growing one as a small standard, twisting it round a stake which can be re-moved when the stem is strong enough to support the head. It gains emphasis in a round or diamond-shaped bed, edged with granite setts and underplanted with primulas, busy lizzies and pansies.

For a more quirky rustic feature, plant mint in a battered bucket sunk into the soil beneath an iron pump. Surround it with the tiny, green leaves of mind-your-own-business (*Soleirolia soleirolii*) trick-ling between slate steppingstones. Dot clumps of lily-of-the-valley or London pride round about.

Awkward areas of deep, dry shade, under the canopy of a greedy-rooted tree for example, present problems. But even here you can make a favourable feature. Grass does not grow here, but paving creates a satisfying feature; if roots pro-trude above the surface, infill that area with pebbles or cobbles.

Some plants grow here, but improve the soil with rotted manure before plant-ing. As feature shrubs, *Aucuba* and the yellow-flowered *Mahonia aquifolium* are happy here. Edge the shrub bed with low-growing ivy, dead nettles (*Lamium*), periwinkles or × *Fatshedera lizei*.

In spring, snowdrops, purple cro-cuses and pink *Cyclamen coum* provide pockets of fresh interest under the bare branches of a deciduous tree. From May to August *Oxalis acetosella* offers white blooms on a low mat of grey-green leaves. Follow with clumps of pink and white *Cyclamen hederifolium* in autumn.

TOOLBOX

MARKING OUT A CIRCLE

TO MARK OUT a circle for paving or planting round a focal point, use a marking line – bought from an iron-monger or made by tying and rolling a length of string round two short, sturdy stakes. Push one stake in firmly at the centre of the circle then stretch out the string to the measurement of the circle's radius. Use the second stake to mark the circle in the soil. Show it up even more clearly by sprinkling sand from a bottle round the circle.

if set within a frame of dark-green trellis-work or within an arch formed by clipped evergreens such as yew or pyracantha.

Less formally, let the plants flow, seemingly at random, round the edges of a paved garden, here jutting out as a peninsula, there ebbing back to the walls, creating a series of hidden, sheltered areas, each containing a surprise as tradi-tional or as quirky as you like. Place a goddess amid camellias, a bronze toad among lilies of the valley or let a carved snake slither across paving.

IMAGINATIVE WAYS WITH RURAL SHADE

Shade is usually easier to deal with in the country garden than in the city: it is un-likely to be so dense and there are proba-bly plants already established.

Never remove mature plants without careful thought, for they have a character that commands attention. With age, many trees and shrubs take on a bold, gnarled form impossible to reproduce

A PLACE IN THE SUN

A SUNNY GARDEN is greatly to be desired. Many plants that do reasonably well in the shade reach their full glory only in the sun, while others barely survive without it. It is far easier to create shade for sun-wary people and plants than it is to let light into a dark garden. The scope for focal point plants is much greater in the sun – as it is for the accompanying furnishings and ornaments.

PLANTS THAT SPEAK OF WARMTH

Plants enjoy the shelter of a warm, walled garden or terrace as much as people do. Many striking, marginally tender plants survive quite far north in a walled south or west-facing garden – especially in towns, where it is warmer than in the countryside. The walls act as storage heaters and give you the chance to display a show-stopping plant of exotic origins or architectural appearance.

The beautiful, crinkled leaves of the tender evergreen honey flower (*Melianthus major*) are a most subtle colour, turning from jade to blue-green. Equally distinctive, the hardy palm *Trachycarpus fortunei* has large, fan-shaped leaves, and it grows well in containers. The swords and strap-leaves of agaves, yuccas, cordylines, phormiums and tender dracaenas also feel at home in sunny, well-drained areas. So do most species of the silver-leaved, spiky *Astelia*, whose rosette of swords makes a dramatic focal point, either on its own or set among plants that have soft, spreading foliage.

CLOTHING A TERRACE WALL

The terrace, usually in a spot that catches the sun, is where family and friends tend to gather on a summer's day. Plants, furniture and ornaments can increase the allure. In a small garden, a feature on the wall may be the focal point.

Some wall plants are imposing enough to hold the attention on their own. In early summer, wisteria cascades with scented white or purple flowers as the leaves are unfurling; in winter, the twisted bare wood has a sculptural value.

The Japanese crimson glory vine (*Vitis coignetiae*), which lives up to its name for autumn colour, the green-leaved *V.* 'Brant' (*continued on p.218*)

SUN-SOAKED ELEGANCE Few people nowadays use a sundial to tell the time, but it adds a classical touch to a white-hot border. All-white delphiniums, roses and *Crambe cordifolia* back up the graceful look of the ornament, and both hard and soft features radiate bleached warmth.

White wedding

Plant the enthusiastic climbing rose 'Wedding Day' to froth like a veil over an old apple tree. Beneath it, grow *Exochorda* × *macrantha* 'The Bride' behind a stone seat, and add groups of delicate *Dicentra spectabilis alba*, whose flowers hang like little heart-shaped lockets.

SOUVENIR GARDENS

It is a pleasure to look back at family anniversaries and happy memories. Why not use the garden as an 'album' and record these special times there?

THERE ARE FEW more charming ways to celebrate a birth or a coming of age than to design a part of the garden so that it will always bring the occasion to mind. By the time slow-growing plants reach maturity, the children should be of an age to appreciate them. And if plants are pot grown, they can be moved on when the young adults set up their own home.

Many wedding anniversaries are conveniently colour related, providing some rich opportunities for souvenir planting schemes. As well as giving the happy couple enjoyment at the time, the plantings make joyful records as they accumulate through the years.

Promised pair

Welcome arrival

Coming of age

To celebrate a birth, plant the standard rose 'Happy Child' to rise from a soft cloud of *Gypsophila paniculata*. Surround these with lavender – white (for innocence), or with blue or pink flowers if you prefer.

For an engagement, make a flowerbed in the shape of two entwined rings. Plant it with the cluster rose 'Dearest', edged with a miniature box hedge of *Buxus sempervirens* 'Suffruticosa'. Clipped cotton lavender (*Santolina chamaecyparissus*) fills the interlocking centre.

Instead of laying down a vintage wine for an 18th or 21st birthday present, give something that will mature just as magnificently. *Magnolia grandiflora* 'Galissonière' is a beautiful evergreen that takes about ten years to begin producing its waxy, fragrant flowers. Grow it in a pot for portability, ready for planting out when its owner settles down.

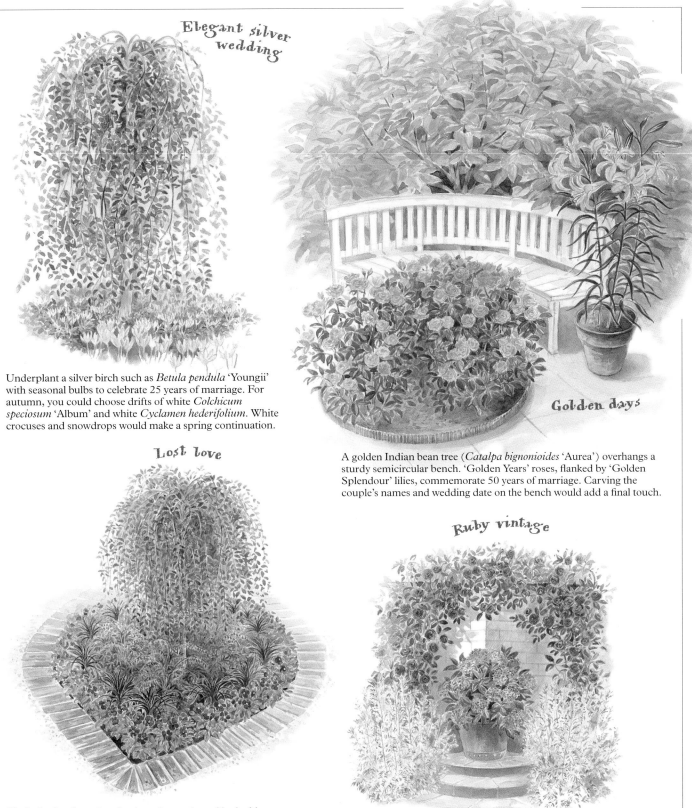

Elegant silver wedding

Golden days

Lost love

Ruby vintage

Underplant a silver birch such as *Betula pendula* 'Youngii' with seasonal bulbs to celebrate 25 years of marriage. For autumn, you could choose drifts of white *Colchicum speciosum* 'Album' and white *Cyclamen hederifolium*. White crocuses and snowdrops would make a spring continuation.

A golden Indian bean tree (*Catalpa bignonioides* 'Aurea') overhangs a sturdy semicircular bench. 'Golden Years' roses, flanked by 'Golden Splendour' lilies, commemorate 50 years of marriage. Carving the couple's names and wedding date on the bench would add a final touch.

Heal a broken heart by planting a heart-shaped bed with a small weeping tree such as *Salix caprea* 'Kilmarnock', whose catkins hang like fat tears. Surround the tree with bleeding-heart (*Dicentra spectabilis*) and edge the bed with clumps of the black grass *Ophiopogon planiscapus* 'Nigrescens'.

Forty years of marriage is aptly marked by trees and shrubs admired for ruby leaves and flowers. Frame the corner with two fragrant roses 'Etoile de Hollande', underplanted with *Artemisia absinthium* 'Lambrook Silver'. Give pride of place to *Hydrangea macrophylla* 'Pia'.

SUNBURST PICTURE UNDERFOOT The ground itself can be a talking point, performing double duty with an imaginative use of hard surfacing. A mosaic of cobbles gives an Italianate character to the courtyard, and the plain paving stones work in practical, restrained harmony.

change all that. Car travellers have plenty of choice. Oil jars, lanterns, statues and garden furniture are often found much more cheaply abroad. Those travelling by plane, train or coach can bring back a few choice ornaments such as conch shells from the beach, brightly painted pots or tiles. Group the souvenirs on the terrace as constant holiday reminders.

COOL IDEAS FOR SUN-DRENCHED BEDS

In a small, sunny garden a silvery-leaved weeping pear (*Pyrus salicifolia* 'Pendula') makes a deliciously icy-looking cascade of downy leaves. A weeping rose could be used instead. Most roses that weep, because they are ramblers, flower only once but 'Awakening' and 'Leverkusen' flower throughout the summer, as does the climber 'New Dawn'. Clematis or sweet peas in tints of mauve clambering up obelisks are also sun-lovers to make a feature of in a tiny garden.

In a narrow part of the garden, painted or stained arches, cut from marine plywood, act as bold punctuation marks when placed along a central shrub-lined stretch of path, both enticing the viewer on and framing the view into a broader, more open area ahead. Using the same tones for fencing and trellis-work, arches and gates creates a peaceful sense of unity. Where you wish to spice things up, choose hot splashes of pink cistus, orange Californian poppies or scarlet nasturtiums – all of them ardent sun-worshippers.

PLANTS TO PROVIDE RELIEF FROM SUMMER'S HEAT

Standing proud in a far corner, to give the garden some much-needed shade, the Indian bean tree (*Catalpa bignonioides*) looks handsome and has huge heart-shaped leaves. Add a circle of clipped box round the trunk for emphasis and winter interest.

If you have room, a sunken rose garden below the terrace will win admiration. You could plant it with that most obliging of pink roses 'Nathalie Nypels' around a standard wisteria.

In a garden of smooth lawns and undulating borders, focal plants that work well from a distance are varieties of Lawson cypress (*Chamaecyparis lawsoniana*) such as 'Green Pillar', 'Columnaris' (blue-grey) and 'Lanei' (yellow). At the end of the garden, a statue of Pan could draw you into the fretted shade of a false

and purple-leaved *V. vinifera* 'Purpurea' all give a romantic look to a wall. Another dramatic and vigorous climber, *Actinidia kolomikta*, has green leaves splashed with pink and white.

If you can make niches in the terrace walls, they will act as a magnet for the eye, whether left plain or with an ornament within. You could make a false niche by fixing a framework of brick or wood on the face of the wall.

Many sun-linked features are as useful as they are decorative. Sundials

are always a fascinating conversation piece, even more so with plants climbing up their sides. Traditionally placed at the centre of knot and herb gardens, sundials are seen to advantage when raised a little on a pedestal of stone or brickwork. To support the weight of such a heavy feature, put it on a solid base of concrete over hardcore or on a sturdy flagstone bedded in sand.

Most people collect souvenirs when on holiday yet neglect them once back home. Buying things for the garden will acacia (*Robinia pseudoacacia* 'Frisia'), which makes a splash of refreshing lime-yellow, rippling in the breeze.

BOLD AND MODERN TOUCHES

Decking looks distinguished on the sunny terrace of a modern house. Use long diagonals, and leave a hole or two in the timber for shade-giving plants. Palms such as *Trachycarpus fortunei*, a fig tree (*Ficus*) and stag's-horn sumach (*Rhus hirta*) all look stunning.

Much can be done to give the lawn impact. Inset sweeps of ground cover such as the silver cotton lavender and its green relative, *Santolina rosmarinifolia*.

Islands of stone on the lawn also make a strong statement. Plant them with clumps of *Pennisetum villosum*, *Stipa pennata* and other ornamental grasses, which come in many sizes and colours and are spectacular when spotlit at night.

For a modern centrepiece, choose an abstract sculpture presenting bold shapes in concrete, wood or metal. Or set a large cogwheel from an abandoned machine on a plinth made from breeze blocks coated with sand and cement.

A NOSTALGIC HAVEN

A sunny cottage garden should be a relaxed miscellany of shapes and colour, from a latticed porch smothered with jasmine to a crab apple in a corner, foaming with blossom in the spring and hung with bright fruit well into the winter.

For a raised attraction, make a circle of bricks or stone and top with a painted tub. In spring, fill the tub with hyacinths or tulips in a mist of forget-me-nots, followed by pelargoniums and petunias.

Millstones make period features, sunk flush with the ground or resting on it. The central hole creates a planter for a small shrub, such as the white *Hebe albicans* or blue-flowered rosemary. To add height, fit a tripod of canes next to it as a support for annuals such as sweet peas, black-eyed Susan (*Thunbergia alata*) or *Convolvulus tricolor* 'Heavenly Blue'.

To make the cottage wall the focus of attention, train a spectacular rose over it, preferably one with an old-fashioned appearance: 'Madame Grégoire Staechelin' is perfect. The large, loosely double, fragrant flowers of deep pink are produced only in early summer, but with unparalleled generosity. Train a clematis – the long-flowering blue 'Mrs Cholmondeley' or sky-blue 'Perle d'Azur' – up through the branches to prolong interest.

WELCOME SHADE-GIVER Pruned into a mop-head, *Pyrus salicifolia* 'Pendula' takes centre stage on the lawn and brings a little shade to a south-facing site. The weeping pear arrests the eye wherever you are in the garden.

HEIGHT ON A BUDGET Different levels of interest add a new dimension but there is no need to buy costly sculptures. Just a length of wood and a stone give a satisfying mix of rough and smooth, round and hard-edged.

BEST PLANTS

ARCHITECTURAL SHAPE

Plants with a strong outline arrest the attention. Their shape often comes from their leaves which, with some species, last all year.

• *Acanthus mollis*: perennial with glossy spires of leaves topped by mauve and white flower spikes in high summer.

• Indian bean tree (*Catalpa bignonioides* 'Aurea'): deciduous tree with large, yellow, heart-shaped leaves, white flowers and long seedpods.

• *Euphorbia characias*: tall, evergreen perennial with bold leaves and yellow flowers in early summer.

• *Gunnera manicata*: a perennial for damp soil, more than head high, with enormous rhubarb-like leaves.

• *Mahonia* × *media* 'Charity': large evergreen shrub with long rows of mid-green, hollylike leaflets and scented yellow flowers in winter.

• Royal fern (*Osmunda regalis*): head-high fern, tinted brownish pink and turning russet as it fades in autumn.

• Stag's-horn sumach (*Rhus hirta* 'Laciniata'): deciduous shrub with ferny leaves turning fiery in autumn.

IN SEARCH OF THE UNIQUE

ONCE YOU HAVE considered the garden's aspect, size, shape and style, it is time for the joyful hunt for the right feature to suit the chosen spot. You may already have a statue that you have been waiting to set out, a favourite plant you are longing to include, or an existing object to find a home for. But it is always worth scouting around for new ideas.

From ancient times, gardens have been embellished by containers and ornaments. Many old styles are still popular, helping to create atmosphere by strengthening both the design and the planting.

GARDEN DECOYS Stone partridges squatting on a sweep of gravel cut out of ground-cover plants introduce an element of wit to the garden. As an added advantage, maintenance of this area is cut to a minimum.

ANIMAL MAGIC AMONG THE PLANTS An inspired position exploits the humorous potential of farmyard statuary to the full. Peeping inquisitively and unexpectedly out of the flowerbed, this pig is likely to cause merriment in anyone strolling round a flowery informal garden.

Antique pieces are still found from time to time, and there are many reproductions about, varying in price and quality. Once weathered, pieces in reconstituted stone make acceptable substitutes for the real thing. Those fashioned from cement are not quite so successful. They lack the texture and take much longer to tone down, although the process can be speeded up by giving them several applications of liquid manure.

TRADITIONAL ORNAMENTS IN STRIKING SETTINGS

Place classic sculptures and period ornaments on the terrace or where the eyes may rest on them at the end of a path, pleached alley or green tunnel. Frame them with recesses, arches, niches, arbours and pavilions, or set them before a semicircle of clipped hedging, at the turn of a path, and between plant groupings of all kinds. Whether a sculpture is of stone, marble, slate, terracotta, metal or wood, there is an appropriate place.

✿ Use wellheads, water cisterns, stone troughs and ancient coppers both as ornaments and containers. Any one of them makes a fine frontispiece to a formal part of the garden.

✿ Wall features include moon windows, masks, plaques, medallions, sundials and panels of relief work, as well as alcoves, niches, recesses and wall fountains.

✿ Weather vanes are decorative on the roof of a house or outbuilding.

✿ In some old gardens, the walls have special recesses for beehives. It would be pleasant to revive the custom or to set hives in niches cut into evergreen hedges.

✿ Ornaments of oriental design – lanterns, Buddhas, dragons – usually look at home in a part of the garden sparsely planted with luxuriant foliage such as small maples or hostas and bamboos, among raked gravel or tiles.

WHEN TO BREAK THE RULES

While there is something reassuring about the traditional and familiar, an element of surprise spices up the garden. Even a formal scheme may benefit from the unexpected – all rules of style and scale can be broken occasionally. A traditional ornament gains extra attention when used in an unusual way; something bizarre, found where least expected, can make you laugh out loud.

Things that are out of scale with their surroundings, though usually to be avoided, can be very dramatic: one large

INGENIOUS FOCAL POINTS

The ornaments that enhance your garden design need not be costly originals – some can be had for a song or even for nothing. Look out for the possibilities about you: auctions and junk shops, car-boot sales and jumble sales all yield treasures.

ARCHITECTURAL SALVAGE
Many firms specialise in searching out decorative pieces. Demolished buildings may provide fragments of stonework, lanterns, columns, pediments and finials, marble and statuary.

IRONMONGERY
Metal wheels, bits of machinery, knife grinders, saucepan holders and rests, horseshoes and pieces of cast or wrought iron all make intriguing and offbeat ornaments for the garden.

HOUSEHOLD ITEMS
Choose from mangles, old saucepans, coal scuttles, milk churns and groups of flagons. Either leave them empty, or use them as unusual pots, if possible drilling holes in the bottom for drainage.

BESIDE THE SEA
Appropriate items for the seaside garden include a lobster pot, toy sailing boat, lengths of rope (neatly coiled), starfish and shells. Make smaller pieces into a wall collage or dot them around the garden.

FARM AND GARDEN
Use the wall of a cottage garden to hang or prop up a plough, cartwheel, beehive, watering can, forcing pot or scythe. Leave them in their weathered state, or paint them to stop rusting.

FROM THE COUNTRYSIDE
Boulders make natural sculptures and dead trees have many possibilities. Whittle them into statues, place plant pots and stones on their truncated branches or carve niches out of them to take a statue.

SPHERE OF SURPRISE The striking plant mix of ghostly sea holly, fleshy leaves of *Crambe cordifolia* and acid-yellow lady's mantle takes a twist with the addition of an armillary sphere, originally used to study the stars.

statue or urn may look magnificent in a small garden. In an L-shaped basement garden, for example, where a narrow leg of the L ends in a blank wall, be daring and fix a metal or wooden arch over the top to make an alcove. Paint the inside a warm colour and place within it a larger-than-life statue. By all the rules this is far too big for such a cramped space, but the effect is powerful.

You achieve a similar effect with a showy plant such as datura, a cordyline or one of the large-leaved ivies trained on a metal frame into a vast cone or spiral. Large plants become even more imposing in a restricted space. In moist, dappled shade, grow a tall bamboo, tree fern, the big rhubarb-like leaves of *Rheum palmatum* or the huge ones of *Gunnera manicata*. In a sunny, well-drained site, grow the sword-leaved dragon tree (*Dracaena draco*) or the fan palm (*Trachycarpus fortunei*). Seen against a light, these form dramatic silhouettes.

THE QUIRKY AND UNEXPECTED

A stone urn, usually seen on a pedestal, empty and sculptural or fully planted, has a wistful charm when found lying on its side among ferns and ivy. If the bowl on its pedestal is filled, not with bedding plants but with flints, fossils, seashells or marble eggs, it has a different impact.

BOAT NOVELTY Seaside gardens sprout the oddest objects, such as a dinghy awash with nasturtiums. Set in the front garden, the cheery, droll greeting brings an instant smile to the lips of the startled visitor.

A SPEEDY BASE

ONE OF THE TASKS that takes up most time in displaying a focal point can be making its ornamental foundation. Rather than laboriously cutting bricks or slabs to fit the required area, set them uncut into the outlined shape – be it round, diamond or square – and fill the gaps with gravel and plants. As the plants grow, they attractively soften the surface, while gravel gives the extra interest of mixed materials.

WATER PUMP AMONG THE FERNS Household aids that no longer fulfil their original function find a new career in the border. A gleaming coat of paint smartens the appearance of metal objects and helps to keep rust at bay.

Enormous stone fruit, scattered over the grass beneath a tree, look plumply beautiful and funny. A smile also comes at the sight of a giant foot on a column, a terracotta head lying at the foot of a seat or a marble baby nestling beneath the gooseberry bushes. Try a classical head among cabbages, a stoneware hot-water bottle at the bare feet of a goddess. Open books in slate or marble, favourites of the funeral parlour, look quite at home in the garden lying among greenery.

Hang small trees with medallions of stained glass that twist and gleam as they catch the sun. It would be fun to hang them on the bare, twisted branches of the corkscrew hazel in winter, before the catkins appear. In similar vein, fat ceramic fruit, say oranges and lemons, give a new character to rather proper mop-headed bay trees.

A copper 'fountain', made from pieces of thin piping, spouting up from a pool of gravel is a conversation piece in a modern setting and an amusing feature in a seaside or cottage garden.

Fix a rubber ball on top of a traffic cone (look in the local telephone directory for stockists) and spray both with metallic paint – copper, silver or gold. The homemade ornament makes a neat, indestructible focal point, at little cost – ideal for shade that is too deep for plants or for plots where children are likely to rampage. Larger balls, set on long lengths of drainpipe, painted or marbled, make impressive columns.

CUNNING DEVICES TO ATTRACT THE EYE

Use height to enhance effects in the garden, whether in the form of a rustic pergola or simply two or three steps.

🖝 A statue or urn gains instant prominence from being raised on some steps.

🖝 Aviaries and small-scale wooden dovecotes can serve ornamental as well as functional needs.

🖝 Hang fanciful birdcages and nesting boxes on walls and trees. If birds spurn them, install china doves or a wire spider.

🖝 A recess in a hollow tree might house a carved dryad, bronze owl, curled snake, Cheshire cat or perhaps gnomes.

🖝 In a wilder part of the garden, mossy logs catch the eye. Bleached and twisted

TRIUMPH OF TOPIARY You can buy wire frames to train plants such as ivy into specific shapes like a bird. Using different sizes turns a lone feature into a themed corner. The architectural bench is included as a stage – set for a cast of living sculptures – rather than a convenient seat.

roots, set on a raised circle, become a satisfying piece of abstract art.

☙ Turn a corner and you may find a green frog in the palm of a giant hand, a bronze butterfly alighting on a mushroom-shaped staddle stone or a willowy nymph resting among the greenery.

☙ Figures of people, plants and animals, cut from marine plywood and painted (the more primitive the better), bring instant height and jollity into a garden. Useful where nothing much will grow, they can be moved about to fill in gaps.

☙ Hang wind pipes or mobiles of stained glass, ceramic fragments, metal discs, shells or scraps of driftwood from a prominently placed arch or branch, to throw flecks of light and attractive shadows as the air currents catch them.

☙ Large shells, fossils and fragments of carved wood or chiselled stone all have their charms and uses. Tuck them here and there, on steps, at the corner of the terrace and among the plants.

SHOW-OFFS AMONG PLANTS

Apart from topiary, with its sculptural qualities and humorous potential, many plants are naturally imposing in form and foliage or curious in habit. Position can emphasise star quality. Dramatise the contrast by placing a pale plant against a sombre background, a column of dark green among light foliage, a spreading plant beside upright and sword-like leaves between low ground cover.

Where space allows, aim for a succession of plants to take pride of place as the seasons change. The first may be a maple (*Acer pseudoplatanus* 'Brilliantissimum') remarkable for its coral spring foliage, heightened by the carpet of *Anemone blanda* at its feet. As it fades the delectable pink-cream shrub rose 'Penelope' takes centre stage. When the rose withers, a hitherto unnoticed *Fothergilla major* flames with scarlet leaves.

Twisted branches, such as those of *Salix matsudana* 'Tortuosa', make intricate patterns against the sky in winter. Plants with yellow leaves and autumn colour reach a climax of beauty with the sun shining through them. Plants that look spectacular when the sun falls on them include the blue conifers, trees with curious or polished trunks – silver birch,

HISSING GEESE The whippy stems of willow are particularly pliable and can be twisted and bent into ornaments light enough to move around the garden at whim. Put them under cover for the winter months.

NOTE OF NOSTALGIA Old horticultural implements such as a lawn roller were made to last and are worth keeping to adorn the garden all year, especially when appropriately placed next to the toolshed. The flowering quince against the wall blooms all spring and bears fruit in autumn.

PENSIVE FIGURE A conversation piece arises partly from the feature itself and partly from where you position it. Seemingly wading in a lake of grey-green hostas, this stone philosopher-poet strikes a whimsical note.

GNARLED WOOD In the countryside, look for twisted roots, branches and mossy logs that will make a garden feature – at no cost. The sedums growing in the crevices draw attention to the interesting texture of the bark.

paper and snake-bark maples – and those with brightly coloured stems, such as willow and dogwood.

Mistletoe never fails to intrigue but is quite tricky to establish. Obtain berries from a known tree, and use the same species as host. Wait until the autumn berries are wholly ripe, make a slit in the bark on the underside of the host branch, insert the berry and seal the cut with clay.

On a bare wall, train climbers up to encircle a round window (real or false), a wall plaque or a piece of metalwork such as a Victorian coal-hole cover or an iron grille. In the shade, use ivy, hop, jasmine or *Clematis montana*. In the sun, try wisteria, golden hop, the semi-evergreen passionflower, evergreen *Solanum jasminoides* 'Album' or *Trachelospermum jasminoides*, with fragrant white flowers.

Make a feature of grass, by setting the mower blades at different heights and cutting it into patterns to surround and highlight a special plant or ornament. In small gardens, a square of lawn does not contribute much to the design but, if you round off the far end into a horseshoe shape or take a bite out of the edge nearest the house, it grows more interesting.

Whatever the size or style of your garden, there is room for at least one feature to stand out, so that the eye has something to home in on before taking in the broad sweep. As in a painting, a few judiciously placed accents encourage your gaze – and, in a garden, your feet – to meander over its length and breadth. The longer you live with a garden, the more your imagination finds scope.

GREAT GARDENS

GREAT COMP

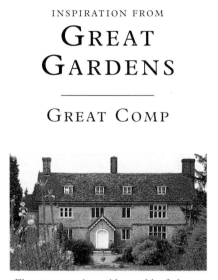

Elegant stone sits amid a wealth of plants.

*An informal mix of trees and
shrubs surrounds the 17th-century
manor house at Great Comp
near Borough Green in Kent,
setting the scene for the unexpected.
Among the many unusual touches
scattered around the grounds
is a bewitching moon gate
at the end of an alley of clipped yew,
which allows a glimpse
of a hidden garden beyond.*

IT IS AN ENDEARING TRAIT of many larger gardens that no matter how grand the general view, there is always room for more intimate corners. In the case of the garden at Great Comp, sinuous paths snake between banks of heathers and potentillas, busts of emperors and sages stare thoughtfully out of the hedges, and a woodland path leads to a weathered Grecian temple.

But the most striking visual feature in the garden is a moon gate, a circular opening in a wall which frames what lies beyond. Moon gates were very fashionable in Britain during the 19th century, and are thought to reflect the influence of Chinese style on English garden design. The wall and moon gate at Great Comp were constructed about 1840.

The gate is approached by a paved path running through a tall, narrow yew alley whose darkness throws the radiance of the scene beyond into relief, with the wall and the gate acting as both a divider and a link between two aspects of the

IN THE FRAME Two soaring conifers act as a focal point behind a broad, sunlit lawn, which is itself framed by a deep herbaceous border.

garden. The moon gate opens out onto an expanse of beautifully tended lawn which is edged with a colourful border of tiger lilies, buddleia, pink phlox and geraniums, among other plants.

ON A SMALLER SCALE

A moon gate works just as well in a small garden, adding interest to a dividing wall between a vegetable plot and an ornamental area, for instance. In the example below, a gate 6 ft (1.8 m) high has been cut out of a piece of trellis fence and strengthened on each side with strips of marine plywood. The trellis acts as a climbing aid for plain, dark ivies, grown up both sides of the trellis to give it a dense, solid appearance.

The significance of a moon gate lies in the subject it frames, however. Here, a colourful sycamore *Acer pseudoplatanus* 'Brilliantissimum', whose leaves are shrimp-pink in spring and bright yellow in autumn, grows out of a frame of unmown grass in a shaven lawn. Behind lies a border of bold lime-green *Euphorbia characias*, plump, upright conifers and irises whose sword-shaped leaves form fans below the late May blooms.

SCREEN THAT REVEALS A dense, small-leaved ivy grows up both sides of a trellis moon gate, its dark foliage making the perfect frame for a sycamore with brilliant spring and autumn leaf.

CREATIVITY WITH CONTAINERS

W HETHER YOU WANT a vibrant splash of colour, year-round pleasure from shapely clipped evergreens, or a bloom-laden camellia when your garden soil is against it, plants grown in containers are a boon. Put them where you will, on grass or concrete, to enliven a dull corner, flank an entrance or to stand in groups in a paved courtyard. Whatever container you choose – old wheelbarrow, black plastic bucket, simple wooden trough, well-used terracotta pot or graceful stone urn – imaginative planting will make it into a small-scale garden that constantly delights.

*Decorative clay pots give added interest to
a lush summer planting of pelargoniums and verbenas.*

THE POTENTIAL OF POTS

GROWING PLANTS in containers is the one activity most gardeners share, whether they own broad acres, a mere pocket handkerchief in town, or a single windowsill. Almost all gardeners do it, and most gardens would benefit enormously if it were done more.

Holidays abroad often inspire the first interest in containers – perhaps when a Mediterranean village delights with a blaze of bloom in every small courtyard or in the tiny space between door and pavement. No empty space is wasted, and any opportunity to bring growth to an otherwise bare spot is eagerly taken.

Often there is no natural soil, so every possible container capable of holding some is brought into play. There are old pots and dishes from the kitchen, and dented tins still faintly proclaiming the virtues of the olive oil they held in an earlier life. The very profusion of containers, and the insouciant tumble of their pelargoniums, basil or marjoram against faded ochre walls, lifts the spirits.

Inspiration may also begin in the totally different world of the great British gardens that attract visitors by the thousand. Elegant urns lining a terrace and large pots guarding a gateway spark off ideas for enhancing the garden at home.

COUNTING THE VIRTUES

Containers offer an instant effect that even the most patient gardener finds hard to resist. A young oak planted in the earth takes years to make an impact. But if your plant is an evergreen shrub in a container, its lush foliage immediately gives the air of a mature garden.

When your containers are light enough to be moved, you can put them where they are most needed – to hold up a fragrant nosegay beside a favourite summer seat or to give welcome winter bloom outside a window. Set a striking container in a prominent position and it makes a dramatic focal point; or you can use lesser pots to draw the eye to an interesting combination planting. Containers are equally effective in distracting from an eyesore or bare patch, or in simply covering the problem.

Many plants give more value for less outlay when you grow them in containers. Half a dozen petunias in a large pot spill out liberally, and – so long as they are well looked after – provide an effect that five times the number is hard-pressed to achieve in a bed. And these same petunias reveal their little-known scent simply by being lifted closer to you.

If you garden on chalk or limestone, you need no longer do without rhododendrons or camellias. Put them in large pots or tubs of lime-free soil, and bend nature to your will.

POSITIONED TO PERFECTION A wonderfully healthy hosta in a simple terracotta pot transforms a shady pathway. Its large leaves with subtle variegations capture any rays of sunlight, intensifying them and making a dazzling focus for the play of light and dark in this cool scheme.

CHOOSING CONTAINERS

W HILE IT IS POSSIBLE to use anything that holds a handful of soil, so long as it has a drainage hole, you gain the greatest effect by carefully suiting a container to its site and the job it has to do. The happy miscellany of old pots and tin drums that gives joy in a sun trap abroad soon palls in a wintry Yorkshire.

Over the years most people accumulate sundry containers, some fit to take on star roles in a group, some more utilitarian and better placed in the back row or masked by nearby plants and their own cascades of growth. Hanging baskets, flat-backed pots and half baskets are invaluable where space is limited.

As far as possible, choose containers whose style, material and colour are in keeping with the overall design of the house and garden. They should not jar. Classical urns outside a simple cottage or a planted dinghy in the middle of a town can look comical rather than pleasing. For prominent display, choose a container that will never bore. It is part of the garden's permanent scene with the power to transform any green space.

HIGH STYLE AT VARIED COST

Anyone with a fat purse need fear no shortage of choice. There is always a wide range of antique pieces, including urns in stone or cast iron, lead cisterns and the terracotta jars which ancient Greeks and Romans used for storage. Many specialist dealers keep large stocks.

Look for reproductions to bring the cost down but still get a piece grand enough for a major focal point. Often, reproductions are made from glass fibre or 'reconstituted stone' (virtually a superior concrete). The best have crisp moulding and develop a patina of age.

A thin coat of live yoghurt or liquid manure speeds the weathered look, proving irresistible to algae and mosses. The pot's location influences the finish. One left in the sun develops grey-white patches of lichen, while one in the shade takes on a green film of moss.

TRADITIONAL AND MODERN

Few shapes have been more successful or more practical than that of the humble flowerpot. Until 20 or 30 years ago, large and small potteries around the country

MAKING IT MORE SHAPELY

With their strong architectural shape, urns lend themselves to bold and profuse planting. Think in terms of shape – height and depth – as well as colour when selecting flowers and foliage.

Plantings in urns look meagre without height.

URNS ARE among the most stately of all containers, and look beautiful even when left empty. However, they lend themselves so well to plants that it is a delight to plant them up. If you have a rather straggly arrangement (left), it is easy to improve upon it and create two totally different images. For summer, aim for an exuberant, lively look, with frothy cascades of pretty pastel flowers surrounding a bushy centrepiece.

For spring you can create something bolder. This arrangement of trailing ivy framing the nodding heads of the small pansies, which form a ruff round the upright tulips, is ideal. It has plenty of style and makes a balanced shape. The combination of deep green and rich purple-black, offset by the white, looks striking without being stark.

Spring contrasts

The tall *Tulipa* 'Diana' and white-flowered forget-me-nots (*Myosotis*) contrast dramatically with the dark pansies (*Viola × wittrockiana* 'Black Beauty'). Ivy (*Hedera helix* 'Eva') cascades round the elegant grouping.

Summer froth

The delicate, trailing stems of *Sphaeralcea munroana* are balanced by the bushy dense white daisylike flowers of *Argyranthemum foeniculaceum*.

POTS, TUBS AND BASKETS

Grand or humble, real or imitation, elaborate or plain, containers offer more scope to spend or save money and stimulate the senses of sight and touch than many garden features. The pleasure of obtaining a treasure is only the start – planting up a pot adds the next dimension.

GLAZED CERAMICS

Oriental-style storage jars transform a balcony but need to be brought indoors before winter frosts. Choose simple plants that do not compete with the pattern.

STRAWBERRY PLANTERS

Place a tall pot with bulbs or fruit growing out of the sides among a group of plainer containers so it stands out. Put your most precious or hardest-to-grow plant at the top, where growing conditions are kindest. Alternatively, grow several herbs in one strawberry pot by the kitchen door.

IMPROVISING, MIXING AND MATCHING

Part of the fun of container gardening comes from pressing bizarre planters into service. Track down an old zinc bath, a butler's sink, a galvanised bucket, a wicker basket, a castellated chimney pot, a terracotta bowl on a pedestal, some old paint pots, or even a worn-out hiking boot. Other possibilities are car tyres, watering cans, teapots and jugs, a wooden wheelbarrow – let your imagination soar.

HANGING BASKETS

Invaluable for maximising growing space, hanging baskets or wall-mounted fixtures raise plants to eye level. Let annuals overspill and cascade down the edges in summer – some models come with built-in water reservoirs to prevent plants from wilting – and fill with pansies in winter, or choose foliage plants for a sophisticated town look. A climber such as morning glory decorates the suspending wires, too.

TERRACOTTA ELEGANCE

Some terracotta pieces have charm enough even without plants. In the ancient Greek style, choose amphorae or pithoi (originally for oil and grain) for a prime place, perhaps flanking steps or an arch. Swagged pots are easier to plant but still deserve a formal spot in keeping with their stately grace, while duck shapes suit a more quirky setting.

STYLES IN WOOD

More than any other material, wood can reinforce the style of its setting. A Versailles box planted with an evergreen clipped into shape lends gravitas to a smart town patio, while a half-barrel or trug brimful of petunias and pinks adds rustic charm to the ordered chaos of a cottage garden. Most wooden tubs are broad and deep. Take advantage of this by planting a shrub – possibly a lavatera or a hydrangea.

TOP OF THE RANGE

Urns in natural or reconstituted stone give a sense of maturity to the garden – not least because they are too solid to move easily. They may be designed with classically inspired patterns such as dolphin motifs or basketwork relief, or come in exotic tangerine or pineapple shapes. A stone trough is ideal for holding an alpine garden or an array of succulents.

CLAY FLOWERPOTS

Every container garden needs flowerpots to suit plants at each stage of growth and to set off more dramatic wares. For a hint of variation, buy one with a coloured ceramic rim. A matching saucer helps to keep the soil moist. Plastic imitations copy the mellow tones of clay at a lower price.

CISTERNS

An antique lead cistern, weathered over the centuries, adds to a planting of bright colours or feathery foliage. Glass fibre planters mimic the real thing and are lighter on the purse and for moving.

were using local clay to turn pots out by the million in every size from tiny 'thumbs' to huge two-footers. A group in different sizes holding a profusion of healthy plants, lining a patio wall, clustered around a seat, or marching down a flight of steps – with the height of pot and planting descending with the steps – is guaranteed to look good.

As more gardeners appreciate the charms of clay pots, examples that appear in the garden sundries section of country house sales are eagerly snapped up. In fact the demand has stimulated a renaissance in clay-pot manufacture.

Besides being attractive and having a shape that makes it easy to turn out a plant and its rootball, clay flowerpots have the advantage of being porous. Water evaporating from them helps to keep plant roots cool during hot weather.

In recent years clay pots have been ousted from favour by plastic. Despite the dire forecasts of gardeners wedded to tradition, plants grow just as well in plastic pots as in clay. Indeed plastic pots do not dry out as quickly, so need watering less often, and the slight flexibility of the plastic withstands frost well.

Brown and muted green plastic pots usually look most appropriate in a garden, reflecting the colours of nature; however in dark areas a light colour is often welcome. Decorating pots is easy and works remarkable transformations.

VERSATILE WOOD

Whether revealing its natural beauty or painted for elegance, wood always enhances its surroundings. There are few smarter containers than a Versailles box.

This was invented in the 17th century for the formal gardens of Louis XIV's palace of Versailles. The orangerie held a couple of thousand citrus trees in boxes, all of which were trundled out every summer to grace the terrace and line the walks. Scaled down to a size suitable for the more typical garden, this pattern of box still holds good – basically a cube with feet and finials at the corners. A pair of boxes painted to match the woodwork of the house and holding clipped evergreens adds formality to a doorway or the top of steps leading to a patio.

The half-barrel is cheap, easily available and deep, providing attractive opportunities for planting.

Check how the wood has been treated before you buy, as many wooden tubs have been coated with creosote,

POT GARDEN A cluster of different sized pots, whether placed on paving stones or gravel, looks superb in a tiny town courtyard or the corner of a larger country garden. For a stunning effect, aim for a variety of leaf shapes and textures, and arrange the tallest pots and plants at the back.

traces of which can damage root tips. Keep your barrels moist; if they dry out the wood shrinks, allowing the metal hoops that hold them together to slip off.

OFFBEAT PLANTERS

Many containers not originally intended for plants work very well. Try to find those which are nearly as broad as they are high, as the proportions are more pleasing and they will be easy to plant up.

Most plants appreciate being in a large container with enough space for their root run. Look out for pieces with sturdy handles which help when moving them.

There are numerous alternatives to the rather grand containers. In fact almost any hollow objects can be planted up from baby baths to discarded boots. If the container is of a material susceptible to frost use it only for short-lived annuals or put it in a sheltered area for the winter.

DECORATING POTS

INEXPENSIVE PLASTIC containers are easily transformed with a coat of matt-finish acrylic paint to give splashes of cheery colour or to create more formal and elegant plant-holders.

If the plant you intend to grow in the container is flowery, decorate the pot discreetly with sponging.

A foliage-interest plant will have added impact in a patterned pot. Six or eight broad stripes in alternate subtle colours always look good, and if you want a little more exuberant detailing add a stencilled design.

SPONGING Put on the base coat of paint and wait for it to dry completely. Dip a sponge in the second colour and dab to give an even, light covering.

STENCILLING Cut out a simple repeated motif from card. Tape it in place and paint over the holes. Remove the card carefully to avoid smears.

SIMPLE STYLE Tall *Lilium regale* against a backdrop of green foliage look sumptuous even in the plainest pots when close set in a group. The frothy flower heads of *Alchemilla mollis* clustered around their base soften the hard lines of the pots and accentuate the lilies' spiky leaves.

MOVABLE CONTAINER *Argyranthemum frutescens* in an old wheelbarrow are trundled to a bare area of gravel to make an informal showpiece. Pink pelargoniums, brilliant yellow calceolaria and trails of ivy foliage set off the dazzling white display.

UNUSUAL POTENTIAL OF TILES Houseleeks (*Sempervivum*) come in a wide range of colours and textures, and are able to grow in very little soil. Their fleshy leaves and curious shapes give them an alien air suited to such an eccentric container as an upturned roof tile.

From a valuable Roman sarcophagus to a chipped enamel bathtub there is only a matter of degree.

What makes each pot or curiosity effective in the garden is a combination of siting and associated planting both in and around the container. Old wooden wheelbarrows, stone sinks, decorative chimney pots, washroom coppers, iron cauldrons and galvanised hip-baths all serve as containers. Even vessels that initially look unappealing soon take on a more attractive appearance when profuse trailing plants cover their sides with flowers and foliage.

Of course not all unusual containers need be old, for many countries still follow time-honoured methods when making utilitarian storage items. Earthenware containers from the Mediterranean and pickled-cabbage crocks from China are especially attractive, but some need drilling with drainage holes. From nearer home, wicker baskets coated with floor sealant, big builders' buckets and storage bins work very well.

☛ Old chimney pots, which sometimes have attractive patterns around the rim, look wonderful with plants spilling over

MINIATURE LANDSCAPE A sink garden is the perfect spot to experiment with alpines and dwarf plants which would be lost elsewhere in the garden. Set among fern fronds of *Dryopteris*, the bell-shaped heads of blue *Aquilegia bertolonii* contrast with the narrow leaves of *Iris graminea*.

CHOOSING THE PLANTS

WHEN CHOOSING PLANTS, strike a balance between container size and plant size; a tiny plant looks ridiculous in a vast urn or tub. The container's shape, too, makes a difference to the ratio between plant and pot. A profusion of leaf and flower tumbling from a narrow, tapered pot is most pleasing to the eye, but this abundance will be short-lived when there is not enough soil for the roots to run freely.

Avoid meanness in the planting and aim for luxuriance and extravagance. Compose a harmonious shape, with the taller plants at the back or the centre, and a gradual descent to a frill of foliage or bloom at the rim. For a makeshift container, choose plants such as nasturtiums and periwinkle that will quickly tumble out and over its edges to create a dense, concealing curtain.

Every type of plant – bulb, tender annual, sturdy perennial, shapely shrub or even small tree – offers its particular benefits and with a bit of planning you can enjoy container plants in flower all year round. Containers have such eye-catching potential that successes or failures are particularly noticeable, but mistakes are easily rectified.

GETTING THE BEST FROM EVERGREEN SHRUBS

Where containers are a principal part of a garden – in a town courtyard or on a balcony, for example – a permanent framework such as evergreen shrubs can provide is a boon. Fortunately, with proper care and the right size of pot, almost any shrub grows happily.

The 'instant garden', every gardener's dream, is attainable with containers and container-grown shrubs, indeed this is how most plants are sold in nurseries and garden centres. When you want only two or three plants, it is not too extravagant to buy items of a considerable size and to pick the best available.

Whether left to develop informally or clipped and trained into topiary shapes, evergreen shrubs can be attractive. But make your choice carefully; while topiary shrubs maintain their desirable characteristic – their strong shape – through the year, many flowering shrubs have several undistinguished· months. When

the sides, and can add valuable height to the back of an arrangement.

🌱 Wheelbarrows are best suited to a rustic site in the country and look pretty bursting with simple flowers such as the trailing, tumbling blooms of nasturtiums.

🌱 Decaying dinghies by the seaside are given new life when planted with unpretentious poppies, such as the yellow horned poppy (*Glaucium flavum*) or tansy (*Tanacetum*).

🌱 Superannuated car or even tractor tyres at the garage look cheerful ablaze with pelargoniums and salvias.

🌱 A shallow sink makes a perfect home for bonsai (miniature trees), or tiny alpines and dwarf bulbs, or plants needing very little soil such as sedums or houseleeks (*Sempervivum*).

🌱 Old-fashioned kitchen equipment – bread crocks, iron cauldrons and earthenware pots for preserving eggs – make wonderful one-off containers. These are all particularly suitable for growing herbs in, and look attractive, as well as being practical, placed beside a kitchen door.

🌱 A beautiful old washroom copper can provide dramatic spring colour when planted with bright red tulips.

BEST PLANTS

SUITED TO SINKS

Alpines and other dwarf plants show up best in a shallow sink.

• *Androsace sempervivoides*: evergreen rosettes with pink flowers in spring.

• Fairy foxglove (*Erinus alpinus*): semi-evergreen with white, pink or purple flowers in late spring.

• *Campanula waldsteiniana*: saucer-shaped blue flowers in summer.

• Rockrose (*Helianthemum lunulatum*): Tiny shrublet with many bright yellow flowers in summer.

• *Achillea* × *lewisii* 'King Edward': semi-evergreen with lacy grey leaves and yellow flower heads all summer.

• Gentian (*Gentiana verna*): bright blue trumpet flowers in spring.

• *Oxalis adenophylla*: grey leaf rosettes with mauve-pink flowers in spring.

• *Phlox caespitosa*: evergreen with white or lilac flowers in summer.

UNDERSTATED SPLENDOUR Even the simplest planting looks stylish in such an elegant container as this stone urn. This variegated ivy appears almost golden in the sunshine, and will maintain its good looks throughout the year with almost no attention or effort on the part of the gardener.

up in summer after a few years' growth.
🌢 New Zealand cabbage palm (*Cordyline australis*), ideal for city courtyards and the mild west, has statuesque, swordlike leaves all year.
🌢 Red-hot pokers (*Kniphofia*), with tall spikes of bright tubular flowers, look spectacular. Swordlike leaves of some, such as *K. caulescens*, are evergreen.
🌢 Conifers that are suitable for containers and give year-round interest are the rugged mountain pine (*Pinus mugo*) and dwarf Siberian pine (*Pinus pumila*).

SMALL DECIDUOUS TREES AND SHRUBS

Even a diminutive garden gains enormously from a beautiful tree carefully placed. Many trees thrive happily in a container, although pot-grown trees cannot be very large or heavy. More important than size is an interesting structure and branching-pattern. Japanese maples – which make excellent container specimens – develop these virtues naturally, but careful pruning develops such character in other plants.

Look for trees which provide year-round interest. Maples, especially Japanese maple (*Acer palmatum* 'Rubrum') and *A. japonicum* 'Aureum', are attractively shaped and offer foliage in dramatic shades of red, orange and gold in autumn. The weeping purple beech (*Fagus sylvatica* 'Purpurea Pendula') also offers vivid coloured leaves – deep purple which turns to orange and gold before they are shed in autumn.

A tree that lights up any corner is the Scotch laburnum (*Laburnum alpinum*). Old plants develop strange, twisted branches and produce cascades of golden-yellow flowers in late spring.

For a mass of frothy blossom, *Prunus* offers a huge choice. A couple of the best dwarf species are the Japanese apricot (*Prunus mume*), which flowers in late winter or early spring, and the small ornamental almond shrub *P. tenella* 'Fire Hill', which has delicate willowy stems and is smothered in pink flowers in April.

Many deciduous shrubs are quite at home in a container. For spectacular spring blooms nothing surpasses a magnolia. The dwarf *Magnolia stellata* is especially suitable for a container as even in open ground it grows to a maximum height and spread of 8-10 ft (2.4-3 m).

Hydrangeas are popular pot shrubs, and deservedly so, for the full flower heads last for a long time and come in a

placed prominently in a container, they cannot merge into the background as border plants do. Choose shrubs that have more than one brief moment of glory.
🌢 *Rhododendron* Cilpinense has a display of pink-and-white flowers in April. A mahogany polish develops on the bark of old plants and the hair-fringed leaves are attractive all year.
🌢 *Rhododendron* Temple Belle carries pink bells in loose clusters, and when

spring is over still draws the eye with shiny, heart-shaped leaves.
🌢 *Pieris formosa forrestii*, a lime-hater like the rhododendrons, drapes itself in late spring with chains of little white bells. Drama follows with brilliant scarlet shuttlecocks of new leaves.
🌢 *Yucca gloriosa* has long, narrow leaves that make a striking architectural statement, especially in the variegated form. A spire of white flowers may be thrown

EASTERN SOPHISTICATION Bonsai trees are a fascinating blend of the minute and the mature. This beautiful Hinoki cypress in a handsome china pot is the product of years of painstaking work, all aimed at making the tree appear ancient – an impression increased by its gnarled trunk.

wide range of colours from the purest white through brilliant pink to cool blue. Other useful shrubs are forms of bush mallow – *Lavatera* 'Rosea' and the blush pink *L.* 'Barnsley'. Among the many roses that grow well in containers are repeat-flowering hybrids or patio roses such as 'Drummer Boy'.

Winter interest comes, surprisingly, from some deciduous shrubs. *Viburnum farreri* has delicate, pink-budded white winter flowers on the bare stems, and the dogwood *Cornus alba* 'Westonbirt' glows with clustered straight red stems.

THE MATURE CHARMS OF BONSAI

Bonsai takes pruning and controlled growth to extreme lengths, with normally full-size trees and shrubs being dwarfed to create beautiful miniatures that suggest great age. A bonsai collection makes a specialised pot garden, which needs persistent care as well as a long time span; some famous specimens are several hundred years old but there are short cuts to the bonsai effect.

The hardy dwarf conifers used in rock gardens make excellent pseudo-bonsai, and offer solid evergreen foliage in a range of colours from the dark green upright *Juniperus chinensis* 'Stricta' to the paler shade of the spreading *Picea pungens* 'Montgomery'.

Use a cotoneaster or a pyracantha for quicker growing bonsai. These shrubs allow you to experiment with pruning and training the shoots into the characteristic gnarled shapes.

The choice of container is vital as it should be in keeping with both the shape and the aged appearance of bonsai. The shallow, glazed traditional Japanese containers always look the most elegant, as well as being perfectly in keeping with the proportions of the trees. A stone, or stone-effect, sink also looks suitably ancient, and is a perfect depth.

UNTROUBLED BY WINTER

There really are no over-wintering annuals or biennials equivalent to the tumbling plants of summer, so winter is a good time to bring on the single most valuable evergreen for containers – the native British ivy (*Hedera helix*). Easy to grow, it has big or tiny leaves – rounded,

YEAR-ROUND VALUE Pretty pansies sit perkily in a wall-mounted terracotta pot. This takes only minutes to plant up and hang, yet can transform a bare patch of wall, making a charming focal point in summer and winter.

heart-shaped, arrowhead, bird's-foot – and comes in plain green, gold, and with cream variegations. Few hardy plants immediately give such an established look to newly planted containers. On top of this, ivy can cope with all but the very worst that winter sends.

Periwinkles (both *Vinca major* and *V. minor*), with their green or variegated leaves, do not have (continued on p.240)

A GARDEN CONTAINED

With a half-barrel and a pair of pots you can prepare a floral feast that will brighten the dullest niche. Each recipe can be adjusted to suit the aspect and the season.

AS THE EGYPTIANS, the Persians and the Moors long ago discovered, the answer to a tough climate and a thankless terrain is containers. With their help, a disregarded corner can be transformed into an ornament of the garden.

Containers, being raised, catch the eye more readily than flowerbeds, and will accommodate plants to cheer nearly any aspect. Almost anything can be grown in them. In the manner of flower arrangers, container gardeners can quickly change the display to suit the season, a mood or an occasion. And, providing they underplant with spring bulbs, they can look out on gardens that are in near-permanent bloom.

White for Maytime

Provided the site is sheltered, adorn late May with the white tree peony 'Joseph Rock' and give it a daphne with cream-edged leaves for company. Thyme and blue-flowered 'Severn Sea' rosemary make a darker contrast. Later, the rose flowers of thyme will look well against the mixed colours of love-in-a-mist.

Colour in April shade

Leading a late spring display in this shadowed site are the white flowers and red leaves of *Pieris* 'Forest Flame' together with blue sprays of *Brunnera macrophylla*. Neither *Iris foetidissima* nor periwinkles mind shade and their variegated leaves look well against the yellow flowers of *Berberis candidula*. At present, the knotweed (*Polygonum affine*) 'Darjeeling Red' beneath the berberis is no more than a leafy mat, but in July will pay for itself with a mass of pink spikes.

Promise of spring

Sunshine is not plentiful in February, but even in half shade, the site can be made sprightly by the catkins of contorted hazel, some bright narcissi, the long-lived white of *Arabis caucasica*, the pale green flowers of Corsican hellebore and the blue of *Chionodoxa luciliae*. The approach of spring is confirmed by the budding dwarf pink *Rhododendron* Cilpinense.

Warm touch in March

In March the camellia 'J.C. Williams' is still in flower behind the early spring flowering *Tulipa kaufmanniana*. Gold narcissi flower shortly after and the evergreen *Abutilon* 'Ashford Red' will produce salmon red flowers from May onwards. In summer, the myrtle bears aromatic white flowers while perennial scarlet tropaeolum scrambles through the camellia.

Ripe September glow

In a part-shaded patch in September, the back of the stage is held by autumn crocuses supported by a purplish Japanese maple. A pair of aucubas hold the centre – a female 'Salicifolia' with berries and, across the steps, a male 'Lanceleaf' without. In the foreground is *Yucca gloriosa* 'Variegata'.

Midsummer gold

In July, a partly shaded corner suits the blue-leaved *Hosta tokudama*, now in flower. *Rhododendron concatenans* also has blue foliage, emphasised by the grey green of Swiss willow, some narcissus spears and a gold-leaved spirea. Nemesias supply the cream and orange highlights.

October fire

Full autumnal sun rouses imperial tints in the spiky *Cordyline australis* 'Purple Tower'. Its richness is accentuated by mauve *Liriope muscari* and some deep red *Sedum* flowers. The few bright *Corokia cotoneaster* fruits will be replaced soon by rosy winter pansies mixed with silver-leaved *Senecio cineraria*.

Summer pastels

June brings full sun to bathe the soaring new leaves of *Aralia elata* 'Variegata', and coax out the first flowers of 'Heavenly Blue' morning glory. The white flowers of the small shrub *Sorbus reducta* are just ending, giving way to white candytuft and the pale pink rock rose *Cistus × skanbergii*.

239

WARM WINTER SHOW *Pyracantha* 'Orange Glow' is a wall shrub for year-round interest. It comes into its own in winter when it is covered in orange-red berries, making it an ideal choice for training against a white wall.

SPRING SHOW A mass of delicate pansies tumbling over each other cannot fail to draw the eye. Here the pretty pastel colours of *Viola* 'Antique Lace' look fragile but flourishing against the sombre brown of the rustic basket.

the bulk of the ivy, but they do have some of its desirable weeping habit in gracing a pot, with the bonus of a sprinkling of blue, purple or white flowers. The double-flowered forms of *Vinca minor* are even more effective.

Invest in some shrubs that will give touches of brighter colour to the winter container display.

- *Daphne odora* 'Aureomarginata' has cream edges to its evergreen leaves and in late winter every twig bears a cluster of fragrant white-and-pink flowers.
- *Skimmia japonica* 'Rubella' has crimson buds among the evergreen leaves on the male plants in winter before the white flower heads open up in March.
- *Mahonia japonica* is crowned with perfumed lemon sprays of bloom through the winter; its ranks of mid-green holly-like leaflets are striking all year, and some of them take on crimson tints in winter.
- Set some empty pots among your group of container shrubs so that you can pop in a succession of pots of bulbs as they come into flower.
- Put some of the tougher indoor pot plants outside. Winter cherries (*Solanum pseudocapsicum*), set with scarlet marble-like fruits amid the evergreen leaves, and chrysanthemums will brighten up a frost-free spot for a couple of weeks.

Colour in Spring

You need relatively few plants to create a feast of colour for spring, so buy the best. A typical half-barrel needs only a dozen fine wallflowers, supported with bulbs, to spill out colour and scent.

Pots undoubtedly take centre stage when in flower but they give pleasure long before, for the swelling buds and

promise of beauty is often as exciting as the real thing. Pots let you cheat nature and bring spring forward a month or so. Start the plants in a greenhouse, cold frame or porch to speed their growth.

For your plants to give a good spring display, you must look after them well through the previous summer, never letting them dry out completely, as this is when the flower buds are formed.

Spring bulbs, quietly biding their time just out of sight during the dullest months, provide a wonderful tonic when they eventually burst forth. Plant tulips, hyacinths, and daffodils 8 in (20 cm) deep, with leafy plants above them; the bulbs' pointed shoots have no problem finding their way through.

Deep containers will hold two layers of bulbs. Plant bulbs of the same kind and you will have a spectacular display

TOOLBOX

NARROW TROWEL

BE SURE TO USE a transplanting trowel when it is time to spruce up containers for the new season. Its narrow, pointed scoop is suited to the confined working space and lets you lift out each spent plant that needs replacing without disturbing any of its more permanent neighbours.

when they all flower together. However, planting layers of different bulbs (such as winter-flowering crocus and fritillaries) will extend the flowering season.

After the bulbs have had their season, non-bulbous plants, if looked after, continue to flower almost into early summer, and certainly until their successors are big enough to make a show. The quality of these wallflowers, forget-me-nots, polyanthuses and pansies, planted in October when the first frosts have done for summer's exotics, must be superb for they have to be able to respond quickly to spring's increased temperatures and extended daylight.

SUMMER BLOOMING

The ideal plant for a summer container should flower from May to October. Avoid plants that are bred for compact habit as they do not provide the lushness and profusion you want. Experiment with tender sub-shrubs such as fuchsias, osteospermums and marguerites (*Argyranthemum frutescens*), which are very fashionable grown as formal standards. They give a suitable height for the centre of a pot. Tall summer annuals with a long flowering period – *Salvia coccinea* 'Lady in Red' or blue *S. farinacea* – are also good centrepieces.

For a profusion of flowers with lower growth few plants are better than the summer classics petunias and nemesias, which come in almost every colour of the spectrum – ranging from red, orange and yellows into the purples and blues.

Round the rim of the pot grow trailing plants, such as begonias, nasturtiums, lobelias, ivy-leafed pelargoniums and verbenas, to cascade over the sides.

Try planting a collection of containers with the same type of plant filling each one. In the summer, when there is so much mixed colour in the flowerbeds, single-planted containers provide a welcome rest for the eye.

LATE SUMMER INTO AUTUMN

The most striking effects can be obtained from sub-shrubs grown on short stems as low standards – and there is much satisfaction in training them yourself. Fuchsias, pelargoniums (both the Regal and Zonal types) and orange-flowered

COOL COORDINATION Shapely glazed and Chinese pots are grouped together in spring for a softly toned display. Cream tulips pick up the acid yellow of the euphorbia, while white pansies harmonise with variegated ivy.

BARREL OF ROSES The fine spreading shape and crowded blooms of the tumbling rose 'The Fairy', combined with daisy-headed *Erigeron*, makes a glorious splash of colour. The plants are guaranteed to brighten the garden and with regular deadheading will flower over a long period.

FIRST-YEAR IMPACT Mauve *Felicia amelloides*, purple *Verbena* 'Loveliness', white *Argyranthemum foeniculaceum* and variegated, scented-leaf pelargonium give immediate height and colour in a new garden while a parterre is being established.

or the coral-barked Japanese maple (*Acer palmatum* 'Seṅkaki'). Plant a shrub such as Chinese witch hazel (*Hamamelis mollis*), which turns golden-leaved in the autumn as well as having red-centred yellow flowers in January, and *Caryopteris* x *clandonensis* 'Kew Blue', which has true blue flowers in September.

Hydrangeas, with large mopheads in a wide range of colours, are excellent for autumn. The bonus is the metamorphosis of the colours: the blue of *H. macrophylla* 'Ayesha' or 'Blue Bonnet' fades to pale turquoise and green, while the pinks and reds, such as *H. serrata* 'Preziosa' deepen to purple and burgundy. The white hydrangeas, such as *H. macrophylla* 'Madame Emile Mouillière', tend to become pale pink.

Tall, stately flowers always look dramatic in containers, and contrast well with bushy plants such as hydrangeas. The crinum, a relative of amaryllis, is elegant and carries as many as ten large pink-and-white trumpet-shaped blooms

Lantana camara take to this form. You need a season to train a bushy head and clear stem and the plants have to be overwintered out of reach of frost.

Every gardener loves the mellow atmosphere which abounds as summer slips into autumn. This is the time when reds and oranges make such pleasant contrasts to the blues, pinks, yellows and whites of the summer, and many plants bridge the seasons.

The maples come into their own in autumn. Look for *Acer griseum*, with its scarlet leaves and colourful peeling bark,

WINTER GLORY The handsome *Viburnum tinus* is evergreen and produces white flowers from winter to spring when so much else in the garden is dull and bare. Its glossy, dark green leaves are a vigorous contrast to all the naked shrubs and the remains of autumn foliage.

PLACING AND CARE

PLANTS IN CONTAINERS are usually cared for more readily then plants in the ground. Because they are closer to eye level and often easier to reach, their needs are soon noticed and attended to; deadheading, for example, is promptly done and any pests are quickly spotted and dealt with. In return for such diligence the plants fulfil their potential.

Grand pieces may need no care at all, for their beauty gives them the quality of pieces of sculpture, requiring only the right position to give lasting pleasure. The satisfying shapes of pithoi – and indeed the narrow necks that make some of them tricky to plant – are dramatic standing empty in a border. Urns work well placed high up. They are not easily accessible for maintenance in such positions but fortunately look imposing left empty. If they are to be seen close up, they are better planted – and with plants that match their elegance.

COMPOSING POT GARDENS

While those gardeners with only a balcony or roof garden have always known the advantages of 'pot gardens', these advantages apply just as much to any size of garden. When an area houses nothing but plants in pots, gardening is rather like flower arranging.

Pots let you compose a picture and experiment. There is also the advantage that the components can be moved about

---

SAFETY FIRST

KEEPING POTS IN THEIR PLACE

A CAREERING CHILD or an adult leaning too heavily on one of your pots to admire the planting could capsize the vessel if it is not firmly fixed. Not only could the culprit be hurt; your precious lilies, fuchsia or petunias could be damaged beyond recovery.

Before filling the pot, drive a strong metal stake or a piece of narrow piping through the draining hole into the ground. Let it reach about halfway up the pot, with at least an equal length in the ground. On paving, drill a hole in the mortar to receive the stake.

---

on a stem, often all through October. For light, delicate flowers choose the African lily (*Agapanthus africanus*). Sitting on thin, erect stems the rounded flower heads composed of bells of white or pale to deep blue float above the strappy leaves and add a graceful touch to the late summer scene. Hunt out *A. praecox* subsp. *orientalis* and *A.* 'Ben Hope'.

Having carefully chosen the containers and decided what to grow, find the best position for them, for display and for sunshine and shelter, then tend them well to enjoy the best they can give.

A COURTYARD GARDEN

A garden is a place to be used, a room outside. Even if you have hardly any space and no flowerbeds at all you can still create a wonderful garden with the help of containers.

ALMOST EVERYONE, it seems, wants a bit of garden – even if they live right in the centre of the busiest city. There are thousands of such little gardens – not much more than courtyards – some enjoying full sun, but others getting only a gleam in high summer. Nevertheless they will all make homes for plants.

In a small space, you cannot afford to waste any corner, so you need plants which tolerate a wide range of aspects.

Owners of little urban courtyards can make good use of the microclimate. Indeed, wherever the courtyard is, it will enjoy the protection provided by the walls and fences.

PAMPERING THE PLANTS

As everything is grown above ground in pots, there is no natural soil at all, and all your plants' fads can be met. For less fussy plants there is all-purpose, grow-virtually-anything compost. Of course the plants must be happy to cope with the container's restricted root-runs, but controlled feeding works wonders for overall plant health.

Furnish your green room to be inviting, and to offer the right balance of relaxation and stimulus. Placing the seat facing south ensures that it catches

Evergreen clematis gives the walls year-round colour

choice conifers make a constant green focus

Blue convolvulus softens clipped bays

every ray of sunshine. This is just the place to sit, bathed in the fragrance of the rose and the jasmine. The delicate fronds of artemisia in the Chinese jars beside the seat are soft and strokable, releasing a delicious fragrance as you brush against them.

In spring and early summer, floral interest comes from the climbers trained against the walls, and from the permanent shrubs. As these shrubs are evergreen they provide a finished effect throughout the year.

The two Versailles boxes with their elegant obelisk bay trees add a touch of formality which sharpens the overall relaxed feel. They can be moved around to frame seasonal colour or to hide plants that are at a less attractive stage. The

PICK A SPRIG Pots of herbs such as thyme, rosemary, marjoram and parsley make an aromatic addition, handy for keen cooks.

pretty group of conifers can also be moved and rearranged as the mood takes you. Their different shapes provide variety and, being evergreen, the trees are interesting all year.

ADAPTABLE PLEASURES

In high summer the warm evenings accentuate the scents of tobacco flowers and mignonettes, while the slightest shower of rain brings a sharp aroma from the leaves of cistus and ceanothus.

Herbs are another possibility, and versatile for those with really small gardens. One large pot of mixed herbs or a selection of small pots looks attractive and is strongly aromatic.

The concept will be particularly useful for all gardeners with no more than a small patch, but the ideas can all be adapted to a larger garden. The glory is that you get instant results – just the thing for all impatient gardeners.

Fragrant climbers frame the seat

Nicotiana and mignonette scent the evening air

1. *Clematis armandii* 'Apple Blossom'
2. Sweet bay (*Laurus nobilis*)
3. *Convolvulus tricolor* 'Blue Ensign'
4. Ivy (*Hedera helix* 'Goldheart')
5. Japanese cedar (*Cryptomeria japonica* 'Elegans Aurea')
6. Mountain pine (*Pinus mugo* 'Gnom')
7. Cypress (*Chamaecyparis lawsoniana* 'Ellwood's Pillar')
8. Maidenhair tree (*Ginkgo biloba*)
9. Cypress (*Chamaecyparis pisifera* 'Filifera Aurea')
10. Spreading juniper (*Juniperus sabina* 'Blue Danube')
11. Common juniper (*Juniperus communis* 'Compressa')
12. *Clematis alpina* 'Frances Rivis' and *Ceanothus impressus*
13. Climbing rose (*Rosa* 'Bloomfield Abundance')

14. Jasmine (*Jasminum × stephanense*)
15. *Viburnum × burkwoodii*
16. *Helichrysum petiolare* and *Petunia* 'Celebrity Ice'
17. *Artemisia absinthium* 'Powis Castle'
18. Rock rose (*Cistus aguilari*)
19. Tobacco plants (*Nicotiana* 'Domino' and *N.* 'Sensation')
20. Mignonette (*Reseda odorata*)
21. Ivy (*Hedera helix* 'Glacier')

to show off at their best, with those in decline going to less important spots.

Tubs and troughs exploding with busy lizzies, fibrous-rooted begonias and brilliant annuals such as petunias, nicotianas and nemesias are especially valuable, being tolerant of moves in and out of sun and shade.

Put tender plants from the conservatory or indoors in a protected spot for the summer, and arrange your especially cherished plants where they can be seen and admired from the house.

BUILDING IN SOME HEIGHT

Any group of containers needs height towards the back. Chimney pots are ideal, or you could invert surplus pots to act as stands. A very effective way of creating height is to place a small pot at the centre of a planted-up slightly larger pot, which in turn is then set on an even larger planted-up pot. Plants tumbling over the rim of each pot will give the effect of a cascade of growth.

A chimney pot is much too big to fill with compost, and in any case is open at the bottom. To grow plants in chimney pots, find a plain plant pot whose rim

MAKING·IT·EASIER

MOVING POTS

ONCE FULL of crocks, soil and fully grown plants, even moderate-sized containers are surprisingly heavy, but you can avoid back strain by moving pots on a dolly. You can buy a dolly or make your own model from rigid marine plywood with castors bolted on sturdy wooden struts under it.

Fix ropes through two opposite sides for more pulling power or for a helper to steady the dolly on a downslope. When moving the dolly over soft or slightly uneven ground, spread the route with flattened cardboard boxes from your grocer or a supermarket.

BUSHY TOP Mediterranean pots are well suited to architectural plants, such as this bromeliad, *Fascicularia bicolor*. The vertical foliage of the *Dasylirion* in the foreground contrasts with the soft horizontal ridges of the pot.

BEST PLANTS

BASKETS FILLED WITH COLOUR

Choose bushy trailing plants for the rim and base of the basket and taller, upright ones for the central planting.

BUSHY AND TRAILING
• Sweet alyssum (*Lobularia maritima*): greyish leaves and white or pink scented flowers all summer.

• *Lobelia erinus* 'Colour Cascade': masses of lilac, pink or white flowers in summer and early autumn.

• *Fuchsia*: late summer flowers in white, pink and bright red or mauve.

• *Pelargonium* 'Mini Cascade': ever-green leaves and masses of red flowers.

• Creeping Jenny (*Lysimachia nummularia*): long stems lined with little evergreen leaves and yellow flowers in midsummer.

• Common ivy (*Hedera helix*): ever-green with plain or variegated leaves.

UPRIGHT
• *Pelargonium* 'Dale Queen': pink flowers from summer to autumn.

• Petunias (*Petunia* 'Resisto Series'): strong blue, trumpet-shaped flowers from summer to autumn.

• Busy lizzies (*Impatiens walleriana* 'Novetter Series'): evergreen with red flowers from spring to autumn.

• Pansy (*Viola × wittrockiana*): range of colours in summer and winter.

• *Verbena × hybrida* 'Showtime': dark leaves and flowers in white, pinks, reds and purples through summer into autumn.

---

rests securely on a lip near the top of the chimney pot. Alternatively, jam crumpled chicken wire into the chimney pot to block it, and put a thick wad of newspaper over it to prevent the compost from falling through the wire when you water the plants.

A half-barrel is very expensive in terms of potting compost. To cut down on the cost, place crumpled balls of newspaper above the layer of crocks. Besides providing bulk, it prevents the compost from being washed away. And as newspaper is so good at retaining moisture, you will save on the watering.

Tall containers in vulnerable or ex-posed positions, as at the top of a flight of steps for example, should be weighed down with a few stones in the base or se-cured with a loop of wire to a handrail or to bricks on the step above to prevent them from being knocked or blown over.

Valuable height is also achieved by growing climbers up supports set into the containers. These come in all shapes, sizes and materials – from the basic bean pole and bamboo wigwam, to the more sophisticated and elegant wooden or metal obelisk, sometimes topped with a little ball. Some have a disc at the base to ensure they stay upright, others flare out at the bottom so that they press against the side of the pot. Without such built-in stabilisers, supports need to be pushed into deep compost or held in crumpled chicken wire. Plants develop a most inelegant list if their support is wobbly.

For vibrant colour and a mass of foliage grow sweet peas, passionflowers

CASCADE OF COLOUR Fuchsia and lobelia are well suited to hanging and wall-mounted baskets as they tumble over the sides, completely hiding the utilitarian container with a riot of blooms and foliage.

(*Passiflora*), or runner beans up a wigwam made of bamboos. A clematis climbing up an obelisk shows itself to advantage. You can create spectacular effects if you grow two clematis plants with different flowering times in the same container – a half-barrel is an ideal size. There is a profusion of blooms from spring through to early autumn. A good early-flowering clematis for a warm garden is *Clematis armandii* – a vigorous evergreen with scented white flowers which first appear in early spring. For later in the year, *C.* 'H.F. Young', with its violet blooms, is free-flowering.

POTS ON WALLS AND CHAINS

Flat-backed pots, free-standing or wall-mounted, semicircular and round hanging baskets – all are ideal for framing windows, embellishing walls and gracing positions impossibly awkward for ordinary containers. They are easy to put up, needing only rustproof hooks, and they look dramatic in a very short time.

Hanging baskets and wall-mounted pots are especially useful for balconies and roof gardens, where floor space is limited. In more conventional gardens, set hanging baskets high on the walls of a house or dangle them from an arbour or tree to give colour. Change the baskets each season and take advantage of the plants appropriate for that time.

To brighten a frost-free corner in winter line a basket with sphagnum moss and fill it with plants such as Christmas

PLANTING A HANGING BASKET

WHERE SPACE for growing plants is limited or when your garden needs a visual boost, hanging baskets are the perfect solution for providing a feast of foliage and colour. Do not worry about packing the plants in; they seem to flower better when massed together. Hessian is a convenient lining for baskets, but you could use sphagnum moss, real or synthetic turf, capillary matting, synthetic whalehide or preformed bowls of wood pulp, or textile fibre.

1. Set the basket on a firm surface, preferably at waist height. Line it with hessian and then with plastic. Jab six or seven draining holes through the lining at the base then fill the basket a quarter full with damp compost.

2. Make seven or eight slits for the first layer of trailing plants. Wrap a plant's foliage in a corner cut from a plastic bag. Feed the point into a slit from inside and ease the plant into place, then remove the bag. Complete the layer in the same way.

3. Fill the basket to halfway with compost. Make another set of slits and feed in the second layer of trailing plants. Press in compost mixed with water-retaining and food granules to 1 in (2.5 cm) from the rim, for the top plants.

4. Plant a circle of bushy plants near the rim of the basket then put upright plants in the centre. Firm the compost well and water the basket thoroughly. Leave it to drain for an hour before hanging it up. Water it every day in hot, dry weather.

cactus (*Schlumbergera bridgesii*), shoots of variegated eleagnus, berried pernettya and holly or flowering stems of heathers.

Ferns, with their arching fronds, are unusual in summer hanging baskets, as are strawberries and alchemillas. In spring a basket crammed with small daffodils is an irresistible sight.

THE KNACK IN MOVING

One virtue of containers is that they are movable – but they are very heavy when filled with compost and plants. To avoid

a strained back you can buy a barrow specifically made to ease the moving. A homemade dolly on castors, to make manoeuvring simpler, may be just as effective. It is also worth looking for containers with handles through which you could slip a couple of broom handles. These would enable you and a helper to carry the pot like a sedan chair. You can bolt handles onto wooden containers, but they must be sturdy.

As a last resort broom handles make very effective rollers, while the problem

COOL ELEGANCE Shapely and stately arum lilies (*Zantedeschia aethiopica*) rise uncluttered from a perfect grey green foil of trailing *Glechoma hederacea* 'Variegata'. The radiating circle of bricks set in the gravel round the base of the pot adds a subtle emphasis to the positioning.

insulating them. The thicker the insulation you provide the better.

The size of the container is a constraint: while smaller containers are at greater risk from the elements, internal insulation is a problem as you must not reduce soil content by too much. Where this is a risk, you may have to resort to the less attractive option of insulating the containers from outside by wrapping them with hessian sacking or bubble wrap. Make sure they are raised slightly off the ground as good drainage is vital.

PROTECTION FOR POTS

If it is not possible to move the container to a garage or cool greenhouse there are various means of protection. Put insulation in before you fill the container with compost – the pressure of which will keep the insulation in place.

🌢 Line large Versailles boxes with expanded polystyrene panels 1 in (2.5 cm) thick and cut to size (make drainage holes to correspond with those of the box). Half-barrels can take the thickest insulating material that will curve to fit.

🌢 Line small containers with a layer or two of bubble wrap.

🌢 Cover the container with a frame made of straw sandwiched between two layers of wire netting.

🌢 To protect tall, delicate shrubs, place a circle of twine-linked canes round them and wrap with hessian or garden fleece.

🌢 Place small containers in a cold frame sunk in sand or bark mulch. If the weather is especially bitter cover the frame with pieces of old carpet or bubble wrap, opening it up for an airing when the temperature rises.

🌢 Place dead bracken or fern fronds around the plant and cover with chicken wire secured to the compost with wire loops to stop the fronds blowing away.

🌢 Protect climbers, which obviously cannot be moved if they are scaling a wall, by carefully threading ferns through the stems. Wrap plenty of insulation round the container and base of the plant, and mulch well with coarse bark.

It is not only the cold which can wreak havoc with plants. Extremes of heat can make them wilt through lack of moisture. To combat this, keep roots cool by covering the compost with gravel, or sink the pots into gravel to conserve moisture.

Inanimate features of the garden are also in danger from frost and the wind. The idea of embellishing gardens with elaborate urns and pots developed in

of steps can be overcome with the aid of a couple of planks and a stout rope. Wrap the rope round the container to prevent slipping, then place the planks on the steps and slide the container down them.

DEALING WITH DRAINAGE

Whatever container you choose, remember that handsome looks are not everything. It is crucial for containers to have enough drainage holes in the base. Plants usually recover remarkably quickly from drying out, but few survive the root rot which accompanies waterlogging.

Drainage holes are easy to make; all you need for terracotta or ceramic pots is a drill, set at a low speed, and a masonry bit. Make a circle of nearly-meeting small holes then knock out the centre with a sharp blow. For wooden containers use a normal wood bit to drill the hole. The container should then be raised off the ground on stones, bricks, or pot feet to make sure water can drain away.

Ceramic pots left outside all winter without drainage holes and full of soil,

will crack if the soil freezes. You can prevent cracked pots from becoming a pile of shards by wrapping wire tightly round them. Plenty of foliage that tumbles over the rim conceals the wire very effectively. If the pots do break apart due to frost, you can still repair them if you have all the pieces (see box, p. 142).

HOW TO AVOID DAMAGE IN SEVERE WEATHER

Once you put your plants outside, you lose the ability to control their environment. When, on top of this, plants are put in containers set apart from the insulating effect of the soil in garden beds, they are even more at the mercy of capricious elements than other plants. They face drying winds, affecting top growth and – through the containers' sides – the roots, while frosts have greater access to the root balls and tips.

The savage effects of wind and cold, which frequently lead to fatal freezing of the roots, can be countered by grouping containers tightly in a sheltered spot and

SCULPTURAL SPLENDOUR Greek pithoi are becoming more widely available in this country and are worth seeking out as they make outstanding architectural focal points. Even left unplanted they will rise from the surrounding plants and add a feeling of immense weight and solidity.

southern Europe where climates are normally a great deal warmer in winter than Britain's. And yet this has not prevented such garden ornaments from becoming favourite features of gardens throughout the country.

In the past, when garden ornaments were displayed only in grander estates, there was no lack of staff to do outdoor work and all significant artefacts were boxed up from autumn to spring.

It still makes sense to protect vulnerable and valuable pieces in the winter. You can move them into a conservatory or frost-proof shed, or you can wrap them with sacking or plastic.

But the garden in winter should still be capable of giving pleasure, and looking out at plastic-draped figures is no joy. Indeed, when most of the herbaceous plants and deciduous shrubs are in eclipse, the inanimate, architectural features become even more important in decorating the dormant garden.

A far better solution is to make sure that containers with permanent plantings are in containers robust enough to withstand all weathers. And there are both plants and pots aplenty to meet the most exacting requirements.

Look for pots with frost-proof guarantees, which many now have. Low-fired terracotta is the most vulnerable material, so it is best kept solely for spring and summer displays. The colour of the clay gives a clue as to the strength of the terracotta – the reddest has been fired at the highest temperatures, so is the toughest, and the palest is the least frost resistant and liable to crack in the cold.

Containers allow you to be adventurous, to take chances and experiment in a way not possible with the more static elements of a garden. They also give the less patient the rare satisfaction of seeing ideas translated into reality instantly. They can provide solutions to the most intractable problems and challenging sites, liven up a gloomy spot or alternatively provide welcome peace in the midst of abundant colour. No garden is complete without them.

REVIVING FROM DROUGHT

DURING THE SUMMER, containers often need watering daily, or even twice on the hottest days. Unless you have installed an automatic watering system, this is quite a chore – and one that may be shirked if time is short – so it would not be surprising if you occasionally ended up with a dried-out container of drooping plants.

Even if the container cannot be moved, do not despair. Water it well then heap moist gravel high round it and water the gravel frequently so that the constant evaporation surrounds the plants with moist air. Many wilted plants will revive remarkably quickly and trimming off any damaged parts will encourage new growth to fill out the plant again.

The gravel looks attractive enough to be a permanent feature of the summer scene if you mound it skilfully. It conserves moisture particularly well when heaped round a cluster of pots, creating a microclimate for them.

INSPIRATION FROM
GREAT GARDENS

POWIS CASTLE

Terraces scale the precipitous castle walls.

A glance across the Severn Valley in Powys to the distant Breidden Hill reveals the impregnable position of this 13th-century castle. Today, it is the formality of its orangery, the classical statuary and a series of impressive views that attract the visitor to the sweep and grandeur of the castle's hanging gardens and terraces.

ALTHOUGH ORIGINALLY the mighty Powis Castle stood atop a naked crag, visitors today are greeted by tier upon tier of plantings, clipped evergreens and urn-topped balustrades surrounding the castle's ancient, rose-red retaining walls.

Towards the end of the 17th century, the Herbert family who owned the castle – and who still live there – decided that it would be much improved by a garden. Five terraces, each stretching 200 yd (183 m), were built, probably under the direction of William Winde, who also designed the gardens at Cliveden in Buckinghamshire.

The terraces were amply furnished with a loggia, pavilions, fountains, statuary and clipped yews, the last of which have now grown to impressive sizes and shapes. But a more recent addition is a number of large, identical terracotta pots containing identical plantings, which are used to give emphasis and cohesion to a balustraded terrace, itself a grandly emphatic feature.

The repeated pattern of the terracotta pots, each of which overflows with the carmine and rose-pink fuchsia 'Display', picks up the colours of the lichened walls

ABUNDANT SKYLINE Luxuriantly planted pots of fuchsia adorn the dramatic stone skyline above one of the terraces at Powis Castle.

and adds even greater height and dignity to the balustrade. The pots also frame an early summer border of ceanothus, hostas and heucheras.

CREATING A FRONTIER

The concept of using a series of identical pots and plantings translates well to a lesser terrace, or to the edge of a patio or stretch of wooden decking. The row of pots effectively divides a terrace from the rest of the garden, or might lead the eye to a favourite border.

It is also effective when there is no choice but to employ containers – to provide a garden on a roof, to bring lustre to a dull corner or to grow acid-loving plants in an alkaline area, for example.

Containers echoing the style used at Powis would be fine in a smaller garden, and are easy to obtain, but even imitations are quite expensive. An alternative is to use 15 in (38 cm) plastic half-pots painted a uniform colour – here, an unusual and discreet French navy blue.

The pots on the terrace below are brimming over with a bold display of mixed plants, despite making a smaller feature than the example at Powis. Each one holds two *Helichrysum petiolare*, which trail over the edges, a ruff of three plants of the fuchsia 'Display', and a pale mauve *Heliotropium arborescens* 'Lord Roberts' to give central height.

The colours echo those used to such effect at Powis, and a fragrant lavender (*Lavandula angustifolia* 'Loddon Pink') under the wall completes the picture.

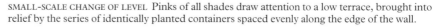

SMALL-SCALE CHANGE OF LEVEL Pinks of all shades draw attention to a low terrace, brought into relief by the series of identically planted containers spaced evenly along the edge of the wall.

ILLUSIONS AND DISGUISES

EVER LOSE HEART if your garden is marred by a clutter of dustbins, intrusive drain covers, an oil storage tank or even the sight of your neighbour's caravan. Turn each problem into an asset with some ingenious design ideas and well-chosen plants. Sometimes it is more than a localised eyesore that needs disguising; but even if the whole garden is flawed by its awkward shape or ugly proportions, you can work skilful deceptions with dense borders, trellises dressed with trailing plants, and even mirrors. Seize the opportunity to make a path wind out of sight to illusory extra space and transform a gloomy spot into a secret corner that entices with its mystery.

SPECIAL FEATURES

Honeysuckle is fast growing and fragrant, and some varieties are evergreen, making it a beautiful ally in a campaign to conceal unattractive objects.

THE ART OF TRICKERY

PART OF GARDENING'S enduring fascination, even for those who have made it their lifetime hobby, is the fact that it operates on so many different levels. There is the great joy to be gained from creating a pleasing display through an appropriate choice of plants, a display to satisfy the eyes, ears and nose. But on another level altogether there is the attraction of a garden which engages the intelligence with humour and surprise.

Whether these elements are introduced to carry out a more complex and satisfying design or for the sheer fun of playing tricks on the unwary visitor, prolonging the enjoyment of a garden as it unfolds slowly is always worthwhile.

The magnificent landscape garden at Stourhead in Wiltshire is a perfect example of how to keep the visitor guessing. It looks entirely natural, set around a lake, but is in fact very carefully contrived so that if the correct route is followed – anticlockwise round the lake – new views open up at particular points, some from high vantage points, others from low down at water level.

Though few people have room to create anything so grand, there is really no need to reveal all in a single glimpse. A measure of imaginative trickery benefits most gardens, no matter what their size, if only in disguising an unsightly dustbin.

TROPICAL OR TEMPERATE? A touch of light paint, *Campsis* 'Madame Galen' clambering over the roof and pots of pelargoniums, spiky agaves and yucca cloak this garage with a sun-drenched character that is more reminiscent of Mediterranean and other southern climes than of Britain.

CREATING AN ILLUSION

PERHAPS ALL GARDENING is an illusion – the stamping of personal wishes and ideas on a plot of land and thinking that it is transformed. But such achievements are only ever transient, because it is never long before nature adapts them – and if left alone, restores the plot almost to its original state.

Since many gardens are smaller than their owners would like, any device that gives an illusion of greater space has much to recommend it and is worth incorporating into a garden design.

One of the first steps to take is to lower the surrounding boundaries, thus bringing more sight of the sky into the garden and making it feel less enclosed. But while open space overhead makes a garden feel bigger, at ground level things work differently.

CREATING GARDEN ROOMS

A garden seen in its entirety at one glance seems smaller than one where some parts are out of immediate view. Many people also like a feeling of intimacy in gardens, and dividing a single space into sections is a way of creating this feeling as well as increasing the apparent size. It gives more scope for employing a variety of themes in the garden, and for providing areas for different uses, popularly referred to as garden rooms. A number of smaller areas such as this can be delineated by hedges, by tall shrubs, or by fences perhaps of decorative trelliswork lightly dressed with climbers.

Such areas can be furnished with seats, which are best placed against a wall or hedge, as people instinctively prefer to sit with their backs to something solid.

THE PITFALLS OF PERSPECTIVE

The effect of perspective is to make distant objects appear smaller than those in the foreground and to make two parallel lines appear to draw closer together as they recede into the distance.

When considering any illusion that makes use of perspective, bear in mind that these 'tricks' have a major disadvantage. They usually work in one direction only and must be planned carefully so that the illusion is seen from the main viewing area. A device that makes the garden appear longer, shorter or even

CREATING PRIVATE SPACE Outdoor 'rooms', such as this one surrounded by a shapely box hedge, are a way of adding a touch of mystery and a feeling of space in a garden. The enclosed room welcomes anyone who enters, through an opening in the hedge, into its calming seclusion.

twice the size from one angle is pointless if the illusion is destroyed when seen from, say, a favourite seat in the centre.

When the illusion is good enough, it remains just as convincing after the trick is discovered to be just that. One way to avoid any disappointment is to ensure that the planting and design in the garden are sufficiently varied to hold the interest.

Planting to achieve an illusion may restrict the choice of plants, and particular favourites may not easily fit into the overall plan. But a little discipline in the basic structure is often good for the keen gardener who is in danger of turning a plot into a collection of plants rather than an area well designed for use and pleasure.

ALTERING PERSPECTIVE WITH LAWN SHAPES

The traditional treatment of a central lawn with beds running the length of the sides is the most practical way of giving the maximum play area for children. The beds are often too narrow to allow satisfying planting, however, and taller plants get buffeted as winds swirl over fences.

You can still keep the arrangement of beds, lawn and paths so that they all run parallel and accentuate the length of the garden, but the path need not be solid. A series of slabs laid as stepping-stones in the centre of the lawn and leading to the far end will draw the eye to the distance and will not interrupt the play area.

You can improve the beds even without widening them. Establish some taller bushes towards the front of the border instead of at the back. This creates more interest and gives shelter to smaller and more delicate plants beneath and behind them. When the children have grown up, the beds can be widened.

Changing the shape of the lawn is another option. Widen the borders but make the lawn narrower at the far end to increase the apparent length. But beware – regular slabs in the lawn, or a regular central path which does not narrow in the same way, spoil the effect.

A combination of stretching the view and creating compartments at the sides surprisingly makes a long, narrow garden appear wider, while increasing the height of planting and making a path slim makes a garden seem narrower.

Not everyone wants to lengthen the appearance of their garden, however. To lose the long, linear shape, divide the garden into distinct sections that have their own identity, making the dividers run across the site. Paved areas with circular and curved shapes, and paths that cross the site diagonally are also effective.

PLANTING TO ALTER THE SENSE OF SPACE

Some plants are naturally architectural and demand attention, while others fade into the background. Exploit these qualities to shorten or lengthen the garden.

❧ To arrest the eye, plant cordylines, yuccas and phormiums either close to the viewer or far away. When they are used in the middle distance, they destroy the impression of length.

❧ Keep small-leaved plants such as bush honeysuckle (*Lonicera nitida*) and privet unclipped when you want them as lesser features in a border; when clipped, their dense habit draws the eye and breaks up the border.

❧ To emphasise length, place bold and large-leaved plants close to the viewing point, with a progression of smaller-leaved plants used as the borders recede.

❧ Put exotic evergreens that have large, dramatic leaf shapes on a patio to draw you instantly to a sitting area and to give it a tropical feel. The rest of the garden, noticed more slowly, will seem larger.

❧ To create a sense of distance, plants at the end of the garden should be airy and ethereal with tiny foliage. The fennels are ideal for this purpose, with diaphanous foliage that appears almost transparent.

❧ Placing tall trees, and especially a row of dark green conifers, at the far end of the garden brings the garden end forward and seems to shorten the plot.

TOPIARY PERSPECTIVE

A less subtle, simpler use of perspective is to place clipped plants deliberately to punctuate the view. To achieve this, clip privet, box, or yew or other conifers in the borders into symmetrical pyramids or cones. The height and width of the cones should be reduced as they recede into the distance, but gradually or the effect is curious – and is also lost when you are walking towards the house.

Even in a small garden, clipped shapes are useful, especially if a plant is chosen that has a smaller-leaved form to use for the distance. Box is good for this, with common box (*Buxus sempervirens*) used in the foreground and the dwarf hedging form (*B. s.* 'Suffruticosa'), with its smaller habit and leaves, used for the distance. If you prefer, the box can be

ALTERING PERSPECTIVE One way of increasing the impression of length in a rectangular plot is to introduce beds which narrow at the far end of the garden; a pathway of paving slabs of decreasing size reinforces the illusion.

SUGGESTING LARGER SIZE Clipped shapes in the border attract and hold the eye, making the viewer take longer to cover the area, while planting small-leaved foliage plants at the garden's end makes it seem further away.

DECEPTIVELY EXPANSIVE The luxuriant planting in this generous border along the edge of the lawn suggests that it is a quiet corner in a large, spacious garden. But closer study shows that the boundary wall of the garden lies just behind the tall blue flower heads of *Campanula lactiflora*.

CHIPPED BARK

REDESIGNING A GARDEN from scratch is a costly business, so it helps to spread the expense over several years.

Until you are ready to lay a permanent path, cheat with bark chips, which are easy to lay over a firm base of well-rolled earth. Use different sizes of chip to create an illusion of distance, with larger chips near the house and smaller ones further away. To enhance the illusion, narrow the path's far end a little.

pot-grown and stand in terracotta pots in the border or on slabs set into the lawn to create a mini avenue.

Apart from box, there is a wide choice of plants trained as standards to pick from, ranging from restrained evergreens through to colourful fuchsias. You could use fuchsias in graduated heights in the summer months and then replace them during the winter with box cones.

A SUBTLER FUNCTION OF COLOUR

Every gardener is interested in colour, but its effect in a garden landscape is not always appreciated. Any bright colour that clamours for attention has the potential to destroy a larger overall effect, and quieter tones are often preferable through most of the garden.

Red is one of the potential problems. It is the colour of danger and excitement, and all eyes are drawn to it. But even in great gardens, red can destroy both a restful landscape and the perspective – when blatantly coloured rhododendrons, for example, are in bloom.

Since red seems to leap forward, it always shortens the perspective. Restrict it to the foreground where its warmth can be enjoyed without destroying any illusion. At dusk, red disappears before other colours, so having red flowers close allows them to be appreciated longer.

In complete contrast, white flowers glow at dusk. During the day, however, some gardeners find their pristine whiteness too severe in the garden. Like red, white should not be used at the far end of a view, except to shorten it. The many other flowers in creamy and lavender tints give the effect of whiteness without actually being so stark and icy.

Blue is a valuable colour to use for suggesting distance because it naturally recedes and disappears, although the strong shades are sometimes too vivid. Misty grey-blues and pale blues are the ideal choice for the far end of the garden, especially if you are fortunate enough to be able to 'borrow' the surrounding countryside as a backdrop, when the colours blend in with the sky.

AN IMAGINATIVE TREATMENT FOR THE GARDEN'S END

Unless you have a pretty or dramatic view beyond the bottom of the garden, which it would be unthinkable to hide, you can choose how the garden should end. One solution is to pretend that it does not actually end at all, but that there is something beyond just out of sight.

This is most easily achieved by planting a dense, clipped hedge across the garden near the end with an arched opening through the centre. In the short gap between this hedge and the actual end of the garden, run a path crossways to give the impression that there is more to come. The archway can frame some eye-catcher, perhaps a statue, a large urn or a piece of sculpture set against the boundary. Behind the hedge, numerous essential but unsightly features – compost bins, potting shed, wheelbarrow and the like – can be hidden, providing that they can also be easily got at.

The same deceit works as a divider in the garden at any stage along its length, perhaps to hide a play area with goalposts or a playhouse. Alternatively, the hedge can frame an attractive fruit tree or vegetable bed, with less attractive beds tucked away to the sides.

Framing a view with an arch or a series of interrupted hedges is theatrical, giving the same impression as a stage set with scenery in the wings, and it has the same effect. The layered appearance convinces the viewer that there is some feature of interest 'offstage', while simultaneously focusing the attention on centre stage. In the garden, a statue or sculpture, an exceptional plant or even a painted scene could be framed by the archway or break in a hedge.

AN ARTFUL TROMPE L'OEIL

The term 'trompe l'oeil' refers to a two-dimensional optical illusion that gives a false sense of depth. For gardeners, however, it often refers to a form of trellis known as treillage, which is made up of adjoining arches to suggest a colonnade, or of concentric arches or rectangles that give the illusion of a tunnel. Set onto a wall or a fence, treillage is most effective at giving the impression of depth.

In most gardens, a trompe l'oeil device works best when at least partially obscured by foliage and framed by a pair of upright matching plants. Formally trained plants such as conifers or bays match the elegant character of trellis-work. Do not paint newly acquired trellis a stark white; the effect is usually better with a slightly understated shade such as sea green or dove grey, especially with ivy or some other climber obscuring the outer edges. Setting the trellis in shade enlists the help of soft lighting to enhance the illusion.

Place a pot of flowers in the window at the centre of the trompe l'oeil tunnel, or if you have a talent for art, paint a rural scene. This borrows from the tradition of leaving gaps or windows in walls through which views of the surrounding countryside could be seen. Because these deceits work best at a distance, great skill as a painter is not necessary. Colours should be kept muted so that the view seems to be far in the distance.

In modern gardens, a rural landscape is not necessarily the most appropriate of views; add a touch of fantasy with a glimpse of the Eiffel Tower or St Paul's Cathedral dome.

TRICKS WITH LIGHT AND SHADE

It is not necessary to incorporate a multitude of elaborate features into a garden to make awkward proportions or dingy conditions seem better. Restraint is often a surer route to a successful design. An area of light and an area of shade, for example, can both create intriguing contrasts and bolster an illusion.

In Britain, which is not renowned for its sun, it is tempting to shun shade and to treat it as a problem. But shade can be

THEATRICAL TIPS Theatre design has many ideas to offer the imaginative gardener. Here, clipped hedges of box work similarly to wings in a stage set, discreetly screening less attractive parts, such as a play area tucked away at the sides, while leading the eye to a beautiful focus.

A ROAD TO NOWHERE An archway is enticing to the least curious garden stroller, implying sights unseen and further delights. But it can also work effectively as a screen to hide a wheelbarrow and the compost heaps.

an effective way to emphasise those areas of the garden that are in sun, the darkness of the one concentrating attention on the brightness of the other.

In many of the great gardens, shady tunnels of ancient yews lead visitors past hidden areas of the garden to another viewpoint where an unexpectedly sunny scene opens up before them. On a smaller scale, you can grow tall hedges to make quite short corridors linking unrelated areas, with a statue or a blaze of colour at the far end to act as a 'draw'. The ground beneath the hedge need not be wasted; you can plant it with shade-loving, ground-covering cyclamens, colchicums, bergenias and ivy.

Shady areas are refreshingly cool on a hot day, especially when overhung by the gently moving branches of trees or by a pergola clothed with climbers. A well-planted pergola can be both fragrant and romantic. Some of the loveliest foliage

---

BRINGING LIGHT TO A DARK CORNER

DO NOT DESPAIR of improving a dingy corner of your garden that receives little light. Taking any one or all of these five simple steps can liven up the area, introducing flashes of lighter colour that lift the mood and brighten the corner.

If you have an outdoor electricity supply, train a spotlight onto the holly for a glowing evening display.

Paint the walls a light, summery colour – not white, because it is quite cold, but a sunny yellow, ochre or buff.

Train the variegated ivy *Hedera helix* 'Goldheart' up a trellis fixed on one wall to introduce touches of lightness all year round.

Add a midgreen circle to the light-coloured wall and place a lollipop-shaped variegated holly (*Ilex* 'Silver Queen', for example) against it.

Lighten the ground surface by flanking soft grey cobbles, or stone or cream gravel, with the silver-spotted woodland plant *Pulmonaria officinalis* (left) and evergreen variegated *Arabis ferdinandi-coburgi*.

LUSH CONTRAST If your garden receives a restricted amount of sun, open up the area where it strikes and intensify the effect with a ground cover of light gravel. The plantings around then contribute a welcome lushness.

plants for it are the vines, and a mixture of edible and ornamental varieties gives a plentiful cover of green and purple foliage and frequently bunches of fruits in just a few years. Twine some honeysuckle and jasmine among the vines for rich fragrance.

Shade allows you to add character and mystery to the garden. A rocky grotto can drip water into an echoing cistern, a pool never becomes green with algae and the imagination can run riot with Gothic and romantic themes. This is the place for fanciful follies, or for ancient-looking broken urns and statues half hidden by large foliage plants.

Frothy cow parsley or spring-flowering bulbs will transform a semi-screened corner into a delightful secret place, reached by a single path. In a spot which is too dark to plant with sun-seeking flowers, create a mass of colour in spring with woodland bulbs and primroses. In

summer, the corner becomes the back-cloth for a planting of bright flowers and a rustic trellis each side of an arch to support a lemon-coloured climbing rose. The arch creates the illusion of a pathway leading into the secret woodland.

A tunnel designed as a straight line can lead directly into another section of the garden, which you glimpse from the tunnel's entrance. But you can create a private sunspot for yourself if the exit from the tunnel is not visible from the entrance but opens through its side onto a surprise area bathed in afternoon sun and sheltered by rose-covered fences.

SKILFUL USE OF MIRRORS

Mirrors are the adventurous gardener's great ally, but they have to be used with care to be effective. With proper placement a mirror seems to extend the garden in a number of directions, although the view above the mirror and the supporting structure must be masked or the magic is broken.

🍂 Large pieces of mirror are not necessary, and are more difficult to fix than smaller pieces, which are just as effective.

🍂 Frame the mirror with evergreen climbers such as ivy and *Akebia quinata*.

🍂 Ensure that the mirror is perfectly upright if you wish to reflect a level

---

TOOLBOX

CUSHIONS FOR A MIRROR

IF YOU PLAN to use a piece of mirror in your garden, it is important that it is securely fixed. Insert rubber grommets into the corner holes of the mirror before screwing it into drilled and plugged holes in the wall. The grommets cushion the mirror like shock absorbers and prevent it from cracking.

Get a glazier to drill holes in the corners of the mirror or buy one ready drilled. Most drilled mirrors come with rubber grommets and with mirrored screw covers to hide the fastening.

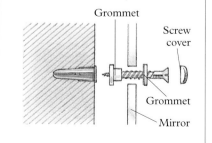

Grommet

Screw cover

Grommet

Mirror

EXTENDING A SMALL GARDEN VIEW

There is one way to extend a garden without buying an extra plot of land. A carefully placed mirror is the key, drawing the eye to a fresh view that is nothing but illusion.

ONE OF THE MOST ATTRACTIVE aspects of using illusion in the garden is that it can be employed in all manner of subtle ways to give an impression of space, of a larger expanse than is in fact there.

A careful choice and positioning of plants helps to draw the eye away from the foreground, on towards the undiscovered delights of the garden's end. Pots of bold foliage, in this case the expansive *Trachycarpus fortunei* and slightly taller *Cordyline australis*, serve a double purpose, highlighting the start of a garden path while simultaneously hiding what lies beyond.

The evergreen nature of this planting ensures that the intrigue of a curved path such as this is never lost but still during the coldest winter months invites the intrepid visitor to investigate even while there is a crisp layer of frost on the circle of lawn.

BEYOND THE FENCE

In the far corner, a delicate trelliswork arch frames what appears to be the start of yet another path. In the distance is an elegant piece of garden statuary but, as anyone who tries to reach it quickly finds out, the true position of the stone figure is elsewhere.

It lies behind the evergreen *Photinia* 'Red Robin' on the left of the garden, and is in fact reached by following the mysterious curved path to its end. A closer look at the original glimpse of the statue reveals that it is actually a reflection, caught in a piece of mirror that is artfully framed by the trellis. During the summer months, climbers swathe the trellis and disguise the mirror further.

A small patch of cobbles at the foot of the mirror appears larger when added to its reflection. It is enough to stop anyone from walking into the glass.

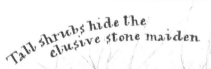

Tall shrubs hide the elusive stone maiden

1. *Sarcococca hookeriana* var. *digyna*
2. *Euphorbia characias*
3. *Skimmia japonica* subsp. *reevesiana*
4. *Camellia* 'Donation'
5. *Photinia* × *fraseri* 'Red Robin'
6. Autumn cherry (*Prunus* × *subhirtella* 'Autumnalis')

A mirror arch extends
the garden view

A curving path
adds tempting
mystery

7. *Miscanthus* 'Silver Feather'
8. Japanese cherry (*Prunus* 'Amanogawa')
9. Chusan palm (*Trachycarpus fortunei*)
10. Cabbage palm (*Cordyline australis*)
11. Daffodils (*Narcissus*)

12. Peach (*Prunus persica*)
13. *Coronilla valentina* subsp. *glauca*
14. *Rubus idaeus* 'Aureus'
15. *Viburnum* × *bodnantense* 'Deben'
16. New Zealand flax (*Phormium tenax*)
17. *Heuchera* 'Palace Purple'
18. *Fatsia japonica*

garden, otherwise it gives the impression of a slope up or down.

- It is rarely necessary to bring the mirror down to ground level, except when a semicircular pond is set against a mirror to give the illusion of a complete circle of water.
- Never position a mirror where you approach it head on. It is best at an angle of 45° so that the illusion holds until you have almost reached the mirror.
- Set a piece of mirror at the end of a pergola at an angle and frame it with plants. That way, it reflects a part of the garden to the right or left, and makes it appear to be beyond the mirror.
- A small mirror fitted in the centre of a trompe l'oeil wall feature is very effective when the angle of approach is right. Screen the mirror from view with plants until your path reaches the spot where the mirror shows an open scene apparently beyond the wall.
- Use small pieces of mirror to reflect light from sunny parts of the garden into a shady corner. In a shady part of a patio, bounce shafts of light onto the floor, a pool or a fountain by fixing pieces of mirror high up on a wall.
- Fragments of mirror set into a wall are effective at night when they reflect and so double the light from candles and flares.

It is best to use toughened mirror glass in the garden, rather than just an ordinary mirror intended for indoor use. To extend the life of an outdoor mirror, test a small area of the silvered reverse with varnish, and then varnish the rest. The mirror must be fixed to a firm surface – a wall is best, or seasoned wood. Clean the mirror regularly or the effect is spoiled by rain, bird droppings or splashed soil on the surface.

Creating Space with a Change of Levels

Another way of making a garden seem more spacious than it is in reality, is by introducing steps leading to a sunken garden surrounded by hedges. Even a couple of steps up or down clearly separate one area from another and make it easier to give each part a convincingly different character. Having distinct sections increases the feeling of space.

Low retaining walls divide areas even more strongly and if the walls are double they can hold soil and serve as raised beds. Where a garden you take over has been constructed with ugly low walls, use plants to disguise them. Coarse alpines

CONFUSING PATHWAYS This ingenious use of a mirror is barely perceptible, a small arc of frame being the only giveaway that there is not really a long path nor a doorway at its end. To create this effect, the mirror starts from ground level and nothing is set in front of it to break the reflection.

THROUGH THE KEYHOLE A small, carefully placed mirror arch introduces a sliver of bright light to this heavily planted corner, engaging the viewer with a false scene before the illusion is slowly disentangled.

CHANGING LEVELS Introducing a change of level is often a good way of expanding a small garden. No more than a couple of steps are needed to give the feeling of a journey of discovery, and clever planting which hides one section of the garden from another adds to the overall effect.

such as aubrietia, arabis and cerastium improve loosely constructed dry-stone walls in summer, and low wall shrubs, *Cotoneaster horizontalis* and *Chaenomeles japonica*, perhaps, add winter interest.

Climbers such as everlasting pea (*Lathyrus latifolius*) and the lower growing clematis – varieties of the early flowering *Clematis alpina* and *C. macropetala*, for example – make good cover where it is difficult to plant in the wall. Fix wide mesh chicken wire or plastic netting over the top of the wall to encourage climbers.

In a garden with a natural slope there is a change of level but not one that adds apparent space. The slope foreshortens the view and also reveals the whole garden at a glance, which shrinks it. One solution is to make a series of terraced areas and create a hedge or screen along the lower side of one of them. This hides the lower garden and an opening near one end of the screen leads you into a different area. Such a screen also provides an effective backdrop for plants when they are seen from below.

PLANTING ILLUSIONS

Viewed from the upper levels of the garden, an area which has been divided up by changes in level may actually appear smaller. Much depends on the planting, however. The height and the spread of the plants, and the size of their foliage, can have a dramatic effect on how big the garden seems. Tall hedges around its borders make a garden feel claustrophobic, and a small garden with a large specimen tree in the centre of its lawn is dominated by the one plant.

To introduce a feeling of space, avoid large-leaved plants and set out several slow-growing bushes or trees of reasonable size towards the boundaries. This way, they do not block off too much light from the centre of the garden. The

Mount Etna broom (*Genista aetnensis*) is perfect, its green branches almost leafless and casting little shade and its habit elegantly semi-weeping when it is young.

Plants with a light and airy appearance also give a sense of space, as do small plants which, when used in groups, do not create a bitty, untidy appearance.

USING PATHS AND OPENINGS FOR A SENSE OF MYSTERY

A curving path rounding a bed in the garden always entices and few people can resist following one, especially if the plants in the bed are tall enough to hide the destination. When the starting point of the path is marked with an arch of foliage or framed with sentinel conifers, the journey is all the more irresistible. Passing through a simple arch adds to the path's mystery and effectively divides one area of the garden from another.

The arch need not be elaborate and may simply be a group of carefully chosen shrubs. The unusual habit of bamboos, which are narrow at the base and open up at the top, makes them form natural arches. Some are hardy, with small leaves ideal for distant planting. If their base needs thickening up, aucubas and bush honeysuckles suit the shade and dryness that bamboos sometimes create at the roots.

Although paths are essentially practical, they can contribute to illusions if artfully planned. Paths look longer if their

THE ALLURE OF CURVES A very gently curved path is best for suggesting further areas of garden that are as yet unseen. A sudden bend, on the other hand, can appear to be nothing more than a disappointing dead end.

KEEP ILLUSIONS WITHIN BOUNDS

PLAYING TRICKS with the senses is part and parcel of a garden but do not go too far. The aim is to create an environment that enchants with its fancies, not to fool any visitors so completely that they harm themselves.

In order to ensure this, plant a couple of low shrubs or a small flowerbed in front of any potential hazard such as a pool or a hidden drop.

Use a smooth surface underfoot to draw people along the safe route, and border it with shifting shingle to deflect them from danger.

COVERING A CLUMSY WALL A change of levels creates space but can be irritating rather than helpful when the structure is unattractive. To cover an ugly low wall, fill the cracks and crevices with rockery plants or disguise its overall shape with distractingly distinctive foliage plants.

PLANTING TO DISGUISE The neat box edges to this curved path seem to propel the visitor along the route, while tall plants in the border obscure what lies round the next corner and so prolong the sense of discovery.

texture is varied – and may slow you down, which makes them feel even longer. Slabs set in gravel or pebbles in concrete, for instance, make the gaze travel along the pathway more slowly.

You can use a path to create a visual diversion. A path of stepping-stones set in grass and curving away to the left draws the eye along it and helps an ugly object on the right to go unnoticed, especially if it is partially covered by unobtrusive plants with medium-sized leaves.

ILLUSORY SOUND AND SCENT

If illusion can fool the eyes, other senses such as hearing can be misled. A garden is usually regarded as a peaceful place, a place to relax and to entertain. But sound does not travel in straight lines, and even the most solid wall cannot give protection from noisy neighbours.

An impression of serenity is created by introducing peaceful sounds to the garden. The most obvious of these is the sound of running water, although wind-chimes stirred by the breeze, the cooing of doves or a thread of birdsong also contribute a mellow touch.

Nothing stirs the emotions like scent. Many strongly fragrant plants have small flowers which are easily worked into elaborate planting plans, while dramatic plants with heavy perfume, especially those that release their scent at night, help to create an air of tropical lushness.

ON TO THE UNKNOWN A canopy of trees and tall flowering shrubs enclose this path, giving it an appealing air of mystery. The unswept nature of the path, and the way the plants billow over its edges, add to the feeling that you are finding the way to a rarely visited secret garden.

265

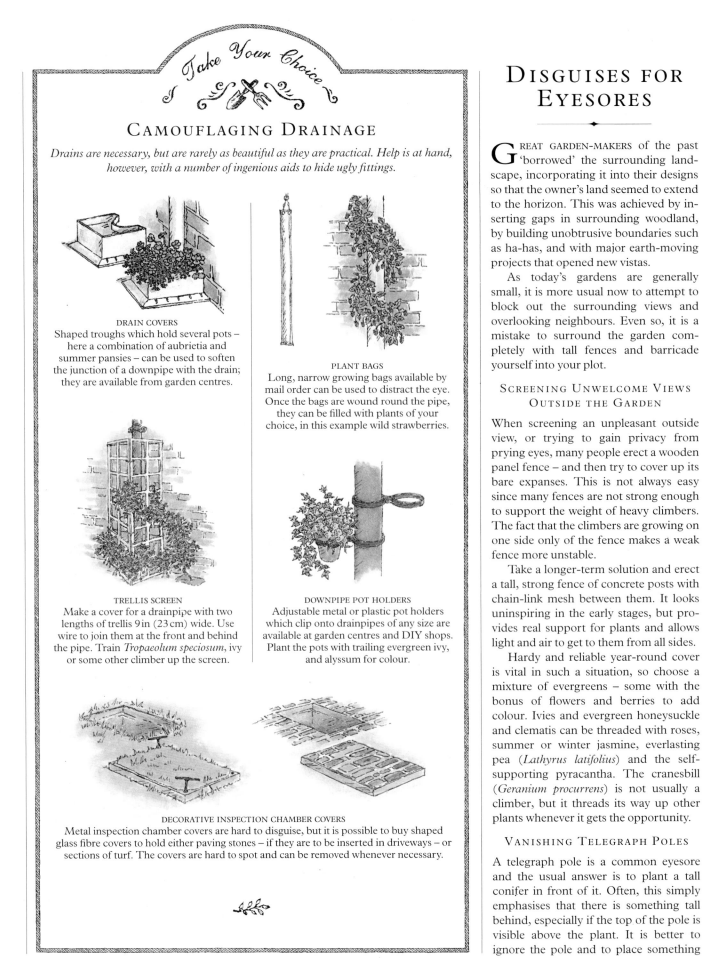

CAMOUFLAGING DRAINAGE

Drains are necessary, but are rarely as beautiful as they are practical. Help is at hand, however, with a number of ingenious aids to hide ugly fittings.

DRAIN COVERS
Shaped troughs which hold several pots –
here a combination of aubrietia and
summer pansies – can be used to soften
the junction of a downpipe with the drain;
they are available from garden centres.

PLANT BAGS
Long, narrow growing bags available by
mail order can be used to distract the eye.
Once the bags are wound round the pipe,
they can be filled with plants of your
choice, in this example wild strawberries.

TRELLIS SCREEN
Make a cover for a drainpipe with two
lengths of trellis 9 in (23 cm) wide. Use
wire to join them at the front and behind
the pipe. Train *Tropaeolum speciosum*, ivy
or some other climber up the screen.

DOWNPIPE POT HOLDERS
Adjustable metal or plastic pot holders
which clip onto drainpipes of any size are
available at garden centres and DIY shops.
Plant the pots with trailing evergreen ivy,
and alyssum for colour.

DECORATIVE INSPECTION CHAMBER COVERS
Metal inspection chamber covers are hard to disguise, but it is possible to buy shaped
glass fibre covers to hold either paving stones – if they are to be inserted in driveways – or
sections of turf. The covers are hard to spot and can be removed whenever necessary.

DISGUISES FOR EYESORES

GREAT GARDEN-MAKERS of the past 'borrowed' the surrounding landscape, incorporating it into their designs so that the owner's land seemed to extend to the horizon. This was achieved by inserting gaps in surrounding woodland, by building unobtrusive boundaries such as ha-has, and with major earth-moving projects that opened new vistas.

As today's gardens are generally small, it is more usual now to attempt to block out the surrounding views and overlooking neighbours. Even so, it is a mistake to surround the garden completely with tall fences and barricade yourself into your plot.

SCREENING UNWELCOME VIEWS OUTSIDE THE GARDEN

When screening an unpleasant outside view, or trying to gain privacy from prying eyes, many people erect a wooden panel fence – and then try to cover up its bare expanses. This is not always easy since many fences are not strong enough to support the weight of heavy climbers. The fact that the climbers are growing on one side only of the fence makes a weak fence more unstable.

Take a longer-term solution and erect a tall, strong fence of concrete posts with chain-link mesh between them. It looks uninspiring in the early stages, but provides real support for plants and allows light and air to get to them from all sides.

Hardy and reliable year-round cover is vital in such a situation, so choose a mixture of evergreens – some with the bonus of flowers and berries to add colour. Ivies and evergreen honeysuckle and clematis can be threaded with roses, summer or winter jasmine, everlasting pea (*Lathyrus latifolius*) and the self-supporting pyracantha. The cranesbill (*Geranium procurrens*) is not usually a climber, but it threads its way up other plants whenever it gets the opportunity.

VANISHING TELEGRAPH POLES

A telegraph pole is a common eyesore and the usual answer is to plant a tall conifer in front of it. Often, this simply emphasises that there is something tall behind, especially if the top of the pole is visible above the plant. It is better to ignore the pole and to place something

SOFTENING SOLID SHAPES Oil tanks can be hard to disguise, but are more easily 'lost' if painted a sympathetic colour. Striking foliage plants may soften straight edges more effectively than shape-hugging climbers.

eye-catching nearby to draw the eye, ousting the previous dominant feature.

With careful design, similar unsightly objects at the edge of a view are upstaged by something attractive and become less obvious. An elegant piece of topiary, an obelisk or an arbour swathed with climbers are permanent distractions.

Another possibility is to make a negative feature into a positive one by planting an ivy or other fast-growing climber up a pole. This is not a possibility with most telegraph poles unless you have permission to do so (this is often refused because telegraph poles require regular inspection and maintenance) but could be used with a similarly shaped eyesore.

HIDING BINS AND OIL TANKS

An eyesore that nearly everybody has to cope with is the dustbin. Gardeners have compost bins too, but these pose an easier problem; they are usually at the far end of the garden where there is scope

CAPTURING THE INTEREST A successful way of pulling the attention away from unsightly dustbins is to place a bold plant nearby. Here, a light-coloured ground cover of gravel and the ribbed, blue-green leaves of *Hosta sieboldiana* var. *elegans* deter the eye from straying behind.

MOVABLE HEDGE

IF YOU HAVE DUSTBINS on a hard surface, plant a movable hedge. A wooden trough at least 15 in (38 cm) wide and deep and filled with a heavy compost is suitable for a hedge of conifer or beech.

Beech hedges that mix green and copper colours are particularly pretty. Clip the sides once a year, in August, to promote bushy growth. Once the hedge reaches about 4 ft (1.2 m) or the desired height clip the top as well.

MASKING A GREENHOUSE A trellis façade breaks up the substantial outline of a greenhouse in winter. When it is not covered in foliage, the trellis allows a significant level of light to reach the plants inside. In the summer, when the sun is brighter, it can support climbing annuals.

for screening by fencing or plants. It may be a satisfying DIY project to build a dustbin compound, but the building rarely achieves its aim because of its solid and obvious outline. Take a leaf out of nature's book. The stripes of a zebra break up its outline, making it difficult to recognise, especially in shifting vertical grass stems. It is not actually hidden, but it is hard to see.

Similarly, plants and screens in the garden can break up the outline of an unsightly object. Evergreens are the best choice as screening material, because the effect is there all year round.

A screen of open-textured evergreens of various heights works well. Ferns and hebes are discreet; the grass *Miscanthus sinensis* keeps its shape in winter and quickly puts up new growth after being cut back in March; *Brachyglottis* 'Sunshine' has loose growth and loves the sun, while *Mahonia japonica* is upright in its growth and tolerant of shade and wind.

Climbers can be great disguisers, but they will give the game away if they follow the contours of a solid, square object. A climber-coated oil tank, for example, remains an unlovely oddity on its own, but surround it with shrubs clipped into blocks and together they make a sort of modern Cubist feature.

Many oil tanks and solid-fuel bunkers are in a prominent position because of the need for access. Screen the object with decorative trellis, or grow a climber as cover. When the surface is smooth so that plants cannot grip, a covering of netting is essential. This also helps when the object needs maintenance such as painting; the netting peels back with care, leaving the plants undamaged.

Once fitted, netting enables almost any climber to scramble up it but make sure you consider the ultimate heights of the plants. They can quickly become a nuisance if they foam too vigorously over the top of the supporting structure.

INSPECTION CHAMBER COVERS

The art of disguise is a difficult one. Great restraint is needed or the disguise itself becomes so artful that it attracts the eye, actually drawing attention to the object you want to lose. This is sometimes a drawback of devices on sale which can be used to hide eyesores. The standard inspection cover found in many

COVERING UP A TREE STUMP

IF IT IS TOO DESTRUCTIVE to remove the stump of a dead tree for some time – because of beloved plants around it, perhaps – smother it with fast-growing annuals such as nasturtiums or dwarf sweet peas until it can be taken out.

One solution often seen is to leave a knee-high stump, drill out the centre and plant it with flowers, but plants in the ground give more vigorous growth and form a more luxuriant cover.

SUMMER SCREENING Make the best use of plants that winter in the greenhouse by bringing them outside in late spring and placing them to hide an unattractive structure. As the sun sinks lower in the sky towards summer's end, return them to their place of warmth and let in more light.

drives, paths and lawns is hardly a thing of beauty, and yet it has to be lived with. In a drive it does not always look too unpleasant, but in a lawn it spoils the whole garden view. A common solution is to place plants on the cover, making a feature in itself. But does such treatment really disguise the cover?

The answer must be no, for in what other circumstance would a gardener place a tub full of flowers in the middle of a lawn? But turn the surrounding area into a hard surface with paving or gravel, and pots or trailing plants are more easily incorporated.

Where the cover is not too far from the edge of a lawn, extend a flowerbed to engulf the offending object and plant periwinkles for ground cover, an ornamental bramble such as the nonfruiting pink-flowered *Rubus ulmifolius* 'Bellidiflorus' and prostrate *Cotoneaster dammeri* to throw long arms of growth over it. When the time comes to open the cover, peg back the plants or, if necessary, cut them back. They will soon recover.

BLOCKING SIGHT NOT LIGHT

One of the most difficult garden features to screen effectively is a greenhouse, because it is essential that light reaches it at all times, especially in the winter when the sun is low in the sky. The problem does not arise if you choose a greenhouse that is attractive in itself, with shapely windows and an elegant frame, rather than one held together with a web of utilitarian struts and frames of metal.

Even when you take over a garden with an ugly greenhouse, there are ways to lessen its impact.

🌢 A tall summer screen of herbaceous plants in a flowerbed will cover the sides but rarely the roof. *Rudbeckia laciniata*, *Macleaya microcarpa*, *Helenium autumnale*, and perennial sunflower (*Helianthus decapetalus*) are all suitable.

🌢 Tall plants in pots, such as standard fuchsias, which winter inside, earn their keep by covering the sides in summer.

🌢 In summer, cover a trellis barrier with annual climbers such as sweet peas and morning glory to give a complete screen. Ornamental, painted trelliswork fitted to the greenhouse itself provides effective shading in summer.

🌢 A temporary screen of canes and runner beans is especially effective when combined with a few flowers such as climbing nasturtiums, morning glory or black-eyed Susan.

🌢 An informal planting of trees and shrubs such as fatsia, broom, lilac and mock orange (*Philadelphus*) provides an effective screen. You can incorporate your favourite plants.

MAKING FANCIFUL FEATURES FROM SHEDS

Disguise need not always be a low-key operation. Putting on a bold front sometimes creates the most convincing appearance of genuine beauty so that few observers ever notice the plainness of the features beneath.

The lean-to greenhouse, for example, is a workaday, practical way to grow plants, enjoy winter sunshine and keep the house warmer. But why not make it a visual asset as well. When the lean-to greenhouse is elaborately framed and equipped with graceful and mobile tiered

IMPROVING DARK CORNERS Overhanging trees can create a dark, dank corner in the garden which is hard to plant. To counter this, construct an archway to trick the viewer into thinking it leads somewhere, and plant light, bright colours in the foreground. The dark corner fades away.

trolleys to act as staging, it becomes a conservatory and is then proudly displayed to the whole world.

With a similar positive approach, you can make a shed become almost anything you want. Use a small quantity of marine plywood and a liberal application of imagination to transform it.

🌰 With pierced wavy eaves and shutters, and some pots of pelargoniums it becomes a chalet.

🌰 Pointed arches at the windows and door and a turret on the roof make it a Gothic lodge.

🌰 Create a grotto with a crenellated roofline, slit windows peering from ivy, a deep porch housing a trickling water feature, a grotesque wall mask and moss-covered rocks flanked by ferns.

🌰 Painted classical columns and a portico round the door make it a temple. Add standard bays or topiary cones for greenery of equal formality.

🌰 Give the shed a Chinese look, with a pagoda-style gable and a coat of bright red paint.

🌰 Paint the shed white and fix black beams to the outside to give it the air of a Tudor-style cottage.

🌰 If there are young children in the family, paint the shed in candy colours and add barley-sugar banister rails to make a gingerbread cottage.

🌰 Decorate the sides of the shed with split larch poles and grow dwarf pines round it for a woodland cabin.

GUILE WITH PAINT

Colour is an essential aspect of disguise and paint in the garden is a great asset, though it may take some experimenting to get just the right effect. Because paint has to be renewed regularly, or can be painted over almost immediately if a mistake is made, any indiscretions are not long-term blots on the scene.

It is common to paint objects in the garden brown, as though that makes them more attractive or more natural and therefore less obvious. But, in fact, very few items in the garden are brown; even the soil and tree trunks lean strongly from brown towards grey.

The other temptation is to paint them green, but there is a huge variety of shades when it comes to choosing a green. Particular care is needed when choosing one for painting a solid shape such as an oil tank, since little natural greenery has such a rigid shape.

Green can be suitable in some cases, but it is better to avoid bright green and choose a dull, mossy shade, a blue-green or a subtle dark grey-green. Place plants around it that have interesting foliage texture so that the tank or other object acts as a foil for the plants.

COLOUR DISGUISE IN SHADE

When an object for hiding is in a dim corner of the garden, perhaps overhung by trees, with a predominantly sombre background, dark paint makes it disappear – black or deep green work best.

The planting around and in front may have to be largely evergreens if the lack of light restricts the planting choice, but even here there are plants with bold leaves, such as fatsia, ferns and bergenias, to contrast with the smaller foliage of those stalwarts, privet and skimmia.

The evergreen euonymus has bright variegated forms, and if the front of the bed is in better light, yellow-flowered rose of Sharon (*Hypericum calycinum*), lilies, sparkling white-flowered *Trillium grandiflorum* and primulas add colour.

Avoid the temptation to position a tall variegated or white-flowered plant against any object you want to hide

DISTRACTING THE EYE To disguise a large object in a shady part of the garden, paint it black or a deep green to make it disappear and then use it as a backdrop to colourful plants placed well forward in the light.

BEST PLANTS

LEAFY DISGUISERS

Whatever the season, there are plants whose eager growth covers an eyesore.

- *Euonymus fortunei* 'Emerald 'n' Gold': yellow and green leaves form excellent wall or ground cover all year.

- *Cotoneaster horizontalis*: small-leaved with pink flowers, copious red berries and herringbone growth.

- Winter-flowering jasmine (*Jasminum nudiflorum*): a good scrambler with yellow winter flowers before the leaves.

- Boston ivy (*Parthenocissus tricuspidata*): a vigorous plant that provides excellent extensive leaf cover.

- *Akebia quinata*: a small-leaved twining evergreen with small, deep-purple, scented flowers in spring.

- Tree poppy (*Romneya coulteri*): fast-spreading and bluish-leaved, with large white, poppylike summer flowers.

- *Humulus japonicus* 'Variegatus': fast-growing annual with white markings.

- Plume poppy (*Macleaya cordata*): tall, herbaceous plant with large leaves.

- Persian ivy (*Hedera colchica*): huge-leaved, glossy evergreen that will swarm anywhere.

---

because the result is to draw attention to it and make it more obvious. White flowers are beautiful in any garden, but pure white is too much of a contrast against dark green when the idea is to blend an object into the shadows. Employ subtlety and avoid clashes and contrasts of colour that clamour for notice.

COLOUR DISGUISE IN LIGHT PLACES

Matching the planting scheme colours to the paintwork or the colour of an object that needs to be disguised is a very effective way of making the two work as a harmonious whole in a bright area.

To achieve this sense of harmony, first choose the type of plants to go around the object as a key for the colour theme. This theme suggests what colour to paint the object in full sun. Black is rarely the answer, as it is the most difficult colour to hide in bright light.

One effective scheme is to plant a collection of conifers around the object, choosing mainly golden-leaved varieties. Painting the object a shade of earthy ochre or a neutral yellow that is duller than the conifers helps it to recede gently into the background. It is the brightly coloured conifers that hold the eye.

Similarly, a steely blue colour for the object would be effective with a fronting of grey conifers, blueish *Hosta sieboldiana* 'Elegans', and grey-leaved lavender.

Light colours, especially misty blues and lavenders, make objects fade into the distance. These colours are especially effective in winter, when the cold, thin light matches their pale tone.

If an object to be hidden is large – a shed or a bunker, for example – make it work as scenery. Bands of bronze and gold shades painted around the base of the object with blue above makes a background for the sun-loving, silver-leaved *Santolina chamaecyparissus*, *Brachyglottis* 'Sunshine', *Artemisia schmidtiana* and *Stachys byzantina*. Frame the sides of the shed or bunker with *Yucca gloriosa* and tall grasses set in silver-grey gravel.

With imaginative use of paint, screening, plants and layout, you can improve the most unpromising scene, concealing its bad points, enhancing its virtues and increasing your pleasure in the garden.

REFLECTING SUNLIGHT Use variegated and yellow ivies to give a sunny covering to an inexpensive wire-netting fence. Behind it you can discreetly hide a barrow, compost bin, or any other unattractive odds and ends.

INSPIRATION FROM

GREAT GARDENS

HAM HOUSE

Formality is cherished, inside and out.

*Ham House, situated on the banks
of the River Thames just west of
London, is one of the least altered
17th-century houses in the country.
The gracious formality of the
original garden, established in the
1670s, is being restored by the
National Trust, who have brought
back to life its eight geometrically
placed lawns, a wilderness and
a classic parterre enclosed by a
series of arboreal tunnels.*

I N A LARGE GARDEN, a tunnel of trees such as those in the grounds at Ham House serves two purposes. It works as a feature in its own right, and also gently focuses the visitor's attention on other attributes of the place.

The tunnels at Ham, for example, define the parterre, crisp rectangles of miniature box hedging punctuated by taller cones. The rectangles are filled alternately with blue lavender and the pale grey and gold of cotton lavender.

The proper way to view the parterre is through the eye-level gap in the sides of the tunnels. These are made from solid yew hedge to chest height, above which pleached hornbeams trained on steel frames make curved roofs overhead. In summer, the tunnels are cool, green and dim, contrasting with the brightness of the parterre outside. When autumn turns the roof yellow, it seems as sunny within as a bright summer's day, while in winter, the bare branches weave an intricate pattern against the pearly sky.

Throughout the year, the tunnels' exits, far off down a dwindling perspective, beckon strollers to view the rest of the garden – some 20 acres, bounded by walls of stone. The current layout of the

ARCHED PATHWAYS The tunnels serve a double purpose at Ham, attractive in their own right and drawing the eye to the distance.

with wild flowers, and edged with hornbeam. Throughout, the gardens are filled with plants that were popular in the 17th century, and it is for this reason that the tunnels at Ham are made with hornbeam and cherry, often featured at the time.

CREATING DISTANCE IN A RESTRICTED SPACE

In the 17th century, illusion was often employed as part of a decorative effect – perhaps on a ceiling covered with gods cavorting in cloudscapes of apparently infinite depth. A similar juggling with perspective is one way to add greater dimension to a small plot of land.

The blank wall rearing up at the end of a small garden can give an illusion of greater openness. Make use of false perspective trelliswork, or 'treillage', which is available from garden centres.

The trellis is attached to a brick wall. Once further strips are added to extend the angled bars, you can begin to see how the trellis is going to provide a sense of distance similar to that of a tunnel. From

this point on, it is the planting around the trellis which is going to give the mock tunnel its illusion of depth. The effect is achieved by growing evergreen plants whose leaf sizes dwindle from front to rear. The larger-leaved plants bring themselves into the foreground, while those with smaller foliage seem far away.

The false tunnel is given an emphatic frame by a pair of *Chamaecyparis lawsoniana* 'Green Hedger', planted one on each side in the 2ft (60cm) strip of soil that runs along in front of the wall. Between them, and at the front of the bed, is *Bergenia cordifolia*, whose broad, red-rimmed foliage draws the eye, as well as differentiating it from the uniformly green, smaller-leaved plants behind.

For these, ivies are an obvious choice, easy to train, and with a wide number of varieties with differing leaf size to select from. Here, the large-leaved ivy *Hedera colchica* 'Dentata' is trained along the wall and creates the first two vertical lines of the mock tunnel, and the small-leaved ivy *H. helix* 'Deltoidea' is trained within it.

Once established, the tunnel will please all year round, requiring only an occasional trim to maintain the lines of perspective, and thus the illusion.

grounds is formal and serene, though not intimidating. It has been re-created, after some persistent detective work and reconstruction by the National Trust, to a design shown in a bird's eye view painting of the house in 1675.

The main part of the garden consists of a geometric arrangement of eight lawns, with gravel paths in between to be adorned with Versailles boxes. A central path leads to the wilderness, a popular 17th-century garden feature which at Ham sports grass paths radiating from a central clearing. The triangular pieces of ground between the paths are planted

ILLUSION OF SPACE The large leaves of bergenia and two different-sized ivies are combined with trellis to contribute a touch of formality and a sense of depth on a small garden's flat wall.

BEAUTY WITH A PRACTICAL PURPOSE

GARDENS CAN BE BOUNTIFUL as well as beautiful. Decorative fruit and vegetables will look handsome in the borders and be delicious to eat, while herbs that flavour your food brighten the garden as they grow. Make some space in the garden for flowers and foliage that not only look beautiful out of doors but please equally in arrangements indoors, whether fresh or dried. And remember that your perfumed plants can blend into a potpourri to bring the garden's freshness into the house. With a little planning and know-how you can double the pleasure from your garden.

Adaptable pansies mirror the deep purple foliage of beet,
making a fine edging to a vegetable plot.

COMBINING USE AND BEAUTY

LETTUCES AND LAVENDER In this potager garden, patterned brick paths run between neatly laid-out, box-edged beds that combine vegetables, flowers, fruits and herbs in a subtle colour blend.

WITH SOME FRESH IDEAS, the right plant varieties and careful planning, it is easy to combine a beautiful garden with a productive one, and all without tying yourself to the labour of the traditional style of allotment or vegetable garden. There are no rules to curb your imagination about the shapes of beds or about plant combinations. In fact the only restraints are physical – what the fruit, flowers and vegetables require in the way of light, space and soil type.

The key to such gardening satisfaction is to give up the utilitarian idea of sowing a crop in a block, watching it mature, and then harvesting it. There is no reason why food crops cannot be grown alongside flowers although in the flowerbed they must, like flowers, perform attractively for an extended period to justify their prominent position.

There is plenty of decorative potential in food crops if you look at them with a fresh eye. What could be more effective than an edging of frilled lettuce to set off a colourful flowerbed? Or perhaps a towering silvery-grey globe artichoke plant as a central feature?

You can grow fruit, vegetables and herbs in containers, or train them into interesting shapes to make a feature of them instead of hiding them away. Grow gooseberries as cordons for a bumper crop from a small area or train apples as step-overs for a space-saving display.

FLOWERS FOR THE HOUSE

Flower arranging is a passion with many people – sometimes to such a degree that the garden's main role is as a resource for arrangements. The passion can be an expensive one if all the materials have to be bought, but fortunately an average garden can provide most of what is needed. A little prudent planning ensures that raiding the beds for flowers to arrange indoors does not spoil the garden's appearance. You can use hedging space to grow a varied supply of desirable foliage, and find plenty of choice items for display in an informal bed of mingled flowers, shrubs and vegetables.

The garden is not just a source of fresh materials. You can preserve flowers and leaves for winter arrangements, or capture their essence in potpourri.

VEGETABLES AND FRUIT

IN PLANNING a useful garden, concentrate on crops that are luxury items, difficult to buy or of poor flavour in the shops. It is best to avoid staple crops such as potatoes; these are always easy to buy and they are greedy for garden space.

The current fashion for combining cropping plants and decorative ones owes something to the old cottage garden miscellany of vegetables and flowers, and a good deal more to the French tradition of a rather formal, ornamental vegetable garden. Indeed, it is the French word 'potager' that is generally used now for such vegetable gardens.

Make your potager in full sun, as most vegetables dislike shade. Prepare the soil well, incorporating garden compost, and keep the beds liberally mulched as a sure way of raising vegetables successfully. Ensure a steady flow of vegetables and

ORDERLY ABUNDANCE Vegetables, flowers and fruit trees flourish within a precise, symmetrical design. Its beauty stems from the lush profusion of the plants and the clipped neatness of the harmonious layout.

avoid too many cropping at once by planting in succession. For example, sow lettuces in batches of four every two weeks from early April until late July, putting three seeds at each of the four spots and thinning out the seedlings as they grow and fill the space.

DESIGNS FOR POTAGERS

A potager usually consists of a number of beds arranged in a geometric pattern, most often rectangular although it can take the form of diamond or even triangular beds radiating from a central point. The beds are edged with wood, brick or stone, and are frequently raised, with quite narrow paths of stone, bricks, grass, or even stepping-stones in gravel between them.

The simplest design is a square plot divided into four with a cross-shaped path. In large gardens there is room for a more elaborate plan, with more beds and a smart but space-consuming edging of

LOOKING GOOD ENOUGH TO EAT The visual pleasure gained from mingling crops, flowers and herbs is apparent here where mauve chive flowers are fronted by lettuce seedlings interspersed with feathery fennel foliage – and all these are in turn bordered by richly coloured pansies and frilly rue.

DECORATIVE CROPS Well-thought-out planting with varied leaf tone, shape and height makes rows of strawberries, parsley, onions, lettuces and cabbages a pleasure to look at even without the bonus of picking for the table.

clipped dwarf box, lavender or santolina. In a small potager define the beds with a quick, narrow hedge of ivy trained over a push-in plastic-covered wire fence.

Try to arrange the beds so that none is more than 5 ft (1.5 m) wide. This allows you to work from the edge of the bed without treading on the soil and compacting it. All the soil remains usable and a surprisingly large amount of food is harvested from a small area.

The juxtaposition of colours, textures and shapes – such as tall fluffy fennel and low, broad-leaved lettuce or silver beet all contribute towards the beauty of the potager, yet a great deal of its attractiveness lies in the overall pattern.

MAKING THE RIGHT CHOICES

The choice of vegetables is a personal one but where space is short, stick to good croppers with ornamental value. Runner beans are high performers that look as good as they taste, and red cabbages are certainly not out of place in the flowerbed. Chives or thyme make a pretty edging to a garden path and are equally decorative for planting under standard roses in the border.

Groups of vivid ruby chard and beetroot, whose green tops are crisscrossed with strong red veins, make striking focal points. Even the brussels sprout has an ornamental version, 'Rubin', which besides glowing with crimson-red leaves has a delicious nutty flavour.

It is best to exclude maincrop potatoes, onions – and probably peas except for mangetout (sugar peas), which are easy to grow, crop over a long period, and are delicious cooked or raw. If you want to grow potatoes, bring on a few new potatoes early under cloches or grow the unusual knobbly salad potato 'Pink Fir Apple', which is rarely on sale.

WAYS TO ADD HEIGHT

Potagers look somewhat flat unless you include plants that provide vertical points of interest. Add height and decorative value with a cane pyramid smothered

ORNAMENTAL CABBAGES With frilled leaves coloured grey-green or red, or with vivid splashes of pink, ornamental cabbages and kales add richness to a planting scheme. Varieties crop through autumn and winter.

TRAIN A STANDARD REDCURRANT

WHEN IT IS LADEN with its glistening red chains of ripe fruits, a redcurrant bush is the ideal combination of beauty and usefulness. It is often grown as a low bush or as one of a row of cordons, but it is shown off to perfection when trained as a standard in either a potager or a flowerbed so that its head is held above the surrounding plants. It needs no more care than other styles of bush.

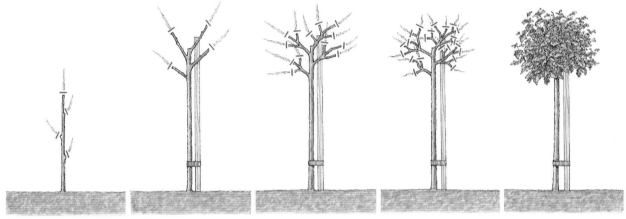

1. Plant a vigorous one-year-old rooted cutting and remove all its sideshoots. The main stem will reach about 3 ft (1 m) during the season – about the right height for a standard. In the autumn cut the tip off the main stem and remove any further sideshoots.

2. The following year three or four sideshoots will arise near the top. Leave them to develop as leaders but cut out all other shoots. When the growing season is over, cut back each leader by half to two-thirds, cutting just above an outward-pointing bud.

3. In the third February, keep about seven of the shoots at the top to form a framework of main leaders, well spaced to admit light and air. Cut half to two-thirds off the length of these leaders and cut out entirely any other shoots that have arisen on the trunk.

4. By the fourth February, each cut-back leader will have produced two new leaders and some laterals (sideshoots). Keep one or two laterals on each branch to add to an even shape; remove the others, then trim all shoots by a third, cutting above outward-pointing buds.

5. In subsequent years, cut back the leaders by half in February and cut laterals back to two or three buds to produce fruiting subsidiary shoots. Every June trim back the subsidiary shoots to about six leaves to open up the head and encourage the fruit to ripen.

with runner beans or sweet peas as a centrepoint in each bed, a rose arch at the entrance to each path, fruit bushes at all the corners or small topiary shapes spaced out along the paths.

As a single tall feature in a small potager, make an arbour at the centre where two paths cross. Keep the structure simple – four wooden posts with crossbeams over the top. Clothe it with peas, beans, ornamental gourds, runner beans, marrows or the purple-podded climbing French beans, which change to green when cooked.

Do not separate your flowers from these climbing vegetables. Plant morning glory (*Ipomoea*), *Mina lobata*, canary creeper or sweet peas to grow through them. The flowers attract pollinating insects, ensuring good crops, although a little extra feeding and room are necessary because the different plants are competing for the same nutrients.

For a spectacular entrance to the potager, grow a pair of standard roses to serve as ornamental gateposts, or be more original with a pair of standard redcurrants. The lobed leaves are decorative on their own but the main glory comes with the chains of glistening ruby fruits in June. From the practical viewpoint, the compact head at shoulder height is easy to net if birds are a problem, and the formal shape makes a focal point all year.

Globe artichokes can do the same job for a single season. These imposing grey-green plants are like giant thistles with huge flower heads to pick at bud stage for a table delicacy.

HEIGHT WITH SCREENS AND EDGINGS

A screen of vegetables or fruit is useful and ornamental for separating the potager from the rest of the garden. It is even more useful in blocking an ugly view or hiding one particular eyesore, such as your valuable but unlovely compost heap. As a temporary screen, staple netting to a stout row of canes and let runner beans or a vigorous variety of pea scramble up it. Runner beans come with flowers in a range of shades from white to red, or both in the case of the ancient but incomparably flavoured 'Painted Lady'.

As a denser screen, erect a double row of 6 ft (1.8 m) canes and cover them with a thick mixed planting of runner beans, French beans, peas and climbing flowers such as black-eyed Susan (*Thunbergia alata*), and even cranesbills and Peruvian lilies, which reach up remarkably when they are given a support.

A lacy screen for summer is created by a well-nourished permanent bed of asparagus. Young asparagus shoots are a culinary treat in early summer, and later the ferny foliage grows more than head high, providing a pretty background to flowers and looking dainty in arrangements, especially with sweet peas.

Jerusalem artichokes, a relative of the sunflower, are very easy to grow. Their tall stems clothed in rough green leaves make an effective windbreak, and are so tough that even after they are dead the strongest serve as temporary stakes for small plants. The knobbly tubers of this artichoke are delicious boiled or made into soup. Sunflowers have similarly tough stems, and a row of these large-flowered hardy annuals makes an attractive hedge in summer – especially if you choose one of the multistemmed varieties with smaller blooms in shades of white, gold or even deep red.

Sweetcorn, another tall, large-leaved crop, makes a thick screen in a sunny spot. It is usually planted in blocks for the best pollination of cobs, but a double row planted as a screen crops well. Look for unusual varieties with variegated foliage or cobs of different coloured grains.

As a more permanent woody screen along the potager's boundary, grow cordon apples, pears, gooseberries or currants; or train loganberries, blackberries or Tayberries on horizontal wires. Such screens are best for the northern side of the plot, where they cast no shade.

Gooseberries are a productive edging for paths. Train them as slim, low cordons so that their scratchy branches do not encroach. The knobbly shapes make a strong outline through the winter.

Colourful summer edgings for the beds are purple-podded peas and French beans with yellow and purple pods.

CROPS IN CONTAINERS

For gardeners with a space problem who long to grow vegetables, there is an easy solution. Many types of vegetable do well in containers. Besides growing new potatoes in tubs, try putting leeks, carrots and even the luxurious asparagus in builders' big black buckets with several drainage holes pierced at intervals round the base.

There is no need to confine yourself to ground-level containers. Raised or hanging ones will give some rewarding results – and at a convenient height.
- Mix courgettes and nasturtiums in a hanging box for display as well as a crop.
- Suspend miniature tomatoes and bush basil or New Zealand spinach in deep hanging baskets.
- Raise herbs in a handy window box outside the kitchen to provide instantly accessible flavourings when cooking.

A cheap and easy container for bringing vegetables, fruit and flowers into growth in unpromising spots is the growing bag. Anywhere you can reach with water becomes a potential growing site. Tomatoes, peppers, aubergines, courgettes, lettuces and beans all thrive in growing bags – in fact the only limit to your success is the amount of water and

STANDING TALL Training a fruit bush as a standard adds height to a flat planting scheme and utilises space well. This gooseberry standard is set off by pink alliums which are easy to grow from bulbs planted in autumn.

feed you supply. Brighten up a bag by putting a few extra plants along its edges as decoration. Lobelia and petunias will quickly smother the bag, as well as attracting pollinators for crops. In the sheltered areas that suit tomatoes, the perfect bagshare is basil, which combines with them so well for the table.

TRY SOMETHING DIFFERENT

Experiment with unusual vegetables for the sheer sparkle they bring. Ruby chard, a plant closely related to beetroot and spinach beet, gives double value with the long thick stalks and midribs to serve like asparagus and the leaves like spinach. The plant is easy to grow and the stalks can be pulled throughout summer and into autumn. Rainbow chard is white and yellow as well as red.

Endive and chicory are both very decorative, endive with frilly, lacy leaves and chicory with the red-tinged leaves and striking red and white hearts that are often known as radicchio.

Chinese vegetables include a variety of greens besides the white barrel-heads of Chinese cabbage. Some greens run to

PRETTY AND PRODUCTIVE Even a trough of flowers has potential for food crops. You can grow a few cabbages among the brightly coloured nasturtiums for foliage that is decorative as well as edible.

seed if sown too early, but since the young flowering shoots of all are tasty both raw and cooked, none need go to waste. They are fast growing with most ready to harvest in 8-10 weeks, but some varieties can be picked after 3 weeks and are ideal for filling gaps between other crops or in flowerbeds. Look for mizuna greens, pak choi and komatsuna.

Peppers and chillies are both neat plants, and though the flowers are not large, the glossy green fruits – changing to red, yellow or purple – are long lasting. Choose those suited to outdoor culture and tuck them in the warmest spot.

Tomatoes, so often thought of as a greenhouse crop, do well in sheltered

BE YOUR OWN SEEDSMAN

SAVE MONEY not only by growing your own crops but also by saving their seeds for the next season's production.

Runner bean and tomato seeds are good candidates as the characteristics bred into the parent reappear consistently in the offspring. Do not save seeds of F1 hybrids, because they do not breed true.

Let a few runner beans hang on one of the best plants until frosts are likely, then take the seeds from the pods and keep the unblemished ones.

Choose a large, fully ripe tomato, cut it open and scoop the seeds into a fine-meshed strainer. Hold it under running water while you gently clean every bit of pulp from the seeds. Spread out the seeds on newspaper until they are dry.

Put each kind of seed in its own clearly labelled paper bag and store in an airtight tin kept in a cool place until you are ready to sow them in spring.

places outside, and the outdoor fruits often have the best flavour. Grow those that you cannot buy easily or cheaply, for example the tiny sweet cherry types, yellow and orange varieties and large, red, full-flavoured beefsteak tomatoes.

OLD-FASHIONED FRUITS

Although most gardeners who grow fruit choose apples and pears, raspberries and strawberries, there are other fruits that are particularly worth growing because they are difficult to buy.

One such fruit is the old-fashioned medlar, which is rarely eaten nowadays, mainly because it is inedible until bletted (nearly rotten). The strong, winy flavour was appreciated with a glass of port at the end of elaborate Victorian dinners. The fruits also make a sharp jelly which is excellent for serving with rich, gamy meat. They are borne on a small tree whose large white flowers in May are beautiful and whose leaves turn yellow, purple and scarlet in many autumns.

The edible quince (*Cydonia oblonga*) is neglected, too, owing to the universal

GROWING UP Purple sage and calabrese front the long narrow leaves of sweetcorn. These, together with the round-leaved, clambering squash plants, add vertical interest to the beds of a densely planted potager.

DUAL-PURPOSE PLANTING Brilliantly coloured ruby chard and red *Nicotiana* growing together show how attractive cropping and flowering combinations can be. They are also handy – you can pick blooms for displaying in the house while gathering vegetables for the kitchen and table.

is closely related to the native bilberry, whortleberry or blaeberry, a plant which thrives in acid highland soils and has tangy small fruits hiding under the ground-hugging leaves.

Blueberries, from the United States, are larger and the main sort is the easy-to-pick highbush blueberry. The white, globular flowers develop into deep purple fruit that ripen as summer ends; the leaves assume brilliant autumn tints of scarlet and crimson.

Plant blueberries in any bed of the very acid soil they require, underplanted with heathers, gaultheria, azaleas and dwarf rhododendrons. If your soil is not acid, grow them in large tubs of erica-ceous compost, which is prepared for heather (*Erica*) and other acid-lovers. Although there are not many blueberry varieties available, it is worth growing two different types to ensure good crops.

GET THE BEST FROM BERRIES AND CURRANTS

If you do not want to grow red or white currants as showpiece standards, buy bushes with several stems coming from the root system. Prune these as open-centred bushes for a mixed bed, or plant them against a wall or screen and train them into fans. Look for well-flavoured 'Rovada' and 'Stanza' redcurrants and 'White Versailles' white currants.

Blackcurrants are easy to train as hedging to frame a potager's beds. They are long-lived plants that thrive in heavy soil. The tough 'Ben Sarek' is particularly suitable but new varieties of soft fruit are introduced each year.

The key to success is to cut the stems back to buds within 2 in (5 cm) of the ground as soon as you plant them. Most of the fruits are produced on the previous year's growth, so as soon as the leaves fall each year cut out a third of the stems, choosing the oldest ones. New fruiting shoots spring from just below the cuts.

Blackberries and raspberries are natu-rals to train as a hedge or screen but there are also more decorative things to do with them. Blackberries are attractive grown over a pergola or arch, especially if you choose the ferny-leaved 'Oregon Thorn-less' which does not scratch you as you pass beneath it.

Make a stunning centrepiece to your potager by planting four or five raspber-ries together and training them up canes. They display the startling white under-sides of the leaves whenever breezes stir

planting of the ornamental quince (*Chaenomeles*), which is a shame as the large white flowers look so attractive among the dark, white-backed leaves. In autumn the golden, round or pear-shaped fruit hang heavy on the slender twigs till the frost strikes. They have a powerful aroma that makes them doubly delightful to display in the house. Do not store the fruits touching other foods though, or they will pass on their taste.

A small tree to grow in a stretch of grass is the crab apple. Resist the most showy flowering varieties and plant the old 'John Downie' whose scarlet and yellow fruits make delicious jelly to spread on scones or to use as the base for a range of mint jellies, adding your own chopped apple-mint, orange-mint or other kind of mint.

NEW VERSION OF AN OLD FAVOURITE

While these were favourites in Britain centuries ago, a new taste that is quickly becoming a favourite is the blueberry. It

PREPARE A COLOURFUL HARVEST

Plant fruit and vegetables that please the eye as well as the palate. You can choose a decorative variety of a favourite and familiar crop such as red-leaved brussels sprouts, or grow exotic plants whose brilliance of colour or unusual form adds interest to the garden and at the table.

CAPE GOOSEBERRIES
These golden yellow fruits from Peru are the size of a cherry and enclosed in papery outer cases, which look like Chinese lanterns and make decorative clusters on the plant.

KOHLRABI
Some varieties of this quick-growing root vegetable have purple skin and flushed leaves; others are all green. It takes only 10 or 12 weeks to mature and produces crops late into autumn.

ORNAMENTAL SWEETCORN
Grow this sweetcorn, *Zea mays japonica* 'Multicolor', for its mixed seed colours. It is not served as a vegetable but makes a vivid garnish, is dried for arrangements and may be dried for cornflour.

ASPARAGUS PEAS
A low-growing plant with cinnamon scarlet flowers and grey-green leaves, this pea is pretty enough to grow in a flowerbed. The edible pods, which have four wavy flanges, should be eaten when they are very small.

RED BRUSSELS SPROUTS
The late-maturing 'Rubin' variety with dark purplish-red leaves bears well-flavoured sprouts for gathering from early winter. Plant a row for a welcome addition of colour at a bleak and bare time of year.

HIGHBUSH BLUEBERRIES
This bushy plant, native to North America, has abundant crops of sharp-flavoured slate-blue fruit in August. In autumn the foliage takes on vivid colours, which contributes to its ornamental value.

STRIPED TOMATOES
Tomatoes always look decorative growing on canes, and the 'Tigerella' variety has the added interest of ripening to red with golden stripes. The plant grows tall and has fruits ready for picking in August.

CUSTARD SQUASHES
Yellow 'Patty Pan' squashes, with their curious flying-saucer shape and frilled edging, look rather like huge creamy flowers. They are best eaten young while the flesh is tender.

them. Extend the season for enjoying fresh raspberries from the garden by growing some autumn-fruiting varieties; 'Fallgold' and 'Zeva', for example, are excellent. Cut all the varieties down to ground level once they finish fruiting.

STRAWBERRY NOVELTIES

Few plants can outdo the strawberry in combining productivity with prettiness. But beware; unless you remove stray runners regularly, the plants are apt to take over huge areas with leafy growth and not be particularly heavy cropping.

To make them even more suitable for the flowerbed, breeders have crossed the strawberry with the marsh cinquefoil. A recently developed variety is 'Serenata', which has pink blooms and gives a good crop of fruit.

Alpine strawberries make a decorative and fruitful edging. These are easily raised from seed, give reasonable crops of small fruit and are now bred to form clumps without producing runners. The fruits are produced over a long period and, although rather laborious to pick, have a fragrance and full flavour that is lacking in many of the larger kinds. The usual variety of alpine that is grown is 'Baron Solemacher'.

Lovers of two-coloured leaves sometimes choose a variegated strawberry but this is best treated as an ornamental plant since it rarely sets much fruit. It does make wonderful ground cover for semi-shade with lamium and periwinkle.

Strawberries are far more adaptable to different situations than used to be thought, so use every stratagem to extend both the space and the season for this most eagerly anticipated summer fruit.

- Grow strawberries in stacking towers, traditional strawberry pots, growing bags and even hanging baskets.
- Extend the season until the first frosts by planting one of the new varieties which fruit throughout the summer – 'Aromel' or 'Pegasus', for example.
- Propagate new plants by rooting the plantlets in pots while still attached by the runner to the parent plant.
- Use your home-raised plantlets for experiments to see how they grow in a variety of containers and composts.
- Look for the yellow fruited 'Alpine Yellow', said to taste of pineapple. Birds have trouble finding the fruits.
- Search for delicious old varieties such as 'Late Pine' and 'Royal Sovereign'.
- For ground cover make a mixture of

APPLE EDGINGS Training apple trees into narrow step-overs uses space well and makes for easy picking. The neat linear pattern formed by the branches is in harmony with the formalised layout of a potager.

alpine strawberries, violets and London pride (*Saxifraga × urbium*).

- Plant alpine strawberries round rose-beds for dainty, productive edgings.
- Place straw or grass mowings around each strawberry plant as soon as the fruits start to form to keep them clean.
- Surround strawberries with a little sawdust to deter slugs and snails, which cannot bear its texture and stay away.

SPACE-SAVING TREES

The small gardens of most modern homes have put many people off growing the old-style fruit trees. Now, however,

FRUITFUL RUFF A generous edging of strawberries is spangled with creamy-white flowers in early summer and follows them with luscious fruit. Put the plants in a sunny, sheltered spot for the most successful crops.

SECATEURS TO CUT IN STAGES

A STRAINED FOREARM and bruising on the ball of the thumb all too often follow an afternoon's pruning. It is the prolonged squeezing on secateur handles that does the damage.

Ratchet secateurs take much of the hard work out of cutting. You can apply pressure on the handles in short bursts, and handles and blades will lock in place after each squeeze.

This allows you to let go, relax the hand and then take up the hold afresh. Tough woody growths yield bit by bit to the blades.

STRAWBERRY PINK Pink-flowered strawberries are pretty enough to grow in a container to set among ornamental plants. Developed from crossing strawberries with cinquefoil, some varieties are more decorative than fruitful.

you can have a mini-orchard without broad acres. New varieties of fruit need little ground space, and now cordons, step-overs, Ballerinas and Minarettes are being grown in many suburban and small country gardens. Dwarf plants suffer badly when starved or too dry, so you must plant them in rich soil and keep them well fed and watered.

STEP-OVER APPLE TREES

Apples are ideal for training as step-overs along the edges of beds in the potager. Cut back the leading shoot of the dwarf tree at about 8 in (20 cm) high and train the two main sideshoots in opposite directions along wires. Remove any other sideshoots from the main stem. This controls the growth and ensures that short, fruit-bearing spurs develop evenly along the two sideshoots. Further pruning is not usually needed because there is very little growth of leafy shoots. Another method is to let two shoots grow upright, then carefully lower them to the horizontal and tie them to the wires.

Despite their name, step-over apple trees are suitable for edging only where they are not likely to be brushed against. Knocking them may damage the buds or developing fruit. They are easy to reach for picking (and netting if necessary) and the trees look good all year round, presenting rows of delicate blossom, then of developing fruits, and even in winter they make an interesting pattern.

CORDONS AND ESPALIERS

More productive than step-overs, though needing no more ground area, are cordons – single-stemmed plants grown slantwise at 45° and tied to four horizontal wires with about 2 ft (60 cm) between tiers. Because many trees fit into a small area, you can easily mix suitable pollinators. A long succession of apples will be produced by 'Discovery', 'George Cave', 'Golden Delicious', 'Crispin' and 'Tydeman's Late Orange'.

Be just a little bolder and you can train your apples or pears as espaliers to make a striking formal screen across one end of your potager – or, indeed, anywhere in the garden. Espaliers are trained as a series of horizontal layers coming out from a vertical stem, in much the same way as pleached trees (see p.49). They can line a bed or path or be grown against a wall to give them more shelter.

In the early stages make sure there is no serious competition for nutrients and

FRUITING ARCHES TO WALK UNDER Apple trees can be trained over strong metal supports to form a beautiful tunnel. As well as bearing generous crops of delicious fruit, the tunnel provides a focal point in the garden from spring blossom through to leaf fall in autumn.

light. Later on, a few annuals round their feet – some knee-high sweet peas, for example – do no harm.

An arch formed by two trees of restricted growth fits in a surprisingly small space, and a short tunnel with perhaps three trees on each side takes no more space than one full-size tree.

BALLERINAS AND MINARETTES

An alternative to carefully pruned apple trees are Ballerinas. These have all been bred from a single shoot on one tree, which showed a desire to grow strong and tall but produced few sideshoots.

The resulting trees make columns of foliage, flowers and fruit that serve as accents where you need a tall specimen that casts little shade. However, only a limited number of varieties have been bred in this form so far, and these do not include many favourite apples.

Minarettes were developed to provide a wider choice of trees with characteristics similar to Ballerinas. The usual apple varieties are grown on dwarfing rootstocks and trained as a column. Unlike Ballerinas, Minarettes have the potential to grow into normal bushes and need simple pruning to keep them in shape. Both Minarettes and Ballerinas do well in containers as well as in flowerbeds.

LUXURIES AND CURIOSITIES

The fig is an unjustly neglected fruit for it has a luscious honeyed sweetness when fresh and ripe. Grow 'Marseilles' or 'Negro Largo' as a compact bush or a full

TO THE RESCUE

SAVING FRUIT

FRUIT CROPS are reduced or lost entirely if a late frost strikes at blossom time. Take action quickly when frost is forecast. Use clothes pegs to hold a sheet of garden fleece or a lightweight net curtain across a row of cordons. Peg a large sheet or old tablecloth over bushes and small trees. At ground level, give insulation with sheets of newspaper held down by light plastic netting held in place by short canes.

---

standard. The leaves, resembling large hands, are always striking, and because the fruits develop without pollination there are no problems with fertilisation. Figs crop best when their roots are restricted, so make perfect pot plants for a sheltered patio. Put them under cover only during the worst frosts.

If you grow a fig in a mild garden, put it by a warm wall and restrict the roots by digging a planting pit 2-3 ft (60-90 cm) square. Line the pit with bricks or paving slabs before filling it with soil.

Grapes make striking ornamental plants as well as producing fruit, but they do not need to be grown in the traditional way – on walls or horizontal wires. All varieties climb up and over pergolas and arbours. Once the leading shoot has reached the desired height, pinch out the tip to encourage branching. In winter reduce each sideshoot to just one or two buds; when these grow in spring and a

flower cluster opens, nip off the shoot one or two leaves beyond the cluster.

You can grow dessert grapes as standards in pots, pruning to develop a small round head which will bear up to a dozen bunches of grapes. 'Black Hamburgh' and 'Bacchus' are suitable varieties.

If you have a sunny conservatory to move the grapes to in autumn, give yourself a treat and grow the fine-flavoured muscat grapes that require longer to ripen than British summers allow.

Some fruits are so unusual in Britain that they have curiosity value. The most impressive of them is the banana. True bananas (*Musa*) are not often seen but try 'Dwarf Cavendish' and you stand a real chance of getting some fruit – as long as you have a sunny conservatory. Once a stem has produced fruit, it slowly dies, but by then new stems have grown.

Occasionally the most unexpected plants give crops of fruit. This can

HERB GARDENS

FEW PLANTS OUTDO herbs for the number of uses they can be put to. Herbs have been popular since Roman times for flavouring food, in cosmetics and to make medicines; some also repel insects and are used to dye clothes. And if all that were not enough to guarantee them a place in the garden, they look good and give out invigorating scents when you brush against them.

Almost everyone must have grown a few chives or some mint in a corner of the garden at some time. The recent enthusiasm for growing herbs is part of a general move towards well-flavoured food and an eagerness to re-create dishes enjoyed on trips abroad. Many herbs are easy to grow, being very undemanding plants which thrive when they are neglected, and actually prefer poor soil to rich. Their only requirements are good drainage and plenty of hot sunshine.

DESIGNS FOR HERB GARDENS

Herbs thrive in containers, and a selection in pots outside the kitchen door is the simplest herb garden, conveniently placed and Mediterranean in style. However, there are countless alternative arrangements. When you grow herbs together as a collection, a 'ladder' of alternate paving slabs and blocks of herbs is attractive along the sunny side of a fence or even the drive.

There is a satisfying formality in a chequered layout with the herbs as dark squares and paving as the light ones. Work out your own pattern to give larger spaces to the herbs you use most.

A wheel design has a beautiful symmetry. A real cartwheel is not big enough for most people's herbs but it is easy to mark out a wheel with bricks or little

happen with the passionflower (*Passiflora caerulea*), whose lovely blooms may be followed in hot summers by a crop of pale orange, egg-shaped fruits. They add colour to fruit salads or can be halved when ripe and wrinkled and sprinkled with sherry before being eaten.

Cape gooseberries (*Physalis peruviana*) are half-hardy annuals to start on a windowsill then plant out in June in the shelter of other plants. They resemble the invasive herbaceous Chinese lantern (*Physalis alkekengi*) but are taller and furry. The lanterns turn a straw colour when the acidic berry within each is ripe. Make an edible garnish for the table by turning back the papery cases and dipping the fruits in chocolate or sugar.

For sheer oddity grow strawberry spinach, a true spinach with fleshy red berries among the leaves. Although the fruit is bland, the plant is so strange that it is worth growing at least once.

BLEND OF COLOUR, AROMA AND TASTE Contrasting foliage spills out onto brick paving in a profuse herb bed. Chives and purple-leaved sage add height and colour variation behind golden-leaved marjoram and thyme, while a spider plant in a pot brought out for summer adds height.

A PATCHWORK OF HERBS

Herbs look attractive, taste delicious and have invigorating aromas – and, as if that were not enough, almost all of them are easy to grow.

HERB GARDENS require only a sunny position to flourish, so this south-west-facing garden is ideal. Shown here at the height of summer, it is bursting with colours and scents that stimulate and satisfy the senses.

Most herbs are quite tough, thriving in conditions that would kill off more demanding plants. They love poor soil and heat – hence their success in Mediterranean countries – so growing them in small beds among paving stones is easy. Besides looking lovely, the paving stones hold the warmth, make it easier to separate and contain the different types of herbs, and contribute to the pretty patchwork of colours.

PRACTICAL PLACING

Keeping the beds small allows easy access to all the plants, while placing the most commonly used herbs along the edges of the beds ensures they are convenient for picking.

Putting the different mints together in one bed looks attractive and provides you with a variety of garnishes and flavourings. The paving restrains the questing stems that run about just below the surface if left unchecked. You can push tiles between the different varieties if you want to prevent them from mingling and to save the less vigorous ones from being swamped.

Lemon-scented verbena is not hardy, so is grown in a pot which is moved indoors in winter. A pot of basil, a tender annual, is brought on early in a glass porch and put outside in June when the garden warms up.

As in every other part of the garden, colours are important. Having a few small beds makes it easy to separate clashing colours. The main colours are purple and pink, but the orange marigolds and yellow lemon balm in the front corner provide a cheerful contrast.

Similarly the blue and white of the borage and coriander stand out against the pink of the roses.

The bay is grown in a pot so that the bold vertical accent it provides can be moved about. Bay is usually listed as hardy but in a pot it is at risk from frost in many areas. Move it to a warm corner for the winter or, better, take it into a light, frost-free porch.

The dill and fennel beside the bench also give height, while the thyme and prostrate rosemary beneath are placed where they are frequently stepped on and so release their glorious aromas.

Tender bay stands outside in summer

Paving restrains rampant mints

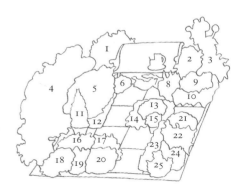

Crushed thyme smells sweet underfoot

Cheerful colours brighten the corner

1. Bronze fennel (*Foeniculum vulgare* 'Purpureum')
2. Dill (*Anethum graveolens*)
3. Angelica (*Angelica archangelica*)
4. Rose 'Ispahan'
5. Borage (*Borago officinalis*) and coriander (*Coriandrum sativum*)
6. Prostrate rosemary (*Rosmarinus officinalis* Prostratus Group)
7. Creeping thyme (*Thymus serpyllum*)
8. Lemon-scented verbena (*Aloysia triphylla*)
9. Purple sage (*Salvia officinalis* 'Purpurascens')
10. Chives (*Allium schoenoprasum*)
11. Sweet bay (*Laurus nobilis*)
12. Golden marjoram (*Origanum vulgare* 'Aureum')
13. Sage (*Salvia officinalis*)
14. Parsley (*Petroselinum crispum*)
15. Basil (*Ocimum basilicum*) and purple basil (*O. b.* 'Purpureum')
16. Black peppermint (*Mentha piperita*)
17. Variegated apple mint (*Mentha suaveolens* 'Variegata')
18. Apple mint (*Mentha suaveolens*)
19. Curled spearmint (*Mentha spicata* 'Crispa')
20. Common mint (*Mentha spicata*)
21. Golden-leaved lemon balm (*Melissa officinalis* 'Aurea')
22. Pot marigold (*Calendula officinalis*)
23. Common (or garden) thyme (*Thymus vulgaris*)
24. Hyssop (*Hyssopus officinalis*)
25. French tarragon (*Artemesia dracunculus*)

hedges of box, dwarf lavender or santolina as the spokes between beds of parsley, thyme, sage, chives, marjoram, tarragon, basil, mint, fennel, coriander, lemon balm and dwarf rosemary. Set a sundial or a pot of bay in the centre. In a more informal style the spokes could be paving wide enough to work from and the centrepiece a whirligig clothes dryer.

One way of giving different amounts of space to the herbs without disturbing the pattern is to make a spiral, widening the farther it is from the centre.

The ultimate in herb garden designs is a knot with the loops and streamers of bows marked in clipped box and herbs growing in the loops. Use string and pegs to mark out the shapes, adjusting them until you are satisfied they are right, then define them with a line of sand poured from a bottle before planting.

Herbs Among the Flowers

Many herbs are easily integrated into the flower border – convenient in a small garden – although mints need to have their spreading underground stems contained by roof tiles or bottomless buckets or plastic sacks sunk into the ground.

Mix purple and curled leaf spearmint with variegated apple mint in a bed left in a patio where you can pick at them and enjoy the aroma from a deck chair.

Grow creeping herbs – camomile, Corsican mint, pennyroyal (*Mentha pulegium*), and lemon-scented thyme – in the cracks between paving stones. They look pretty and release delicious fragrance when trodden on.

Sow seeds of coriander, fennel, dill, sweet cicely and angelica among other tall flowers and encourage borage, too. It will self seed, and though the flowers are not big, they are of such a bright blue that errant seedlings can be forgiven.

Herbs provide some of the best silver and gold foliage in the garden. Among silver-greys are the curry plant (*Helichrysum angustifolium*), thymes, sages and rosemary, which also smothers itself in blue flowers in spring. The yellow-leaved plants include golden marjoram and the gold-tipped form, both of which make bright edging plants. Yellow lemon balm makes a bushy plant in summer and has an intense, fresh scent. Cut off the flowers before seed is set or you end up with a forest of seedlings. Rosemary adds a touch of gold in its gilded form, and both the 'Icterina' and 'Kew Gold' forms of sage stand out in summer.

PLANTS FOR FLOWER ARRANGERS

CUT FLOWERS bring the scent, colour and freshness of the garden into your home, but before you rush to plant the best flowers for cutting, remember that foliage makes an equally valuable contribution. Every bloom makes more impact, and fewer are needed, when partnered by plenty of foliage. In florists' shops it is leaves, not flowers, that are expensive and in short supply.

You can grow foliage in the hedge, in screens within the garden and as shrubs scattered in the borders. Do not restrict yourself to green foliage; other colours – especially silver – are just as valuable. Make careful plans for a range of leaf size, from tiny conifers to bold fatsias and hostas. Vegetables, too, provide useful leaves and this is one of the best reasons to grow asparagus; even when crops are sparse, the feathery leaves in summer are perfect with cut flowers.

ESSENTIAL GREENERY

The commonest foliage in shops is eucalyptus and pittosporum, both of which are evergreen and grow happily in gardens provided they have a sheltered site. The easiest eucalyptus is grey *Eucalyptus gunnii*. Clipped back to ankle height each spring once the danger of frosts is over, it forms a low bush, producing wands of round leaves, the youngest flushed with pink. *Pittosporum tenuifolium* has small and glossy green, variegated or purple wavy-edged leaves, depending on the cultivar, clothing the black stems. In spring there is a bonus of chocolate brown, sweetly scented blooms.

One quick-growing Leyland cypress (× *Cupressocyparis leylandii*) supplies all you need by way of mid-green foliage. For small gardens the slower-growing *Chamaecyparis* 'Green Hedger' is better.

Other shrubs that fit comfortably into borders and are tolerant of cutting are the evergreens Mexican orange blossom (*Choisya ternata*), *Coronilla glauca* and *Elaeagnus*. *Choisya*, with its shiny deep-green leaves in sets of three, makes a

STRIKING SPECIMENS Gain the double benefit of height and drama in the garden with outstanding foliage for flower arrangements. Grey-green, toothed *Melianthus major* grows behind sword-shaped *Phormium* leaves.

strong foil for all flowers, while *Coronilla glauca* provides blue-grey leaves that complement blue, mauve and pink flowers. *Elaeagnus pungens* 'Maculata' has generous splashes of yellow in the leaves, but *E. × ebbingei* is faster growing. Though it is plain green, it has a form 'Limelight' with a yellow splash and scented, silvery autumn flowers, followed by orange berries in some seasons.

DOUBLE-VALUE FOLIAGE PLANTS

When your garden needs a hedge, make sure you plant one that has foliage attractive enough for flower arrangements. For a low hedge, consider *Euonymus fortunei* and *E. japonicus*. Both are evergreen and best known with yellow or white variegations. Euonymus does well in shade as long as it is well fed and watered there.

Another low-growing evergreen is *Viburnum davidii* whose handsome large leaves have three deep grooves from stem to tip. With both male and female plants mingled in a hedge, you get a bonus of unusual turquoise berries after the flat heads of white midsummer flowers.

A loose, open screen is formed by the evergreen fatsia, whose large leaves are prized by flower arrangers. The stems are rather sparse and the leaves need to be removed individually. An underplanting of periwinkles fills out the bare base and gives extra evergreen foliage.

Garrya elliptica is quick-growing and bushy, with crinkled evergreen leaves and long grey catkins in winter. Plant the scented, winter-flowering *Viburnum × bodnantense* 'Dawn' beside it – and use the two together in arrangements as well.

Rather similar to garrya is *Itea ilicifolia*, which produces its long, scented, greenish catkins in midsummer. It needs a sunny wall, while garrya will tolerate one facing north or north-west.

COLOURFUL SPECIMEN PLANTS

Just because privet (*Ligustrum*) is widely grown, do not overlook its virtues. Golden privet (*L. ovalifolium* 'Aureomarginatum') is a bright spark in border or vase to accompany fiery *Crocosmia* 'Lucifer', *Dahlia* 'Bishop of Llandaff' or *Lilium* 'Enchantment'; alternatively, aim for a contrast with cool blue delphiniums, lupins or anchusa.

The common hollies *Ilex aquifolium* and the bolder *Ilex × altaclerensis* are valued for their shapely, glossy leaves which, with the addition of white or gold variegations and brilliant scarlet berries,

BOLD BACKDROP Evergreen *Fatsia japonica* grows as an open shrub with large, glossy leaves. Picked individually and brought indoors, the leaves make a stunning backdrop to choice flowers.

WARM TINTS *Cotinus coggygria* 'Royal Purple' adds depth and contrast to pink *Alstroemeria* flowers in the garden or in a vase.

SHADES OF RED The young leaves of *Photinia × fraseri* 'Red Robin' are shiny red and make an interesting variation in foliage colour.

WINTER STYLE The white-veined, arrow-shaped leaves of *Arum italicum* 'Pictum' are prized for winter arrangements – as are the green flowers and toothed foliage of *Helleborus argutifolius*.

PALE BEAUTIES The honesty (*Lunaria annua* 'Alba Variegata') may have the background role while the tulip 'White Triumphator' blooms in spring, but honesty's smart leaves persist after tulips fade – and it has papery silver seed-discs for autumn arrangements.

look superb when they are mixed with luminous white flowers. Do not clip the bushes into small dumplings. Instead, cut out long stems as you need them; this keeps a more open bush and provides more stems suitable for arrangements.

New Zealand flax (*Phormium*) has swordlike leaves up to 6 ft (1.8 m) long – and even taller flower spikes. The common forms have green or bronze leaves, but there are varieties striped in yellow, pink, red and orange. The leaves last for weeks in water. In a border they go well with hebes and prostrate conifers.

Senecio cineraria, formerly known as *Cineraria maritima*, is a silvery leaved ferny plant popular in summer bedding schemes. In all but the coldest gardens, however, it survives the winter and it is excellent for winter picking. *Brachyglottis* 'Sunshine' makes long stems of oval, grey leaves that fit into any scheme.

DECIDUOUS BEAUTY

Shoots of many deciduous shrubs wilt quickly so are rarely seen in shops. You must use them quickly after cutting or condition them before use by standing them in deep cold water overnight. The red-berried elder (*Sambucus racemosa*) in the yellow-leaved form 'Plumosa Aurea' has divided leaves of a rich butter-yellow with a purplish flush. The common elder is parent to some desirable garden plants that do well in the poorest soil and almost any conditions. The best is *Sambucus nigra*, especially 'Guincho', which is purple when grown in the sun. It has the added bonus of pretty, pale pink flower heads in early summer.

The purple forms of the smoke tree (*Cotinus coggygria*) have become more popular than the green. When pruned hard every second year the bushes make compact growth with long stems for cutting; the green forms have vivid scarlet autumn colour. Vines offer rich purple leaves with extra autumn fire. For the biggest leaves on the biggest plant try *Vitis coignetiae*, or in small gardens grow *V. vinifera* 'Purpurea'.

The most admired herbaceous leaves must be the hostas. Leaves vary from just a few inches long to broad plates in green, grey or yellow; in autumn and

winter the firmest ones take on a golden translucence and last for weeks before hard frosts fell them. More substantial for winter arrangements are the leathery, round, evergreen leaves of bergenia, which are tinged red at the rim.

FERNS, GRASSES AND ANNUALS FOR DISPLAY

Ferns, especially the hardy *Dryopteris filix-mas* and *Athyrium filix-femina*, are excellent for cutting. Common Solomon's seal (*Polygonatum × hybridum*) grows well with ferns and its arching stems holding up rows of paired leaves like wings add grace to arrangements.

Though annuals are usually grown for their flowers some, such as *Euphorbia marginata*, are valued for their foliage. The leaves are rimmed and veined with white. *Kochia scoparia*, a mass of feathery growth, is a perfect foil for sculptured blooms. Cosmos and larkspur also produce dainty, finely cut leaves.

Allow your imagination to spread to the unorthodox. Variegated maize plants, and many other grasses, are easy to incorporate in arrangements. Cabbages,

kales and beetroot are among the many vegetables that have strikingly ornamental foliage worthy of display.

CUT BLOOMS FROM THE BORDER

Establishing a long succession of flowers for cutting is quick, easy and not costly. Grow quantities of perennials such as achilleas, aquilegias, delphiniums, campanulas, lupins and lobelias from seed and you have flowers from their second season, increasing in number each year.

Before the perennials occupy their full space, fill it up with hardy annuals such as larkspurs, pot marigolds and Italian white sunflowers – all fast growers with plenty of flowers. Half-hardy annuals add to the choice with, for example, orange and bronze French and African marigolds, scarlet salvias and blue ageratums. All last well in water. Once you have planted your range of quick-to-establish flowers, fine-tune with particular colours and improve the succession.

FLOWERS TO CUT IN SPRING

Tulips and daffodils are always available in the shops in spring, but the varieties tend to be rather limited. Grow a few of the newer shades and forms, in particular the split-corona or 'orchid-flowered' daffodils such as *Narcissus* 'Cassata', or the miniature *N.* 'Tête à Tête' which puts up several stems from each bulb.

Double, parrot and lily-flowered tulips such as white 'Schoonord', rosy 'China Pink' and brilliant 'Orange Parrot' are superb in arrangements. Prick the stem below the flower before use so that it does not bow down.

Plant out hyacinth bulbs from pots in the garden after flowering. They usually make a cluster of small stems that are perfect for picking. Choose the salmon-pink 'Gypsy Queen' and deep purple 'Distinction' as well as the commoner pastels. 'Gypsy Queen' goes particularly well in both garden and vase with the blues of scilla and chionodoxa.

COOL OR WARM FOR SUMMER

Summer blues make subtle arrangements used with foliage alone. Mixed with white, they are cool and elegant, with lemons they are fresh, and they temper exuberant flames and pinks.

In early summer, the dainty blooms of Siberian iris (*Iris sibirica*) are excellent for cutting. The leaves are easy to use too, being long and grassy. To follow, grow the blue lily of the Nile (*Agapanthus*) in a warm, sheltered spot. The narrow-leaved Headbourne Hybrids are the hardiest and produce many slender flower spikes. A more homely source of blue is the tall *Campanula persicifolia*, with large, pale blue flowers.

Delphiniums often have main stems that are too big for cutting. However, if you remove them you bring on a forest of more useful sideshoots. 'Belladonna' types with sparse flowers on branched stems are best for arrangements.

If you prefer warmer colours, the Peruvian lily (*Alstroemeria*) is among the

FIXING A CANE WIGWAM

TYING CANES into a pyramid for runner beans or sweet peas is a tricky business – and often insecure, as the canes can easily shift within the twine.

With a purpose-made clip, sound fixing is easy. Each cane is held in its own slot on an unobtrusive disc or ring; there are similar versions made in plastic or metal.

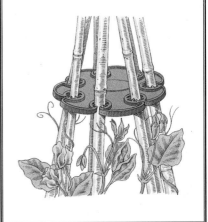

TRIPLE CROP Fast-growing, fragrant sweet peas are trained on a trellis pyramid with ruby chard at the base. The beautiful blend provides spinach-type leaves for harvesting and abundant flowers for cutting.

PINK TRUMPET FLOWERS A tempting array to gather for the house is composed of pink-flushed creamy-white *Lilium regale*, clusters of pink alstroemeria and clouds of starry gypsophila. All are easy to grow in the garden and last well in water once they have been cut.

very best cut flowers – long-lasting and long-stemmed, light in form and full of interesting detail for close scrutiny. The tall spires of foxgloves rival it for close-up interest, with intricate freckling inside the sculpted flower tubes. The plants are so easily grown from seed that you can plant lots. Select the smallest for cutting and leave a few main spikes to seed.

Another self-seeder that no gardener or flower arranger should be without is *Alchemilla mollis*. The rounded leaves are pretty in themselves and the froth of tiny yellow flowers makes it doubly valuable.

SUMMER SPECIALS

For pure luxury, grow silky-petalled, fragrant peonies. The later-flowering *lactiflora* types have three or four buds on each stem and once the crown bud has opened, you can cut the smaller buds for arrangements. The pale pink, double 'Sarah Bernhardt' and the rosy 'Bowl of Beauty' filled with golden stamens are both exquisite.

A few lilies can transform arrangements, especially the heavily scented trumpet types such as 'Pink Perfection', 'African Queen' and *Lilium regale*. The bulbs are not expensive so plant double quantities – half for cutting. For variety try bright yellow 'Connecticut King', an upward-facing hybrid, and dramatic 'Casablanca' with huge white blooms.

Once, roses were set apart in their own formal bed but it is common now to use them anywhere and there are roses for mixed borders, patios, rockeries, rough banks and tubs. The choice of colours is vast, but white is the most useful. Though it is old, 'Iceberg' is hard to beat for vigour; in some years it is still bearing flowers at Christmas.

Try some of the more unusual shades, particularly when you are mingling roses with other flowers. The greenish-tinged 'Peppermint Ice' emphasises the purity of white flowers.

The 'blue' roses, actually lilac and mauve shades, should be used more often in pink, silver and grey schemes. Most of them have an intense perfume. Try the grey and brown roses, too, such as 'Edith Holden' and 'Nimbus'. In the flowerbed they tend to fade from view

but in an arrangement they are moody and subtle used with grey leaves and show up well against glossy, dark foliage.

FROM SUMMER INTO WINTER

Dahlias are the most eye-catching border flowers as summer fades, and indispensable as cut flowers. Those with bronze foliage and copper or red blooms, such as 'David Howard' and 'Bishop of Llandaff', make a superb hot-colour arrangement with cotinus and rudbeckias.

For more delicate schemes, *Anemone hupehensis* var. *japonica* gives tall stems whose buds open to wide discs of pink or white. Masterwort (*Astrantia major*) has a cottage garden charm, with white flower bracts, sometimes flushed pink, round little green flowers on long, strong

AN UNASSUMING ASSET In a partly shaded spot grow *Astrantia major* and *Campanula lactiflora*. The simple beauty of the flowers shows to advantage in a vase.

PRETTY AS A PICTURE Summer flowers cut to bring colour and scent inside the house are best picked early in the morning or in the evening and placed straight away into a deep bucket of cold water for several hours before they are trimmed again and arranged.

stalks. One of the best forms is 'Shaggy'. *A. maxima* has brighter pink shades.

The best of the Michaelmas daisies are the forms of *Aster amellus* in pink, mauve and violet, and *A. × frikartii* 'Mönch'. Sedum's flat heads of pink flowers make perfect companions for asters. As they age, sedums turn crimson then rust. The most spectacular forms have purple leaves and deep pink flowers.

Foliage and berries take pride of place in winter but flowers add sparkle. The Christmas hellebore (*Helleborus niger*) and the green-flowered hellebore species excel, and if you work in miniature, grow snowdrops, winter aconites, crocuses and the honey-scented *Iris danfordiae*.

MAKE CUT FLOWERS LAST

Pick flowers and foliage early in the morning or, failing this, in the evening. Cut newly opened flowers, using sharp secateurs or scissors, and put them in water immediately. Cut most stems again once indoors, cutting under water and at a slant. This gives more stem cells access to water and stops them being blocked by resting flat on the bottom of the vase. Put the trimmed flowers in deep cold water in a cool place for several hours.

Narcissi, euphorbias, bluebells and other flowers that exude a slimy or milky sap when cut need different treatment. Hold the stem ends in a flame for 30 seconds or protect the flower heads with a paper bag and plunge the stem ends into boiling water for 20 seconds. Immediately after treatment put the flowers into deep water for two or three hours.

Add a couple of drops of bleach or proprietary flower food to the vase water to help the flowers stay fresh. Remove any leaves that would be below water or they rot and sour the water. Every other day change the water, trim the stems and remove any wilting flowers. Put the display in a cool, but not draughty, place.

RANUNCULUS Brilliantly coloured and long lasting when cut, ranunculus flowers dry well using the silica gel method.

HELICHRYSUM Pick the papery flowers before the bracts are fully open and hang them in bunches in an airy spot out of bright sunshine.

STATICE Delicate sprays of assorted coloured papery statice (*Limonium* species) look well in the garden and are dried by hanging.

PRESERVING FLOWERS

PLAN AHEAD for winter flower arrangements and preserve blooms and leaf shoots. Some require very little effort; simply put the flowers and foliage of late summer and early autumn, such as sedums, in buckets or bowls with about 2 in (5 cm) of water in the bottom, then allow that to dry out naturally. This method preserves their colour well.

Hydrangeas are even easier to preserve. Many mop-head Hortensia types (*Hydrangea macrophylla*) take on burnished copper and green tones if left to age on the plant and then hung to dry. The tiny 'Pia' and the neat, deep red 'Prezioza' age to rich colours but for something different try the hardier *H. paniculata*, whose pyramidal white heads age to pink. Leave some hydrangea flowers even longer to skeletonise into pale, delicate globes.

Other means are needed to preserve spring and summer flowers. The key to drying them successfully is speed, which retains the shape and colour. Pick the plants when there is no moisture on them. Look for well-coloured flowers that are just opening and for grasses that have not started to drop their seeds.

Prepare flowers immediately after picking them. Strip the leaves off the stems. Wire plants with large heads and thin stems or the heads would be too heavy for the dried stems. Cut off the stem 1 in (2.5 cm) below the flower. Make a hook on a piece of florists' wire and push it down through the centre of the flower until the hook grips it.

The easiest drying medium is simply air. Tie the prepared flowers into small bunches, using a slipknot which you can tighten with minimum disturbance as the stems shrink. Hang the bunches upside down in an airy place, preferably dim and shady, until the flowers are crisp.

Instead of drying the plants in air you can use silver sand, borax, or silica gel powder or crystals (sold by chemists). Sprinkle a thin layer of drying agent in an airtight tin or plastic box, place the flowers on top, then sprinkle more drying agent over the flowers and between the petals. Close the box, seal it with sticky

FOR WINTER COLOUR A late summer gathering of flowers to dry from the border includes blue sea hollies (*Eryngium*) with feathery ruffs, and globe thistles (*Echinops*) with their steely blue spherical heads. Both are tall plants adding height and interest to a bed and an indoor display.

tape then put it in a warm spot such as an airing cupboard until the flowers are crisp – usually 2-3 days in silica, 3-4 days in sand and 3-4 weeks in borax. Do not leave it too long or the flowers become brittle. Lift them out carefully. You can use the drying agent again and again, drying it between uses.

There is a huge selection of plants and flowers that are easy to preserve. Lark-spur, delphiniums, foxgloves, achilleas, thistles and white daisylike helipterum are all easy to dry and for a spectacular display choose the opium poppy *Papaver somniferum* and *Allium giganteum*, both of which have huge dramatic seed heads. Among roses, choose red and orange ones for drying, because they maintain their colour especially well.

For preserving sprays of foliage, stand the stems in a mixture of two parts hot water to one part glycerine. Beech, eleag-nus and eucalyptus are reliable. The leaf colour often changes as the glycerine is absorbed into the stems and leaves.

Try drying anything you fancy; noth-ing is lost if you fail and there is always a chance of some subtle colour giving a new character to a familiar flower.

Be bold when it comes to arranging the preserved material. For example, an unusual winter decoration is made by combining beech leaves with the papery orange seedpods of Chinese lantern. There is no bar to mixing dried and fresh flowers. Whether dried ones have their own stems or wires, protect the parts that will be in water with coating of varnish or dip them in melted candle wax.

CAPTURE SUMMER'S ESSENCE

Potpourri stores the unique perfumes of summer for you to enjoy in the house during winter. It is simple to make from a mixture of petals and aromatic leaves; they are preserved with a fixative oil or essence, both available from garden centres and some craft shops.

Adjust the ingredients to make the scent that pleases you. Be ready to experi-ment with whatever flowers you have available. Among the leaves you can use are balm, hyssop, mint, thyme, santolina, marjoram, cranesbill, angelica, artemisia, and sweet bergamot (*Monarda*).

As a basic recipe, try using: 10 dried pot marigold heads, 6 dried pelargonium leaves, the dried petals of 5 roses, 2 tea-spoons of dried lavender and 2 drops of rose fixative. Mix all the ingredients well in a large bowl. Seal the potpourri in a

FLOWERS FOR DRYING

Grow a selection of flowers for drying that will give you a varied palette of colours and an assortment of textures and shapes.

- Yarrow (*Achillea filipendulina* 'Coronation Gold'): large flat heads of deep yellow flowers. Air dry by hanging or standing.

- Straw flower (*Helichrysum bracteatum*): large daisylike flowers in a range of red, orange, pink, white and yellow. It is among the easiest flowers for air drying.

- Hare's-tail grass (*Lagurus ovatus*): grows in tufts with slender stems bearing soft, fluffy white flower spikes; hang to dry.

- Globe thistle (*Echinops*): easily air dried globular, spiky flower heads with a steely blue metallic sheen.

- Honesty (*Lunaria*): purple flowers followed by flat and silvery moon-shaped seedpods that are easily dried by hanging.

- Bells of Ireland (*Moluccella laevis*): erect spikes of small fragrant flowers, surrounded by bell-shaped pale green papery calycles. Dry with silica gel.

- Love-in-a-mist (*Nigella damascena*): many-petalled flowers, generally blue, with feathery foliage; hang dry for their balloon-shaped seedpods.

- Sunflower (*Helianthus annuus*): the dramatic large heads of dark seeds, set in concentric circles, look spectacular when dried for flower arrangements. Use silica gel.

dry airtight jar for two weeks before putting it out in bowls.

For a more bracing perfume, follow the method above but combine: 16 table-spoons of snipped balsam needles, about 20 miniature pine cones, 8 tablespoons of rose hips and 2 drops of pine-scented fixative. If any potpourri's scent fades, add a drop more fixative.

Lavender makes a particularly fresh-scented potpourri. Mix 4 cups of dried lavender, 6 drops of lavender essential oil, and 1 tablespoon each of ground cin-namon, allspice and mace. Mix all the ingredients then put in paper bags and fold over loosely. Keep in a dark, cool place to cure for about 7 weeks before putting the potpourri out in bowls.

TEASEL Dry the prickly heads of teasels (*Dipsacus*) and keep them their natural colour or spray them ornate silver and gold.

LAVENDER As well as adding colour to dried flower arrangements, lavender adds fresh fragrance to potpourri and scented sachets.

INSPIRATION FROM
GREAT GARDENS

PITMEDDEN

Reconstructed 17th-century formal garden.

Situated just north of Aberdeen, Pitmedden is a grand garden in the manner of a French palace. What started out as a sturdy Scottish castle surrounded by mossy moorland is now a model of the formal layout.

The precision of the evergreen hedging is echoed in the perfectly trained fruit trees that adorn the mellow walls and, in their sheltered position, provide a generous crop of apples and pears.

THE FORMAL GARDEN, which is really the grand reception room moved out of doors, was a child of the Italian Renaissance that grew to maturity in 17th-century France. It ornamented the grounds of palaces such as Versailles as well as those of many lesser houses.

In Britain, too, vast expanses round grand houses were laid out in terraces and vistas. Knot gardens of low hedging filled with flowers were planted in intricate arabesques, heraldic designs and even family mottoes. Water was brought in as fountains and canals, and trees, rigidly trained and drilled, stood decorative guard along boundary walls. All reflected how unruly Nature was improved by the orderly will of Man.

ONE MAN'S GARDEN VISION

Sir Alexander Seton, who unexpectedly became owner of Pitmedden in 1667, after the death of his elder brother, resolved to transform his inheritance into a French-style dream of formal beauty. He was aided by the fact that the moor slopes away to the east. This inspired him to create a split-level layout that enabled visitors, then as now, to stroll along the upper terraces and admire the entire garden spread out below them.

The plant patterns admired by today's visitors are not the same as those enjoyed by Sir Alexander's guests. The massive stone walls that he built still stand, as do his elegant, two-storey pavilions whose roofline is repeated in the buttresses of the yew hedges. There is still the graceful sweep of the double flights of steps, too. But the castle burned down in 1818 and was replaced by a house and farm. For many years the three-acre plot was used as a kitchen garden, with the earth that once carried Seton's intricate patterns of box and flowers raising potatoes.

Rescue arrived in 1952 when the National Trust for Scotland undertook the tidying up of the stone framework of

ELEGANCE IN LIVING FORMS The backdrop of trained fruit trees sets the tone for orderly buttresses of yew and trim low box hedges.

the garden and began replanting. Seton's plan was long lost, so three of the four knot gardens were modelled instead on the planting at the Palace of Holyroodhouse. The fourth one, with its thistle emblems, its crosses of St Andrew and its Seton mottoes and heraldry, was designed as a salute to the garden's founder.

RETAINING A SENSE OF PERIOD

The patterns laid out required 3 miles (5 km) of box hedging which, by 1958, was well enough established for the colours to be blocked in. This is done afresh each year, using tens of thousands of bedding plants, among them yellow-flowered alyssums, waxy begonias and dwarf wallflowers.

There was a break with tradition in the creation of some large herbaceous borders, but they are at once recalled to a sense of period by the fruit trees, trained with rigorous symmetry on the walls behind them. Some of these trees are espaliered, with horizontal tiers of branches coming off a central stem, while others are fan trained, with the main branches radiating out from the trunk like the ribs of a fan. Surprisingly, the effect of such precision is to soften the lines of the old stone walls with a tracery of branches in winter and rays of greenery in summer, making a satisfying backdrop through the year.

FAN-TRAINING TODAY

Just a single fan-trained tree can perform a similar service in a much smaller garden, where it brings interest to a bare fence or a dull garage wall. The tree is practically two-dimensional and so takes up little garden space, but it produces clouds of spring blossom and a crop of fruit. A south-facing wall will help to protect the flowers from frost damage and to encourage the fruit to ripen. A peach or a nectarine is excellent for a warm, sunny spot. On a north-facing wall you can grow a morello cherry.

Fan-training a tree requires a stout framework of canes secured to horizontal wires stretched across a wall about 8 ft (2.4 m) high. Apart from this, the tree's needs are fairly modest: medium loam, good drainage and a planting position about 9 in (23 cm) out from the wall.

SPRING BLOSSOM FOR SUMMER FRUIT A fan-trained tree lends beauty to a plain brick wall. Tuck *Tulipa* 'Peach Blossom' and *Hyacinthus* 'L'Innocence' under a 'Peregrine' peach tree.

WATER IN THE GARDEN

W ATER GENTLY TRICKLING into a pond, or a fountain's droplets sparkling in the sun give a garden movement and music that never palls. No matter what size or shape of plot you have, there is a water feature that can enhance it – whether your choice is a wall fountain, an overflowing pitcher, a jet bubbling through shingle, or a more formal pool, tranquil and shimmering, reflecting the graceful goblets of water lilies. Keep the feature ultrasimple or install a pumped, circulating arrangement – and if you do, why not lay on an automatic watering system to end forever the need to carry cans or rely on leaky hoses. It is easy once you have the right idea.

Clear water spills over weathered rocks, studded with ferns, flowers and grasses, onto intricately coiled and textured fossils.

THE ALLURE OF WATER

THE SENSUAL QUALITY of water is a pleasure which never fades, and there is seldom a garden, no matter what size, that is not the better for its inclusion. Even where the concept, construction, colour and scent of a garden appear to give all that could be asked, water introduces a play of light and movement in what can be an immediate and sometimes dramatic change.

The soothing effect of still water's steady reflections, the cool clear sound as it runs and the crystal sparkle of a fountain plume all contribute to making water a constant centre of attraction, irresistible both to people and wildlife. Even a town pool is visited by birds, butterflies, frogs, newts and the occasional toad; and since such creatures are increasingly under threat in the wild, some kind of water feature in the garden provides a valuable haven for them, no matter what its size.

Many people are fortunate enough to have some form of natural water in or around their garden. An overgrown pond, a disused well, a bubbling spring, a small stream or even the banks of a canal or river are a delight to the gardener, all providing an opportunity to develop a natural water garden or a bog garden, and extend the garden's range of plants. Others may take over a garden where a water feature has already been installed – a formal pool, perhaps, or a cascade or graceful fountain.

MAKING THE MOST OF THE EXTRA ELEMENT

Those who have such luck can use judicious planning and planting to integrate the water source into a design of their own making, or even rework the existing feature. A pond might be enlarged as part of a new overall scheme perhaps or, more ambitiously, a stream could be diverted to form a new feature altogether. This might take the form of an island, with a pool large enough to provide a home for fish.

If you are adding a water feature to the garden for the first time, you will find that the size and style of the house and garden largely determine the feature you choose. Where there is very limited space, small container pools, birdbaths, fountains and wall masks may be the best way to introduce water to the garden, and ready-made, simple-to-fit examples are on sale in many garden centres.

These are among the easiest of water features to maintain. People who are less mobile, very busy or away frequently might also consider installing a watering system for the garden. With water conservation and costs now a concern for gardeners it makes sense to use water prudently and avoid wasting it.

TIME FOR REFLECTION Water lilies form the centrepiece of this tranquil pool, its perfect circle interrupted by *Primula florindae*, bogbean, iris and water forget-me-not. The pool lends serenity to this corner of a country garden, where a seat beneath a tree promises secluded leisure.

SIMPLE WATER FEATURES

IT IS PERHAPS in the very smallest gardens that water is most appreciated. In a restricted space every inch counts, and the shallowest saucer-pool or trickling wall fountain makes an impact quite disproportionate to its size. Even a balcony or the tiniest of roof gardens is enlivened by a container pool planted with a miniature water lily, or by the soft murmuring of a bubble fountain in a ceramic bowl.

CREATING AN INSTANT POOL

Birds love to perch on the edge of a dish and dip their beaks in water, or plunge in for an energetic splash. Birdbaths and saucer pools are the simplest way to bring water into the garden. Any shallow container serves the purpose, even an upturned dustbin lid with its edges disguised by plants and pebbles.

Simple designs which you can empty and scrub clean are the most practical, because such containers quickly become green with algae. Part-fill a dish with pebbles if it is a little too deep, to raise the water level and give the birds' feet a firmer grip.

The bowl of a garden urn makes a charming mossy pool if the drainage hole is plugged, and you can create an unusual bath out of large, coiled fossils, giant clamshells, sculpted hands, ceramic leaves or leaden water-lily pads.

Try a variety of containers in different positions to see which looks the best. Arrange a collection of low bowls or shallow dishes as a collage to catch and reflect the light, or scatter flowers on the water to imitate miniature water lilies. Alternatively, sink a plain, saucer-shaped birdbath into the lawn to serve as a pool. Set it just below the surface of the ground, so the mower can skim over the rim without making contact.

UNLIKELY CONTAINER POOLS

Practically anything that holds water or will support a liner can be used as a trough or a small, sunken pool. Ceramic sinks, half-barrels, galvanised water cisterns, plastic domestic water tanks, tin

MINIATURE POOLS Even the smallest gardens benefit from a mini-pool. The lilies and hostas round this pool disguise how tiny it really is, but even so it has room for water-loving sweet galingale (*Cyperus longus*) to flourish.

PROTECTING TODDLERS

IF YOU MOVE to a house with a pond in the garden and you have small children, make the pond safe at once. Turn a shallow pool into a sandpit, but make sure it has a cover if it has no drainage holes. Fill larger pools with sand or chipped bark to use as a play area.

If you want to keep the pool, cover it with a strong, ornamental metal grille or a homemade cover of timber decking. Leave the odd small hole for taller water plants to grow through. A temporary frame of extra-strong trellis with a small mesh is useful for placing over the pool when you have occasional young visitors. The frame can be fixed in place quickly with wooden pegs or metal tent pegs.

Larger pools and natural streams must be fenced off, and any gates padlocked. Well-made fencing screened by cornus, golden elder, rhododendrons or bamboos is unobtrusive and easy to live with while the children are small.

Older children should be safe with an informal pool with sloping sides.

SIMPLE POOL Water in a shallow stone bowl resting in heaped cobbles reflects sunlight and foliage, bringing a different quality to a garden. It would also be appreciated by birds.

trunks and even the polystyrene casing that protects newly bought goods such as microwave ovens can be fitted with a liner or sealed.

Some metals are poisonous to plants, and it is important that metal containers are coated inside with a nontoxic paint or a sealant such as bitumen.

The humble origins of more mundane containers are easily disguised with paint to imitate lead, marble, terracotta or verdigris-coated copper, or masked by an outer shell of loose bricks, log-roll

RURAL TOUCH A stone trough nestling among golden balm and a crowd of pelargoniums looks at home in cottage gardens, and is large enough to grow irises, mimulus and glyceria.

edging, tongue-and-groove panelling or timber offcuts. Do not stifle your imagination – one garden is adorned with a small and ancient, open-topped car, its interior lined and filled with water in which a number of goldfish, water lilies and irises have a spacious home.

POSITIONING MINI-POOLS TO ADVANTAGE

Mini-pools look their best when their shape and materials are sympathetic to the style of the garden – a Chinese jar standing among bamboo, for example. Pots and bowls make excellent mini-pools, suitable both for outdoors and for a small conservatory. Pots with drainage holes can be sealed with mastic.

If frequent top-ups are necessary in hot weather, make certain there is always water available that has stood for a few days in a watering can. This ensures that the water is not too cold and allows some of the chemicals in tap water to evaporate.

Half-barrels or tubs look well in most gardens, even on a formal terrace. They can be used singly in a very small garden.

Where there is a little more space, put them in a group with each one holding a different variety of the same plant – a miniature water lily, for example.

TUMBLING MOVEMENT IN A CASCADE

Where water runs from an old iron tap or pump into a container below, it can also be made to spill over the edge of the first container and into another.

A pretty development of this idea is a sunken cluster of overlapping wooden tubs set into the ground at various depths, or perhaps into a slope. The water spills from one tub to the next to form an attractive cascade and then down into a concealed reservoir, from where it is pumped back up to the tap to start its fall again.

Surround the sunken tubs with stones, pebbles and shells, and edge them with ferns and hostas, bright blue *Brunnera*, creeping Jenny (*Lysimachia nummularia*), and a clump of *Iris sibirica*.

Grow suitable water plants in the tubs. Water lilies should be in the sun for at least half the day to flourish. Varieties that do well in a small space include the two smallest, *Nymphaea × helvola*, which grows in 4-9 in (10-23 cm) of water and has tiny yellow flowers, and the similar

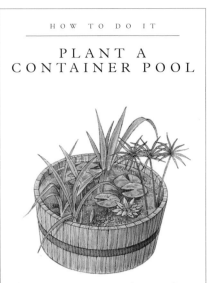

HOW TO DO IT

PLANT A CONTAINER POOL

SUCCESSFUL PLANTING of a container pool depends in part on filling the pool without disturbing the compost and gravel on the base. Spread a 6 in (15 cm) layer of water-plant compost in the empty container and cover it with 2 in (5 cm) of lime-free gravel or shingle.

Cover the gravel with a wad of newspaper and add the water in a gentle trickle with a hosepipe or watering can. Remove the paper carefully and leave the pool to settle for a day or two before planting.

To plant, carefully press the small water lilies, marginal plants, floaters and oxygenators through the gravel and into the compost, and firm them in. In a slightly deeper pool, plant marginals in plastic containers and place them on up-ended bricks to keep them at the right level, as they like to have their roots in shallow water.

Each tub or similar sized container will hold one miniature water lily, a couple of marginal plants and two or three underwater oxygenators.

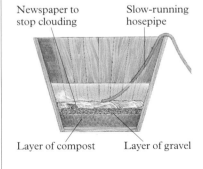

Newspaper to stop clouding

Slow-running hosepipe

Layer of compost   Layer of gravel

MULTIPLYING THE IMPACT Grouping similar containers of differing sizes is an easy way of creating striking effects. Fill them with irises and dwarf water lilies for a water garden display that costs less than building a pond.

CIRCULATING WATER

MANY WATER FEATURES, such as fountains, cascades and artificial streams, require a pump to circulate the water. A submersible pump hidden in the trough below a fountain or under a cascade is the most practical, and surprisingly easy to install.

Choose the right pump for the feature you want to build. A small, low-voltage pump with a transformer is all that is needed for a millstone bubble fountain, for example, while a taller jet requires a more powerful pump.

GENTLE TRICKLE A fish seems to leap from pool to pool, a trickle of water escaping from its mouth onto the *Houttuynia cordata*.

RING OF BOX Gleaming, coloured stones at the base of this simple spray fountain are encircled by box hedging. The tank and pump mechanism are hidden underground.

N. tetragona. The white-flowered *N. candida*, scented *N.* 'Odorata Minor', pink *N.* 'Pygmaea Rubra', and wine-red *N.* 'Laydekeri Purpurata' are also suitable.

Among the most attractive floaters are frogbit *Hydrocharis morsus-ranae*, which is similar to a tiny white water lily, and the ivy-leaved duckweed, *Lemna trisulca*, with its delicate green fronds.

Oxygenators are sometimes invasive, but are easily controlled in small pools by removing surplus growth when necessary. The water buttercup (*Ranunculus aquatilis*) is one of the less invasive oxygenators, whereas *Elodea canadensis* and *Lagarosiphon major* should only be introduced in pools where it is possible to thin them out in autumn because they can get out of hand if left to grow unchecked.

EASY-TO-FIT MOVING WATER

Simple wall fountains are especially suited to shady corners, where few water plants flourish. They are also among the

CLASSICAL FORMALITY Clipped box topiary and banks of lavender, with *Rosa rugosa* behind, combine to create a feeling of timelessness in this quiet corner. A cherub fountain stands in a small formal pool, whose brick surround is softened by the elegant flowers and foliage of *Iris laevigata* 'Alba'.

safest features to install if your garden is used or visited by young children, to whom water is an irresistible magnet.

Traditional designs for wall fountains include the heads of lions, gods and goddesses, or cherubs, dolphins and seashells. Such a feature is all the more effective when it is surrounded by an arch, an alcove or an 'illusion' trellis suggesting an alcove.

Some striking contemporary garden features have water running over a series of chutes, or spurs, of brick, slate, timber, metal, glass or even glass bottles.

A simpler variation on this idea is made by setting a row of outlets along a wall with the water flowing from them into a long, narrow trough, with a concealed pump returning it to flow from the outlets continually. The choice of outlets includes masks, spouts, short pipes of clay or metal, or V-shaped chutes of stone, tiles or slate. Such a feature has great visual impact in gardens of all sizes, and yet the sound is gentle.

In a small garden, set a freestanding fountain in a flowerbed or on a raised circle of brickwork, or on a low plinth in one corner. In a slightly bigger garden, a freestanding fountain makes an attractive centrepiece for a larger pool.

REGULATE THE FLOW

In general, the larger the pool, the better a fountain looks, so allow a reasonable surface both for the play of falling water, and for plants beyond. Water plants, and especially lilies, dislike being splashed.

The height and spread of any fountain spray needs to be appropriate. If the spray is too wide, it wastes water and leaves surrounding surfaces wet and perhaps slippery. As a rough guide, you should have a pool that is at least twice as wide as the height of the water jet.

With a narrow-mouthed container such as a Mediterranean oil jar, on the other hand, you can let the water brim over to trickle down the sides. This looks cool and soothing, whereas a bubble or spray jet is busier and more contrived.

Small fountains and wall cisterns have to be turned off and drained in winter, unless they are in a spot guaranteed frost free; the water trickle can freeze if left on and damage the fitting. And always bear in mind that, while the sound of water might be soothing to you, neighbours may not share your enthusiasm for an uncontrollable noise close by so choose and site a fountain carefully.

FOUNTAIN DESIGNS

There is a remarkable range of fountain designs available in garden centres. Most of them come with their own pump and electrical fittings. Installing them is generally straightforward and certainly rewards the small effort with ample pleasure.

FORMAL WALL FOUNTAINS
Simple wall fountains can be fitted almost anywhere, from roof gardens to basements. Most spout water from a pipe or an ornamental feature, such as a mask or the mouth of a fish, into a container below.

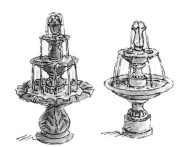

TIERED FOUNTAINS
Although they can be installed as free-standing features, tiered fountains look best when placed in the centre of a larger pool with the overflow spilling out of the bowl and into the surrounding water.

SMALL FOUNTAINS
Freestanding fountains sitting in their own bowl are useful in a limited space and look good set in flowerbeds. They range in style from traditional bowls, with or without pedestals, to tall terracotta jars.

WATER CISTERNS
Cisterns are similar to wall fountains but have a tap in place of the waterspout. Like wall fountains, they are made in a variety of materials, and many designs are safe if young children use the garden.

BUBBLE FOUNTAIN
The safe, low jet of water runs over pebbles held in a container. Bubble fountains are sold with their own pumps and reservoirs, both of which are hidden.

CLASSICAL FOUNTAINS
Fountains come in many shapes, some humorous, some quirky, others more classically beautiful. A number of risqué designs follow a robust tradition – a dog with a lifted leg, for example.

INFORMAL PONDS

A NATURAL-LOOKING POND is a still sheet of reflective water, its only movement a gentle rippling as fish rise or the wind ruffles the surface. Perhaps soft eddies mark the spots where a small stream meanders in and out.

Most man-made pools and ponds can be divided loosely into formal features and informal ones which are generally more natural looking. A large garden could employ both, with perhaps a classical wall fountain or formal pool near the house and an irregular pool or a small stream set in a wilder corner, but in smaller gardens you generally have to decide upon one or the other.

Though apparently artless, informal streams and ponds need meticulous care in design and placing. The pond in particular should be as large as possible; the more generous its proportions, the more convincing it will be, and curves must look natural from all aspects.

GETTING THE SHAPE RIGHT

In the wild, most ponds are roughly circular or elliptical, with a few indentations here and there, while streams dawdle between sloping banks or gush through rocky, fern-lined gorges. In a garden, such ponds or a simulated stream work

BRIDGE WITH A PURPOSE Bridges always look best where they are really needed, not simply decorative. Here the bridge leads across the banks of a small stream planted with water irises, rhododendrons and *Hosta undulata*.

BEST PLANTS
IN THE SHALLOWS

Marginal plants, found in the shallows of ponds, are good for softening the edges of an artificial pool. Put the plants in plastic boxes of aquatic plant compost and place them so the box rim is just below the surface.

• Bog arum (*Calla palustris*): glossy leaves, and arum-like sheathed flowers in late summer followed by red berries.

• Bowles golden sedge (*Carex elata* 'Aurea'): foliage plant which grows to 16 in (40 cm) in very shallow water.

• Loosestrife (*Lythrum virgatum* 'Rose Queen'): bears purple spires from June to September; grows in water or mud.

• Bogbean (*Menyanthes trifoliata*): broad leaves, pink buds and white fringed flowers in May.

• Golden club (*Orontium aquaticum*): waxy leaves and yellow and white sheathed flowers in May.

• Japanese rush (*Acorus gramineus* 'Variegatus'): tiny, invasive semi-evergreen with grasslike leaves.

• Miniature reed mace (*Typha minima*): a dainty bulrush with round, velvety heads from midsummer.

• *Iris laevigata* 'Variegata': hardy iris which flowers in June and July.

RED BLAZE Evergreen azaleas in flower add glowing colour to the dense green foliage that leans down to the water. Rough stone boulders circle the pool, giving a natural edging that blends with the plants.

best some way from the house and in the sort of spot a natural feature might occur, coiling round the land's contours, for example, or settling in dips and hollows.

To help a stream look more natural, make it seem to run out from under a bridge, or perhaps rise as a spring bubbling up among stones and plants. On fairly flat ground, the flow of a stream can be altered by placing rocks on the stream bed, while on a sloping site, the water might run briskly down over a ledge or a series of falls and pools.

A small pond or short stream appears larger when its edges are in part concealed by carefully placed plants, so the water seems to disappear round a corner. A similar effect is achieved by placing a low bridge at one end so that the water appears to flow out from under it and then disappear into a group of plants at the other end, suggesting further reaches on either side.

PLANTING UP
AN INFORMAL POND

At the planting stage a little cheating is allowed, for a truly natural pond contains only native water plants. Most gardeners want a little variety, however – a few cultivated and more showy plants, perhaps, or at least some goldfish.

It is tempting to combine water and trees, which are so beautiful when reflected in still water. But trees often throw too much shade and their dead leaves entail quite a lot of clearing up in autumn. Rotting leaves give off gases that will kill fish if trapped when the water freezes over, so you should either cover the pond with mesh to catch the leaves as they fall or scoop them out daily.

If you are set on planting a tree nearby, try the neat little weeping willow *Salix caprea* 'Kilmarnock' for tiny ponds, and the graceful *S. purpurea* 'Pendula' for a medium-sized pond. These have all the grace of the more common ones but are half the size or less. Another willow, *Salix exigua*, is not a weeper but its elegant habit and silver leaves make it an excellent centrepiece for a group of grey, white and blue plants.

The many varieties of Japanese maple have an affinity with water. Their lobed foliage, reddish flowers, brilliant autumn

CONVINCING STREAM Astilbes and hostas adorn one bank and a birch surrounded by forget-me-nots the other beside this artificial stream. Its authentic appearance comes from following what seem to be natural curves.

HIGH NOTES AND LOW In a small garden a pond is often the major decoration. Give it splashes of colour as in this planting where bright flowers are set among contrasting foliage – ribbed hostas, sword-shaped leaves and the graceful plumes of pampas grass (*Cortaderia richardii*).

LOG BARRIER

TO MAKE a pleasing psychological barrier and to protect the pond margins from impetuous children and heavy-footed adults, drive a number of logs or short lengths of wood into the ground about 8-10 in (20-25 cm) apart, a short way from the edge of the pond. Stagger the height a little if you prefer. A run around roughly a third of the pond's circumference looks best, with taller plants guarding the rest.

You can prevent children from walking along the top of the logs by rounding off the sawn wood. To deter herons use a staple gun to fix fishing line along the posts, about 8 in (20 cm) high. The line will not hurt the long-legged birds, but it will keep them away from any fish.

the bronze leaves and red flowers of *Lobelia cardinalis*. In a garden where there is much shade and muted colour, the pond may be the main feature and one you want to draw attention to.

CHOOSING MARGINALS

Attractive plants for the margins include the flowering rush, *Butomus umbellatus*, and marsh marigolds, surely the essence of spring. *Caltha palustris*, the familiar king-cup, has bright buttercup flowers while the double form, *C. p.* 'Plena', is smothered with yellow pompoms.

Iris kaempferi, mimulus, primulas and the twisted corkscrew rushes, *Juncus effusus* 'Spiralis' and *J. inflexus* 'Afro' are also good for pond edges.

Where there is room, grow the invasive sweet galingale *Cyperus longus* or the less rampant *C. eragrostis*. Most people want a water lily or two, and goldfish appreciate their shady leaves. Excellent lilies for a small to medium pond are the red-flowered *Nymphaea* 'Froebelii',

colour and intriguing winter outlines make them attractive trees to have in the garden no matter what the season.

With the choice and placing of shrubs and other plants in or near water, much the same considerations apply as for the rest of the garden. Climate and soil, contrasts of size, shape and tones of foliage, and the subtle groupings of colours with

occasional 'hot spots' all need to be taken into account when working out the planting round a pond.

Plants are the most natural adornments to use in an informal water garden and muted colours blend more easily. Foliage plants are ideal, with a few splashes of colour – the blues and yellows of irises and king-cups for instance, or

N. 'James Brydon' (which is pinkish-red and scented and will stand a little shade), the pink *N.* 'Firecrest' and *N.* 'Rose Arey', white *N.* 'Marliacea Albida' and yellow *N.* 'Marliacea Chromatella'.

When planting directly into compost, use smooth stones to hold new plants in position. If the plants are in containers, top the compost with smooth shingle and if necessary weight with pebbles or use larger stones to wedge them in place.

POND SURROUNDS AND FINISHING TOUCHES

Informal ponds and streams, edged in part with shrubs and marginal plants, are set off best by a verge of shingle and cobblestones. Grass laid right up to the water's edge can become muddy.

If you wish to transform a formal pool into an informal one, a good way is to establish a shallow, irregularly shaped bog garden round the straight edges of the pool and to fill it with moisture-loving plants. Such a garden would quickly disguise the earlier formality.

Bridges, stepping-stones, seats and buildings all give character to a garden. Bridges especially are best placed where really necessary – not in an arbitrary and unconvincing fashion over a tiny stream you could step across, for example.

🍃 A stone slab, a pair of railway sleepers or a couple of thick, weathered planks make a strong, attractive bridge.

🍃 Place a staggered run of roughly hewn stones or cylinders of tree trunk to use as stepping-stones. They look natural, but make sure they are both level and stable.

🍃 Keep seating simple. Seats by an informal pond or stream should have a casual, weathered look, with nothing so new that it spoils the effect.

🍃 A deck chair or an ancient bench, a swing or a string hammock under an apple branch, some mossy logs, a plank or a slab of stone supported on bricks all provide seating that does not jar.

🍃 Buildings must be unpretentious – a rustic arbour of larch logs, for example, with a roof of thatch or brushwood.

Any number of ideas can be used to give a water garden its own character. A garden shed next to the pond could turn into a 'boathouse' if given a verandah and a dash of bright paint and surrounded with exuberant plants. And sculpture, 'found' objects – driftwood, stones and shells – and figurines such as a stone frog or a pair of stately cranes add interest to ponds of all sizes.

CREATING A WATERFALL To seem convincing, waterfalls need a considerable drop over a wall or an outcrop of rock; here, maples frame the tumbling water and stand out against the stone around it.

RELAXING THE FORMALITY To soften the regular outline of a formal pool, replace some of the paving with cobbles. Thick planting with evergreens, yellow irises and corydalis also helps.

OVER THE WATER If you have a large body of water, create a quiet jetty from which to enjoy it. Wooden decking can provide a seating area among bamboos, gunnera and reedmace.

FORMAL POOLS AND FEATURES

A FORMAL POOL may lie bare and still as a dark mirror, or be enlivened by water spurting up from the surface, or brim with water plants beneath which fish silently glide.

The pool might be at the centre of a terrace or small garden or, where there is a little more space, it might divide one area of the garden from another and be crossed by a bridge or stepping-stones.

Whatever their size and shape, formal pools and other formal features look best near the house, or in paved areas, or in any part of a garden that is laid out with a geometric design.

In many gardens, one component of a formal water design is often linked to another – a pool is fed from a cascade or wall fountain, for example, or is set at the far end of a narrow canal. The pool may be in virtually any geometric shape – oval, round, semicircular, rectangular, square, hexagonal, octagonal and even, occasionally, triangular.

BEING INVENTIVE WITH SHAPE

Where space is at a premium, an L-shaped pool at the boundary or at the corner of a paved area is very useful, leaving the centre of the garden free as a seating area. A pool of this shape is composed of two adjoining or overlapping rectangular shapes.

Other devices which serve to make a garden more interesting include turning the whole design of the garden at an angle to the plot. A square pool becomes diamond-shaped, for example, and an area of paving becomes diagonal and runs between the long sides of two triangular pools. As the plantings around the garden boundary and the pool are thus swung into the garden, they too become diagonal and create hidden areas that give a feeling of extra space. A set of interlocking circles, one containing water, can be swung to create similar effects.

Circular or semicircular pools have a less rigid feel to them than other geometric designs, and work in both formal and informal settings. A semicircular pool is

MODERN LINES Contemporary materials, designs or sculptures often look stunning in a formal garden. Here, low jets in the mini-pool and the sprays falling from it add gentle ripples to the strong, still, angular forms.

ROPES TO HELP PLANT A POOL

A SIMPLE SOLUTION to placing a large container of water plants in a large, filled pool is to thread two lengths of rope or clothes line through the holes in the container. With one person on each side of the pool, use the ropes to suspend the plant over the water.

When it is correctly positioned, lower the container into the water. Once the container is firmly on the bottom of the pool, pull the ropes through the holes and out of the water.

SPLASH OF COLOUR A fountain adds movement to this pool, the height of the spray kept low so as not to disturb the water lilies. Softening the formal pool shape and paved terrace is a scattering of cranesbills, rose campions, sisyrinchiums, alchemillas, campanulas and helianthemums.

often used against a garden wall as the basin of a fountain. If the garden is fenced, build a free-standing wall to back the pool and support a wall mask. Give the wall an arched or stepped top and frame the edges with foliage to complete a pleasing and self-contained feature.

WISE CHOICES FOR POOL SURROUNDS

The materials that surround a formal pool, whether level, raised or at the centre of a sunken garden, should complement the materials used to build the house and employed elsewhere in the garden. Local stone, slate and brickwork are all possible edging materials, and where they tie in with the house walls, the paths and any terracing, the whole gives a restful and unifying impression.

Concrete, engineering bricks, substantial timbers and decking all go well with contemporary architecture, while frost-proof quarry and terracotta tiles fit in happily with most types and periods of brick houses. An added advantage to terracotta tiles is that they can be laid both inside and outside the house and conservatory, so providing a link between the garden and house interior.

The surround of a level pool might be made of paving, gravel (which is slightly less formal) or grass. Grass looks very attractive laid up to the water but its edge will sink under frequent treading unless it is laid over a firm rim of some kind, such as chamfered concrete.

HOW TO CREATE ATMOSPHERE

Whatever pool shape and type of edging you choose, the planting radically alters the feel of any stretch of water in the garden. A rectangular pool, edged by stone flags and unadorned on a terrace or a fine, level lawn for example, is an austere but handsome sight.

Purists insist that no plants should rise above the rim of such a pool to detract from its symmetry, but you can add a fountain for its plume to give movement. Framing the pool with pleached hornbeams heightens the formality and gives a hint of mystery, while a Versailles box at each corner holding strappy-leaved, blue-flowered agapanthus makes it less severe. Replace the agapanthus with generously planted urns and a few pots at each corner for an atmosphere altogether warmer and more welcoming.

In a tiled courtyard garden, a similar unplanted pool, quite shallow, lined with matching tiles and with a central fountain, brings a Mediterranean air. Grow plenty of plants such as figs, plumbago,

CHANGING THE MOOD OF A POOL

ELEGANT SIMPLICITY A low hedge of clipped box surrounds the pool, level with the stone coping, and is in turn surrounded by a formal area of gravel. A magnificent water lily takes pride of place.

SOFTER CHARM The pool frame is almost hidden by profuse planting spilling over its edges. White petunias flank the large-leaved *Bergenia cordifolia* while alchemillas foam along the sides.

REPAIRING A CONCRETE POOL

A CONCRETE POOL that is leaking can usually be repaired with a flexible liner. As the damage was probably caused by subsidence or a weak mix of concrete, fresh cracks are likely to appear if you simply fill existing ones.

Drain out the pool. Any cracks should be filled with mortar and then left to dry before the pool is relined.

It is possible to order a preformed or flexible liner direct from the manufacturers in the correct size for your pool. This is slightly more expensive than fitting one yourself, but does save time and ensures a neat finish.

---

vines, jasmine and trachelospermum as wall cover, with lilies, daturas, pelargoniums, palms, oleanders and yuccas in containers to create a lush, southern mood. Put the foliage plants in the shade and the bloomers in the sun. Mosaic, marble, slate, stable pavers, granite setts or terracotta tiles all work well as lining materials for the pool, especially with matching or similar surrounds.

THE BEST SHAPES FOR RAISED POOLS

Most raised pools belong near to the house or in formal parts of the garden, since natural ponds – with the exception of some rock pools – are seldom above the surrounding ground level.

Stone troughs and lead cisterns (or glass fibre reproductions) make handsome raised pools, and are perhaps the

---

simplest way of introducing a sculptural element into the garden. They are particularly suited to small spaces, tucked away in a corner.

If a trough or similar container is not available, you can build a raised pool of any size quickly and inexpensively. Most raised pools are about 18 in (45 cm) high, but if you want a deeper pool – to accommodate fish, perhaps – sink it partly into the ground or the rim becomes inconveniently high. Any excavated soil can be used in raised beds.

Reclaimed stone, old bricks, rendered and painted concrete blocks or railway sleepers are all suitable materials for such a pool, which is then lined with a preformed or flexible liner. A raised pool is safer than a ground-level one for very small children and people with impaired sight, and is easy to care for.

For a central pool in a restricted space, choose a round, hexagonal or octagonal shape. These take up less room, have no sharp corners and combine well with raised, triangular beds in each corner. Alternatively, use a space-saving triangular pool across one corner of a small garden or basement area, adding a wall fountain above or a bubble fountain within the pool. Surround the pool with large containers of fatsia, choisya and bamboo, underplanted with ferns and some trailing ivy. And if you long for flowers, add summer pots of white busy lizzies frothing round tall tobacco plants.

Fish thrive in a raised pool as long as you provide them with a good depth of water and some shade. Short pieces of clay drainpipe lying on the base, or slates supported on bricks make good hides, while lily pads and floating aquatics also provide cover.

MORE UNUSUAL FORMAL FEATURES

The term 'rill' or 'canal' sounds a touch grand, but refers to a long, narrow pool or channel, usually with straight edges. The most elaborate ones link a series of small, formal pools or lead into a larger pool, adorned by two or more fountains, perhaps. Two rills, set one each side of a path, lead the eye most effectively to a view, a garden seat or an ornamental building of some kind.

Rills, whether plain or planted, alter a garden considerably, giving an impression of different proportions. In a long, narrow garden, for example, a rill cutting across from one side to the other, with a

Water gently trickles from an elegant urn

Fish dart beneath delicate scented lilies

A border of bricks circles the pool

A PLACE FOR REFLECTION

*Broad slabs of stone offer a tempting place to sit, trail a hand
through the water of this raised hexagonal pool, and enjoy
the gentle sound and motion in a few minutes of contemplation.*

A FLASH OF GOLD darting out of sight under the broad, gleaming leaves of a water lily, a splash of purple from a cluster of irises, the sound of trickling water – all draw the young and the old to the edges of this pool. Scent, sight and sound merge to form a harmonious whole, with the plants and edgings around the pool creating a flattering frame for the water-loving plants inside it. As water trickles from the mouth of the urn into the pool, a few lazy ripples shiver on the surface.

PLANTS FOR THE POOL

The open gravel surround invites an approach to the pool from any of its six sides. Small ferns, alchemillas and grasses soften the meeting of low brick walls and ground, while a circle of matching brick edging defines the pool area and keeps at bay the enthusiastic foliage of hostas, irises and bergenias.

Within the pool, a small scented water lily (*Nymphaea* 'Rose Arey') takes pride of place while an elegant *Zantedeschia aethiopica* 'Crowborough' rises serenely above the pool's broad stone coping, each small yellow flower spike wrapped protectively in a sculptured white sheath.

No matter what the shape or size of a garden, the reflective quality and movement of water add an extra dimension to the design, as well as giving scope for water-loving plants.

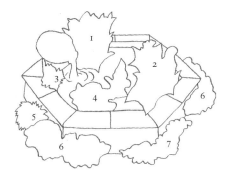

1. *Iris* × *robusta* 'Gerald Darby'
2. *Zantedeschia aethiopica* 'Crowborough'
3. *Lobelia siphilitica*
4. Water lily (*Nymphaea* 'Rose Arey')
5. Sedge (*Carex oshimensis* 'Evergold')
6. *Alchemilla mollis*
7. *Blechnum penna-marina*

DISCREET RAISED POOL Timber decking flanks this unusual pool, adding a change of level to the small garden. A trickle of water falls from the fish's mouth, while a pot of pink *Nerium oleander* softens an awkward corner.

SIMPLE AND PRACTICAL Slabs of paving stone placed at regular intervals serve as attractive bridges across an extended rill. The lush *Lysichiton*, hostas and *Ligularia* on either bank obscure the hard lines of the rill's edges.

T O T H E R E S C U E

CONTROLLING POND INVADERS

ALGAE AND PONDWEED can become troublesome, but there is a simple and unusual solution. Organically grown straw, and particularly barley straw, will control it.

Tie a handful of straw in a bundle and attach it to a brick or other weight. Put the straw in the pond and leave it until the water has cleared. For best results, treat the pond every spring and autumn – and keep it free of dead leaves and decaying vegetation.

To remove blanket weed algae (an aptly named green slime), use a forked branch or rake. Simply twirl the branch or rake in the weed, which will wrap itself around it ready for lifting out.

The floating common duckweed (*Lemna minor*) can be removed from a large pond by two people holding a long rope. Skim the rope across the pond's surface and lift out the weed.

---

stone slab laid across here and there to bridge it, effectively shortens and widens the garden. The impression is reinforced if each end is blurred by bamboos and evergreen plants and the water seems to flow out of sight beneath an arch in each of the side walls.

Circular or semicircular rills can be used to create most unusual designs. They might be used to border a seating area or enclose a flowerbed, or simply to surround a statue on a circular pedestal. As long as the water is still and at least 18 in (45 cm) deep, the rill can be stocked with fish.

Where a bridge is needed to cross a formal pond or canal, match the bridge's design to the period of the house or the style of the garden. Stepping-stones are another alternative; they should stand slightly above the water's surface and be laid securely on their supports of brick or concrete. Again, they work best when they match the style of the pool and its surrounds, but above all they should always be absolutely level so that they appear to be floating on the water.

RUNNING WATER ON A SLOPE

One formal design feature that is often combined with a pool is a cascade, or a series of cascades. Although these are most often associated with the gardens of great country houses, a small garden – where the sound of falling water has a tremendous impact – will easily accommodate a miniature version.

The water might fall from a chute, flow over a straight lip or run down a ramp or two or three steps into a pool or trough below. It is then returned to the top of the cascade by a submersible pump hidden in the pool or trough.

Where a garden is on two levels, set a short, wide flight of steps into a sloping bank and edge the steps with a cascade on either side. More ambitiously, construct a ramp or fall of steps to carry a rush of water from a pool in the upper level into another below.

Although it appears complicated to construct, the building of a cascade is a relatively simple affair – its construction is similar to that of a recessed flight of garden steps. It may well be set into a sloping site and lead into a pool below, faced with materials as diverse as bricks, granite kerbstones, slabs of stone or slate, or railway sleepers. The steps of the cascade can be edged with either a hard surface or a green one of lawn or plants. A cascade is one of the few formal features that also works successfully in an informal setting, looking at home, for example, in an unmown grassy slope planted with a few bulbs.

MAKING A POND MORE FORMAL

If you inherit an irregular, informal pool from previous owners of the garden and would like to give it a more geometric, formal look, there are a number of ways in which you can achieve this without removing the feature totally.

Timber decking is particularly attractive when used with water features. Decking can be laid over the existing curves of a pool, leaving a rectangular or L-shaped opening that harmonises with the rectangular lines of a terrace or patio made of more decking, or of bricks, stone or concrete slabs, or gravel. Small changes of level add interest, while the raised and overhanging edges of the decking work to make a pool feel larger because the water seems to continue underneath it further than it really does.

Where you are adapting a larger pool, treat the part nearest the house in this way, or create a straight line along the nearside with slabs, planks or railway sleepers. Blur the edges at the pool's far end with bold, shapely plants; clumps of bamboo and the enormous leaves of *Gunnera manicata* are good for this, as is the giant rhubarb, *Rheum palmatum*, especially *R. p.* 'Bowles' Crimson' and red-leaved *R. p.* 'Atrosanguineum'. *Rodgersia aesculifolia* also has impressively large, sculptural leaves.

Closer to the house, and particularly where there are awkward angles as the curves join the straightened edges, the attractive, rather formal and upright *Iris kaempferi* and *I. sibirica* work well. The sweet flag *Acorus calamus*, in particular the attractive *A. c.* 'Variegatus' and the stately *Zantedeschia aethiopica* 'Crowborough', are striking or you can obscure any abrupt angles with a large, elegant container or two planted with an architectural fatsia or a strappy leaved, white or blue flowered agapanthus.

TESTING BEFORE DIGGING

Before spending anything on a water feature for the garden, draw a plan of the garden's current layout on graph paper. Make a tracing of the layout and then use cut-outs from a catalogue to try out various sites, sizes and shapes for the water feature, remembering that all pools

UNDISTURBED CORNER Water lilies love still water and sun, and a scattering of *Cistus* petals at the margin indicates how undisturbed the water is in this brick-edged round pool. *Cistus*, too, is a sun-lover and the perfect abundant companion to set off the sculpted formal air of water lilies.

should be sited out of the wind, away from frost pockets and in the sunlight for at least half the day, especially if they are going to contain fish. If you live in an area of very heavy rainfall or frequent flooding, site a pond where there is no danger of pollutants seeping into it. If you have no choice about where the pond is to be placed, avoid all risk of pollutants by building a raised pool.

Next, try out your design in the garden by marking out possible shapes, using battens for the straight lines and homemade plywood set squares for the corners. Circles and semicircles can be drawn with a string-and-peg compass.

MOCK-UP PLANTING

Place containers of plants and pots of house plants in and around the outlined pool for a rough idea of planting possibilities, and try out an assortment of objects to represent rocks, boulders or cobbles.

Push in bamboo canes to indicate reeds and clumps of irises, while opened umbrellas of various sizes, tied to stakes, represent weeping trees and shrubs. All this preparation is well worth while, for mistakes made when the feature is built irritate for ever or are costly and time-consuming to correct.

ELECTRICITY AND WATER SUPPLIES

Lights transform any garden at night, but when set under water, beneath pools, fountains and cascades, or playing over the surface of a pond and nearby plants, the garden becomes magical, the darkly gleaming water adding a certain mystery.

Outdoor lighting and recirculating pumps both require an outdoor electricity supply, and very bright lights and powerful water jets need to be connected to mains electricity, installed by an electrician with cable laid in conduits to guard against damage by garden tools. A residual circuit breaker is essential.

A few lights and a standard fountain or small waterfall will run off a low voltage transformer (12 or 24 volts), which can be fitted to a socket inside the house. Again, both protected cabling and a circuit breaker are needed.

A water supply near a pool is useful for top-ups, although most sound pools will survive without, except in very hot summers. Water lost through evaporation is mostly replaced by rain, and too much tap water added at one time can upset the ecological balance of the pool.

PRACTICAL WATER USE

SAVING WATER becomes more urgent every year as prices rise and supplies cannot meet the growing demand. It makes sense to reduce non-essential water consumption in the garden.

Install water butts, with lids, to catch rainwater from all roofs. It is simple to insert a rainwater diverter by cutting out a section of downpipe with a hacksaw. The diverter sends the water from the pipe into the butt but when this is full lets it continue down the pipe to the normal outlet. If you have room, and a secluded corner, install a row of butts. Where space is limited, set up a slimline, wall-mounted butt with a built-in diverter. Slimline butts have a capacity of 22 gallons (100 litres), and are easily fitted to all standard downpipes.

Most well-established plants survive quite long periods of drought without coming to much harm. However, if you live in a low-rainfall area and are choosing new plants, consider those which tolerate some weeks of dry soil and baking sun. These include artemisia, broom, buddleia, cacti, ceanothus, cistus, *Convolvulus cneorum*, cotoneaster, eleagnus, euphorbia, genista, *Geranium macrorrhizum*, ivy, lavender, lilac, oriental poppy, periwinkle, pinks, *Rosa rugosa*, rosemary, salvia, santolina, tamarisk and yucca, among many, many others.

Even these drought-tolerant species need water until their root systems become established, however. Rig up a temporary shade in sunny weather and mulch the soil with gravel.

MINIMUM CARE FOR MOISTURE-LOVERS

Save moisture-lovers for naturally damp or shady places, digging in plenty of organic matter before planting.
- Puddle in new plants and apply a 2 in (5 cm) mulch of compost.
- Use black plastic, old carpet or newspaper as a mulch, and cover it with grass clippings, shingle or bark chips.
- Plant thick ground cover to help the soil stay moist and keep down weeds,

CUTTING BACK ON WASTE Install a water butt, or more than one, to collect rainwater from the roof rather than letting this valuable source go to waste. Rainwater is slightly acid, so reserve it for your acid-loving plants.

ECONOMICAL LUSHNESS This tiered fountain, recessed into an alcove, uses the minimum of water. A mere trickle is needed by the tenacious mosses and liverworts, flanked by maidenhair ferns, clinging to the stone and giving it a velvet texture. A pot of *Zantedeschia* completes the scene.

MONEY·SAVERS

PERFORATED HOSE SYSTEM

LAYING ON a watering system need not be expensive and can save both water and money by directing water only where it is needed. Use a perforated hose fitted to an outside tap and laid along the surface of flowerbeds or a lawn, to be turned on and off as required. The similar seep hose leaks water from a seam to soak an area 18 in (45 cm) wide along its length.

them, in their pots, in a larger container filled up with damp compost or gravel.

🍂 Line hanging baskets with black plastic and push a pierced plastic beaker or small plastic bottle into the compost to fill with water for slow release.

🍂 Provide constant moisture for plants in pots by mixing water-retentive granules with the compost.

You need to water a lawn only in long periods of very hot, dry weather. In dry spells, simply let the lawn grow to about 1½ in (4 cm) and leave the cuttings on the ground. When absolutely necessary, give the lawn a good soak once or twice a week at the most, and if possible, leave some areas unmown and unwatered.

WHICH HOSE TO USE WHEN?

A watering can gives you the best control for watering, but if you are using a hose, always check taps and hose connections for drips and leaks, and use a hose with a trigger nozzle, spray-gun or a lance extension (useful for hanging baskets) to save waste. Feeding attachments can be connected to both lances and hose-ends.

It is now a legal requirement to fit any type of hose to a tap with a double check-valve. This cuts out all risk of polluted water siphoning back into the mains.

Tangled hoses are likely to split and leak. In a small garden, keep the hose coiled away in a tub or terracotta pot which has been drilled to allow one end of the hose through to the tap connection. Or install a wall-mounted hose reel, which is a tidy way to store a hose.

Small accessories that are also helpful are hose guides – small plastic spools with a zinc spike that sticks into the ground. These are also sold as cable guides and allow the hose to swivel freely as it is used, so preventing both kinks in the hose and damage to plants.

which compete for moisture, by hoeing or hand weeding. Hoeing loosens the soil so that moisture penetrates more easily.

🍂 Do not water unnecessarily or too often. Give water to plants that really need it. Most prefer an occasional thorough soaking to a daily sprinkling.

🍂 Any especially thirsty or fragile plants can have their own watering system. Cut off the end of a plastic bottle, stick it neck downwards into the soil just above the roots, and then fill the bottle with water.

🍂 The same direct watering works for trees and shrubs. Use a short piece of drainpipe instead of a bottle and drill holes in the sides. Fill the pipe with gravel so that it does not become blocked by soil and insert it above the roots of the plant.

🍂 During a very hot spell, group pot plants together in a shady spot or put

INSPIRATION FROM
GREAT GARDENS

HESTERCOMBE HOUSE

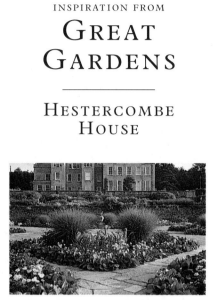

A formal parterre sets off Victorian grace.

The sprawling mansion at Hestercombe, near Taunton in Somerset, is made remarkable by its breathtaking garden. This fine product of the Edwardian partnership between Sir Edwin Lutyens and Gertrude Jekyll was completed in 1908, although it later fell into disrepair. Restoration started in the 1970s, and among the garden's majestic features brought back to life are an orangery, a rotunda with a round, still pool, and two most unusual rill gardens.

As THE 19TH CENTURY drew to its end, Edwin Lutyens, who was to become the most fashionable architect of the age, met the artist-turned-gardener Gertrude Jekyll. From the moment they met, their shared interest in gardens became clear and a long-term collaboration began. The gardens at Hestercombe are a fitting tribute to their complementary tastes and interests. The fragrance and sumptuousness of the plantings owe much to Gertrude Jekyll's imagination, while the layout reflects Lutyens's preoccupation with natural materials and geometric form.

Nowhere is this more apparent than in the Rill Gardens at Hestercombe. The raised terraces which contain the West Rill and East Rill flank the paved and richly planted Plat, or parterre, situated below the house.

Each of the rills – long, narrow, water-filled channels – emerges from a recessed half-dome set into a wall above half a globe that holds a pool. Water falls into the pool from a stone god above and feeds the rill. The pleasing symmetry of the design is heightened by the sound of falling water and the play of sunlight on the surface of the two pools.

The rills are edged with slabs of the warm grey local slate, and every few yards their parallel sides are diverted into symmetrical, ribbon loops of stone. These create decorative beds for water forget-me-nots, irises, arrowhead and other water plants.

More of the same plants grow in the rills themselves, which in fact double as watery borders. They are outlined by stretches of lawn, further slab paths and, in the case of the West Rill, shrubs and roses. The East Rill has a surround of bright herbaceous borders filled with poppies, red-hot pokers, irises and other traditional plants.

In each instance, the view spread out before the vine-crowned stone god that

PERFECT SYMMETRY Local stone flanks the sides of this rill. The narrow channel of water leads the eye to an unusual circular pool set under a half-dome in an ivy-covered wall.

spouts water into the pool is splendid indeed, for beyond the rill's end, where it falls over a brink into a lily pond, the eye is carried out over Taunton Vale to the blue rim of the Blackdown Hills.

A SPECTACULAR SETTING FOR WATER PLANTS

Although many gardeners would be hard pushed to find space for both a rill and a lily pond, there is no doubt that a smaller variation on Lutyens's rill could make a strikingly simple feature in any garden.

In the example below, the rill serves as a long, narrow garden pool. The water does not emerge from a spouting stone god but seems to come from underneath a paved semicircle of imitation York stone fringed with London brick.

Standing on the semicircle is an unpretentious garden seat framed by a vine, *Vitis vinifera*, trained to form an arch against the brick wall at the end of the garden, while to the front and sides of the seat stand pots filled with *Plecostachys serpyllifolia*, *Verbena* 'Hidcote Purple' and the purple pansy *Viola* 'Maggie Mott'. The three plants combine beautifully, the silvery-grey helichrysum leaves adding a shimmer to the purples.

Echoing the slate ribbon curls at Hestercombe, the straight edges of this rill are relieved by two 3ft (1m) circles of London stock brick. They are linked by a tiny bridge consisting of a slab of imitation York stone supported on flat iron bearers. The circles make handsome frames for beds of purple *Campanula portenschlagiana* and mirror the edging of the semicircular seat surround.

The rill is framed with the same paving as that used under the seat. The watery bed of the rill itself is filled with clumps of *Iris laevigata* 'Snowdrift' interspersed with *I. l.* 'Dorothy' and *I. versicolor* 'Rosea'. All three flower in June, as do the dainty blue water forget-me-nots, *Myosotis scorpioides* 'Sapphire' and 'Mermaid'. On the far side of the little bridge is an arrowhead, *Sagittaria sagittifolia* 'Flore Pleno'.

The lawn flanking the rill is enclosed by a box hedge at one side and a bed of *Hebe pinguifolia* 'Pagei' on the other, both making a quiet contribution to this garden's air of peaceful privacy.

POOL WITH A DIFFERENCE The rill – here simply an unusually shaped garden pool – brings harmony and character to this small garden, drawing a framed seat at one end into the design.

Making Wildlife Welcome

ENDLESS ENTERTAINMENT is provided by the small creatures that find the food and shelter they need in your garden. It is easy to entice by your choice of cultivated and wild plants – an evergreen hedge, a luxuriant climber and a small tree all attract birds, while a densely planted border mixing nectar-rich flowers and plentiful foliage invites insects and offers cover for small animals. Welcome wild plants as well as creatures and give your garden an informal corner that is full of character.

A golden daisylike inula with its open flower head attracts the attention of the peacock butterfly.

WILDLIFE IN YOUR GARDEN

SIMPLY IMAGINE a spring garden without birdsong or a summer garden without butterflies and you realise how much pleasure would be gone. Wildlife adds an extra dimension that all too often is taken for granted. Watching the activities of birds – belligerent robins defining their territory, acrobatic bluetits feeding as they swing upside-down from a twig and blackbirds quelling the insistent squawks of their voracious young – is an entertainment that can captivate even those who are not nature lovers.

Although every garden has some wildlife, it is easy to draw in a much greater variety – and without turning the garden into an untamed wilderness. With just a few changes, you will provide food or homes not only for butterflies and birds, but also for many small animals.

Take a more relaxed attitude to uncultivated flowers and fruit, pests and weeds. These are foods for butterflies and moths, as well as for ladybirds, frogs, bats and hedgehogs. Let nature's predators work for you and your work will lessen while the pleasure grows.

WILD COLOUR A stretch of garden cultivated as a minimeadow provides a habitat for wildlife and is easy to maintain as it needs infrequent cutting. The pink corn cockles and red poppies are typical of annuals that flourish in such an environment, preferring disturbed soil.

APPEALING TO THE BIRDS

TOP OF THE BILL for entertainment are birds, which are active in the garden all year long from the flurry of spring courtship and nest-building, to the struggle for survival in winter. You can watch wrens flitting in and out of the honeysuckle, sparrow-parties squabbling, and robins impatiently waiting for you to turn over the next forkful of soil. Blackbirds delight with their evening songs in the summer, and thrushes create another typical sound of summer as they swing snails vigorously onto stones to crack open the shells. Food is one of a garden's chief attractions for birds, with water and shelter equally enticing. Even a tiny garden can offer all three.

VALUE FROM HEDGES

Most gardeners mark some of their boundaries with hedges, walls, fences or railings. Living boundaries such as hedges are valued as decorative backdrops but they also make perfect wildlife havens without taking up any extra garden space. They provide nest sites and dense cover where birds can roost and hunt, and winter berries give much-needed food in the colder months.

While evergreen hedges are a strong garden feature and provide good nest sites through the winter, mixed hedges of native plants are better as they offer a variety of food, be it insects or fruits. They give varied pleasure to the gardener, too, with flowers from spring to early summer, autumn fruits, and some evergreen foliage for the winter.

Make your own blend of hedge characteristics or concentrate on just one.
🦜 For the best effect, make sure that at least a quarter of the hedge is evergreen and choose plants that thrive in most conditions, such as holly, cherry laurel and *Berberis darwinii*.
🦜 Let a few plants in the hedge grow without clipping to give more blossom, more fruit and more food and accommodation for birds. Good candidates are hawthorn and common crab apple.
🦜 Prickly, intruder-proof hedges make excellent nest sites. Berberis, holly and hawthorn are all ferociously spiny, pyracantha less so.
🦜 Many conifers are good for nesting in. Yew and juniper grow dense and can be

FEEDING ON SEEDS After pollination, female catkins of the alder tree form conelike fruits which protect ripening seeds. In autumn and winter the cones split open to disperse seed and are a favourite food source for siskins which in the colder months like to flock together in the tree.

close-clipped, but are best for the birds when they are allowed to develop a fair height and spread.

☛ Cotoneaster and pyrancantha are easy to grow and their scarlet autumn fruits are a magnet for thrushes and blackbirds.

HOSPITABLE WALLS AND FENCES

Climbing or trailing plants draped over walls and fences liven up the tiniest space and make ideal nest sites for birds. When the plants produce autumn berries too, they are twice as attractive to many birds. In a small garden, a fence clothed with a variety of climbers or with a flat, wide-spreading plant makes better use of space than a hedge does.

Many space-saving boundary plants are just as pleasing to the gardener as they are to the birds.

☛ The herringbone-pattern shoots of *Cotoneaster horizontalis* keep close to the supporting wall or fence, especially when judicious pruning is applied. The vivid red autumn leaves and berries are very striking, and even when the plant is bare of leaves, the branching pattern is still a satisfying sight.

☛ The flowering quince (*Chaenomeles japonica*) is hardy, tolerant and easily trained to grow on wires against a wall or fence. The wide cups of white, pink or scarlet blossom smother the spiny shoots and are followed by autumn fruits that look like golden apples.

☛ Several species of clematis provide good sites for nesting and produce an unsurpassed display of flowers. *Clematis montana*, with pink or white flowers, is deciduous but quickly forms a mass of dense growth. Even more vigorous is the white-flowered *C. armandii*, which has the added advantage that its glossy foliage is evergreen.

☛ Ivies are tolerant, go-anywhere plants, and their evergreen leaves provide excellent cover for nesting. Those that have

A CHARM OF GOLDFINCHES These little birds delicately extract seeds from spear thistles; they also use thistledown for their nests. Dainty in movement, they are colourful birds with black and yellow wings and red faces.

TO THE RESCUE

OUT OF THE NEST

IT IS WORTH TRYING to rescue a young nestling – one with few or no feathers – by putting it back in the nest if you can reach it safely. The parent birds will often tend it as if nothing had happened. Do not be too hasty if you find a fully feathered young bird on the ground. Keep the cat away and watch from a good distance. The parent is usually foraging nearby and will return in time if you do not frighten it off.

STATELY STEMS The tall plumes of the evergreen pampas grass (*Cortaderia selloana*)
are popular with birds such as sparrows. The
silky heads, formed in late summer, make
excellent nesting material for birds.

a boundary plant, but its flowers look
cheerful and bright against a wall or
fence and its ripe seeds are irresistible to
finches and other seed-eaters.

TREES TO TEMPT THE BIRDS

A well-chosen tree gives a feeling of
maturity to a garden, as well as adding
height, movement, a play of light and
shade, and colour. As a wildlife feature, it
provides vital lookout perches and song
posts for birds and will support a scarcely
believable variety of insects for birds and
animals to feed on.

Even for a small space, there is a
choice of trees with more than one period
of interest, so be sure to choose one
which has decorative spring flowers as
well as autumn fruits.

Crab apples (*Malus*) and rowans
(*Sorbus*) are the two best groups of trees
for birds. The spring blossoms of crab
apples in particular make a beautiful
show, followed in autumn by an abundance of fruit. Among the dozens of
excellent varieties available are 'John
Downie', 'Evereste' and 'Profusion'.
'Golden Hornet' and 'Red Sentinel' are
among those with fruits that hang on the
tree during winter, attracting redwings
and fieldfares that are driven south in
January and February by harsh weather.

Red-berried rowan, also called mountain ash, is the birds' favourite of the
Sorbus family. It is sheer enjoyment to see
a rowan quivering all over as a crowd of
mistle thrushes tear avidly at the fruits.
The ground under the tree is scarlet with
fallen fruits for a time, but these are taken
when the tree has been stripped bare.

Mature robinia trees, graceful with
green or golden ferny leaves, have the
same addictive hold on pigeons and
doves, which set the branches trembling
as they probe into the bunches of seeds
hanging down in midsummer.

Where there is more space there is
more choice. Few can surpass these small
trees for beauty, although some may
outdo them as hosts for insects.

PUTTING OUT FOOD FOR BIRDS

The acrobatic and territorial displays of
birds feeding on nuts, bread or pieces of
fruit make an absorbing show, and you
can watch them from indoors in winter.

BEST PLANTS

NATIVE TREES FOR WILDLIFE

If you have room for only one tree in
the garden, choose one of the beautiful
native species. These are the food
supply for the largest number of insects. Both the insects and the trees'
seeds or fruits draw birds to feed. Small
mammals, and rodents such as squirrels, will also use the habitat.

• Oak (*Quercus robur* or *Q. petraea*):
284 insect species recorded; choose for
large gardens only.

• Silver birch (*Betula pendula*): 229
insect species recorded.

• Downy birch (*Betula pubescens*):
more than 200 insect species recorded.

• White willow (*Salix alba*): more than
200 insect species recorded.

• Alder (*Alnus glutinosa*): 90 insect
species recorded.

• Aspen poplar (*Populus tremula*):
more than 90 insect species recorded.

• Beech (*Fagus sylvatica*): 64 insect
species recorded; choose for large
gardens only.

• Ash (*Fraxinus excelsior*): 41 insect
species recorded.

• Rowan, or mountain ash (*Sorbus
aucuparia*): 28 insect species recorded.

AN UNEXPECTED WINDFALL Fallen fruit is a
valuable source of food in the hard winter
months. Blackbirds and thrushes especially
enjoy it, but you may spot a visitor from
further away, such as this fieldfare.

two-coloured, variegated leaves, such as
Hedera helix 'Glacier', add extra colour
and cheer up a shady corner.

☙ Honeysuckle and summer jasmine,
both with spectacular flowers and heady
scent, provide dense cover for birds.

☙ Given a sunny, south-facing wall
or fence and a wire mesh to climb, the
blue-centred passionflower (*Passiflora
caerulea*) will flower from late summer
until the first frosts of autumn and hide
nesting birds in its tangle of growth.

☙ The sunflower is an unusual choice as

Providing food when natural sources are scarce can also mean the difference between life and death for birds.

There are many more visitors in cold weather when birds from woodlands and open country come to gardens in search of food, and winter migrants swell the numbers. Birds quickly come to depend on the food you provide, and may die if the supply fails for even a day.

Put out food from late autumn to around the end of March. Judge when to start and finish by the weather – do not stop feeding in the middle of a cold snap, for example. If you continue to feed during a cold spring, the food is an easy source for parents feeding fledglings, so avoid peanuts or large pieces of food which could choke young birds.

In a normal spring, it is best to let the adults gather natural food such as caterpillars. However, if there is a spring or summer drought, birds may need some fruit for moisture and grated cheese or very finely chopped nuts for protein.

MAKING UP THE MENU

Some birds have particular needs but most widen their diet when times are hard. For smaller birds, crumble large chunks of food into tiny pieces or chop nuts, bread and other foods finely.

Avoid spicy and salty foods, raw meat, which can cause food poisoning, and desiccated coconut, which swells up dangerously in the stomach.

Catering for special tastes needs very little effort.

🐦 Many birds like to feed on peanuts in hanging feeders. If buying nuts in bulk, watch out for damp, dusty or mouldy nuts, which could contain aflatoxin – a fungus poisonous to birds.

🐦 A fresh coconut cut in half and hung upside-down from a branch or clothes post is especially popular with tits.

🐦 Hang a cooked poultry carcass from a branch – out of reach of foxes – to be picked clean by small birds. Gather up any fallen bones, which can choke cats and dogs.

🐦 Grated cheese is a particular favourite with robins. They also relish mealworms, which are sold in specialist pet shops.

🐦 Pour the fat from grill and roasting pans over chopped kitchen scraps. Pack the mixture into a cup feeder, or empty a half-coconut or margarine tub to hang in a tree for tits and robins to feed on.

🐦 Table scraps such as cooked potatoes, dried fruit, cereal, rice, bacon rinds and

Take Your Choice

BIRDFEEDERS

Bring pleasure to the garden with a birdfeeder during the bleak winter months. Site it away from predators such as cats and, for maximum entertainment, within view from indoors.

NUT TOWER
Peanut feeders must have mesh fine enough to prevent birds pulling out whole nuts. Models with perches let several birds feed at once. A stainless steel construction makes the feeder strong and rustproof.

SQUIRREL RESISTANCE
A caged nut feeder keeps out larger birds as well as squirrels, allowing tits and other small birds to feed at leisure. For a feeder as sturdy as this, use a strong hanging bracket to secure it.

POST-MOUNTED BOX
A flat-backed feeder is easy to screw or tie to a post, fence, wall or tree. The overhanging lid stops rain falling on the nuts, and a ledge at the base gives somewhere for birds to perch.

FINCH FEEDER
Entry holes let in only finches or smaller birds; models are available with smaller entrances for tits and tree-creepers. The outer cage is squirrel proof. The feeder has fine mesh for seeds rather than nuts.

DIY MODEL
Make your own birdfeeder with an old cup or mug suspended by a length of wire. Put scraps of food, seeds and melted fat in it, but not peanuts, unless chopped, as whole ones can choke small birds.

WINDOW FIXTURE
Supple but strong suckers hold the feeder against the window in all weathers. The birds soon get used to people moving about indoors, and you can watch the feeding from the comfort of an armchair.

pastry are welcomed by most birds. Soak dry bread before putting it out.

🐦 Chopped-up apples attract blackbirds, thrushes, redwings and fieldfares. If you have an apple or crab apple tree, store some of the fruit in boxes to put out in midwinter.

🐦 Seeds are sought out by many birds, especially finches. Black sunflower seeds are particularly popular.

THE BEST PLACES TO PUT BIRD FOOD

You can attract a greater variety of birds by putting food in several places. A feeding station near the house is great fun to watch from the sink or your armchair, but to draw the shyer birds put some food further away, and keep your binoculars beside you for a closer look. Having several feeding sites gives the less aggressive birds the chance to feed away from the hurly-burly at the bird table.

Put food well away from places where cats can hide and put it out by early afternoon, so that it has been eaten by the time night falls; otherwise rats, mice and foxes may become regular visitors.

You can encourage birds to eat overwintering pests and their eggs by hanging a feeder in a tree where the pests collect; or by pushing fat, suet and nuts into cracks in the bark.

When snow is settling on the ground, put the birds' food on a broad piece of wood or hardboard so that it does not sink out of their reach.

Food is kept out of reach of most predators when it is put on a bird table. Do not have a table with a built-in nestbox or territorial disputes will break out frequently. The table is best when at least 18 in (46 cm) across, with a rim to prevent food from blowing off and a couple of holes to encourage rainwater to drain away. A roof is useful to keep off the worst of the weather.

Mount the table on a post 4-5 ft (1.2-1.5 m) high, or hang it from a stout branch. If squirrels are a problem, use a smooth post and fit a wide collar of metal or strong plastic halfway up to prevent them from climbing it, and site the table well away from trees.

If squirrels are not a problem, site the table only two or three strides from a tree or large shrub. Birds like to approach the table gradually, making sure it is a safe place to feed, and knowing they can return to cover quickly.

Give the bird table a thorough scrub every month or so to reduce the risk of spreading disease.

ENCOURAGING BIRDS TO NEST

Watching a bluetit flying in and out of its nest to feed its young is an engaging sight. You are more likely to see this when you provide suitable nesting sites in the garden. Thick hedges and wall shrubs are all that many birds need but others have particular preferences.

Robins often nest in an old jug, kettle or teapot thrust into a dense hedge or shrub. Many other birds will use a nestbox or other artificial nests, but if you buy a nestbox, make sure that the design is approved by the Royal Society for the

SETTING UP A SAFE NESTBOX

A NESTBOX in the right position, protected from predators, attracts hole-nesting birds such as tits, flycatchers and nuthatches. Put the box up in winter before the breeding season, at least 10 ft (3 m) from the ground. The box should be at least 4 in (10 cm) square inside for tits, and about 6 × 4½ in (15 × 11.5 cm) for slightly larger birds. The wood should be at least ½ in (1.3 cm) thick, treated with wood preservative on the outside only. Fix the box securely to a tree with pieces of cord threaded through four holes and tied round the tree. Tilt the box slightly forward to avoid rainwater channels that run down the trunk. Face the entrance north through to south-east, away from most of the wettest winds and the midday sun. For extra protection from predators such as cats and squirrels, surround the trunk with a collar of prickly plants above and below the nestbox.

Hinged lid opens up box for cleaning.

Sloped lid with overhang to throw off rain.

Metal strip to prevent squirrels from enlarging the hole.

Hole 1⅛ in (2.9 cm) across for bluetits.

Holes for cord to tie the box to the tree.

At least 5 in (12.5 cm) from hole to base so that predators cannot reach fledglings.

Protection of Birds or the British Trust for Ornithology.

All birds are on the lookout for nesting material in spring, so when you clean up the garden borders, leave small heaps of dry grass and twigs at the edge of the lawn – and add the soft hair from grooming your dog or cat.

When you clean out a nestbox at the end of the season, take care not to inhale the dust from the nesting material. Once the box is clean and dry, put in a handful of dry grass or wood shavings to make a cosy winter roost for birds such as wrens.

The same style of nestbox suits all hole-nesting birds. A box for nuthatches and tree sparrows should be slightly wider and about 2 in (5 cm) deeper than a box for tits.

The size of the entrance governs which birds can enter. A hole that is 1 in (2.5 cm) across lets in marsh and coal tits, 1 1/16 in (2.9 cm) across suits bluetits and 1 1/4 in (3.2 cm) across is big enough for great tits, nuthatches and tree sparrows. Avoid having a perch outside the box; predators can keep watch from it and frighten off potential nesters.

SAFETY FOR WIDE-OPEN NESTS

Birds such as flycatchers and robins prefer open-fronted boxes, where the front panel covers only the bottom half of the box. These boxes are more vulnerable to attack and need to be placed with particular care. They are best fixed on sheer walls, preferably among climbing plants for concealment. An old shed, garage or outbuilding with permanent access through a high, open window also gives protection.

Fix the boxes securely, avoiding any place where rainwater tends to stream down the wall. Fix two battens down the back of the box so it stands away from the wall a little and is less likely to rot.

Artificial nests for swallows and house martins are easily made to imitate the cup-shaped nests the birds build from mud. Nail two strips of wood together to make a right-angled support and fix half an empty coconut shell to it with wire netting. Nail the support under a garage beam or the house eaves.

To help swallows and martins build their own nests during a dry spell, make a muddy puddle to give them a supply of building material.

PROTECTING LOW NESTS FROM PREDATORS

Siting a nestbox carefully spares it from many predators, but you can provide extra protection by surrounding a threatened nest made in a hole or box on the ground with a circle of dark wire netting.

Use 2 in (5 cm) mesh to cover nests of small birds, and 3 in (7.5 cm) mesh for larger birds. Fix the wire netting when the nestboxes are put in place or maintained in winter, or after the eggs have been laid and before they hatch. Use a piece about 3 ft (1 m) across and make sure its high point is at least 1 ft (30 cm) above the nest and well supported with ties, nails or a forked stick so that predators cannot press it down.

VIVID VISITOR Trees with rough bark have plenty of grubs in the crevices, which the great spotted woodpecker extracts with its beak and long tongue. The bird also takes seeds and nuts from birdfeeders.

MOUTHS TO FEED Robins will readily nest in a kettle thrust into a hedge, hung from a tree or even, as here, lodged on a wire fence covered with ivy. Make sure that the spout is not facing upwards or the nest will be flooded.

WATER TO BENEFIT WILDLIFE

IF YOU WANT to make only one addition to turn your garden into a magnet for wildlife, it must be water. Birds, frogs, toads, newts and insects will be attracted even by a birdbath or tiny pond. If your pond is on a larger scale, a whole new range of plants is open to you, as well as the welcome opportunity to spot animals such as hedgehogs and foxes. Water irises, lily pads and king-cups thrive in the water, while dense and dramatic moisture-lovers crowd round it if you let an overspill drench the soil.

THE BOON OF BIRDBATHS

Birds need water not only for drinking, but for keeping their feathers clean and in a weatherproof condition. Even an old roasting tin half filled with water will soon attract a cluster of regular visitors to entertain you with their antics.

A birdbath with a gradually sloping base is best as different birds like to bathe

A DUSTBIN DIP

BIRDS WILL SPLASH vigorously in an expensive ornamental birdbath – but just as readily in an upturned old dustbin lid. Prop it in place with bricks to ensure it is stable and put some gravel in the bottom to give the birds something to grip underfoot. Change the water every few days and in the winter be sure to break any ice which forms. Give the lid a brisk scrub occasionally to keep it clear of algae.

at varying depths. There are many designs on the market, some simple and geometric, some more ornately modelled as leaves or scallop shells.

Although the water is only shallow, it can be dangerous if toddlers play in the garden; they can drown in as little as a couple of inches. One solution is to set the bath on a pedestal, maybe even in a fenced-off area for full peace of mind.

Scrub out the birdbath occasionally, especially if a large number of birds are using it, to avoid spreading pests and diseases. In freezing weather, make sure that there is always fresh water available, but never keep the water ice-free by adding salt or antifreeze; this would prove fatal for the birds.

FROGS, TOADS AND NEWTS

Amphibians breed in water and spend much of their time close to it, but they venture into other parts of the garden to find food. They eat slugs, flies and other pests, so are a boon to gardeners.

Long and lively courtships in spring are as interesting to observe as the fascinating gradual development of tadpoles into young adults. It is much more interesting to watch this mysterious process of metamorphosis take place in your own garden than in the clinical surroundings of the school science lab.

To speed up the arrival of toads or frogs at a new pond, put in some spawn from a nearby garden pond. Avoid spreading disease and unbalancing local populations by introducing spawn only from garden ponds within a half-mile radius – never take it from the wild.

Encourage amphibians to stay in your garden over winter by preparing a few hibernation sites. Favourite places for toads and newts are under rockery stones or in logpiles – preferably not too far from the pond – while most frogs prefer

VALUED FRIEND Toads breed in water in spring then live on land nearby. Encourage their beneficial feeding habits – they eat snails – by providing hibernation sites on dry land under stones or logs near to a pond.

MAKE AN ORNAMENTAL POND SAFER FOR WILDLIFE

A TRADITIONAL GARDEN POND is usually designed for decorative plants and fish. Birds and insects may be attracted to it, but its steep sides and paved rim can make it a deathtrap for many small creatures. With a few inexpensive changes, however, you can quickly make the pond friendly to wildlife.

Make a temporary escape route by propping a heavy wooden board from the base or shelf of the pond to the rim. Weight the wood at the bottom with a brick.

Put a slender branch across a corner. Birds can perch on it to drink and dip into the water.

To replace the board, collect or buy enough large smooth pebbles to heap in a corner right up to the rim so that frogs and other creatures can get out onto the paving.

As an alternative to removing paving, grow plants such as cotoneaster, periwinkle, creeping Jenny and purple bugle to arch and trail over it into the water.

Take up some of the paved rim and let grass or other plants spread to the water's edge to make a covered green corridor to the pond.

Put aquatic plants in the pond to oxygenate the water, shade it and give extra ways in and out.

to hibernate in mud at the bottom of the pond itself. Amphibians also hide in compost heaps, so take care when you are forking out and turning the compost.

A MINIATURE WILDLIFE POND

A wooden half-barrel makes a quick and easy miniature pond to fit in the tiniest corner. Just dig a hole the same size as the barrel, sink it in the ground with the rim flush with the soil and fill it with water. Any cracks seal as the wood swells.

Barrels are treacherously steep-sided, and should be fitted with an escape route for wild creatures. Compact marginal plants or a ramp of wood fixed to the inside of the rim serves the purpose. King-cups and water irises are suitable

marginal plants. Place them on bricks so that their heads are in air.

Plant the centre of the barrel with a small water lily such as the scented pink *Nymphaea* 'Odorata Turicensis' and an oxygenating plant – perhaps the water violet, *Hottonia palustris*. Around the barrel, grow plants to lean over and provide shade. Hostas, dwarf bamboos and *Alchemilla mollis* are suitable.

Instead of buying perforated pots to hold pond plants, use brussels sprouts bags from a greengrocer or supermarket. The close mesh defeats fish and other nibblers, but the plants' roots can spread out through the holes.

If you already have an ornamental pond, it may not be safe or welcoming to

many creatures. Steep sides, fish that eat insects and tadpoles, and a barren paved surround make many ponds quite hostile to wildlife.

Frogs, toads and hedgehogs are likely to drown if there is no easy way out of the pond, and on an open, sunbaked approach frogs and toads could die of dehydration. Rather than going to the trouble and expense of remaking the whole pond, apply a few measures – some instant, some taking a little longer – that will make it much safer and more attractive for small creatures.

Ease of access can be planned from the start when you make a pond from scratch. Site the pond in a sunny position and put in enough (continued on p.334)

A WILDLIFE POND AND BOG GARDEN

Generously sized leaves and more delicate flowers clothe a pond, giving you as much satisfaction as the wildlife that skilful planting encourages.

TO CREATE a successful wildlife pond, make sure that there is easy access to the water for small amphibians such as frogs and newts. Cobbles and gravel on the gently sloping side make a beach where creatures can easily reach the water. When the pond is bordered by lawn, lay the turf so that it just projects over the edge to make a cool hiding place for animals in the summer. Plenty of planting both in and around the pond is also a sure way to attract wildlife.

MOISTURE-LOVING PLANTS

Creatures are much readier to approach the water if there is some natural cover. A lush bog garden of moisture-loving plants is sought by toads, hedgehogs and many insects that like to shelter under the cool, damp leaves. All you need is a lined cavity filled with soil containing plenty of water-retentive, bulky organic matter. Placed next to the pond, it makes an ideal transition from garden to water. It is easy and cheap to make and can be any size you wish. To cut down on

Rodgersia leaves provide a canopy

New dragonflies spread their wings on tall iris stems

Hostas give dense cover for small animals

maintenance, plant the pond with a mixture of species that quickly achieves a natural balance. In a small garden, mingling cultivated plants with wild species may 'lift' the ornamental value.

Try to select plants that have a direct wildlife benefit, such as flowers that produce nectar and pollen for butterflies and bees. Oxygenating plants are vital to keep the water clear and free from green algae. Start in the deepest water with some water violets, which have delightful spikes of pink and white flowers, and water hawthorn, with daintier blooms.

To keep the sun off the pond, and so reduce the growth of algae, make sure that there are enough plants in the middle of the water. For a healthy, well-balanced pond, about a third should be covered with foliage. Plants such as water lilies, with their fleshy leaves and glorious flowers, luxuriate on the surface, and they grow well in deep water. Newts shelter from the sunlight under the plants and perch on the leaves, too, to bask.

Frogs hop from leaf to leaf in their quest for food, and range in colour from large and bright green to small and brown depending on variety. They are partial to snails, and so perform a useful task by ridding the garden of some of the most persistent pests, inevitably attracted to fleshy-leaved plants such as hostas. Toads are another welcome amphibian attracted by the water, both to breed and find food.

WILDLIFE MAGNETS

Many plants that flourish in shallow water at the pond's edge are magnets for wildlife – and add beauty as well. Water forget-me-not and king-cup have pretty flowers that attract bees and other pollinating insects, and they also provide essential undergrowth for frogs and toads to take cover in.

Upright or tall-stemmed plants such as irises and grasses are ideal for encouraging dragonflies and damselflies to breed. They lay their eggs near the roots, and the nymphs hatch and climb up the stems to shed their skins and dry their wings for an hour or two before flying off to look for a mate.

The iridescent emerald and royal blue colouring of the fully fledged insects is as alluring to larger forms of wildlife as to humans. Predators such as swallows descend to skim the water's surface, swooping and dipping to catch their prey or take a sip to drink.

1. *Rodgersia podophylla*
2. Meadowsweet (*Filipendula ulmaria* 'Aurea')
3. *Iris laevigata* 'Variegata'
4. Brooklime (*Veronica beccabunga*)
5. Water forget-me-not (*Myosotis scorpioides*)
6. Dwarf reedmace (*Typha minima*)
7. Water violet (*Hottonia palustris*)
8. Ragged robin (*Lychnis flos-cuculi*)
9. Lady's smock (*Cardamine pratensis*)
10. Water avens (*Geum rivale*)
11. King-cup (*Caltha palustris*)
12. Water lily (*Nymphaea alba*)
13. Water lily (*Nymphaea* 'Solfatare')
14. *Hosta crispula*
15. Bugle (*Ajuga reptans* 'Purpurea')
16. *Lagarosiphon major*
17. *Glyceria maxima variegata*
18. Water mint (*Mentha aquatica*)
19. Water hawthorn (*Aponogeton distachyos*)
20. *Cotoneaster dammeri*
21. *Astilbe simplicifolia* 'Sprite'
22. Creeping Jenny (*Lysimachia nummularia* 'Aurea')
23. Lesser periwinkle (*Vinca minor*)

Frogs need a shallow way in and out of water

Waterlily leaves shade the water

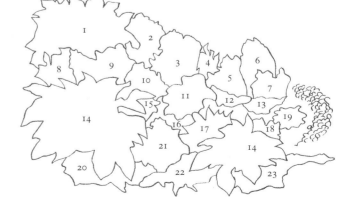

ANIMALS IN YOUR GARDEN

NATURAL RAFT A frog suns itself on a water lily pad. Plant water lilies in a sunny spot to encourage vigorous flowering. The large leaves shading the water help to prevent harmful algae from forming.

plants to shade about a third of the water. Too much sun on it encourages algae to grow and clog the pond.

To reduce the amount of algae that spreads in your pond (which requires some effort to remove) make sure that many of the plants you choose are efficient oxygenators. If you have to refill the pond, use rainwater rather than tap water, as tap water is rich in nutrients that encourage algae.

Unless you have a large garden, the pond is likely to be a prominent feature, close to the house so that you can enjoy it fully, and an integral part of the decorative garden you are developing.

Cultivated plants are what many gardeners choose for such a situation, but purists on wildlife matters prefer to grow only native plants in and around their ponds. Native plants attract the largest number of insects, and consequently of the creatures that feed on them. Whether you choose decorative plants, native plants or a mixture, you can make a beautiful pond.

You can speed up the naturalisation of a newly made wildlife pond by putting in a bucket of mud from a neighbour's wildlife-rich pond. It will be full of larvae, including the eggs of water snails, which help to keep the pond clean.

BEST PLANTS

A PURIST'S WILDLIFE POND

Many indigenous plants that grow in wetlands or ponds can create a flowering habitat for wildlife in the garden.

• Yellow flag (*Iris pseudacorus*): large, bright yellow flowers and swordlike leaves from May to July.

• Purple loosestrife (*Lythrum salicaria*): pink-purple flower spikes from June to August.

• Flowering rush (*Butomus umbellatus*): pink flowers with red stamens from July to September; almond scent; razor-sharp leaves.

• Hemp agrimony (*Eupatorium cannabinum*): tall and bushy, soft pink flower heads from July to September.

• Bogbean (*Menyanthes trifoliata*): pink buds, then white starlike flowers from May to July.

• Marsh marigold (*Caltha palustris*): yellow flowers from March to May.

• Common valerian (*Valeriana officinalis*): pink flowers from June to July.

• Common water crowfoot (*Ranunculus aquatilis*): white buttercup-like flowers with yellow centres from May to June; floats on water.

• Grass of Parnassus (*Parnassia palustris*): cream blooms with green veining from July to October.

M OST ANIMALS that feed, live or breed in your garden are hardly ever seen. Field mice, moles, voles and shrews – and even deer such as muntjac in some areas – may spend much of their time in gardens, but are all very shy and prefer to stay under cover. Even so, during quiet contemplation of your garden you could spot one of these creatures feeding unawares.

Grey squirrels are more common and bolder, and their acrobatic displays are an endless source of amusement. They are much less amusing when they dig up your bulbs. It is often food put out for the birds that attracts squirrels, so if you do not want to encourage them, make sure you put food in squirrel-proof feeders.

Foxes, too, arouse mixed feelings but many people enjoy the sight of a sleek, sharp-faced fox slipping alongside the hedge. Foxes are now common in town as well as country. Dustbins are one attraction, low birds' nests and fallen fruits are others, so protect nests with wire netting and pick up crops of windfalls if you see the fox as a foe.

Hedgehogs and bats arouse many prejudices, but gardeners usually welcome both since they are enormously beneficial for the garden.

HAVENS FOR HEDGEHOGS

Hedgehogs are active at night, when they eat slugs, snails, caterpillars, insects and other pests. Avoid using slug pellets and insecticides because these poison much of their food and can often prove fatal. Hedgehogs may be short of food during dry spells in summer, particularly later in the season when the young hedgehogs need to put on weight quickly before winter. Put out some tinned cat or dog food and water, not milk, to see them through the most critical times.

Providing nest sites helps hedgehogs to survive, especially through their hibernation from late autumn to about the end of March. Compost heaps or any undisturbed pile of dry leaves or grass mowings are likely nesting spots. Try to avoid turning or emptying a compost heap during winter, and check bonfire rubbish carefully before setting light to it.

An upturned washing-up bowl, camouflaged with twigs and leaves, quickly

NIGHT LIFE A pipistrelle bat chases a caddis fly on one of its nightly hunting expeditions. Pipistrelles, Britain's smallest bats, are widespread, and feed on caddis flies, gnats and tiny moths.

makes a hedgehog home. Cut a hole in the side and, for a safer entrance, lead a 3 ft (1 m) tunnel to it made of three lengths of wood 4 in (10 cm) wide. Nail them together using two for the sides and one for the roof.

INSECT-HUNTERS SUPREME

Twilight on a summer evening is the likeliest time to notice bats, but they are on the wing nearly all night, hunting flying insects which they eat in prodigious numbers. Even the smallest species of bat can eat hundreds of insects a night.

Bats' numbers are steadily declining as insecticides kill off their food supply, and suitable spots for roosting become rarer. Bats roost in lofts, old buildings, holes in trees, and even in old tunnels. If you are planning any building work or timber treatment which could affect a suspected roost, consult English Nature on how to avoid harming the bats.

The best way to encourage bats to come into your garden is to make sure it offers insects and roosting sites. Local conservation groups give advice on choosing and siting bat boxes for roosting. You can help to boost the supply of insects by gardening without pesticides, planting a diverse range of plants and having a pond.

BY-PRODUCT OF PERFUME

Strongly scented plants add an exquisite pleasure to summer evenings, when most people can relax and really appreciate the garden. The scents that delight us exist to lure moths and other insects to pollinate the plants, which in turn draw hunting bats. Two of the most heavily perfumed plants are climbing summer jasmine and honeysuckle – *Lonicera × heckrottii* 'Gold Flame', and *L. periclymenum* 'Belgica' and 'Serotina' are especially fragrant.

Among the loveliest of night-scented plants are the white-flowered tobacco plant (which can attract colourful hawkmoths), night-scented stock and sweet rocket. Many other plants intensify their fragrance on warm evenings – among them Mexican orange blossom, lavender, philadelphus and lilac.

Grow some of these near the house and, if you leave an outside light on, you may catch sight of bats in action.

WINTER SUPPLIES Hawthorn berries provide winter food for many birds, and for small mammals such as this bank vole. These creatures are particularly dependent on garden supplies as hedgerows disappear.

GARDENER'S HELPMATE Hedgehogs eat slugs, beetles and caterpillars. They hibernate among piles of dead leaves in sheltered places under shrubs or brambles, so leave some piles to encourage them.

ATTRACTING BUTTERFLIES

GENERATION GAP The holly blue butterfly lays its eggs on holly in spring and ivy in autumn. The two generations of caterpillars prefer to eat the flower buds and young fruits of their host plants rather than the leaves.

WAVY WINGS The comma butterfly has distinctive wings with ragged edges. It prefers to bask in sheltered sunshine, so plant flowers for it in a protected spot. Ivy flowers give an autumn supply of nectar.

WHILE WE REGARD many garden insects as prey for other creatures, we accord a higher status to some. Bees, for example, are the very image of industry, with a strong community sense into the bargain. Dragonflies have a certain rarity value and never fail to amaze as nature's steely-blue helicopters, infinitely more skilled than the man-made imitations, and beautiful too.

Far ahead in the insect beauty parade are butterflies. With their handsome markings and delicate, dancing flight, they are a delight to watch. A glimpse of the first one each year gives a promise of summer. Through midsummer into early autumn different species visit the garden to seek the food they need, or plants to lay their eggs on, or sheltered spots where they can spend the winter.

There are some easy lures to attract more butterflies into the garden.
- Grow plenty of the nectar-rich blue flowers that many adults feed on.
- Butterflies always make for the sun and dislike being buffeted by the wind, so grow the nectar-rich plants they like in a sheltered, south-facing spot.
- Leave a shed window ajar in autumn, so that butterflies can enter and hibernate under cover.
- Some butterflies hibernate in evergreens, such as ivy, but a few prefer dry, dead leaves, so delay cutting back dead herbaceous perennials until spring.
- Leave windfall apples, pears and plums on the ground, and butterflies such as red admirals will feast on the fermenting fruit.
- A patch of nettles left to flourish in a sunny corner makes an ideal nursery for butterflies. Red admirals, peacocks, small tortoiseshells and commas all lay their eggs on nettles.

NECTAR FROM SHRUBS AND PERENNIALS

The aptly named butterfly bush (*Buddleia davidii*) must be the gardener's first choice for attracting butterflies. Its long panicles of flowers from mid to late summer are white, blue, pink and mauve. Plant several buddleias together if you have space, and prune them back in late February or early March. For a longer succession of flowers, prune some bushes hard, and others lightly. Deadheading after flowering brings on another flush of flowers.

Lilac is another shrub whose profuse blooms attract butterflies. Its fragrant white flowers appear in late spring, and are blue, deep lavender, creamy-yellow or white. For extra colour in summer, thread a large-flowered clematis through the lilac plant once it is well established.

Another scented spring beauty, with large white flower heads, is *Viburnum × burkwoodii*, which can be grown as a free-standing bush or trained against a wall or a fence – as can ceanothus, which has exquisite deep blue flowers.

Rosemary is also happy to grow against a sunny wall. Choose the narrow 'Miss Jessopp's Upright' where space is restricted. Blue flowers are especially popular with butterflies and with bees as well. *Caryopteris × clandonensis* is a good small shrub with fluffy blue flowers that appear in August and September.

Lavender and hyssop, old favourites, are ideal for edging, as is common thyme, an excellent aromatic ground-cover plant. Your own herb patch is a great bonus in the garden. Not only does it provide flavours for cooking, but the plants themselves are decorative and their flowers attract many butterflies, as well as beneficial bees and hoverflies.

GOSSAMER WINGS Damselflies lay eggs in incisions made in the stems or leaves of plants just beneath the surface of the water. Tall-stemmed plants, such as flag iris, let the emerging nymphs climb to the surface.

A SUNNY BUTTERFLY BORDER

The butterfly bonanza is from high to late summer, when the nectar-sipping beauties stock up on food to see them through the winter.

MAKE THE BORDER in a sheltered and sunny spot as butterflies are attracted by the warmth. Indispensable as a taller, back-of-the-border plant is buddleia; it forms the framework of this bed. Choose a white form as a change from the more familiar purple, especially to give a lighter, more airy look to the border.

Ceanothus impressus, with its exquisite deep blue flowers that appear in April and May is a useful source of nectar in spring. It does well as a free-standing bush or trained against a wall or fence. Nectar-rich smaller shrubs include *Caryopteris clandonensis*, which can be covered with so many clusters of flowers from midsummer that the whole bush is a haze of blue-purple. Late-flowering herbaceous perennials take over as the shrub blooms fade.

Perennials such as globe thistles, Michaelmas daisies and *Clematis heracleifolia* are generously adorned with the blue-purple flowers so irresistible to butterflies. The ice plant (*Sedum spectabile*) makes a contrast with its flat, pink flower heads maturing to rusty red; they are especially popular with small tortoiseshell butterflies.

Buddleia is a favourite with butterflies into late summer

Evening primrose opens at sundown

Sedums offer nectar into autumn

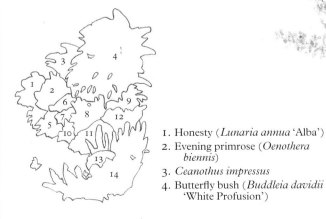

1. Honesty (*Lunaria annua* 'Alba')
2. Evening primrose (*Oenothera biennis*)
3. *Ceanothus impressus*
4. Butterfly bush (*Buddleia davidii* 'White Profusion')
5. Lesser periwinkle (*Vinca minor*)
6. Michaelmas daisy (*Aster × frikartii*)
7. *Caryopteris clandonensis*
8. Globe thistle (*Echinops ritro*)
9. *Berberis verruculosa*
10. Viper's bugloss (*Echium vulgare*)
11. Ice plant (*Sedum spectabile*)
12. *Clematis heracleifolia* 'Wyevale'
13. Thyme (*Thymus serpyllum coccineus* 'Major')
14. Catmint (*Nepeta mussinii*)

NIGHT FLIGHTS An elephant hawk-moth with delicate pink-flushed wings and body rests on a tobacco plant in the summer dusk. This nocturnal feeder is seen from June to August in gardens with tempting plants.

Most herbs flourish in sunny spots where the soil is well drained.

Late-flowering herbaceous perennials extend the food supply for butterflies. Globe thistles, Michaelmas daisies and *Clematis heracleifolia* are all good choices with their blue-purple flowers. An ice plant (*Sedum spectabile*) makes a colour contrast with its flat, rusty-pink flower heads, which are especially popular with small tortoiseshells.

Add a few evergreens to your butterfly border and it will please you throughout the year, as well as enticing more birds. *Berberis verruculosa* is an evergreen shrub with leaves that are glossy dark green on top and blue-white underneath, and yellow flowers that are especially

ESSENCE OF SPRING Growing lots of spring flowers provides food for butterflies before the summer abundance of nectar. Orange-tip butterflies are to be seen dancing lightly over the flowers from the beginning of May, when forget-me-nots are a source of nectar.

valuable since they come out in spring, when fewer plants are flowering. Lesser periwinkle makes dark evergreen ground cover with the bonus of sporadic flowers, either white or bluish-mauve, over a long period, certainly from March to July and sometimes even into October.

FAST AND EARLY FOOD

In the two or three years it takes for shrubs and perennials to develop and make a show, you can fill the spaces and get short-term splashes of colour with some annuals and biennials. For a cheap and cheerful display of annuals to attract butterflies, grow night-scented stock, mignonette, viper's bugloss, candytuft, blazing star (*Mentzelia aurea*) and tidy tips (*Layia elegans*).

Spring flowers are also invaluable, since they provide vital nourishment for peacocks, small tortoiseshells, brimstones and other butterflies that rouse early from hibernation. Crocuses, snowdrops, *Anemone blanda*, aubrietia and *Alyssum saxatile* all open their flowers early in the year.

Do remember when planning your planting that the feeding needs of the adult butterflies differ from those of the larvae – for while butterflies need nectar, larvae require vegetable or plant fodder, such as nettles.

PLANTS FOR A WILD CORNER

ONE OF THE BEST WAYS of attracting wildlife is to let part of your garden grow more freely – and an extra bonus is the time you save on maintenance. By just spending less time on mowing, you can let a flower-spangled meadow or a natural-looking woodland area develop. But you can also make more of the wild flowers that gardeners often disregard.

WILD FLOWERS IN BORDERS

Freed from competition with grasses and other vigorous plants, wild flowers established in a border give a wonderful display. Take care to avoid invasive plants such as buttercups and thistles. Make a start with familiar wild flowers.

❧ Plant primroses, sweet violets, oxlips and bugle under deciduous shrubs.

❧ Foxgloves and evening primrose look lovely in a cottage-garden border, as does thrift – an ideal edging plant, with its neat hummocks studded with pink flowers.

❧ For a dry bank or rockery, yellow

MAKING · IT · EASIER

SHORT CUT TO A WILD GARDEN

GET YOUR WILDLIFE PATCH off to a quick start by making import-export deals with neighbours who already have well-established wild gardens.

In late spring, cut and lift a few small squares of your turf and replace them with squares of meadow from your neighbours. Your turfs will fill the gaps left in their gardens.

flowers such as toadflax, horseshoe vetch and bird's-foot trefoil make a striking contrast with red valerian, maiden pink and bloody cranesbill.

RAISING FROM SEED

Do not take plants or seeds from the wild. Specialist suppliers stock both seeds and plants, while most garden centres sell wild-flower plants. Growing wild flowers from seed is an economical way of raising a large number of plants. You will be most successful if you treat them like cultivated plants.

To encourage seeds of primrose, cowslip, oxlip, clustered bellflower and violet, which need a period of cold before germinating, sow them in autumn and put the trays outside. Alternatively trick the seeds; mix them with damp sand in a polythene bag and put them in a refrigerator for six to eight weeks.

To ensure the best germination for hard-coated seeds, such as those of trefoil and cranesbill, rub the seeds between two sheets of fine sandpaper so that vital moisture can penetrate the seeds easily.

DEVELOPING A MEADOW

One of the most striking ways of making your garden look more natural is to create a wild-flower meadow. Either start from scratch by sowing a mixture of grass and flower seeds onto bare soil, preferably in the early autumn, or sow wild flowers in part of your lawn. Pull a sturdy, fixed-tine rake firmly over a lawn you are converting into a meadow. The rake will quickly scrape off some grass, making shallow bare patches where you can sprinkle seed. Do not feed the meadow or let cut grass lie on it and enrich it. Wild flowers are ousted if greedier feeders are encouraged. You need mow only twice a year – in late spring and late autumn.

A surprising range of flowers appears once you stop mowing a lawn frequently. Many of the plants traditionally treated as weeds – daisies, clover, speedwell and self-heal – have pretty flowers and can be left to flourish, while invasive ones, such as dandelions and thistles, should be deadheaded after flowering.

Let a fringe of long grass grow round the edge of a lawn and plant a selection of primrose, cowslip, bird's-foot trefoil, meadow cranesbill, harebell, columbine, oxeye daisy, bugle and campion in it. Either buy them ready-grown or raise them from seed.

In a larger area of taller, rough grass, you can plant tough herbaceous perennials. For a sunny site there is plenty of choice, including bear's breeches (*Acanthus mollis*), goatsbeard (*Aruncus sylvester*), *Crambe cordifolia*, globe thistle (*Echinops*), soapwort (*Saponaria officinalis*) and *Senecio tanguticus*.

Create a gently winding mown path through your wild-flower meadow. This will give it some structure and tempt you to wander along it, looking at the butterflies and insects that will congregate.

In a very small garden, grow your wild flowers in containers, some for meadow flowers and some for woodland flowers. Give each meadow pot a good layer of pebbles for easy drainage, cover this with garden subsoil or used seed compost, and finish off with an inch of topsoil. For woodland pots use rich but well-drained soil and put them in a shady position.

BRIGHT CORNFIELD COLOUR

A sunny corner of well-drained soil gives you the opportunity to make a glorious blaze of summer colour with annual wild

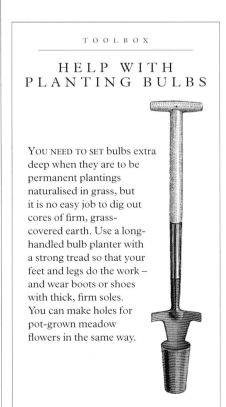

CORNFIELD FLOWERS A planting of corn camomile, cornflowers and corn marigolds not only looks pretty but also creates an environment that attracts butterflies and many other meadow insects.

ENCHANTED WAY Encouraging a garden corner to develop into a secluded glade is an excellent way to make wild flowers such as oxeye daisies and tall grasses look at home in a cultivated setting.

flowers. These are traditionally called cornfield flowers because they flourish in freshly disturbed ground, such as fields sown with annual grain crops. These flowers are simple but spectacular – bright red field poppies, golden corn marigolds, rich blue cornflowers, pink corn cockles, white, yellow-centred oxeye daisies and white campions.

Cornfield flower seeds are sold by specialist suppliers, either as a prepared mixture or as individual varieties. In autumn or early spring, dig over the ground or rake it to a fine tilth, then rake the seed in lightly to cover it.

To keep the flowers coming year after year, leave them to set seed. Pull them up in autumn, shake the seed out onto the ground, then rake it vigorously.

NATURALISING BULBS

In patches of rough grass, verges or under trees, plant bulbs to give colour year after year. Choose natural-looking plant varieties: daffodils, snowdrops and winter aconites are perfect. Plant daffodils by the end of September, but snowdrops and winter aconites establish best when planted at the end of winter.

Autumn crocuses will give colour in September and October. Look for the blue *Crocus speciosus* and the lilac *Crocus kotschyanus* syn. *C. zonatus*.

Let bulbs' leaves die back before cutting them off as this is how the plants build up energy for next year's flowers.

DAPPLED WOODLAND GLADES

With just one or two trees and well-chosen underplanting, you can give the feeling of a woodland glade to your garden. Aim for a combination of shelter and open space, sunshine and shade.

Plants for a woodland glade need to be a variety of heights to provide vegetation at all levels. Choose a tree that forms a fairly light or high canopy of foliage so that a wide range of plants will grow underneath. For well-drained soils, the best trees are silver birch and rowan. On loamy to heavy soils, hawthorn, wild cherry and bird cherry do well, while apple and crab apple trees also make suitable centrepieces.

Below the trees, make a middle layer of berrying, shrubby plants such as

PERILS OF CLOVER

TURF THREADED with clover is a pretty sight when the flowers are in bloom, but do not let clover grow if babies who are at the crawling stage, toddlers or people with bare feet are likely to be on the lawn. Clover nectar is irresistible to bees, which may sting if bare flesh threatens to crush them.

PERENNIAL DELIGHT The English bluebell (*Hyacinthoides non-scripta*) is daintier than the common Spanish bluebell. Naturalised bulbs give colour year after year and their flowers attract nectar-seeking insects.

common elder, blackthorn, holly and hawthorn. Alternatively choose *Cornus alba* 'Westonbirt', *Exochorda macrantha* 'The Bride', *Spiraea × arguta*, *Daphne mezereum*, snowy mespilus (*Amelanchier canadensis*), and dog rose (*Rosa canina*). Underplant them with dense swathes of shade-loving hellebores, pulmonarias, *Iris foetidissima* and winter aconites.

Honesty, foxglove and Welsh poppy like the conditions, and ground carpeters such as forget-me-nots, primroses, woodruff, celandines, lilies-of-the-valley and violets are essential. Use small spring-flowering bulbs to fill any gaps. For summer, bluebells are happy in semi-woodland conditions.

A Place for Takeovers

Rather than waging constant war on rampant plants, discover what benefits they offer. In the right place, their over-enthusiasm can be a boon for reducing maintenance and attracting wildlife. Put them in the awkward corners and let them flourish where you will never have success with border plants.

- To make a nettle patch much more suitable for butterflies, cut a third of the plants back to ground level in mid June, and another third a month later. Check the undersides of leaves for eggs or caterpillars first. The site must be sunny.
- *Euphorbia amygdaloides* var. *robbiae* forms handsome evergreen clumps with bright lime-yellow bracts in spring, and it quickly spreads by underground stems.
- Comfrey (*Symphytum officinale*) is excellent for ground cover and bears pretty white and pink spring flowers. It is also a speedy compost activator.
- Rampant ground-cover roses such as 'Pheasant', 'Grouse', 'Partridge', 'Max Graf' and 'Pink Drift' sprawl rapidly over a sunny bank.
- Brambles, with their berries and nesting possibilities, make the most of a drab or hidden corner.

There is really no need to slave in the garden. By allowing nature to take its course, while always keeping a watchful eye on developments, you can have a beautiful garden, and one which will attract more wildlife. On top of this you have the bonus of actually having the time to observe all these extra visitors.

UNDER THE APPLE TREE Intermingle wild and cultivated flowers in the dappled shade cast by a blossoming apple tree. Hellebores near the shed lead to blue forget-me-nots and yellow primulas, with comfrey circling the trunk.

INSPIRATION FROM
GREAT GARDENS

BENINGTON LORDSHIP

Georgian grace suits an ancient Saxon site.

Just to the east of bustling Stevenage in Hertfordshire lies a garden whose past and present are cunningly intermingled. Well-planned herbaceous borders climb to the castle bailey, once-productive fishponds now serve as gracious lily pools, and ever-multiplying winter bulbs swathe the grassy moat.

Among the finest features of Benington Lordship's unfussy garden is the annual display of snowdrops, soon joined by winter aconites, which dress historic ruins around the handsome, red-brick house. In February of each year, the owners open the garden before the main season so that visitors can enjoy the flood of delicate white blooms which weave in between buttercuplike flowers with smart green ruffs.

Between them, these small plants create a crowd puller to rival even the garden's famous summer borders, as rivers of white and gold flow down the banks of the old moat and rush in spate alongside paths and under trees.

A Glimpse of Spring

The purpose of such a planting is to brighten the garden on days when summer is virtually forgotten, to form a cheerful carpet beneath trees whose bare branches frame only leaden, scudding clouds. At Benington Lordship, colour is extended into March by flowering scillas as blue as Mediterranean skies, and by the emergence of naturalised daffodils. By the time these begin to fade away, spring has arrived.

This idea is easily transferred to a smaller garden, where a grassy verge alongside a path or perhaps beneath a skeletal tree can be called into service as a flowery glade for late winter. As the flowers push up through the grass, they look equally well against an open stretch of ground, a hedge, a wall with or without ivy, or woven fencing panels.

To create the impression of a natural swathe of flowers, scatter alternate handfuls of snowdrop and winter aconite bulbs over the grass in autumn. Plant them where they fall using a dibber or thick stick to make a hole about 3 in (7.5 cm) deep for each bulb, and then trickle in fine soil from an old jug or other container to fill the holes.

As Simple as Nature

Another appealing trait of snowdrops and aconites is that, once established, they can be left more or less to their own devices, and will obligingly multiply, year by year. All they ask is that their leaves are allowed to die back before the area is mown. The bulbs cease to bloom long before the deciduous trees come into leaf, but shrubs and trees that look their best in winter and spring are used to extend the season of interest.

This backup for the snowdrops and aconites is just as appropriate for a small garden as it is in a larger expanse. You might plant nearby a Japanese cherry that flowers between November and April and follows up with coppery red young leaves – *Prunus subhirtella* 'Autumnalis', perhaps – or introduce *Betula albo-sinensis,* a Chinese birch whose orange-red bark is particularly striking in winter. Alternatively, surround the base of a silver-barked or canoe birch with a ruff of colourful bulbs.

For a long-running show, ideal for a small garden, plant the bulbs under and about a snowy mespilus, *Amelanchier lamarckii.* This tree bears a profusion of white flowers at just about the time the bulbs are ending, and then provides black, edible berries in June and a blaze of foliage in autumn.

The Art of Timing

When planting the drifts of bulbs, consider whether they are to be your sole display or the first of a parade of blooms that lasts until the pink and white cyclamens of autumn. If you have room, plant narcissi and bluebells round the margins and crocuses for spring and autumn too. Bear in mind the background hues and shapes of the house or driveway.

And while it might be an advantage to possess a backdrop of Norman fortification, the pleasure that such bulbs bring enhances any garden and brightens the winters for all who see them.

UNDER WINTRY SKIES Brilliant eddies of snowdrops and winter aconites swirl about the stony remains of the Norman keep.

EARLIEST BLOOMS A carpet of bulbs planted beneath a snowy mespilus in a small garden introduces a succession of late winter flowers that returns each year.

In Tune
with Nature

RESPECT FOR NATURE'S PROCESSES is strong in gardeners, and many feel a growing reluctance to risk causing long-term damage by unnecessary applications of chemicals. Friendly persuasion is much more in tune with the times. Whether the problem concerns improving soil fertility, banishing weeds, or controlling pests, there are plenty of 'green' methods that work, and let you be more organic without being eccentric.

Poppies, feverfew and sage flourish in an informal bed. Growing a wide variety of plants together makes them less susceptible to attack by a particular pest.

TAKING A GREENER LINE

Rather than worry that pesticides are harming plants and creatures in your garden, why not attempt 'greener' methods? Even without trying out-and-out organic techniques – though you may wish to do so – you can take a few easy steps towards plant care that does no harm to the environment.

In the long term, chemical-free or almost chemical-free gardening leads to stronger and more self-sufficient plants.

Most pesticides do not distinguish between friend and foe, killing both the pests and the beneficial creatures that feed on them, so they may even increase the number of garden pests. Some weed-killers may leave poisonous residues and weaken the plants they are intended to protect. Storing and using chemicals safely also causes concern, especially where there are children or pets about.

STEPS TO GREENER GARDENING

Fortunately, there are ways to maintain the quality of your plants without using chemical preparations. Use home-grown green manures and compost made from garden and household waste to improve soil structure, keep in moisture and replenish vital nutrients.

Help to reduce the number of pests by growing plants that attract their natural predators – such as frogs and birds – or by changing to more varied planting schemes. As a last resort, use biological pest controls, which are more narrowly targeted and much less harmful to the garden than chemical ones.

Give your plants the best chance of success by giving them a little attention every year and by acting in sympathy with the natural balance between plants, soil, bacteria, insects and their predators.

TOP-LEVEL DISPLAY Adopting simple green techniques such as growing ground-cover plants rather than using weedkillers is not just kind to the environment. It also cuts down your labour and leads to a lovely garden packed with healthy roses and pinks (*Dianthus*).

LOOKING AFTER THE SOIL

THE BEST WAY to keep plants strong and healthy, and produce a fine display of flowers and healthy crops of fruit and vegetables, is to improve the soil. Because gardening tends to involve growing many plants in a confined space, it is inevitable that they take more out of the soil than they give back. Adding bulky decayed vegetable matter and natural fertilisers replaces the lost nutrients and keeps the soil in good condition.

To manage your soil to the best advantage, you need to know whether it is light or heavy. Sand is lightest and coarsest in texture. It feels harsh and gritty, and the particles scarcely hold together at all, even when moist. Chalk also has a light texture. Clay is heaviest and finest in texture. It feels sticky like putty when wet and dries out into rocklike clods. In between the two extremes, silty soils feel smooth, soft and floury.

WHAT YOUR SOIL NEEDS

Light soils such as sand and chalk are free draining and need organic matter such as garden compost or well-rotted manure incorporated to improve their capacity to hold water and nutrients.

Heavy soils such as clay and silt need to be opened up, as in their natural state they are poor draining and hard to work. Adding organic matter again helps to improve the soil. With very heavy soil, it is also worth digging in coarse grit at the rate of two buckets per square yard or metre. Use the weather to your advantage. Do heavy work such as breaking in new ground or digging over a plot in autumn. Leave the earth rough in large clods; the frost will get into it and help to break it down to a crumbly texture.

Garden compost is one of the most effective materials both for feeding the soil and improving its structure. Others are rotted manure, leaf mould, and materials available at a garden centre such as finely chipped or composted bark.

TURN WASTE INTO COMPOST

You can make compost at home. Kitchen and garden waste is an immensely valuable source of nutrients and soil conditioners, so it is worth making use of it rather than throwing it all away or burning it. To make the best compost, you

COMPOST BINS FOR CONVENIENCE

Inside a bin, garden debris heats up rapidly, the rotting process is faster, the amount of water in the heap can be controlled and everything stays neatly in one place. You need more than one container to make enough compost, unless your garden is small.

SECTION BOX
Cheap and easy to make, each square is made from four pieces of floorboard nailed to four battens. You can add sections as the heap builds up, then take them away to mix or remove compost or move the heap.

DOUBLE ACTION
Some metal bins are divided into two sections for the most convenient use of space. One side 'cooks' while the other is being filled.

INSULATED PANELS
Metal bins with insulated panels help debris to heat up and rot rapidly. These bins are raised off the ground with bricks and mesh to improve air circulation, and are easy to take apart for emptying.

NEW ZEALAND BOX
With a slotted front for easy access, a New Zealand box is solid and long lasting. Either buy one, or make one from 3 ft (1 m) planks. If you make two bins, stand them side by side, so they share one wall and save wood and heat.

CHICKEN WIRE AND CARPET
Make your own cheap compost bin by stapling wire mesh round four posts. Line the inside with old carpet. An unlined container is best for making leaf mould.

COMPOST TUMBLER
Made of plastic on a metal frame, a tumbler saves the job of emptying, mixing and reloading the heap. The compost rots down fast because you can aerate it frequently by turning it.

MAKE THE BEST COMPOST

THE RICHEST COMPOST comes from a mixture of soggy debris, such as lawn mowings and kitchen waste, and prunings. Strawy manure, nettles or mowings all speed up the process, but any material rots in the end. Most heaps take about six months to 'cook'. Once the mixture is brown and crumbly it is ready to use.

1. Spread a thick layer of coarse, woody prunings in the base. Push it into the corners but do not press down. This layer raises the heap slightly off the ground, helping air to circulate so that the compost rots down more quickly.

2. Fork a layer of weeds (but not the roots of perennial types), ornamental plant trimmings and old bedding plants onto the heap. If you are using an open-fronted container put another slat in place to stop material spilling out.

3. To speed the rotting process as you fill the bin, mix the weeds with grass clippings or comfrey leaves. Combining coarse material with fine aerates the grass clippings which might otherwise become slimy and smelly.

4. If the heap seems dry, sprinkle it with water. It is better to water as you go along rather than at the end, to get an even consistency. The material needs to be damp enough to encourage the bacteria that make it rot, but not soaking wet.

5. Cover the heap so that you can prevent moisture loss but keep out rainwater. A lid also helps it to heat up more quickly. A piece of old carpet does the job splendidly, coupled with a sheet of polythene to keep the rain out.

6. Once the bin is full, leave it for a month or two. If you have enough space, turn the compost to mix it. Empty the material out and fork it back in. Turn the heap sides to middle as it goes back in. The centre is hotter and rots faster.

need the right balance of air, water and garden debris. The tidiest way to combine the three elements is in a container, although you can simply make a heap on the ground and cover it with a thick sheet of pegged-down black plastic while it slowly rots into usable compost.

Virtually any waste can go on the heap except diseased plant material and perennial weed roots, which will continue to grow there unless the mixture becomes very hot indeed.

Collect kitchen scraps, such as vegetable and fruit peelings, coffee grounds and teabags, for the heap, but avoid cooked food and raw meat which encourage rats and mice. Eggshells can go on the heap, but take a long time to rot. Large amounts of orange and lemon peel make the compost too acidic.

Cardboard boxes, waste paper and old newspapers can be scrunched up or shredded and mixed into the heap.

Ideally, add a nitrogen-rich material at about every 1 ft (30 cm) depth as the heap builds up, to increase the compost's fertility and speed the rotting process. This could be fresh manure, nettle shoots or comfrey leaves. There is also a range of compost activators on sale.

Worms burrow in and out, breaking down the material. Bacteria also work on the compost. To increase their activity and improve drainage, stand the bin on soil rather than paving. If possible, site the compost where you are going to grow vegetables in future. Then you make the most of nutrients that may seep out from the bottom of the heap. This natural feeder makes the soil very fertile.

Make sure your bin is easily accessible with a wheelbarrow. You may be adding heavy material such as manure and large quantities of weeds too awkward to carry.

SETTING UP A WORMERY

A wormery is a container for kitchen and garden waste inhabited by a colony of worms that break down organic material into extremely fertile compost. It takes up less room than a compost heap and debris in it rots down faster.

You can buy a wormery, but it is very easy to make your own from a bin with holes drilled through the bottom. Raise the bin just off the ground and slide a drip tray under it because liquid will drain out. To start the colony, put into the bin about 100 brandling worms bought from a fishing shop. You need to add the waste slowly at first so that the

MONEY·SAVERS

A HOMEMADE WORMERY

MAKING YOUR OWN WORMERY is a dual money saver – garden compost is free, and you save on the price of a shop-bought wormery.

Make a few holes in the bottom of a dustbin, kitchen bin or old barrel big enough to hold at least a month's waste. Place it on bricks either side, with a drip tray underneath. Put a layer of gravel in the bottom to improve drainage, then a layer of well-rotted compost or manure about 3 in (7.5 cm) deep. Tip in the worms. Cover with a thinner layer of compost or manure. When the colony has become established, after a couple of weeks, start adding kitchen peelings.

Lid secured with brick

Fresh kitchen waste

Processed material

Layer of gravel

Bin raised on two bricks

Drip tray to catch liquid

worm population has time to build up. Do not add fresh waste until the last amount is almost digested and starts to resemble ready-to-use compost. The worms will work their way up, processing the waste. As the drip tray beneath fills up, collect the liquid which is rich in nutrients, dilute it with ten times as much water and use it as plant food.

Once the bin is full, take out the processed material to use on the garden. The worms will be in the top layer. Skim the layer off and set it aside while you empty out the rest of the compost, then put it back in the bottom of the wormery. Alternatively, push the compost through a garden sieve to sift out the worms.

During severely cold weather, move the wormery into a greenhouse or garage

THE PRIDE OF THE BORDER The bark of a flowering cherry (*Prunus serrula*) glistens with health above the perennials. The cherry's leaves are used for leaf mould and the spent border plants for compost, both returned to the border to sustain its fertility.

LEAVES TO IMPROVE SOIL

AUTUMN HARVEST Collect your deciduous autumn leaves to make leaf mould – one of the best soil conditioners. To see its effect, go for a woodland walk and, as your feet rustle through the leaves, look at the rich, crumbly soil under the trees, the result of decades of fallen foliage.

MAKING LEAF MOULD Tree and shrub foliage needs to rot down separately from the waste on your compost heap, because leaves are fibrous and they decompose more slowly than annuals, light stems and kitchen peelings.

READY TWO YEARS LATER When the leaves have crumbled to a flaky soil-like consistency, spread the leaf mould onto bare ground as a mulch or fork it into the top layer of soil, where it greatly improves the structure.

HIRING A SHREDDER

IT IS OFTEN BETTER to hire a shredder than to buy one. A shredder is expensive, especially the large models which enable you to put in thick sections of wood. The smaller models can be laborious to use as you can only feed in a couple of woody growths at a time. Shredders are also noisy, and a large one does the job more quickly. Check costs with a tool hire shop, and see if neighbours are interested in sharing a weekend's hire. Wear stout gloves and safety goggles when shredding.

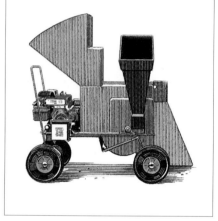

where the temperature is at least 15°C (59°F), as the worms do not function well at lower temperatures.

HOW TO MAKE LEAF MOULD

A container to hold leaf mould is cheap and quick to build. Hammer four 4ft (1.2m) posts into the ground to make a square about 3ft (1m) across and run wire netting around them, securing it with galvanised metal staples. Make sure that the netting can be removed easily from one side of the square for emptying out the leaf mould.

Use smaller containers if you are not likely to have a large number of leaves. Make a compact version by hammering just one post into the ground and fixing both ends of the netting to it, forming a cylinder. Alternatively, store the leaves in stout, black polythene sacks with a few holes pierced in them.

In autumn, gather up the leaves every few days, because they soon form a solid layer that smothers and kills any grass or other plants underneath. Put the leaves in the container and press them down well;

it is surprising how many can be packed in. Water them if they are dry. Check the heap from time to time to make sure it is damp enough, as rotting slows down if there is not enough moisture. Patches of white, thread-like fungus are a typical symptom of dryness.

Leaves take one or two years to rot down, so it is best to keep each year's fall separately. For a labour-saving alternative to gathering and storing leaves, take a tip from nature and let them rot down where they fall, but only on bare soil. Rake the leaves off any plants or the lawn and put them on the ground under shrubs or trees, and between herbaceous plants, where worms and other insects will take them into the soil during winter.

Choose a way to collect the leaves that you find easiest according to the amount.
🌢 Use a springtine rake with plastic, rubber or metal tines for small areas.
🌢 If you have large areas to clear, consider a hand-pushed leaf collector.
🌢 Leaf vacuums suck up the leaves into a large bag. Blowers quickly blow the leaves into heaps and corners where they can be picked up.
🌢 You can wait for a strong autumn wind to blow leaves into heaps, provided they are not left for very long.

Uses for Waste Wood

Use a shredder to cut your unwanted tree prunings and branches to a manageable size. Then add them to the compost heap or save them for a mulch. Shredding avoids the waste of valuable material on a bonfire or taking it to a tip.

Safety is a prime concern when using a shredder. Follow the instructions, and always use a residual current device (see p.108), which cuts off the power supply immediately any electrical fault occurs. Keep children and animals at a safe distance, and always switch off and unplug the machine when leaving it unattended.

Never put fresh shreddings directly onto the borders as a mulch, because they take nitrogen from the soil as they rot down. Instead, stack them in a heap, cover it and leave for at least six months.

Animal Manures as Soil Improvers

If you are breaking in new ground, dig rotted organic matter such as manure into the soil. Around established plants in borders, put a thick layer of rotted material as a mulch on the bare soil, where worms will gradually drag it below the surface. Take care the organic matter does not directly touch plant stems or leaves because it will scorch them.

There are many different sources, apart from homemade garden compost. Animal manure is the most common. Some farms and stables deliver manure in bulk for a reasonable charge, and many sell it cheaply to callers. Make sure that your bags are strong and the car boot is well lined with newspaper.

Horse, cow or pig manure is usually mixed with straw or wood shavings, which are good soil improvers. Poultry manure is too strong to go direct onto the borders, so it is best mixed into the compost heap. It makes a speedy activator.

It is vital that all manure is well rotted – preferably a year old – before being dug in or it will scorch the plants' roots and even kill them. Stack fresh manure in a heap, covering it with polythene so that the nutrients are not washed out by rain, until it stops smelling and is ready to use.

Ready-made Soil Conditioners

Mushroom compost is useful for opening up the dense structure of clay soil, although it contains few nutrients. But avoid placing it around rhododendrons, camellias and other acid-loving plants as it contains lime, which they dislike. Mushroom compost is usually sold in bags by local growers (check the classified advertisements in your local paper), though it is sometimes available more cheaply in bulk.

Prepacked soil conditioners are on sale at garden centres and nurseries but can be expensive. Bags of concentrated manure or composted materials are usually available and contain nutrients to enrich the soil. Composted bark can be dug in to improve soil structure, although it has little nutrient value. Coarser grades of bark are not for digging in. They are best used as a surface mulch.

Tree and shrub planting composts are also on sale. These contain fertiliser and are specially prepared to get new plants off to a good start. Planting composts and soil conditioners may be sold alongside potting composts, which have a totally different function, being prepared for growing plants in containers.

Growing Green Manures

Do not allow areas of earth to stay bare for weeks or months, particularly over the winter or if you are breaking in new

SOIL-IMPROVING PLANTS So-called 'green manure' is provided by plants such as mustard that grow quickly and are then dug into the soil, where they rot down to release nutrients and open up the soil structure.

BREAKING HEAVY GROUND Italian rye grass has deep roots that break down heavy soils and improve sandy ones. While still standing, it prevents weed growth and holds nutrients that are otherwise washed out of bare soil.

SOURCE OF NITROGEN Sow clover seed from April to August in rows, or scatter it on the ground and rake it in lightly. As well as cheering up the look of bare ground, it adds nitrogen to the soil when the crop is over.

GROWN FOR GREEN MANURE

Some of the most popular choices for green manures – crops that put nutrients back into the soil – are common plants attractive in their own right:

• Alsike clover (*Trifolium hybridum*): good source of nitrogen, tolerating very damp or acid soils. Sow from April to August.

• Mustard (*Brassica nigra, B. rapa* and *Sinapis alba*): quick-growing plants that mature in 3-6 weeks. Very good nitrogen provider for the next crop. Do not grow where club root is a problem as it is susceptible to the disease. Sow March to September.

• *Phacelia tanacetifolia*: sow in spring to mature in 4-8 weeks, or sow in summer to overwinter. If left to flower, it attracts beneficial insects such as hoverflies and bees.

• Perennial rye grass (*Lolium perenne*): deep-rooting plant which is tremendously beneficial to soil structure. Sow August to October and dig in the next spring.

• Winter tares (*Vicia sativa*): excellent for heavy soils. Sow in spring to dig in later in summer, or in late summer to overwinter.

• Bitter lupin (*Lupinus albus*): good plant for adding nitrogen to light, acid soils. Sow from March to June and dig in 2-3 months later.

PRACTICAL BUT PRETTY Comfrey hybrids, for example *Symphytum* 'Hidcote Pink', make vigorous ground cover. Though the common comfrey is most beneficial for making manure, the hybrids have showier flowers.

ground. Sow a green manure crop to improve the soil and dig it in before it becomes woody, usually just before flowering. Trouble-free choices include mustard, clover and rye. One of the gardener's best friends is comfrey (*Symphytum officinale*). It is an attractive plant and has large leaves rich in the nutrient potash. You can harvest and use the leaves in several different ways.

For the compost heap, they make an ideal activator – add them in a layer every 1 ft (30 cm) or so. Alternatively, shear down the plants and place the leaves directly on the ground as a nutrient-rich mulch. This is especially good for vegetables, soft fruit bushes and flowering plants, which all have a high potash requirement. Or you can add the leaves to organic material in runner bean and sweet pea trenches.

You can also make a convenient and cheap liquid fertiliser from comfrey. Take a barrel or a large bucket, drill a couple of holes in the bottom, pack it full of comfrey leaves and put on a cover. Place a brick on top of the cover to weigh the leaves down and stand the container on a couple of bricks with a tray underneath. Dilute the liquid that seeps out with ten times as much water before applying it to any plants as a liquid feed.

Comfrey is also traditionally used as a medicinal plant. Its old country name is 'knitbone' because a poultice of the leaves is said to speed the healing of broken bones, bruises and sprains, and to offer balm to the overworked gardener.

OTHER WAYS TO DISPOSE OF GARDEN DEBRIS

Sometimes, despite compost heaps, wormeries, shredders and the like, you just have too much unmanageable garden debris to handle at home. Refuse collectors are often reluctant to take away large woody prunings and perennial weeds, but the material can be of use somewhere, so there is no need to burn it.

Many councils are now separating and composting garden debris to put this valuable source of nutrients to good use, so take household or garden waste that you cannot recycle yourself to municipal waste tips. Some councils have gone one step further and provide ready-shredded waste, which you can take in exchange for your unshredded material.

An increasing number of garden centres have a large shredder on site early in the New Year for recycling Christmas trees. Take your tree along for shredding, and you may be able to take a free bag of chipped material in return. Stack the chippings for six months, then use them as a mulch to suppress weeds and improve the soil structure.

PRECAUTIONS TO OBSERVE WITH BONFIRES

Bonfires are useful when there is no easy alternative way to dispose of garden waste – if you are clearing a wilderness, for example, and if bonfires are permitted in your area.

To avoid getting on bad terms with the neighbours, bear a few points in mind before lighting a bonfire.

🜚 Check with your council that bonfires are allowed. Some places, especially in towns, are 'clean air' zones. Bylaws in your area may stipulate minimum distances from roads.

🜚 Site the bonfire well away from any buildings, fences or plants.

🜚 Stack and cover the bonfire material until it is completely dry. It will burn much faster and give off less smoke than green, damp waste.

🜚 Choose a still day as strong winds could easily blow the fire out of control. Keep a spade and a couple of buckets of water or a hosepipe close by, in case the fire gets out of hand.

🜚 Have the bonfire late in the evening, not during the day on a fine weekend when neighbours are outside in the fresh air enjoying their gardens.

🜚 Do not leave a fire still burning when you go to bed.

🜚 It is courteous to tell your neighbours before you light a fire, so that they can close their windows and take in any washing if they wish.

🜚 Check that there are no creatures such as hedgehogs or toads hiding in your bonfire heap, especially in autumn when they tuck themselves away to spend the winter there.

🜚 Scatter the ash from the bonfire on the garden soil – it contains potash and other useful minerals.

Fallen leaves are gathered for leaf mould

Stored logs make mulch when shredded

Comfrey is used for nutritious plant feed

RECYCLING IN A WILDLIFE CORNER

With a little ingenuity, most plants can be recycled for the garden's next generation. A sheltered spot in the dappled shade of a deciduous tree is a perfect site.

THE WIDER THE RANGE of plants, the less they are plagued by pests. A mass planting of a single species – in a rose bed, for example – acts as a magnet for swarms of its very own pest and drains the soil of its favoured nutrient, leaving you reliant on ever-increasing amounts of pesticide and fertiliser to maintain the status quo. It is far less trouble to plant a range of species. The plants attract a rich diversity of insects and wildlife that help to keep pests in check.

Mixing native flowers of the area with introduced plants can also help the whole garden by attracting useful pest predators and cutting down the risk of disease. Birds, bees and butterflies add to the beauty of the plants themselves.

A few logs provide a harbour for beneficial ground beetles, which eat slugs and snails. If you hire a shredder, you can grind the wood down to go onto the compost heap or to be used as a weed-smothering mulch. A bird feeder completes the natural idyll.

1. Lime (*Tilia cordata*)
2. Foxglove (*Digitalis purpurea*)
3. Ivy (*Hedera helix*)
4. Comfrey (*Symphytum officinale*)
5. Herb Robert (*Geranium robertianum*)
6. Forget-me-not (*Myosotis sylvatica*)

BEATING THE WEEDS

THE TREND TOWARDS informal and densely planted mixed borders is a great help in combating weeds. The weeds are crowded out by ornamental plants and there is less bare soil where they could otherwise flourish.

One of the joyous aspects of gardening today is a relaxed 'live and let live' attitude to weeds in the lawn. A more informal style gives a new outlook on many so-called weeds, so long as they are not too invasive.

Many gardeners no longer wish to clear the lawn of daisies, speedwell, self-heal and other native plants, preferring to create a flower-studded carpet. Similarly, some people simply leave moss in the lawn. It provides a smooth green carpet, which is the chief point of having a lawn. However, moss can gradually eliminate grass and cannot take hard wear.

PREVENTING WEEDS

If you do not wish to leave 'weeds' in the lawn or border, be ruthless. However keen on the natural look, few gardeners wish to be plagued by aggressive perennials such as ground elder. Such weeds are hard to get rid of once they have taken hold, so make conditions as unfriendly for them as possible and act immediately you spot an unwanted plant.

There is a clear line between a well-groomed lawn dotted here and there with native flowers, and an uneven patch alternating bare earth with rampant weeds. Make sure you stay on the right side of the line by following a few good practices. This is especially important when you are taking over a neglected lawn or beginning with a bare plot.

LAWN KNOW-HOW

For a new lawn, prepare the ground well. The soil needs the same attention whether you are making a lawn from turf or from seed. The best times to begin are autumn and spring, when seed germinates and establishes quickly, and the soil is not likely to dry out. Remove all perennial weeds and dig or rotavate the soil. Firm and level the area thoroughly, or you will end up with a lumpy lawn.

Dig up weeds by hand, taking care to remove all the roots of deep-rooted weeds such as dandelions. Use a fork for

AERATING A TIRED LAWN

IF THE DRAINAGE is bad or the lawn is too large to spike with a garden fork, buy or hire a tool that pulls out cores of soil. For a medium-sized lawn, a foot-powered aerator is adequate, although it is hard work – rather like jumping on a pogo stick. For a large lawn, hire an electrically powered aerator. After aerating, brush in sharp sand to fill the holes and keep the soil well drained.

this, or a special weeding tool that grips the roots deep down to haul the weed out of the ground. If you have to use chemicals, it is best to treat the weeds with a 'touch-weeder', rather than to spray the whole area indiscriminately.

GIVE THE LAWN SOME AIR

Good drainage encourages healthy grass. Even on well-drained ground, the soil under an established lawn can become compacted by years of foot traffic. In autumn, when the ground is slightly moist but not wet, spike the lawn with a garden fork, pressing it into the ground to the depth of its tines and rocking it to and fro to open the holes. Do this in rows about 6 in (15 cm) apart. Shovel some sharp sand onto the grass and brush it in so that the holes stay open.

In early spring, before mowing, scarify the lawn. This means going over the whole lawn with a springtine rake or a powered raking machine to take out the dead grass that builds up at the base of the stems, impeding drainage. Scarifying also lifts up the spreading stems of weeds such as buttercups and clover, which are then cut off by the mower.

🌱 Scatter any worm casts on the surface with a rake or brush before mowing, or

you will be left with little patches of bare soil. Never kill worms – they help to aerate the soil and to pull decomposing organic matter into the ground.

🌱 Mow frequently – about once a week. Regular mowing discourages the growth of weeds and coarse grasses.

🌱 Do not compost clippings if the lawn has just been treated with weedkiller.

🌱 Do not cut the grass too short, or you will scalp the lawn and create bald patches that are ideal weed and moss beds. About 1 in (2.5 cm) is a good length, although that can be halved for a very fine, well-kept lawn.

🌱 For the first two cuts in spring, adjust the blades so the grass is not so short.

🌱 Keep your mower clean, and with its blades sharpened and correctly adjusted.

PRETTY BUT INVASIVE The creeping buttercup lives up to its name, building up a network of plants once it takes hold in the soil. Despite the prettiness of its flowers, it is best to fork it out before it puts out runners or sheds seeds.

PERENNIAL PERIL Greater bindweed can get the better of garden plants if left. In autumn or spring, dig up clumps of weed-infested decorative perennials. Divide them, remove and destroy all the weed roots, then replant.

VIBRANT BORDER Healthy plant growth is the best weed suppressor. A layer of stone chippings between plants makes extra ground cover to help tagetes and gazania hybrids and *Portulaca grandiflora* to crowd out weeds.

❦ Send the mower for servicing or repair in autumn or winter – do not wait for spring to discover it is not working properly, as the repair shops then have a long waiting list.

For the average lawn, feeding is not necessary. If you mow regularly without a box, the fine mowings act as a natural mulch and provide adequate 'feed'.

In areas where the grass never grows satisfactorily, such as in deep shade or where the ground is full of tree roots, set out shade-tolerant plants such as pulmonaria instead.

HOW TO DEAL WITH WEEDS

There are several ways to tackle weeds, in lawn or border, depending on whether they are annual or perennial. Deal with perennial weeds as soon as they appear among established plants in your borders, or they can quickly get out of control. Hand weeding is simplest. Use a fork to dig out every little bit of root, otherwise any remaining pieces will regrow. The stems can be composted, but leave them in the sun for several weeks to dry out first. Do not put the roots on the compost heap as they will probably carry on growing. Throw them away or burn them.

Annuals are straightforward to control because they grow fresh from seed every year, and the whole plant dies once the top growth is hoed off or pulled up. But perennial weeds such as ground elder and bindweed are more persistent. They continue to grow from year to year from tough root systems and spread by means of underground shoots which go beneath paths and fences into your borders, where both roots and stems exert a stranglehold on plants.

Hiring a rotavator to cultivate overgrown ground is a good plan so long as the weeds are annuals. Do not rotavate if there are any perennial weeds, because the spinning blades will chop the roots into dozens of pieces and each piece will produce a new plant.

MODERN METHODS OF CONTROLLING WEEDS

Where you cannot dig out the weed roots, perhaps because they are entwined in established shrubs, you may be forced to use a weedkiller. A compromise is to

DECORATIVE MULCHES

LEAVES UNDER POTENTILLA Spread an organic mulch around newly planted or established shrubs to moderate extremes of temperature and suppress weeds. Apply when the soil is damp and do not let it touch the stems.

WOODCHIPS ROUND CRANESBILLS Wood chippings suit a rustic-style garden. Mulches derived from wood range from fine sawdust to roughly shredded bark. Either shred the wood yourself or buy prepared bark.

COMPOST AROUND GAILLARDIAS Most annuals produce their best display in fertile, compost-rich soil. It is easiest to mulch when sowing or when seedlings are put in their flowering positions. Use only fully rotted compost.

PEA SHINGLE WITH SAXIFRAGE Gravel of all grades makes a suitable mulch for alpines to grow through as they thrive in shallow, stony soil reminiscent of mountain shale. Gravel drains freely but does not provide nutrients.

spray just the perennial weeds with weed-killer. Wait until they are dead, then dig or rotavate the ground. The weedkiller must be a systemic type (absorbed by the plant) such as glyphosate. Spray it onto the leaves and the plant will absorb it down to the roots. Long-established weeds may need several applications to kill them. Remember it can also kill your garden plants if any chemical gets on their leaves.

Systemic weedkillers are available in gel form which you can brush on the weed foliage. Alternatively, wear strong rubber gloves, coat the palms with gel and pull the weed through your hands.

Bindweed is particularly hard to deal with among shrubs. One trick is to put bamboo canes near its base so the weed climbs up them. When there is plenty of growth, slip the bindweed off the canes, soak it in a bucket of weedkiller and lay it carefully on some polythene so that the liquid does not drip onto other plants.

More recent safe weedkillers have been developed from fatty acids, which destroy by dissolving the waxy coating of the plant's leaves.

HOW TO REPEL INVADERS

Perennial weeds do not recognise boundaries such as garden fences. Weeds invading your garden from outside first need to be killed, then prevented from repeating the attack. Ideally, you should tackle the weeds at their source. When

MAKING·IT·EASIER

CARPET CONTROL

STARVING WEEDS of light will kill an infestation within a year without your having to lift a finger. Just put down an opaque covering. Old pieces of carpet, sheets of cardboard or black polythene, or thick layers of newspaper all do the job admirably. Ensure that the edges are buried in the soil and that separate pieces are well overlapped, so that not a scrap of light gets through.

this is a neighbour's garden you will need to make a tactful approach and perhaps offer to do the work.

Should you prefer not to approach your neighbour, tackle the weeds from your side, either by digging out as much root as possible or by treating the top growth with systemic weedkiller. Once the ground is clear on your side of the boundary, prevent a fresh invasion by sinking corrugated iron or paving slabs into the ground to a depth of 12-18 in (30-46 cm). If that is not possible, run a 6-12 in (15-30 cm) wide strip of black polythene along the lower rim of the fence, stapling it securely and burying the bottom edge in your border soil.

SMOTHERING WEEDS

Taking on a weed-infested plot does not have to mean using weedkillers. Blotting out the light kills even the toughest weeds and requires nothing from you except patience. Provided you want to kill all the plant growth in an area, cover the ground with a layer of material such as black plastic that excludes all light. Leave it in place for six months to a year.

Deprived of all daylight, even the strongest weeds eventually succumb. Once they are dead, remove the covering material. The ground underneath should be reasonably dry and in an ideal state to dig over, ready for cultivating ornamental plants of your choosing.

MULTIPURPOSE MULCHES

Mulching – spreading a layer of vegetable matter or polythene on the ground to prevent weeds from growing – brings many other benefits. It slows down water loss by evaporation from the soil and insulates the plant's roots so that they stay cooler in summer and warmer in winter, ensuring better growth. Some mulches add vital organic matter to the soil – and look good too.

Mulches can be organic – consisting of rotted plant material – or artificial sheeting. Organic mulches add plenty of bulky matter and some nutrients to the soil. Spread them on bare soil in a layer about 2 in (5 cm) thick, and keep them away from any plant stems which might otherwise rot. There is a wide range of materials to choose from: many are the same as the rotted organic matter you dig into the soil to condition it.

CHOICES FOR ORGANIC MULCHES

Rotted manure and garden compost are particularly beneficial, though they often contain some weed seeds. Mushroom compost is useful except around acid-loving plants as it contains some lime.

Shredded woody material is good. Stack it for six months to a year first, or buy composted bark, otherwise the mulch will take nitrogen from the soil as it rots down. Chipped bark can be bought in several grades from coarse to fine. Bark is sold in bags or sometimes loose in bulk, which is much more economical if you need a large quantity of material. It sets off plants well.

The only disadvantage is that birds love to forage for insects and often throw bark onto the lawn. There is little you can do to deter them, but the benefits of the mulch and the birds far outweigh the small chore of sweeping up.

Coir (coco-shell) mulch is similar to bark products, and it is also said to repel slugs and snails.

GETTING THE BEST FROM ARTIFICIAL MULCHES

There is a range of materials that you can place on the soil as a single layer like a blanket, securing the edges by burying them in the ground. An artificial mulch warms the ground and promotes root

PROTECTION UNDER PLANTS A mulch of well-rotted, strawy manure under roses adds nutrients to the soil and keeps moisture in as well as smothering weeds. The naturally abundant flowers and robust growth of *Rosa* 'Iceberg' are a tribute to the fertility and balanced structure of the soil.

growth. Lay it before planting and cut holes in the material for the plants to grow through. Materials include plastic or polythene, woven plastic matting, thick layers of newspaper and even recycled materials such as wool.

All artificial mulches look better when cunningly disguised with a thin layer of chipped bark, soil or other material, unless used in an out-of-the-way part of the garden.

White mulches can reflect light up from the ground, which is useful for ripening fruit. Use clear plastic mulches in late winter or early spring, so that early crops can be sown with some protection from frost. Black polythene mulches absorb the sun's heat and so quickly warm the soil, but they block out light.

With the exception of wool, which adds some nitrogen to the soil, artificial mulches have no nutrient value.

Mulch sheeting is particularly effective around fruit and vegetables: it keeps weeds at bay and protects the crops from a coating of rain-splashed soil or from rotting through touching the ground. Always use an artificial mulch, straw or matting with strawberries. Because the fruits are on or near the ground, they are particularly susceptible to pest damage, mud splash and rotting.

KEEPING PLANTS HEALTHY

O NE OF THE ESSENTIALS for having thriving plants is to choose robust ones in the first place. Shops, garden centres and mail order firms vary enormously in the quality of their plants, so it is as well to know what to look for.

Garden centres that belong to the Garden Centre Association (GCA) are usually reliable as they require certain standards of performance, and they also guarantee to replace hardy plants that die within a certain period, unless they have suffered from obvious neglect.

LOOK HARD BEFORE BUYING NEW PLANTS

Choose plants that look vigorous and free from pests, diseases and weeds. All plants should be clearly labelled, but avoid those with faded labels as they have clearly been on sale for a long time. Reject any plants that are pot-bound – their pots bulging with roots – as their growth will have been impeded and they may not recover fully. The exception is herbaceous perennials, which can be rejuvenated by division. During the growing season, do not buy any plants obviously suffering from lack of water.

The ideal time to buy roses, fruit trees and bushes is in late autumn when the new season's stock has just come on sale, though it is possible to buy container-grown plants all year round. You can often buy roses, shrubs, trees and plants for hedging more cheaply in autumn when they are sold as bare-rooted or field-grown plants, just as they have been lifted from their nursery field rather than grown on in containers.

Buy disease-resistant varieties whenever possible, particularly of roses. Some varieties, especially the newer ones, are selected for resistance to common diseases such as black spot, mildew and rust. If you are buying fruit bushes, check that the stock is certified virus-free.

THE BEST PLANT FOR THE SITUATION

Rather than trying to force plants to do what you want, be led by their needs. Putting plants in suitable conditions and soil – be it sun or shade, acid or alkaline – ensures they flourish. It also saves you money because a plant may sicken and

LEAFY SPLENDOUR The leaves of a variegated hosta and reddish tints of a Japanese maple provide as much beauty of shape and colour as a bed of flowers. As a bonus, hostas are ground-cover plants, so they keep the weeds down. But there is one drawback: slugs relish the fleshy leaves.

die if the conditions are wrong. Although there are some tolerant, unfussy plants that grow equally well almost anywhere, most have particular preferences as to site and light. For instance, rhododendrons must have acid soil and abutilon needs a warm and sheltered situation.

Select plants suitable for where you want to put them. Seek out information given at garden centres and nurseries, both on plant labels and from staff, who are usually happy to help. Going armed with as much detail as you have on the site and type of soil in your garden helps to pinpoint the ideal plants. You can easily test your soil if you are not sure about what type it is (see p.62).

THE RIGHT MOVES TO PREVENT DISEASE

Sturdy plants are unlikely to succumb to disease. A plant under stress from lack of food, water, or just from poor growing conditions is much more liable to fall prey to sickness. If you practise good garden hygiene, disease is less likely to take hold. Diseases are spread by spores which may continue to breed on dead material, so pick off or gather up any diseased leaves, flowers or fruit and put them in the dustbin or burn them – do not put them on the compost heap. A little tidying saves you time and money on replacing weakened plants.

When a plant keeps suffering from the same disease year after year, get rid of it. The plant could be old, or it may not like the conditions in your garden.

When you are replacing a dead plant, choose a different species. Diseases specific to the former plant can remain in the soil to attack the new arrival. Rose sickness is a prime example – new roses may not thrive in soil that has previously grown roses at any point over the past ten or even 15 years. The reason is unsure,

BENEFICIAL PREDATORS Hoverflies prey on aphids, so aim to encourage as many of these wasp-like insects as possible. They are drawn to the garden by open blooms rich in pollen and nectar such as single-flowered roses. You can also set out French marigolds to attract them.

SLUG DAMAGE There are several measures you can take to reduce the slug population. One is to sink small bowls or cartons into the ground and fill them with beer. They are irresistible to slugs, which fall in and drown.

LACEWING HOTEL Lacewing larvae feed on aphids, so encourage the adults to lay eggs by hanging a 'hotel' in a tree in winter. Cut the bottom off a plastic bottle and line the inside with corrugated paper, secured with wire.

NATURAL PEST CONTROL Ladybirds are the most efficient aphid predator. The aphids suck the sap of young growth and flower buds, disfiguring and weakening the plant and sometimes spreading viral diseases.

COMMON DISEASE Roses may be afflicted by black spot, except in industrial areas where air pollution works to your advantage, keeping the disease at bay. Look for rose varieties bred to resist black spot if it is rife in your region.

but it seems that the roots of new roses are more vulnerable than the older, more robust roots of long-established roses.

MAKE FRIENDS OF PREDATORS

The most time-saving way to control pests is to let nature do the work for you. Many birds, frogs, toads and hedgehogs, eat pests. There are insect predators too: ladybirds, hoverflies, lacewing flies and ground beetles are your friends.

Encourage these creatures to live and flourish in your garden by providing a friendly habitat for them. Beetles and other ground-living insects like long grass, so it is worth having a meadow area, however small. Leave some stones and pieces of wood on the ground for a daytime hiding place.

Ladybirds hibernate in dry crevices or on leaves and stems of dead herbaceous perennials, so do not cut these down until early spring. If you have to burn garden prunings and debris shake the stems out first to dislodge any ladybirds. You can even buy 'lures' which are impregnated

SAFETY FIRST

CARE WITH CHEMICALS

SPRAY ONLY on a still day so that there is no danger of the chemicals drifting on the breeze. Spray insecticides in the evening when there are fewer beneficial insects, such as bees, ladybirds and hoverflies, around.

Use as little of the chemicals as possible by treating only the plants which are directly infected, rather than spraying indiscriminately. Keep chemicals away from ponds and watercourses. Label them and keep them locked up.

HERB AS REPELLANT The strong smell of chives is said to repel pests that are attracted by scent, so try growing the herb near susceptible plants. The flowers appear in the summer and you can use the leaves in salads.

with a pheromone that attracts ladybirds and other aphid-eaters.

Hoverflies home in on flowers full of nectar. They also love carrot flowers, so if you have any carrots past their best for eating, plant them instead. They produce heads of white flowers on tall stems.

COMPANION PLANTING

Planting nectar-rich flowers to attract pest-controlling insects is just one form of companion planting, which is the use of plants to benefit each other. Some plants are said to prevent pests and diseases in the first place. Strong-smelling ones such as onions and garlic deter pests. Interplanting rows of carrots with onions masks the carrot smell that attracts carrot root fly.

Planting marigolds is believed to help to prevent pests, thanks to the strong, pungent smell of the flowers and foliage.

Bee-attracting plants are especially useful with runner beans, fruit trees and tomatoes, which need to be pollinated to set a crop of fruit. Bees home in on blue-flowering plants in particular, such as viper's bugloss, phacelia, globe thistle, hyssop, lavender and rosemary. They are drawn to the fragrant flowers of sweet peas, so plant them to grow up canes alongside canes of runner beans.

DISADVANTAGES OF CHEMICALS

If you use chemical pesticides, you may also kill the pests' natural predators, so the next infestation will have a better chance to flourish. Spraying roses with a general insecticide, for instance, may kill the ladybirds and hoverflies which feed on destructive greenfly.

The knock-on effect of killing the beneficial garden creatures can make the problem worse in the long run. Widespread chemical use has also made some pests more resistant, and as a result new or stronger chemicals have to be formulated to combat them.

Gardening without chemicals saves you money, time, perhaps potential damage to your health and certainly harm to the health of the garden's natural pest controllers. Most horticultural problems can be efficiently tackled using safe, alternative methods.

GUIDELINES FOR THE USE OF CHEMICALS

If there is no choice but to use a chemical, there are guidelines you can follow for maximum safety and minimum impact on your garden.

🌸 Choose safer chemicals that are derived from natural sources, such as derris and pyrethrum, but remember that they may still kill beneficial insects, including bees, as well as pests.

🌸 Always follow the manufacturer's instructions and wear protective clothing if recommended.

🌸 Store chemicals in a safe place away from children and animals.

🌸 Spray only infected plants or parts of plants. Blanket spraying, apart from the expense, can harm wildlife in the garden.

🌸 Keep pets away from the treated area for a couple of days.

SCIENCE FOR THE GARDENER

Introducing a natural predator that will attack one type of pest without harming another is called biological control. Many large-scale commercial food and plant producers are using biological controls instead of chemicals, with such success that gardeners are taking up the idea, too. Such controls are mostly available by mail order. One of the commonest is the nematode, a tiny parasitic worm used against slugs and vine weevils.

Most biological controls are best used in a protected environment such as a greenhouse or conservatory. Do not use chemical sprays as well or you will kill the introduced predator.

Biological controls are perfectly safe to use and extremely effective, provided that you follow a few rules. The environment needs to be reasonably warm – but the minimum temperature requirement varies according to the type of predator. As soon as you notice a growing pest population, introduce the predator. Once all the pests have been consumed, the predator will die out and you will have to reintroduce it for any future infestations.

Make sure that you use the correct predator for each pest.

🌸 The tiny but effective parasitic wasp called *Encarsia formosa* for whitefly.

🌸 The predator *Phytoseiulus* for red

Hoverfly grubs devour aphids on roses and broad beans

Hoverflies gather on fennel flowers in midsummer

Blue phacelia and poached-egg plant feed hoverflies all summer

A BORDER OF COMPANION PLANTS

In a border of mixed species, each plant attracts a different predator to its pests and draws on different nutrients. Companion planting takes this natural scheme a step further.

TO MAKE MIXED PLANTING effective, place species that are susceptible to a particular pest close to plants that attract the natural predators of that pest.

Aphids infest many garden plants. Blackfly have a special fondness for broad beans, lettuce have their own lettuce aphid and roses are often smothered in greenfly. Lupins also attract aphids but, like broad beans, they put nutrients back into the soil.

ATTRACTING THE DEFENCE

Aphid eaters such as hoverflies and ladybirds follow supplies of their food, but may not gather until pest numbers have built up. Speed up the process with judicious planting.

The best way to attract hoverflies is with nectar-rich flowers. Among their favourites are the poached-egg plant (*Limnanthes douglasii*), an easily grown hardy annual that makes a lovely path or border edging. It self-seeds easily so, if you plant it once, you will have it for years to come. Its delicately scented flowers appear from June to August.

Phacelia, another annual good for edging, and the tall fennel, which bears flat heads of flowers, also attract predators. The purple-leaved form of fennel is especially beautiful.

A cottage border is the perfect site for a well-balanced, informal planting of ornamental plants, herbs, and vegetables handsome enough to deserve a place in full view. Choose a sunny, sheltered, well-drained site, and watch the beneficial insects come and do the job of pest control for you.

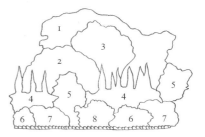

1. Japanese honeysuckle (*Lonicera japonica* 'Halliana')
2. *Rosa* Alexandra Rose
3. Fennel (*Foeniculum vulgare* 'Purpureum')
4. Lupin (*Lupinus* Russell 'Blue Jacket')
5. Broad bean (*Vicia faba*)
6. Poached-egg plant (*Limnanthes douglasii*)
7. Lettuce 'Salad Bowl', green and bronze forms
8. *Phacelia tanacetifolia*

CONTROLLING SNAILS AND SLUGS

GARDEN FRIEND Hedgehogs prey on the slugs and snails that are so destructive to garden plants, so they are welcome visitors. These spiny mammals sniff through garden litter to nose out food, which is all the more reason to use chemicals sparingly, and avoid poisoning beneficial creatures.

PLANT DESTROYERS Snails have shells and slugs do not, but both eat plants, particularly those with fleshy leaves. At night they emerge from dense vegetation to feed. The pests also lurk behind pots and in crevices and holes.

HOMEMADE CLOCHE PROTECTION As soon as you put in young plants, protect them from slugs and snails with covers made from clear plastic bottles. Leave the lid of the bottle off so that air can circulate around the plant.

SLUG SOLUTION

A BIOLOGICAL SLUG CONTROL is provided by a microscopic nematode that attacks and kills only slugs. The nematode culture can be ordered and is delivered in sachets by post. The contents are added to a watering can and watered onto the ground. Nematodes are an effective control but not cheap.

slugs and snails and other common pests from attacking your crops with simple traps or by putting up a barrier.

WILY MEANS TO KEEP PESTS OFF YOUR CROPS

Keep birds off with netting. They often peck at young plants and seedlings in winter, and at ripe strawberries in summer. The best way to deter them is to cover the crop with horticultural fleece or netting, but make sure the edges are secure so the birds do not get caught up in the material. Alternatively, string homemade bird scarers such as strips of foil or the tape from old cassettes on canes to flutter in the breeze.

Control codling moth larvae, which burrow into apple cores, with a sticky pheromone trap.

Use a similar trap to control plum fruit moths. They tunnel into young fruits, causing them to drop prematurely.

Defeat winter moths, pests of apple buds and shoots, by fixing grease bands round the trunks of apple trees in autumn, ideally by early October. The flightless females are caught when they crawl up the trunk to lay their eggs.

WAYS OF DETERRING PETS AND WILD ANIMALS

Not all creatures are welcome in the garden. It depends very much on your own view – some people are overjoyed to see a heron by their pond, for example, while fish-keepers certainly are not. However, a bit of strategic planning usually keeps unwelcome visitors at bay.

Cats visit most gardens, so site the bird table and bath away from potential hiding places from where cats can pounce. Put any nest boxes at least 10 ft (3 m) off the ground.

Fit your own cat with a collar and bell which warns birds of its approach. Having a cat flap pays dividends – most

spider mite, a nuisance in conservatories.
🐾 Australian ladybird beetle (*Cryptolaemus*) for mealy bugs.
🐾 The predatory midge *Aphidoletes aphidimyza* for greenfly, blackfly and other aphids under cover in a greenhouse or conservatory.
🐾 The predatory midge *Metaphycus* for scale insect.
🐾 The miniature mite *Amblyseius cucumeris* for thrips.
🐾 The bacterium *Bacillus thuringiensis* for cabbage white caterpillars.

TRAPPING SLUGS AND SNAILS

Slugs and snails are a nuisance in most gardens but you can combat them without resorting to slug pellets, which are harmful to birds, hedgehogs, toads and other creatures that will eat the poisoned slugs. Cats are also at risk, because the

damp pellets can get into the cracks between the pads on their feet, and they will swallow the poison while grooming. Children also have to be kept away.

Certain plants are delicacies for slugs and snails, especially runner beans, hostas, delphiniums and lilies, all of which often need protection throughout the season. In dry weather, try surrounding the plant with a layer of gravel or crushed eggshells to deter the pests.

Lay old carpet, paving slabs or planks on the ground overnight. Slugs and snails gather in such cool, dark places during the day. Turn the trap over in the morning to provide a feast for the birds.

Catch slugs and snails by hand if you are not squeamish. Go hunting with a torch in the evening after dark, preferably in damp weather when slugs and snails are most active. You can prevent cats enjoy snoozing indoors and so spend much less time stalking birds. There are ways to deter cats: see which works best.

❧ A cat of your own usually keeps out the neighbours' cats.

❧ Scatter prickly prunings of trees and shrubs such as holly, roses and berberis where cats enter the garden.

❧ Lay commercial, purpose-made spiky mesh just under the soil with the spikes sticking up.

❧ Chemical deterrents in powder and liquid form are on sale. Buy makes which state on the label that they are safe for use around children and other creatures. Apply frequently.

❧ Some cats detest citrus fruits, so try leaving out half-lemons or orange peel.

PROTECTING PLANTS FROM DEER AND SQUIRRELS

Rural gardens are often visited by deer, particularly the little muntjac, sometimes called the barking deer because its call is like a loud, hoarse bark. A fence at least 6 ft (1.8 m) high is the only sure defence against deer. Surround new plants with wire netting for a couple of years or until they are well established. There are tree guards available which are biodegradable and decompose after the plant is big enough to fend for itself.

Grey squirrels consume bird food and can damage young shrubs and trees. Wire netting makes a good shield, but keeping food away is more difficult.

Site bird tables several yards away from trees, posts and roofs, from where squirrels can make a flying leap. Make feeding sites harder to reach by running a clothes line between two trees or posts, with a biscuit tin at each end as a baffle. Hang bird feeders and a table in the middle. The squirrels are bound to reach the food eventually, but at least their antics will keep you entertained.

OUT OF BOUNDS FOR BIRDS

Keep dust-bathing birds off newly prepared seedbeds by covering the ground with netting or horticultural fleece. Protect winter vegetable crops, especially brassicas, from hungry birds with netting. The same applies to fruit trees and bushes which can be stripped of their buds by bullfinches. If you like to grow large quantities of soft fruit, it is worth buying or making a fruit cage.

Small birds are sometimes attacked and killed by larger ones such as magpies and sparrowhawks. Give the little birds a greater chance of survival by creating dense plantings of prickly shrubs so that they have somewhere they can hide, and leave a shed or garage window open for the same reason.

Bird tables provide rich pickings for sparrowhawks so, if their attacks are frequent, surround the bird table with 3 in (7.5 cm) wire mesh. This allows only small birds to slip through.

Herons can pick off all the fish in a garden pond unless the water is covered with a net. A more attractive alternative to netting as a deterrent is to run a thin wire around the pond about 1 ft (30 cm) high and the same distance from the pond's edge. The wire will catch the bird's legs and scare it off. Create hiding places in the pond for fish, such as large stones raised on bricks, and large-leaved aquatics such as water lilies.

Whatever your views on environmental matters, taking a greener approach can often offer short cuts to keeping the garden in tiptop condition. The rewards for using green ideas instead of chemicals are peace of mind on health and safety, natural beauty, and the satisfaction and low cost of recycling.

MAKING·IT·EASIER

CODLING MOTH TRAP

THE EASIEST WAY to trap the common apple-tree pest called a codling moth is with a pheromone trap. It contains a piece of sticky card and the pheromone given off by female moths. This attracts males, which are trapped, and so cannot fertilise the females.

One trap is enough for up to five trees within a radius of about 50 ft (15 m). Hang it in the branches at about head height in mid May, or earlier if the weather is warm.

RODENT ALERT Grey squirrels attack birds' nests, eating eggs and fledglings. They also devour leaves, shoots, buds and flowers and dig up juicy taproots. Wire netting is the best protection for both plants and nests.

VISITOR TO RURAL GARDENS Muntjac deer are shy, dainty creatures which are beautiful to watch, although they do eat and destroy plants, especially young ones. Protect young trees with wire guards or biodegradable tubes.

FISH-EATING BIRDS Herons in flight are handsome birds, but they can clear a pond of fish. Putting a net over the entire pond is the most reliable and effective defence if these large, patient hunters frequent your area.

INSPIRATION FROM
GREAT GARDENS

SNOWSHILL MANOR

Golden house stands above garden courts.

*When Charles Wade laid out
Snowshill Manor's relatively modest
two acres in Gloucestershire
in the 1920s, he created a series
of walled 'rooms' or 'courts'
running down the hillside,
each with its own style
and mood. Today, these areas
are the site of the National Trust's
first organic garden. The result
is flourishing, sturdy
plantings which are seldom
troubled by pests and diseases.*

IN EARLY JUNE the steep borders at Snowshill Manor are a glorious jostle of poppies, phloxes, peonies, Canterbury bells, penstemons, catananches, lady's mantle, hollyhocks, cranesbills of various sorts and a host of other perennials, with half-hardy annuals tucked in to fill the gaps. Climbing roses, purple vines and figs scramble over the lichen-clad walls, while a year-round link between springtime bulbs and the Michaelmas daisies of early autumn is provided by a purple glow of sage.

Four wooden compost bins provide mulch for the garden; they are filled with lawn mowings and other garden debris, and activated by droppings taken from the medieval dovecote that overlooks the big herbaceous border.

The bins produce a friable material which is used from each in turn. It is well broken down and full of nourishment. Since the start of the organic regime six years ago, the plants have flourished.

OPULENT ORGANIC BORDERS

The same plants will thrive in an organically fed herbaceous border of your own. The one below is fronted by a gravel path and backed by a wattle fence that hides the wooden backs of the compost bins, as well as providing support for a climbing vine, *Vitis vinifera* 'Purpurea'. A modest dovecote is set among the compost bins. Eye-catching, blood red oriental poppies light up the bed where hollyhocks and verbascum soar, while blue penstemons and campanulas merge with purple sage at the front of the bed.

As at Snowshill, regular mulching ensures lush growth, giving nourishment for both flowering and foliage plants.

ORGANICALLY IN TUNE The inhabitants of the ancient dovecote at Snowshill provide the vital activator for homemade compost, which is produced in bins hidden by the wall at the back of this luxuriant herbaceous border.

CONCEALED COMPOST Perennials benefit from compost – made, as at Snowshill, just behind the bed, but on a more compact scale.

CHOOSING PLANTS FOR YOUR GARDEN

THIS CHART SUMMARISES the characteristics and needs of the garden plants recommended in the body of the book. Plants are listed in alphabetical order under their botanical name. The number(s) immediately after a name refers to the page where the plant is mentioned. Several familiar botanical names have changed recently as plants have been reclassified: wallflower is no longer *Cheiranthus* but *Erysimum*, for example, and *Senecio* 'Sunshine' is *Brachyglotttis* 'Sunshine'. The former name is listed and directs you to the current name.

Sometimes plants are referred to in the text by common name only; their botanical names are given on p.377 so that you can easily trace them in the chart. Vegetables, fruits and wild flowers or plants are not included in this chart of cultivation details, but the general index (pp.377-83) shows where they are mentioned in the text.

The abbreviations used in the chart are explained in the key below. In the column for plant type, the designation refers to how the plant should be treated rather than to strict botanical type; some plants that are tender or short-lived perennials, for example, have to be grown as annuals in the British climate. The column on soil requirements has an entry only where a plant has particular needs; most plants will grow in most soils.

A

	PLANT TYPE	SOIL	SITUATION	PERIOD OF INTEREST	HEIGHT
Abies pinsapo 162	E Tr	-	☼	1-12	20ft(6m)
Abutilon 'Ashford Red' 239	E Sh	-	◑	5-10	10ft(3m)
vitifolium 166	Sh	-	◑	5-6	12ft(3.7m)
'Veronica Tennant' 119	Sh	-	◑	5-6	12ft(3.7m)
Acacia dealbata 42	E Tr	-	☼	12-3	25ft(7.5m)
Acanthus mollis Latifolius Group 41, 119, 219, 255, 339	P	-	◑	7-8	3ft(90cm)
spinosus 117	P	-	☼	6-8	3ft(90cm)
Acer griseum 162, 242	Tr	-	☼	1-12	10ft(3m)
japonicum 'Aureum' 236	Tr	-	☼	5-10	30ft(9m)
negundo 'Auratum' 189	Tr	-	☼	5-10	30ft(9m)
'Flamingo' 189, 192	Tr	-	☼	5-10	30ft(9m)
palmatum 98, 162	Tr	-	☼	5,9-10	20ft(6m)
'Bloodgood' 209	Tr	A	◑ S	4-9	10ft(3m)
'Rubrum' 236	Tr	-	☼	5-10	20ft(6m)
'Senkaki' 242	Tr	-	☼	5-10	20ft(6m)
pseudoplatanus 'Brilliantissimum' 224, 227	Tr	A	◑ W	4-9	20ft(6m)
rubrum 'Scanlon' 147	Tr	A	◑ S	4-9	20ft(6m)
Achillea filipendulina 'Coronation Gold' 297	P	-	☼	6-8	4ft(1.2m)
× *lewisii* 'King Edward' 235	Rc	-	☼	6-8	4in(10cm)
'Moonshine' 29, 75	P	-	☼	6-8	4ft(1.2m)
'Schwefelblüte' ('Flowers of Sulphur') 156	P	-	☼	6-8	2ft(60cm)
taygetea 156	P	-	☼	6-9	18in(45cm)
Acidanthera murieliae (now *Gladiolus callianthus* 'Murieliae')					
Aconitum carmichaelii 174	P	-	◑	8-9	4ft(1.2m)
Acorus calamus 317	P	M	☼	5-9	3ft(90cm)
'Variegatus' 317	P	M	☼	5,4-9	2½ft(76cm)
gramineus 309	P	M	☼	5-9	10in(25cm)
Actinidia chinensis (now *A. deliciosa*)					
deliciosa 134, 209	Cl	-	◑	6-9	30ft(9m)
kolomikta 14, 189, 196, 218	Cl	-	◑ S	6-9	20ft(6m)

	PLANT TYPE	SOIL	SITUATION	PERIOD OF INTEREST	HEIGHT
Adiantum raddianum 'Kensington Gem' 201	E P	-	◑/●	1-12	12in(30cm)
venustum 93	P	-	◑	5-10	9in(23cm)
Aethionema 'Warley Rose' 42	Rc	-	☼	4-5	6in(15cm)
Agapanthus africanus 243	P	-	☼	6-8	4ft(1.2m)
'Ben Hope' 243	P	-	☼	6-8	3ft(90cm)
Headbourne Hybrids 119, 293	P	-	☼	6-8	3ft(90cm)
praecox subsp. *orientalis* 243	P	-	☼	6-8	12in(30cm)
Ajuga reptans 72	E P	-	◑/●	6-7	9in(23cm)
'Purpurea' 333	E P	-	◑/●	6-7	8in(20cm)
Akebia quinata 260, 271	Cl	-	☼	5,6-9	30ft(9m)
Alcea rosea 25	P	-	☼	7-9	6ft(1.8m)
Alchemilla mollis 111, 125, 131, 173, 234, 294, 315, 331	P	-	◑	4-9	18in(45cm)
Allium giganteum 297	Bu	-	☼	6-8	6ft(1.8m)
schoenoprasum 289	Bu	-	☼	6-8	12in(30cm)
Alnus glutinosa 67, 326	Tr	M	☼	4-7	30ft(9m)
Aloysia triphylla 189, 289	Sh	-	☼	5-6	4ft(1.2m)
Alstroemeria Ligtu Hybrids 157, 158	P	-	☼	6-8	3ft(90cm)
psittacina 155	P	-	☼	6-8	2ft(60cm)
Althaea rosea (now *Alcea rosea*)					
Alyssum montanum 42	Rc	-	☼	5-6	6in(15cm)
saxatile (now *Aurinia saxatilis*)					
Amaranthus caudatus 117, 162	An	-	☼	6-8	3ft(90cm)
Amelanchier canadensis 340	Sh	-	◑	4-5,9	10ft(3m)
lamarckii 94, 343	Sh	-	◑	4-5,9	20ft(6m)
Androsace sempervivoides 235	Rc	-	☼	4-5	3in(7.5cm)
Anemone blanda 214, 224, 338	Bu	-	◑	2-4	4in(10cm)
'Radar' 135	Bu	-	◑	2-4	4in(10cm)
hupehensis var. *japonica* 294	P	-	◑	7-9	4ft(1.2m)
nemorosa 66	P	-	●	5-6	6in(15cm)
sylvestris 156	P	-	◑	4-9	18in(45cm)
Anethum graveolens 289	P	-	☼	7	3ft(90cm)

PLANT TYPE An annual; Aq aquatic; Bam bamboo; Bi biennial; Bu bulb, corm, rhizome, tuber; Cl climber; E evergreen; P perennial; Rc rock plant; Ro rose; Sh shrub; Tr tree.

SOIL A needs acid soil; L needs alkaline soil; M needs moist to wet soil; D needs dry soil.

SITUATION ☼ does best in full sun; ◑ thrives in full sun or light shade; ● does best in full shade; ◑/● grows well in full sun, light shade or full shade; ●/◑ does best in full shade or light shade; S needs shelter; W tolerates wind.

PERIOD OF INTEREST numbers 1-12 represent the months when the plant has, for example, flowers, fruits or colourful bark.

HEIGHT represents height at maturity (or 20 years for trees and shrubs).

Plant	Plant Type	Soil	Situation	Period of Interest	Height
Angelica archangelica 289	P	-	◐	7-8	6ft(1.8m)
Anthemis cretica 160	P	-	☼	5-6	12in(30cm)
cupaniana (now A. punctata subsp. cupaniana)					
nobilis (now Chamaemelum nobile)					
punctata subsp. cupaniana 156	An	-	☼	6-8	9in(23cm)
Anthriscus sylvestris 'Ravenswing' 173	P	-	◐	5-9	4ft(1.2m)
Antirrhinum 162	An	-	☼	6-7	18in(45cm)
Aponogeton distachyos 333	Aq	-	☼	6-8	3in(7.5cm)
Aquilegia bertolonii 235	Rc	-	☼	6-7	12in(30cm)
canadensis 158, 174	P	-	☼	5-6	2ft(60cm)
formosa 174	P	-	☼	5-6	2ft(60cm)
viridiflora 155	P	-	☼	5-6	2ft(60cm)
Arabis caucasica 238	Rc	-	☼	5-8	6in(15cm)
ferdinandi-coburgii 21, 259	Rc	-	☼	5-8	3in(7.5cm)
Aralia elata 98, 255	Tr	-	◐	8-9	20ft(6m)
'Variegata' 239	Tr	-	◐	8-9	20ft(6m)
Araucaria araucana 96	ETr	-	☼	1-12	20ft(6m)
Arbutus menziesii 163	ETr	-	☼	6,9	20ft(6m)
unedo 192	ETr	-	☼	9-2	15ft(4.5m)
Argyranthemum foeniculaceum 231, 242	EP	-	☼ S	6-8	3ft(90cm)
frutescens 201, 214, 234, 241	EP	-	☼ S	6-8	3ft(90cm)
Armeria maritima 69	Rc	-	☼	5-7	9in(23cm)
Artemisia abrotanum 167	P	-	☼	6-8	4ft(1.2m)
absinthium 167	P	-	☼	5-10	3ft(90cm)
'Lambrook Silver' 119, 196, 217	P	D	☼	7-10	2½ft(76cm)
dracunculus 289	P	D	☼ S	6-10	18in(45cm)
'Powis Castle' 148, 245	EP	-	☼	1-12	3ft(90cm)
schmidtiana 271	P	-	☼	5-10	12in(30cm)
'Nana' 162	Rc	-	☼	5-10	6in(15cm)
Arum italicum 'Pictum' 291	Bu	M	◐	5-10	12in(30cm)
Aruncus sylvester 339	P	-	◐	6	2½ft(76cm)
Asparagus setaceus 'Nanus' 201	EP	-	◐	1-12	2ft(60cm)
Aspidistra elatior 37	EP	-	◐	1-12	12in(30cm)
Asplenium nidus 191	EP	M	●	1-12	2-4ft(1.2m)
scolopendrium 19, 139, 173, 205	EP	M	◐/●	1-12	2ft(60cm)
Astelia 215	EP	-	◐	4-9	2ft(60cm)
Aster amellus 295	P	-	☼	8-9	2ft(60cm)
× frikartii 337	P	-	☼	8-9	2½ft(76cm)
'Mönch' 295	P	-	☼	8-10	2½ft(76cm)
novae-angliae 'Andenken an Alma Pötschke' 38	P	-	☼	7-9	2½ft(76cm)
'Harrington's Pink' 138	P	-	☼	8-9	4ft(1.2m)
Astilbe simplicifolia 'Sprite' 333	P	M	◐	8	6in(15cm)
Astrantia major 294	P	-	◐	6-9	2ft(60cm)
'Shaggy' 294	P	-	◐	6-9	2ft(60cm)
maxima 294	P	-	◐	6-9	2ft(60cm)
Athyrium filix-femina 292	P	M	◐/●	4-9	4ft(1.2m)
Aubrieta deltoidea 111, 119	Rc	-	☼	4-5	3in(7.5cm)
Aucuba japonica 'Crotonifolia' 211	ESh	-	◐	1-12	8ft(2.4m)
'Lanceleaf' 239	ESh	-	◐	1-12	8ft(2.4m)
'Salicifolia' 239	ESh	-	◐	1-12	8ft(2.4m)
Aurinia saxatilis 14, 338	Rc	-	☼	5-6	9in(23cm)
var. citrina 119	Rc	-	☼	5-6	9in(23cm)

B

Plant	Plant Type	Soil	Situation	Period of Interest	Height
Ballota pseudodictamnus 154	EP	-	☼	7-8	6in(15cm)
Bassia scoparia 292	An	-	☼	4-9	3ft(90cm)
Begonia 'Allan Langdon' 201	Bu	-	☼	6-9	2½ft(76cm)
Berberidopsis corallina 37, 210	ECl	A	◐ S	7-9	12ft(3.7m)

Plant	Plant Type	Soil	Situation	Period of Interest	Height
Berberis candidula 238	ESh	-	◐	5-7	6ft(1.8m)
darwinii 324	ESh	-	◐	4-5,10	8ft(2.4m)
× stenophylla 50, 51	ESh	-	◐	4	8ft(2.4m)
thunbergii 38	Sh	-	◐	4-10	4ft(1.2m)
verruculosa 337, 338	ESh	-	◐	5-6	6ft(1.8m)
Bergenia cordifolia 94, 273, 314	EP	-	◐	4-5	18in(45cm)
'Silberlicht' 119, 205	EP	L	◐	4-5	15in(38cm)
Betula albo-sinensis 343	Tr	-	◐	1-12	20ft(6m)
pendula 75, 326	Tr	-	◐	4-10	30ft(9m)
'Youngii' 217	Tr	-	◐	4-5	10ft(3m)
pubescens 326	Tr	-	◐	3	30ft(9m)
utilis var. jacquemontii 162, 163	Tr	-	◐	1-12	20ft(6m)
Blechnum penna-marina 315	EP	-	◐/●	1-12	6in(15cm)
Borago officinalis 289	An	-	☼	6-9	2½ft(76cm)
Brachyglottis 'Sunshine' 14, 54, 75, 113, 154, 268, 271, 292	ESh	-	☼	6-9	4ft(1.2m)
Briza media 169	An	-	☼	7-9	18in(45cm)
Brugmansia candida 'Knightii' 194	ESh	-	◐	6-9	12ft(3.7m)
Brunnera macrophylla 156, 238, 305	P	M	◐	4-5	18in(45cm)
Buddleia alternifolia 189	Sh	-	☼	6	12ft(3.7m)
davidii 336	Sh	-	☼	7-10	9ft(2.7m)
'White Profusion' 337	Sh	-	☼	7-10	9ft(2.7m)
fallowiana var. alba 119	Sh	-	☼	7-10	6ft(1.8m)
Butomus umbellatus 310, 334	PAq	-	☼	7-9	3ft(90cm)
Buxus sempervirens 256	ESh	-	◐	1-12	10ft(3m)
'Elegantissima' 14	ESh	-	◐	1-12	6ft(1.8m)
'Handsworthensis' 197	ESh	-	◐	1-12	10ft(3m)
'Suffruticosa' 45, 216, 256	ESh	-	◐	1-12	3ft(90cm)

C

Plant	Plant Type	Soil	Situation	Period of Interest	Height
Calceolaria 56	An	-	☼	6-8	10in(25cm)
Calendula officinalis 289	An	-	☼	5-9	2ft(60cm)
'Art Shades' 117	An	-	☼	5-9	12in(30cm)
'Orange King' 56	An	-	☼	5-9	12in(30cm)
Calla palustris 309	P	M	☼	5,9	12in(30cm)
Calluna vulgaris 'Cramond' 89	ESh	A	☼	8-9	18in(45cm)
'Darkness' 89	ESh	A	☼	8-10	12in(30cm)
'H.E. Beale' 89	ESh	A	☼	8-10	18in(45cm)
'Serlei' 89	ESh	A	☼	9-11	2ft(60cm)
Caltha palustris 310, 333, 334	P	M	☼/◐	3-5	12in(30cm)
'Plena' 310	P	M	☼/◐	3-5	12in(30cm)
Camellia 'Contessa Lavinia Maggi' (now C. japonica 'Lavinia Maggi')					
'Freedom Bell' 135	ESh	A	◐ S	4-5	10ft(3m)
japonica 'Lavinia Maggi' 205	ESh	A	◐ S	4-5	15ft(4.5m)
× williamsii 'Donation' 260	ESh	A	◐ S	11-5	10ft(3m)
'J.C. Williams' 239	ESh	A	◐ S	1-5	12ft(3.7m)
Campanula lactiflora 257, 294	P	-	◐	7-8	4ft(1.2m)
'Alba' 94	P	-	◐	7-8	4ft(1.2m)
persicifolia 94, 293	P	-	◐	6-8	3ft(90cm)
portenschlagiana 321	Rc	-	◐	6-8	6in(15cm)
poscharskyana 42, 76	Rc	-	◐	6-11	6in(15cm)
waldsteiniana 235	Rc	-	☼	7-8	6in(15cm)
Cardamine pratensis 333	P	M	☼/◐	4-5	12in(30cm)
Carex elata 309	P	M	◐	5-9	2ft(60cm)
'Aurea' 212	P	M	◐	5-9	2ft(60cm)
flagellifera 162, 171	EP	-	☼	1-12	12in(30cm)
oshimensis 'Evergold' 315	EP	-	☼	1-12	12in(30cm)
Carpinus betulus 45, 51	Tr	-	☼/◐	4-5	20ft(6m)
'Fastigiata' 71	Tr	-	☼/◐	4-5	20ft(6m)
Caryopteris × clandonensis 336, 337	Sh	-	☼ S	8-9	4ft(1.2m)
'Kew Blue' 71, 115, 242	Sh	-	☼ S	8-9	4ft(1.2m)

	PLANT TYPE	SOIL	SITUATION	PERIOD OF INTEREST	HEIGHT
Cassia didymobotrya (now *Senna didymobotrya*)					
Catalpa bignonioides 189, 218, 255	Tr	-	☼	7	20ft(6m)
'Aurea' 217, 219	Tr	-	☼	7-10	12ft(3.7m)
Ceanothus arboreus 'Trewithen Blue' 189	ESh	-	☼S	5-6	15ft(4.5m)
× *delileanus* 'Gloire de Versailles' 119	Sh	-	☼	7-9	5ft(1.5m)
impressus 66, 245, 337	ESh	-	☼	4-5	10ft(3m)
thyrsiflorus 'Repens' 14	ESh	-	☼	5-6	5ft(1.5m)
Cedrus atlantica 'Pendula' 198	ETr	-	☼	1-12	15ft(4.5m)
Centaurea cyanus 117	An	-	☼	6-9	18in(45cm)
montana 117	P	-	☼	5-6	18in(45cm)
Cercis siliquastrum 66, 94, 137, 147	Tr	LD	☼	5	20ft(6m)
Chaenomeles 'Geisha Girl' 12	Sh	-	☼	3-5	4ft(1.2m)
japonica 43, 263, 325	Sh	-	☼	3-5,9	3ft(90cm)
'Pink Lady' 12	Sh	-	☼	3-5	4ft(1.2m)
'Rowallane' 12	Sh	-	☼	4-5	5ft(1.5m)
speciosa 12, 170	Sh	-	☼	3-5	15ft(4.5m)
Chamaecyparis lawsoniana 45	ETr	-	◐	1-12	40ft(12m)
'Columnaris' 218	ETr	-	◐	1-12	15ft(4.5m)
'Ellwood's Pillar' 245	ETr	-	◐	1-12	10ft(3m)
'Fletcheri' 52	ETr	-	◐	1-12	25ft(7.5m)
'Gimbornii' 17	ETr	-	◐	1-12	3ft(90cm)
'Green Hedger' 273, 290	ETr	-	◐	1-12	20ft(6m)
'Green Pillar' 218	ETr	-	◐	1-12	20ft(6m)
'Lanei' 218	ETr	-	◐	1-12	30ft(9m)
'Nana Gracilis' 22	ETr	-	◐	1-12	6ft(1.8m)
'Pembury Blue' 75	ETr	-	◐	1-12	25ft(7.5m)
obtusa 'Nana' 101	ESh	-	◐	1-12	5ft(1.5m)
pisifera 98	ETr	-	◐	1-12	30ft(9m)
'Filifera Aurea' 245	ETr	-	◐	1-12	15ft(4.5m)
Chamaemelum nobile 187	EP	-	☼	6-8	4in(10cm)
'Treneague' 90, 108	EP	-	☼	1-12	4in(10cm)
Chamaerops humilis 199	ETr	-	☼	1-12	5ft(1.5m)
Cheiranthus (now *Erysimum*)					
Chimonanthus praecox 42, 165, 166, 168	Sh	-	☼	12-2	10ft(3m)
Chionodoxa luciliae 238	Bu	-	◐	4	6in(15cm)
Choisya ternata 17, 53, 75, 189, 198, 210, 290	ESh	-	☼S	4-5	8ft(2.4m)
'Sundance' 157	ESh	-	☼S	1-12	3ft(90cm)
Chrysalidocarpus lutescens 191	Tr	-	◐	1-12	15ft(4.5m)
Chrysanthemum (now *Argyranthemum, Dendranthema*)					
Cimicifuga racemosa 117	P	-	◐	6-7	5ft(1.5m)
Cineraria maritima (now *Senecio cineraria*)					
Cistus × *aguilari* 245	ESh	-	☼	6-8	5ft(1.5m)
corbariensis (now *C.* × *hybridus*)					
hybridus 13, 209	ESh	LD	☼	5-7	4ft(1.2m)
skanbergii 239	ESh	-	☼	6-8	5ft(1.5m)
Citrus limon 'Meyer' 143	ESh	-	☼S	4-6	6ft(1.8m)
Clarkia unguiculata 117	An	-	☼	6-8	18in(45cm)

	PLANT TYPE	SOIL	SITUATION	PERIOD OF INTEREST	HEIGHT
Clematis alpina 193, 263	Cl	L	◐	4-5	6ft(1.8m)
'Frances Rivis' 245	Cl	L	◐	4-5	6ft(1.8m)
armandii 12, 16, 247, 325	ECl	-	☼	4-5	15ft(4.5m)
'Apple Blossom' 245	ECl	-	☼	4-5	15ft(4.5m)
chrysocoma 209	Cl	-	◐	6-7	10ft(3m)
cirrhosa var. *balearica* 209	ECl	-	◐	2-4	10ft(3m)
'Ernest Markham' 43	Cl	-	◐	6-9	12ft(3.7m)
'Etoile Violette' 154	Cl	-	◐	7-9	15ft(4.5m)
flammula 209	Cl	-	◐	8-10	10ft(3m)
florida 'Sieboldii' 143, 170	Cl	A	◐	4-5	10ft(3m)
heracleifolia 64, 165, 337, 338	P	-	☼	7-8	3ft(90cm)
'Wyevale' 337	P	-	☼	7-8	3ft(90cm)
'H.F. Young' 247	Cl	-	◐	5-6,9	12ft(3.7m)
'Huldine' 134	Cl	A	◐	7-10	13ft(4m)
× *jackmanii* 40, 138	Cl	-	◐	7-10	12ft(3.7m)
'Superba' 12	Cl	-	◐	7-9	15ft(4.5m)
macropetala 140, 193, 195, 263	Cl	-	◐	5-6	8ft(2.4m)
'Markham's Pink' 137	Cl	A	◐	5-6	12ft(3.7m)
'Madame Julia Correvon' 138	Cl	-	◐	7-8	6ft(1.8m)
montana 170, 199, 210, 225, 325	Cl	L	◐	5-6	20ft(6m)
'Elizabeth' 134	Cl	-	◐	5-6	30ft(9m)
'Mrs Cholmondeley' 219	Cl	L	◐	5-8	12ft(3.7m)
'Nelly Moser' 36, 37	Cl	L	◐	5-9	12ft(3.7m)
'Perle d'Azur' 219	Cl	-	◐	6-9	12ft(3.7m)
tangutica 35, 162	Cl	L	◐	8-10	20ft(6m)
texensis hybrids 40	Cl	A	◐	6-9	10ft(3m)
viticella 40	Cl	L	◐	7-9	12ft(3.7m)
'Alba Luxurians' 137	Cl	L	◐	7-9	12ft(3.7m)
'Minuet' 52	Cl	-	◐	7-8	8ft(2.4m)
Cobaea scandens 53, 196	Cl	-	☼S	8-10	12ft(3.7m)
Colchicum 'Lilac Wonder' 144	Bu	-	◐	9-11	10in(25cm)
speciosum 142	Bu	-	◐	9-11	10in(25cm)
'Album' 89, 144, 217	Bu	-	◐	9-11	10in(25cm)
'Rosy Dawn' 89	Bu	-	◐	9-11	8in(20cm)
Convallaria majalis 139	Bu	L	●	4-5	8in(20cm)
Convolvulus althaeoides 193	P	-	☼	5-9	trailing
cneorum 14, 97, 172, 199, 318	ESh	-	☼S	6-9	2ft(60cm)
tricolor 'Blue Ensign' 245	An	-	☼	6-9	12in(30cm)
'Blue Flash' 159	An	-	☼	6-9	12in(30cm)
'Heavenly Blue' 219	An	-	☼	6-9	12in(30cm)
'Royal Ensign' 117	An	-	☼	6-9	12in(30cm)
Cordyline australis 236, 255, 260, 261	ETr	-	☼	6-9	15ft(4.5m)
'Purple Tower' 239	ETr	-	☼	6-9	10ft(3m)
'Purpurea' 24	ETr	-	☼	6-9	10ft(3m)
Coriandrum sativum 289	An	-	☼	6-9	2ft(60cm)
Cornus alba 75	Sh	-	◐	11-4	10ft(3m)
'Aurea' 134	Sh	-	◐	11-4	8ft(2.4m)
'Elegantissima' 55, 192, 205	Sh	-	◐	6-10	8ft(2.4m)
'Spaethii' 22	Sh	-	◐	6-10	8ft(2.4m)
'Westonbirt' 55, 237, 340	Sh	-	◐	11-4	8ft(2.4m)
controversa 'Variegata' 147	Tr	-	◐	6-7,9	15ft(4.5m)
Corokia cotoneaster 239	ESh	-	☼S	5,9	10ft(3m)
Coronilla glauca (now *C. valentina* subsp. *glauca*)					
valentina subsp. *glauca* 261, 290, 291	ESh	-	☼	5-7	5ft(1.5m)
Cortaderia richardii 310	P	-	☼	7-8	8ft(2.4m)

PLANT TYPE **An** annual; **Aq** aquatic; **Bam** bamboo; **Bi** biennial; **Bu** bulb, corm, rhizome, tuber; **Cl** climber; **E** evergreen; **P** perennial; **Rc** rock plant; **Ro** rose; **Sh** shrub; **Tr** tree.

SOIL **A** needs acid soil; **L** needs alkaline soil; **M** needs moist to wet soil; **D** needs dry soil.

SITUATION ☼ does best in full sun; ◐ thrives in full sun or light shade; ● does best in full shade; ◐/● grows well in full sun, light shade or full shade; ●/◐ does best in full shade or light shade; **S** needs shelter; **W** tolerates wind.

PERIOD OF INTEREST numbers 1-12 represent the months when the plant has, for example, flowers, fruits or colourful bark.

HEIGHT represents height at maturity (or 20 years for trees and shrubs).

	PLANT TYPE	SOIL	SITUATION	PERIOD OF INTEREST	HEIGHT
Corylus avellana 'Contorta' 154, 162, 238	Sh	-	◐	11-3	15ft(4.5m)
Cosmos atrosanguineus 165	P	-	☼	8-9	2½ft(76cm)
Cotinus coggygria 157, 292	Sh	-	☼	6-7	10ft(3m)
Purpureus Group 117, 147	Sh	-	☼	5-10	10ft(3m)
'Royal Purple' 119, 291	Sh	-	☼	5-10	10ft(3m)
Cotoneaster dammeri 64, 76, 269, 333	ESh	-	☼	6,9-10	12in(30cm)
horizontalis 92, 137, 174, 263, 271, 325	Sh	-	☼	5,9-10	2ft(60cm)
salicifolius 'Pendulus' 205	ESh	-	◐	6,9	10ft(3m)
× *watereri* 'Cornubia' 192	Sh	-	☼	6,9-10	15ft(4.5m)
Crambe cordifolia 93, 215, 222, 339	P	D	◐	6	6ft(1.8m)
Crataegus monogyna 51	Tr	-	☼	5,9	15ft(4.5m)
Crocosmia 'Lucifer' 291	Bu	-	☼	8-9	3ft(90cm)
Crocus ancyrensis 134	Bu	-	☼	2-3	4in(10cm)
kotschyanus 340	Bu	-	☼	9-10	4in(10cm)
'Pickwick' 146	Bu	-	☼	3	4in(10cm)
speciosus 89, 340	Bu	-	☼	10-11	4in(10cm)
zonatus (now *C. kotschyanus*)					
Cryptomeria japonica 'Elegans Aurea' 245	ETr	-	☼	1-12	6ft(1.8m)
Cupressocyparis leylandii 46, 93, 290	ETr	-	☼	1-12	50ft(15m)
Cyclamen coum 31, 134, 135, 214	Bu	LD	● S	12-3	3in(7.5cm)
Cyclamen hederifolium 52, 66, 89, 135, 156, 214, 217	Bu	LD	●	8-10	4in(10cm)
Cyperus eragrostis 310	EP	M	☼	6-8	2ft(60cm)
longus 303, 310	EP	M	☼	6-8	3ft(90cm)
Cytisus battandieri 42, 189	Sh	D	☼	5-6	15ft(4.5m)
× *kewensis* 119, 140	Rc	D	☼	5	2ft(60cm)
× *praecox* 116	Sh	D	☼	4-6	5ft(1.5m)

D

	PLANT TYPE	SOIL	SITUATION	PERIOD OF INTEREST	HEIGHT
Daboecia cantabrica 89	ESh	A	☼	5-10	18in(45cm)
Dahlia 'Bishop of Llandaff' 157, 291, 294	P	-	☼	8-10	3ft(90cm)
'David Howard' 294	P	-	☼	8-10	3ft(90cm)
'Ellen Houston' 159	P	-	☼	8-10	3ft(90cm)
Daphne laureola 165	ESh	L	◐/●	2-3	4ft(1.2m)
mezereum 166, 340	ESh	L	◐	1-3,9	5ft(1.5m)
odora 'Aureomarginata' 240	ESh	L	◐	1-4	5ft(1.5m)
retusa 21, 141	ESh	-	◐ S	5-6	2ft(60cm)
Datura inoxia 143	An	-	☼	7	3ft(90cm)
Delphinium elatum hybrids 75, 94	P	-	☼	6-8	6ft(1.8m)
Dendranthema 'Mei-kyo' 173	P	-	☼	9-10	18in(45cm)
Dianthus barbatus 160	Bi	-	◐	6-9	16in(40cm)
'Dad's Favourite' 160, 165	P	L	☼	6-7	10in(25cm)
deltoides 42, 66, 111	Rc	LD	☼	6-7	9in(23cm)
'Doris' 14, 160, 165	P	L	☼	6-9	10in(25cm)
'Gran's Favourite' 177	P	L	☼	6-7	10in(25cm)
'Houndspool Ruby' 197	P	L	☼	6-8	12in(30cm)
'Mrs Sinkins' 177	P	L	☼	6-7	9in(23cm)
'Show Pearl' 14	P	L	☼	6-7	12in(30cm)
'Sops in Wine' 165, 167	P	L	☼	6-7	6in(15cm)
Dicentra spectabilis 217	P	M	◐	4-6	2½ft(76cm)
alba 213, 216	P	M	◐	4-6	2ft(60cm)
Digitalis purpurea 175, 353	An	-	◐	6-7	5ft(1.5m)
'Sutton's Apricot' 173	P	-	◐	5-6	3ft(90cm)
Dorotheanthus bellidiformis 14	An	-	☼	7-10	3in(7.5cm)
Dracaena draco 222	ETr	-	◐	7-9	10ft(3m)
Dryas octopetala 134	ERc	LD	☼	5-6	3in(7.5cm)
Dryopteris filix-mas 292	P	M	◐/●	5-10	4ft(1.2m)

E

	PLANT TYPE	SOIL	SITUATION	PERIOD OF INTEREST	HEIGHT
Eccremocarpus scaber 53	Cl	D	☼ S	6-10	10ft(3m)
Echinops 297	P	-	☼	8-9	4ft(1.2m)
ritro 337	P	-	☼	8-9	4ft(1.2m)
Echium vulgare 337	Bi	-	☼	6-8	12in(30cm)
Elaeagnus × *ebbingei* 50, 291	ESh	-	◐	10	15ft(4.5m)
'Gilt Edge' 211	ESh	-	◐	9-10	15ft(4.5m)
'Limelight' 71, 291	ESh	-	◐	1-12	10ft(3m)
pungens 'Maculata' 209, 211, 291	ESh	-	◐	10-11	12ft(3.7m)
Elodea canadensis 306	Aq	M	☼	1-12	-
Embothrium coccineum 145	ETr	AM	◐ S	5-6	12ft(3.7m)
Epimedium alpinum 134	P	-	◐	4-5	18in(45cm)
perralderianum 94	P	-	◐	4-5	12in(30cm)
× *youngianum* 'Niveum' 139	P	-	◐	4-5	9in(23cm)
Eranthis hyemalis 72	P	-	◐	2-4	4in(10cm)
Erica arborea 89	ESh	-	☼ S	1-5	12ft(3.7m)
× *darleyensis* 89	ESh	-	☼	11-5	18in(45cm)
Erigeron karvinskianus 111	P	-	☼	7-9	4in(10cm)
Erinus alpinus 42, 235	Rc	D	☼	3-7	3in(7.5cm)
Erysimum 'Bowles' Mauve' 174	P	-	☼	4-10	2ft(60cm)
cheiri 'Harpur Crewe' 167	P	-	☼	3-4	18in(45cm)
'Tom Thumb Mixed' 14	Bi	-	☼	5	9in(23cm)
'Cloth of Gold' 117	Bi	-	☼	5-7	18in(45cm)
Escallonia 'Iveyi' 193	ESh	-	◐ S	6-8	10ft(3m)
'Red Hedger' 50	ESh	-	◐	7-8	8ft(2.4m)
rubra var. *macrantha* 193	ESh	-	◐	6-8	10ft(3m)
Eschscholzia californica 117, 153	An	-	☼	7-9	12in(30cm)
Eucalyptus gunnii 22, 290	ETr	-	☼	1-12	40ft(12m)
pauciflora subsp. *niphophila* 119	ETr	-	☼	1-12	20ft(6m)
Eucryphia 'Nymansay' 144	ETr	-	● S	8-9	15ft(4.5m)
Euonymus fortunei 291	ESh	-	◐	5-7	15ft(4.5m)
'Emerald 'n' Gold' 212, 271	ESh	-	◐	5-6	2ft(60cm)
'Silver Pillar' 99	ESh	-	◐	1-12	5ft(1.5m)
'Silver Queen' 21	ESh	-	◐	1-12	3ft(90cm)
japonicus 193, 291	ESh	-	◐	1-12	12ft(3.7m)
Eupatorium cannabinum 334	P	-	◐	7-9	4ft(1.2m)
Euphorbia amygdaloides var. *robbiae* 145, 170, 341	P	L	◐	5-6	18in(45cm)
characias 13, 29, 260	EP	L	☼	3-5	4ft(1.2m)
subsp. *wulfenii* 219	P	LD	☼ S	3-7	4ft(1.2m)
dulcis 'Chameleon' 173	P	-	☼	5-10	12in(30cm)
griffithii 174	P	-	☼	6-8	3ft(90cm)
'Dixter' 158	P	-	☼	6-8	3ft(90cm)
'Fireglow' 158	P	-	☼	6-8	3ft(90cm)
marginata 292	An	-	☼	6-8	2ft(60cm)
polychroma 158	P	-	☼	4-5	18in(45cm)
Exochorda × *macrantha* 'The Bride' 216, 340	Sh	-	☼	4-6	10ft(3m)

F

	PLANT TYPE	SOIL	SITUATION	PERIOD OF INTEREST	HEIGHT
Fagus sylvatica 45, 326	Tr	LD	☼	9-10	30ft(9m)
'Purpurea Pendula' 197, 236	Tr	-	☼	4-10	10ft(3m)
Fargesia murieliae 171	Bam	-	◐	1-12	13ft(4m)
Fascicularia bicolor 246	EP	-	☼ S	6-8	18in(45cm)
× *Fatshedera lizei* 24, 214	ESh	-	◐	9-10	6ft(1.8m)
Fatsia japonica 37, 98, 206, 208, 210, 261, 291	ESh	D	●/◐	10	10ft(3m)
Felicia amelloides 242	P	-	☼ S	5-9	12in(30cm)
Festuca glauca 64, 207	P	-	☼	6-7	9in(23cm)
Ficus carica 255	Sh	-	☼ S	1-12	12ft(3.7m)
Filipendula ulmaria 'Aurea' 173, 333	P	M	☼	6-8	2½ft(76cm)

	PLANT TYPE	SOIL	SITUATION	PERIOD OF INTEREST	HEIGHT
Foeniculum vulgare 'Purpureum' 162, 289, 361	P	D	☼	7-8	6ft (1.8m)
Fothergilla major 224	Sh	A	☼	5	6ft (1.8m)
Fraxinus excelsior 67, 326	Tr	-	◑	1-12	40ft (12m)
Fritillaria imperialis 174	Bu	-	◑	4-5	3ft (90cm)
Fuchsia 'Display' 201, 251	Sh	-	◑	8-9	3ft (90cm)
'Gay Fandango' 201	Sh	-	◑	8-9	3ft (90cm)
magellanica 53, 147	Sh	D	◑	6-10	6ft (1.8m)
var. *molinae* 53	Sh	-	◑	7-10	6ft (1.8m)
'Rose of Castile Improved' 200	Sh	-	◑	7-10	15ft (4.5m)

G

	PLANT TYPE	SOIL	SITUATION	PERIOD OF INTEREST	HEIGHT
Galanthus elwesii 146, 205	Bu	-	◑	1-4	10in (25cm)
nivalis 72	Bu	-	◑	2-3	6in (15cm)
Galium odoratum 195	P	-	◑	6-8	6in (15cm)
Galtonia candicans 119, 125	Bu	-	☼	8-9	4ft (1.2m)
Garrya elliptica 40, 42, 145, 291	ESh	-	◑ S	12-3	9ft (2.7m)
Gaultheria procumbens 108	ESh	A	◑	1-12	6in (15cm)
Genista aetnensis 264	Tr	-	☼	6-7	15ft (4.5m)
Gentiana septemfida 156	Rc	-	☼	7-8	6in (15cm)
verna 235	Rc	-	☼	4	3in (7.5cm)
Geranium pratense 75	P	-	☼	5, 8-9	2½ft (76cm)
macrorrhizum 318	P	-	◑	4-8	18in (45cm)
'Bevan's Variety' 21, 148	P	-	◑	4-8	18in (45cm)
× *oxonianum* 'Claridge Druce' 36, 37	P	-	☼	5-8	18in (45cm)
procurrens 266	P	-	☼	5-8	12in (30cm)
robertianum 353	P	L	☼	5-8	9in (23cm)
sanguineum 64, 154	P	L	☼	5-8	12in (30cm)
Geum 'Lionel Cox' 134	P	-	☼	5-6	18in (45cm)
rivale 333	P	M	☼	5-9	18in (45cm)
Ginkgo biloba 245	Tr	-	◑	9-10	20ft (6m)
Gladiolus callianthus 'Murieliae' 147, 166	Bu	-	☼	7-8	3ft (90cm)
Glaucium flavum 235	Bi	-	☼	8-9	12in (30cm)
Glechoma hederacea 'Variegata' 248	EP	-	☼	1-12	trailing
Glyceria maxima 'Variegata' 333	P	-	☼	6-8	3ft (90cm)
Griselinia littoralis 50, 193	ETr	-	◑ S	4-5	10ft (3m)
Gunnera manicata 142, 219, 222, 255, 317	P	M	◑ S	4-6, 10	8ft (2.4m)
Gypsophila paniculata 216	P	-	☼	6-8	3ft (90cm)
repens 106	Rc	-	☼	6-8	6in (15cm)

H

	PLANT TYPE	SOIL	SITUATION	PERIOD OF INTEREST	HEIGHT
Hakonechloa macra 'Aureola' 161, 170, 171	P	-	◑	5-9	12in (30cm)
Hamamelis mollis 166, 242	Sh	-	◑	2-3, 9-10	12ft (3.7m)
Hebe albicans 219	ESh	-	☼	6-7	2ft (60cm)
'Autumn Glory' 94, 119	ESh	-	☼	8-11	5ft (1.5m)
brachysiphon 123	ESh	-	☼	7-8	6ft (1.8m)
buxifolia 'Nana' 21	ESh	-	☼	1-12	6in (15cm)
× *franciscana* 'Blue Gem' 123	ESh	-	☼ S	7-11	3ft (90cm)
'La Seduisante' 53	ESh	-	☼ S	8-9	3ft (90cm)

	PLANT TYPE	SOIL	SITUATION	PERIOD OF INTEREST	HEIGHT
'Midsummer Beauty' 53, 71	ESh	-	☼	7-9	6ft (1.8m)
pinguifolia 'Pagei' 108, 321	ESh	-	☼	6-7	6in (15cm)
salicifolia 53, 123	ESh	-	☼ S	6-8	6ft (1.8m)
Hedera algeriensis 'Gloire de Marengo' 196, 205	ECl	-	◑	1-12	20ft (6m)
canariensis 208	ECl	-	◑	1-12	20ft (6m)
colchica 208, 271	ECl	-	◑	1-12	20ft (6m)
'Dentata' 273	ECl	-	◑	1-12	20ft (6m)
'Dentata Variegata' 71, 196	ECl	-	◑	1-12	15ft (4.5m)
'Sulphur Heart' 196	ECl	-	◑	1-12	15ft (4.5m)
helix 52, 196, 212, 237, 246, 353	ECl	-	◑	1-12	30ft (9m)
'Deltoidea' 273	ECl	-	◑ S	1-12	15ft (4.5m)
'Eva' 231	ECl	-	◑	1-12	4ft (1.2m)
'Glacier' 75, 197, 205, 245	ECl	-	◑	1-12	6ft (1.8m)
'Goldheart' 196, 245, 259	ECl	-	◑	1-12	20ft (6m)
var. *hibernica* (now *H. hibernica*)					
'Pedata' 134	ECl	-	◑	1-12	12ft (3.7m)
'Tricolor' 14	ECl	-	◑	1-12	6ft (1.8m)
hibernica 53, 196, 213	ECl	-	◑	1-12	20ft (6m)
Helenium autumnale 269	P	-	☼	8-10	5ft (1.5m)
Helianthemum lunulatum 235	Rc	-	☼	6-7	9in (23cm)
'Mrs Earle' 134	Rc	-	☼	6-7	12in (30cm)
'Wisley Primrose' 134	Rc	-	☼	6-7	12in (30cm)
Helianthus annuus 117, 297	An	-	☼	7-9	3-15ft (4.5m)
decapetalus 269	P	-	☼	7-9	6ft (1.8m)
Helichrysum angustifolium (now *H. italicum*)					
bracteatum 297	An	-	☼	8-10	2½ft (76cm)
italicum 289	ESh	-	☼	1-12	2ft (60cm)
petiolare 245, 251	ESh	-	☼ S	1-12	12in (30cm)
Helictotrichon sempervirens 115, 161	EP	-	☼	1-12	3ft (90cm)
Heliotropium arborescens 'Lord Roberts' 251	ESh	-	☼ S	5-10	5ft (1.5m)
Helleborus argutifolius 119	EP	M	●/◑	3-4	2ft (60cm)
foetidus 38	EP	M	●/◑	3-5	2ft (60cm)
niger 142, 295	P	M	●/◑	12-3	12in (30cm)
orientalis 13, 135, 156	P	M	●/◑	2-3	18in (45cm)
Hemerocallis citrina 188	P	-	☼	7	2½ft (76cm)
Hepatica transsilvanica 135	Rc	-	◑	3-4	6in (15cm)
Hesperis matronalis 167, 190	P	-	◑	5-8	3ft (90cm)
Heuchera micrantha 'Palace Purple' 261	P	-	◑	6-9	12in (30cm)
Hibiscus rosa-sinensis 'Holiday' 201	ESh	-	☼ S	5-9	8ft (2.4m)
Hippophae rhamnoides 193	Sh	-	☼	5, 9	12ft (3.7m)
Hordeum jubatum 162	P	-	☼	7-9	2ft (60cm)
Hosta crispula 333	P	-	◑	6-7	2ft (60cm)
fortunei var. *albopicta* 156	P	-	◑	5-7	18in (45cm)
sieboldiana 75, 142, 156, 267	P	-	◑	6-7	2ft (60cm)
var. *elegans* 271	P	-	◑	6-7	2½ft (76cm)
'Snowden' 168	P	-	◑	5-9	4ft (1.2m)
'Sum and Substance' 168	P	-	◑	5-9	18in (45cm)
'Thomas Hogg' 156	P	-	◑/●	5-9	2½ft (76cm)
tokudama 239	P	M	◑	6-9	18in (45cm)
undulata 308	P	M	◑	6-7	2ft (60cm)

PLANT TYPE **An** annual; **Aq** aquatic; **Bam** bamboo; **Bi** biennial; **Bu** bulb, corm, rhizome, tuber; **Cl** climber; **E** evergreen; **P** perennial; **Rc** rock plant; **Ro** rose; **Sh** shrub; **Tr** tree.

SOIL **A** needs acid soil; **L** needs alkaline soil; **M** needs moist to wet soil; **D** needs dry soil.

SITUATION ☼ does best in full sun; ◑ thrives in full sun or light shade; ◑/● grows well in full sun, light shade or full shade; ● does best in full shade; ◑/● does best in full shade or light shade; **S** needs shelter; **W** tolerates wind.

PERIOD OF INTEREST numbers 1-12 represent the months when the plant has, for example, flowers, fruits or colourful bark.

HEIGHT represents height at maturity (or 20 years for trees and shrubs).

	PLANT TYPE	SOIL	SITUATION	PERIOD OF INTEREST	HEIGHT
Hottonia palustris 331, 333	P Aq	-	☼	5-7	12in (30cm)
Houttuynia cordata 306	P	M	☼	5-9	9in (23cm)
Howeia forsteriana 191, 201	E Tr	-	◑/●	1-12	15ft (4.5m)
Humulus japonicus 'Variegatus' 53, 271	Cl An	-	☼	6-9	20ft (6m)
lupulus 'Aureus' 41	Cl P	-	☼	6-8	20ft (6m)
Hyacinthoides non-scripta 340	Bu	-	◑/●	5	12in (30cm)
Hyacinthus 'Distinction' 293	Bu	-	☼	12 or 4	9in (23cm)
'Gipsy Queen' 145, 293	Bu	-	☼	12 or 4	9in (23cm)
'L'Innocence' 299	Bu	-	☼	12 or 4	9in (23cm)
'Myosotis' 146	Bu	-	☼	12 or 4	9in (23cm)
orientalis 166	Bu	-	☼	12 or 4	9in (23cm)
'Ostara' 135	Bu	-	☼	12 or 5	9in (23cm)
Hydrangea arborescens 'Annabelle' 75	Sh	M	◑	7-10	3ft (90cm)
'Grandiflora' 71	Sh	M	◑	7-10	3ft (90cm)
macrophylla 211	Sh	M	◑	7-9	6ft (1.8m)
'Ayesha' 242	Sh	M	◑	7-9	5ft (1.5m)
'Blue Bonnet' 242	Sh	M	◑	7-9	5ft (1.5m)
Hortensia Group 296	Sh	M	◑	7-10	5ft (1.5m)
'Madame Emile Mouilliere' 242	Sh	M	◑	7-9	6ft (1.8m)
'Pia' 217, 296	Sh	M	◑	7-9	4ft (1.2m)
paniculata 296	Sh	M	◑	7-9	10ft (3m)
petiolaris 12, 17, 42, 44, 75, 76, 208	Cl	-	◑	6	30ft (9m)
'Preziosa' 242, 294	Sh	M	◑	7-9	4ft (1.2m)
Hydrocharis morsus-ranae 306	Aq	M	☼	6-8	3in (7.5cm)
Hypericum calycinum 64, 120, 270	E Sh	-	☼	7-9	18in (45cm)
Hyssopus officinalis 289	E P	-	☼	7-9	12in (30cm)

I

	PLANT TYPE	SOIL	SITUATION	PERIOD OF INTEREST	HEIGHT
Iberis sempervirens 42, 134, 154	E Rc	-	☼	5-6	9in (23cm)
Ilex × altaclerensis 291	E Tr	-	◑	1-12	15ft (4.5m)
'Camelliifolia' 213	E Tr	-	◑	1-12	20ft (6m)
'Golden King' 174	E Tr	-	◑	1-12	15ft (4.5m)
'Lawsoniana' 99	E Tr	-	◑	1-12	15ft (4.5m)
aquifolium 45, 291	E Tr	-	◑	1-12	15ft (4.5m)
'Argentea Marginata' 209, 211	E Tr	-	◑	1-12	15ft (4.5m)
'Argentea Marginata Pendula' 205	E Tr	-	◑	1-12	12ft (3.7m)
'Handsworth New Silver' 144	E Tr	-	◑	1-12	15ft (4.5m)
'J.C. van Tol' 31, 144	E Tr	-	◑	1-12	20ft (6m)
'Madame Briot' 139	E Tr	-	◑	11-2	20ft (6m)
'Silver Queen' 259	E Tr	-	◑	1-12	15ft (4.5m)
Impatiens 'Accent White' 144	An	-	☼	5-9	10in (25cm)
'Novetter Series' 246	An	-	☼	5-9	6in (15cm)
walleriana 246	An	-	☼	5-9	10in (25cm)
Inula magnifica 158	P	-	☼	8-9	8ft (2.4m)
Ionopsidium acaule 111	An	-	◑	7-9	3in (7.5cm)
Ipomoea 'Heavenly Blue' 219, 239	An	-	☼	6-9	10ft (3m)
Iris danfordiae 135, 295	Bu	-	◑	1-2	4in (10cm)
ensata 77, 310, 317	P	M	◑	5-7	2½ft (76cm)
foetidissima 238, 341	E P	D	◑	5-7, 11	2ft (60cm)
graminea 235	P	-	◑	5-6	18in (45cm)
kaempferi (now *I. ensata*)					
laevigata 'Alba' 306	P	M	◑	5-7	2½ft (76cm)
'Dorothy' 321	P	M	◑	5-7	2½ft (76cm)
'Snowdrift' 321	P	M	◑	5-7	2½ft (76cm)
'Variegata' 309, 333	P	M	◑	6-7	2ft (60cm)
pseudacorus 334	P	M	◑	5-7	5ft (1.5m)
'Variegata' 173	P	M	◑	5-7	4ft (1.2m)
pumila 14	P	-	☼	5	6in (15cm)
× *robusta* 'Gerald Darby' 315	P	-	◑	6	3ft (90cm)
sibirica 75, 136, 293, 305, 317	P	M	◑	5-7	3ft (90cm)
variegata 66	P	-	☼	6	18in (45cm)
versicolor 'Rosea' 321	P	M	◑	6-7	2ft (60cm)
Itea ilicifolia 143, 291	E Sh	-	◑ S	8-9	10ft (3m)

J, K

	PLANT TYPE	SOIL	SITUATION	PERIOD OF INTEREST	HEIGHT
Jasminum grandiflorum 'De Grasse' 191	E Cl	-	☼	8-9	6ft (1.8m)
nudiflorum 31, 42, 271	Cl	D	◑	11-3	10ft (3m)
odoratissimum 190	E Sh	-	◑	6-8	6ft (1.8m)
officinale 42, 116, 143, 167	Cl	D	◑	6-10	10ft (3m)
'Aureo-variegatum' (now *J. o.* 'Aureum')					
'Aureum' 125	Cl	D	◑	6-10	10ft (3m)
sambac 'Maid of Orleans' 190	E Cl	-	◑	6-8	10ft (3m)
× *stephanense* 245	Cl	-	☼	6-8	12ft (3.7m)
Juncus effusus 'Spiralis' 310	E P	M	☼	1-12	12in (30cm)
inflexus 'Afro' 310	E P	M	☼	5-9	12in (30cm)
Juniperus chinensis 'Stricta' 237	E Tr	-	☼	1-12	15ft (4.5m)
'Pfitzeriana' (now *Juniperus × media* 'Pfitzeriana')					
communis 'Compressa' 245	E Sh	-	☼	1-12	2½ft (76cm)
× *media* 'Pfitzeriana' 21, 79, 99	E Sh	-	☼	1-12	10ft (3m)
'Pfitzeriana Aurea' 66	E Sh	-	◑	1-12	3ft (90cm)
recurva 99	E Sh	-	◑	1-12	12ft (3.7m)
sabina 'Blue Danube' 245	E Sh	-	◑	1-12	12ft (3.7m)
'Tamariscifolia' 21, 76	E Sh	-	◑	1-12	2½ft (76cm)
'Skyrocket' 99	E Tr	-	◑	1-12	12ft (3.7m)
Kerria japonica 116	Sh	-	◑	4-5	6ft (1.8m)
'Pleniflora' 43	Sh	-	◑	4-5	6ft (1.8m)
'Variegata' 37	Sh	-	◑	4-5	4ft (1.2m)
Knautia macedonica 154	P	LD	☼	6-9	2½ft (76cm)
Kniphofia caulescens 24, 236	E P	-	☼	9-10	4ft (1.2m)
Kochia scoparia (now *Bassia scoparia*)					

L

	PLANT TYPE	SOIL	SITUATION	PERIOD OF INTEREST	HEIGHT
Laburnum alpinum 236	Tr	-	☼	5-6	15ft (4.5m)
Lagarosiphon major 306, 333	Aq	-	☼	1-12	-
Lagurus ovatus 162, 297	An	-	☼	6-9	15in (38cm)
Lamiastrum galeobdolon (now *Lamium galeobdolon*)					
Lamium galeobdolon 120	P	-	◑	6-8	12in (30cm)
maculatum 175	P	-	◑	5-8	6in (15cm)
'Album' 28	P	-	◑	5-8	6in (15cm)
'Beacon Silver' 64	P	-	◑	5-8	6in (15cm)
Lantana camara 242	E Sh	-	☼ S	4-9	6ft (1.8m)
Lathyrus latifolius 12, 52, 263, 266	Cl P	-	☼	7-9	8ft (2.4m)
odoratus 193	Cl An	-	☼	7-9	3-10ft (3m)
'Painted Lady' 168	Cl An	-	☼	7-9	6ft (1.8m)
Laurus nobilis 245, 289	E Tr	-	◑ S	1-12	15ft (4.5m)
Lavandula angustifolia 'Hidcote' 54, 115	E Sh	-	☼	7-9	2ft (60cm)
'Hidcote Pink' 167	E Sh	-	☼	7-9	2ft (60cm)
'Loddon Pink' 251	E Sh	-	☼	7-9	2ft (60cm)
'Munstead' 54, 119, 197	E Sh	-	☼	7-9	3ft (90cm)
Lavatera 'Barnsley' 192, 206, 237	P	-	☼	6-9	5ft (1.5m)
'Rosea' 192, 237	P	-	☼ S	7-9	6ft (1.8m)
thuringiaca 'Barnsley' (now *L.* 'Barnsley')					
'Rosea' (now *L.* 'Rosea')					
trimestris 117	An	-	☼	7-9	2ft (60cm)
'Silver Cup' 66	An	-	☼	7-9	2ft (60cm)
Layia elegans 338	An	-	☼	5-9	18in (45cm)
Lemna minor 316	Aq	-	☼	1-12	--
trisulca 306	Aq	-	☼	1-12	--
Leucojum vernum 135, 144	Bu	-	◑	2-3	9in (23cm)
Liatris spicata 41	P	-	☼	9	2½ft (76cm)
Ligularia przewalskii 195	P	M	◑	7-8	6ft (1.8m)

	PLANT TYPE	SOIL	SITUATION	PERIOD OF INTEREST	HEIGHT
Ligustrum lucidum 213	ETr	-	☽ S	8-9	15ft(4.5m)
'Excelsum Superbum' 189, 211	ETr	-	☼	8-9	20ft(6m)
ovalifolium 45	ESh	-	☽	7	12ft(3.7m)
'Aureo-marginatum' (now *L. o.* 'Aureum')					
'Aureum' 211, 291	ESh	-	☽	1-12	12ft(3.7m)
sinense 'Variegatum' 212	ESh	-	☽	7,9	12ft(3.7m)
Lilium 'African Queen' 294	Bu	-	☽	7-8	5ft(1.5m)
auratum 167, 174	Bu	A	☽	8	5ft(1.5m)
candidum 166	Bu	L	☽	6-7	4ft(1.2m)
'Casablanca' 294	Bu	-	☽	8	4ft(1.2m)
'Connecticut King' 294	Bu	-	☽	7	2½ft(76cm)
'Enchantment' 291	Bu	-	☽	7-8	2½ft(76cm)
'Golden Splendour' 217	Bu	-	☽	7-8	5ft(1.5m)
hansonii 75	Bu	-	☽	6-7	5ft(1.5m)
lancifolium 158	Bu	-	☽	8-9	4ft(1.2m)
longiflorum 197	Bu	-	☽	6-8	12in(30cm)
monadelphum 75	Bu	-	☽	6-7	3ft(90cm)
Pink Perfection 189, 294	Bu	-	☽	8	4ft(1.2m)
regale 164, 166, 234, 294	Bu	-	☽	6-8	4ft(1.2m)
speciosum 166	Bu	-	☽	8	4ft(1.2m)
Limnanthes douglasii 147, 361	An	D	☼	5-8	6in(15cm)
Liriodendron tulipifera 137	Tr	-	☼	7-11	20ft(6m)
Liriope muscari 239	EP	-	☼	9	12in(30cm)
Lobelia cardinalis 310	P	M	☽	7-9	2½ft(76cm)
erinus 'Colour Cascade' 246	An	-	☼	6-9	6in(15cm)
siphilitica 315	P	M	☼	7-9	2½ft(76cm)
Lobularia maritima 246	An	-	☼	6-9	6in(15cm)
Lonicera × *americana* 166	Cl	-	☽	6-7	20ft(6m)
fragrantissima 165	Sh	-	☽	2-3	6ft(1.8m)
× *heckrottii* 'Gold Flame' 335	Cl	-	☽	6-8	15ft(4.5m)
japonica 'Aureoreticulata' 37	Cl	-	☽	6-10	20ft(6m)
'Halliana' 40, 146, 166, 196, 361	Cl	-	☽	6-9	30ft(9m)
nitida 45, 51, 187, 197, 256	ESh	-	☽	4-5	6ft(1.8m)
'Baggesen's Gold' 51	ESh	-	☼	4-5	6ft(1.8m)
periclymenum 188	Cl	-	☽	6-8	20ft(6m)
'Belgica' 91, 167, 209, 335	Cl	-	☽	7-8	20ft(6m)
'Early Dutch' (now *L. p.* 'Belgica')					
'Graham Thomas' 134, 167	Cl	-	☽	6-8	20ft(6m)
'Serotina' 91, 197, 209, 335	Cl	-	☽	6-9	20ft(6m)
× *tellmanniana* 125	Cl	-	☽	6-8	15ft(4.5m)
Lotus berthelotii 143	EP	-	☼ S	7-9	6in(15cm)
Lunaria annua 297	Bi	-	☽	4-6,10	2½ft(76cm)
'Alba' 337	Bi	-	☽	4-6,10	2½ft(76cm)
'Alba Variegata' 292	Bi	-	☽	4-6,10	2½ft(76cm)
Lupinus Russell 'Blue Jacket' 361	P	-	☽	5-6	3ft(90cm)
Lychnis flos-cuculi 333	P	M	☽	5-7	2½ft(76cm)
Lysimachia nummularia 246, 305	P	-	☽	6-8	3in(7.5cm)
'Aurea' 117, 333	P	-	☽	6-8	3in(7.5cm)
Lythrum salicaria 334	P	-	☽	6-8	4ft(1.2m)
virgatum 'Rose Queen' 309	P	M	☼	6-9	2ft(60cm)

M

	PLANT TYPE	SOIL	SITUATION	PERIOD OF INTEREST	HEIGHT
Macleaya cordata 271	P	-	☼	6-8	6ft(1.8m)
microcarpa 269	P	-	☼	6-8	6ft(1.8m)

	PLANT TYPE	SOIL	SITUATION	PERIOD OF INTEREST	HEIGHT
Magnolia grandiflora 'Galissonière' 216	ETr	A	☽ S	7-9	20ft(6m)
stellata 205, 236	Sh	-	☽ S	3-4	10ft(3m)
Mahonia aquifolium 53, 75, 116, 214, 268	ESh	-	☽	3-4	5ft(1.5m)
japonica 24, 166, 240, 255, 268	ESh	-	☽	11-4	6ft(1.8m)
lomariifolia 99	ESh	-	☽ S	9-10	8ft(2.4m)
× *media* 'Charity' 27, 145, 198, 210, 219	ESh	-	☽ S	11-2	10ft(3m)
'Lionel Fortescue' 36, 37	ESh	-	☽	11-2	10ft(3m)
Malus 'Evereste' 282, 326	Tr	-	☼	5,9-10	18ft(5.5m)
'Golden Hornet' 326	Tr	-	☼	5,9-10	20ft(6m)
'John Downie' 326	Tr	-	☼	6,9-10	20ft(6m)
'Profusion' 189, 326	Tr	-	☼	5,9-10	20ft(6m)
'Red Sentinel' 174, 326	Tr	-	☼	5,9-10	20ft(6m)
sargentii 66	Tr	-	☼	5	8ft(2.4m)
sylvestris 67	Tr	-	☼	5	30ft(9m)
Matteuccia struthiopteris 173	P	-	●/☽	5-10	3ft(90cm)
Matthiola bicornis 188, 190	An	-	☼	7-8	18in(45cm)
incana 117	Bi	-	☽	6-7	18in(45cm)
Meconopsis betonicifolia 156	Bi/P	A	☽	6	3ft(90cm)
cambrica 175	P	-	☼	6-9	18in(45cm)
× *sheldonii* 115	P	A	●	6	5ft(1.5m)
Melianthus major 215, 290	ESh	-	☼	5-8	10ft(3m)
Melissa officinalis 'Aurea' 289	P	-	☼	6-7	2½ft(76cm)
Mentha aquatica 333	P	M	☼	6-8	2ft(60cm)
piperita 289	P	-	☼	4-9	2ft(60cm)
× *piperita citrata* 165	P	-	☼	4-9	2ft(60cm)
pulegium 289	P	-	☽	4-9	9in(23cm)
requienii 111	Rc	M	☽	4-9	½in(1.3cm)
spicata 289	P	-	☽	6-10	2ft(60cm)
'Crispa' 289	P	-	☽	6-10	12in(30cm)
suaveolens 289	P	-	☽	4-9	18in(45cm)
'Variegata' 289	P	-	☼	4-9	18in(45cm)
Mentzelia aurea 338	An	-	☼	5-8	18in(45cm)
Menyanthes trifoliata 309, 334	Aq	-	☼	5-7	9in(23cm)
Mesembryanthemum criniflorum (now *Dorotheanthus bellidiformis*)					
Milium effusum 'Aureum' 173	P	-	☽	5-9	12in(30cm)
Mina lobata 53, 279	Cl	-	☼	6-8	15ft(4.5m)
Miscanthus sacchariflorus 53	P	-	☼ W	8-9	10ft(3m)
'Silberfeder' ('Silver Feather') 261	P	-	☽	5-10	6ft(1.8m)
sinensis 170, 268	P	-	☼ W	5-9	6ft(1.8m)
Moluccella laevis 155, 297	An	-	☼	6-9	2ft(60cm)
Montia sibirica 153	An	-	●/☽	5-7	6in(15cm)
Muehlenbeckia complexa 134	ECl	-	☽	9-11	2ft(60cm)
Muscari armeniacum 156	Bu	D	☽	4-5	9in(23cm)
Myosotis alpestris 12	P	D	☼	4-6	4in(10cm)
scorpioides 333	P	M	☽	4-6	6in(15cm)
'Mermaid' 321	P	M	☽	4-6	12in(30cm)
'Sapphire' 321	P	M	☽	4-6	12in(30cm)
sylvatica 353	P	M	☽	4-6	6in(15cm)
'White Ball' 231	Bi	-	☽	6	9in(23cm)

PLANT TYPE **An** annual; **Aq** aquatic; **Bam** bamboo; **Bi** biennial; **Bu** bulb, corm, rhizome, tuber; **Cl** climber; **E** evergreen; **P** perennial; **Rc** rock plant; **Ro** rose; **Sh** shrub; **Tr** tree.

SOIL **A** needs acid soil; **L** needs alkaline soil; **M** needs moist to wet soil; **D** needs dry soil.

SITUATION ☼ does best in full sun; ☽ thrives in full sun or light shade; ● does best in full shade; ☽/● grows well in full sun, light shade or full shade; ●/☽ does best in full shade or light shade; **S** needs shelter; **W** tolerates wind.

PERIOD OF INTEREST numbers 1-12 represent the months when the plant has, for example, flowers, fruits or colourful bark.

HEIGHT represents height at maturity (or 20 years for trees and shrubs).

N

	PLANT TYPE	SOIL	SITUATION	PERIOD OF INTEREST	HEIGHT
Nandina domestica 98	E Sh	-	◑ S	7,9	6ft(1.8m)
Narcissus 'Cassata' 293	Bu	-	◑	4-5	18in(45cm)
poeticus var. recurvus 105, 156, 167	Bu	-	◑	6	18in(45cm)
'Tête à Tête' 293	Bu	-	◑	4-5	9in(23cm)
'Thalia' 10	Bu	-	◑	4-5	9in(23cm)
Nepeta mussinii (now N. racemosa) racemosa 176, 337	P	-	☀	5-9	18in(45cm)
Nerium oleander 316	E Sh	-	☀	6-10	15ft(4.5m)
Nicotiana alata 167, 197	P	-	☀	7-8	12in(30cm)
'Evening Fragrance' 188	P	-	☀	7-9	2ft(60cm)
'Domino' 245	An	-	☀	6-9	12in(30cm)
langsdorffii 155	An	-	☀	7-8	5ft(1.5m)
'Sensation' 245	An	-	☀	6-9	2½ft(76cm)
Nigella damascena 162, 175, 297	An	-	☀	6-9	18in(45cm)
'Persian Jewels' 117	An	-	☀	6-9	18in(45cm)
Nymphaea alba 333	Aq	-	☀	6-8	-
candida 306	Aq	-	☀	6-8	-
'Firecrest' 310	Aq	-	☀	5-9	-
'Froebelii' 310	Aq	-	☀	6-8	-
× helvola 306	Aq	-	☀	6-8	-
'James Brydon' 311	Aq	-	☀	6-8	-
'Laydekeri Purpurata' 306	Aq	-	☀	6-8	-
'Marliacea Albida' 311	Aq	-	☀	6-8	-
'Marliacea Chromatella' 311	Aq	-	☀	6-8	-
'Odorata Minor' 306	Aq	-	☀	6-9	-
'Odorata Turicensis' 331	Aq	-	☀	6-8	-
'Pygmaea Rubra' 306	Aq	-	☀	6-8	-
'Rose Arey' 311, 315	Aq	-	☀	6-8	-
'Solfatare' 333	Aq	-	☀	6-8	-
tetragona 306	Aq	-	☀	6-8	-

O

	PLANT TYPE	SOIL	SITUATION	PERIOD OF INTEREST	HEIGHT
Ocimum basilicum 289	An	-	☀	6-9	2ft(60cm)
'Purpureum' 56, 289	An	-	☀	6-9	2ft(60cm)
Oenothera biennis 337	Bi	-	☀	6-10	3ft(90cm)
Olearia virgata 209	E Sh	-	☀	5-6	15ft(4.5m)
Onoclea sensibilis 93	P	M	◑/●	4-5,10	18in(45cm)
Onopordum nervosum 153	Bi	-	☀	7-8	6ft(1.8m)
Ophiopogon planiscapus 'Nigrescens' 217	E P	-	☀	5-6	9in(23cm)
Origanum vulgare 'Aureum' 197, 289	P	-	☀	7-8	6in(15cm)
Orontium aquaticum 309	Aq	-	☀	7-8	2in(5cm)
Osmanthus × burkwoodii 46, 144	E Sh	-	◑	4-6	15ft(4.5m)
delavayi 165	E Sh	-	◑	4-6	6ft(1.8m)
Osmunda regalis 93, 219	P	M	◑	9-10	5ft(1.5m)
Oxalis acetosella 214	P	-	●/◑	3-5	3in(7.5cm)
adenophylla 235	Rc	-	◑	5-7	3in(7.5cm)

P, Q

	PLANT TYPE	SOIL	SITUATION	PERIOD OF INTEREST	HEIGHT
Pachysandra terminalis 64, 108	E P	-	●/◑	4-5	6in(15cm)
Paeonia 'Argosy' 171	Sh	L	☀	5-6	4ft(1.2m)
'Bowl of Beauty' 294	P	L	☀	5-6	3ft(90cm)
delavayi 167	Sh	L	◑	5	6ft(1.8m)
'Joseph Rock' 238	Sh	L	◑	5	4ft(1.2m)
'Sarah Bernhardt' 138, 165, 294	P	L	☀	5-6	2ft(60cm)
Papaver orientale 160	P	-	☀	6-7	2ft(60cm)
'Beauty of Livermere' 138	P	-	☀	6-8	3ft(90cm)
rhoeas 'Fairy Wings' 117	An	-	☀	6-9	12in(30cm)
somniferum 117, 297	An	-	☀	6-8	2½ft(76cm)
Parahebe lyallii 42	E Sh	-	☀	6	6in(15cm)
Parnassia palustris 334	P	M	◑	7-10	9in(23cm)

	PLANT TYPE	SOIL	SITUATION	PERIOD OF INTEREST	HEIGHT
Parthenocissus henryana 139, 198, 209	Cl	-	●/◑ S	6-10	15ft(4.5m)
quinquefolia 44	Cl	-	●/◑	9-10	20ft(6m)
tricuspidata 44, 271	Cl	-	◑	9-10	20ft(6m)
'Lowii' 209	Cl	-	◑	9-10	20ft(6m)
'Veitchii' 71, 209	Cl	-	◑	9-10	20ft(6m)
Passiflora caerulea 190, 287, 326	Cl	-	☀ S	6-9	20ft(6m)
Paulownia tomentosa 255	Tr	-	☀ S	5	15ft(4.5m)
Pelargonium 'Chocolate Mint' 168	E P	-	☀	6-9	2ft(60cm)
'Dale Queen' 246	E P	-	☀	6-9	12in(30cm)
'Ecco' 146	E P	-	☀	6-9	12in(30cm)
'Eroica' 146	E P	-	☀	6-9	12in(30cm)
'Fragrans' 168	E P	-	☀	6-9	2ft(60cm)
'Graveolens' 168	E P	-	☀	6-9	2ft(60cm)
'Mexican Beauty' 197	E P	-	☀	6-9	12in(30cm)
'Mini Cascade' 246	E P	-	☀	6-9	12in(30cm)
peltatum 'La France' 191	E P	-	☀	6-9	5ft(1.5m)
'L'Elegante' 143, 191	E P	-	☀	6-9	5ft(1.5m)
quercifolium 168	E P	-	☀	6-9	18in(45cm)
Pennisetum villosum 162, 219	P	-	☀	6-7	2ft(60cm)
Petroselinum crispum 289	An	-	◑	6-9	12in(30cm)
Petunia 'Celebrity Ice' 245	P	-	☀	6-8	9in(23cm)
'Resisto Series' 246	P	-	☀	6-8	9in(23cm)
Philadelphus 'Beauclerk' 51, 167	Sh	-	◑	6-7	6ft(1.8m)
coronarius 'Aureus' 41, 173, 212	Sh	D	◑	6-7	8ft(2.4m)
'Sybille' 189	Sh	-	◑	6-7	4ft(1.2m)
Phlox caespitosa 235	E P	-	☀	6-8	3in(7.5cm)
paniculata 175	P	-	☀	6-8	3ft(90cm)
Phormium 'Dazzler' 205	E P	M	☀ S	6-8	3ft(90cm)
tenax 24, 174, 255, 261	E P	-	☀ S	7-9	10ft(3m)
'Aurora' 147	E P	-	☀	1-12	2ft(60cm)
'Bronze Baby' 174	E P	-	☀	1-12	2ft(60cm)
Photinia × fraseri 'Red Robin' 260, 291	E Sh	-	◑ S	1-12,5	10ft(3m)
Phyllitis scolopendrium (now Asplenium scolopendrium)					
Phyllostachys aurea 192	Bam	-	☀	1-12	20ft(6m)
Physalis alkekengii 162, 287	P	-	◑	7,9	18in(45cm)
peruviana 287	P	-	☀	7,9	2ft(60cm)
Physocarpus opulifolius 'Dart's Gold' 134, 157	Sh	M	☀	4-5	10ft(3m)
Picea pungens 'Montgomery' 237	E Sh	-	☀	1-12	3ft(90cm)
Pieris 'Forest Flame' 238	E Sh	A	◑	6,1-12	6ft(1.8m)
formosa var. forrestii 236, 237	E Sh	A	◑ S	6,1-12	12ft(3.7m)
Pinus mugo 98, 113, 236	E Sh	-	☀	1-12	10ft(3m)
'Gnom' 245	E Sh	-	☀	1-12	6ft(1.8m)
pumila 236	E Sh	-	☀	1-12	6ft(1.8m)
sylvestris 67	E Tr	-	☀	1-12	30ft(9m)
Pittosporum tenuifolium 290	E Tr	-	☀	1-12,5	20ft(6m)
Plecostachys serpyllifolium 321	An	-	☀	6-10	12in(30cm)
Plectranthus coleoides 'Variegatus' 143	E P	-	◑ S	6-8	2ft(60cm)
Pleioblastus auricomus 154, 171	Bam	-	◑	1-12	6ft(1.8m)
variegatus 171, 173	Bam	-	◑	1-12	4ft(1.2m)
Plumbago auriculata 190	E Sh	-	☀ S	7-11	10ft(3m)
Polygonatum × hybridum 292	P	-	◑	5-6	4ft(1.2m)
Polygonum affine 65, 177, 238	P	-	◑	7-8	3ft(90cm)
Polystichum setiferum 19, 173	E P	L	●/◑	1-12	3ft(90cm)
'Acutilobum' 139	E P	L	●/◑	1-12	2ft(60cm)
Populus tremula 67, 326	Tr	-	☀	4-9	20ft(6m)
Portulaca grandiflora 355	An	D	☀	6-9	9in(23cm)
Potentilla pallida 136, 156	P	-	☀	6	2ft(60cm)
recta 'Citrina' (now P. r. pallida)					

	PLANT TYPE	SOIL	SITUATION	PERIOD OF INTEREST	HEIGHT
Pratia angulata 111	P	M	◑	5,9	½in(1.3cm)
Primula bulleyana 174	P	M	☼	7	2ft(60cm)
elatior 139	P	-	◑	4-5	9in(23cm)
florindae 174, 302	P	M	☼	7-9	3ft(90cm)
juliana 'Wanda' 173	P	-	◑	4	6in(15cm)
sikkimensis 174	P	-	☼	7-8	2ft(60cm)
vulgaris 175	P	-	◑	3-4	6in(15cm)
Prunus 'Amanogawa' 261	Tr	-	☼	4-5	15ft(4.5m)
avium 'Plena' 94	Tr	-	☼	4-5,9	20ft(6m)
cerasifera 'Pissardii' 47	Tr	-	◑	2-3 +	20ft(6m)
laurocerasus 46, 197	ESh	-	◑	4	15ft(4.5m)
'Otto Luyken' 206	ESh	-	◑	5 +	20ft(6m)
lusitanica 37, 71	ESh	-	◑	6	15ft(4.5m)
mume 168, 236	Tr	-	☼	2-3	10ft(3m)
persica 261	Tr	-	☼	1-4	12ft(3.7m)
sargentii 144	Tr	-	◑	3,9	15ft(4.5m)
serrula 75, 144, 147, 162, 163, 349	Tr	-	☼	5,11-4	15ft(4.5m)
serrulata 349	Tr	-	◑	4-5	15ft(4.5m)
spinosa 51	Sh	-	☼	4	15ft(4.5m)
× *subhirtella* 'Autumnalis' 135, 260, 343	Tr	-	◑	11-4,9	15ft(4.5m)
'Tai Haku' 10	Tr	-	◑	4	20ft(6m)
tenella 'Fire Hill' 236	Sh	-	☼	5-6	5ft(1.5m)
Pulmonaria officinalis 64, 259	P	-	●/◑	4-5	12in(30cm)
saccharata 135	P	-	●/◑	3-4	12in(30cm)
'Cambridge Blue' 156	P	-	●/◑	3-4	12in(30cm)
Pulsatilla vulgaris 162	P	L	☼	6-7	12in(30cm)
Pyracantha atalantioides 75	ESh	-	◑	6,9-3	10ft(3m)
'Aurea' 71	ESh	-	◑	6,9-3	10ft(3m)
'Orange Glow' 240	ESh	-	◑ S	6,9	15ft(4.5m)
Pyrus salicifolia 'Pendula' 197, 218, 219	Tr	-	☼	4-5	15ft(4.5m)
Quercus petraea 326	Tr	-	◑	10	30ft(9m)
robur 67, 326	Tr	-	◑	10	30ft(9m)

R

	PLANT TYPE	SOIL	SITUATION	PERIOD OF INTEREST	HEIGHT
Ramonda myconi 42	Rc	-	●/◑	4-5	6in(15cm)
Ranunculus aquatilis 306, 334	Aq	-	☼	4-7	-
Reseda odorata 167, 245	An	-	☼	7-9	2ft(60cm)
Rhamnus alaternus 'Argenteovariegatus' 92	ESh	-	◑	6-8,9	6ft(1.8m)
Rheum palmatum 142, 153, 168, 222, 317	P	-	◑	6	6ft(1.8m)
'Atrosanguineum' 171, 195, 317	P	-	◑	6	6ft(1.8m)
'Bowles' Crimson' 317	P	-	◑	6	6ft(1.8m)
Rhododendron bureavii 89	ESh	A	◑	5	10ft(3m)
calophytum 89	ESh	A	◑ S	4	20ft(6m)
Cilpinense 236, 238	ESh	A	◑	3-4	5ft(1.5m)
concatenans 239	ESh	A	◑	5	8ft(2.4m)
'Lemonora' 89	Sh	A	◑	5	5ft(1.5m)
luteum 116, 189	ESh	A	◑	4-5,9	8ft(2.4m)
'Mars' 116	ESh	A	◑	4-6	10ft(3m)
obtusum 89	ESh	A	◑	5-6	3ft(90cm)
Temple Belle 236	ESh	A	◑	4-5	8ft(2.4m)
Rhus hirta 162, 219	Tr	D	◑	6-7	15ft(4.5m)
'Laciniata' 219	Tr	D	◑	9-10	15ft(4.5m)
typhina (now *R. hirta*)					

	PLANT TYPE	SOIL	SITUATION	PERIOD OF INTEREST	HEIGHT
Ribes sanguineum 'Brocklebankii' 134	Sh	D	◑	3-5	8ft(2.4m)
Ricinus communis 159	An	-	☼	5-10	6ft(1.8m)
'Impala' 159	An	-	☼	5-10	6ft(1.8m)
Robinia hispida 42	Sh	D	☼ S	5-6	10ft(3m)
pseudoacacia 'Frisia' 71, 93, 96, 212, 219	Tr	D	☼	6	15ft(4.5m)
Rodgersia aesculifolia 317	P	M	◑	5-7	3ft(90cm)
pinnata 'Superba' 154	P	M	◑	5-7	4ft(1.2m)
podophylla 333	P	M	◑ S	5-7	4ft(1.2m)
tabularis 153	P	M	◑	5-7	3ft(90cm)
Romneya coulteri 116, 119, 271	P	-	☼ S	7-8	6ft(1.8m)
Rosa 'Alba Semiplena' 91	Ro	-	☼	5-6	8ft(2.4m)
'Albéric Barbier' 134	Ro	-	☼	6-9	15ft(4.5m)
'Albertine' 14, 16, 41, 138	Ro	-	☼	6-7	15ft(4.5m)
Alexandra Rose 361	Ro	-	☼	6-9	6ft(1.8m)
Allgold 71	Ro	-	☼	6-8	2½ft(76cm)
'Aloha' 197	Ro	-	☼	6-9	10ft(3m)
'Awakening' 218	Ro	-	◑	6-9	10ft(3m)
banksiae 'Lutea' 42, 69	Ro	-	☼	5-6	20ft(6m)
'Bantry Bay' 214	Ro	-	☼	6-9	12ft(3.7m)
'Blanc Double de Coubert' 206	Ro	-	☼	6-9	5ft(1.5m)
'Bloomfield Abundance' 245	Ro	-	☼	6-9	6ft(1.8m)
'Buff Beauty' 125, 173	Ro	-	◑	6,9	7ft(2m)
canina 61, 340	Ro	-	☼	6,9	10ft(3m)
'Cécile Brunner' 177	Ro	-	☼	6-9	3ft(90cm)
centifolia 91	Ro	-	☼	6-8	4ft(1.2m)
'Chinatown' 36	Ro	-	☼	6-9	5ft(1.5m)
'Complicata' 55	Ro	-	☼	6-9	10ft(3m)
'Dearest' 216	Ro	-	☼	6-9	2½ft(76cm)
'Debutante' (weeping standard) 205	Ro	-	☼	6-9	5ft(1.5m)
'Drummer Boy' 237	Ro	-	☼	6-8	3ft(90cm)
'Edith Holden' 294	Ro	-	☼	6-10	2½ft(76cm)
eglanteria 189	Ro	-	☼	6-7,9	6ft(1.8m)
'Emily Gray' 138	Ro	-	☼	6-8	15ft(4.5m)
'Etoile de Hollande' 217	Ro	-	☼	6-8	12ft(3.7m)
'Felicia' 36	Ro	-	☼	6-9	4ft(1.2m)
'Félicité Perpétue' 214	Ro	-	☼	6-8	15ft(4.5m)
'Fragrant Cloud' 165	Ro	-	☼	6-9	5ft(1.5m)
'Francine Austin' 177	Ro	-	☼	6-9	3ft(90cm)
foetida 'Persiana' 98	Ro	-	☼	6-7	6ft(1.8m)
'Fru Dagmar Hastrup' 206	Ro	-	☼	6-9,10	3ft(90cm)
gallica 'Versicolor' 160, 177	Ro	-	☼	6-7	2½ft(76cm)
'Glamis Castle' 205	Ro	-	☼	6-9	3ft(90cm)
glauca 117	Ro	-	☼	6-9	6ft(1.8m)
'Golden Showers' 13, 36	Ro	-	☼	6-10	10ft(3m)
'Golden Years' 217	Ro	-	☼	6-9	2½ft(76cm)
'Grouse' 341	Ro	-	☼	6-9	2ft(60cm)
'Guinée' 177	Ro	-	☼	6-7	15ft(4.5m)
'Happy Child' 216	Ro	-	☼	6-9	3ft(90cm)
'Iceberg' 101, 157, 205, 294, 357	Ro	-	☼	6-9	4ft(1.2m)
'Ispahan' 289	Ro	-	☼	6-9	5ft(1.5m)
'Königin von Dänemark' 160	Ro	-	◑	6-7	4ft(1.2m)
'Lady Hillingdon, Climbing' 165	Ro	-	☼	6-10	18ft(5.5m)
'La Reine Victoria' 167	Ro	-	☼	6-9	4ft(1.2m)
'Laura Ford' 38	Ro	-	☼	6-8	7ft(2m)
'Leverkusen' 218	Ro	-	☼	6-9	10ft(3m)
'Madame Alfred Carrière' 144, 188	Ro	-	☼	6-9	20ft(6m)
'Madame Grégoire Staechelin' 219	Ro	-	☼	6-8	20ft(6m)
'Maiden's Blush' 160	Ro	-	◑	6-7	6ft(1.8m)

PLANT TYPE **An** annual; **Aq** aquatic; **Bam** bamboo; **Bi** biennial; **Bu** bulb, corm, rhizome, tuber; **Cl** climber; **E** evergreen; **P** perennial; **Rc** rock plant; **Ro** rose; **Sh** shrub; **Tr** tree.

SOIL **A** needs acid soil; **L** needs alkaline soil; **M** needs moist to wet soil; **D** needs dry soil.

SITUATION ☼ does best in full sun; ◑ thrives in full sun or light shade; ● does best in full shade; ◑/● grows well in full sun, light shade or full shade; ●/◑ does best in full shade or light shade; **S** needs shelter; **W** tolerates wind.

PERIOD OF INTEREST numbers 1-12 represent the months when the plant has, for example, flowers, fruits or colourful bark.

HEIGHT represents height at maturity (or 20 years for trees and shrubs).

Name	PLANT TYPE	SOIL	SITUATION	PERIOD OF INTEREST	HEIGHT
'Maigold' 17	Ro	-	☼	6-7	15ft (4.5m)
'Masquerade, Climbing' 40	Ro	-	☼	6-9	18ft (5.5m)
'Max Graf' 341	Ro	-	☼	6-7	2ft (60cm)
'Meg' 11	Ro	-	☼	6-7	12ft (3.7m)
'Mermaid' 209	Ro	-	☀ S	6-9	30ft (9m)
moyesii 147	Ro	-	☼	6-7,9	10ft (3m)
'Mundi' (now R. gallica 'Versicolor')					
'Nathalie Nypels' 218	Ro	-	☼	6-9	3ft (90cm)
'Nevada' 181	Ro	-	☼	5-6	8ft (2.4m)
'New Dawn' 166, 167, 214, 218	Ro	-	☼	6-9	10ft (3m)
'Nimbus' 294	Ro	-	☼	6-8	3ft (90cm)
× odorata 'Mutabilis' 36	Ro	-	☼	6-10	5ft (1.5m)
'Viridiflora' 155	Ro	-	☼	6-10	3ft (90cm)
'Parade' 197	Ro	-	☽	6-9	10ft (3m)
'Partridge' 341	Ro	-	☼	6-9	2ft (60cm)
'Paulii' 64	Ro	-	☽	6-7	3ft (90cm)
'Penelope' 36, 224	Ro	-	☼	8-10	6ft (1.8m)
'Peppermint Ice' 294	Ro	-	☼	6-8	3ft (90cm)
'Pheasant' 341	Ro	-	☼	6-9	2ft (60cm)
'Pink Drift' 341	Ro	-	☼	6-8	2ft (60cm)
'Pink Perpétué' 197	Ro	-	☼	6-9	12ft (3.7m)
'Pompon de Paris, Climbing' 43	Ro	-	☼	6-9	12ft (3.7m)
'Princesse Louise' (weeping standard) 205	Ro	-	☼	6-7	6ft (1.8m)
'Prosperity' 157	Ro	-	☼	6-8	6ft (1.8m)
'Queen Elizabeth' 36	Ro	-	☼	6-10	6ft (1.8m)
'Queen of Denmark' (see Königin von Dänemark)					
'Rambling Rector' 36	Ro	-	☼	6-7,9	20ft (6m)
'Roseraie de l'Hay' 165, 167	Ro	-	☼	6-7	7ft (2m)
rubiginosa (now R. eglanteria)					
rugosa 38, 66, 306, 318	Ro	-	☼	6-10	7ft (2m)
'Seagull' 36	Ro	-	☼	6-7	15ft (4.5m)
'Surrey' 41	Ro	-	☼	6-9	2ft (60cm)
'Tall Story' 79	Ro	-	☽	7-9	3ft (90cm)
'The Fairy' 148, 242	Ro	-	☼	6-9	2ft (60cm)
'Wedding Day' 216	Ro	-	☼	6-7	30ft (9m)
xanthina 'Canary Bird' 206	Ro	-	☼	5-6	8ft (2.4m)
'Zéphirine Drouhin' 13, 146, 162	Ro	-	☼	6-9	9ft (2.7m)
Rosmarinus officinalis 75	ESh	-	☼	4-9	6ft (1.8m)
'Miss Jessop's Upright' 336	ESh	-	☼	4-9	6ft (1.8m)
Prostratus Group 289	ESh	-	☼	4-9	18in (45cm)
'Severn Sea' 238	ESh	-	☼	4-9	3ft (90cm)
Rubus idaeus 'Aureus' 261	Sh	-	☽	5-9	2½ft (76cm)
ulmifolius 'Bellidiflorus' 269	Sh	-	☽	6-9	8ft (2.4m)
Rudbeckia laciniata 269	P	-	☼	8-9	7ft (2m)
Ruta graveolens 161	ESh	-	☼	5-10	2ft (60cm)

S

Name	PLANT TYPE	SOIL	SITUATION	PERIOD OF INTEREST	HEIGHT
Sagina subulata 111	Rc	-	☼	4-9	2in (5cm)
Sagittaria sagittifolia 'Flore Pleno' 321	Aq	-	☼	7	2½ft (76cm)
Salix acutifolia 'Blue Streak' 134	Sh	M	☼	10-4	15ft (4.5m)
alba 326	Tr	M	☼	5	20ft (6m)
'Chermesina' 51	Tr	M	☼	10-4	20ft (6m)
apoda 162	Sh	-	☼	3-4	3in (7.5cm)
caprea 67	Sh	-	☼	3-4	15ft (4.5m)
'Kilmarnock' 162, 217, 309	Sh	-	☼	3-4	6ft (1.8m)
daphnoides 51	Sh	-	☼	11-4	25ft (7.5m)
exigua 309	Sh	-	☼	6-10	12ft (3.7m)
fargesii 162	Sh	-	☼	5-10	10ft (3m)
fragilis 67	Tr	-	☼	3	15ft (4.5m)
hastata 'Wehrhahnii' 162	Sh	-	☼	4	6ft (1.8m)
lanata 135	Sh	-	☼	4-5	4ft (1.2m)
matsudana 'Tortuosa' 224	Tr	-	☼	4	20ft (6m)
'Melanostachys' 154	Sh	-	☼	4	10ft (3m)
purpurea 'Pendula' 309	Sh	-	☼	3-4	8ft (2.4m)

Name	PLANT TYPE	SOIL	SITUATION	PERIOD OF INTEREST	HEIGHT
Salvia coccinea 'Lady in Red' 241	An	-	☼	8-9	2ft (60cm)
farinacea 241	An	-	☼	6-8	2ft (60cm)
officinalis 289	ESh	-	☼	6-8	3ft (90cm)
'Icterina' 289	ESh	-	☼	5-9	2ft (60cm)
'Kew Gold' 228, 289	ESh	-	☼	5-9	2ft (60cm)
'Purpurascens' 119, 289	ESh	-	☼	6-8	2ft (60cm)
'Tricolor' 197	ESh	-	☼	6-8	2ft (60cm)
patens 143	P	-	☼	8-9	2ft (60cm)
rutilans 164	Sh	-	☼ S	8-9	2ft (60cm)
Sambucus nigra 51, 292	Tr	-	☽	6,9	15ft (4.5m)
'Guincho' 292	Tr	-	☽	6,9	15ft (4.5m)
racemosa 'Plumosa Aurea' 22, 212, 292	Sh	-	☽	5-9	10ft (3m)
Santolina chamaecyparissus 75, 216, 271	ESh	-	☼	7	2ft (60cm)
'Nana' 14	ESh	-	☼	7	9in (23cm)
rosmarinifolia 26, 219	ESh	-	☼	7	18in (45cm)
virens 101	ESh	-	☼	7	2ft (60cm)
Saponaria officinalis 339	P	-	☼	7-8	3ft (90cm)
Sarcococca confusa 21, 141	ESh	-	☽	1-3	5ft (1.5m)
hookeriana var. digyna 260	ESh	-	☽	12-3	5ft (1.5m)
var. humilis 166	ESh	-	☽	1-3	18in (45cm)
humilis (now S. h. var. humilis)					
Saxifraga cotyledon 42	ERc	-	☽	6-8	2ft (60cm)
× urbium 13, 284	EP	-	●/☽	6-9	12in (30cm)
Scabiosa caucasica 'Clive Greaves' 66	P	-	☼	6-8	2ft (60cm)
'Mount Cook' 136	P	-	☼	6-9	2ft (60cm)
Schisandra rubriflora 210	Cl	-	☽ S	8-9	20ft (6m)
Schizophragma hydrangeoides 44	Cl	-	☽	6-8	30ft (9m)
Scilla non-scripta (now Hyacinthoides non-scripta)					
siberica 115, 205	Bu	L	☽	3	6in (15cm)
Scrophularia aquatica 'Variegata' 154	P	-	☽	6-10	3ft (90cm)
Sedum 'Ruby Glow' 14	P	-	☼	7-9	12in (30cm)
spectabile 154, 337, 338	P	-	☼	7-9	18in (45cm)
Sempervivum montanum 42	ERc	-	☼	1-12	6in (15cm)
Senecio cineraria 154, 239, 292 'Sunshine' (now Brachyglottis 'Sunshine')	ESh	-	☼	6-10	2ft (60cm)
tanguticus 339	P	-	☽	9-10	5ft (1.5m)
Senna didymobotrya 164	ESh	-	☼	1-12	10ft (3m)
Shibataea kumasasa 17	Bam	-	☽	1-12	2ft (60cm)
Skimmia japonica 211	ESh	-	☽	4-5, 10	5ft (1.5m)
subsp. reevesiana 260	ESh	-	☽	4-5, 10	2ft (60cm)
'Rubella' 213, 240	ESh	-	☽	4-5	5ft (1.5m)
Smilacina racemosa 139	P	-	●/☽	5-6	3ft (90cm)
Solanum crispum 40, 115	Cl	-	☼ S	8	20ft (6m)
'Glasnevin' 42, 134	Cl	-	☼ S	6-8	20ft (6m)
jasminoides 'Album' 225	Cl	-	☼ S	7-9	20ft (6m)
pseudocapsicum 240	ESh	-	☼	9-12	2ft (60cm)
Soleirolia soleirolii 110, 214	ERc	-	☽	1-12	1in (2.5cm)
Sollya heterophylla 190	ECl	-	☽ S	6-10	10ft (3m)
Sorbus aucuparia 89, 326	Tr	-	☽	6,8-9	20ft (6m)
cashmiriana 189	Tr	-	☼	6,9	10ft (3m)
hupehensis 28, 189	Tr	-	☼	5,9-10	20ft (6m)
reducta 239	Sh	-	☼	8-10	12in (30cm)
vilmorinii 189	Tr	-	☼	6,9-10	10ft (3m)
Spartium junceum 116	ESh	-	☼	6-9	10ft (3m)
Sphaeralcea munroana 231	P	-	☼	6-10	18in (45cm)

	PLANT TYPE	SOIL	SITUATION	PERIOD OF INTEREST	HEIGHT
Spiraea × arguta 340	Sh	-	☽	6-7	4ft(1.2m)
japonica 'Goldflame' 41	Sh	-	☼	6-8	5ft(1.5m)
Stachys byzantina 29, 110, 119, 160, 162, 271	EP	-	☼	1-12	6in(15cm)
'Silver Carpet' 108	EP	-	☼	1-12	6in(15cm)
macrantha 154	P	-	☼	7-8	2ft(60cm)
Stephanotis floribunda 201	ECl	-	☼ S	4-9	15ft(4.5m)
Sternbergia lutea 142	Bu	-	☼	9	6in(15cm)
Stipa gigantea 208	P	D	☼	6-8	6ft(1.8m)
pennata 161, 219	P	D	☼	6-8	2½ft(76cm)
Symphytum 'Hidcote Pink' 352	P	-	☽	6-7	2ft(60cm)
officinale 341, 352, 353	P	M	☽	6-7	4ft(1.2m)
Syringa vulgaris 189	Sh	-	☼	5-6	15ft(4.5m)

T

	PLANT TYPE	SOIL	SITUATION	PERIOD OF INTEREST	HEIGHT
Tagetes erecta 157	An	-	☼	6-9	2½ft(76cm)
patula 157	An	-	☼	6-9	12in(30cm)
Tamarix pentandra 51	Sh	-	☼	5-10	12ft(3.7m)
Tanacetum parthenium 'Aureum' 173	P	-	☼	6-9	12in(30cm)
Taxus baccata 45, 148	ETr	L	☽	1-12	15ft(4.5m)
'Fastigiata' 31, 79	ESh	L	☽	1-12	10ft(3m)
Teucrium chamaedrys 106	EP	-	☼	8	9in(23cm)
Thunbergia alata 13, 195, 219, 279	An	-	☼ S	6-9	10ft(3m)
Thymus × citriodorus 163	ESh	-	☼	6-8	6in(15cm)
serpyllum 108, 187, 197, 289	ERc	-	☼	6-8	2in(5cm)
coccineus 'Major' 337	ERc	-	☼	6-8	2in(5cm)
vulgaris 289, 336	ESh	-	☼	6-8	12in(30cm)
Tiarella cordifolia 29	EP	-	●/☽	6	12in(30cm)
Tilia cordata 49, 353	Tr	-	☽	7	25ft(7.5m)
Trachelospermum jasminoides 134, 166, 189, 195, 225	ECl	A	☼ S	7-8	12ft(3.7m)
Trachycarpus fortunei 96, 98, 138, 199, 215, 219, 222, 260 261	ETr	-	☼	5-6	6ft(1.8m)
Tradescantia 'Isis' 14	P	-	☽	7-9	2ft(60cm)
zebrina 'Purpusii' 56	EP	-	☽	4-9	trailing
Trillium grandiflorum 270	P	A	☽	4-6	12in(30cm)
Triteleia laxa 66	Bu	-	☼	5-6	9in(23cm)
Tropaeolum majus 52, 53, 56	An	-	☼	6-9	8ft(2.4m)
peregrinum 35, 52	An	-	☽ S	7-10	12ft(3.7m)
Tulipa 'Apricot Beauty' 117, 173	Bu	-	☼	4	15in(38cm)
'Black Parrot' 117	Bu	-	☼	4-5	2ft(60cm)
'China Pink' 293	Bu	-	☼	4	2ft(60cm)
'Clara Butt' 160	Bu	-	☼	5	2½ft(76cm)
'Couleur Cardinal' 158	Bu	-	☼	4	15in(38cm)
'Diana' 231	Bu	-	☼	4	15in(38cm)
'Greenland' 160	Bu	-	☼	4-5	2½ft(76cm)
kaufmanniana 239	Bu	-	☼	4-5	10in(25cm)
'Negrita' 173	Bu	-	☼	4-5	18in(45cm)
'Orange Parrot' 293	Bu	-	☼	4-5	2ft(60cm)
'Peach Blossom' 299	Bu	-	☼	4	15in(38cm)
'Purissima' 10, 214	Bu	-	☼	4	18in(45cm)
'Queen of the Night' 155	Bu	-	☼	5	2½ft(76cm)
'Red Riding Hood' 12	Bu	-	☼	3-4	6in(15cm)

	PLANT TYPE	SOIL	SITUATION	PERIOD OF INTEREST	HEIGHT
'Schoonord' 293	Bu	-	☼	4	15in(38cm)
'Spring Green' 156	Bu	-	☼	4-5	3ft(90cm)
'Springtime' 173	Bu	-	☼	4	2ft(60cm)
'White Triumphator' 292	Bu	-	☼	5	2½ft(76cm)
Typha minima 309, 333	P	M	☼	6-9	2½ft(76cm)

U, V

	PLANT TYPE	SOIL	SITUATION	PERIOD OF INTEREST	HEIGHT
Ursinia anethoides 159	An	-	☼	6-9	18in(45cm)
Valeriana officinalis 334	P	-	☼	6-7	4ft(1.2m)
Veratrum nigrum 147	P	-	☽	7-8	6ft(1.8m)
Verbascum bombyciferum 162	Bi	L	☼	6-7	6ft(1.8m)
Verbena 'Hidcote Purple' 321	P	-	☼	8-9	6in(15cm)
× hybrida 'Showtime' 246	P	-	☽ S	8	3ft(90cm)
'Loveliness' 242	P	-	☼	7-9	6in(15cm)
'Sissinghurst' 208	P	-	☼ S	7-9	9in(23cm)
Veronica beccabunga 333	P	M	☽	7-8	9in(23cm)
Viburnum × bodnantense 165, 213	Sh	-	☽	10-3	12ft(3.7m)
'Dawn' 37, 291	Sh	-	☽	10-3	12ft(3.7m)
'Deben' 261	Sh	-	☽	1-5	12ft(3.7m)
× burkwoodii 26, 245, 336	ESh	-	☽	3-5	8ft(2.4m)
carlesii 152	Sh	-	☽	4-5	7ft(2m)
davidii 17, 21, 291	ESh	-	☽	6,10-1	4ft(1.2m)
farreri 135, 165, 237	Sh	-	☽ S	11-3	8ft(2.4m)
rhytidophyllum 75, 137	ESh	-	☽	5-6	15ft(4.5m)
tinus 53, 94, 137, 210, 243	ESh	-	☽	2-4	12ft(3.7m)
Vinca major 237	EP	-	☽/●	5-9	18in(45cm)
'Variegata' 21, 197	EP	-	☽/●	5-9	18in(45cm)
minor 237, 240, 333, 337	EP	-	☽/●	4-8	6in(15cm)
'Aureovariegata' 64	EP	-	☽/●	3-7,10	6in(15cm)
Viola 'Antique Shades' 240	An	-	☼	5-9	6in(15cm)
cornuta 'Alba' 148	P	-	☽	7-9	9in(23cm)
'Maggie Mott' 321	P	-	☽	5-9	6in(15cm)
'Mollie Sanderson' 155	P	-	☽	5-9	6in(15cm)
odorata 'Coeur d'Alsace' 165, 166	P	-	☽ S	5-6	9in(23cm)
'Admiral Avellan' 165	P	-	☽ S	5-6	9in(23cm)
'Quatre Saisons' 166	P	-	☽	5-9	9in(23cm)
tricolor 'Bowles' Black' 155	An	-	☽	5-9	6in(15cm)
× wittrockiana 246	An	-	☽	5-9	6in(15cm)
'Black Beauty' 231	An	-	☽	5-9	6in(15cm)
Vitis 'Brandt' 215	Cl	-	☽	6-10	20ft(6m)
coignetiae 215, 292	Cl	-	☽	10	30ft(9m)
vinifera 321	Cl	-	☼	6-10	20ft(6m)
'Purpurea' 41, 197, 201, 218, 292, 365	Cl	-	☽	6-10	20ft(6m)

W, Y, Z

	PLANT TYPE	SOIL	SITUATION	PERIOD OF INTEREST	HEIGHT
Weigela florida 'Aureovariegata' 94	Sh	-	☽	5-6,5-9	6ft(1.8m)
'Foliis Purpureis' 41	Sh	-	☼	5-6	6ft(1.8m)
'Florida Variegata' 154	Sh	-	☽	5-6,5-9	6ft(1.8m)
Yucca filamentosa 86, 117	ESh	-	☼	7-8	5ft(1.5m)
flaccida 17	ESh	-	☼	7-8	5ft(1.5m)
gloriosa 236, 255, 271	ESh	-	☼	7-9	8ft(2.4m)
'Variegata' 239	ESh	-	☼	7-9	8ft(2.4m)
Zantedeschia aethiopica 248, 319	EP	-	☽	6-8	3ft(90cm)
'Crowborough' 315, 317	EP	-	☽	6-8	3ft(90cm)

PLANT TYPE **An** annual; **Aq** aquatic; **Bam** bamboo; **Bi** biennial; **Bu** bulb, corm, rhizome, tuber; **Cl** climber; **E** evergreen; **P** perennial; **Rc** rock plant; **Ro** rose; **Sh** shrub; **Tr** tree.

SOIL **A** needs acid soil; **L** needs alkaline soil; **M** needs moist to wet soil; **D** needs dry soil.

SITUATION ☼ does best in full sun; ☽ thrives in full sun or light shade; ● does best in full shade; ☽/● grows well in full sun, light shade or full shade; ●/☽ does best in full shade or light shade; **S** needs shelter; **W** tolerates wind.

PERIOD OF INTEREST numbers 1-12 represent the months when the plant has, for example, flowers, fruits or colourful bark.

HEIGHT represents height at maturity (or 20 years for trees and shrubs).

COMMON AND BOTANICAL NAMES

The chart on pp.366-76 lists plants by their botanical names; below are the botanical names of plants mentioned in the text by common name only, so that you can look them up in the chart.

aconite, winter *Eranthis hyemalis*
alder *Alnus*
arrowhead *Sagittaria sagittifolia*
ash *Fraxinus excelsior*
aspen, quaking *Populus tremula*
aubrietia *Aubrieta*
autumn crocus *Colchicum autumnale*, *Crocus nudiflorus*
azalea *Rhododendron*
balm *Melissa officinalis*
bamboo *Nandina, Phyllostachys, Pleioblastus, Shibataea*
basil *Ocimum basilicum*
bay *Laurus nobilis*
beech *Fagus sylvatica*
bellflower *Campanula*
birch *Betula*
black-eyed Susan *Thunbergia alata*
blackthorn *Prunus spinosa*
bluebell *Hyacinthoides non-scripta*
bogbean *Menyanthes trifoliata*
borage *Borago*
box *Buxus*
broom *Cytisus, Genista*
bugle *Ajuga reptans*
busy lizzie *Impatiens*
cabbage palm *Cordyline*
camomile *Chamaemelum nobile*
canary creeper *Tropaeolum peregrinum*
candytuft *Iberis*
Canterbury bell *Campanula*
catmint *Nepeta*
cherry *Prunus*
cherry, autumn flowering *Prunus × subhirtella* 'Autumnalis'
cherry, Japanese *Prunus* 'Amanogawa'
cherry pie *Heliotropium arborescens*
cherry, wild *Prunus avium*
Chinese lantern *Physalis alkekengi*
chives *Allium schoenoprasum*
chrysanthemum *Argyranthemum, Dendranthema*
columbine *Aquilegia*
comfrey *Symphytum*
coriander *Coriandrum sativum*
cornflower *Centaurea cyanus*
cotton lavender *Santolina chamaecyparissus*
cow parsley *Anthriscus sylvestris*
cowslip, giant *Primula florindae*
crab apple *Malus*
cranesbill *Geranium*
creeping Jenny *Lysimachia nummularia*
curry plant *Helichrysum italicum*
cypress *Chamaecyparis, Cupressus*
daffodil *Narcissus*
dill *Anethum graveolens*
dog rose *Rosa canina*
dogwood *Cornus*
elder *Sambucus*
evening primrose *Oenothera biennis*

fennel *Foeniculum vulgare*
fern *Asplenium, Athyrium, Dryopteris, Matteuccia, Onoclea, Polystichum*
fern, maidenhair *Adiantum venustum*
fern, royal *Osmunda regalis*
feverfew *Tanacetum parthenium*
flax, New Zealand *Phormium tenax*
forget-me-not *Myosotis*
forget-me-not, water *Myosotis scorpioides*
foxglove *Digitalis*
fritillary *Fritillaria*
gentian *Gentiana*
globe thistle *Echinops*
golden rod *Solidago*
grape hyacinth *Muscari*
hawthorn *Crataegus*
hawthorn, water *Aponogeton distachyos*
hazel, corkscrew *Corylus avellana* 'Contorta'
heath *Erica*
heather *Calluna vulgaris*
heliotrope *Heliotropium*
hellebore *Helleborus*
holly *Ilex*
hollyhock *Alcea*
honesty *Lunaria*
honeysuckle *Lonicera*
honeysuckle, bush *Lonicera nitida*
hop *Humulus*
hornbeam *Carpinus betulus*
hyacinth *Hyacinthus*
hyssop *Hyssopus officinalis*
ice plant *Sedum*
iris, water *Iris laevigata*
ivy *Hedera*
jasmine *Jasminum*
jasmine, winter *Jasminum nudiflorum*
juniper *Juniperus*
king-cup *Caltha palustris*
lady's mantle *Alchemilla mollis*
lamb's tongue *Stachys byzantina*
laurel, cherry *Prunus laurocerasus*
laurel, Portugal *Prunus lusitanica*
laurel, spotted *Aucuba*
lavender *Lavandula*
lemon *Citrus limon*
lilac *Syringa*
lily *Lilium*
lily, Madonna *Lilium candidum*
lily-of-the-valley *Convallaria majalis*
lily, water *Nymphaea*
ling *Calluna vulgaris*
London pride *Saxifraga × urbium*
love-in-a-mist *Nigella damascena*
lupin *Lupinus*
mallow *Lavatera*
maple *Acer*
marigold, African *Tagetes erecta*
marigold, French *Tagetes patula*
marigold, marsh *Caltha palustris*
marigold, pot *Calendula officinalis*
marjoram *Origanum*
Mexican orange blossom *Choisya ternata*

Michaelmas daisy *Aster*
mignonette *Reseda*
mint *Mentha*
mock orange *Philadelphus*
morning glory *Ipomoea*
mullein *Verbascum*
nasturtium *Tropaeolum majus*
oak *Quercus*
oleander *Nerium oleander*
oxlip *Primula elatior*
pampas grass *Cortaderia*
pansy *Viola*
parsley *Petroselinum crispum*
passionflower *Passiflora*
peach *Prunus persica*
pearlwort *Sagina*
peony *Paeonia*
periwinkle *Vinca*
pine *Pinus*
pink *Dianthus*
pink, maiden *Dianthus deltoides*
poppy *Papaver*
poppy, Californian *Eschscholzia californica*
poppy, Himalayan blue *Meconopsis betonicifolia*
poppy, Welsh *Meconopsis cambrica*
potato vine *Solanum jasminoides*
primrose *Primula vulgaris*
privet *Ligustrum*
quince, flowering *Chaenomeles*
red-hot poker *Kniphofia*
reed *Juncus*
reedmace *Typha*
rose *Rosa*
rosemary *Rosmarinus officinalis*
rowan *Sorbus aucuparia*
rue *Ruta*
sage *Salvia officinalis*
saxifrage *Saxifraga*
scabious *Scabiosa*
sedge *Carex*
silver birch *Betula pendula*
snowdrop *Galanthus*
Solomon's seal *Polygonatum*
speedwell *Veronica*
spirea *Spiraea*
stock *Matthiola*
stock, night-scented *Matthiola bicornis*
sunflower *Helianthus*
sweet briar *Rosa eglanteria*
sweet pea *Lathyrus*
sweet pea, everlasting *Lathyrus latifolius*
sweet rocket *Hesperis matronalis*
sweet william *Dianthus barbatus*
sycamore *Acer pseudoplatanus*
thrift *Armeria maritima*
thyme *Thymus*
tobacco plant *Nicotiana*
tulip *Tulipa*
vine *Vitis*
violet *Viola*
violet, water *Hottonia palustris*
viper's bugloss *Echium vulgare*
Virginia creeper *Parthenocissus quinquefolia*
wallflower *Erysimum*
whitebeam *Sorbus aria*
willow *Salix*
witch hazel *Hamamelis*
yew *Taxus baccata*

INDEX

A number in *italics* indicates that the reference is to a caption only.

ACKNOWLEDGMENTS

The publishers would like to thank the following people, gardens, companies and organisations for their help during the preparation of illustrations for *Good Ideas for Your Garden*.

Advance Moulding Components Ltd, Southall, Middlesex. Agriframes Ltd, East Grinstead, W Sussex. Airport Aquaria, West Drayton, Middlesex. Allibert (UK) Ltd, Droitwich, Hereford and Worcs. Atlas Stone Products, Chipping Camden, Gloucs. David Austin Roses, Wolverhampton, W Midlands. Barnsley House GDF, Cirencester, Gloucs. Gillian and Kenneth Beckett. Bel Mondo Garden Features, London. Bressingham Gardens, Diss, Norfolk. Bulrush Peat Co Ltd, Magherafelt, Co Londonderry, N Ireland. Cannock Gates Ltd, Cannock, Staffs. Capital Garden Products Ltd, Ticehurst, E Sussex. Chatsworth Carpenters, Bakewell, Derbyshire. The Chelsea Physic Garden, London. The Clarke Tinwhistle Co Ltd, Five Oak Green, Kent. J.B. Corrie and Co Ltd, Petersfield, Hants. Andrew Crace Designs, Much Hadham, Herts. The Dale Stone Co Ltd, Escrick, N Yorks. Darlac Products, Datchet, Berks. Dobies, Torquay, Devon. Duct and Access Covers Ltd, Crosskeys, Gwent. Earlfarm Ltd, Woodbridge, Suffolk. East Malling Research Station, East Malling, Kent. Forest Fencing Ltd, Stanford Court, Stanford Bridge, Hereford and Worcs. Forsham Cottage Arks, Ashford, Kent. Mr Fothergills Seeds, Kentford, Newmarket, Suffolk. Geebro Ltd, Hailsham, E Sussex. Grosfillex (UK) Ltd, London. Habitat UK Ltd, London. HanD-I-Yman, Wickford, Essex. R. Harkness and Co Ltd, Hitchin, Herts. Harvest Ironcraft, Tenterden, Kent. Heals, London. Hozelock Ltd, Aylesbury, Bucks. Jackson & Sons (Fencing) Ltd, Ashford, Kent. C & K Jones, Tarvin, Cheshire. Kootensaw Dovecotes, Totnes, Devon. Leisure and Outdoor Furniture Association (LOFA), Surbiton, Surrey. Lotus Water Garden Products Ltd, Burnley, Lancs. Marley Extrusions Ltd, Maidstone, Kent. Marshalls Mono Ltd, Halifax, W Yorks. Mattocks Roses, Oxford. M & M Timber Co Ltd, Kidderminster, Hereford and Worcs. Mid Wales Rustic, Llandrindod Wells, Powys. Netlon Ltd, Blackburn, Lancs. Ollerton Engineering Services Ltd, Preston, Lancs. Ornamental Heritage, Coventry Rd, Kingsbury, Warks. J. Parker Dutch Bulbs Ltd, Old Trafford, Manchester. Parlamast Ltd, Driffield, N Yorks. Past Times, Witney, Oxford. Allen Paterson. Photos Horticultural Picture Library. Pots and Pithoi, Turners Hill, W Sussex. Price's Patent Candle Co Ltd, London. Proper Gates, Ludlow, Shropshire. Rapitest Ltd, Corwen, Clwyd. Redwood Stone Ltd, Wells, Somerset. Rockways Water Garden Features, Chelmsford, Essex. The Royal Horticultural Society's Garden, Wisley, Surrey. Sainsbury's Homebase Ltd, Wallington, London. Savill and Valley Gardens, Windsor Great Park, Berkshire. Harry Smith Collection. Stapeley Water Gardens Ltd, Nantwich, Cheshire. Stuart Garden Architecture, Wiveliscombe, Somerset. The Stewart Company, Croydon, Surrey. Standard Manufacturing Co, Derby. Suttons Seeds Ltd, Torquay, Devon. Thompson and Morgan (Ipswich) Ltd, Ipswich, Suffolk. Trackwork Ltd, Doncaster, S Yorks. Traditional Garden Supply Co Ltd, Cranleigh, Surrey. Thos Trevis Smith Ltd, Cradley Heath, W Midlands. Unwins Seeds Ltd, Histon, Cambridge. Van Tubergen UK, Diss, Norfolk. Verdigris Ltd, Stevenage, Herts. Westlanz Swags Ltd, Carmarthen, Dyfed. Whitehouse Ivies, Fordham, Colchester, Essex. C J Wildbird Foods, Hereford and Worcs. Wolf Tools, Ross-on-Wye, Hereford and Worcs.

PICTURE CREDITS

Pictures are identified by their position on the page. This is abbreviated as *t* top, *c* centre, *b* bottom, *l* left, *r* right, and combinations such as *cl* centre left and *br* bottom right. A name in brackets indicates the name, designer or owner of the garden in the picture.

8 S & O Mathews. 10 Clive Nichols. 11 *t* Eric Crichton, *b* S & O Mathews. 13 *t* Juliette Wade, *b* Will Giles. 14 Eric Crichton. 15 *t* and *b* Photos Horticultural Picture Library. 18 *t* John Glover, *b* Neil Holmes. 19 Eric Crichton. 20 *t* George Leveque, *br* Andrew Lawson. 21 *l* Eric Crichton, *r* Clive Nichols (Jill Billington). 24 Biofotos. 25 Andrew Lawson. 26 Elizabeth Whiting. 28 *t* Juliette Wade, *b* Susanna Brown. 29 *t* Tania Midgley, *c* Photos Horticultural Picture Library, *b* Ardea, London. 30 *l* The Garden Picture Library/Stephen Jury. 30-31 Biofotos. 32 Jerry Harpur. 34 Hugh Palmer. 35 Jerry Harpur. 38 Jerry Harpur. 40 Jerry Harpur. 42 Royal Botanic Garden, Edinburgh. 43 *t* Clive Nichols, *b* Eric Crichton. 44 *t* Elizabeth Whiting/Dennis Stone, *b* Photos Horticultural Picture Library. 45 Jacqui Hurst. 47 *t* Biofotos, *c* Eric Crichton, *b* Photos Horticultural Picture Library. 48 *l* and *r* Photos Horticultural Picture Library. 50 The Garden Picture Library/John Fero Sims. 51 *t* Harry Smith Collection, *bl* S & O Mathews, *br* Eric Crichton. 52 Clive Nichols. 53 *t* Photos Horticultural Picture Library, *b* Harry Smith Collection. 54 *tl* Tania Midgley. 54-55 Clive Nichols. 55 The Garden Picture Library/Marijke Heuff. 56 *l* Harry Smith Collection. 56-57 Andrew Lawson. 58 Planet Earth Pictures/Wayne Harris. 60 *l* Jerry Harpur. 61 *t* and *b* Elizabeth Whiting. 62 *bl* S & O Mathews. 62-63 John Glover. 64-65 Ardea, London/Bob Gibbons. 65 *tr* Jonathan Buckley, *bl* The Garden Picture Library/John Glover. 66 *t* Biofotos, *bl* Photos Horticultural Picture Library. 67 *t* Beckett Picture Library, *bl* Ardea, London/Ian Beames. 68 Ardea, London/Bob Gibbons. 69 *t* Eric Crichton, *cl* Christine Ternynck. 70 Harry Smith Collection. 72 *t* Biofotos, *cl* Clive Nichols. 74 Martin Thompson. 76 *b* Tania Midgley. 76-77 S & O Mathews. 77 *bl* Bruce Coleman Ltd/Eric Crichton. 78 *l* The National Trust/John Bethell. 78-79 Photos Horticultural Picture Library. 80 The Garden Picture Library/Marijke Heuff. 82 George Leveque. 83 Elizabeth Whiting. 84-85 Clive Nichols (Myles Challis). 86 *bl* Elizabeth Whiting, *br* Andrew Lawson. 86-87 The Garden Picture Library/John Glover. 87 Harry Smith Collection. 90 *b* Clive Nichols (Jill Billington). 90-91 Elizabeth Whiting. 91 *tl* and *l* Elizabeth Whiting. 92 *bl* The Garden Picture Library/Marijke Heuff. 92-93 S & O Mathews. 93 *tr* Andrew Lawson, *bl* Ardea, London/A.P. Paterson. 94 Juliette Wade. 95 The Garden Picture Library/John Miller. 97 Juliette Wade. 98 Jerry Harpur. 99 *t* Jerry Harpur, *c* The Garden Picture Library/Ron Sutherland, *b* Elizabeth Whiting.

100 *l* S & O Mathews. 100-1 S & O Mathews. 102 The Garden Picture Library/Jane Legate. 104 George Leveque. 105 *t* Marijke Heuff, *b* Andrew Lawson. 106 *b* Andrew Lawson. 106-7 Andrew Lawson. 108 *cl* John Glover, *br* The Garden Picture Library/Ron Sutherland. 109 *t* Clive Nichols (J. Billington), *b* The Garden Picture Library/Ron Sutherland. 110 *br* Andrew Lawson. 110-11 S & O Mathews. 111 Brian Chapple. 112 *b* George Leveque. 112-13 The Garden Picture Library/John Glover. 113 *t* Clive Nichols, *c* John Glover, *b* Jerry Harpur. 114 Will Giles. 115 *t* Brian Chapple, *b* Jerry Harpur. 116-17 Clive Nichols. 120 *t* Elizabeth Whiting, *c* Eric Crichton, *b* Juliette Wade. 121 *t* Jerry Harpur, *l* Christine Ternynck, *c* Elizabeth Whiting, *b* Jerry Harpur. 122 *b* Elizabeth Whiting/Jerry Harpur. 122-3 The Garden Picture Library/Jerry Parvia. 123 Jerry Harpur (Rofford Manor). 124 *l* Eric Crichton. 124-5 Biofotos. 126 Jacqui Hurst. 128 Jacqui Hurst. 129 Jerry Harpur. 130-1 S & O Mathews. 132 The Garden Picture Library/Clay Perry. 137 John Glover. 138 *tl* and *tr* S & O Mathews. 140 *tr* Harry Smith Collection. 140-1 Harry Smith Collection. 144 The Garden Picture Library/Karin Craddock. 145 Andrew Lawson. 146 *t* Jerry Harpur, *b* Tim Sandall. 147 Marijke Heuff. 148 *l* The National Trust/Nick Meers. 148-9 Patrick Taylor. 150 Clive Nichols. 152 Clive Nichols. 153 George Leveque. 154 John Glover. 156 *tl* Andrew Lawson. 156-7 Clive Nichols. 157 *t* Clay Perry, *bl* Christine Ternynck. 158-9 Clive Nichols. 159 *t* S & O Mathews, *b* Eric Crichton. 160 *t* and *b* S & O Mathews. 161 Eric Crichton. 162 *t* John Glover, *c* Andrew Lawson, *b* Tim Sandall. 164 Tania Midgley. 166-7 George Leveque. 167 Photos Horticultural Picture Library. 168 Andrew Lawson. 169 The Garden Picture Library/Brian Carter. 170 Photos Horticultural Picture Library. 172 *b* Clive Nichols. 172-3 S & O Mathews, *b* Elizabeth Whiting. 173 George Leveque. 174 *tl* Christine Ternynck. 174-5 Clay Perry. 175 *br* Clive Nichols. 176 *l* S & O Mathews. 176-7 The National Trust/Stephen Robson. 178 Jerry Harpur. 180 Photos Horticultural Picture Library. 181 *t* Elizabeth Whiting, *bl* Harry Smith Collection. 182 *t* Jonathan Buckley, *b* Elizabeth Whiting. 184 The Garden Picture Library/Linda Burgess. 185 Andrew Lawson. 186 S & O Mathews. 187 *t* The Garden Picture Library/Anthony Paul, *bl* Photos Horticultural Picture Library, *br* Harry Smith Collection. 188 Jerry Harpur. 189 *t* The Garden Picture Library/Geoff Dann, *br* The Garden Picture Library/David Secombe. 190 *b* Elizabeth Whiting. 190-1 Jerry Harpur. 192-3 Jerry Harpur. 193 *bl* The Garden Picture Library/Brian Carter, *br* Harry Smith Collection. 194 *t* Harry Smith Collection, *b* The Garden Picture Library/John Glover. 195 George Leveque. 198 *t* Eric Crichton, *b* Elizabeth Whiting. 199 *t* Jerry Harpur, *b* The Garden Picture Library/Neil Holmes. 200 *l* The National Trust/Matthew Antrobus. 200-1 *l* Brian Chapple. 202 Harry Smith Collection. 204 The Garden Picture Library/Lamontagne. 207 *t* Eric Crichton, *bc* Clive Nichols (Anthony Noel). 208 *t* Tim Sandall, *b* Neil Holmes. 209 *t* George Leveque, *b* Clive Nichols. 210 *b* Eric Crichton. 210-11 S & O Mathews.

211 Clive Nichols (Anthony Noel). 212 *t* Tania Midgley, *bl* Eric Crichton. 213 *t* Elizabeth Whiting/Jerry Harpur, *b* Andrew Lawson. 214 Clive Nichols. 215 Jerry Harpur. 218 John Glover. 219 *t* George Leveque, *b* Andrew Lawson. 220 *t* Harry Smith Collection, *b* Elizabeth Whiting. 222 *t* The National Trust/Neil Campbell-Sharp, *b* The Garden Picture Library/John Glover. 223 *t* Harry Smith Collection, *b* Clive Nichols. 224 *b* The Garden Picture Library/John Glover. 224-5 Harry Smith Collection. 225 *t* Jacqui Hurst, *b* Biofotos. 226 *l* Stephen Robson. 226-7 Stephen Robson. 228 Eric Crichton. 230 Christine Ternynck. 231 S & O Mathews. 233 Juliette Wade. 234 *t* S & O Mathews, *c* Photos Horticultural Picture Library, *bl* Marijke Heuff. 235 George Leveque. 236 Harry Smith Collection. 237 *t* Marijke Heuff, *cr* Andrew Lawson. 240 *tl* The Garden Picture Library/John Glover, *bl* Juliette Wade. 240-1 Marijke Heuff. 242 *t* Andrew Lawson, *b* Juliette Wade. 243 Marijke Heuff. 246 Juliette Wade. 247 Photo Lamontagne. 248 Photos Horticultural Picture Library. 249 S & O Mathews. 250 *l* Jerry Harpur. 250-1 The National Trust/Mike Warren. 252 Juliette Wade. 254 *b* Clive Nichols. 255 *t* John Glover. 256 *t* Marijke Heuff, *b* John Glover. 256-7 S & O Mathews. 258 *b* Jerry Harpur. 258-9 John Glover. 259 Tania Midgley. 262 Clive Nichols. 262-3 The Garden Picture Library/Marianne Majerus. 263 Elizabeth Whiting. 264 *t* Elizabeth Whiting, *b* Clive Nichols. 265 *tl* Eric Crichton, *r* Elizabeth Whiting. 267 *t* The Garden Picture Library/John Glover, *b* Tania Midgley. 268 The Garden Picture Library/Jerry Pavia. 269 Photos Horticultural Picture Library. 270 *l* Harry Smith Collection. 270-1 The Garden Picture Library/Marijke Heuff. 271 Andrew Lawson. 272 *l* The National Trust/Nick Meers. 272-3 *t* The National Trust/Stephen Robson. 274 Jacqui Hurst. 276 Eric Crichton. 277 *t* Juliette Wade, *b* Jerry Harpur. 278 *t* John Glover, *b* Jacqui Hurst. 280 *t* Juliette Wade. 280-1 Clive Nichols (Daniel Pearson). 281 Eric Crichton. 282 Andrew Lawson. 284 *br* Eric Crichton. 284-5 *t* Jerry Harpur. 285 Marijke Heuff. 286-7 The Garden Picture Library/John Glover. 287 The Garden Picture Library/Brian Carter. 290 Tania Midgley. 291 Elizabeth Whiting/Jerry Harpur, *cl* S & O Mathews, *cr* and *b* Eric Crichton. 292-3 Andrew Lawson. 293 Clive Nichols (Nigel Colborn). 294 *b* Andrew Lawson. 294-5 S & O Mathews. 295 Jacqui Hurst. 296 *t* S & O Mathews, *cl* Tania Midgley, *bl* The Garden Picture Library/Vaughan Fleming, *br* Eric Crichton. 297 *t* and *b* Elizabeth Whiting. 298 The National Trust for Scotland/JMF. 298-9 Royal Botanic Garden, Edinburgh/Brinsley Burbidge.

300 Eric Crichton. 302 Christine Ternynck (De Kempenhof). 303 Elizabeth Whiting. 304 *t* Eric Crichton, *c* The Garden Picture Library/Ron Sutherland. 305 Eric Crichton. 306 *t* Clive Nichols, *c* Eric Crichton, *b* Jerry Harpur. 308 *b* Christine Ternynck. 308-9 John Glover. 309 Eric Crichton. 310 John Glover. 311 *t* The Garden Picture Library/Ron Sutherland, *c* and *b* Christine Ternynck. 312 *b* The Garden Picture Library/Gary Rogers. 312-13 *t* Jerry Harpur. 314 *t* Jerry Harpur, *c* George Leveque. 316 *t* Jerry Harpur, *b* Andrew Lawson. 317 S & O Mathews. 318 *b* S & O Mathews. 318-19 George Leveque. 320 *l* Jerry Harpur. 320-1 Charles Mann. 322 Andrew Lawson. 324 Jacqui Hurst. 325 *t* Bruce Coleman Ltd/Konrad Wothe, *cr* Bruce Coleman Ltd/Dennis Green. 326 *tl* Harry Smith Collection, *c* Bruce Coleman Ltd/Ume Walz. 328-9 Mike Read. 329 Aquila Photographics/K.A. Linnard. 330-1 NHPA/Stephen Dalton. 334 Biofotos. 335 NHPA/Stephen Dalton, *c* and *b* Ardea, London/Anthony & Elizabeth Bomford. 336 *t* NHPA/Stephen Dalton, *c* Neil Holmes, *b* Bruce Coleman Ltd/Bob Glover. 338 *t* Bruce Coleman Ltd/Jane Burton, *cl* Photos Horticultural Picture Library. 339 Andrew Lawson. 340 *t* The Garden Picture Library/Mayer/Le Scanff, *b* Ardea, London/Ian Beames. 342 *l* and *r* Brian Chapple. 344 The Garden Picture Library/Didier Willery. 346 Photos Horticultural Picture Library. 349 Eric Crichton. 350 *t* Brian Chapple. 351 *c* The Garden Picture Library/Brian Carter, *b* Henry Doubleday Research Association. 354-5 Clay Perry. 355 *t* Ardea, London/A.P. Paterson, *b* Holt Studios Ltd/Nigel Cattlin. 356 *cr* Photos Horticultural Picture Library. 357 Photos Horticultural Picture Library. 358-9 Jerry Harpur. 359 *t* NHPA/Stephen Dalton, *cl* The Garden Picture Library/Brian Carter, *c* Ardea, London/Ian Beames, *bl* Holt Studios Ltd/Nigel Cattlin. 360 Harry Smith Collection. 362 *t* Biofotos/Jason Venus, *cl* Holt Studios Ltd/Nigel Cattlin, *b* Henry Doubleday Research Association. 363 *t* Biofotos, *c* RSPCA Photolibrary/Colin Carver, *b* Aquila Photographics/R. Glover. 364 *l* The National Trust/Nick Meers. 364-5 The National Trust/Nick Meers.

ORIGINATION Wace Corporate Imaging, London, England   PAPER Smurfit Condat, Neuilly, France
PRINTING Maury Imprimeur SA, Malesherbes, France   BINDING Reliures Brun SA, Malesherbes, France
40-438-1